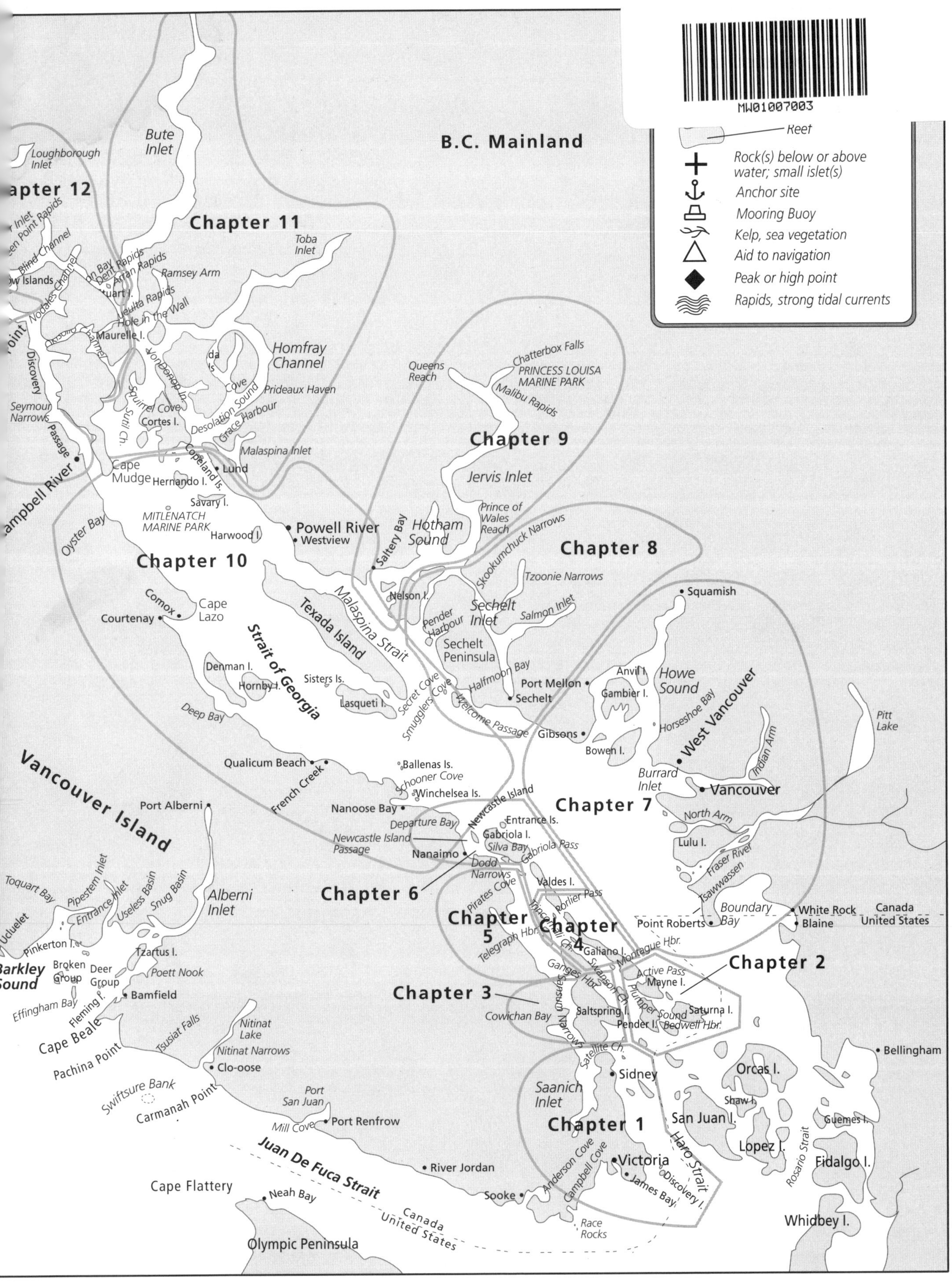

MW01007003
Reef
Rock(s) below or above water; small islet(s)
Anchor site
Mooring Buoy
Kelp, sea vegetation
Aid to navigation
Peak or high point
Rapids, strong tidal currents
B.C. Mainland
Chapter 12
Chapter 11
Chapter 10
Chapter 9
Chapter 8
Chapter 7
Chapter 6
Chapter 5
Chapter 4
Chapter 3
Chapter 2
Chapter 1
Vancouver Island
Strait of Georgia
Juan De Fuca Strait
Bute Inlet
Loughborough Inlet
Toba Inlet
Homfray Channel
Campbell River
Cape Mudge
Powell River
Westview
Comox
Courtenay
Cape Lazo
Texada Island
Malaspina Strait
Jervis Inlet
Sechelt Inlet
Squamish
Howe Sound
West Vancouver
Vancouver
Burrard Inlet
Nanaimo
Gabriola I.
Valdes I.
Galiano I.
Mayne I.
Saturna I.
Pender I.
Saltspring I.
Sidney
Victoria
Sooke
Port Alberni
Alberni Inlet
Barkley Sound
Bamfield
Cape Beale
Port Renfrow
Cape Flattery
Neah Bay
Olympic Peninsula
Orcas I.
San Juan I.
Lopez I.
Fidalgo I.
Whidbey I.
Bellingham
White Rock
Blaine
Point Roberts
Boundary Bay
Canada
United States

Exploring the South Coast of British Columbia

Gulf Islands and Desolation Sound to Broughton Archipelago and Blunden Harbour

Third Edition

By Don Douglass & Réanne Hemingway-Douglass

Fine Edge
Nautical & Recreational Publishing
Anacortes, Washington

Quotations from Canadian *Sailing Directions*

Quotations from the Canadian *Sailing Directions, Vol. 1* and *Vol. 2* are used with permission of the Canadian Hydrographic Service. Information from *Sailing Directions* is for illustrative purposes only and does not meet the CHS requirements; such information is not to be used for navigation. The appropriate *Sailing Directions* and CHS charts required under the Regulations of the Canada Shipping Act must be used for navigation.

Important Legal Disclaimer

This book is designed to provide experienced skippers with planning information for cruising Southeast Alaska. Every effort has been made, within limited resources, to make this book complete and accurate. There may well be mistakes, both typographical and in content; therefore, this book should be used only as a general guide, not as the ultimate source of information on the areas covered. Much of what is presented in this book is local knowledge based upon personal observation and is subject to human error.

The authors, publisher and local and governmental authorities make no warranties and assume no liability for errors or omissions, or for any loss or damage of any kind incurred from using this information.

Library of Congress Cataloging-in-Publication Data

Douglass, Don, 1932–
Exploring the South Coast of British Columbia : Gulf Islands and Desolation Sound to Broughton Archipelago and Blunden Harbour / by Don Douglass & Réanne Hemingway-Douglass. — 3rd ed.
p. cm.
Includes bibliographical references and index.
ISBN 978-1-932310-23-8 (pbk.)
1. Pilot guides—British Columbia. 2. Yachting—British Columbia—Guidebooks.
I. Hemingway-Douglass, Réanne, 1933- II. Title.
VK945.D683 2009
623.89'2971131--dc22 2009028628

ISBN 978-0-938665-23-8

Address requests for permission to:
Fine Edge, 14004 Biz Point Lane, Anacortes, WA 98221
www.FineEdge.com

Printed in the United States of America

Dedicated to the Memory of Juanita Pacifico Clark
Loyal Friend, Adventurer, Crewmate
who composed the following poem on board *Baidarka*
Port Neville, B.C.

At Sea

Where Caspian terns rest, wet silhouettes

And Arctic waves rush to their secret rendezvous,

The *Baidarka* skipper smiles, watchful and beholden,

Two strangers bent on his fair passage,

One warning of dangers lurking in the weed,

The other murmuring deeply

Godspeed.

Acknowledgments

We wish to express our gratitude and appreciation to the many people who, over the years, have given us encouragement and support in our research projects.

A special thanks to Captain Kevin Monahan with the Canadian Coast Guard, Pacific Region, for his Foreword and sidebar; his impact can be felt throughout this book.

To fellow skipper and adventurer, Roderick Frazier, Professor Emeritus UCSB—a descendant of legendary explorer Simon Roderick Fraser—for his sidebar.

To John deBoeck, Nanaimo—researcher, explorer, and captain of *Clavella*—for sharing years of recollections with us; Captain Dave Young of Royston, for twenty-eight years Captain of the *Uchuck III*—for his sidebar.

Thanks to Ian Douglas, Quadra Island for his photographs; to Linda Schreiber, Tonnae Hennigan, Tom Shardlow and Colin Jackson for their sidebars; and to Anne Vipond for her sidebars and photographs.

To the many professionals of service agencies who took took time to help us with innumerable details: in particular, Brian M. Watt, Canadian Hydrographic Service, Pacific Region, for providing photographs; to Mike Woods, C.H.S., for information on horizontal datum; to the Ministry of Environment, Lands and Parks, Geographic Data B.C., for permission to reproduce B.C. Government air photos; to Cheryl Noble of B.C. Parks for help in updating our files; and to the many harbour masters, park rangers, marina managers, and others who were kind enough to answer questions as we completed our research. To our many readers who wrote to share their insights and experiences, and to the many local residents, resort operators, and crews of fishing and cruising boats who, along the way, have shared meals, coffee and stories with us.

We couldn't have done this book, either, without the *Baidarka* crew members, who over the years have pulled up the anchor, taken the helm, stood innumerable bow watches, kept the galley stove going, helped us record raw data, and provided photographs: Tom and Gloria Burke; Herb Nickles; Seth Nickles; Frank and Margy Fletcher; Bob and Annamae Botley; Geza and Russlyn Dienes; Katherine Wells and Lloyd Dennis; Jane and Gary Gillingham; Ward Clark and the late Juanita Pacifico Clark; Dick Walls; and our son and daughter-in-law, Sean Collins and Margaret Walls.

We are indebted, also, to Bill Wolferstan and John Chappell, modern-day explorers of this south coast of British Columbia whose classic guidebooks set a high standard in cruising information.

And last, to our land "crew"—whose efficient and competent help through many "foggy" months brought this project to final fruition—a rousing thanks: Melanie Haage, book design; Faith Ann Rumm, Rick Jones, and Sue Athmann diagrams and computer graphics; Pat Eckart, typing and copyediting; and Cindy Kamler, our "eagle eye" editor.

Contents

Foreword

by Kevin Monahan

It is almost forty years now since I arrived at Vancouver Airport, an awestruck five-year-old from the heart of London, England. I remember the wide streets, the huge trees, and the awesome rock-bound coast. Even the moderate mountains in my new backyard were larger than life. Thus began an enchantment which has lasted till this day. I confess to feeling an intense passion for the great waterways, mountains, and islands that litter Canada's west coast. This rich environment, which has nurtured humans since the first Asiatic settlers arrived here tens of thousands of years ago, has nurtured me also. I came here a foreigner, yet I now belong to this coast.

Throughout my time at sea, it has been the tiny harbours that appealed to me the most. No matter how stimulated by the drama of the coast, one must eventually find refuge. Diminutive but secure, such places are scattered throughout this coastline in vast numbers, providing privacy and contentment for the spirit. Indeed, after beating my way through gale-force winds or worse, weaving my boat into a quiet anchorage brings on a kind of euphoria, a joy that cannot be understood without the experience.

Don and Réanne Douglass have spent a large part of their lives exploring new places, be it on land or at sea. An attempt at Cape Horn almost ended in disaster. Their 42-foot sailing boat, *le Dauphin Amical,* was pitchpoled by a breaking sea at Fifty South latitude. Still they managed to hold their vessel together and make the Strait of Magellan, limping into Punta Arenas after thirty-seven days. Réanne's account of their journey is both a candid portrayal of a couple surviving under extreme duress and a wildly exciting sea story. I read the book in one sitting, and today I marvel at their seamanship and fortune in enduring the almost unendurable.

In this book, *Exploring the South Coast of British Columbia—Gulf Islands and Desolation Sound to Broughton Archipelago and Blunden Harbour,* as in their previous publications, Don and Réanne present an atlas of local knowledge for the amateur and professional alike. Together they have systematically recorded the details of numerous anchorages including such important information as exposure to various winds, the quality of the bottom, and the character of the local topography.

These guidebooks are designed to be constant wheelhouse companions, and they easily fill our expectations. But they are also truly friendly books bursting with the personalities of the authors. When referring to a particular bay or passage, I can hear Don giving his advice or recounting his experience in such and such a location during a storm and a large ebb tide. It is a reassuring presence that passes along these detailed notes and maps, recommends the best routes, and brings us safely to our destination.

May you all have safe and eventful voyages.

Kevin Monahan is with the Canadian Coast Guard Pacific Region.

Introduction

Welcome to *Exploring the South Coast of British Columbia!*—a guidebook to help you enjoy some of the finest cruising grounds in the world. With this book in hand, you are seldom more than 30 minutes from a lovely, sheltered cove or a place to drop your hook and get out of the wind, fog or current—no need to push your vessel and crew to make a major port or marina when conditions indicate you should stop and wait.

In providing up-to-date pilothouse information, we have tried to address general and navigational concerns that might arise as you plan and execute your cruise. In particular, we provide the "local knowledge" often referred to in Canadian *Sailing Directions* as necessary for safe navigation.

This local knowledge is subjective in nature. While we have made every effort to present the information in a consistent manner to allow you to compare details about one cove with another, as skipper you must use your own judgment in matters concerning safe navigation. Excerpts from the official Canadian Hydrographic Service data, as well as details drawn from our own experience, have been incorporated to give you a basis on which to form your judgment.

How This Book is Organized

Each chapter in this book covers a separate cruising area, proceeding usually from south to north; an area map at the beginning of each chapter serves as a quick reference to the location of channels, passages and coves found within the text. The inside front and back cover-maps provide an overview of the entire area featured in the book.

Each geographical entry in this new edition follows the same user-friendly layout. *Place Name* comes first, followed by *the Island or Major Body of Water* on which it is located, then *General Location* and distance from a prominent place.

Next follows the *Nautical Chart Number(s)* for that place, with the *largest scale chart* mentioned first. To help you locate a place in poor visibility, in this new edition we have provided an *Entrance Waypoint* (the Lat/Long for the center of the preferred channel when approaching from seaward). The *Anchor Position(s)* we have personally used or recommend are given, followed by the *Horizontal Datum (NAD 83)* which is the same as WGS 84, the GPS system default and the datum we used to derive these waypoints.

Be aware that the route from an Entrance Waypoint to an Anchor Waypoint is normally curvilinear so you must choose your route by visual means and using a depth sounder. If you blindly follow a straight-line course between the entrance and anchor waypoints, you may find intervening land in your path!

The text in indented italics is excerpted from *Sailing Directions*; this feature gives you the official viewpoint (if it is available) to help you judge the value of our local knowledge.

The main body of the text describes the *Local Knowledge* we have discovered by personal observation or in conjunction with sources we believe to be reliable and knowledgeable.

The last entry under each place-name is specific *Anchoring Information* for the Anchor Site Waypoint identified in the heading and/or on the detailed diagram for that place. If you should find widely different conditions than those described, double-check your position on the chart and make your own judgment about suitability for the particular conditions.

Canadian Charts and Symbols

Canada is in the process of converting all of its navigational charts from traditional British naval units to the metric system. Anyone navigating in British Columbia must pay close attention to every chart used since a large part of Canadian charts are now metric with the exception of some out-of-the-way places. The metric charts may or may not have "Metric" printed in red in the lower right-hand corner. Please note that several of the charts issued in the late 1980s and 1990s, although metric, do not use the new 1983 horizontal datum.

These metric changes involve more than just a substitution of numbers—the symbols for depth and height have changed as well. For instance, [1_3] on old Canadian charts and on American charts means a depth of 1 fathom and 3 feet, for a total depth of 9 feet (1.5 fathoms). On the metric charts, the symbol [1_3] means 1.3 meters or about 4 feet. The elevation of an island or islet is usually shown as a number followed by a dot [57•]; the elevation at the top of trees is a number with a line over it [$\overline{57}$]; a number preceded by a dot indicates spot elevation, such as the elevation of a peak [•57]. Since many of these differences can be confusing, be sure to purchase and study Canadian Chart 1 (Symbols, Abbreviations and Terms) to familiarize yourself with current Canadian symbols.

Unnamed islands and islets are indicated in the text by their elevation enclosed in parentheses [e.g. island (45)]. In some cases, where more than one chart covers an area, the numbers in parentheses may be either in feet or meters and may change from chart to chart.

Sample Layout Selection

Place name

Wootton Bay (Lancelot Inlet)
Charts 3559, 3312, 3538; at the extreme N end of Lancelot Inlet; 1.9 mi N of Isabel Bay
Entrance: 50°04.64'N, 124°42.85'W
Anchor: 50°05.00'N, 124°43.14'W

Largest scale chart listed first; distance from known place

All GPS coordinates adjusted to NAD83

> *Wootton Bay, at the head of Lancelot Inlet, affords anchorage in about 20 m (66 ft.).* (SD)

Excerpts from (SD) Sailing Directions— always in italics

Wootton Bay is barely 200 yards from Portage Cove in Desolation Sound. This isthmus was an excellent portage for canoers and kayakers before the No Trespassing signs went up from the inholding. This can be a very quiet, calm anchorage. It is partially exposed to southerlies.

Our own recorded local knowledge based on personal experience

Anchor in 6 fathoms over mud, shells and some rocks with fair-to-good holding.

Describes depth(s), bottom material and holding power

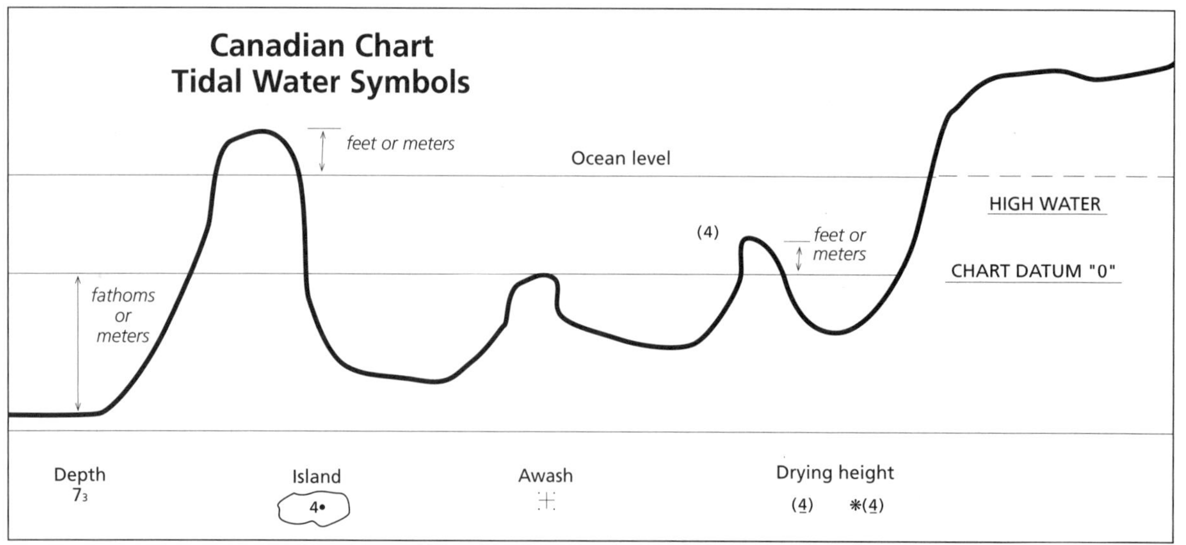

Northwest Anchoring

Northwest cruising is all about anchoring; once you get beyond marinas and fishing resorts, the feeling of being safely anchored in your own secluded cove is unforgettable. Finding an anchorage is one of the challenges and pleasures of cruising; we hope this book will help you find your *own* special site!

A well-set, over-sized anchor assures a good night's sleep. A conventional cruising anchor (not a lightweight folding version), a boat-length of chain, and good nylon rode are indispensable equipment. We always carry a smaller lunch hook to use during temporary stops or to restrict our swinging room. Sometimes for security—in close quarters or in deep, steep-to anchorages—we use a stern tie to shore. Although we usually prefer to swing on a single CQR anchor, in marine parks or popular anchorages, we try to minimize our impact by matching the mooring technique and swinging radius of other boats. Note that larger vessels frequently use an all-chain rode which gives a unique turning radius.

Choosing our site carefully and setting our anchor well assures us that *Baidarka* will rock us to sleep even in occasional downslope winds or williwaws.

Definitions Used for Holding Power

Excellent—very good holding

Anchor digs in deeper as you pull on it—the preferred bottom in a blow, but a rare find—usually thick sticky mud or clay.

Good holding

Generally sufficient for overnight anchorage in fair weather—anchor digs in but may drag or pull out on strong pull. Common in mud/sand combinations or hard sand.

Fair holding

Adequate for temporary anchorage in fair weather, but boat should not be left unattended. Bottom of light sand, gravel with some rocks, grass or kelp. Anchor watch desirable.

Poor holding

Can be used for a temporary stop in fair weather only. Bottom is typically rocky with a lot of grass or kelp, or a very thin later of mud and sand—insufficient to properly bury anchor. Anchor watch at all times is recommended.

Steep-to

Depth of water may decrease from 10 fathoms to 1/2 fathom in as little as one boat length! (Approach at dead-slow recommended.) Use shore tie to minimize swinging and to keep anchor pulling uphill.

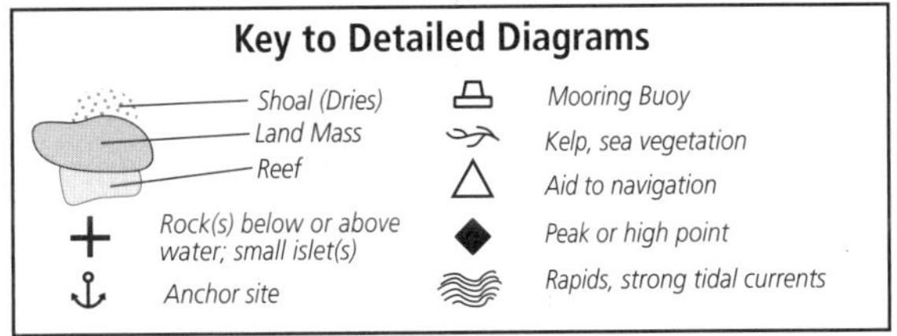

Anchor Diagrams

We have included anchor diagrams for sites we feel would be helpful. These diagrams are non-representational and not to scale; they do not include all known or unknown hazards—they simply show the approximate routes we took, the typical depths we found, and the places we anchored.

We always keep a vigilant bow watch when entering a new cove because we like to keep "one foot on the beach" to get the feel of a cove and to partake of the sights, sounds and odors of the land. Larger vessels or those with deep-draft may want to anchor in deeper water to provide a greater margin of safety.

Measurements and Other Conventions Used in this Book

Spelling and usage of place names follows, as closely as possible, local traditions and the lead of the Canadian *Sailing Directions.*

For the time being, we have chosen to continue using fathoms, nautical miles, yards, feet, degrees in Fahrenheit, etc. in our guidebooks.

(Canadians are more adept at making conversions than Yankees are.) We urge both local and visiting navigators to double-check each chart, echo sounder readings, and GPS initial settings for consistent use of measurement units (i.e. fathoms, meters, feet, hundredths of minutes, etc.).

Unless otherwise noted, the depths listed in the text or shown on diagrams are always given in fathoms, regardless of the measurement units on cited charts; depths are also reduced to approximate zero tide. In Canada, zero tide data is given as the lowest expected tide for the year; therefore tide tables almost always appear as a positive number rather than the frequent minus tides of the United States. When you use the depth numbers on our diagrams, you should add the amount of tide listed in the corrected tide tables.

Bearings and courses, when given in this book, are generally magnetic and identified as such. Courses are taken off the chart compass rose; they are approximate and are to be "made good." No allowances have been made for deviation, current or drift. When compass cardinal points are used (e.g. NW or SE), these refer to true bearings and should be taken as approximate only.

Distances are expressed in nautical miles and speed is expressed in knots unless otherwise stated. Scales on the diagrams are expressed in yards, meters, and miles as noted and are approximate only. Time is given in four-digit 24-hour clock numbers, and all courses are given in three digits.

Latitude and longitude in the text are cited in degrees, minutes, and decimal minutes to the nearest hundredth of a minute and are taken from the largest scale chart available. (Seconds are not used.) These Lat/Longs (GPS positions) are to be treated as approximate only. Many of the referenced charts are not accurate—nor can they be read accurately—to one-hundredth of a minute. We have approximated this last digit to provide as complete a picture as possible.

We generally find very good correlation between the charts and GPS readings when we take the average of a series of readings. Universal coverage of Differential GPS or the eventual demise of Selective Availability, along with improved charts, will make accuracy to one-hundredth of a minute (plus or minus 60 feet) commonplace.

For optimum accuracy in charting you must set your GPS receiver to the correct horizontal datum for the chart you are using. The horizontal datum for Canadian charts for the south coast of British Columbia is either NAD 83 or NAD 27; be alert for changes in the datum between the different editions of a given chart. (NAD 27 differs from NAD 83 by about 0.011 minutes in latitude and 0.089 minutes in longitude, a difference of about 300 feet.)

The default datum in GPS receivers is generally WSG 84 which, for all practical purposes, is equivalent to NAD 83. For all waypoints in this Second Edition, we use NAD 83 as the horizontal datum. If you want to plot these positions on an NAD 27 chart, each waypoint must be corrected by the amount indicated on each chart. We have been told by Canadian Hydrographic Service (CHS) that, if a horizontal datum is not specified on a particular chart, it can be assumed to be NAD 27. To see the graphic difference in these two horizontal datums, please see the Sidebar "Horizontal Datum Makes a Difference!" in Chapter 4, page 108.

This guidebook documents many small, unnamed coves and bays, and in all cases, we tried to use local names. However, where we could find no reference, we used a new name that seemed appropriate. Local names and new names are enclosed in quotation marks upon their first use.

The Bibliography lists a number of publications that are useful or required on board, including *Sailing Directions* and *Small Craft Guide*.

Exploring the South Coast of British Columbia covers inside waters where summer weather is usually fairly stable and well-predicted, and ocean swells are diminished to almost zero.

VHF weather forecasts are given for all parts of B.C.'s South Coast where you are seldom out of range of good reception. You can also receive B.C. marine weather forecasts by visiting links on our website (www.FineEdge.com) or by telephoning 604-664-9010. Vessels that intend to circumnavigate Vancouver Island or travel to areas where weather becomes a major concern, may refer to *Exploring Vancouver Island's West Coast,* Second Edition, for a more detailed discussion of weather, sea conditions, marine hazards, and the "outside" environment.

Border Crossings

On either side of the border, there are different jurisdictions and protocols. As you cross back and forth between the Canada-U.S. border in either direction, you need to follow a few simple Customs regulations. A vessel must be cleared by Customs at a designated Port of Entry. Generally this is done by the skipper or his designee who reports in person or by telephone. All other crew members must stay aboard (along with baggage and goods) until Customs issues a clearance number. (For more information, please see Appendix D or telephone Revenue Canada at 800.461.9999 or 604.666.0545.)

Cruising Ethics

"Leave No Trace" must be the goal of every cruising boat. Always try to leave a place cleaner than you found it and take away only great photos and warm memories. Leave nothing but echoes of laughter and a fading, gentle wake.

Errata and Updates

Please note that dynamic changes occur frequently these days, particularly in urban areas

---

Cruising Etiquette

The waters of Southern B.C. are among are among the busiest cruising areas on our coast. We rub shoulders not only with each other, but with kayakers, campers and a variety of other users. It is critical that, while enjoying the area, we remember to respect others' rights to enjoy them and that we preserve them for future generations to enjoy as well. A little cruising etiquette is in order:

- Respect the flora, fauna and marine environment of these waters, as well as the privacy of the people who live here.
- Don't discharge raw sewage into bays, harbors, or anchorages. Use shoreside facilities, a holding tank, or an appropriate MSD.
- Manage your trash. Under any circumstances, don't stash it ashore or sink it in the chuck. Sort out recyclables and recycle them. Dispose of the rest at a suitable garbage drop or pack it with you until you find one. Note that fewer and fewer marine parks in the Canadian Gulf Islands have garbage bins these days.
- When choosing a spot to anchor, respect the swinging room and privacy of those who got there before you and leave room for those who may arrive later. Arrange your "swinging circle" to coincide with boats around you. Use a stern line to limit your swing where necessary.
- Remember that most boaters come to B.C. for peace and quiet. In anchorages or marinas, keep noise down. If you have a genset or portable generator, use it discreetly. Don't run it during everyone else's cockpit cocktail hour or when people are trying to sleep; don't turn it on and flee in your tender or retreat below because you can't stand the noise. Sailors, tie those halyards away from the mast. Don't "buzz" the anchorage in your tender or PWC, and don't let your crew do it either. If you really want to party, find the nearest pub on shore—there are lots of good ones, especially in the Gulf Islands.
- Keep your wake down in anchorages, restricted passages and waterways.
- Leave nothing behind but your wake. Your fellow cruisers, both now and in years to come, will thank you for it.

Welcome to British Columbia!

—Duart Snow, Editor, *Pacific Yachting*

Publisher's Note: In 1999, Canadian Coast Guard instituted a policy of "no discharge zones" for certain areas of British Columbia where there is high boat usage and where the exchange of tidal waters is limited. For more information, please visit CCG website: www.pacific.ccggcc.gc.ca

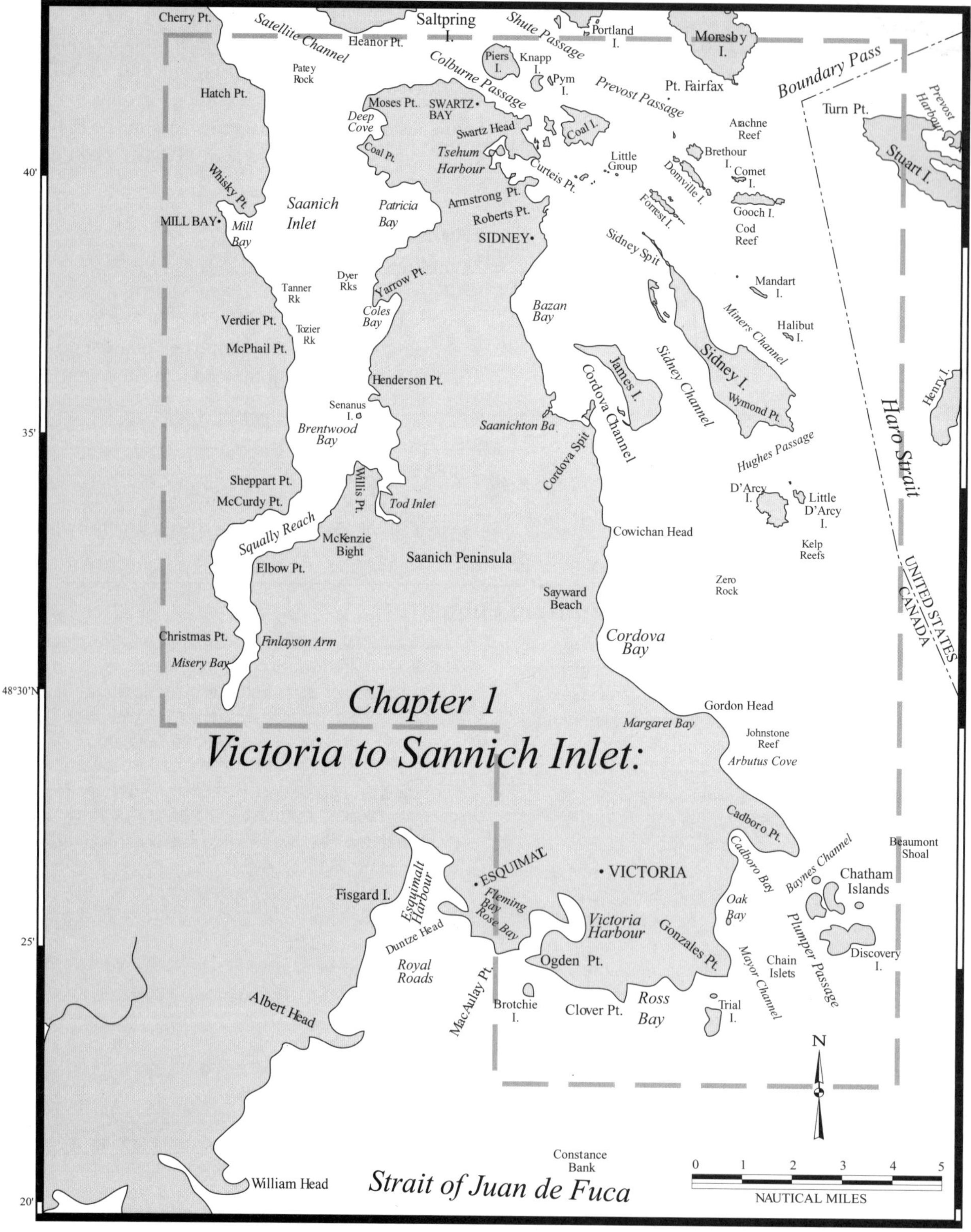
Chapter 1
Victoria to Sannich Inlet:
Cherry Pt.
Satellite Channel
Saltpring I.
Eleanor Pt.
Shute Passage
Portland I.
Moresby I.
Boundary Pass
Patey Rock
Colburne Passage
Piers I.
Knapp I.
Pym I.
Prevost Passage
Pt. Fairfax
Prevost Harbour
Turn Pt.
Stuart I.
Hatch Pt.
Moses Pt.
SWARTZ BAY
Deep Cove
Swartz Head
Coal I.
Arachne Reef
Coal Pt.
Tsehum Harbour
Little Group
Brethour I.
Comet I.
Curteis Pt.
Domville I.
Whisky Pt.
Saanich Inlet
Patricia Bay
Armstrong Pt.
Roberts Pt.
Forrest I.
Gooch I.
MILL BAY
Mill Bay
SIDNEY
Cod Reef
Sidney Spit
Dyer Rks
Tanner Rk
Yarrow Pt.
Mandart I.
Coles Bay
Bazan Bay
Miners Channel
Verdier Pt.
Tozier Rk
Halibut I.
McPhail Pt.
James I.
Sidney Channel
Sidney I.
Henderson Pt.
Cordova Channel
Henry I.
Senanus I.
Wymond Pt.
Haro Strait
Brentwood Bay
Saanichton Ba
Hughes Passage
Cordova Spit
Sheppart Pt.
Willis Pt.
D'Arcy I.
Little D'Arcy I.
McCurdy Pt.
Tod Inlet
Cowichan Head
Squally Reach
McKenzie Bight
Kelp Reefs
Saanich Peninsula
Elbow Pt.
UNITED STATES
CANADA
Zero Rock
Sayward Beach
Cordova Bay
Christmas Pt.
Finlayson Arm
Misery Bay
48°30'N
40'
35'
25'
20'
Gordon Head
Margaret Bay
Johnstone Reef
Arbutus Cove
Cadboro Pt.
Cadboro Bay
Beaumont Shoal
Baynes Channel
Chatham Islands
ESQUIMALT
VICTORIA
Fisgard I.
Esquimalt Harbour
Fleming Bay
Rose Bay
Oak Bay
Victoria Harbour
Gonzales Pt.
Plumper Passage
Duntze Head
Royal Roads
Ogden Pt.
Mayor Channel
Chain Islets
Discovery I.
MacAulay Pt.
Albert Head
Brotchie I.
Clover Pt.
Ross Bay
Trial I.
N
Constance Bank
William Head
Strait of Juan de Fuca
0 1 2 3 4 5
NAUTICAL MILES

1

VICTORIA TO SAANICH INLET

Victoria—British Columbia's capital sometimes called the "City of Gardens"—is historic and lovely with an old-world charm. First settled in 1843, the original Hudson's Bay fort has become a sophisticated city, home to the Provincial Legislature, the famous Empress Hotel, and the Maritime and Royal British Columbia museums. With its Thunderbird Park totems, Chinatown, rose gardens and horse-drawn buggies, Victoria captivates all her visitors.

Marine parks are scattered throughout the Gulf Islands to the east of Vancouver Island. Discovery Island is almost due east of Oak Bay, while D'Arcy Island is to the north as you cruise along the Saanich Peninsula. Still further north is Sidney Island with Sidney Spit Marine Park. This picturesque park, with its white sand beach and lagoon, is popular for wildlife viewing. Don't miss the great blue herons and fallow deer. A well-developed park, Sidney Spit has campsites, picnic areas, and a float.

The port town of Sidney lies north of Victoria on Vancouver Island. There are many excellent marinas in Tsehum Harbour, Sidney, and Canoe Bay. Sidney offers all amenities, including the Sidney Museum with its wonderful whale murals, a racetrack, golf course, restaurants and shops. For adventurous small boats, Rum Island—the tiny site of Isle-de-Lis Marine Park, six miles northeast of Sidney Spit—makes a nice picnic stop. As you can guess, the island was named for rum-runners who once frequented this coast.

Rounding the northern tip of the Saanich Peninsula to the west, you head into the famous fishing grounds of Saanich Inlet which has numerous coves and bays to explore. Don't miss magnificent Butchart Gardens near Brentwood Bay where on Saturday evenings in summer you can view fireworks after touring the lighted gardens.

For boaters who like to bicycle, the Galloping Goose Regional Trail is a part of a growing network of multiuse trails in B.C. It runs on an abandoned railway bed for 60 kilometers

Peter Fromm

Wooden Boat Festival draws sailboats from both sides of the border

Peter Fromm

The J boat Endeavor *heads north*

between downtown Victoria and Sooke on the west coast of Vancouver Island. The first nine kilometers after leaving the city centre is paved for bicycle commuters. The rest of the trail is for horseback riding, hiking, and recreational bike riders.

Leading north out of Victoria is the Lochside Trail, a 29-kilometer ride down the Saanich Peninsula from the B.C. Ferry Terminal in Swartz Bay. This picturesque trail is a combination of paths, bike lanes, and country roads, sometimes with views of the coast and passing through the town of Sidney.

Please note: effective January 1, 2004 all marinas below Courtenay, B.C. began using VHF Channel 66A. Some marinas may continue to monitor both their original channel and VHF Channel 66A during a transition period.

Approaches to Victoria Outer Harbour

(Vancouver Island)

Charts 3415, 3440, 3313
Entrance (200 yds W of breakwater light): 48°24.81'N, 123°23.78'W
Entrance (100 yds W of Shoal Pt light): 48°25.41'N, 123°23.41'W

Natural History of the Gulf Islands

Eons ago, these islands were probably part of Vancouver Island. Then rising water and glacier action created myriad islands. Consisting primarily of sedimentary rock—sandstone, shale or conglomerate—they lie in a roughly northwest/southeast direction; ridges and valleys run in the same direction.

Summer temperatures usually range from 50 to 70 degrees F, earning the islands the name, "Canada's Hawaii." Moderate temperatures and rainfall have created dry woodlands on the islands. Douglas firs dominate, along with coppery-barked, gnarled, evergreen arbutus (madrone); prickly pears can even be found on some of the southernmost islands!

The waters are rich with colorful marine life: spiny red urchins, green anemones, ochre stars, and blue mussels. Orcas are frequently spotted here. Along the shores and rocks, harbor seals and Steller sea lions feed and bask, while otters, mink and raccoons forage along shores and streams. Thousands of migratory seabirds fill the sky with sound and grace; cormorants, and gulls nest in the wave- and wind-carved sandstone cliffs; great blue herons and bald eagles nest on the islands.

Marine parks, provincial parks, ecological reserves, and Indian reserves are scattered throughout the area. Access to all or parts of some lands may be restricted, and regulations apply to camping, fires, and gathering shellfish. Please respect these regulations and help to protect these fragile areas for future generations.

The larger islands have substantial populations while many of the smaller islands are uninhabited. A multitude of bays, coves, and inlets invite you to enter and explore, to stay the night lulled to sleep by gentle winds and the cries of seabirds. The history of First Nation's people, explorers, early pioneers, miners, loggers, and fishermen is written in ancient petroglyphs, decaying cabins, and rotting wrecks.

Summer weather usually brings mornings with gentle winds and calm seas. By late afternoon, however, brisk westerly winds and chop usually develop. If you plan a crossing, start early in the morning to avoid these uncomfortable conditions. Southeast gales occasionally blow through the area, but you can find many good places to shelter until the front passes.

Victoria Harbour ...is entered between Macaulay Point and the Ogden Point breakwater. East of a line joining Colvile Island and Shoal Point up to the Johnson Street Bridge is known as Inner Harbour.

The harbour entrance is easily recognized by the breakwater and a long, low grey building close north on the east side of the entrance....

Regulations for Victoria Harbour are Practices and Procedures for Public Ports with the addition of several special rules that govern fuelling procedures, towing and the length of tow, speed limits in specific areas, prohibited anchorages, prohibited fishing areas, sewage discharge and mooring....

Approaching Victoria Outer Harbour

The Harbour Master's office and the harbour patrol craft are equipped with VHF radios and monitor Channel 18A.

...Sailing is prohibited in the Middle, Inner and Uper Harbour. All sails must be lowered even when under power.

...Anchoring is prohibited without permission of the Harbour Master. (SD)

Cruising vessels approaching Victoria from the north generally use Baynes and Mayor channels. Boats approaching from Cattle Pass and Rosario Strait pass either north or south of Trial Islands. Boats leaving from the west or from Port Townsend can take a tack directly for the harbor entrance.

Peter Fromm

The yawl Zulu *enjoys summer in the islands*

Warning: Be on the alert for seaplanes. There has been an increase in the number of aircraft that land in Victoria Harbour waters. Two major traffic areas or runways lie east-west and north-south of Shoal Point in the Fisherman Bay area. Contact the Victoria Harbour Office for information on docking.

⚓ **Victoria Harbour Office** tel: 250.363.3273

Fleming Bay (Vancouver Island)

Charts 3415, 3419, 3440, 3313; 0.25 mi NW of Macaulay Pt; 8 mi NW of Victoria Hbr bkw

Entrance (outer, 0.1 mi NW of Macaulay Pt): 48°25.08'N, 123°24.84'W

Entrance (breakwater): 48°25.19'N, 123°24.82'W

Fleming Bay, protected by a breakwater, is only used by small craft. It has several floats and a launching ramp. (SD)

Fleming Bay, a tiny bay west of the entrance to Victoria Harbour, is strategically located to provide shelter for small craft that may have difficulty entering Victoria Harbour. Shelter can be found in the lee of Gillingham Islands or behind the breakwater. Swinging room is tight, so if you need to anchor temporarily, it's a good idea to use a stern tie to the breakwater. In an emergency, shallow-draft boats can tie to the launch ramp float. When entering, avoid the Gillingham Islands, many of which are underwater reefs marked by substantial kelp beds.

There are picnic facilities along shore and you can walk to Saxe Point Park and English Village on Lampson Street where you can visit a replica of Anne Hathaway's cottage.

Anchor in 2 to 3 fathoms.

Rose Bay (Vancouver Island)

Charts 3415, 3440, 3313; 0.28 mi NE of McLoughlin Pt
Entrance: 48°25.32'N, 123°23.73'W

Rose Bay, between McLoughlin Point and Work Point, has a rockfill breakwater protecting some floats extending from its west side. (SD)

Rose Bay is a shallow bay on the west side of Victoria Harbour. Work Point Boat Club, behind a breakwater, may offer emergency shelter for small craft.

West Bay (Vancouver Island)

Charts 3415, 3440, 3313; N side of Berens I; 0.1 mi NE of Work Pt
Entrance to dredged channel: 48°25.48'N, 123°23.53'W

West Bay is entered between Berens Island and Colvile Island. A channel, dredged to a depth of 1.5 m, leads NW through West Bay to the marinas. The outer end of the channel is marked by port hand buoy "V23" and the north side of this channel is marked by dolphins. (SD)

West Bay is entered through a dredged channel on its southwest side, avoiding a shallow booming area to the north of the channel. West Bay Marina, on the inner bay, has moorage for small craft. Just west of the marina there is a marine ways, with a store and pub nearby. West Bay has been newly developed with high-rise apartments, a unique float home area for up to 30 homes, and walkways that connect several parks along the north shore of the bay all the way to the Johnson Street bridge (about a 40-minute walk). The Victoria Harbour ferry offers convenient transportation across Victoria Harbour to the Empress Hotel.

⚓ **West Bay Marine Village** tel: 250.385.1831; fax: 250.385.2274; monitors VHF Ch 66A; website: www.westbay.bc.ca; email: info@westbay.bc.ca; open year-round; reservations recommended

⚓ **Hidden Harbour Marina** tel: 250.388.4666; fax: 250.414.5149; website: www.hiddenharbour.ca; email: info@hiddenharbour.ca; open year-round; reservations recommended

Lime Bay (Vancouver Island)

Charts 3415, 3440, 3313; 0.25 mi N of Shoal Pt
Entrance: 48°25.57'N, 123°23.21'W

Several condominiums and a hotel are along the north shore between Lime Bay and Songhees Point. Tuzo Rock, close east of Songhees Point, dries. The area between Tuzo and Discovery Rocks is a booming ground. (SD)

Spinnakers, at the head of Lime Bay, is a popu-

Peter Fromm

Haulout time for a Pinkeye schooner

Anne Vipond

Parliament House seen from Victoria Inner Harbour

lar gathering place for meals and beer. For reservations, telephone 250.384.2112.

Victoria Inner Harbour

Charts 3412, 3415, 3440, 3313; btwn Shoal Pt & Johnson St Bridge
Entrance (Inner Hbr btwn Laurel & Songhees Pts): 48°25.41'N, 123°22.38'W

Victoria, one of the most beautiful and welcoming cities accessible by pleasure craft, has all the charm of an English town. (Residents have told us that it's more British than England!) The public floats in James Bay offer some of the finest city docking anywhere in North America. From the Inner Harbour, everything is within easy walking distance—restaurants, art galleries, gift shops, museums, marine supply stores, and markets.

Since the non-profit organization, Greater Victoria Harbour Authority, took over ownership of Causeway Floats (Empress Floats) and Wharf Street Marina, great improvements have already been made in the public moorage facilities and will continue to be made into the future. The Causeway Floats were extended and upgraded. Power was increased to 30 amp and security improved. The dock along Ship Point was extended, boater-only restrooms, showers and laundry (located south of the Customs Dock) opened, and a service kiosk at both the Empress Floats and Wharf Street Marina will be installed. A pumpout station near the Customs Dock is planned for the future, along with concierge service for pleasure craft. Boaters wishing to call at Victoria during winter months should contact the Harbour Authority regarding moorage specials; during holiday periods and special events, please call the Harbour Office to inquire about reservations. To keep abreast of all changes in Victoria Harbour, please check www.victoriaharbour.org.

⚓ **Victoria Harbour Authority Office**
tel: 250.383.8326; fax: 250.383.8306;
VHF Ch 66A; website:
www.victoriaharbour.org

⚓ **Victoria Customs Office** tel: 888.226.7277

Erie Street Government Wharf, locally Fishermen's Wharf (Victoria Harbour)

Charts 3415, 3440, 3313; S side Victoria Hbr; 0.1 mi E of Shoal Pt
Fuel dock: 48°25.44'N, 123°23.11'W
Wharf Street public floats: 48°25.43'N, 123°23.06'W

Ten public finger floats, east of [Shoal Point] *are generally used by the fishing fleet; between May*

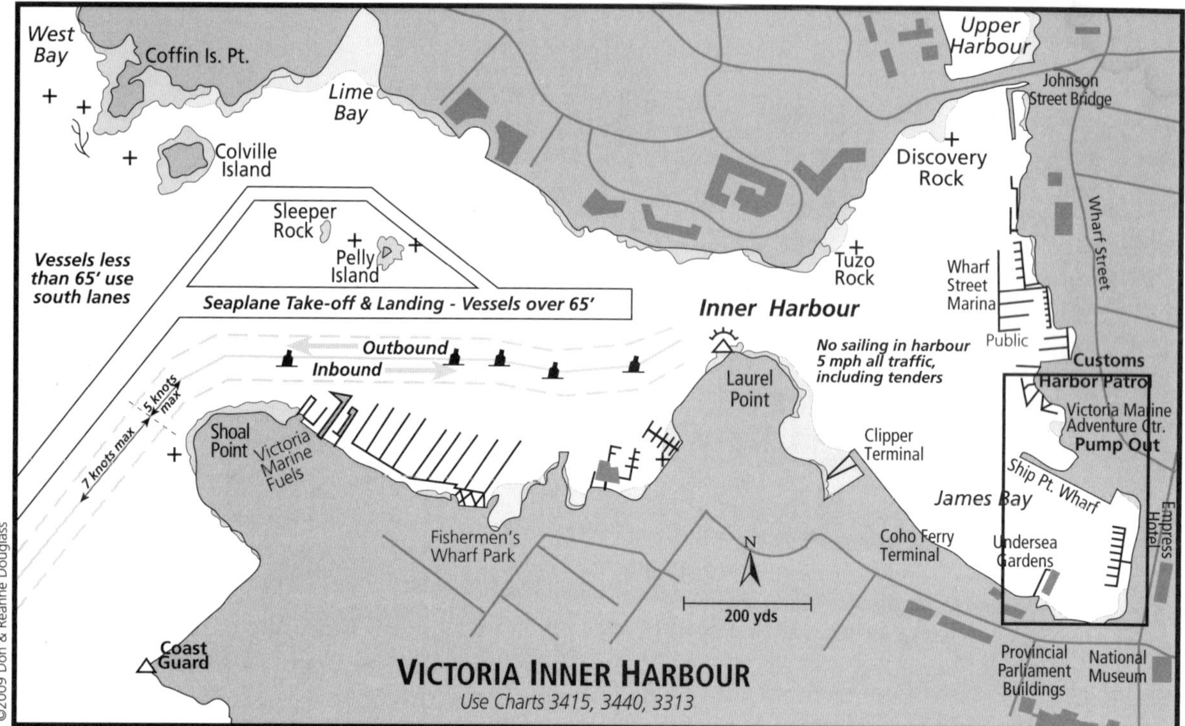

30 and August 31, when the fishing fleet is at sea, they are used by pleasure craft. (SD)

Fishermen's Wharf—the public floats just east of the fuel dock—may offer transient moorage for pleasure craft, depending on commercial fishing activities. The floats are usually quite crowded and rafting may be required. Power, water, and shower facilities are available. Call on VHF Channel 66A for space availability.

⚓ **Erie Street Government Wharf** tel: 250.383.8326 (Fishermen's Wharf); fax: 250-383-8306; monitors VHF Ch 66A; website: www.victoriaharbour.org; email: moorage@victoriaharbour.org; power; water; shower; overflow moorage only

⚓ **Coast Harbourside Hotel and Marina** tel: 250.360.1211; fax: 250.360.1418; full amenities with hotel facilities available to marina guests; reservations recommended; open year-round

⚓ **Victoria Marine Fuels** tel: 250.381.5221; this is the only fuel dock in the inner harbor; also carries food items, snacks and fishing supplies; open year-round

James Bay (Victoria Inner Harbour)

Charts 3415, 3440, 3313; 1.2 mi NE of the hbr entrance
Entrance: 48°25.40'N, 123°22.36'W
Causeway Floats (Empress Floats): 48°25.31'N, 123°22.17'W

James Bay, SE of Laurel Point, has the Provincial Parliament Buildings near its south end and the Empress Hotel near its east end. Ferry wharves

Passenger ferry, Victoria Inner Harbour

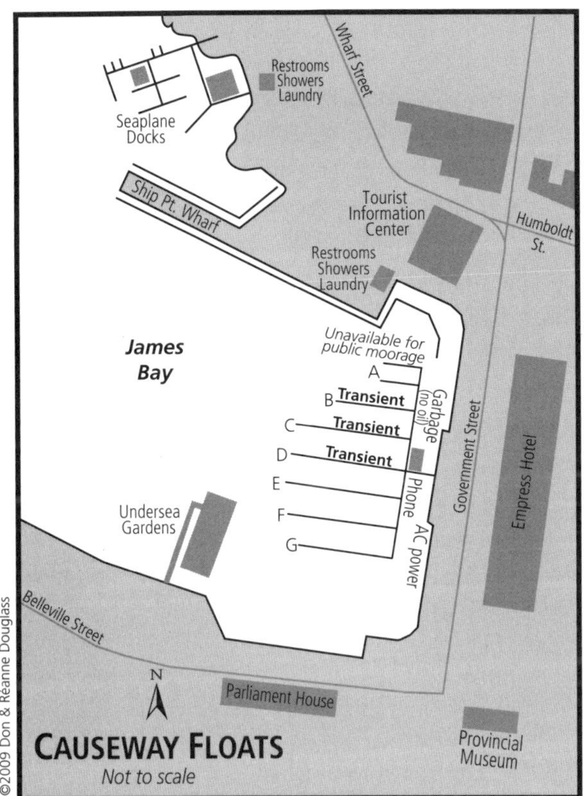

Wharf Street Government Public Floats

form the SW side of James Bay, NW of the Undersea Gardens. Public floats along the east side of James Bay provide facilities for pleasure craft. Ship Point wharf is on the north side of James Bay.

North of Ship Point wharf are small craft floats, a seaplane terminal, the Fisheries Protection wharf and the Customs wharf; a little farther north are public finger wharves with facilities for pleasure craft and seaplane floats. A public wharf is on the east side of the harbour, close south of the Johnson Street Bridge. (SD)

The public dock just below the Empress Hotel in James Bay is our favorite urban port of call, particularly in the winter when space is less restricted. Moorage in high-season is usually limited to two days. Water and power (20 amp) are available for vessels up to 57 feet; restrooms, showers, and laundry facilities are located below the InfoCentre on the lower quay. The facilities, which used to be open during summer season only, have been open year-round in recent years (with the exception of certain holidays).

Food provisions can be purchased at Thrifty Foods, 475 Simcoe, three blocks from the harbor; open seven days a week from 0800 to 2100 hours, the supermarket includes an in-house bakery and deli (tel: 250.544.1234). Thrifty charges a reasonable fee to deliver to your boat.

Although we leave it to you to scout out your own favorites among Victoria's many fine restaurants, shops, boutiques and art galleries, we list a few of our favorites. Murchies' for cappuccino, teas, coffees, sandwiches and pastries, is at 1110 Government Street. (We've been ordering their products for over twenty years!) Munro's Books, right next door, has a terrific selection of books on British Columbia, as does Crown Books at 521 Fort Street. Wells Book Group at 832 Fort Street has one of the best selections of used nautical books we've run across in the Northwest. The Provincial Museum across from the Parliament House is well worth a visit. And don't miss the

Victoria

Victoria – a vibrant, cosmopolitan city; a study in contrasts as old English charm mixes with contemporary world. You immediately feel the rhythm and the beat of this energizing Garden City of Canada – it buzzes with activity and the year-round mild climate in conducive to sight-seeing.

If you arrive from the States you must clear Customs in Victoria before docking. Docking at the government's Causeway Floats is a great place to be – a front seat on all the action and the action is plentiful. Be prepared to have other boats rafted to yours during busy summer season.

Whether by sea or air, this city is very accessible. With daily ferries and high-speed catamarans to mainland British Columbia and Washington State, the Victoria International Airport only half an hour from downtown, this is one port your guests can arrive or depart with ease. And there are those marvelous ubiquitous float planes that journey almost anywhere, anytime.

Stroll Government Street, overlooking the Causeway Floats, for a great panoramic view of the harbor. It is an audible and visual feast. Float planes, ferries, quaint water taxies, whale watching craft and private boats form the backdrop as musicians,, mimes and lively dancers entertain the audience on the waterfront promenade. In mid-summer the sidewalk teems with tourists snapping photos of the scenery and each other.

Anne Vipond

Victoria's Maritime Museum on Bastion Square

Just the other side of Government Street, where late model cars share space with horse-drawn carriages and red, double-decker sight-seeing busses, stands the regal Empress Hotel. While the hotel is renowned for its elegant Afternoon High Tea, you might opt to exchange the scones-crumpets-tarts and silver tea service of late afternoon for lunch in the Kipling room on the lower level. Whether you choose the buffet or order from Kipling's menu you will definitely enjoy and relax. Be sure to explore the hotel shops.

The Royal British Columbia Museum, with its unique and beautifully presented exhibits, is a short walk from the Empress. Plan to add a fantastic experience in their IMAX Theater. Suggestion: You may want to visit these fascinating places of discovery before lunch – a great way to build up an appetite.

Wander down Government Street, past book sellers, restaurants and gift shops to Bastion Square. Every boater should visit the Maritime Museum, housed in Victoria's first court house. Afterwards, meander leisurely through the arts and crafts booths in the Square flanking the museum. There's something for everyone.

Caution: on the way to Bastion Square you'll approach Murchie's Tea and coffee Ltd. Enter at your own risk. This bustling shop is best described in two words: taste sensations. You will be tempted by glorious quiches, scrumptious lasagnas, tantalizing sandwiches, and irresistible pastries. Try one of each. The food is exquisite. Here's a tip: bring a variety back to the boat. Eat and rejoice. Once you've tasted a Murchie's Opera Slice, you may decide to stay in Victoria another day. It's that good.

Prepare yourself for more things to see and do than time in which to do them. Victoria is one of the ports you'll put on the must return list.

Did you know...

Those colorful entertainers who perform in public places for donations are called buskers.

The folks who manage the docks and wharves are wharfingers.

There are 762 restaurants in Greater Victoria.

Canada comes from the Iroquois word Kanata, meaning village or settlement.

Coast Victoria Harbourside Hotel and Marina in the inner harbour is the only marina in Victoria that accepts docking reservations.

Each summer 950 lampposts in downtown Victoria are adorned with flower baskets.

Maritime Museum at 28 Bastion Square where you can see Captain Voss' Tilikum, John Guzzwell's *Trekka* owned by the Maritime Museum. The little sailboat has recently been reconditioned and occasionally participates in water events in the greater Victoria-Puget Sound area.

The Customs dock in Victoria is located just south of Wharf Street floats, at the end of James Bay. Have your ship's identification papers, and information on your crew available, to expedite clearance. Your clearance number must be displayed from a dockside port light or window.

⚓ **Victoria Harbour Authority Marina (office)** tel: 250.383.8326; fax: 250.383.8306; for moorage, call on VHF Ch 66A; website: victoriaharbour.org; restrooms; showers; laundry; up to 57-foot vessels; 2-day limit, if full; open year-round

⚓ **Victoria Harbour Master** tel: 250.363.3578

⚓ **Canadian Customs** tel: 888.226.7277

Peter Fromm

Glaucous-winged gull, a Vancouver Island resident

Wharf Street Marina (Victoria Inner Harbour)

Charts 3415, 3440, 3313; 0.2 mi NW of James Bay floats
Position: 48°25.48'N, 123°22.30'W
Customs dock: 48°25.46'N, 123°22.27'W

Public floats, close north of the Customs wharf, consist of a large T-shaped float with numerous finger floats extending from it. (SD)

The Wharf Street Marina provides convenient transient and long-term moorage for visiting pleasure boats. Showers, electricity, and garbage collection are available near the wharf (showers and laundry are closed during winter season). All amenities are within walking distance, and Bastion Square, the home of the B.C. Maritime Museum, lies just east of these floats.

⚓ **Wharf Street Marina** tel: 250.383.8326; fax: 250.383.8306; monitors VHF Ch 66A; website: www.victoriaharbour.org; email: moorage@victoriaharbour.org; power; water; shower; reservations recommended.

Broughton Street Customs Float (Victoria Inner Harbour)

Chart 3415; S of Wharf St Government Marina; N of the seaplane terminal
Position: 48°25.46'N, 123°22.27'W

The Broughton Street Float is reserved for vessels clearing Customs.

Johnson Street Bridge (Victoria Inner Harbour)

Charts 3415, 3440, 3313; 0.38 mi NW of James Bay public floats
Position: 48°25.68'N, 123°22.32'W
Position (Upper Hbr): 48°25.94'N, 123°22.4'W

Johnson Street Bridge, at the NE end of Inner Harbour consists of separate road and rail spans. It is manned 0800 to 1600 hours daily. It will not be opened except for an emergency between 0700 to 0900 hours and 1600 to 1800 hours on weekdays. Communication with the bridge is made on Channel 12, 156.6 MHz, call sign VAH20, telephone (250) 385-5711. Application

> *for bridge openings outside these hours must be made in advance. A fee is charged for this service. Give as much notice as possible through the City Fire Department telephone (250) 385-5711. The signal for opening the bridge is three blasts on a ships horn.* (SD)

The Johnson Street bascule bridge, which dates to 1925, is a vehicle and railroad bridge; it was designed by the same engineer who designed the Golden Gate and the Vancouver Gate bridges, dates to 1925. The bridge leads to Upper Harbour, Rock Bay, Selkirk Water, Gorge Water, Gorge Park, and Portage Inlet. Ebb currents under the bridge reach 2 knots. Upper Harbour is a busy industrial area. North of Upper Harbour, where the water becomes shallow and there are a number of bridges, the inlet is used for recreation only.

Ross Bay (Vancouver Island)

Charts 3424, 3440, 3313; 2 mi E of Ogden Pt breakwater
Position: 48°24.40′N, 123°20.60′W

> *Abandoned submarine cables cross the entrances to Ross Bay and Gonzales Bay.*
>
> *The flagstaff on Beacon Hill is prominent.* (SD)

Ross Bay, which has Clover Point to its west and Gonzales Bay to its east, is directly open to southeast weather. Between Ogden Point and Holland Point, on the south side of Beacon Hill, there is a nice walkway where you can watch colonies of seals playing in the water and hauling out on the rocks.

Gonzales Bay (Vancouver Island)

Charts 3424, 3440, 3313; W of Harling Pt; E of Ross Bay
Entrance (.075 mi NW of Templar Rock): 48°24.43′N, 123°19.79′W

The eastern part of tiny Gonzales Bay is filled with rocks. An observatory open to the public is located on Gonzales Hill, 0.2 mile northeast of the bay.

McNeill Bay (Vancouver Island)

Charts 3424, 3440, 3313; 0.9 mi NW of Trial I Light
Position: 48°24.63′N, 123°18.74′W

McNeill Bay is open to the full force of southerlies. The area immediately to the southeast, around the Trial Islands (an Ecological Reserve), has strong tide rips. While we don't recommend McNeill Bay for anchoring, kayaks can haul out on several beaches in the vicinity.

Enterprise Channel (Trial Islands)

Charts 3424, 3440, 3313; btwn Trial & Vancouver Is
Entrance (W): 48°24.19′N, 123°19.04′W
Center of narrows: 48°24.53′N, 123°18.43′W
Entrance (E): 48°24.36′N, 123°17.86′W

> *Enterprise Channel [is] locally known as Trial Island Pass...local knowledge is advised before attempting this channel. The fairway is tortuous and less than 0.1 mile wide in its narrowest part; tidal streams run at 3 kn and there is a considerable amount of kelp.*
>
> *Mouat Reef, which dries 0.9 m, lies on the north side of the east entrance and has a depth of 1.5 m about 0.1 mile SW of it. The reef is marked by south cardinal buoy "VE" and by kelp in summer and autumn.*
>
> *Brodie Rock is a pinnacle with 5.5 m over it rising from a ridge in 20 m of water.* (SD)

Enterprise Channel is a short passage on the north side of the Trial Islands along the Victoria shore. At spring tides, currents run up to 3 knots in Enterprise Channel; off the south end of Trial Islands, they run 6 knots or more. Whenever strong currents oppose local winds, the Trial Islands are known for turbulent waters and rough seas. Standing and breaking waves have been observed close to the Trial Islands.

Enterprise Channel is used by small craft and kayakers under favorable current and sea conditions.

Mayor Channel

Charts 3424, 3440, 3313; 0.6 mi NE of Gonzales Pt; the S entrance to Oak Bay
Entrance (S): 48°24.81′N, 123°17.00′W
Entrance (N, 0.20 mi E of Fiddle Reef): 48°25.78′N, 123°16.80′W

Mayor Channel...is the passage generally used by coastal vessels. It is entered south between Thames Shoal and the reefs extending south from Great Chain Island; the north entrance is between Lewis Reef and Fiddle Reef.

Tidal streams follow the fairway of Mayor Channel at 2 and 3 kn. The flood sets north and the ebb south.

Mouat Channel, on the west side of Mayor Channel, separates Thames Shoal from Lee Rock.

Chain Islets, a group of scattered rocks and islets on an extensive shoal, lie 1 mile NE of Gonzales Point.... Chain Islets and the surrounding area are an Ecological Reserve. (SD)

Mayor Channel, which lies to the west of Chain Islands and Oak Bay, leads eventually to Baynes Channel and then into Haro Strait.

Oak Bay (Vancouver Island)

Charts 3424, 3440, 3313; 0.87 mi NW of Gonzales Pt
Entrance (Mary Tod I Light): 48°25.55′N; 123°17.92′W
Marina: 48°25.55′N, 123°18.05′W

Oak Bay, to the west of Mayor Channel, has a large marina on its south side; it is entered between the breakwater at Turkey Head and the breakwater projecting south from Mary Tod Island.

Prohibited boating area, at the north end of Oak Bay fronting Willows Beach, is reserved for bathers and power boating is prohibited. (SD)

The preferred entrance to Oak Bay is on the south side of Mary Tod Island; the entrance northwest of Mary Tod Island is not recommended due to shallow depths. Cruising vessels from the Gulf and San Juan islands that want to avoid entering the Strait of Juan de Fuca can take moorage in Oak Bay; downtown Victoria is just a twenty-minute bus ride.

Oak Bay Marina, open year-round, has full facilities for pleasure boaters that include fuel, power, showers and laundry, a repair shop and a small chandlery. During summer season it's a good idea to phone ahead for availability of slips. The marina is within walking distance of Oak Bay Village and convenient bus service to downtown Victoria.

Willows Beach, 0.7 mile due north of the marina, has restricted boating.

⚓ **Oak Bay Marina** tel: 250.598.3369 or 800.663.7090 ext. 247; fax: 250.598.1361; monitors VHF Ch 66A; website: www.oakbaymarina.com; email: obmg@obmg.com; fuel; power; showers; laundry; repairs; launching ramps; restaurants; fishing supplies; a small chandlery; open year-round

Chatham Islands

Chart 3424; 1.2 mi NW of the Sea Bird Pt Lighthouse
Position (Puget Cove): 48°26.38′N, 123°14.66′W
Position (Alpha Islet Cove): 48°25.90′N, 123°13.83′W

Oak Bay

Oak Bay is one of Victoria's most established and exclusive neighborhoods, many of its turn-of-the-century mansions designed by the British architect Francis Rattenbury. When entering Oak Bay, visitors are said to be going "behind the Tweed Curtain," for the area's British traditions of cricket, golf and afternoon tea are as solid as the stately homes built on granite and volcanic bedrock.

The historic Oak Bay Beach Hotel is now under redevelopment to include private residences and vacation suites. The Marina Restaurant, overlooking the Oak Bay Marina, is another popular dining spot with views of Haro Strait, an elegant atmosphere, and featuring fresh seafood and a sushi bar. A few blocks inland, the local shops are located on Oak Bay Avenue. Lit with replica gas lanterns, this shopping district is reminiscent of an English village's high street, its Tudor-style buildings housing tea rooms and boutiques. **—AV**

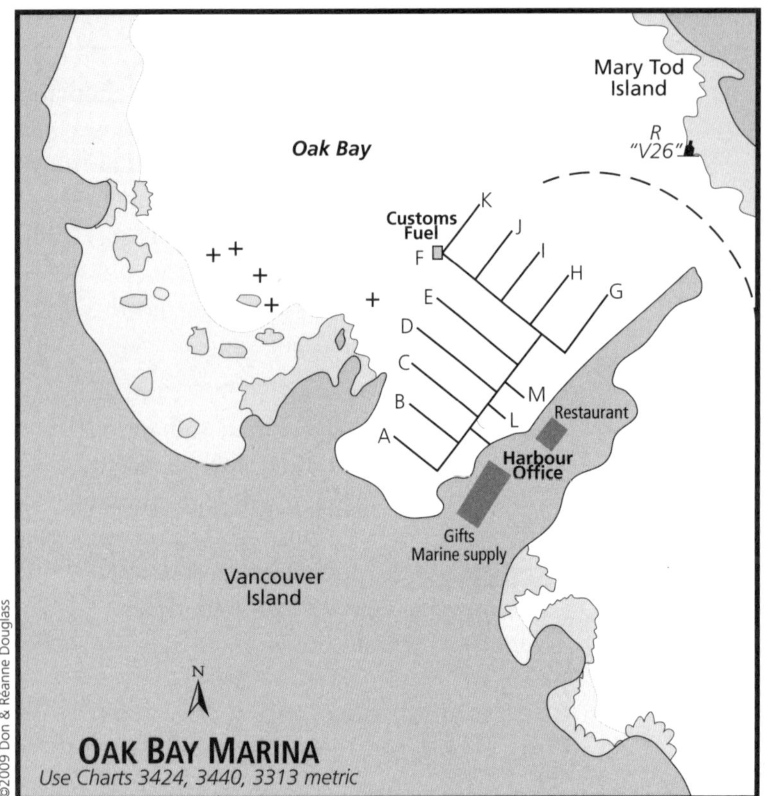

In settled weather, small craft can find temporary anchorage in Puget Cove in 1 to 2 fathoms in the northeast corner of the largest of the Chatham Islands; in Alpha Islet Cove between Discovery Island and Alpha Islet; at the west end of Alpha Islet Cove, due south of Griffin Island; or in a larger 6-meter hole south of Alpha Islet.

Chatham Islands, on the east side of Baynes Channel, are a compact group of islands and rocks. The islands are low, wooded and almost connected to one another at LW. Alpha Islet, Griffin Island and the surrounding area are an Ecological Reserve. (SD)

[Editor's note: Puget Cove is incorrectly located in SCG; its entrance is on the northeast part of the island.]

A favorite destination of kayakers and other small boaters, the Chain Islets and Chatham Islands lie at the convergence of Juan de Fuca and Haro straits. Due to the numerous rocks and reefs surrounding Chain Islets, Discovery Island, and Chatham Islands, the area is best explored by small boat. The Chathams, which are low-lying with grassy areas and arbutus trees, are Indian Reserves, as is the northern part of Discovery Island; please respect these reserves and do not go ashore. The southern part of Discovery Island is a Marine Park with shore access.

Discovery Island Provincial Marine Park, Rudlin Bay

(Strait of Juan de Fuca)

Charts 3424, 3440, 3313; 2.7 mi E of Oak Bay

Position: 48°25.15'N, 123°13.77'W

Discovery Island lies at the junction of Juan de Fuca and Haro Straits. The island is wooded and rises to 38 m at Pandora Hill. Discovery Island Provincial Marine Park consists of the south half of the island.

Heavy tide-rips, often dangerous to small craft, are formed in the vicinity of Discovery Island,

The schooner Trader *profits from good weather*

particularly near Sea Bird Point, and off the foul ground fronting Commodore Point. (SD)

Discovery Island Provincial Marine Park, the southern two-thirds of the island, is maintained in a relatively wild and natural condition with a few primitive campsites; fires are forbidden. The park is a good place from which to visit the rocky shores and reefs, home to many shore birds.

The bottom in Rudlin Bay and around the island is uneven with many rocks and reefs, some of which are marked by kelp in summer. Exposed to the south, the bay is not recommended as an overnight anchorage. Although there is no all-weather protection from winds that sometimes whip through the area, temporary anchorage in fair weather can be found 0.3 mile southwest of Seabird Point. For more protection from southwest winds, Alpha Islet Cove, on the north side of Discovery Island, may be a better choice. Be careful to avoid the turbulent waters off Sea Bird Point.

Anchor in the center of the bay, clear of the rocks in about 1 to 3 fathoms; irregular and rocky bottom with kelp.

⚓ **Discovery Island Provincial Marine Park**
toilets; picnic area; no fires; kayaking; camping; fishing; swimming; hiking; open year-round

Cadboro Bay, Royal Victoria Yacht Club (Vancouver Island)

Charts 3424, 3440, 3313; 1.1 mi W of Cadboro Pt
Entrance (Bay): 48°26.67'N, 123°17.01'W
Entrance (RVYC): 48°27.19'N, 123°17.66'W
Anchor: 48°27.37'N, 123°17.66'W

Cadboro Bay, though open to the SE, is not subject to heavy seas; tugs and rafts frequently shelter here. A rock breakwater on the west side of the bay, shelters the Royal Victoria Yacht Club. Cadboro Bay and its approach are often used for yacht races; various buoys and markers for these races are likely to be encountered. Several private mooring buoys are in the bay. (SD)

Cadboro Bay is a good place to anchor if you need to wait for fog to dissipate or an unfavorable current to change. There is ample room for anchoring north of the Royal Victoria Yacht Club. The yacht club itself has reciprocal moorage and Customs clearance.

Peter Fromm

Folk Song *in a calm Strait of Juan de Fuca*

Anchor in 3 fathoms over mud and sand; good holding.

⚓ **Royal Victoria Yacht Club**
tel: 250.592.2441; Customs clearance

Baynes Channel

Charts 3424, 3440, 3313; S of Cadboro Pt; N of the Chatham Is
Entrance (SW): 48°26.31'N, 123°16.00'W
Entrance (NW): 48°26.90'N, 123°15.22'W

Tidal streams set along the axis of Baynes Channel at 4 to 6 kn in the north entrance, between Strongtide Islet and Cadboro Point, and at 2 to 3 kn in its south entrance. The flood sets NE and the ebb SW. The winds can be very changeable in Baynes Channel. A strong wind opposing the tide will cause heavy tide-rips with short, steep seas. Due care should be taken in this area. (SD)

Baynes Channel is commonly used as a shortcut for boaters wishing to avoid a passage outside

Discovery Island. The waters in the channel can be turbulent and a wind shift is frequently experienced in the transition from Juan de Fuca Strait to Haro Strait.

Shortcutting through Baynes Channel

Maynard Cove (Vancouver Island)

Charts 3424, 3440, 3313; N of Cadboro Pt
Position: 48°27.11′N, 123°15.93′W

> *Submarine cables cross Baynes Channel from Maynard Cove to the Chatham Islands.* (SD)

Small craft should not anchor in tiny Maynard Cove because of a submarine cable.

Haro Strait

Charts 3440, 3313; btwn Vancouver & San Juan Is
Entrance (S, 2 mi E of Discovery I): 48°25.00′N, 123°10.00′W
Entrance (N): 48°41.63′N, 123°16.05′W

> *Haro Strait lies between Juan de Fuca Strait and Boundary Pass, encompassing the waters between San Juan Island and Vancouver Island. The southern limit is between Sea Bird Point (Discovery Island) and Cattle Point (San Juan Island).*
>
> *The main shipping route to Vancouver follows the Traffic Separation Scheme east of Discovery Island, thence through the portion of Haro Strait lying east of Sidney Island, thence through Boundary Pass entering the Strait of Georgia between East Point, on Saturna Island, and Alden Point, on Patos Island.*
>
> *Haro Strait and Boundary Pass are deep and for the most part wide. Great caution and vigilance are necessary because of reefs in some parts and the rate and varying directions of the tidal streams.*
>
> *A ferry crosses the north end of Haro Strait running between Sidney, B.C. and Anacortes, Washington. Charted ferry routes are general indications of the route followed by the ferry. The ferry can be encountered anywhere within the vicinity of the route shown.* (SD)

The Canada-U.S. border runs through Haro Strait, separating Vancouver Island from San Juan Island. Since Haro Strait is the main north-south shipping lane for large vessels, use caution when crossing this body of water, particularly in low visibility.

See *Sailing Directions* for gyre information and diagram.

Telegraph Cove (Vancouver Island)

Charts 3440, 3313; 0.84 mi N of Ten Mile Pt
Position: 48°27.98′N, 123°16.76′W

> *Telegraph Cove, Finnerty Cove and Arbutus Cove lie between Ten Mile Point and Gordon Head, 3 miles NNW.* (SD)

Telegraph Cove is a tiny cove with the above-mentioned rock in the center of its entrance.

Finnerty Cove (Vancouver Island)

Charts 3440, 3313; 0.87 mi NW of Telegraph Cove
Position: 48°28.44′N, 123°17.87′W

> *A submarine pipeline (sewer outfall), close south of Finnerty Cove, extends 0.2 mile offshore. Another pipeline is laid in the south part of Finnerty Cove.* (SD)

Temporary anchorage with marginal protection can be found in fair weather in tiny Finnerty and Arbutus coves.

Arbutus Cove (Vancouver Island)

Charts 3440, 3313; 1.4 mi S of Gordon Head; 0.25 mi N of Finnerty Cove
Position: 48°27.68′N, 123°18.03′W

Arbutus Cove is shallow and exposed to southeast weather.

Margaret Bay (Vancouver Island)

Charts 3440, 3313; S end of Cordova Bay; W of Cormorant Pt
Entrance: 48°30.01′N, 123°18.58′W
Anchor: 48°29.83′N, 123°18.69′W

> *Cormorant Point is 0.3 mile west of Gordon Head. Gordon Rock, 0.15 mile north of Gordon Head, dries 1.5 m.* (SD)

Margaret Bay has easy access to Haro Strait in case you need to wait for fog to lift. Anchorage can be found 0.15 mile west of Gordon Rock. Avoid kelp patches, the charted Gordon Rock, and the foul east end of the bay.

Anchor in 1 to 2 fathoms.

Cordova Bay (Vancouver Island)

Charts 3440, 3313; 5 mi NW of Ten Mile Pt; 2.5 mi SE of Cowichan Head
Entrance: 48°30.21′N, 123°19.28′W
Anchor: 48°29.77′N, 123°19.12′W

> *Anchorage can be obtained in the south part of Cordova Bay, about 1 mile NNW of Gordon Head. The holding ground is good and depths are 15 to 16 m.*
>
> *A torpedo firing area is located in the north end of Cordova Bay and extends north to Cordova Spit.* (SD)

Cordova Bay is a large bight which, at its southeast end inside Cormorant Point, is fairly well sheltered from westerlies as well as southerlies. If you happen to get caught in this vicinity in fog and your experience using radar is not strong, this is a good place to head for shelter. Anchorage can be found 0.25 mile southwest of Cormorant Point. Avoid the kelp beds near shore. During settled weather, the sand and gravel beach affords good access.

Mount Douglas Park, on the south shore of Cordova Bay, is named for the first governor of the colony of Vancouver Island. Mount Douglas (740 feet) has trails and good views of the San Juan Islands to the east, Victoria to the south, and the Gulf Islands to the north.

Anchor in 2 fathoms over sand; fair-to-good holding.

Zero Rock

Charts 3440, 3313; 2.5 mi E of Cordova Bay
Position (half-way btwn Zero & Little Zero rocks): 48°31.59′N, 123°18.11′W

> *Zero Rock, 1.8 miles NNE of Gordon Head, dries 3 m; it lies in the south approach to Cordova and Sidney Channels. Shoal pinnacles and a rock with less than 2 m over it lie within 0.5 mile north of Zero Rock.*
>
> *Little Zero Rock, 1 mile WNW of Zero Rock, dries 2.4 m and is steep-to on its east side. Shoal pinnacles and a rock with less than 2 m over it extend 0.6 mile WNW from Little Zero Rock.* (SD)

When heading north from Victoria toward Sidney, avoid the complex of rocks and reefs off

Peter Fromm

Checking out favorite places

Peter Fromm

Pride in seamanship: a Flemish coil dock line

Cordova Bay in the vicinity of Zero Rock and Little Zero Rock.

D'Arcy Island Marine Park (Sidney Ch)

Charts 3441, 3313; 1 mi SE of Sidney I
Anchor (W side): 48°33.80'N, 123°17.00'W

> *D'Arcy Island is wooded and D'Arcy Island Marine Park is undeveloped. Mooring buoys lie off the north end of the island.* (SD)

D'Arcy Island was a leper colony from the late 1800s to 1925. A Marine Park since 1961, the island is now one of about a dozen South Coast marine parks included in the Gulf Islands National Park Reserve, established in 2004. The wooded island has no overnight shelter and the undeveloped park has a few walk-in campsites. Numerous rocks and shoals (many of which are marked by kelp in summer) surround the island creating an irregular bottom. To explore by dinghy or kayak, you can anchor temporarily in the southwest bight if the weather is fair and stable. Some small craft can anchor in stable weather on the east side of D'Arcy Island; however, the entrance is narrow and the bottom is rocky and uneven. A mooring buoy on the east side of D'Arcy Island is reserved for Park authorities. Note that Little D'Arcy Island, off the northeast of D'Arcy Island is private. Anchor in 2 to 5 fathoms over a rocky bottom with poor holding.

⚓ **D'Arcy Marine Park** toilets; camping; picnic area; hiking; kayaking; fishing; open year-round

Hughes Passage

Charts 3441, 3313; btwn Sidney & D'Arcy I
Entrance (E): 48°34.88'N, 123°15.93'W
Entrance (W): 48°34.55'N, 123°17.93'W

> *Hughes Passage separates D'Arcy Island from Sidney Island to the north and leads west from the main shipping channel of Haro Strait into Sidney Channel. On its south side, it is encumbered with drying and above-water rocks extending 0.3 mile north from D'Arcy and Little D'Arcy Islands.* (SD)

Hughes Passage, 2 miles due west of the south entrance to Mosquito Pass on San Juan Island, is used by many boats headed for Port Sidney. Small craft may find temporary anchorage in fair weather close to shore on either side of Hughes Passage, avoiding the rocks and reefs.

Cordova Channel

Charts 3441, 3313; btwn Vancouver & James Is
Entrance (S): 48°35.10'N, 123°21.49'W
Entrance (N): 48°37.00'N, 123°23.14'W

> *Cordova Channel separates James Island from Saanich Peninsula.*
>
> *Tidal streams in Cordova Channel are weak with a variable rate and direction.* (SD)

In southeast weather, with an option of good anchorage in Saanichton Bay, Cordova Channel offers slightly more protection than Sidney Channel.

Saanichton Bay (Vancouver Island)

Charts 3441, 3313; 3.3 mi S of Sidney Hbr
Entrance: 48°36.00'N, 123°22.81'W
Anchor: 48°35.70'N, 123°22.80'W

> *Saanichton Bay, entered between Cordova Spit and Turgoose Point, affords anchorage open to SE winds. Tidal streams are not significant. The south side of the bay and the south end of Cordova Spit is an Indian Reserve.*

Private mooring buoys are in Saanichton Bay. The charted buoys are for securing logbooms. (SD)

Saanichton Bay affords good shelter from southeast winds and currents in Cordova and Sidney channels. Anchorage can be found 0.4 mile southwest of Cordova Spit, avoiding private buoys.

Anchor in about 4 fathoms over sand, mud and gravel with good holding.

Ferguson Cove (Vancouver Island)

Charts 3441, 3313; 0.8 mi NW of Cordova Spit
Position: 48°36.08'N, 123°23.45'W

Ferguson Cove is a cable crossing area. There is a small public dock on the south side of the cove at Turgoose Point.

Cordova Channel

Bazan Bay (Vancouver Island)

Charts 3441, 3313; 0.8 mi SW of the Washington State ferry dock at Sidney
Position: 48°37.83'N, 123°24.31'W

...two submarine pipelines extend 0.9 mile offshore at Bazan Bay. (SD)

Bazan Bay is a shallow, open bight useful as a temporary anchorage in settled weather only.

Sidney Channel

Charts 3441, 3313; btwn James & Sidney Is
Entrance (S): 48°34.91'N, 123°18.68'W
Entrance (N): 48°37.75'N, 123°21.42'W

Sidney Channel is entered from the south between James Spit and D'Arcy Island; its north entrance is between the north extremities of James and Sidney Islands. (SD)

Strong ebb currents, as well as choppy waters, may be experienced in Sidney Channel when a southeast wind is blowing.

Sidney Spit Marine Park (Sidney Island)

Charts 3441, 3479, 3313; 2.3 mi SE of Sidney Hbr breakwater
Entrance: 48°38.47'N, 123°20.87'W
Float: 48°38.50'N, 123°19.93'W
Anchor: 48°38.58'N, 123°20.16'W

Sidney Spit ...extends about 1 mile north from Sidney Island. Sidney Spit Marine Park has picnic and camping facilities. Mooring buoys and a landing float for small pleasure craft are on the west side of the spit. (SD)

Sidney Spit Marine Park is located on a low, sandy spit about a mile long with a sand, grass and gravel beach. Douglas fir and arbutus grow at its grassy south end. The bottom is shallow and flat over a large area. In summer, you may be able to pick up one of the mooring buoys or tie to a small-craft landing float. The park is open all year, but in winter, with the passage of fronts, strong northwest winds can create an uncomfortable chop. A hiking trail loops around the park and out to the north end of the spit. You can easily land a dinghy inside the spit, comb the outer beach for driftwood, or check out the ruins of an early 1900s' brick factory near the saltwater lagoon on the south side of the park. The park's excellent facilities include picnic table, toilets, campsites and play areas. The area outside the Park boundary to the south, is privately owned.

Anchorage can be found on the west side of Sidney Spit in a small 3-fathom hole northwest of the seasonal dinghy float, or farther west in the channel between the two shoal areas extending south from Sidney Spit light.

Anchor in 2 to 3 fathoms over sand; good holding.

⚓ **Sidney Spit Marine Park** has picnic area; toilets; play area; open year-round

Anne Vipond

Sidney Spit Marine Park

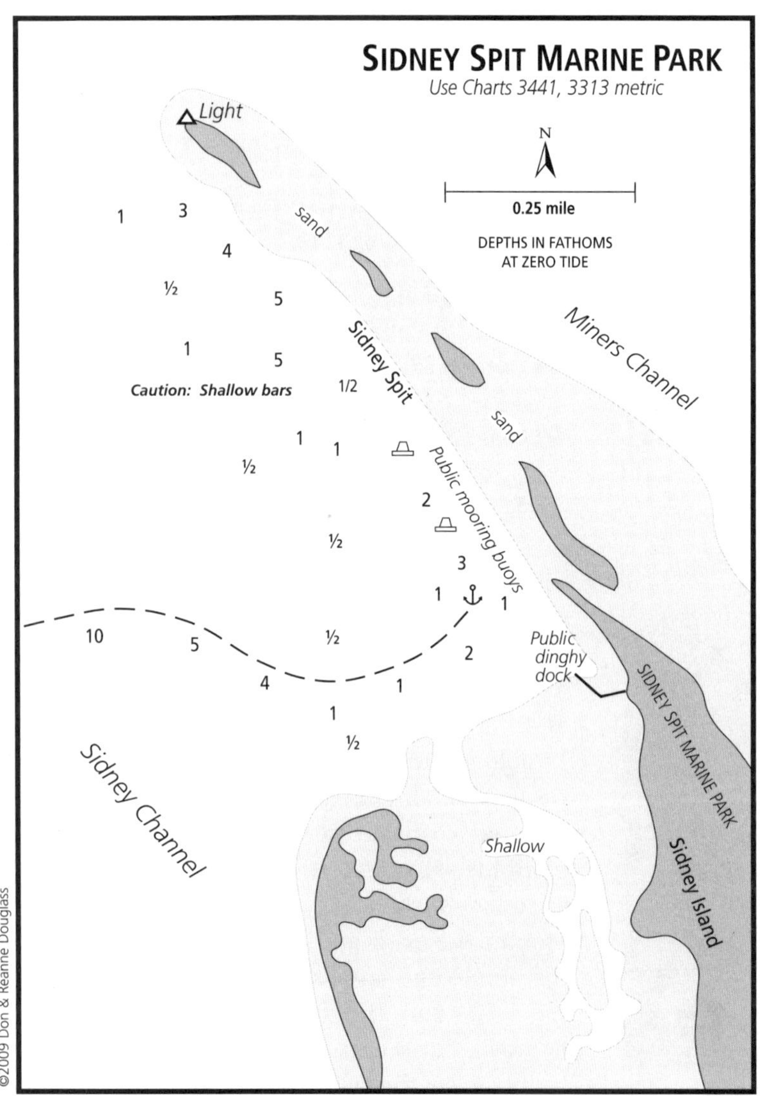

Isle-de-Lis Marine Park (Rum Island)

Charts 3441, 3313; 2.8 mi NE of Sidney Spit
Anchor: 48°39.83'N, 123°16.85'W

Isle-de-Lis Marine Park encompasses Rum Island. (SD)

Undeveloped Isle-de-Lis Marine Park makes a good picnic stop in fair weather. Temporary anchorage can be found along the steep-to shoreline in about 5 fathoms.

⚓ **Isle-de-Lis Marine Park** has pit toilet; picnic area; camping; hiking trails; kayaking; open year-round

Sidney (Vancouver Island)

Charts 3476, 3479, 3441, 3313; 2.3 mi S of the Swartz Bay ferry terminal; 14 mi N of Victoria
Entrance (0.067 mi N of Buoy G"U5"): 48°38.89'N, 123°23.31'W
Public pier: 48°38.96'N, 123°23.56'W
Anchorage (temporary): 48°39.02'N, 123°23.54'W
Breakwater light to Port Sidney: 48°39.15'N, 123°23.52'W

Sidney...is the terminal of the Washington State Ferry that runs to Anacortes. The Victoria International Airport is close west of the town site.

A rock breakwater extending 250 m north from close north of the

public wharf and a second rock breakwater extending south from drying ledges 0.3 mile north of the public wharf, protect a marina. The entrance between the breakwaters is about 30 m wide with two private buoys used for traffic separation and there are depths of about 2 m alongside the floats.

The Washington State Ferry landing is 0.4 mile south of the public wharf. (SD)

Sidney, whose origins date back to the late nineteenth century, has become a major seaside resort. The public pier is used by commercial fishing boats only; there is no sheltered anchorage at Sidney, except for temporary anchorage just north of the public pier in 1 to 3 fathoms as noted in the Sidney Harbour diagram.

Located behind the rock breakwater, Port Sidney Marina is the lovely, large marina entered between green buoy "U5" and red buoy "U6." Reefs that extend between the north breakwater and shore are not visible at high tides, so do not attempt to enter from the north in anything larger than a kayak. You can clear Customs by phone from the outer dock; there is a fee for overnight moorage and facilities are excellent.

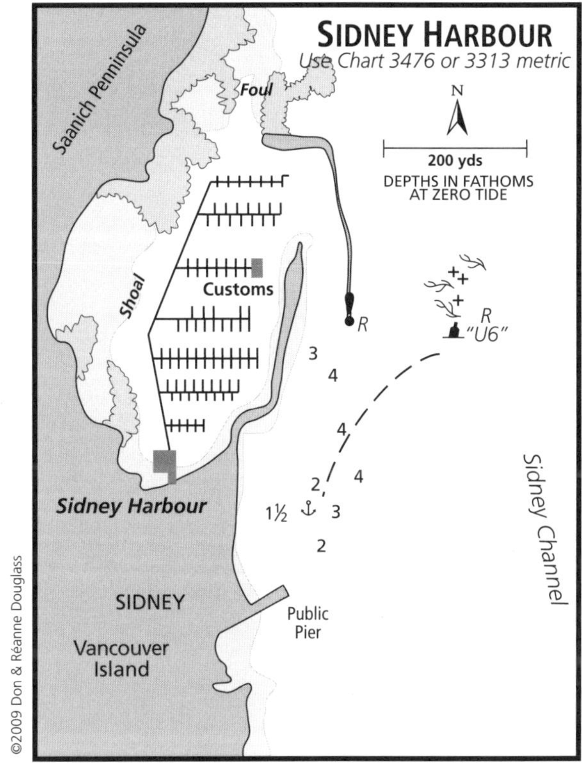

The town of 11,000, just a few blocks from the marina, has full services with many fine stores, chandleries, restaurants, bakeries, and two full-service groceries. There are

Sidney Spit

Sidney Island is part of an interesting collection of small islands strung along Haro Strait. Some are privately owned, others are marine parks, and their shorelines range from rocky bluffs to sandy beaches. Worth millions of dollars in today's recreational real estate market, these islands were not always so highly prized. Back in 1860, when the Hudson's Bay Company held an auction in Victoria for lots on Sidney Island, there were few takers and, as recounted in Walbran's ***British Columbia Coast Names,*** one skeptical settler remarked that "he would not give six-pence an acre let alone six shillings."

Sidney Island has since become the "Pearl of the Gulf Islands," enjoyed each summer by hundreds of boaters and by visitors from Sidney who arrive by passenger ferry. A long spit of soft sand extends from the island's northern tip where a marine park with on-shore trails, picnic facilities and campsites is located.

The sandy beaches of Sidney Island and neighboring James Island are drift deposits left behind by retreating glaciers some 10,000 years ago. These land forms of ground-up sand, gravel and clay are subject to erosion with coastlines that are shallow and constantly shifting, but they provide beautiful beaches such as the one at Sidney Spit which is ideal for sunbathing and swimming in the warm water.

In the early 1900s, before Sidney Island became a vacation playground, the island's clay was scraped from the ground and turned into bricks at a local mill, its ruins located in the meadow that borders a saltwater lagoon at the south end of the park. The rest of Sidney Island is in private hands, as is James Island where an explosives plant once operated. Currently owned by a Seattle billionaire, James Island has become a multi-million-dollar retreat with sandy beaches, a golf course and other amenities. **—AV**

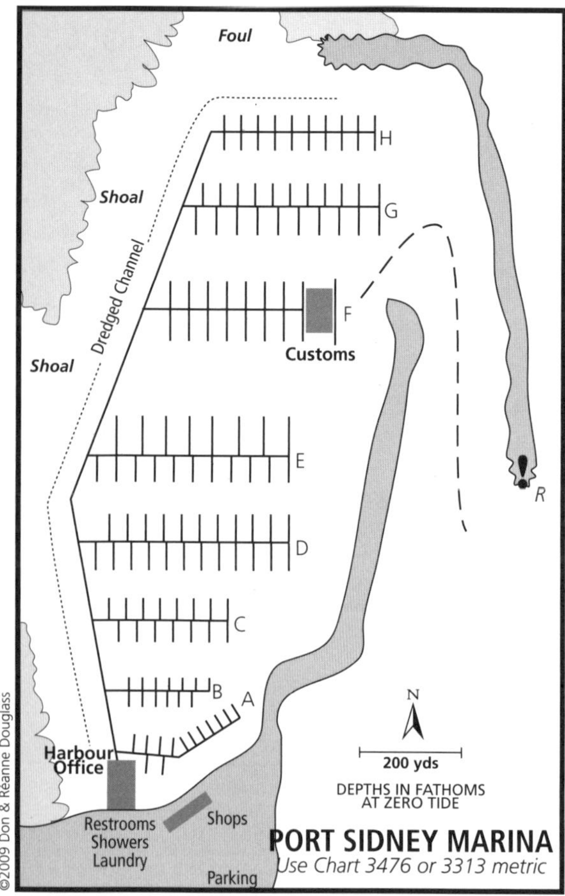

several stores with marine products in town including West Marine. Tanner's Bookstore, on Beacon Street, has a good selection of books and charts. Boaters Exchange at 2426 Buran (250.655.3101) is a "museum" of second hand marine equipment.

⚓ **Port Sidney Marina**
tel: 250.655.3711;
fax: 250.655.3771; monitors VHF Ch 66A; website: www.portsidney.com; power; water; toilets; showers; laundry; pumpout; Customs clearance

Roberts Bay (Vancouver Island)

Charts 3476, 3441, 3313; 0.75 mi N of Sidney Marina
Entrance: 48°40.02′N, 123°23.64′W
Anchor: 48°39.86′N, 123°23.87′W

Graham Rock lies off the entrance to Roberts Bay and on the south side of the approach to Tsehum Harbour. (SD)

If you need to wait for proper tide or current conditions in the area, shallow Roberts Bay, bordered by lovely homes, offers temporary anchorage. *Caution:* Avoid Graham Rock at the entrance and drying mud flats and shoals inside the 1-fathom curve.

Anchor in 2 fathoms over mud and sand with good holding.

Tsehum Harbour (Vancouver Island)

Charts 3476, 3441, 3313; 1.25 mi NW of Sidney Marina
Entrance (Outer): 48°40.25′N, 123°23.85′W
Entrance (0.04 mi NE of Thumb Pt bkw light): 48°40.29′N, 123°24.24′W
Anchor: 48°40.32′N, 123°24.78′W

Tsehum Harbour...is entered between Armstrong Point and Curteis Point. Several marinas are in the harbour and it is used extensively by pleasure craft. The channel into the harbour and to the marinas is well marked by lights, daybeacons and buoys.

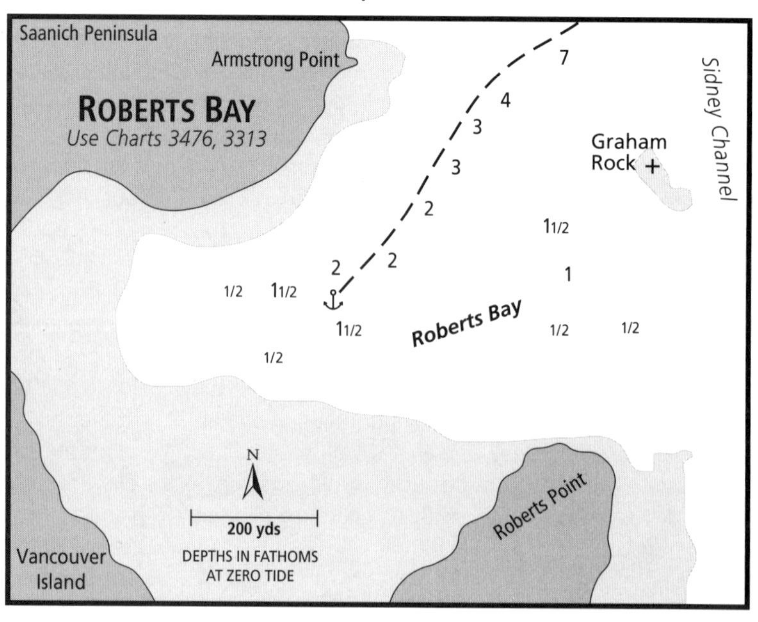

Shoals extend 0.25 mile ESE from Curteis Point. The north shore of Tsehum Harbour, between Curteis Point and Kingfisher Point, is fringed by drying and below-water rocks. (SD)

Tsehum (pronounced "see-'em" from the Cowichan word for "clay") Harbour, an inlet known locally as Shoal Harbour for its shallow depths, has a number of public and private marinas and yacht clubs from south to north the marinas that cater to small craft are Van Isle Marina, North Saanich Marina, and Westport Marina. Several other private marinas and a Royal Victoria YC outstation are located within the harbour.

Anchorage can be found 0.1 mile southeast of Mill Point in the west end of Tsehum Harbour avoiding the rocky shoals.

Anchor in about 1 fathom over mud; good holding.

Van Isle Marina (Vancouver Island)

Charts 3476, 3441, 3313; S shore of Tsehum Hbr; inside the breakwater
Fuel dock: 48°40.25'N, 123°24.41'W

Van Isle Marina is one of the largest and most popular on Vancouver Island for permanent moorage, as well as transient. In addition to the full amenities that include water, power, laundry, showers, fuel, Internet access, launch ramps, pump out and Philbrooks repair facilities, the site is home to two excellent restaurants —Dock 503 and Blue Peter Pub. Because of its popularity the marina advises that you call ahead for reservations. Van Isle has Customs clearance dock on the float west of the fuel dock at the north end of the marina.

⚓ **Van Isle Marina** tel: 250.656.1138; fax: 250.656.0182; monitors VHF Ch 66A; website: www.vanislemarina.com; Customs

---

Sidney

Sidney-by-the-Sea swings in summer with musical concerts at the Centennial Bandstand, parades and festivities on Sidney Days, the Summer Market and a host of other special town events throughout the year. It's a place with big city amenities and small town hospitality and pace.

The Port Sidney Marina is as good as it gets – clear in at the Customs dock first. Then enjoy the marina's fine facilities, wide concrete docks festive with hanging flower baskets and a staff that is friendly and accommodating. Everything shines. And the bonus is a pleasant and easy walk to the downtown business district.

Take a leisurely stroll along Beacon Street lined with a variety of gift shops, restaurants, bakeries, art galleries, grocery and liquor stores – there's even a barber shop on this main street. Safeway is at the far end of town.

It doesn't take long to discover why Sidney is also known as "Booktown" – the town abounds in bookstores with a wide range of specialties, from nautical to mystery, rare to mundane, new to used. Whether you are simply a browsing booklover or a serious collector you'll find friendly and helpful booksellers eager to assist you.

Intersperse your explorations and discoveries with time-out for rest and relaxation. You may find it difficult to escape being drawn into the bakeries.

A must visit: Lunn's Pastries, Deli and Coffee Shop. Say hello to Robert Lunn, enthusiastic third generation Baker and Confectioner who takes great pride in the family business. The moment you enter the shop your olfactory and visual senses are held hostage. Whether it be their rich chocolates, heavenly cakes or scrumptious pies, resign your self to the simple fact that making a decision is problematic. Solution: indulge. Try on e of each dessert - a Vanilla Slice puff pastry, butter or jam tart or perhaps Apricot pie, chock-full of fruit. Lunn's serves delicious home-made soups, sandwiches and savory-meat-pie lunches.

Did you know…

Clearing Customs is easier with a CANPASS. You can call 1-888-CANPASS for an updated list of reporting stations. Check it out.

The free limit is one bottle of wine (1.5 litres), or one bottle of liquor (1.14 litres), or 24 cans of beer or ale (8.5 litres) per person meeting age requirements. If you bring more liquor into Canada than the free allowance of alcohol you will have to pay both customs and the provincial or territorial assessments.

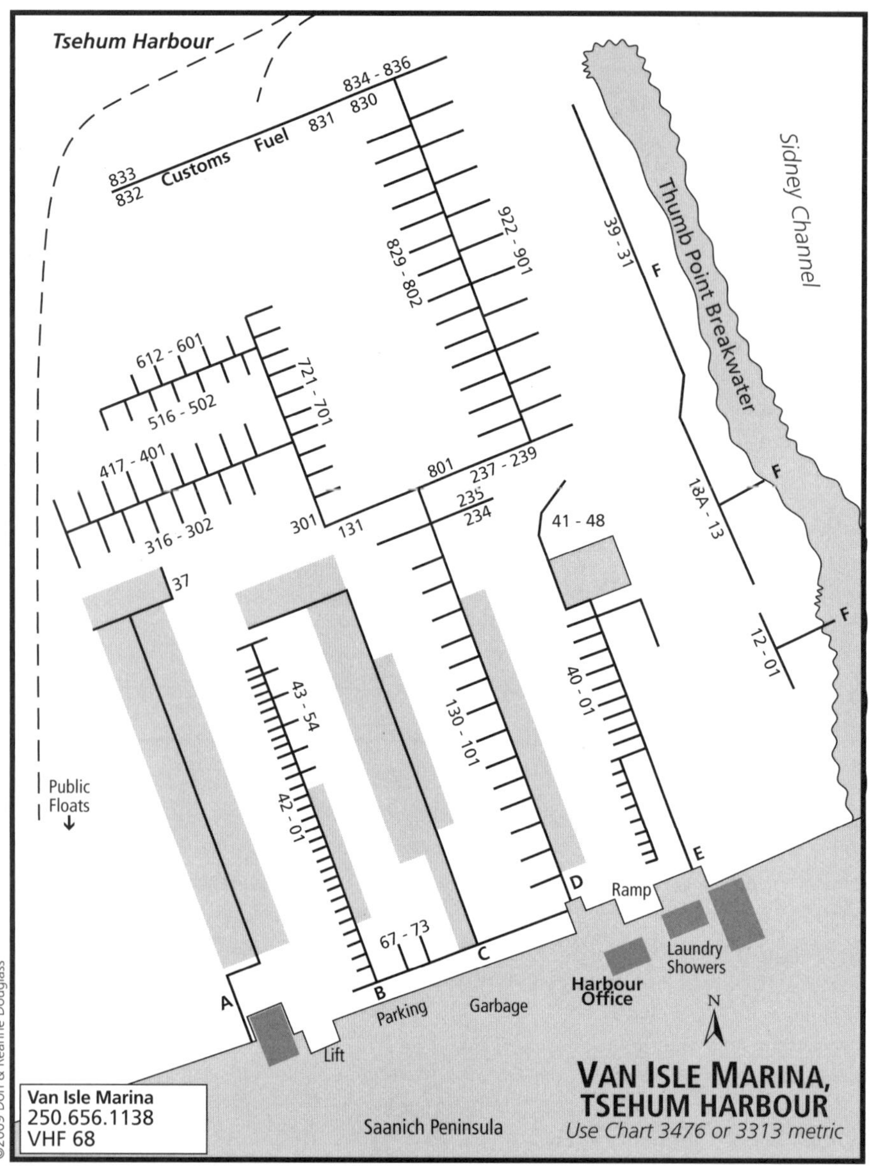

dock; reservations advised

⚓ **Philbrooks Ltd.**
tel: 250.656.1157;
fax: 250.656.1155;
website: www.philbrooks.com;
full-service boatyard

Tsehum Harbour Authority Wharf

(All Bay Public Floats)
Charts 3476, 3441, 3313;
SW of Van Isle Marina
Entrance: 48°40.23'N, 123°24.48'W
Floats: 48°40.10'N, 123°24.47'W

Customs clearance for pleasure craft can be obtained at the customs float in All Bay.

All Bay is on the south side of Tsehum Harbour, west of Thumb Point.

The public wharf, in All Bay, has two wharfheads and three floats with depths of 2.4 m alongside.

Diesel fuel, gasoline, fresh water and provisions can be obtained from the various marinas.

Repairs to hull and engine can be carried out by several boatyards. (SD)

Shoreside at Tsehum Harbour

The public wharf in Tsehum Harbour is essentially used by commercial vessels. Phone ahead for the possibility of pleasure craft moorage in July and August. Water, power, and phones are available; showers are located nearby.

⚓ **Tsehum Harbour Authority Wharf**
tel: 250.655.4496

Anne Vipond

Boathouses in Tsehum Harbour

Blue Heron Basin (Tsehum Harbour)

Charts 3476, 3441, 3313; W of Mile II Pt
Entrance: 48°40.40'N, 123°24.84'W

Blue Heron Basin is at the west end of Tsehum Harbour. (SD)

The marina complex at the north side of Blue Heron Basin is known as North Saanich Marina, Blue Heron Bay, south section.

North Saanich Marina (Tsehum Harbour)

Charts 3476, 3441, 3313; 0.15 mi NW of Kingfisher Pt
Entrance: 48°40.42'N, 123°24.74'W
Fuel dock: 48°40.55'N, 123°24.79'W

North Saanich Marina, with primarily permanent moorage, has a fuel dock with gasoline and diesel and a small store. Phone ahead to inquire about overnight moorage. The entrance to the marina is narrow and intricate, requiring close attention to the buoys and any opposing traffic.

⚓ **North Saanich Marina** tel: 250.656.5558; fax: 250.656.1574; primarily permanent moorage; fuel; open year round

Bryden Bay (Tsehum Harbour)

Charts 3476, 3441, 3313; 0.13 mi E of Kingfisher Pt
Position: 48°40.47'N, 123°24.43'W

Bryden Bay, located on the north side of Tsehum Harbour, is foul. It has a very shallow irregular bottom with many rocks and reefs, some of which are marked by kelp.

Page Passage

Charts 3476, 3441, 3313; btwn Fernie I & Harlock Islet; S of Iroquois Passage
Entrance (S): 48°40.61'N, 123°23.67'W
Entrance (N): 48°40.94'N, 123°23.76'W

Page Passage is entered from the south between Curteis Point and Kamaree Point. Fernie Island and Johnson Islet are on the east side of the passage and Kolb Island, with Harlock Islet close SE, form its west side. Rose Rock lies in mid-channel, at the north end of Page Passage. Three rocks, two with less than 2 m over them and one that dries 0.2 m, lie in or near mid-channel; the north rock is marked by port hand buoy "U7."

A speed limit of 8 km/h (4 kn) is prescribed. (SD)

Tsehum Harbour

This marina-packed harbor is the boating hub of the southern Gulf Islands with its numerous sailing schools, charter operators and boat yards. Van Isle Marina provides guest moorage (and Customs clearance) and on shore is a coffee shop. Waterfront dining can be enjoyed next door at the Blue Peter Pub & Restaurant where guest moorage is usually available right in front of the restaurant. A short walk down Harbour Road toward Armstrong Point will take you to the Latch Restaurant, a timbered building with a huge stone fireplace set among manicured gardens. It was built in 1920 as a summer retreat for a former Lieutenant-Governor and is now a restaurant open daily for dinner and lunch on Sundays.

Curteis Point marks the north entrance to Tsehum Harbour and it was there that Muriel Wylie Blanchett, author of ***The Curve of Time,*** lived with her children on seven wooded acres when they weren't exploring the coast in their cabin cruiser during the summers of the 1930s. Directly north is Canoe Bay (locally known as Canoe Cove), a good spot to tie up when meeting passengers arriving by ferry at Swartz Bay. The marina facilities here are excellent for doing maintenance or repairs, and just up the hill on the edge of the forest is the Stonehouse Pub where you can enjoy lunch, dinner or snacks with your pint of beer.

—AV

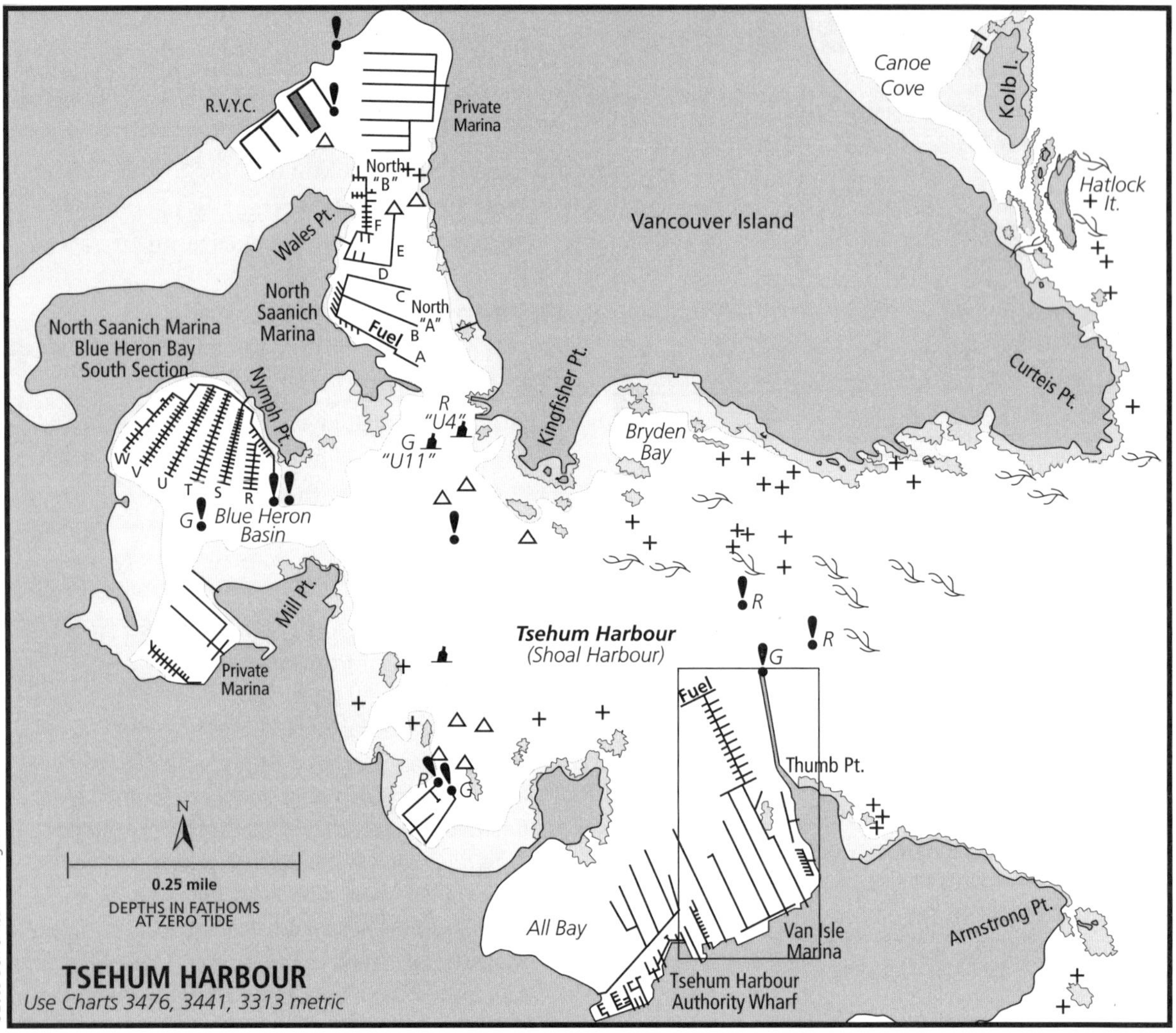

TSEHUM HARBOUR
Use Charts 3476, 3441, 3313 metric

R.V.Y.C.
Private Marina
North "B"
Wales Pt.
North Saanich Marina
North Saanich Marina Blue Heron Bay South Section
Fuel
North "A"
Nymph Pt.
Blue Heron Basin
"U4"
"U11"
Kingfisher Pt.
Vancouver Island
Canoe Cove
Kolb I.
Hatlock It.
Curteis Pt.
Bryden Bay
Mill Pt.
Private Marina
Tsehum Harbour (Shoal Harbour)
Thumb Pt.
All Bay
Van Isle Marina
Tsehum Harbour Authority Wharf
Armstrong Pt.
0.25 mile
DEPTHS IN FATHOMS AT ZERO TIDE

Anne Vipond

Canoe Cove Marina

Page Passage is frequently used by small boats headed for Canoe Bay. The passage is narrow and has several shoals; caution is advised due to strong currents. Refer to Chart 3476. Vessels headed for Colburne Passage can use the less intricate John Passage 0.4 mile to the northeast.

A small canoe passage west of Harlock Islet should be used only by kayaks and canoes; it is clogged with rocks and reefs, and its shallow waters are subject to strong currents and turbulent water.

Canoe Cove (Vancouver Island)

Charts 3476, 3479, 3441, 3313; 0.4 mi SE of Swartz Bay; 0.7 mi NE of Tsehum Hbr
Entrance (from Iroquois Passage): 48°40.98′N, 123°23.82′W
Outer float: 48°40.95′N, 123°24.03′W
Anchor: 48°40.91′N, 123°24.04′W

> *Canoe Bay, locally known as Canoe Cove, is approached between Kolb Island and Musclow Islet. Numerous drying and below-water rocks lie north and west of Musclow Islet.*
>
> *Customs clearance for pleasure craft can be obtained at the float at the east end of the marina....*
>
> *A private daybeacon is in the north part of Canoe Bay.*
>
> *Marina facilities in Canoe Bay afford extensive berthing for small craft. Repairs and supplies are obtainable.* (SD)

Well-sheltered Canoe Cove can be entered from either Iroquois Passage on the east or Page Passage on the south. Both have a number of unmarked rocks and shoals and reference should be made to the large-scale Charts 3313, page 7, or 3476 (both 1:10,000) [3479]. During spring tides swift currents are encountered in the area. Since the cove is small, turning room is limited and a sharp lookout is advised.

Canoe Cove Marina has full services with

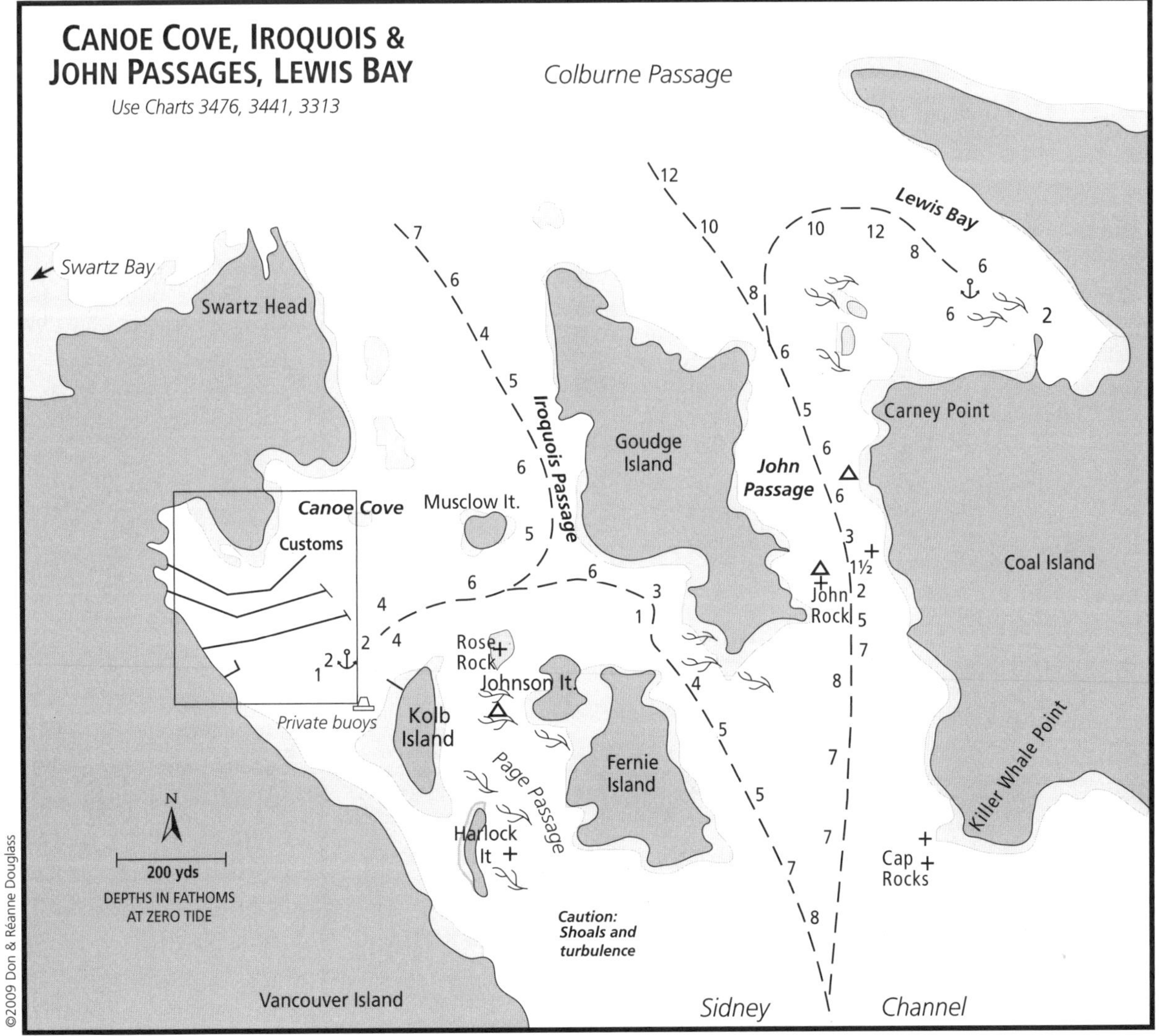

repair facilities and 24-hour Customs check-in by telephone. Limited transient moorage is on a space available basis and they will make every effort to fit you in with adequate notice. From here, it's a half-mile walk to Swartz Bay ferry terminal. You can find temporary anchorage on the south side of the long marina floats where space is available.

Anchor in 3 fathoms over sand and mud; good holding.

⚓ **Canoe Cove Marina** tel: 250.656.5566; fax: 250.655.7197; monitors VHF Ch 66A; website: www.canoecovemarina.com; fuel; power; showers; laundry; repair facilities; Customs clearance

Iroquois Passage

Charts 3476, 3441, 3313; W of Goudge I; 0.5 mi SE of Swartz Bay
Entrance (S): 48°40.81′N, 123°23.45′W
Entrance (N): 48°41.36′N, 123°23.92′W

Iroquois Passage, entered from the south between Goudge Island and Fernie Island, leads NW passing east of Musclow Islet; it enters Colburne Passage between Swartz Head and Goudge Island light. A reef of above-water and drying rocks extends NNW from Musclow Islet to Swartz Head. (SD)

Iroquois Passage is used by pleasure craft for entering Canoe Cove or as a shortcut between Tsehum Harbour and Swartz Bay. As you enter the passage, favor the southwest side of Goudge Island to avoid the submerged mid-channel rock shown on Chart 3476.

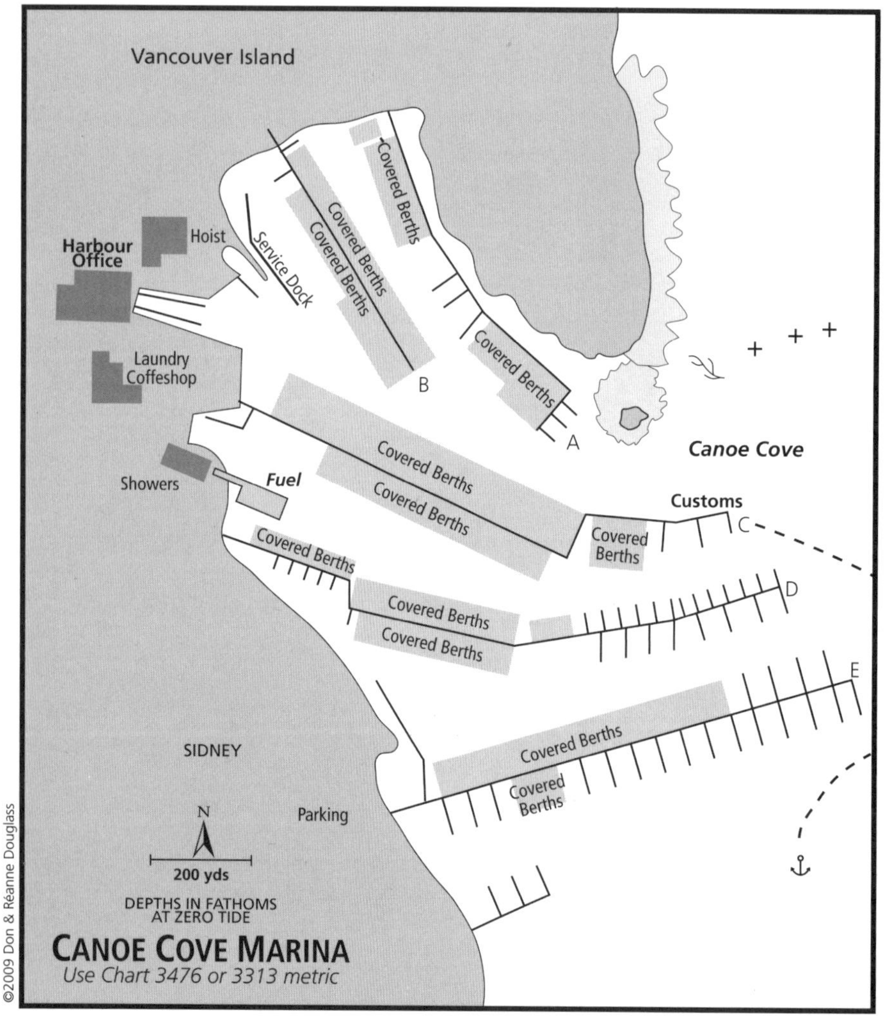

CANOE COVE MARINA
Use Chart 3476 or 3313 metric

John Passage

Charts 3476, 3441, 3313; 0.8 mi SE of Swartz Bay
Entrance (S): 48°40.91′N, 123°23.28′W
Entrance (N): 48°41.27′N, 123°23.41′W

John Passage separates Coal Island from Goudge Island and is entered from the south between Killer Whale Point and Fernie Island. Cap Rocks lie close-off Killer Whale Point and several drying reefs lie in the fairway. (SD)

If you're north- or southbound, John Passage is somewhat easier than Page and Iroquois passages, but it still requires careful piloting.

Lewis Bay (Coal Island)

Charts 3476, 3441, 3313; NW side of Coal I
Entrance: 48°41.35'N, 123°23.31'W
Anchor: 48°41.27'N, 123°23.12'W

> *Lewis Bay, in the north part of Coal Island, is entered between Carney Point and Fir Cone Point. A reef of drying rocks extends 0.1 mile NW from Carney Point. A rock, with 1.3 m over it, lies in the centre of the bay. A breakwater and privately owned floats close east of it are at the head of the bay.* (SD)

Lewis Bay provides temporary shelter in 7 fathoms from southeast weather. Be careful to avoid the cable crossing on the north side of the bay.

Colburne Passage

Charts 3476, 3441, 3313; connects Haro Strait with Satellite Channel
Entrance (E): 48°41.82'N, 123°25.21'W
Narrows (mid-ch, SW of Piers I): 48°41.87'N, 123°25.48'W
Entrance (W, 0.24 mi SW of Arbutus Islet): 48°42.17'N, 123°26.25'W

> *Colburne Passage is entered from the east between Fir Cone Point, the NW extremity of Coal Island, and Pym Island. It leads west to Satellite Channel between Coal Island, Goudge Island and Saanich Peninsula on the south and Pym, Knapp and Piers Islands on the north.* (SD)

Swartz Bay (Vancouver Island)

Charts 3476, 3479, 3441, 3313; 2.2 mi NW of Sidney Marina
Entrance: 48°41.36'N, 123°24.32'W
Public wharf: 48°41.25'N, 123°24.44'W
Anchor: 48°41.29'N, 123°24.38'W

> *Swartz Bay...is on the south side of Colburne Passage, about 1 mile west of Fir Cone Point. It is the site of a large ferry terminal and connected by highway to Victoria.*
>
> *Tidal differences for Swartz Bay (Index No. 7270), referenced on Fulford Harbour, are in Tide Tables, Volume 5.*
>
> *The Swarz Bay Terminal is operated by the British Columbia Ferry Services Inc. Regular and frequent passenger and vehicle service is maintained to and from Tsawwassen, on the mainland, and to places in the Gulf Islands.*

Canoe Cove

Canoe Cove offers good anchoring in Canoe Bay and temporary moorage at the marina. Its northern Saanich Peninsula location is a terrific jumping-off point for cruising the Gulf and San Juan islands. But Canoe Cove is more than just another stopover. It's a marine community with a distinct flavor of its own. Not only do more than 450 boats occupy the long finger docks and ribbed boathouses, but a host of marine-related businesses are fitted into a roughly circular arena next to the wharves. For those who enjoy wandering through boatyards, this one is filled with a jumble of 1940's-style chocolate-brown and seashell-white buildings, huge modern corrugated sheds, and a hundred boats on stilts.

The Cove's enterprises employ a hundred people who build and sell boats, repair pleasure craft with registrations from Portland to Juneau, train marine repair crews and teach boating. The compact area is highly eclectic (Morgan Warren sells her wild-bird paintings from a minute A-frame studio), but the common thread mobilizing the place is, of course, boats. Those who frequent the Cove talk about its sense of community, friendship and intense socializing.

Canoe Cove's epicentre is the Coffee Shop, with its self-serve counter, grey-laminate tables and outside terrace. It serves breakfast, a hearty lunch and endless coffees seven-days-a-week. Boaters are welcomed by the "regulars," who daily eat breakfast or lunch here while hotly debating politics, religion, or "whether the Martians are coming," as one retired police officer said. The Stonehouse Pub, an easy stroll from the dock, serves sensibly-priced lunch and dinner and makes the most of its 1935 charm and English gardens. Besides offering fresh salads and salmon, the restaurant serves such pubby fare as crab cakes, bangers and mash, and shepherd's pie.

Profit making is not new at Canoe Cove. It began, as many of its habitués recount with glee, as a rumrunner's haven during U.S. Prohibition. Contraband booze was stored until a pitch-dark night encouraged transport to the San Juans or Puget Sound's ports. By the late 1920's, it already boasted a small marina. Today, Canoe Cove Marina is the biggest operation.

Canoe Cove occupants work cooperatively. According to one yacht builder, this collaboration characterizes the place and makes it unique: "It's a bit like a neighbourhood where you can borrow a cup of sugar."

—Marianne Scott

The ferry berth close east of the B.C. Ferry terminal is for freight ferries operating from the Fraser River.

Swartz Bay lights at the ferry terminal are private and fitted with radar reflectors. The fog signal is operated by ferry personnel when required for ferry movements.

A public float, east of the ferry landings, is 26 m long at the end of a trestle approach ramp. The outer end of the float has a depth of 0.6 m. The bottom surrounding the float is mainly rock ledges with sand and gravel patches between; a depth of 0.6 m lies 10 m NE of the float. This float is intended for vessels loading and unloading; use of the float is restricted to 2 hours. (SD)

The public wharf, just east of the ferry terminal and north of Dolphin Road, is useful for dropping off or picking up crew who use the Interisland or Tsawwassen ferries.

Satellite Channel

Charts 3441, 3313; the main E-W route btwn Saanich Peninsula & Saltspring I
Entrance (E): 48°45.56'N, 123°21.67'W
Entrance (W): 48°44.71'N, 123°33.57'W

Satellite Channel, ...entered from Swanson Channel at its east end, leads around the south end of Saltspring Island to Fulford Harbour, Saanich Inlet, Cowichan Bay and the south end of Sansum Narrows. Shute and Colburne Passages enter the south side of Satellite Channel....

The east end of Satellite Channel is frequently used by large ferries going between Swartz Bay, at the north end of Saanich Peninsula, and Tsawwassen on the mainland. Smaller ferries cross Satellite Channel between Swartz Bay and Fulford Harbour. Charted ferry routes are general indications of the route followed.

Tidal streams attain 1 to 2 kn in Satellite Channel. In the vicinity of Cape Keppel the flood sets NW and the ebb SE. (SD)

Peter Fromm

Islands disappearing into the sunset

Satellite Channel is used by vessels bound for Saanich Inlet or those northbound via Sansum Narrows.

Saanich Inlet (Vancouver Island)

Charts 3441, 3462, 3313; W of Saanich Peninsula; S of Satellite Channel
Entrance (N): 48°41.52'N, 123°30.35'W

Saanich Inlet, entered between Hatch Point and Moses Point, extends 13 miles south from Satellite Channel.... The head of Saanich Inlet is known as Finlayson Arm.

A deep trough runs down the centre of the inlet, but close offshore there are several isolated rocks and reefs. (SD)

Twelve-mile-long Saanich Inlet is known chiefly for its upscale settlement of Brentwood Bay and—for cruising boats—as the gateway to Butchart Gardens. Most boaters planning to visit the gardens moor at one of the marinas in Brentwood Bay and either walk from the docks or take their dinghy to the dinghy dock in Butchart Cove. Brentwood Bay Lodge and Angler's Anchorage Marina both have full amenities. The public dock in Brentwood Bay has no amenities. The main street of the village directly above the ferry dock is lined with small shops. There is a good ice cream parlor. The ferry runs between Brentwood Bay and Mill Bay.

Deep Cove (Vancouver Island)

Charts 3441, 3313; S of Moses Pt; 6.6 mi N of Brentwood Bay
Position: 48°41.02'N, 123°28.63'W

Deep Cove, entered between Moses Point and Coal Point, has the remains of a public wharf in its south part. A marina is close east of the public wharf.

Several pilings and a rubble breakwater are at the head of the cove.

Several private mooring buoys are in Deep Cove. (SD)

Minimizing Piloting Risks in Hazardous Areas

Crunch! The boat comes to a sudden stop and crew members are thrown forward against bulkheads and fittings. The 35-foot sailing yacht Granite Seeker has hit a rock at full speed. The crew is bruised and sore and the boat is severely damaged—safe enough to get them home, but their holiday is over.

Each year, many boaters find themselves in trouble because of the underwater features of this coastline. Accidents range from a light touch while attempting to get into a shallow anchorage to plowing into a underwater rock at full speed. Unfortunately, many boaters are unaware of the dangers or unaware of the potential severity of this type of accident.

The first step in avoiding the rocks in B.C. waters is to develop a fear of any accident. Fear of rocks shouldn't prevent cruising, but sailors should keep the danger of an unexpected "landfall" in their minds at all times in potentially treacherous areas.

A second step in avoiding rocks is to take preparation time with the charts. I've interviewed many people who have had accidents and was surprised to learn that, while many had spent time with the charts before their trip, they didn't look for potential problems. In planning their passages, some actually drew lines over major hazards then, during their trip, followed their plotted track and collided with a charted obstacle. When looking through charts and planning routes, remember that identifying hazards near your intended course is as important as the actual bearings to steer.

Another important step for avoiding rocks is to give clear instructions to people on the helm. No one can steer within one degree of a compass course, so instructions should include an ideal bearing for a lead mark along with an acceptable range of variance, calculated in advance. A good set of instructions might be: "Steer for the light directly ahead of us with a red band on top. The course should be 250 degrees on your compass, but it could safely range from 240 to 255 without any problem." This kind of instruction is useful to the person steering; he or she would know to alert the navigator if the bearing started to reach the edge of the "safe range."

By establishing clearing bearings in advance, the helmsman knows when to alert the skipper. (Many accidents have occurred when the navigator was not on deck.) The only time a navigator should go below deck is in the middle of open water is when the helmsman needs only to maintain a course bearing and keep an eye for traffic and debris in the water.

Motoring down Saanich Inlet

Navigators should avoid entering areas with unmarked hazards. The B.C. coastline is littered with so many rocks and hazards that it would be impossible to mark them all with navigation aids. However, where navigation aids do exist, it's a good idea to give them a wide berth as they often mark one end of a hazard or the centre of a reef which extends out several hundred yards. This is especially important with fluctuating tides; the potential for danger increases with a low tide, and the chance of disaster comes with a falling tide. Some sailors, with each successful trip, come incrementally closer to danger as their confidence increases. The comment, "But I've been in there many times before without a problem," could indicate that the accident victim probably used progressively less care with each trip.

The final piece of advice is slow down! When entering an area of potential danger, slow to a crawl. Remember: When you are unsure, stop the boat, get a fix, then continue on a safe course. Speed increases damage from minor to major and exponentially adds to the problems created by underwater collisions. A tap at half a knot probably can be fixed with a paintbrush. One knot means a bit of putty and an extra day out of the water for the annual haul-out. But five or six knots could put a modern production boat out of commission for three weeks or more, with repair costs from $5,000 to $30,000 or beyond.

There is nothing that adds misery to a holiday faster than an accident. In my mind, hitting a partially submerged log is an accident. Logs don't appear on the charts but rocks do. Hitting a rock demonstrates poor piloting skills or carelessness on the part of the navigator. When I hear about a boat that has run aground at full speed, I may ask where? or when?, but my real question is *why?* **—Colin Jackson**

Deep Cove can be entered on either side of Wain Rock. The cove is generally too deep and exposed for convenient anchorage. Some small boats anchor tucked in the northeast corner next to shore or over the area of a flatter bottom on the south side of Coal Point. Avoid the rocks and shoals in the southeast portion of the bay by paying close attention to the buoys. Deep Cove Marina, which has limited moorage for visiting boats, is on the south shore of the cove.

⚓ **Deep Cove Marina** tel. 250.656.0060; limited moorage

Towner Bay (Vancouver Island)

Charts 3441, 3313; 0.8 mi SE of Coal Pt; 1 mi NW of Patricia Bay
Position: 48°40.04'N, 123°28.53'W

Towner Bay is a tiny, shallow bight, too small to be of much use as an anchorage.

Pat (Patricia) **Bay** (Vancouver Island)

Charts 3441, 3313; 5 mi N of Brentwood Bay
Position: 48°39.43'N, 123°27.31'W

> *Patricia Bay, known locally as Pat Bay, about 1.5 miles south of Deep Cove, is fringed by drying flats. The Institute of Ocean Sciences is on the SE side of the bay. Victoria International Airport is east of the bay.*
>
> *A rock breakwater extends 100.5 m south from the inner end of the main pier and another rock breakwater, close west, extends 107 m north from the south shore protecting a small boat harbour with floats for berthing small craft.* (SD)

Peter Fromm

Finding a good place to beach a dinghy

Pat Bay is the home of the Institute of Ocean Sciences and the Pacific Geoscience Centre. Temporary anchorage can be found in the north part of the bay, avoiding the government docks and buoys.

Mill Bay (Vancouver Island)

Charts 3441, 3313; 5.7 mi NW of Brentwood Bay
Public wharf: 48°38.82'N, 123°33.02'W
Anchor: 48°38.95'N, 123°32.91'W

> *Mill Bay, on the west side of Saanich Inlet, opposite Patricia Bay, is entered south of Whiskey Point. A shoal pinnacle lies in the centre of the bay and a marina, protected by a floating breakwater, and launching ramp are close north of the public wharf.*
>
> *The public wharf in Mill Bay has a float with 30 m of berthing and depths of 1.2 to 3 m alongside.* (SD)

Mill Bay offers good protection from prevailing summer northwesterlies. During winter months, or low pressure periods, the bay is open to weather from the southeast. Mill Bay Marina, located behind the small breakwater on the west side of the bay, has 15-amp power, showers, fuel, marine supplies, boat ramp, and laundry facilities. The public wharf and float, just south of the marina, is used by fishing boats. Anchorage can be taken over a large part of the bay, avoiding private mooring buoys which lie between the marina and public wharf.

Anchor in 5 to 7 fathoms over sand and mud; good holding.

⚓ **Mill Bay Marina** tel: 250.743.4112; monitors VHF Ch 66A; power; showers; fuel; marine supplies; launch ramp; laundry

Coles Bay (Vancouver Island)

Charts 3441, 3313; 2 mi S of Pat Bay; E of Yarrow Pt
Entrance (N): 48°37.59'N, 123°29.08'W
Entrance (S): 48°36.93'N, 123°29.07'W
Anchor: 48°37.66'N, 123°28.15'W

Coles Bay affords anchorage in 20 to 30 m. Dyer Rocks, 1 m high, lie close SW of Yarrow Point on the west side of Coles Bay. A rock, with 1.8 m over it, lies 0.3 mile WSW of Yarrow Point; it is marked by port hand buoy "U23." Approaching Coles Bay from north give Dyer Rocks a berth of at least 0.5 mile to avoid the shoals extending south from them. (SD)

Coles Bay offers fair-to-good protection in all but stormy weather, tucked in against the northeast shore beneath the tall trees. Avoid Dyer Rocks to make access easy. There is a small park ashore with picnic sites and trails.

Anchor in 5 fathoms over a sandy bottom.

Thomson Cove (Vancouver Island)

Charts 3441, 3313; 1.5 mi N of Brentwood Bay
Position: 48°35.96'N, 123°28.63'W

Thomson Cove has a private warning buoy marked "Electric cables — No anchoring within 50 feet" near its head. A flagpole is on Henderson Point. (SD)

Thomson Cove, the small indentation on the north side of Henderson Point, has good protection from southeast weather. However, due to its depths and limited swinging room, Brentwood Bay or Tod Inlet are better choices for anchorage.

Brentwood Bay (Vancouver Island)

Charts 3441, 3313 7 mi S of Satellite Channel
Entrance (N, 0.19 mi NE of Senanus I): 48°35.71'N, 123°28.99'W
Entrance (S): 48°34.99'N, 123°29.22'W
Public float: 48°34.35'N, 123°27.86'W

Brentwood Bay is entered between Henderson Point and Willis Point; Senanus Island lies in its entrance. Brentwood Bay village, several marinas, numerous private floats and mooring buoys are in the SE corner of the bay.

Starboard hand buoy "U22" marks a drying rock close SW of the ferry landing.

Do not approach the marina close south of the ferry wharf between the above-mentioned buoy and daybeacon; drying rocks lie between the buoy and shore.

The public float, 0.3 mile SE of the ferry landing, is 22 m long with a depth of 4.2 m alongside.

Diesel fuel, gasoline, lubricants, provisions, ice and fresh water are obtainable. (SD)

The village of Brentwood Bay, perched on the hill surrounding the bay, is an upscale residential suburb with lovely shops, restaurants and a first-class marina. The Brentwood Bay Lodge and Spa, completely rebuilt and renovated to the highest standards since our last edition has moorage for over 60 vessels. New docks, upgraded power (15 to 50 amps), showers, laundry, wireless internet connection and full use of the pool and spa facilities. (See Sidebar.) Pleasure craft should plan to make advance reservations. The Lodge is open year-round so take advantage to make reservations in the off season.

Chances are slim for transient moorage these days in Anglers Anchorage Marina; their slips

B.C. Marine Parks

The motto of the B.C. Bureau of Tourism's "Super, Natural British Columbia" applies perfectly to the Marine Parks. Where else can cruising boats find more than 60 marine parks just between Haro Strait and Queen Charlotte Sound? Boaters on both sides of the border have the B.C. government to thank for setting aside the waterways and land for these parks.

Montague Harbour, Rebecca Spit, Plumper Cove, Newcastle Island, and Sidney Spit were the first marine parks to be established more than 40 years ago. Since then, the numbers have increased exponentially. Most of the marine parks are accessible only by boat; many are developed with wharves or floats, water, toilets and camping and picnic sites; some have mooring buoys and charge a reasonable fee; others are primitive and undeveloped and free.

Explore pre-historic middens, pristine beaches, creeks, lakes, forests and rugged mountains. Whether you come by cruising vessel, canoe or kayak, show your appreciation by respecting the parks, other boaters and, leave no trace of your visit. Like the backpackers motto: "Pack it in, pack it out!"

To show your support and appreciation, become a member of the B.C. Parks Forever Association or make a donation to The Nature Trust of British Columbia, especially if you're visiting from the States

Anne Vipond

Tod Inlet

are dedicated mainly to permanent moorage. The Public Wharf has no facilities.

Boats that prefer to anchor, can head south a third of a mile to Tod Inlet.

⚓ **Angler's Anchorage Marina** tel: 250.652.3531; full amenities

⚓ **Brentwood Bay Lodge** tel: 250.652.3151 (marina); monitors VHF Ch 66A; no fuel; full amenities

Tod Inlet (Vancouver Island)

Charts 3441, 3313; extends 0.8 mi S from Brentwood Bay
Entrance: 48°34.41'N, 123°28.34'W
Anchor: 48°33.60'N, 123°28.24'W

Tod Inlet, at the south end of Brentwood Bay, has a narrow entrance, less than 0.1 mile wide. Port hand buoy "U21," on the east side just inside the entrance, marks a rock on the outer edge of a small gravel spit.

Anchorage and shelter for small craft can be obtained inside Tod Inlet in about 5 m, mud bottom. (SD)

Brentwood Bay

Brentwood Bay – a fair wind to adventure, a place to launch an extraordinary journey in the pristine "still waters" of the Sannich Inlet.

The marina staff is friendly and helpful. They'll happily direct you to the Marine & Eco-Adventure Centre for guided eco-cruises, or the PADI Centre for a scuba diving experience. Whether you wish to rent a kayak or have questions about hiking, the staff can assist. Reserve a berth at the marina.

Butchart Gardens is only 10 minutes away from the marina in one of the Lodge's water-shuttles. And Victoria is just 20 minutes away from Brentwood Bay by bus. Be sure to add these destinations to you must see list.

Nestled in the wooded hillside above the marina is the five star oceanfront resort, the Brentwood Bay Lodge & Spa. There's something for everybody with its outdoor heated pool, hot tub, gift shop, gourmet restaurant and a casual pub.

The Marine Pub exudes warmth and comfort with a great view of nature's spectacular scenery. The menu is a mix of traditional and contemporary pub dishes. Be adventurous. They boast a large selection of "craft beers and regional wines," and with live music Friday and Saturday evenings, that's a winning combination. Minors may not eat in the Pub but tables are available outside and you can order from the pub's menu.

The Arbutus Grill, part of the lodge, is dining at its finest, a gastronomical event further enhanced with wines from their award winning cellar. Dinner reservations are strongly recommended.

Be sure to stop in at the Resort's beer and wine store which has an excellent variety of chilled adult beverages; and a few steps away you will be captivated by a tempting assortment of pastries and breads. Eat, drink, savor and be happy.

Surrounded by spectacular scenic beauty, Brentwood Bay is a tranquil respite from life's busy demands. Here the opportunity exists to do something or nothing, your choice.

Did you know...

Butchart Gardens was once the site of rich lime deposits which Robert Pim Butchart mined and used in his business manufacturing Portland cement.

There's a dinghy dock and a boater's entrance to Butchart Gardens in Tod Inlet.

Victoria Butterfly Gardens, near Butchart, features butterflies flying freely about as visitors stroll an indoor tropical rainforest.

The Institute of Ocean Sciences, a major scientific facility, is located about five miles north of Brentwood Bay. Visitors are welcome.

Tod Inlet, an extension of Brentwood Bay, provides excellent shelter from all weather. During high season, multiple boats line the inlet and you may have trouble finding a place to anchor unless you arrive early in the day. Avoid the spit and dangerous rock at the entrance by favoring the west shore and keeping "U21" to port. The narrow, steep sides of the inlet create a sense of isolation from the bustling tourist center nearby. During high season multiple boats line the inlet and you may have trouble finding a place to anchor, unless you arrive early in the day.

Anchor in 2 to 3 fathoms over soft black mud with shells and shale chips; very good holding.

Butchart Cove (Vancouver Island)

Charts 3441, 3313; E side of Tod Inlet; 0.35 mi SW of the Brentwood marinas
Position: 48°34.19'N, 123°28.44'W
Butchart Cove dinghy dock: 48°34.07'N, 123°28.21'W

You can take your boat into tiny Butchart Cove and anchor or pick up one of the four mooring buoys provided for visitors (limit one night). In summer months, however, when it tends to be congested, Tod Inlet is a better alternate anchorage. You can also anchor on the south side of Butchart Cove using a shore tie. There are some shoals in the cove, so check the depths carefully. If you enter gate from above the dinghy dock, you must return via the same gate. The nice dinghy dock can accommodate about 20 dinghies.

The gardens are well worth a visit in summer, particularly at sundown on a Saturday evening when there is a spectacular display of fireworks. It's a good time for a picnic; be sure to bring along a blanket or cushions to sit on and arrive early.

In a severe winter, Butchart Cove may freeze over completely due to the fresh water on its surface. However, we have spent several winter holiday nights in the cove without encountering any ice. Temporary anchorage can be taken just north of the dinghy dock in 2 fathoms, sand, gravel and mud bottom with fair holding and limited swinging room.

Finlayson Arm (Vancouver Island)

Charts 3441, 3313; S end of Saanich Inlet
Marina: 48°29.85'N, 123°33.10'W

> *Finlayson Arm extends 3.5 miles south from Repulse Rock and forms the south end of Saanich Inlet.*
>
> *A marina is on the west side of Finlayson Arm, close north of the mud flats.* (SD)

Finlayson Arm, which extends deep into Vancouver Island, is a beautiful and narrow fjord. The mud flats and delta of Goldstream River lie at the head of the arm. Weather systems rarely reach the end of the inlet. The river, which has a major salmon run in the fall, is a great place to explore by dinghy or kayak. Nearby Goldstream Provincial Park has campsites and trails, including a trail to the top of Mount Finlayson (1,365 feet).

Goldstream Boathouse, at the edge of the drying flats has limited guest moorage. Facilities include water, power, toilets, haulout for boats up to 50 feet, a boat ramp and picnic area.

Misery Bay, the small bay 0.9 mile north of Goldstream Boathouse, is too deep for convenient anchoring.

⚓ **Goldstream Boathouse** tel: 250.478.4407; fax: 250.478.6682; monitors VHF Ch 66A; power; fuel; repair facility and haulout to 50 feet; launch ramp; moorage for four to six boats; water; toilets; picnic area; reservations recommended; open year-round

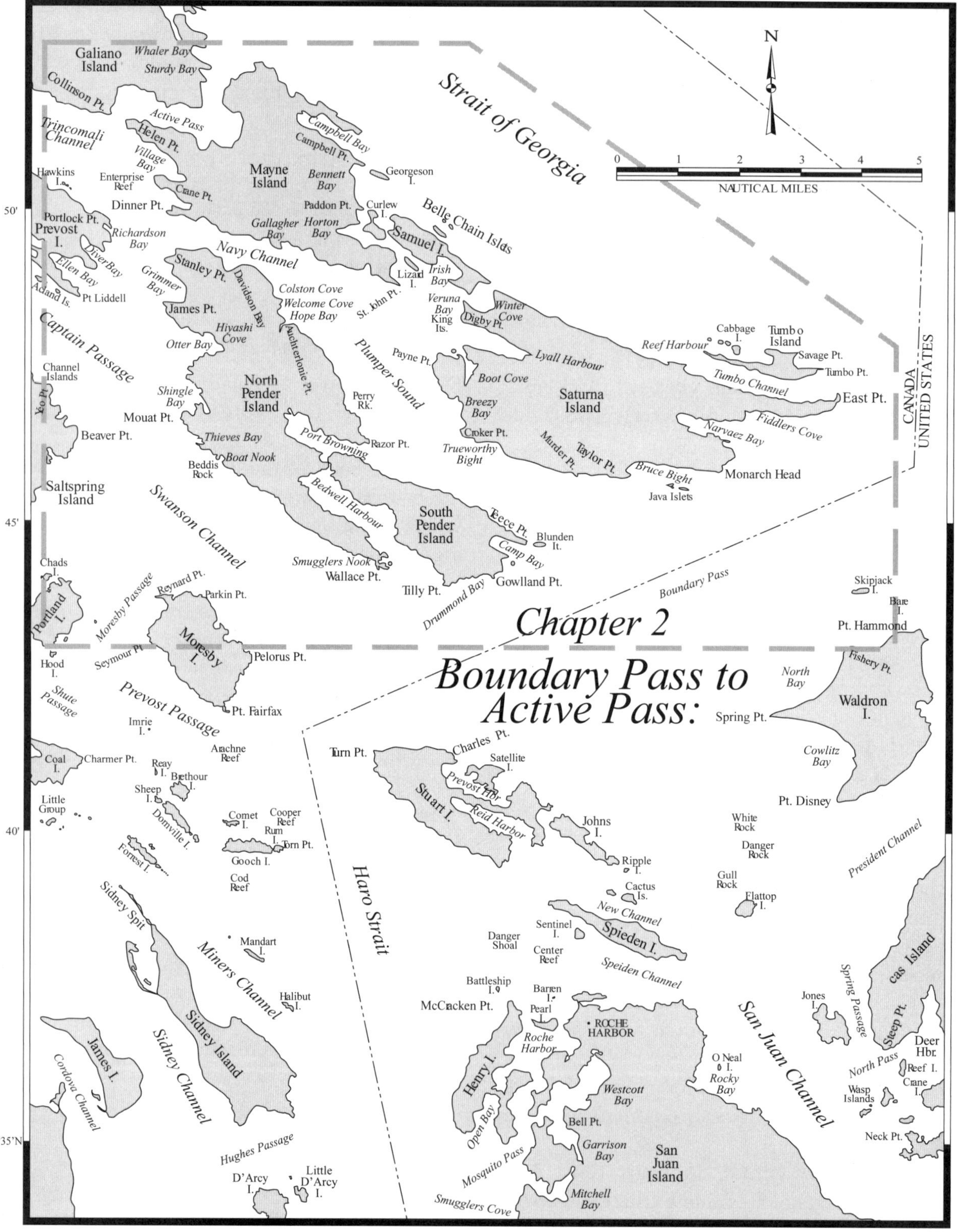
Chapter 2
Boundary Pass to Active Pass:
Strait of Georgia
NAUTICAL MILES
Galiano Island
Mayne Island
North Pender Island
South Pender Island
Saturna Island
Saltspring Island
Moresby I.
Stuart I.
Spieden I.
Sidney Island
James I.
San Juan Island
Waldron I.
Henry I.
Swanson Channel
Navy Channel
Plumper Sound
Captain Passage
Prevost Passage
Haro Strait
Boundary Pass
Miners Channel
Sidney Channel
San Juan Channel
President Channel
Active Pass
Trincomali Channel
ROCHE HARBOR
CANADA
UNITED STATES

2

BOUNDARY PASS TO ACTIVE PASS: Plumper Sound and Swanson Channel

The Gulf Islands surrounding Plumper Sound are sometimes referred to as the lower outer islands; to some boaters, they are the most remote and scenic in the cruising paradise of the Gulf Islands. Life is slow and quiet here, but serious currents and turbulent waters are found in the surrounding waters of Boundary Pass, Active Pass, and the Strait of Georgia. Safe inside Plumper Sound and Swanson Channel, the islands and sheltered coves take on an added charm. When gales are predicted in the area of Boundary Pass, you can head to Bedwell Harbour, Boot Cove or Hyashi Cove.

The northeast end of Boundary Pass brings you to Saturna Island, one of the largest of the Gulf Islands but relatively undeveloped, with a permanent population of less than 300. There are many coves and bays to explore along the shores of Saturna and the smaller nearby islands of Cabbage and Tumbo. Cabbage Island Marine Park is a pretty spot with good crabbing in Reef Harbour between Cabbage and Tumbo.

If you sail southwest, you can visit Bedwell Harbour, a seasonal Customs port-of-entry, and take the Pender Canal toward Port Browning and Plumper Sound, or cruise up Plumper Sound, visiting the west side of Saturna and the eastern shores of South and North Pender islands. Beaumont Marine Park, on South Pender, is a popular park with a beach, drinking water, hiking trails, and campsites. There is a Public Market in Port Browning every Saturday morning from mid-June through October. Come early!

You can hopscotch back and forth, visiting North Pender, Mayne, and Prevost islands, then sail through Active Pass to the southeastern end of Galiano Island. Winter Cove Marine Park, Saturna Island, is a well-protected anchorage with good hiking trails and a great picnic area. Mayne Island is a quiet place of farms and orchards with historic sites such as the Mayne Museum, Church of St. Mary Magdalene, and the Active Pass Light Station.

Anne Vipond

East Point, Saturna Island, looking out on Boundary Pass

Boundary Pass

Charts 3441, 3462; connects Haro Strait with Strait of Georgia
Entrance (W): 48°41.63′N, 123°16.05′W
Entrance (E, 1.6 mi NW of Alden Pt; 1.8 mi NE of East Pt): 48°48.00′N, 123°00.50′W

> *Boundary Pass, between Haro Strait and the Strait of Georgia, encompasses the area from Stuart Island to Patos Island.*
>
> *Between Saturna and Patos Islands tidal streams are strong and somewhat erratic, with tide-rips and eddies; care should be observed when navigating in this area.* (SD)

The international boundary runs down the center of 11-mile Boundary Pass in a northeast-southwest direction and the distances between the Gulf and San Juan islands vary between 2 and 6 miles. Boundary Pass is known for its strong currents, particularly ebb flows which include the outflow of the Fraser River. Tide rips, standing waves, and turbulent waters can be found during spring tides or when strong winds blow against the currents.

East Point light, Saturna Island

Prevost Harbour on Stuart Island and Bedwell Harbour on South Pender Island offer the best shelter on either side of the pass.

In restricted visibility, it is particularly important to cross the shipping channels at right angles and to watch for high-speed vessels.

East Point Light, Saturna Island

(Boundary Pass)

Charts 3441, 3462; 2.9 mi W of Alden Pt on Patos I; 8.6 mi NE of Prevost Hbr
Position: 48°46.99′N, 123°02.76′W

> *Boiling Reef extends 0.4 mile NE from East Point; a rock 2 m high stands in the center of the reef.*
>
> *East Point, the SE extremity of Saturna Island, is moderately steep-to but should be given a wide berth because of heavy tide-rips, overfalls and eddies in its vicinity.* (SD)

Tide rips, standing waves, and turbulent waters are found in the vicinity of East Point. This area is particularly dangerous on strong spring ebb tides when the Strait of Georgia empties its pent-up waters, including the outflow of the Fraser River. Boiling Reef offers good sportfishing in settled weather during neap tides.

East Point is considered one of the better places for sighting orcas.

Tumbo Channel (Strait of Georgia)

Charts 3441, 3462; btwn Tumbo & Saturna Is; W of East Pt
Entrance (E, 0.39 mi NE of Boiling Reef): 48°47.66′N, 123°02.22′W
Entrance (W, 1.0 mi W of Tumbo I): 48°48.09′N, 123°07.54′W

Currents in the Gulf Islands

The tidal currents of the Gulf Islands, as well as the entire Strait of Georgia to Desolation Sound, ebb and flood through Juan de Fuca Strait. These currents are felt most strongly near headlands and in narrow channels and passages. Favorable currents can be used to advantage up to the point where their speed becomes excessive or turbulence becomes threatening. It's always prudent to wait for slack water in narrow passages or off headlands where the currents react strongly with opposing winds.

Driftwood on the Tumbo Island reef

Tumbo Channel is deep but has dangers in both entrances. (SD)

Tumbo Channel, a deep-water route along the north shore of Saturna Island, is largely protected from the Strait of Georgia seas. The currents in the channel flow easterly during both falling tides and rising tides due to the back eddy formed off Boiling Reef. The private mooring buoys found along the Saturna shore, west of East Point, indicate fair shelter during summer weather. The west entrance to Tumbo Channel leads into Reef Harbour.

The south side of Tumbo Island, which is steep-to, can be approached closely to study the interesting sandstone cliffs. This same Chuckanut sandstone is found in Bellingham Bay and extends across the Sucia Islands and northwest along the south side of the Strait of Georgia. The tilted sandstone layers form many of the rocks and reefs which become hazards for boaters; the Belle Chain Islets to the northwest of Saturna Island are an example of this.

Reef Harbour/Cabbage Island Marine Park (Tumbo Island)

Charts 3441, 3462; 1.9 mi NW of East Pt
Entrance (W): 48°48.13'N, 123°06.57'W
Anchor: 48°47.88'N, 123°05.62'W

Reef Harbour, between Cabbage Island and the west end of Tumbo Island, can be used as a temporary anchorage for small craft; local knowledge is advised. (SD)

Reef Harbour is a favorite anchor site for boaters who want a centrally-positioned overnight anchorage at the confluence of the Strait of Georgia and Boundary Pass. Approach Reef Harbour carefully from the northwest, avoiding the rocks and reefs off Tumbo Island. The east end of the harbor is quite shallow with a number of submerged rocks. Do not attempt to enter the harbor without carefully consulting Chart 3441 and posting alert lookouts; not all rocks are marked by kelp.

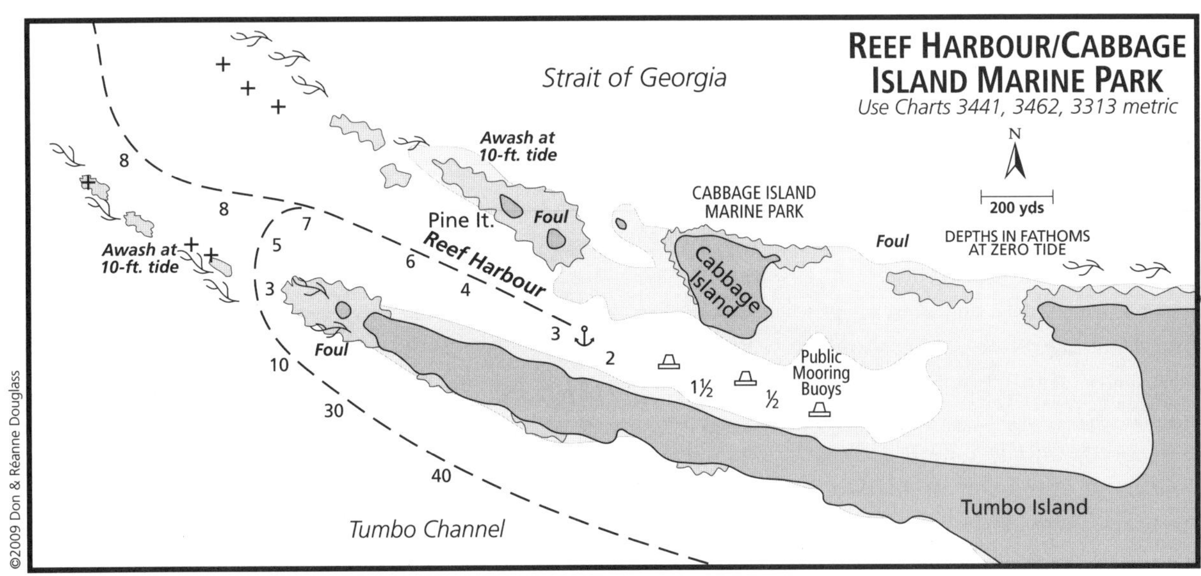

Arne Vipond

Low tide on Cabbage Island, Reef Harbour

Cabbage Island is exposed and windswept

Although Tumbo Island protects the harbor from southeast seas, the low profile of this island, as well as Cabbage Island, allows the wind to whip through the anchorage. Due to exposure to wind and the limited swinging room, Reef Harbour should be used only in settled weather.

Exposed and windswept, undeveloped Cabbage Island Marine Park is surrounded by a large sandy beach with good picnic sites on its south shore. The shoals to the east of Cabbage Island have tide pools that provide fascinating exploration. The trees in the center marsh on the island were either killed by saltwater intrusion or blown down during a winter storm. Driftwood on the island indicates its exposure to Fraser River outflow winds as well as to southeast storms, giving it a sense of isolation and vulnerability.

Cabbage Island Marine Park (open year-round) has pit toilets, camping, picnic area, swimming, fishing, canoeing and kayaking. It's easy to land a dinghy along the lovely beach on the south side of the island and do some exploring. In summer 2004, nine new mooring buoys were installed and the park was incorporated into the new Gulf Islands National Park Reserve, along with most of Tumbo Island. A fee is charged for moorage.

Note that in heavy northwesterlies it can be difficult to pick up a buoy on the outer limits of the buoys.

Anchor in 1 to 2 fathoms over mud and sand with good holding. Be sure to check your anchor set.

⚓ **Cabbage Island Marine Park** has pit toilets; camping; picnic area; swimming; fishing; canoeing: kayaking; open year-round

Fiddlers Cove (Saturna/Boundary Pass)

Charts 3441, 3462, 3313; 1.45 mi SW of East Pt Light
Position: 48°46.82'N, 123°04.93'W

Fiddlers Cove is too small for anything but

Narvaez Bay, a fair-weather anchorage

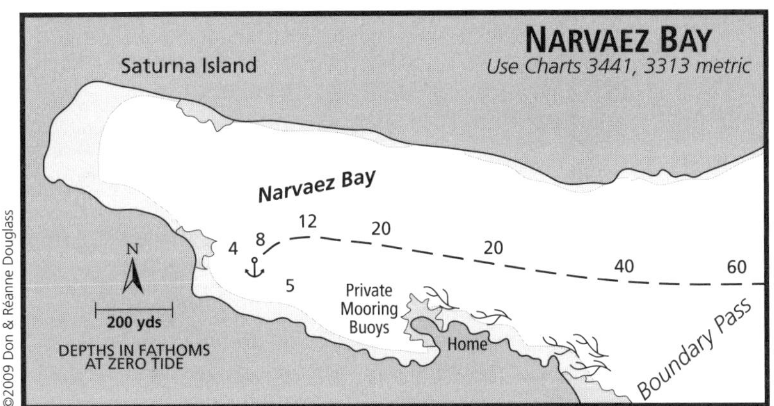

©2009 Don & Réanne Douglass

temporary anchorage for sportfishing boats during prevailing northwest weather.

Narvaez Bay (Saturna/Boundary Pass)

Charts 3441, 3462, 3313; 2.2 mi SW of East Pt
Entrance: 48°46.49'N, 123°05.16'W
Anchor: 48°46.48'N, 123°06.04'W

> *Narvaez Bay, entered east of Monarch Head, is free of dangers. It is not recommended as an anchorage, except in fine weather, as it is exposed to the east; with strong winds from that direction a heavy sea rolls in.* (SD)

Narvaez Bay provides temporary shelter when seas are kicking up in Boundary Pass or it makes a convenient overnight anchorage in fair weather.

Small boats find anchorage off the tiny cove on the south side of the bay with a modicum of protection from southeast winds. Avoid the several private mooring buoys in the cove. Larger boats anchor near the head of Narvaez Bay. Portrions of the Narvaez Bay shoreline were added to the list of Gulf islands National Park Reserve in 2004, and picnic tables and a toilet have been installed.

Anchor in 4 to 5 fathoms over mud; good holding; limited swinging room.

Bruce Bight (Saturna/Boundary Pass)

Charts 3441, 3462, 3313; E of Taylor Pt; 1.4 mi W of Monarch Head; 1.2 mi SW of Narvaez Bay
Entrance (E, 0.3 mi SW Monarch Head): 48°45.70'N, 123°06.02'W
Entrance (S): 48°45.66'N, 123°07.39'W
Anchor: 48°45.90'N, 123°07.71'W

> *Java Islets, 0.8 mile east of Taylor Point, are bare and rocky.* (SD)

Shelter from westerly winds is reported deep in Bruce Bight. Avoid a submerged rock 0.11 mile southeast of Taylor Point.

Anchor in 5 fathoms over a mixed bottom with fair holding.

Camp Bay (South Pender I)

Charts 3441, 3462, 3313; 6.0 mi SW of East Pt; 1.9 mi E of Bedwell Hbr
Entrance: 48°44.43'N, 123°10.64'W
Anchor: 48°44.66'N, 123°11.03'W

Camp Bay is open to the southeast but provides shelter from westerly winds. The passage between Teece Point and Blunden Islet is clear for small craft with 6 fathoms minimum in the fairway. Anchorage can be found at the north side of the bay.

Anchor in about 3 fathoms over mud, gravel and sand with fair holding.

Canned Cod Bay (South Pender Island)

Charts 3477, 3441, 3313; S of Camp Bay; 0.22 mi N of Gowlland Pt
Position: 48°44.35'N, 123°11.00'W

Canned Cod Bay, a tiny bay in the lee of Higgs Point, is used as a temporary anchorage by sportfishing boats. It is exposed to southeast weather and has limited swinging room.

Drummond Bay (South Pender Island)

Charts 3477, 3441, 3313; 0.3 mi SW of Gowlland Pt
Position: 48°44.03'N, 123°11.44'W

Drummond Bay is a shallow bight that offers little shelter. It has a foul bottom.

Peter Cove (North Pender Island)

Charts 3477, 3441, 3313; 0.6 mi SE of Bedwell Hbr; 1.9 mi W of Gowlland Pt
Entrance: 48°44.32'N, 123°13.83'W
Anchor: 48°44.32'N, 123°14.00'W

Private mooring buoys are in Peter Cove and the bay north of it. (SD)

Peter Cove, at the south tip of North Pender Island, has a good view to the southeast that can be used to advantage if you are waiting for conditions to improve before crossing Boundary Pass to the San Juans. It should be used only as a temporary anchorage in settled weather. The small cove is crowded with limited swinging room and private mooring buoys to avoid. *Caution:* The bottom is irregular and there are several unmarked submerged rocks, including a large uncharted rock in the southwest corner of the cove.

Anchor in 2 to 3 fathoms over sand, mud and rock; poor-to-fair holding.

Anne Vipond

Statue of Washington Grimmer, early Pender settler

Bedwell Harbour (North/South Pender)

Charts 3477, 3441, 3313; 4.2 mi N of Prevost Hbr
Entrance: 48°44.09'N, 123°13.32'W
Anchor: 48°45.11'N, 123°14.05'W

Bedwell Harbour, an inlet formed by the overlap of North Pender Island and South Pender Island, is entered between Tilly Point and Wallace Point. The harbour is used mainly by pleasure craft and its facilities are solely for such craft. ... Strong south winds funnel through the harbour, but no heavy sea is raised. Pender Canal, at the north end, connects Bedwell Harbour to Port Browning.

Anchorage, with the exception of in the vicinity of the submarine cable and pipeline, can be obtained almost anywhere in Bedwell Harbour. The best position is 0.2 mile SE of Skull Islet in 13 to 15 m, stiff mud bottom.

Four public floats, attached to the south side of the main public float, are reserved for vessels entering and clearing Customs. They are 12 to 49 m long, in a T-formation, with 4.6 to 7.6 m alongside. (SD)

Bedwell Harbour, between South and North Pender Island, is one of the most popular cruising destinations in the Gulf Islands.

Bedwell Harbour

The ridges that run in a northwest/southeast direction on the Gulf Islands, formed by upthrusting of the earth's crust, now shelter such bays as Bedwell Harbour on South Pender Island. At its head is a large gravel beach backed by a brackish marsh used by a variety of birds. In an effort to protect these wetlands, the Pender Island Conservancy Association acquired Medicine Beach Marsh and it is now a nature sanctuary. The bird life seen here includes Great Blue Herons and ospreys.

Beaumont Marine Park, on the east side of Bedwell Harbour, provides mooring buoys, a beach and beautiful wooded trails. Picnic tables are stationed along the shoreside trail and serious hikers will want to follow the trail to the summit of Mount Norman where a viewing deck provides a panorama of distant islands and mainland mountains. Beaumont Park, established in 1962, occupies land that was donated by philanthropist Captain Ernest Godfrey Beaumont and by the Crown Zellerbach logging company. **—AV**

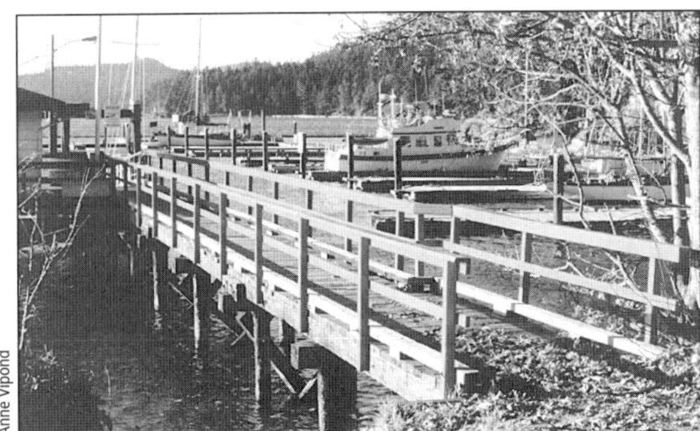

Anne Vipond

Bedwell Harbour in autumn

BEDWELL HARBOUR
Use Charts 3477, 3441, 3313 metric
Breakwater
Marina Office
Fuel
South Pender Island
Pool
Store
Showers
Laundry
Customs
Seaplanes
Hotel
Egeria Bay
©2009 Don & Réanne Douglass

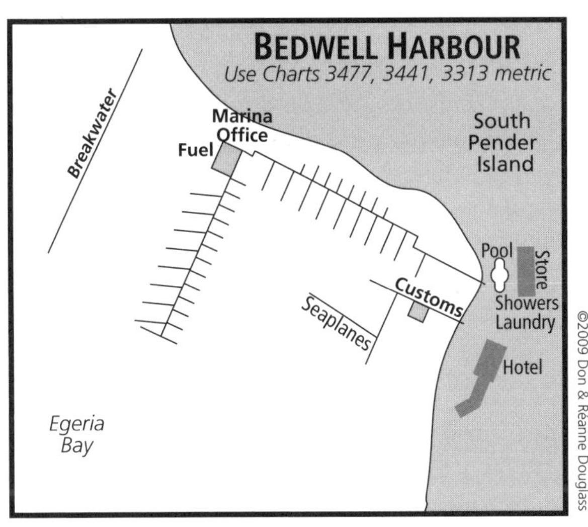

Poets Cove Resort and Spa and Beaumont Marine Park are the two major draws. Since our 2nd Edition was published, the former

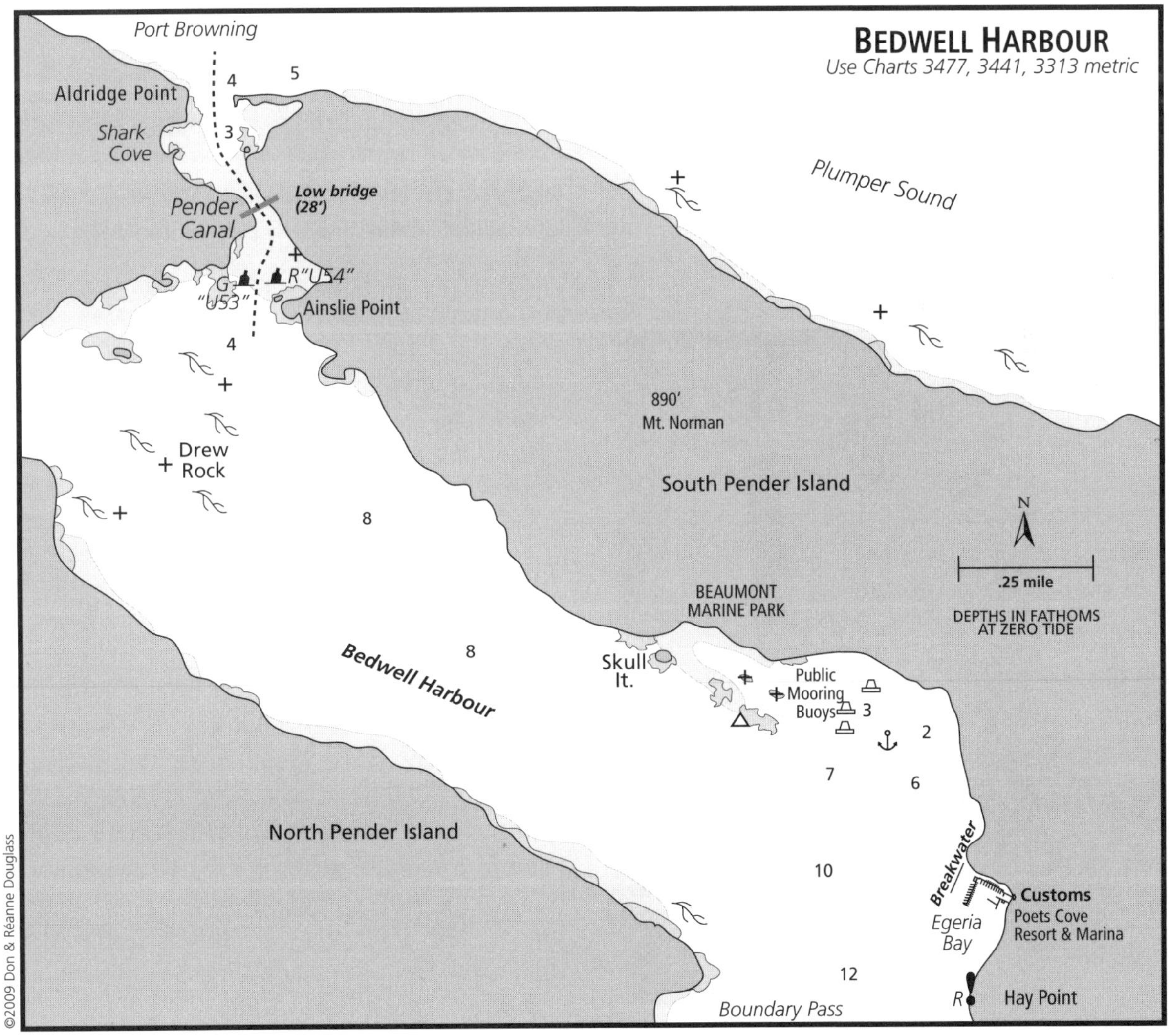

BEDWELL HARBOUR
Use Charts 3477, 3441, 3313 metric
Port Browning
Aldridge Point
Shark Cove
Pender Canal
Low bridge (28')
R"U54"
G "U53"
Ainslie Point
Plumper Sound
890'
Mt. Norman
South Pender Island
Drew Rock
N
.25 mile
DEPTHS IN FATHOMS AT ZERO TIDE
BEAUMONT MARINE PARK
Skull It.
Public Mooring Buoys
Bedwell Harbour
North Pender Island
Breakwater
Customs
Poets Cove Resort & Marina
Egeria Bay
Hay Point
R
Boundary Pass
4
5
3
4
8
8
3
2
7
6
10
12
©2009 Don & Réanne Douglass

Bedwell Harbour Resort and Marina has been completely rebuilt by new owners with luxurious facilities and upgraded docks.

Open year-round, the resort features a pool, spa, laundry, a small store and deli, showers, power, wireless internet and two restaurants. Customs clearance in Bedwell Harbour is by phone only at the dock below the swimming pool.

Mooring buoys can be found at Beaumont Marine Park; boaters preferring to anchor can drop a hook to the southeast of the mooring buoys.

Anchor in 5 fathoms over mud with good holding.

⚓ **Poets Cove Resort and Spa**
tel: 888.512.7638; monitors VHF Ch 66A;
website: www.poetscove.com;
email: marina@poetscove.com

⚓ **Customs Clearance** tel: 888.226.7277

Tight clearance under the bridge in Pender Canal

Beaumont Marine Park (South Pender I)

Charts 3477, 3441, 3313; 0.5 mi NW of Poets Cove Seaside Resort
Anchor: 48°45.14'N, 123°14.09'W

> *Beaumont Marine Park is on the NE shore of* [Bedwell] *harbor.* (SD)

Beaumont Marine Park, now part of the Gulf Islands National Park Reserve, is open all year and has walk-in camping, picnic sites, toilets and drinking water. There are 15 mooring buoys (overnight fee paid at on-shore kiosk), and well-sheltered anchorage can be found east of the mooring buoys. The bottom north of Skull Islet is shallow and foul.

Anchor in 4 to 5 fathoms over sand, mud and gravel with fair holding.

⚓ **Beaumont Provincial Marine Park**
camping; picnic area; fresh water; open year-round

Pender Canal (North/South Pender)

Charts 3477, 3441, 3442, 3313; 1.4 mi NW of Poets Cove Resort
Entrance (N): 48°46.06'N, 123°15.54'W
Entrance (S): 48°45.74'N, 123°15.44'W

> *Pender Canal leads north from the head of Bedwell Harbour into Shark Cove and Port Browning. It is about 23 m wide with a least depth of 2.2 m through it and is fringed on both sides by drying ledges. In the south entrance a drying rock and a rock awash are marked by starboard hand buoy "U54" and port hand buoy "U53."*
>
> *A highway bridge crosses Pender Canal near its north end; it has a vertical clearance of 8.5 m and a width between piers of 12.2 m.*
>
> *Tidal streams in Pender Canal attain 3 to 4 kn at springs; the flood sets north and the ebb south.* (SD)

The route north from Bedwell Harbour through Pender Canal to Port Browning is scenic and interesting, but suitable only for small craft. Boaters are asked to slow down and watch their wake through the canal, especially when powering against the current.

The canal, 0.3 mile long, reaches its narrowest point (40 feet at high water) at the bridge joining the two islands. Since clearance under the bridge is just 26 feet, larger yachts and sailboats must use Swanson Channel to the west or Plumper Sound to the east when heading for Port Browning or points north.

Plumper Sound

Charts 3441, 3477, 3313; btwn Boundary Pass on the S & Navy & Trincomali Channels on the N
Entrance (SE): 48°45.10'N, 123°09.25'W
Entrance (NW, 0.5 mi N of Fane I): 48°48.94'N, 123°16.13'W

Plumper Sound has Saturna, Samuel and Mayne Islands on its east side; North and South Pender Islands form its west side. Ease of access and entered from Boundary Pass between Blunden Islet and Taylor Point it leads NW to Navy Channel which in turn leads to the junction of Swanson and Trincomali Channels.

Georgeson Passage and Winter Cove, on the NW and SE sides, respectively, of Samuel Island, lead into the Strait of Georgia. Port Browning and Pender Canal, between South and North Pender Islands, lead into Bedwell Harbour and Swanson Channel.

Tidal streams flood NW and north through Swanson Channel and NW through Plumper Sound, but a branch flows east into Navy Channel, meeting that flowing through Plumper Sound off Hope Bay, where tide-rips are formed.

The Gulf Island ferries ... pass at frequent intervals through Navy Channel and Plumper Sound.... (SD)

Poets Cove Resort & Spa, Bedwell Harbour, South Pender Island, B.C.

There's something about Poets Cove that smiles. Nestled below the tree lined bluffs of Mount Norman, this marina provides more than merely a place to clear Canadian Customs, fuel up at the accessible fuel dock, or tuck in to escape foul weather. The scenery is breath taking; the staff is warm and welcoming.

You'll definitely want to launch the kayak or tender and explore hidden coves and bays along the coastline. If you long for solitude, venture to the very end of South Pender Island to a pebble covered beach known as Gowlland Point Park – a perfect place to relax.

Whether anchored or moored to buoys in Beaumont Marine Park, you should make a point to dinghy over to the marina for a pleasant hike, bike ride, relaxing meal or, just to investigate the time-share vacation home real estate.

This cruising destination has come a long way from its modest beginnings and roughhewn post office. Now, the simple wooden docks lead to a new luxurious and sophisticated resort replete with world class amenities – heated swimming pool, hot tub, super laundry room, great showers, market, restaurants and spa.

The compact moorings Market offers an opportunity to restock, replace your reading material, pick up a gift or two, or buy sandwiches and ice cream – a place you're likely to bump into fellow boaters and swap sea stories.

At the Poets Cove Resort & Spa, you can choose between the elegant ambience of the Aurora restaurant with its tempting contemporary menu, or the more casual setting of the Syrens Lounge that offers classic comfort food and a local brew, indoors or on the terrace. Whichever eatery you choose you'll find the service efficient and friendly, the food wonderful, the view exquisite. Suggestion: Make reservations if you plan on dining at Aurora. It is a favorite of locals as well as the marina and resort guests.

Wander through the Resort's Susurrus Spa, absorbing the aura. For the more adventurous there are excitingly mysterious experience - the Steam Cave, the Vichy Shower, the Sea Clay massage and more.

During the summer, Bedwell Harbour is a popular port of entry and very busy. Suggest you call ahead and reserve a spot.

Poets Cove beckons – you'll remember it as one of the many beautiful Gulf Island destinations you eagerly anticipate visiting again.

Did you know...

Susurrus means a whispering or rustling sound in Latin.

The Pender Islands were once the haunts of rum running smugglers which may explain names like Smugglers Nook and Thieves Bay.

The Penders have no village or town center.

Pender Island was named in 1857 in honor of Captain Daniel Pender who surveyed the B.C. coast from 1857-1870.

Plumper Sound is a large body of water sometimes used as temporary anchorage for ships waiting to cross over to Vancouver Harbour. A 3-knot ebb current flows southbound in Plumper Sound on spring tides or during heavy runoffs in the Fraser River. Large northbound boats clearing Customs in Bedwell Harbour frequently use Plumper Sound and Swanson Channel as alternatives to Pender Canal.

Anne Vipond

Port Browning

The Pender Islands

With a Mediterranean climate and a perimeter scalloped with bays, coves and public beaches, the Pender Islands are a welcoming spot. To get a mental image of the islands' layout, imagine the head of a salmon about to chomp on a slice of pizza. The salmon is North Pender and the pizza is South Pender.

Originally one island, it became two when a canal was cut across a narrow isthmus more than a century ago. A one-lane bridge built in the 1950s stitches the islands back together.

Only about 2,000 Penderites reside here, although that number swells in the warmer months as vacationers take advantage of a wide range of accommodations and leisure activities. And it's small—about 14 square miles—with a network of roads meandering through farmland, woods and rolling hills. Ferryboats link the Penders to the mainland, Vancouver Island and other nearby Gulf Islands.

You have a choice of three marinas. Otter Bay Marina on North Pender is near the ferry dock. Port Browning Marina is centrally located and closest to shopping. Poet's Cove Marina is the official Customs entry for boats coming from U.S. waters, and fuel is available.

There are no big towns, but a gathering place on North Pender is the Driftwood Centre. Here you'll find a post office, grocery, pharmacy and other shops. If you've been on your boat a while, you might want to visit the fitness center, laundromat and hair salon. Or stock up on fresh produce at the Saturday morning Farmers' Market.

For news of cultural events, pick up a copy of *The Pender Post*, a monthly publication that lists art openings, poetry readings and craft fairs. Plays and concerts are held at the new Community Hall, a handsome timber building on Bedwell Harbour Road. It also hosts a Farmers' Market on Saturday mornings throughout the summer.

On North Pender, visit Roesland, site of a historical museum. Poke around in dilapidated cottages on this former resort nestled in a forest of Douglas fir and arbutus. Roesland and Roe Lake are part of the Gulf Islands National Park Reserve. www.gulfislandsnationalpark.com

On South Pender, see Beaumont Marine Park, a welcoming beach with picnic tables and fresh water. From here you can hike up the Mt. Norman trail. Or walk to the canal that separates, and the bridge that unites, the two Penders. Check out the local residents walking or lounging at Mortimer Spit, then cross the bridge to see the Helisen Archaeological Site where evidence has been found of First Nations settlements going back 5,000 years.

The numerous public beaches invite beachcombing and wildlife viewing. If you are more energetic, you can rent bikes or scooters to explore the terrain, or scuba equipment to investigate the waters. Rental kayaks are available at both Otter Bay and Poet's Cove.

Play a round of golf at the 9-hole Pender Island Golf and Country Club at Otter Bay or plunge into swimming pools at the three marinas. You'll find tennis courts at the Port Browning Marina.

To try your hand at a popular local sport, play disc golf at Disc Park in Magic Lake Estates. It is a 27-hole course where, instead of driving golf balls, players hurl Frisbee-like discs.

Two general stores operate out of renovated historical buildings: the Hope Bay Store (4301 Bedwell Harbor Rd.) and the Port Washington Store at Grimmer Bay.

Tourist information is available at the Pender Island Visitor Info Centre, 2332 Otter Bay Road, tel. 250.629.6541.

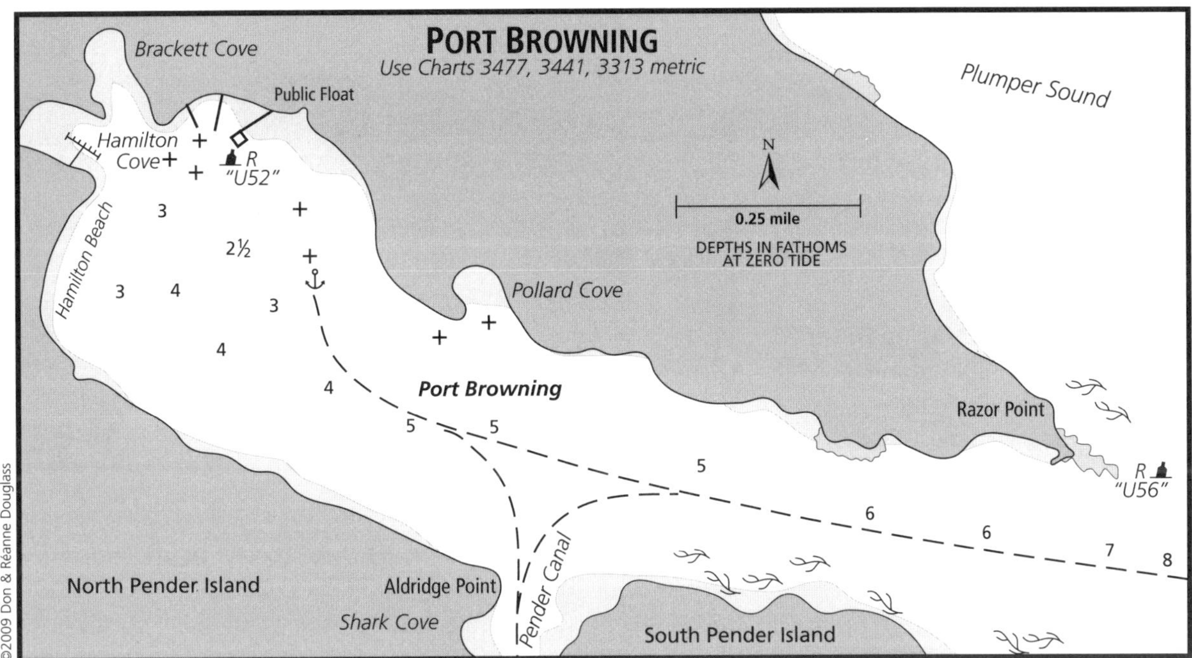

Port Browning (North Pender Island)
Charts 3477, 3441, 3442, 3313; 2.2 mi NW of Poets Cove Resort; 3.8 mi SW of Winter Cove
Entrance (E): 48°46.06'N, 123°14.08'W
Public float: 48°46.65'N, 123°16.12'W
Anchor: 48°46.60'N, 123°16.08'W
Entrance (Brackett Cove breakwater): 48°46.61'N, 123°16.31'W

> *Port Browning, entered south of Razor Point, is an inlet formed by the overlap of North and South Pender Islands. The bottom is mainly mud and a convenient anchorage is 0.4 mile from the head in about 8 m.* (SD)

Port Browning, with its easy access from both Pender Canal and Plumper Sound, has convenient anchorage as well as full-service Port Browning Marina. Has reasonable depths throughout, but care should be taken to avoid any private buoys. Anchorage may be found as shown on the diagram or along the periphery of the bay. Due to the long fetch in Port Browning, chop can build up inside the bay in southeast weather. Port Browning Marina Resort in Brackett Cove is preferable in such conditions. The public wharf on the north side of the bay has very limited space and no facilities.

The Marina, located behind the breakwater in Brackett Cove, has power (15 amp),

Pender Islands

The Penders were once one island, joined by a neck of land over which the natives would portage their canoes. In 1903 a short canal was dredged to accommodate small passenger steamships, and the islands were rejoined by the construction of a bridge in 1957. Thirty years later, an archaeological dig revealed evidence of native occupation at this site which dates back several thousand years. Some of the artifacts found are on display at the Pender Library, located about 2-1/2 miles north of Port Browning on Bedwell Harbour Road.

The canal, which connects Port Browning with Bedwell Harbour, has a least depth of 7 feet and a vertical clearance of about 26 feet at high water. By dinghy is a good way to explore the 'canal zone' while moored in Port Browning. The Helisen Archeological Site lies on the North Pender side of the bridge where roadside plaques recount the history of the area. On the South Pender shore is Mortimer Spit, its shell beach ideal for picnics while watching boat traffic in the canal. **—AV**

water, showers, laundry, swimming pool, pub, liquor store and is within walking of Driftwood Centre, North Pender Island's supply center where you can find a grocery store and post office.

Anchor in 3 to 5 fathoms over mud with good holding.

⚓ **Port Browning Marina Resort** tel: 250.629.3493; monitors VHF Ch 66A; website: www.portbrowning.com; email: portbrowning@gulfislands.com

Shark Cove

Shark Cove (Port Browning/ North Pender Island)

Charts 3477, 3441, 3442, 3313; N of the Pender Canal Bridge
Position: 48°45.95'N, 123°15.55'W

> *Shark Cove, on the south side of Port Browning, is sheltered by Mortimer Spit.* (SD)

Shark Cove offers excellent emergency shelter for small boats, but with very limited swinging room.

Pollard Cove (Port Browning/Pender Island)

Charts 3477, 3441, 3442, 3313; 0.4 mi SE of Port Browning public wharf; 0.5 mi N of Pender Canal Bridge
Position: 48°46.38'N, 123°15.61'W

Hope Bay (North Pender Island, Plumper Sound)

Charts 3477, 3442, 3313; 3.2 mi W of Winter Cove
Entrance: 48°48.24'N, 123°15.95'W
Public float: 48°48.20'N, 123°16.50'W

> *Hope Bay, entered between Auchterlonie Point … and Fane Island, has a public wharf and float. Hope Bay is connected to other settlements on North and South Pender Islands by road.*
>
> *Anchorage can be obtained in Hope Bay, about 0.2 mile south of Fane Island, in 13 to 16 m, mud bottom.* (SD)

Hope Bay provides shelter in westerly weather; it is out of the strong current that flows along the east side of Fane Island and exceeds 3 knots during spring tides. Its bottom has irregular depths with a 25-fathom hole halfway between the public float and Fane Island. Anchorage can be found north of the public float avoiding private mooring buoys. New shops and restaurant on shore.

Welcome Cove (North Pender Island)

Charts 3477, 3442, 3313; N of Hope Bay; 0.22 mi W of Fane I
Position: 48°48.41'N, 123°16.57'W

Welcome Cove is a tiny, shallow indentation that offers temporary shelter to sportfishing boats. Avoid the reef 0.13 mile west of Fane Island.

Colston Cove (North Pender Island)

Charts 3442, 3313; NE side of North Pender I; 0.4 mi NW of Hope Bay
Position: 48°48.61'N, 123°16.66'W

Colston Cove, a tiny cove somewhat out of the current of Navy Channel, provides moderate shelter for sportfishing boats in fair weather. Avoid a rock and reef off its entrance.

Navy Channel

Charts 3442, 3313; 2 mi SE of Active Pass; 3 mi W of Winter Cove
Entrance (E): 48°48.94'N, 123°16.13'W
Entrance (W): 48°49.63'N, 123°19.64'W

> *Navy Channel leads WNW between Mayne Island and North Pender Island and connects Plumper Sound to the north end of Swanson Channel and*

the south end of Trincomali Channel.

The maximum flood tidal stream is 2 to 3 kn, at the east end of Navy Channel; the maximum ebb tidal stream is 2 to 3 kn off Croker Point, and 1 to 2 kn in Navy Channel.

Conconi Reef, about 0.1 mile off the Mayne Isand shore, dries 2.4 m at its highest point. (SD)

Navy Channel has strong currents during spring tides and can be choppy when strong southeast winds occur on an ebb current. Avoid the foul area behind Conconi Reef on the north shore.

Davidson Bay (North Pender Island)

Charts 3442, 3313; 1.4 mi NW of Hope Bay
Position: 48°49.11′N, 123°17.97′W

Davidson Bay, an open bight in Navy Channel, affords temporary anchorage to sportfishing boats in fair weather. Although it is exposed to the wake of passing vessels, it is somewhat protected from prevailing winds.

Gallagher Bay (Mayne Island)

Charts 3442, 3313; S side of Mayne I; 1.7 mi SE of Dinner Pt
Position (0.16 mi E of Conconi Reef): 48°49.45′N, 123°17.30′W

Gallagher Bay, on the north shore of Navy Channel, is a small development in the bight behind Conconi Reef. It is useful only as a temporary anchorage for sportfishing boats in fair weather. *Caution:* North and east of Conconi Reef, Gallagher Bay has a number of isolated rocks.

Saturna Beach (Saturna Island)

Charts 3477, 3442, 3313; S side of Breezy Bay; N side of Croker Pt
Position: 48°46.66′N, 123°12.16′W

Saturna Beach ... has private floats and mooring buoys off it. (SD)

Saturna Beach lies at the south end of Breezy Bay, an open roadstead on the west end of Saturna Island. The water off the beach is shallow, and the land behind is a bench leading southward below nearly-vertical Brown Ridge. Mount Warburton Pike (1,607 feet) is 1.2 miles east of Saturna Beach. The flashing red lights of TV towers on the peak can be seen for many miles in the Gulf and San Juan islands.

Breezy Bay (Saturna Island)

Charts 3477, 3441; 0.4 mi N of Croker Pt
Position: 48°46.90′N, 123°12.23′W

Breezy Bay lies between Croker Point and Elliot Bluff. (SD)

Small craft can sometimes find shelter from easterly winds over the large 1-fathom flat in Breezy Bay. The south end of Breezy Bay, with private floats and mooring buoys, is known as Saturna Beach. Scuba diving is popular at the north end of Breezy Bay and along Elliot Bluff to the north.

Saturna Point (Saturna Island)

Charts 3477, 3441, 3313; 0.5 mi E of Payne Pt; 0.8 mi S of Winter Cove
Public wharf: 48°47.89′N, 123°12.03′W

Saturna community, close east of Saturna Point, has a general store and post office (V0N 2Y0).

The public wharf, on Saturna Point, is 34.4 m long at its outside face with a depth of 7.8 m alongside. Two floats, attached to the east side of the wharf, have a combined length of 59.7 m with a depth of 5.5 m alongside.

The ferry wharf is close west of the public wharf. (SD)

Saturna Point has a small public wharf and a fuel dock just east of the ferry dock; a small village lies east of the point.

⚓ **Saturna Point Wharf** tel: 250.539.5726

Boot Cove (Saturna Island)

Charts 3477, 3441, 3442, 3313; 0.1 mi S of Saturna Pt
Entrance (0.1 mi NE of Trevor Islet): 48°47.82′N, 123°12.19′W
Anchor: 48°47.57′N, 123°11.91′W

A rock, with 3.4 m over it, lies in the approach to Boot Cove, about 0.15 mile west of Saturna Point; it is marked by starboard hand buoy "U58."

Boot Cove, entered between Saturna Point and Trevor Islet, affords anchorage for small craft on

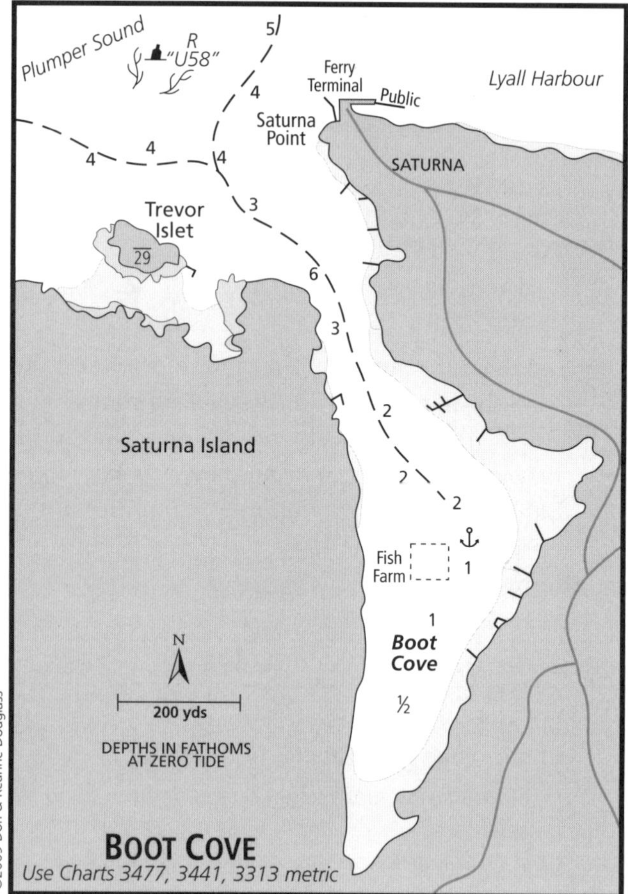

a mud bottom. When entering the cove, favour the starboard side to avoid a rock with 0.6 m over it. (SD)

Boot Cove is a narrow, landlocked inlet with good protection from all but the south from where strong gusts spilling over Brown Ridge may create williwaws. Anchorage can be found in the northeast corner avoiding the aquaculture, private docks, and mooring buoys all of which restrict swinging room.

Anchor in 1 fathom over a mud bottom with good holding.

Lyall Harbour (Saturna Island)

Charts 3477, 3441, 3442, 3313; E of Saturna Pt; 0.7 mi S of Winter Cove
Entrance: 48°48.09'N, 123°12.38'W
Anchor: 48°47.81'N, 123°10.98'W

Lyall Harbour, on the west side of Saturna Island, is entered between Payne Point and King Islets. Anchorage in Lyall Harbour is sheltered from all but west winds and can be obtained, clear of the submarine cable area, in depths of 13 m in the entrance decreasing to 5 m about 0.1 mile from the mud flat at the head. (SD)

Lyall Harbour is easy to enter; anchorage can be found at the head of the bay off a drying mud flat with lots of swinging room. Some southeast gusts enter the harbor from the low pass along Lyall Creek. The public wharf, just east of the ferry dock, caters mostly to fishing vessels. There are no pleasure craft facilities. The fuel dock is run by the Saturna Point Boat Store which offers provisions, fishing licenses and supplies. The Lighthouse Pub is located below the store.

Anchor in 3 fathoms over mud with good holding.

⚓ **Saturna Point Boat Store**
tel: 250.539.5725; fuel; store

Winter Cove (Saturna/Samuel Islands)

Charts 3477, 3441, 3442, 3313; 5.9 mi SE of Active Pass; 4.1 mi NE of Bedwell Hbr
Entrance (outer, 0.08 mi N of Minx Reef): 48°48.91'N, 123°12.60'W
Entrance (inner, 0.14 mi E of Mikuni Pt): 48°48.66'N, 123°11.98'W
Winter Cove Yacht Club float: 48°48.50'N, 123°11.69'W

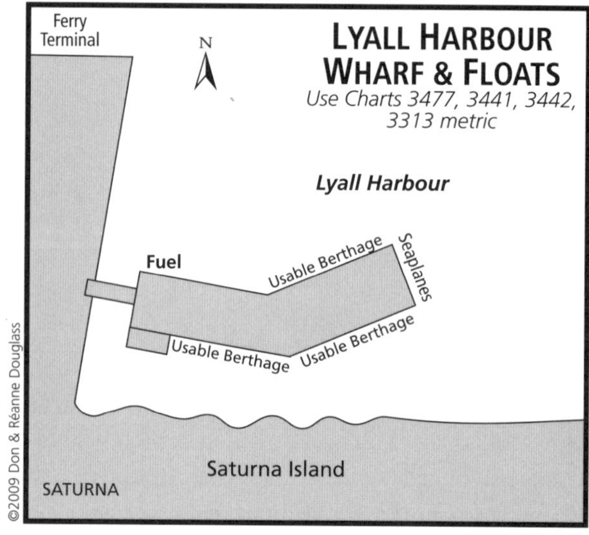

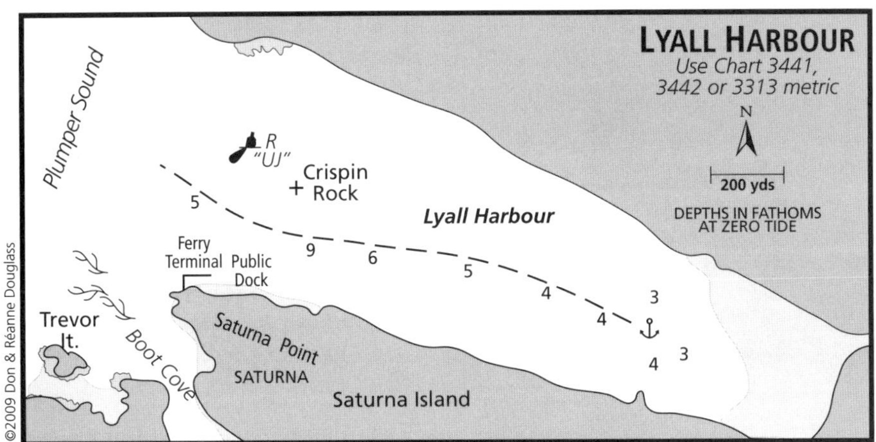

Winter Cove, between the NW side of Saturna Island and the SE side of Samuel Island, is shallow and has several drying reefs and below-water rocks in it. It affords shelter for small craft and a route, from Plumper Sound, to the Strait of Georgia. (SD)

Winter Cove is a popular boating area with its sand and mud beaches and its waters protected from all but northwest winds. When you enter from Plumper Sound, avoid the widespread shoals and isolated rocks inside the cove, especially Minx Reef. Photos of upended sailboats, high and dry in Winter Cove, are legendary, so be sure to check your tide tables and monitor your echo sounder. Because of its proximity to the silt effluent of Fraser River, the water in the cove is opaque and its isolated rocks difficult to see. Mooring buoys along the southwest shore are private.

Lyall Harbour, Saturna Island

Winter Cove Marine Park (Saturna I)

Charts 3477, 3441, 3313; on SE shore of Winter Cove
Anchor: 48°48.68'N, 123°11.56'W

Winter Cove Marine Park is on the east side of the cove. (SD)

Winter Cove Marine Park, now part of the Gulf Islands National Park Reserve, is a good place to limber up and roam around on shore. Anchoring in Winter Cove is the butt of cruising jokes. The east shore is quite shallow and there is a sandbar with 4 feet over it in the center of the cove. Sailboats frequently find themselves listing at odd angles on low water. Using Chart 3477 and a depth sounder will prevent these problems.

The 228-acre marine park has a picnic area, launching ramp, and delightful hiking trails.

Anchor in about 1-1⁄2 fathoms over sand and mud with fair-to-good holding.

⚓ **Winter Cove Marine Park** has a picnic area; launching ramp; hiking trails

William Kelly

Boat Passage viewed from Winter Point

Boat Passage

Charts 3477, 3442, 3313; btwn Winter Pt on Saturna I & Ralph Grey Pt on Samuel I
Position: 48°48.85'N, 123°11.33'W

Boat Passage ... leads into the Strait of Georgia. The passage has a least depth of 2.1 m and two drying rocks lie close-off Ralph Grey Point. It is only suitable for small craft at or near slack water; local knowledge is advised. (SD)

Boat Passage, the narrow slot between Winter Point and Ralph Grey Point, is best observed from land. Rocks and strong currents menace this passage

Lyall Harbour

Steep slopes line both sides of Lyall Harbour where hillside homes sit nestled among the trees. A small valley at the head holds a village with a schoolhouse, playground and two tennis courts for public use. A pair of rubber boots is recommended for hauling your dinghy across the muddy foreshore at low water. Sunset Boulevard leads through the center of the village to East Point Road. If you turn right and follow this road along the harbor's south shore, you will soon reach the island's general store which sells groceries and liquor, as well as freshly-baked cookies and bread from the local Haggis Farm Bakery. Heading in the opposite direction, you can take a scenic, two-to-three mile hike over fairly steep terrain to Winter Cove. For the longer trek to East Point, along the island's north coast, a bicycle is recommended.

The ferry docks at the entrance to Lyall Harbour where a pub/restaurant and store are located just a few steps from the government wharf. From here it's a pleasant walk along the road that rings Boot Cove. Serious hikers will want to tackle Mt. Warbuton Pike, Saturna's highest mountain. It's reached by tracing East Point Road to the Narvaez Bay Road junction (location of the general store) where you take nearby Harris Road which veers to the right. Follow Harris for about half a mile, then turn left onto Staples Road, a packed dirt road that leads through a forest reserve to the mountain summit. Warburton Pike was named for an Oxford-educated and widely-traveled Englishman who arrived on Saturna Island in 1884 to take up sheep farming. Both an adventurer and businessman, he soon owned much of Saturna Island, from Breezy Bay to East Point.

The first light at East Point was constructed in 1888 on land acquired from Warburton Pike. It was built following the 1886 grounding of the barque *Rosenfeld* when the tug towing her ventured too close to East Point. Boiling Reef extends about half a mile northeast of the point, and before a fog horn was installed in 1939, East Point was widely considered the most dangerous point on the route between Vancouver and Victoria. The original lighthouse was replaced in 1967 with a modern house and skeleton tower. Natural attractions at East Point include the eroded sandstone formations, a protected beach and sweeping views across the water where it's not unusual to see a pod of killer whales rounding the point. **—AV**

Anne Vipond

Floats, Lyall Harbour

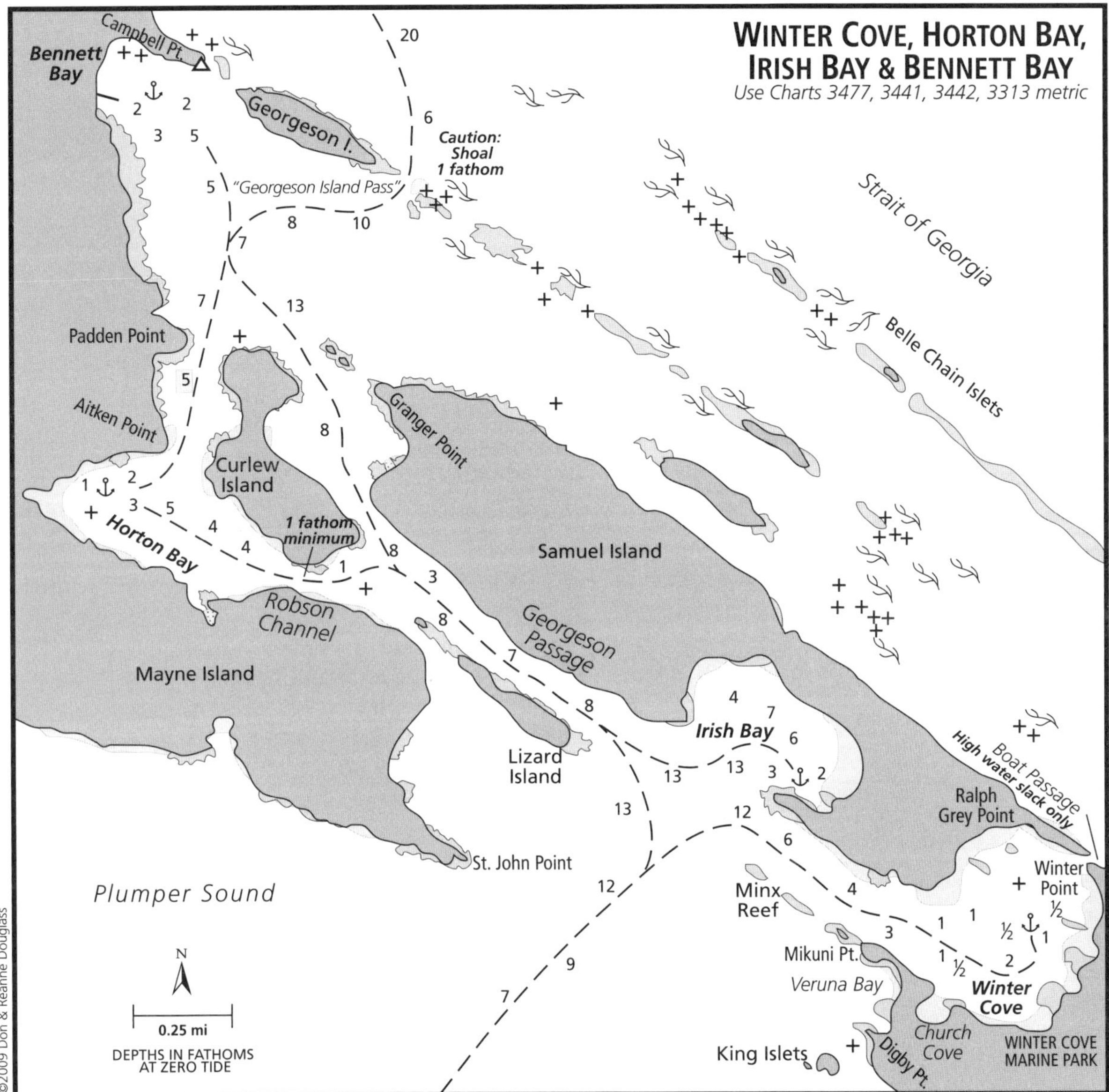

during spring tides with flows of up to 7 knots that create 2-foot high "rooster tails" for 50 yards. Boat Passage is not recommended for anything other than a dinghy or kayak at slack water. When the current is flowing through the passage, there is danger that your boat could be swept through. Although at high-water slack it is sometimes used by local sportfishing boats that cross to the outer coast of Saturna Island or fish the Belle Chain Islets, it is safer to use Georgeson Passage.

Church Cove (Winter Cove)

Charts 3477, 3442, 3313; S end of Winter Cove
Position: 48°48.53'N, 123°11.90'W

Church Cove has a sandy flat which dries at low water. It is sometimes used by local boats.

Irish Bay (Samuel Island)

Charts 3477, 3442, 3313; 0.8 mi NW of Winter Cove
Entrance: 48°49.09'N, 123°12.71'W
Anchor: 48°49.05'N, 123°12.42'W

Irish Bay ... provides good anchorage for small craft. Floats in the bay are private. (SD)

Undeveloped Irish Bay offers good protection just inside its east bight.

Anchor in 3 fathoms; soft bottom with fair holding.

Who checked the tide tables yesterday?

Georgeson Passage

Charts 3477, 3442, 3313; on SW side of Samuel I; from Plumper Sound to the Strait of Georgia
Entrance (S): 48°49.15'N, 123°13.10'W
Entrance (N, 0.20 mi NW of Grainger Pt): 48°50.11'N, 123°14.26'W

Georgeson Passage entered from Plumper Sound between the SE extremity of Lizard Island and the SW side of Samuel Island, leads NW then north between Curlew and Samuel Islands into the Strait of Georgia. The least depth through the fairway is 10.4 m but dangerous shoals and rocks lie in the north entrance.

The flood sets NW and the ebb SE through Georgeson Passage. (SD)

Georgeson Passage provides access to Horton, Bennett, and Campbell bays and the fishing grounds of Belle Chain Islets. The passage is used by small vessels as an alternative to Active Pass. Avoid the shoals and reefs indicated on the charts. While currents on spring tides are strong, they run about half those in Active Pass. The bottom is irregular and turbulence can be encountered.

Winter Cove

Winter Cove Marine Park, now part of the Gulf Islands National Park Reserve, is a great place for walks ashore or for embarking on bicycle rides along the quiet roads of sparsely-populated Saturna Island. A broad sand-and-mud beach beside the boat launch is where most boaters land their dinghies. Nearby lies an open area of lawn with picnic tables overlooking the cove. A trail leads from the edge of the grass clearing into the forest where it loops around Winter Point, with views overlooking the Strait of Georgia. Offshore lie Anniversary Island and the Belle Chain Islets.

At Winter Point you can take a close look at Boat Passage, a narrow gap between Saturna and Samuel Islands. This is a tricky pass with reefs on either side and currents reaching 6 knots. During prohibition it was used by rumrunners when dodging government revenue boats in the Strait of Georgia.

Samuel Island has been owned by a succession of prominent people since the early 1900s, including Ralph Grey, a relative of Earl Grey who was Governor-General of Canada from 1904 to 1911. The island was purchased in the 1930s by the engineer A.J.T. Taylor, builder of Vancouver's Lions Gate Bridge, who leased the island to a resident caretaker named George McRae Thompson and his family.

Taylor had a lodge built overlooking Winter Cove to serve as a private residence whenever he and his friends visited the island, and in summer they often anchored their luxury yachts in Irish Bay. Meanwhile, Thompson raised Jersey cows on Samuel Island and worked at odd jobs on Saturna Island.

The Belle Chain Islets were used for target practice at the beginning of World War II and all day long fighters and bombers would fly over Samuel Island, dropping cartridge cases and, in one instance, mistakenly firing at the lodge. When an officer came to investigate Thompson's complaint, he was shown five paint drums filled with spent shells and clips as well as the path a bullet had taken through the lodge, narrowly missing one of Thompson's daughters and killing three sheep. Damages were paid and the training pilots became more careful about hitting the correct target base.

Saturna Island's July 1st Lamb Barbecue is one of the Gulf Islands' most popular annual events. Formerly held in Breezy Bay, it now attracts dozens of boaters to Winter Cove on the Canada Day holiday. **—AV**

Robson Channel

Charts 3477, 3442, 3313; btwn Mayne I & S shore of Curlew I
Entrance (E): 48°49.57'N, 123°14.04'W
Entrance (W): 48°49.57'N, 123°14.41'W

> *Robson Channel, between the south end of Curlew Island and Mayne Island, leads into the south part of Horton Bay. A rock, with less than 2 m over it, lies in the east entrance to Robson Channel and a drying ledge extends south from the south extremity of Curlew Island.* (SD)

Heading carefully through Robson Channel

Robson Channel, the narrow entrance to Horton Bay, is subject to strong ebb currents. The channel is shallow and has about 1 fathom minimum in the fairway. Avoid the submerged rock south of the entrance point by favoring the north shore, but remain alert to the small reef extending south from Curlew Island. The bottom of Robson Channel is rocky and irregular.

Horton Bay (Mayne Island)

Charts 3477, 3442, 3313; 2.3 mi NW of Winter Cove
Entrance (E): 48°49.57'N, 123°14.41'W
Entrance (N, 0.05 mi E of Paddon Pt): 48°50.10'N, 123°14.62'W
Public floats: 48°49.52'N, 123°14.66'W
Anchor: 48°49.75'N, 123°15.00'W

> *Horton Bay affords snug anchorage for small craft; it should be entered at or near slack water. Entering Horton Bay from the north Paddon Point can be passed reasonably close-to but Aitken Point should be given a reasonably wide berth to avoid the piles extending from it. A rock, with less than 2 m over it, lies 0.1 mile off the head of the bay.*
>
> *The public float, on the south side of Horton Bay, is 24.3 m long with 1.8 to 3.7 m depths alongside.* (SD)

Horton Bay provides good shelter for small craft either at the public dock on the south shore or along the north shore. Strong and unrelenting currents, particularly on spring tides, make anchoring or docking difficult. The public dock is subject to strong currents alongside and is often crowded. The bay should be entered during daylight hours only.

Good anchorage can be found in the northwest corner of the bay, out of the current except for some weak eddies. Avoid the private moorings and drying mud flats.

Anchor in 2 fathoms over sand and mud with good holding.

Bennett Bay (Mayne Island)

Charts 3477, 3442, 3313; 1 mi N of Horton Bay
Anchor: 48°50.72'N, 123°14.84'W

> *Bennett Bay, south of Campbell Point, affords good anchorage for small craft but is exposed to SE winds. ... Private floats are in the bay.* (SD)

Bennett Bay, with its flat, shallow bottom, provides good protection from northwest winds. However, we do not recommend it in southeast gales. (Notice the piles of driftwood on shore!)

Anchor in 1 to 2 fathoms over mud with good holding.

Georgeson Island Pass

Charts 3477, 3442, 3313; 1 mi NE of Horton Bay; 3.9 mi SE of Active Pass
Position: 48°50.49'N, 123°13.89'W

Georgeson Island Pass is what we call the

small-boat passage clear of kelp at the southeast end of Georgeson Island. The narrow passage lies between the reef and kelp beds that extend 0.06 mile southeast of Georgeson Island and the chain of reefs that begin 0.12 mile from Georgeson Island. Use Charts 3477 or 3313 as your guide. The fairway is difficult to gauge during foul weather, limited visibility, or strong currents. The fairway, which carries between 1 and 2 fathoms, should be attempted only in fair weather.

At the west end of Georgeson Island, a small-boat passage with about 1 foot of water at zero tide is frequently used by sportfishing boats at adequate tide levels. Larger boats entering or exiting the Strait of Georgia will find a deep-water route 1.9 miles to the southeast of Georgeson Island along the south side of Belle Chain Islets.

Campbell Bay (Mayne Island)

Charts 3477, 3442, 3313; 2 mi SE of Active Pass
Entrance: 48°51.08'N, 123°14.64'W
Anchor: 48°51.53'N, 123°16.20'W

> *Campbell Bay, entered between Campbell Point and Edith Point, affords temporary anchorage, mud bottom; it is exposed to the SE and has private floats and mooring buoys in it.* (SD)

Campbell Bay offers quiet moorage in fair weather at its head. A number of fine homes with summer docks sit along its south shore. While the bay is open to southeast storms, it does offer protection from prevailing northwest winds. Light southeast winds peter out before reaching the head of the bay.

Anchor in 4 fathoms over sand and mud with good holding.

David Cove (Mayne Island)

Charts 3442, 3313; 0.8 mi SE of Georgina Pt
Position: 48°52.00'N, 123°16.54'W

> *David Cove is fringed by drying ledges and kelp and has depths of 7 to 9 feet (2.1 to 2.7 m) near its head. Anchoring is not recommended because of the submarine cables running through it.* (SD)

David Cove is a small indentation on the outer coast of Mayne Island. Although it is full of mooring buoys, it can be used as a temporary stop to wait for favorable conditions in Active Pass. Avoid the cable crossing area at the north end of the cove.

Swanson Channel

Charts 3441, 3442, 3313; connects Active Pass to Boundary Pass & Satellite Channel
Entrance (S): 48°43.33'N, 123°15.63'W
Entrance (N): 48°49.45'N, 123°20.43'W

> *Swanson Channel leads north from Boundary Pass and Satellite Channel to Trincomali Channel, Active Pass and Navy Channel. North Pender Island forms the east side of Swanson Channel; Moresby, Saltspring and Prevost Islands form its west side. Satellite Channel leads west between Moresby and Saltspring Islands. Captain Passage ... offers no saving in distance to vessels proceeding up Swanson Channel for the upper reaches of Trincomali Channel but by taking this passage the ferry traffic entering and leaving Active Pass is avoided.*
>
> *Tidal streams flood NW and north through Swanson Channel, but a branch flows into Navy Channel; the ebb flows SE. At the north end of Swanson Channel, there is another division of the flood stream, one part going through Active Pass, the other through Trincomali Channel. Toward Enterprise Reef there is a significant increase in the velocity of the flood stream, and, at the entrance to Active Pass 5 to 7 kn can be expected with large tides; 3 to 5 kn on smaller tides.*
>
> *The north part of Swanson Channel is used by ferries operating between Swartz Bay, Tsawwassen, and the Gulf Islands. The tracks are usually mid-channel. However, inter-island ferries cross Swanson Channel between Captain Passage and Otter Bay.* (SD)

Swanson Channel is the main north/south route in the southern Gulf Islands. It is used by boats that are too large to squeeze through Pender Canal. Because the northern section is a main ferry route and fast-moving ferries leave large wakes, use caution throughout the area.

Smugglers Nook (North Pender Island/ Swanson Channel)

Charts 3477, 3441, 3313; 0.27 mi NW of Wallace Pt
Position: 48°44.29'N, 123°14.26'W

Smugglers Nook, a tiny indentation, is used only by small sportfishing boats.

Boat Nook (North Pender Island)

Charts 3441, 3442, 3313; 3.1 mi NW of Bedwell Hbr
Entrance: 48°45.84'N, 123°18.19'W
Anchor: 48°45.93'N, 123°18.18'W

> *Beddis Rock dries 3.7 m and lies off the north entrance point of Boat Nook.* (SD)

Boat Nook is a tiny cove used by sportfishing boats. Open to the south, it provides temporary anchorage in fair weather. Upon entering, avoid the mooring buoys and Beddis Rock and anchor to the west side of the cement piling. Kelp north of Beddis Rock keeps chop to a minimum.

Anchor in 1 to 2 fathoms over sand, mud and shells with good holding.

Thieves Bay (North Pender Island)

Charts 3441, 3442, 3313; 1/2 mi SE of Mouat Pt; 3.6 mi NW of Bedwell Hbr
Entrance: 48°46.30'N, 123°18.95'W
Position: 48°46.26'N, 123°18.79'W

> *Thieves Bay, 0.5 mile NW of Beddis Rock, is shallow with depths of 0.6 m. A rockfill and piling breakwater protects private floats and a launching ramp.* (SD)

Thieves Bay is filled largely by a private marina (members only). Avoid the kelp, rock and reef off the point when entering. Since the small bay has no swinging room, it is useful only in an emergency.

Shingle Bay (North Pender Island)

Charts 3441, 3442, 3313; 0.38 mi NE of Mouat Pt; 4.8 mi SE of Active Pass
Entrance: 48°47.00'N, 123°19.13'W
Anchor: 48°46.88'N, 123°18.64'W

> *Mouat Point ... is fairly steep-to and forms the south side of Shingle Bay. The ruins of an old wharf are on the east side of the bay. A private float is at the head of the bay.*
>
> *Anchorage can be obtained in the centre of Shingle Bay, in depths of 20 to 27 m; it is exposed to west winds.* (SD)

Shingle Bay is a scenic, shallow bay offering good protection from southerly weather off its drying flat. Before you anchor, check the tide tables carefully. The small bay has limited swinging room. Avoid the four rocks off the south entrance point.

Anchor in 1 to 2 fathoms over mud with good holding.

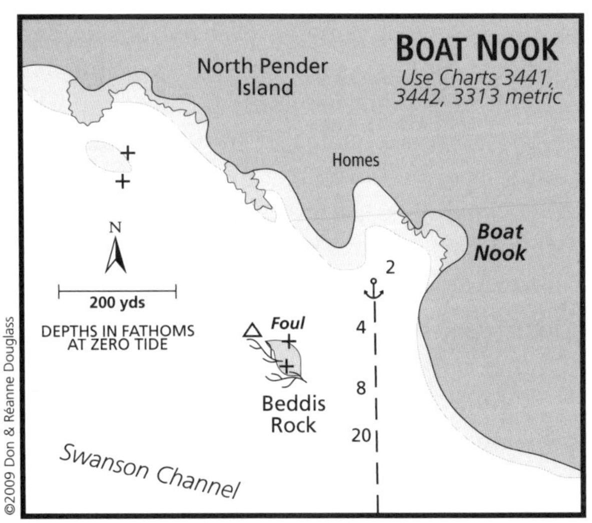

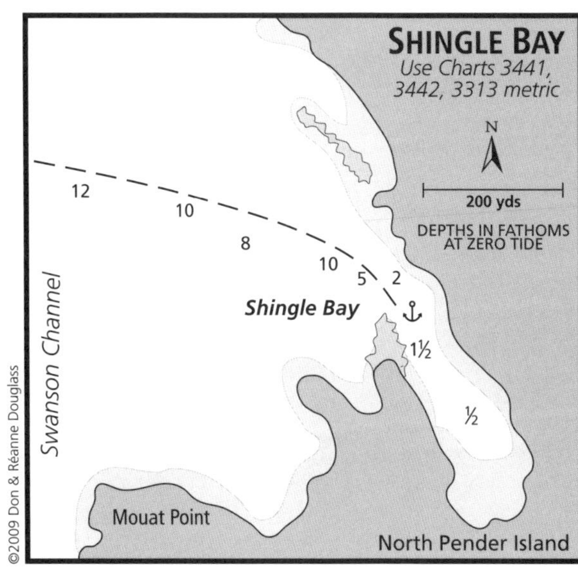

Ella Bay (North Pender Island)

Charts 3441, 3442, 3313; S of Otter Bay on S side of Roe Islet
Position: 48°47.67'N, 123°18.81'W

Ella Bay offers good shelter in its center to small craft in fair weather. Avoid the rocks off the south entrance.

Otter Bay homes

Anne Vipond

Otter Bay (North Pender Island)

Charts 3441, 3442, 3313; 4.0 mi SE of Active Pass; 4.4 mi NW of Bedwell Hbr
Entrance: 48°47.88'N, 123°19.04'W
Anchor: 48°47.82'N, 123°18.43'W

> *Otter Bay has a ferry landing on its north shore. ...*
>
> *Anchorage for small vessels can be obtained in Otter Bay, in 13 to 17 m, mud bottom.* (SD)

Otter Bay is a large bay that offers good protection from southeast weather. The head of Otter Bay or small Ella Bay to the south behind the small islet are popular spots to anchor and have a number of private mooring buoys. Ferry wash is minimal but some afternoon westerly chop is common. Hyashi Cove on the north side of Otter Bay is the site of Otter Bay Marina.

Anchor in 2 to 4 fathoms over mud with good holding.

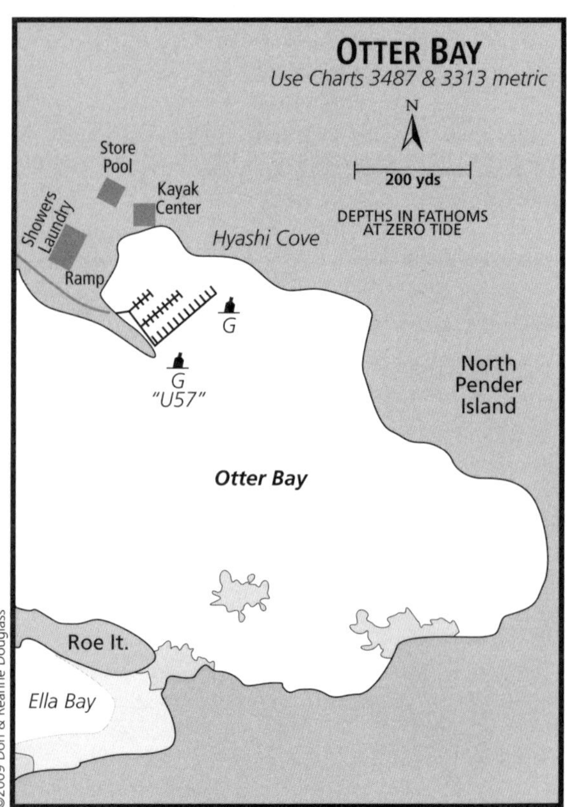

Hyashi Cove (North Pender Island)

Charts 3441, 3442, 3313; in the NW corner of Otter Bay
Marina: 48°47.96'N, 123°18.59'W

> *A marina is on the north side of Otter Bay, in Hyashi Cove. Port hand buoy "U57" is close SE off the point south of the marina.* (SD)

Hyashi Cove is the home to Otter Bay Marina, one of the most popular destinations in the Gulf Islands. Open year-round the marina has full services plus an adult swimming pool and a children's pool, golf course, restaurant, shuttle service to the commercial center and other amenities. Access to the B.C. Ferry is just a short walk. The marina recommends reservations.

⚓ **Otter Bay Marina**
tel: 250.629.3579; fax: 250.629.3589; monitors VHF Ch 66A; power; water; laundry; showers; heated pool; open year-round; reservations recommended

Grimmer Bay/Port Washington

(North Pender Island)

Charts 3442, 3313; 1 mi NW of Otter Bay
Entrance: 48°48.75'N, 123°19.67'W
Public float: 48°48.78'N, 123°19.26'W
Anchor (N): 48°48.72'N, 123°19.24'W

Grimmer Bay, the approach to Port Washington, has a chain of above-water and drying rocks extending 0.2 mile WNW from the middle of its east shore; Boat Islet is the outer extremity of these rocks.

The public wharf is 15.8 m long at its outside face, with 4.6 to 5.8 m alongside. A 21.3-m float is on the south side of the wharf, with a 12.2-m seaplane float attached to it. A 24.4-m float is attached to the north end of the wharf.

Danger.—A rock, with less than 2 m over it, lies about 45.6 m south of the SE end of the public wharf. (SD)

Grimmer Bay is divided into north and south sections by a reef that extends 0.2 mile offshore and is marked by a flashing red light. Quiet anchorage can be found in either the north or south sections of the bay, with the north part providing more protection. There is a lot of swinging room and the bottom is fairly flat. Other than the public wharf and small float on the north shore, there are no facilities here. Port Washington is the small develop-

---

Otter Bay

Around the corner from the B.C. Ferries dock, tucked behind a breakwater in Hyashi Cove, is the Otter Bay Marina —its grounds containing an outdoor swimming pool, small playground, kayak rentals, store and laundromat. Bicycles can be hired at the marina for a tour of North Pender, its hilly and winding roads leading past leafy lanes and country craft shops; a number are located on or near Port Washington Road that leads to Hope Bay where additional studios and craft stores are located.

At the junction of Port Washington Road and Otter Bay Road is Old Orchard Farm, its Victorian farmhouse begun in 1882 by Washington Grimmer, one of Pender's first settlers. Born in London, England, Grimmer married a young local woman named Elizabeth Auchterlonie in 1885. Their second child was delivered in the middle of Navy Channel while Grimmer was rowing Elizabeth to the midwife on Mayne Island. They named the boy Neptune in honor of his waterborne birth and he lived well into his nineties.

Washington Grimmer was the island's first postmaster and once a week he would row the seven miles to Mayne Island to collect the mail. After a government wharf was built at Port Washington in 1890, mail and other goods arrived by steamer. However, the steamer captains disliked the tiny dock and in bad seas they would often signal for Washington to row out and retrieve passengers or supplies.

A short walk north of Otter Bay Marina is the island's nine-hole golf course where you can rent clubs and carts. The course was built in the late 1930s when George Grimmer, a son of Washington, agreed to sell his sheep pasture in Grimmer Valley. The clubhouse serves lunches, snacks and dinner which can be enjoyed outside on the verandah in sunny weather. A bronze sculpture of Washington Grimmer on horseback stands on the edge of the golf course. The Stand at the Otter Bay ferry dock, just down the hill from the marina, is popular for take-out food and provides a small outdoor garden in which to enjoy your milk shakes and seafood burgers.

A Visitor Information Centre is located on Otter Bay Road, about a quarter mile east of the marina. With a map in hand, you can follow South Otter Bay Road to the Malahat Properties park land. Purchased in 1996 by the Pacific Marine Heritage Legacy, this 215-hectare parcel of mostly second-growth forest is, overall, in a natural state with numerous trails, a small lake and some waterfrontage bordering the northeast shores of Shingle Bay. **—AV**

Anne Vipond

Otter Bay pumpkin time

ment at the public wharf on the north shore of Grimmer Bay.

Anchor southeast of the public float in 3 fathoms; sand with fair-to-good holding.

Ellen Bay (Prevost Island)

Charts 3442, 3313; on the S side of Prevost I
Entrance: 48°48.71'N, 123°21.50'W
Anchor: 48°49.18'N, 123°22.60'W

> *Ellen Bay affords fair anchorage near the middle in 27 m, mud bottom, or about 0.1 mile from the head of the bay, in 18 m.* (SD)

Although open to southeast winds, Ellen Bay provides good anchorage with protection from prevailing northwest winds. A shallow 1- to 2-fathom shelf at the isthmus to Annette Inlet can be used as a scenic anchor site (private property, no fires). From your boat at high water you can look into Annette Inlet. Boats wishing more swinging room can anchor farther out in 7 to 8 fathoms. Moderate southerly swell and chop die off along the southern shore before reaching the head of the bay. This can be considered a fair-weather anchorage only—driftwood on the beach indicates this is no place to be caught in a southeast storm.

Anchor in 2 fathoms over a mixed bottom (mud with rocky spots). Holding is fair-to-good if you set your anchor well.

Diver Bay (Prevost Island)

Charts 3442, 3313; 0.5 mi SW of Portlock Pt
Entrance: 48°49.06'N, 123°21.17'W
Anchor: 48°49.48'N, 123°21.85'W

> *Diver Bay is entered between Red Islets and Bright Islet.*
>
> *Small craft can obtain anchorage in 9 to 13 m, sand and mud; it is exposed to the SE.* (SD)

Diver Bay, like Ellen Bay, offers protection in prevailing westerlies, but it is exposed to the southeast and can be considered a fair-weather anchorage only. Anchorage can be found off the small brown house in the north corner at the head of the bay.

Anchor in 4 to 5 fathoms over sand, mud and some rocks.

Richardson Bay (Prevost Island)

Chart 3313; 1.9 mi S of Active Pass
Entrance: 48°49.57'N, 123°21.05'W
Anchor: 48°49.63'N, 123°21.19'W

Richardson Bay, a tiny nook 0.5 mile north of Diver Bay, offers shelter to one or two boats in the lee of a small, unmanned lighthouse on Portlock Point. Rocks and reefs extend 100 yards or more from Portlock Point and an islet with three trees lies off the south shore. Ferry wake, southeast exposure, and the occasional bellowing foghorn are the only concerns in this otherwise natural and quiet place.

Since swinging room is limited, it's a good idea to use a second anchor or a stern tie to shore. Note the rebar stakes and old chain on the north wall.

Anchor in 1 to 3 fathoms over brown sand, mud and sea lettuce with fair holding.

Active Pass

Charts 3473, 3442, 3313; joins the Strt of Georgia with Swanson & Trincomali Channels
Entrance (S, 0.6 mi NW of Enterprise Reef): 48°51.40'N, 123°20.91'W
Entrance (N): 48°52.95'N, 123°17.34'W
Georgina Pt Light: 48°52.40'N, 123°17.49'W
Helen Pt Light: 48°51.46'N, 123°20.70'W

Anne Vipond

B.C. ferry entering Active Pass

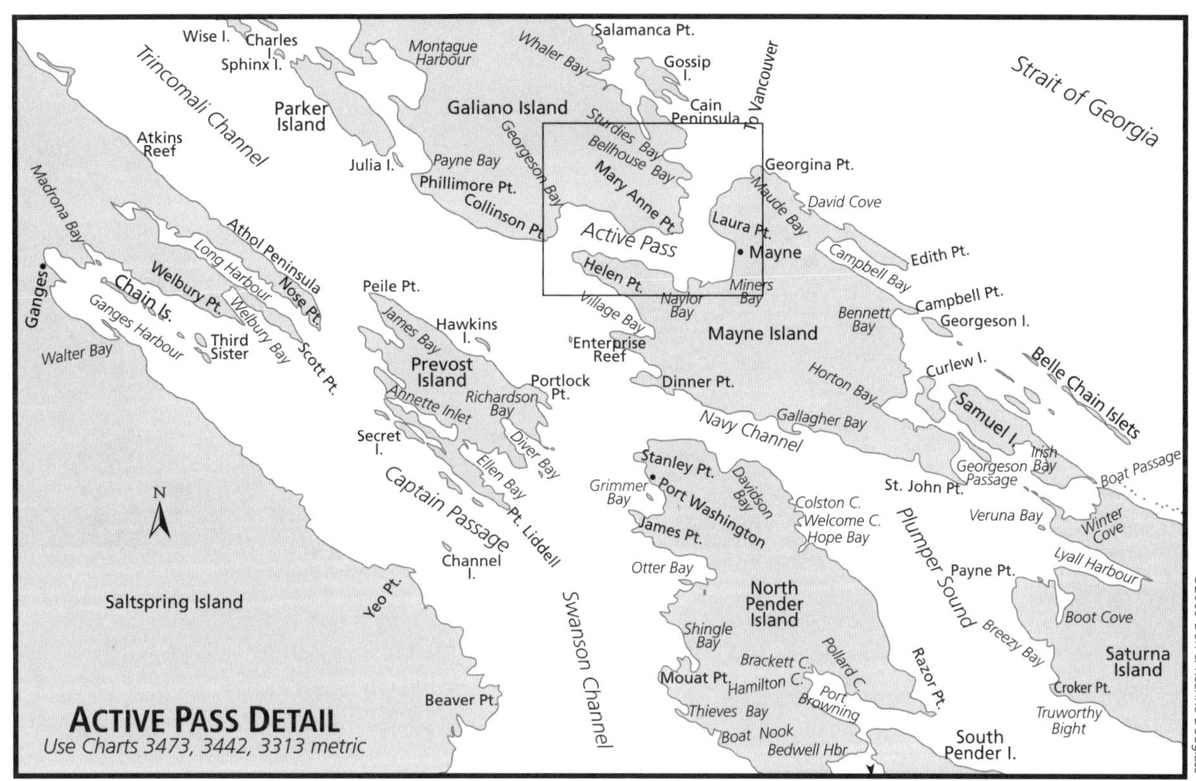

Active Pass ... is a deep, tortuous channel leading from Swanson and Trincomali Channels into the Strait of Georgia. The fairway is about 0.2 mile wide in its narrowest part.

Great care should always be taken to avoid the dangers at the west entrance, as well as Fairway Bank and the shoals, on either side of the north entrance to the pass. Active Pass is

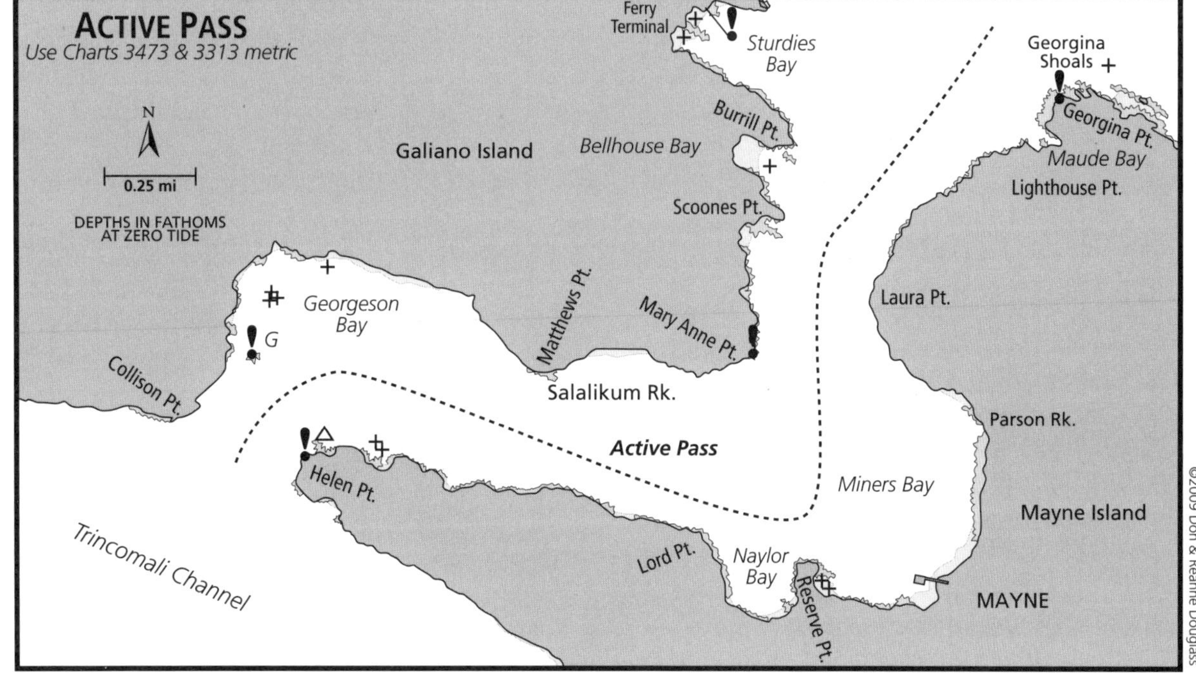

not recommended for attempting under sail.

Predictions of the times and rates of maximum current and the times of slack water are given for Active Pass (Index No. 3000) in the Tide Tables, Volume 5.

On the north-going (flood) tidal stream, there is a strong set into Miners Bay along its north shore, and on the south-going (ebb) tidal stream there is a corresponding set into the bay along its south shore.

On strong flood tides, violent rips, dangerous to small craft, occur over an area extending from mid-channel, south of Mary Anne Point, to Laura Point. Strong rips also occur near Fairway Bank and are increased in violence during strong winds from the north quadrant.

Caution. On the Strait of Georgia side of Active Pass heavy tide-rips occur in the vicinity of Gossip Island, Lion Islets and Salamanca Point, particularly with the flood tidal stream and a strong NW wind. (SD)

Anne Vipond

Looking down on Active Pass from Galiano Island

Active Pass is known for its turbulent waters and strong currents which often reach several knots with breaking waves. Please see the full descriptions in Coast Pilot. *Caution:* It is not recommended that sailboats or low-powered pleasure craft use Active Pass since they cannot maintain normal speeds in the turbulence of spring tides.

The pass carries all ferry and commercial traffic between the Strait of Georgia and the ferry terminal in Swartz Bay. Ferry boats and other large ships announce their pending transit through Active Pass with a security call on VHF Channel 16. If you have restricted maneuverability, respond to their announcement on Channel 16 before they come roaring around the bend.

Within Active Pass, Sturdies Bay and Miners Bay have major facilities in case you need to stop.

Anne Vipond

A passing wake becomes a standing wave in Active Pass

Enterprise Reef

Charts 3473, 3442, 3313; S entr to Active Pass at the confluence of Trincomali, Swanson, & Navy Channels
Enterprise Reef Light: 48°50.70′N, 123°20.90′W

Enterprise Reef consists of two rocky heads about 0.2 mile apart; the west head dries 0.9 m, the other has 0.3 m over it.

Enterprise Reef lights (271), on the west rock, are shown from a white tower with a red band at the top. The upper light, shown at an elevation of 6.4 m, is visible all round the horizon. The lower light, shown at an elevation of 3.8 m, is a sector light.

Port hand buoy "U51" marks the east end of the reef. (SD)

Just west of Enterprise Reef the area is very busy with high-speed ferry traffic that requires alert helmsmanship.

Village Bay (Mayne Island)

Charts 3473, 3442, 3313; 0.9 mi E of Enterprise Reef
Entrance: 48°50.81'N, 123°20.08'W
Anchor: 48°50.59'N, 123°19.53'W

Village Bay, 1 mile SW of Helen Point, affords anchorage in about 15 m north of the submarine cable. A ferry enters the bay at frequent intervals.

A ferry landing is on the north shore of Village Bay. (SD)

Village Bay, the site of the Mayne Island ferry terminal, offers good protection from southeast winds; however, it is subject to ferry wake and open to the northwest. Anchorage can be found in the south side of the bay avoiding the numerous private mooring buoys.

Anchor in 5 fathoms over a mud bottom.

Georgeson Bay (Galiano Island)

Charts 3473, 3442, 3313; 1.25 mi N of Enterprise Reef; 1.9 mi NW of Miners Bay
Position: 48°51.95'N, 123°20.83'W

Georgeson Bay, on the north side of the channel, lies between Collinson Point and Matthews Point. Off the west shore is a drying ledge with Galiano light on it, and farther north there are several shoals and rocks with less than 2 m over them. (SD)

Small craft wanting to get out of the way of ferryboat traffic can anchor temporarily in the 3-fathom shallow north of the submerged rocks.

Naylor Bay (Mayne Island)

Charts 3473, 3442, 3313; 0.5 mi W of Miners Bay
Position: 48°51.10'N, 123°18.80'W

B.C. Marine Trails

The British Columbia Marine Trail Association was established to preserve recreational access to the coast from the water. Using advocacy, education, and stewardship the BCMTA will facilitate the creation and maintenance of a water trail from the 49th parallel to Canada's border with Alaska in the north. Every 8 to 10 miles, wherever possible, will be a site accessible to the public for landing and/or camping. These sites, not solely restricted to human-powered craft, cater to all types of small craft exploring B.C.'s rugged coast. Some sites are already established in the form of existing Marine Parks under various government organizations. Other sites have been licensed to the BCMTA by the private landowners. Depending upon the usage of the site, the BCMTA uses the volunteer initiative of its members to clean up and build any appropriate facilities such as a composting toilet at Blackberry Point on Valdes Island (Gulf Islands).

For a small fee/donation the public can now enjoy this site and all its amenities. It is the long-term goal to have the trail completed by the year 2005. We encourage everyone to participate by joining the Association and volunteering to help out. The recent publication "Kayak Routes of the Pacific Northwest" outlines roughly the current trail and is available from the BCMTA. You can contact the BCMTA by writing to 2000-1066 West Hastings Street, Vancouver, B.C. V6E 3X2, tel: 604.683.5191, www.bctma.com Being a member allows you to participate in this ambitious project plus the newsletters will inform you of new sites being developed. Come to B.C. and enjoy the beauty of our coast.

Miners Bay (Mayne Island)

Charts 3473, 3442, 3313; in the center of Active Pass; on the NW side of Mayne I
Entrance: 48°51.33'N, 123°18.24'W
Public float: 48°51.13'N, 123°18.12'W
Anchor: 48°51.24'N, 123°18.04'W

Georgina Point Light

> *Miners Bay, 0.5 mile SE of Mary Anne Point, affords anchorage in case of necessity. Mariners must go close inshore to obtain a depth of 20 m, and even there are barely out of the whirl of the tidal streams; caution is necessary because of the strong eddies that set into the bay. Numerous private mooring buoys lie close offshore. Anchorage is prohibited in the submarine cable area.*
>
> *Mayne, a settlement in the SE corner of Miners Bay, has a post office (V0N 2J0), heliport and communication with neighbouring ports and communities is maintained ... through the ferry landing at Village Bay.*
>
> *The pub lic wharf has a berthing face of 21.6 m with a depth of 4 m alongside. Three floats are attached to the public wharf. The float on the south side is for small craft.* (SD)

Miners Bay, on the east shore of Active Pass, is off to the side of the traffic and turbulence found in Active Pass; however, a moderately strong countercurrent to Active Pass circulates inside the bay. It is also subject to frequent ferry wake.

The public wharf and fuel dock have limited moorage. Temporary anchorage can be taken north of the public wharf and fuel dock, avoiding private mooring buoys.

Miners Bay gets its name from a local campsite once used by gold miners traveling to the Fraser River from Victoria.

Anchor in 4 fathoms over sand and gravel with fair holding.

Bellhouse Bay (Galiano Island)

Charts 3473, 3442, 3313; 0.35 mi S of Sturdies Bay
Position: 48°52.25'N, 123°18.69'W

> *Bellhouse Bay, between Scoones Point and Burrill Point, has drying reefs in it.* (SD)

Bellhouse Bay is too shallow for convenient anchorage.

Sturdies Bay (Galiano)

Charts 3473, 3442, 3313; N end of Active Pass; E end of Galiano I
Entrance: 48°52.53'N, 123°18.65'W
Public float: 48°52.59'N, 123°18.93'W

> *Sturdies Bay is shallow with some foul ground extending about 0.1 mile from the head. A combined public wharf and ferry landing has a depth of 4.9 m alongside its head. ... The wharf is equipped with a 3-tonne crane. The community has stores and resorts and the B.C. Ferry Corporation makes regular calls.* (SD)

Sturdies Bay, one of the two ferry landings for Galiano Island (the other being Montague), serves the residents of Cain Peninsula and

Whaler Bay. The bay offers moderate and temporary shelter.

A public float is located on the west side of the ferry complex. *Caution:* Beware of strong ferry wake and shallow waters at this float. It is a short walk up the ferry ramp to the Sturdies Bay community. Bellhouse Park, on the south shore of Sturdies Bay, is a good place to picnic and observe the ferryboats plowing through Active Pass.

Anchor (temporarily) in 1 to 2 fathoms south of the ferry terminal.

Maude Bay (Mayne Island)

Charts 3473, 3442, 3313; in the N of Mayne I; at the N end of Active Pass
Position: 48°52.33'N, 123°17.60'W

Maude Bay is a small, shallow indentation on Lighthouse Point 0.1 mile southwest of Georgina Point Light.

Whaler Bay (Galiano, Strait of Georgia)

Charts 3473, 3442, 3313; 0.7 mi NW of Sturdies Bay
Entrance (SE): 48°53.08'N, 123°18.88'W
Entrance (N): 48°53.87'N, 123°19.83'W
Small craft public float: 48°53.02'N, 123°19.57'W
Position (Murchison Cove): 48°53.40'N, 123°20.11'W

The passage between Gossip Island and Cain Peninsula leads to Whaler Bay; it has rocks and shoals in its SE entrance and a least depth of 8.8 m.

The north entrance to Whaler Bay lies between Gossip Island and Twiss Point. Lion Islets, 0.4 mile north of Twiss Point, consist of two islets connected by a drying reef; the passage west of the islets is unusable, even for small craft.

Caution. Heavy tide-rips occur in the vicinity of Gossip Island and Lion Islets, particularly with a flood tidal stream and a strong NW wind.

The public wharf and float are in the south arm of Whaler Bay, about 0.2 mile south of Cain Point. Depths of as little as 0.3 m are found in the vicinity of this wharf. There are numerous private wharves, floats and flag staffs along the shores of Whaler Bay and Gossip Island. (SD)

Whaler Bay, sheltered by Gossip Island on the east and Galiano Island on its south and west, is very shallow with a number of reefs and submerged rocks. Shelter can be found off the coves along the west side of Whaler Bay. Murchison Cove, at the southwest corner of Whaler Bay, dries completely at low water.

The bay, while exposed to winds from the north and northeast, is generally a good place to await favorable conditions in Active Pass. The public float located in the shallow waters of the south arm of Whaler Bay can be used only with careful reference to tide tables.

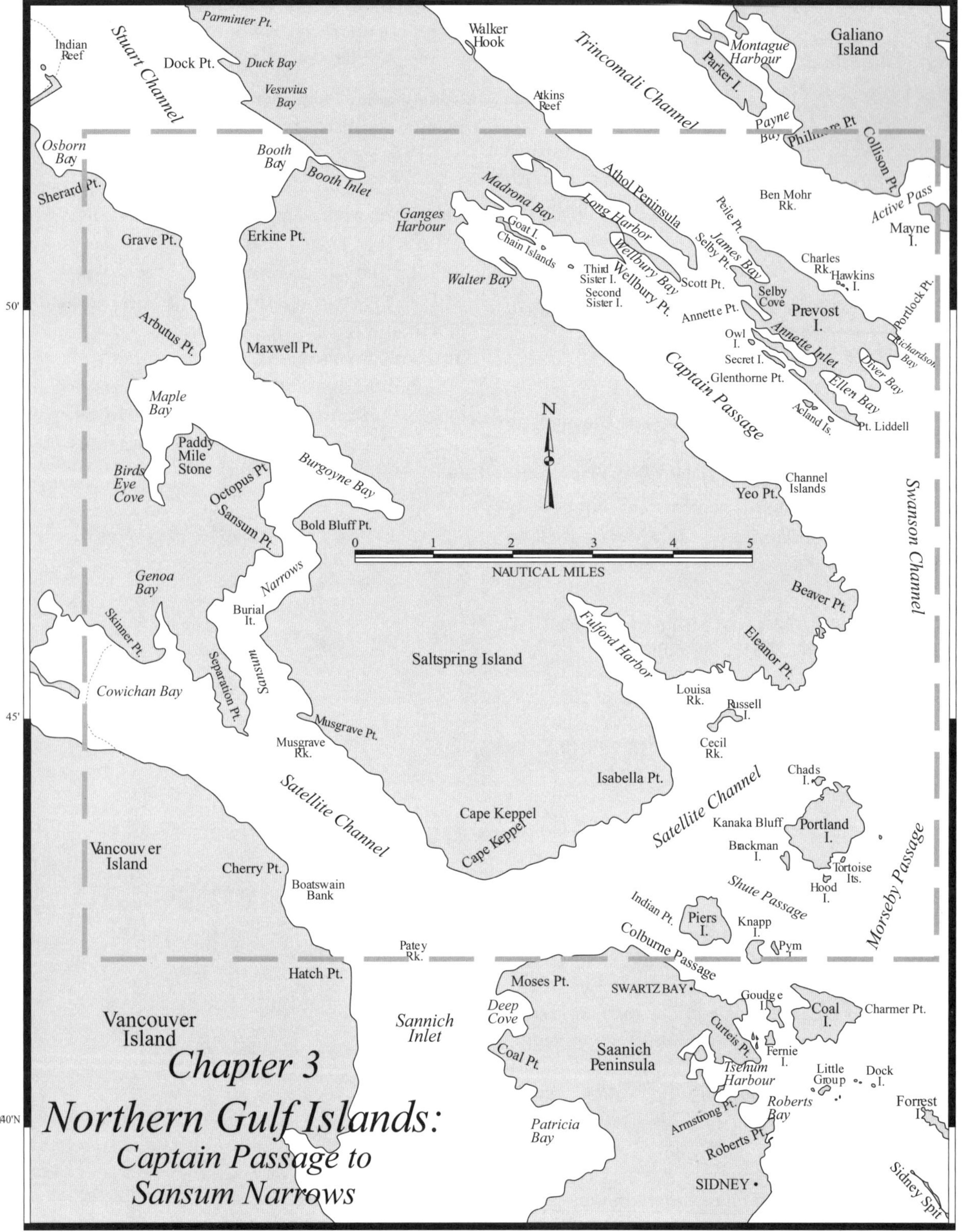

Chapter 3
Northern Gulf Islands: Captain Passage to Sansum Narrows

3

CAPTAIN PASSAGE TO SANSUM NARROWS: Saltspring and Prevost Islands, Portland Island, and Satellite Channel

From the southern end of Galiano Island, it's just a short hop southwest across Trincomali Channel to Prevost Island. Ringed by small inlets offering scenic beauty in intimate settings, Prevost Island is one of the more isolated islands in terms of access and development. It is a beautiful place, a quiet pastoral countryside that has been farmed by the family of Hussey de Burgh since 1924. The seven large indentations in Prevost's shoreline, including James Bay, Selby Cove, Annette Inlet, and Glenthorne Passage, offer isolated anchorages far from the bustle of busier islands.

Saltspring Island, which lies across Captain Passage from Prevost, is the largest and most populous of the Gulf Islands and the center of island enterprise. Known originally by the native peoples as Klaathem, it received its current name from officers of the Hudson's Bay Company because of its brine pools—14 in all—that lie inland. The first permanent settlers were freed black slaves seeking to avoid the prejudice they encountered in the U.S. With its 77 miles of shoreline, Saltspring offers numerous harbors, bays and coves to entice the cruising visitor. Ganges Harbour—a major tourist attraction—is a busy place with several marinas, shops, boutiques, galleries, and restaurants.

Portland Island, site of Princess Margaret Marine Park, and nearby Brackman Island Ecological Reserve are just a short distance south across Satellite Channel.

Portland Island was given to Princess Margaret on her visit to Victoria in 1958, and she in turn gave the island to British Columbia. The Marine Park encompasses the entire island, offering a unique opportunity to explore a complete island in its natural setting. The island is heavily wooded with many hiking trails along its slopes. Portland Island can be easily circumnavigated by dinghy or kayak to observe the tide zone. The east side of the island is a paradise for scuba divers; off the shore, a sunken freighter serves as an artificial reef for divers.

From Portland Island, take Satellite Channel south to Fulford Harbour or the southernmost shores of Saltspring and over to Vancouver Island for a visit to Cowichan and Genoa bays. Cowichan is a picturesque, bustling village with some marvelous inns, restaurants, a great deli, and several marinas and marine supply stores. Genoa Bay is the site of Genoa Bay Marina, with excellent facilities for transients, including showers, cafe, crafts, and a friendly atmosphere. There are some good hikes from Genoa Bay, especially up to Mount Tzuhalem for terrific views down Satellite Channel to the Saanich Peninsula.

Sansum Narrows runs almost due north-south between Vancouver and Saltspring

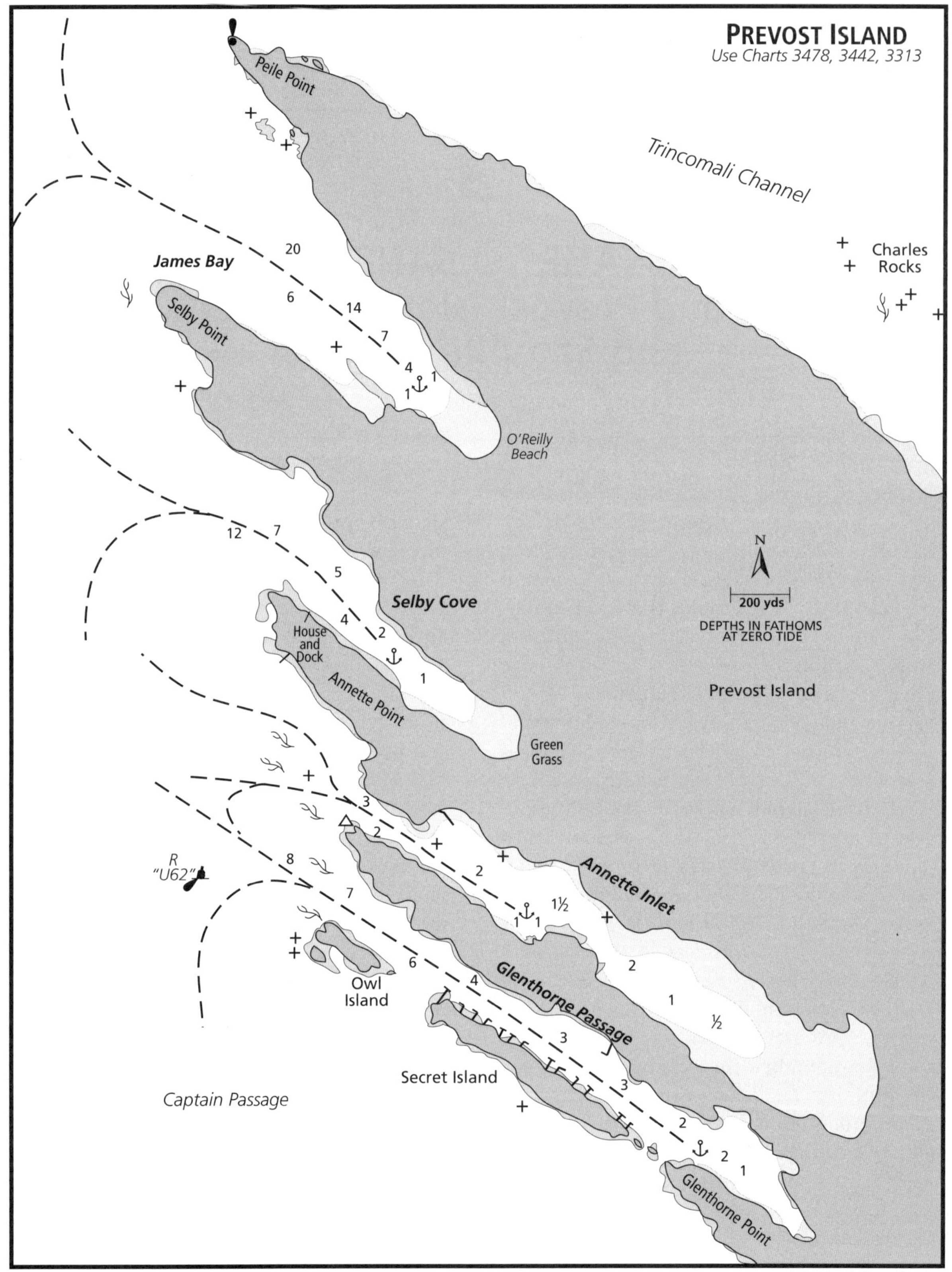
PREVOST ISLAND
Use Charts 3478, 3442, 3313
Peile Point
Trincomali Channel
Charles Rocks
James Bay
Selby Point
O'Reilly Beach
Selby Cove
House and Dock
Annette Point
Green Grass
N
200 yds
DEPTHS IN FATHOMS AT ZERO TIDE
Prevost Island
R "U62"
Annette Inlet
Owl Island
Glenthorne Passage
Secret Island
Captain Passage
Glenthorne Point

Anne Vipond
Good holding over sticky bottom can be found in James Bay

islands. This winding channel is well sheltered and the shortest route between Saanich Peninsula and Dodd Narrows at the north end of the Gulf Islands.

On the Saltspring side of the narrows, Musgrave Landing offers some enticing hikes, beautiful Burgoyne Bay is a good place to swim, and nearby Mount Maxwell Provincial Park offers hiking, picnicking, hidden caves, and spectacular views. Adjoining the park is an Ecological Reserve a great spot for watching the dynamic flights of turkey vultures, peregrine falcons, and bald eagles. On the Vancouver side are Maple Bay and Birds Eye Cove. Popular Maple Bay Marina has showers, laundry, gift shop, groceries, and a restaurant; the beautiful grounds entice most visitors to stroll the garden. At Birds Eye Cove Marina, look for their new mural.

Captain Passage

Charts 3478, 3442; leads from Swanson to Trincomali Chs
Entrance (S, 0.6 mi N of Beaver Pt Lt): 48°46.85′N, 123°21.93′W
Entrance (N, mid-ch btwn Nose & Peile Pts): 48°50.76′N, 123°24.80′W

> *Captain Passage, entered from Swanson Channel between Beaver Point and Point Liddell, leads NW between Prevost and Saltspring Islands to Ganges Harbour and Trincomali Channel.*
>
> *Tidal streams within Captain Passage attain 2 to 3 kn on the flood and 3 to 4 kn on the ebb.*
>
> *The Gulf Islands ferries operating from Tsawwassen, on the mainland, pass at frequent intervals through Captain Passage and call into Long Harbour, at the NW end of the passage.* (SD)

Out of the main ferry traffic lanes, Captain Passage is frequently used by pleasure craft as an alternative to Active Pass. Numerous rocks and reefs in the passage are well marked and charted.

When following the center of Captain Passage, avoid Horda Shoals marked by green-red-green buoy “UD” on the west and the shoal marked by red buoy “U62” on the east; both are off the entrance to Glenthorne Passage.

Prevost Island (Captain Passage)

Charts 3478, 3442, 3313; 2 mi SW of Active Pass

> *Prevost Island is moderately high, thickly wooded and separates Captain Passage from Swanson and Trincomali Channes. Point Liddell, the SE extremity of Prevost Island, has a reef of drying and below-water rocks extending 0.2 mile SE from it.* (SD)

Prevost Island is privately owned and has no regular ferry service. It has several deep coves which afford some good anchor sites, as well as opportunities for fishing and recreation.

(For anchor sites on the east side of Prevost Island facing Swanson Channel, please see Chapter 2.)

James Bay (Prevost Island)

Charts 3478, 3442, 3313; 3.8 mi E of Ganges Hbr
Entrance: 48°50.78′N, 123°24.39′W
Anchor: 48°50.48′N, 123°23.89′W

> *James Bay, north of Selby Cove, is sheltered from the south but open to the NW.* (SD)

James Bay offers very good protection from southeast storms with lots of swinging room

Anne Vipond

James Bay's broad gravel beach

over a rare sticky bottom; a number of boats can crowd in here. Although it is open to the northwest, afternoon chop usually dies off before the head of the bay. However, when strong northwesterlies blow through Trincomali Channel, James Bay can become uncomfortable. In settled weather, it is a quiet anchorage and a favorite of cruising boats.

Avoid the foul ground just south of Peile Point light and the long reef along the south shore. The beach at the head of the drying flat is known as O'Reilly Beach.

Anchor in 4 to 6 fathoms over thick black mud with very good holding.

Selby Cove (Prevost Island)

Charts 3478, 3442, 3313; 0.8 mi S of Peile Pt
Entrance: 48°50.27'N, 123°24.38'W
Anchor: 48°50.05'N, 123°23.96'W

Annette Inlet and Selby Cove ... are narrow and shallow but afford sheltered anchorage to small craft. (SD)

Selby Cove, separated from James Bay by the long peninsula of Selby Point, is protected on its south side by Annette Point. Entered between Annette and Selby points, the cove offers snug anchorage at its head off the drying flat. Avoid the rock at Annette Point and the large private dock just to the southeast. Night or radar approaches to Selby Cove are the easiest of any on Prevost Island.

Selby Cove, although more intimate and sce-

James Bay and Selby Cove

Prevost Island, accessible only by private craft, is one of the least developed of the Gulf Islands, much of it remaining pastoral farmland. To preserve some of this island's pristine scenery, the Pacific Marine Heritage Legacy—a federal/provincial partnership—acquired waterfront property on James Bay and adjacent Selby Cove in 1996.

James Bay is now almost completely surrounded by park land, from its northeast entrance point to its head and halfway along its southwest shoreline where a small orchard has always been an attraction with its springtime apple blossoms. Boaters can head ashore to the broad gravel beach at the bay's head where a cleared valley leads inland and a sheep trail can be hiked to Peile Point. The entire Peile Point peninsula, with views overlooking Trincomali Channel, is part of the park.

About half of Selby Cove's northeast shoreline, opposite the Annette Point peninsula, is now park. Any park services on Prevost will be minimal since it's the natural scenery of this island that the Legacy is striving to preserve. Forest trails and grassy bluffs make these Prevost anchorages ideal for hikes and picnics.

Prevost Island, along with James Bay, was named by Captain Richards in 1859 for Captain James Prevost, commander of the *HMS Satellite*. Captain Prevost was the British commissioner appointed to settle the San Juan boundary dispute between British Columbia and the United States, and was a key witness in the arbitration hearings. He died, an admiral, in 1891.

Prevost Island was acquired by Digby Hussey de Burgh in the 1920s. An Irishman of noble lineage, whose family owned an estate in County Limerick, de Burgh raised sheep, goats and cattle on Prevost's pastures. His son Hubert took over the island property in 1938. His four daughters grew up on this isolated island—one becoming a concert pianist. Upon Hubert's death, his widow Jean, two of their daughters and a son-in-law continued living on Prevost and much of the island remains in the family's hands. **—AV**

Anne Vipond

Looking north from the hilltop at James Bay

nic than James Bay, has more limited swinging room.

Anchor in 1 to 2 fathoms over sand with fair-to-good holding.

Annette Inlet (Prevost Island)

Charts 3478, 3442, 3313; 1.2 mi S of Peile Pt
Entrance: 48°49.94'N, 123°24.21'W
Anchor: 48°49.63'N, 123°23.61'W

Anne Vipond

Using a stern tie to shore in Selby Cove

Annette Inlet has a drying rock in its approach and shoal depths on the north and south sides of its entrance. A private daybeacon is on the south entrance point to Annette Inlet. (SD)

Landlocked Annette Inlet is a quiet and picturesque place to get away from it all. Avoid the dangerous rock and shoal 200 yards off the center of the entrance by favoring either the Annette Point side or the Glenthorne Passage side. There is another submerged rock 250 yards inside the inlet, south of a private dock.

The head of the inlet dries and is shallow throughout—a good environment for birds. You can anchor midchannel off the flat or, for protection from southeast gusts, in the little nook on the south shore. Although Annette Inlet provides very good shelter it has limited swinging room. At high tide you can see across the head of the inlet into Ellen Bay.

Anchor in one-half to 1 fathom over soft mud with very good holding.

Glenthorne Passage

Charts 3478, 3442, 3313; NE of Secret I
Entrance: 48°49.70'N, 123°24.13'W
Anchor: 48°49.28'N, 123°23.22'W

Glenthorne Passage has several private mooring buoys and floats along its shores. (SD)

Nestled in a scenic setting, Glenthorne Passage is a cruising favorite that gives very good protection in all weather. It is entered at its northwest opening by passing on either side of Owl Island. The north shore of Secret Island has many private homes and docks. Anchorage can be taken anywhere along the narrow channel. The southeast entrance, a window off Glenthorne Point, is only 10 yards wide with a half-fathom in the fairway at low water; it is used as a dinghy passage.

Anchor in 2 to 3 fathoms over mud with good holding.

Anne Vipond

Tucked behind the spit in Long Harbour

Saltspring Island

Twenty miles long and eight miles wide, Saltspring Island is the largest of the southern Gulf Islands. Explored by the Spanish and English in the 1700s, and first settled in the 1850s, the island became a major sheep-farming area in the 1900s.

Lying in the rain shadow of Vancouver Island, Saltspring Island has cool, dry summers with lots of sunshine. There are quiet beaches, acres of forest with miles of trails, and an abundance of wildlife. It is a wonderful place for hiking, camping, cycling, riding, diving and kayaking.

Many well-known artists live on Saltspring and the island has become a center for arts and crafts. There are galleries, inns, pubs, restaurants, and shopping to suit everyone.

Note: Although residents of Saltspring Island write the name of their island as Salt Spring, we follow the convention used on the charts except in the case of local names.

Long Harbour (Saltspring Island)

Charts 3478, 3442, 3313; 1.3 mi NE of Ganges Hbr
Entrance: 48°50.48′N, 123°25.30′W
Anchor (Nose Pt Islets): 48°50.83′N, 123°25.69′W
Anchor (in nook; 0.27 mi NW of Clamshell Islet): 48°51.39′N, 123°26.64′W
Anchor (head of hbr): 48°51.64′N, 123°27.90′W

Long Harbour, entered between Scott Point and Nose Point, extends 2 miles NW terminating in a mud flat. A group of islets, connected to the north shore by a drying ridge, lie 0.4 mile NW of Nose Point.

Anchorage can be obtained in Long Harbour, north of the ferry route and midway between the group of islets, near the entrance, and Clamshell Islet in the middle of the harbour, in 17 to 18 m, mud bottom.

Facilities of the Royal Vancouver Yacht Club ... are private. (SD)

Long Harbour, on the south side of Athol Peninsula, extends 2.2 miles deep into Saltspring Island. This long, scenic inlet becomes quiet once past the area of local traffic between the Royal Vancouver Yacht Club outstation and the ferry terminal.

Anne Vipond

Nose Point

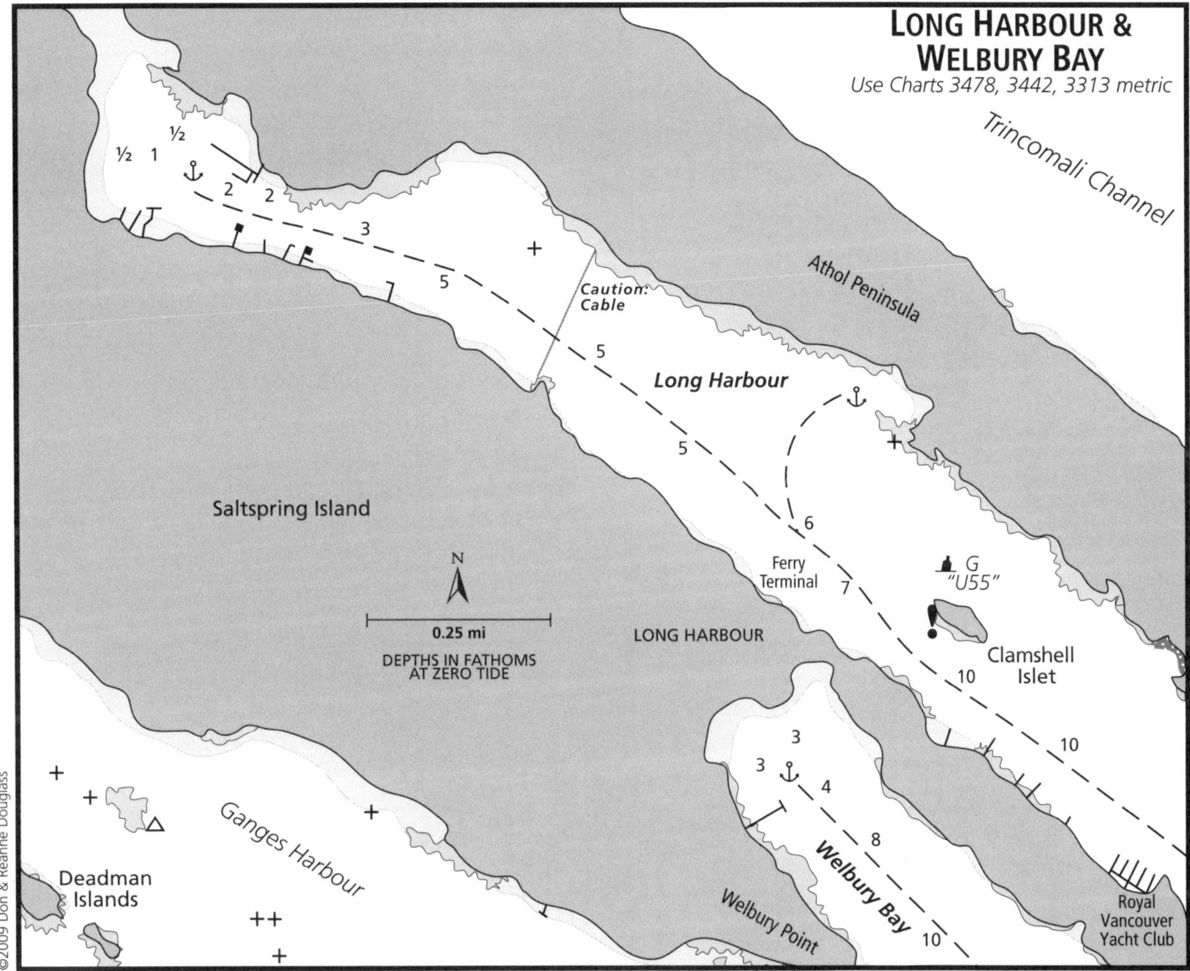

In addition to beautiful private homes along shore, you may frequently see classic wooden schooners moored at the head of Long Harbour. Good protection is afforded in most weather as southeast chop tends to die off the deeper you go into the harbor. The head has numerous private docks and mooring buoys. Avoid anchoring near the cable crossing 0.45 mile northwest of the ferry dock.

Anchor (head of the harbor) in 1 to 2 fathoms over sticky gray mud with very good holding.

Welbury Bay (Saltspring Island)

Charts 3478, 3442, 3313; btwn Long & Ganges Hbrs
Entrance: 48°50.31'N, 123°25.64'W
Anchor: 48°50.94'N, 123°26.21'W

Welbury Bay is entered between Welbury Point and Scott Point. A shoal extending 0.6 mile SE from Welbury Point is marked at its outer end by port hand buoy "U49." (SD)

Welbury Bay is well placed on Captain Passage to offer shelter from north and west winds; it is open to the southeast. Except for the rocky patch northwest of buoy "U49," it has easy access. The northeast corner of the bay is just a few yards from the Long Harbour B.C. ferry dock.

Welbury Bay is surrounded by fine homes along the tree-covered shore and does not have the local and commercial traffic found in Long Harbour and Ganges Harbour.

Anchor in 3 to 4 fathoms over mud with good holding.

Madrona Bay (Saltspring Island)

Charts 3478, 3442, 3313; 0.5 mi NE of Ganges, inside Chain Islets
Entrance (E): 48°50.49′N, 123°26.91′W
Entrance (S): 48°51.19′N, 123°29.11′W
Anchor: 48°51.46′N, 123°29.17′W

Madrona Bay is the small bay protected by and separated from Ganges Harbour by the Chain Islets. Away from the bustle of Ganges Harbour, Madrona Bay offers a quieter anchorage for cruising boats with a view of attractive homes among the trees.

The deep-water channel to Madrona Bay starts 0.23 mile southwest of Welbury Point and 0.38 mile northeast of Second Sister Island. Stay north of the reefs and rocks and favor the Saltspring Island shore until you have passed Money Makers Rock and the reef north of Deadman Islands. Once past these reefs, favor the north shore of Goat Island to avoid two rocks near the center of the channel.

The south entrance between Powder Islet and the west corner of Goat Island is marked with a navigational aid; however, use caution in transiting this narrow passage—the fairway carries just 2 fathoms and has reefs on either side.

Anchor in 2 to 3 fathoms over grey mud with very good holding.

Ganges Harbour (Saltspring Island)

Charts 3478, 3442, 3313; 5.9 mi W of Active Pass
Entrance (0.15 mi SE of Second Sister I Lt; 0.12 mi NE of Ganges Shoal): 48°50.05′N, 123°27.24′W
Entrance (Government Boat Basin, 0.13 mi SW of Grace Islet Lt): 48°51.04′N, 123°29.76′W
Public floats (NW of Coast Guard wharf): 48°51.27′N, 123°29.91′W
Anchor (0.14 mi NE of Coast Guard wharf): 48°51.33′N, 123°29.78′W
Ganges Marina (N end of breakwater): 48°51.36′N, 123°29.92′W
Salt Spring Marina (harbor's end): 48°51.45′N, 123°30.03′W

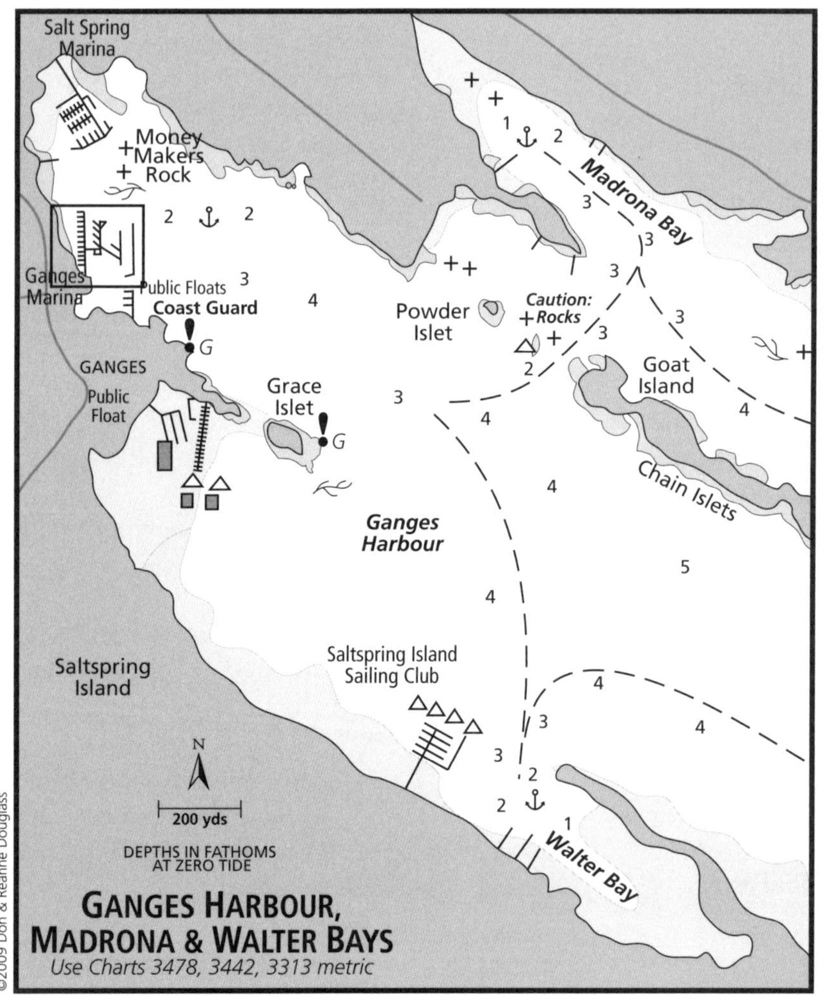

Ganges Harbour, entered from Captain Passage, is free of dangers in the fairway, with the exception of Ganges Shoal, which has 4 m over it.

The public wharf, 0.2 mile NW of Grace Islet light, has a berthing length of 41 m and depths of 2.8 to 4.7 m alongside.

Public floats for small craft are about 45 m NW of the public wharf.

The boat basin, west of Grace Islet, is protected on its east side by a breakwater. . . . Three

Gulf Island hideaway

public floats with a common connection to shore are at the north end of this boat basin; they provide a total berthing space of 300 m. Power is laid on the floats; garbage and used oil disposal facilities are at the head of the floats.

Marinas are near the head of Ganges Harbour.

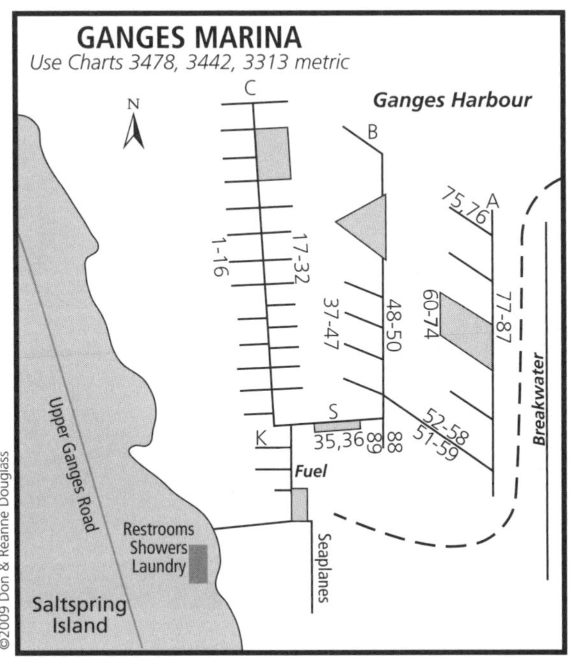

On approaching the marina at the head of the harbour take extra caution to avoid Money Makers Rock, which has less than 6 feet (1.8 m) over it.

The approach to Ganges is without danger or difficulty provided it is made south and west of the Chain Islands; but a good lookout should be kept for seaplanes landing and taking off in the harbour.

Money Makers Rock, close-off the marina near the head of Ganges Harbour, has less than 2 m over it. (SD)

Ganges Harbour, the largest of the settlements on Saltspring Island, is a quaint town with a variety of gift shops, restaurants, galleries and a market, all within a short walking distance of the boat harbor.

The public Ganges Boat Harbour Wharf has power, showers, garbage and waste disposal, launch ramp, and telephone; transients are welcome. Salt Spring Marina at the head of the bay offers guest moorage, power (15 and 30 amp), showers, laundry and a launch ramp. A chandlery, gift shop and haulout up to 40 feet is also available. The Rogue Café is open for breakfast lunch and dinner and take-out lunches, or dine at the well-known Moby's Oyster Bar. During the summer months a harbor shuttle is available to cross the harbor into town. Ganges Marina, just north of the public floats next to the Coast Guard pier, was recently renovated with new marina offices, bathrooms, showers and an area for internet connections. The docks are capable of handling boats of all sizes with 15, 30 and 50 amp power. Complimentary muffins and coffee every morning at the marina office provides an interesting opportunity to meet your fellow cruisers.

For reading matter and charts, we like to head to Volume II Bookstore in Mouat's Mall near the public dock (open seven days a week in summer).

Ganges Harbour can be very busy in the summer, but you can usually find fair-weather anchorage across the bay off the northeast shore. Walter Bay, 0.85 mile southeast of Ganges, provides shelter from southeast winds; Madrona Bay, 0.5 mile northeast of Ganges, offers a quiet escape from the traffic and bustle of Ganges.

Money Makers Rock (mentioned above in the quotation from SD) is sometimes marked by kelp; it lies 400 feet north of the Ganges breakwater and 300 feet southeast of Saltspring Marina.

Ganges

Ganges – village by the sea – is a great place to unwind, and stock up. Whether at anchor, tied up at one of several marinas, or the public dock, it is only minutes away by dinghy or on foot to the town center. Of course, it could take longer if you get sidetracked and wander into one of many interesting diversion along the way. Operative words: relaxing, hospitable, convenient.

The business hub of the village, Mouat's Center, has just about everything you ever wanted but never expected to find: supermarket, bank, post office, hardware/general store, liquor store, book vendors, clothing shops, art galleries, and restaurants. The challenge will be where to go first.

For provisioning, Thrifty Foods is one terrific supermarket which prides itself on the personal touch and, get this – Thrifty delivers to boats! Be sure to check out the bakery, deli and cheese sections. Enjoy the great Saltspring cheese!

Mouat's Store, opened in 1907, combines old fashioned hospitality and ambience with 21st century trends. Whether buying or browsing, this place is pure fun. There's something for everyone from hardware to housewares, toys to deck furniture, and, of course, boating supplies.

Tasty eateries abound – many with outdoor café-like settings. Whatever the choice, you'll have a fantastic view of the water and float planes in action. Keep those sturdy flying machines in mind; they are handy transportation should guests wish to join you, or jump ship.

Beyond Mouat's Center, at Ganges Lower Village, the streets teem with temptation. Bakeries and an ice cream parlor are within easy strolling distance. There's a drugstore, dry cleaner, clothing store, shoe repair, book store, and quaint shops. Saturday mornings between mid-April and mid-October, meander through the Farmer's Market at Centennial Park – an adventure that tantalizes the senses.

While Ganges may appear to be a simple, charming village, rest assured it has all the necessary services and facilities a traveler might need, including a Canadian Coast Guard station, RCMP detachment, fire department, hospital, ambulance, doctors, dentists and churches.

There are galleries galore. Don't miss visiting Artcraft, a building filled with a wide variety of art by talented Saltspring artists – pottery, watercolors, wood carvings, jewelry and more, directly across the street from the Ganges Marina. Heading out from Ganges Marina toward the Mouat Center, you'll probably notice Alan Crane outside his gallery, creating one of his fine stone sculptures. He's always ready with a smile and greeting and never too busy to chat as he works.

Ganges is more than merely a destination to tuck in overnight. Spend a few days and you'll discover when you leave that it's like saying, "Good-bye" to an old friend... you'll want to return again and again.

Anne Vipond

Ganges village

Anne Vipond

Anchorage in Ganges Harbour, northeast of Chain Islets

⚓ **Ganges Boat Harbour Wharf** tel: 250.537.5711 (Harbour Authority of Salt Spring Island); monitors VHF Ch 66A; power; showers; garbage; waste disposal; launch ramp; telephone; transients welcome

⚓ **Salt Spring Marina** tel: 800.334.6629 or 250.537.5810; monitors VHF Ch 66A; website: www.saltspringmarina.com; cafe and pub; full amenities

⚓ **Ganges Marina** tel: 250.537.5242; fax: 250.538.1719; monitors VHF Ch 66A; website: www.ganges-marina.com; email: gangesmarina@shaw.ca; full amenities

⚓ **Coast Guard** pier tel: 250.537.5242

Walter Bay (Ganges Harbour)

Charts 3478, 3442, 3313; 0.55 mi SE of Ganges public wharf
Entrance: 48°50.77'N, 123°29.22'W
Anchor: 48°50.66'N, 123°29.15'W

Walter Bay, on the SE shore of Ganges Harbour, has private floats and a mooring buoy. The Saltspring Sailing Club floats, protected by a floating breakwater, are close NW of Walter Bay. (SD)

Walter Bay offers good shelter east of the Saltspring Island Sailing Club facilities and west of the drying mud flat, avoiding the private mooring buoys.

Anchor in 1 to 2 fathoms over mud with good holding.

Satellite Channel

Charts 3441, 3313; joins Swanson Channel & Sansum Narrows
Entrance (0.24 mi SE of Eleanor Pt): 48°45.05'N, 123°22.93'W
Entrance (NW, 0.69 mi E of Separation Pt): 48°44.47'N, 123°33.15'W

Satellite Channel, entered from Swanson Channel at its east end, leads around the south end of Saltspring Island to Fulford Harbour, Saanich Inlet, Cowichan Bay and the south end of Sansum Narrows. Shute and Colburne Passages enter the south side of Satellite Channel.

The east end of Satellite Channel is frequently used by large ferries going between Swartz Bay, at the north end of Saanich Peninsula, and Tsawwassen on the mainland; these ferries use Active Pass. Smaller ferries cross Satellite Channel between Swartz Bay and Fulford Harbour.

Tidal streams attain 1 to 2 kn in Satellite Channel. In the vicinity of Cape Keppel the flood sets NW and the ebb SE. (SD)

Satellite Channel and Sansum Narrows provide the fastest route to Nanaimo from Saanich Peninsula; northbound vessels can use a favorable flood current all the way through Stuart Channel to Dodd Narrows.

Anne Vipond

Walter Bay offers shelter from southeast weather

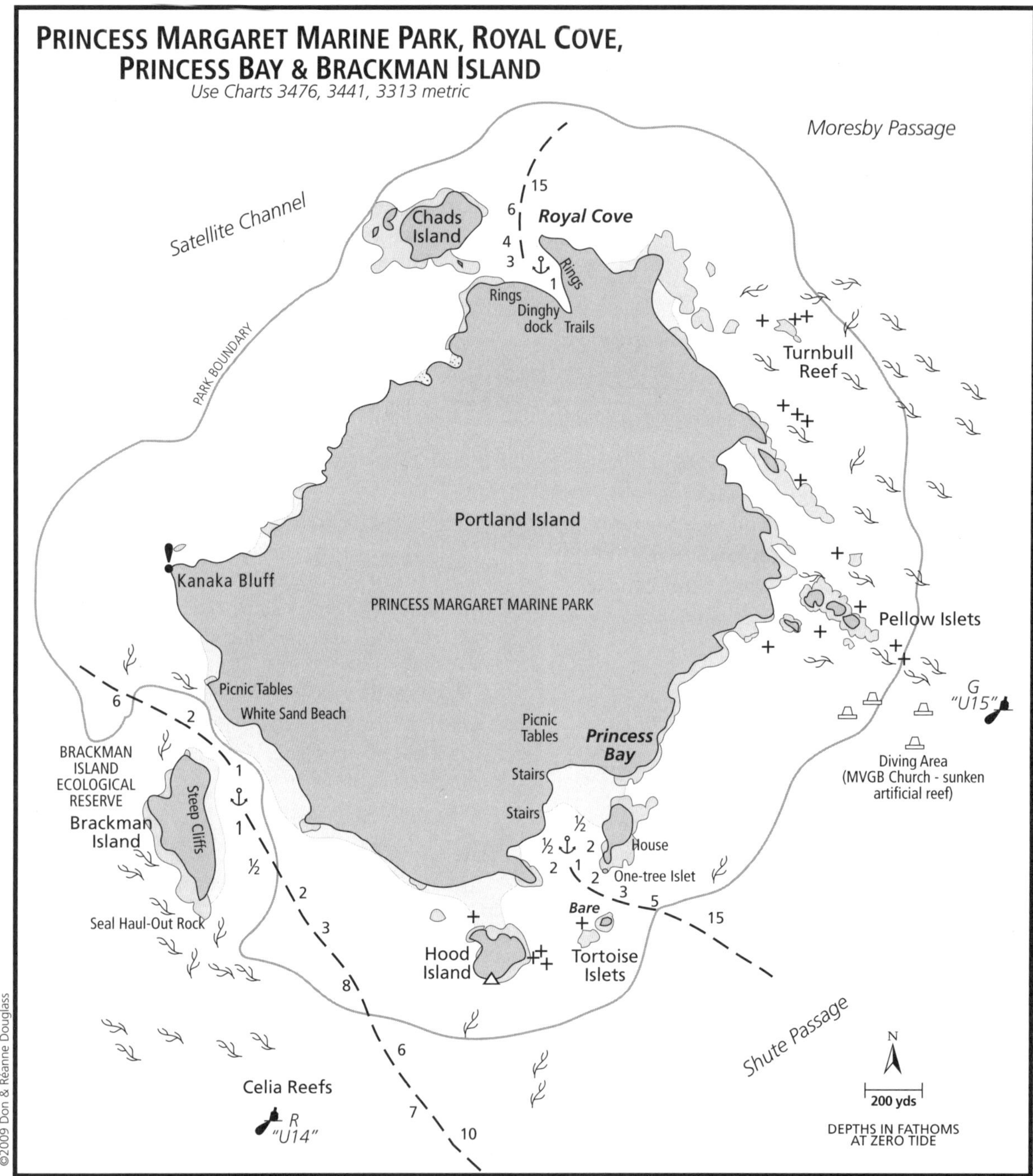

Princess Margaret Marine Park

(Portland Island)

Charts 3476, 3441, 3313; 4 mi N of Sidney Marina
Entrance (Princess Bay): 48°43.03'N, 123°22.00'W

Princess Margaret Marine Park encompasses the whole of Portland Island. (SD)

Anchor sites can be found on Portland Island in Royal Cove, Princess Bay, Pellow Islets, and in the channel adjacent to Brackman Island. An artificial reef used by scuba divers lies on the east side of Portland Island.

Originally given to Princess Margaret Windsor to commemorate her visit to British Columbia during the province's Centennial in 1958, Portland Island was returned to the province to be designated as a Marine Park. The 450-acre island has drinking water, camping and toilet facilities, and a nice trail that leads through an abandoned apple orchard.

Anne Vipond

Royal Cove, Portland Island

In fair weather, you can anchor in Royal Cove behind Chad Island and in Princess Bay near Tortoise Island, at the southeast side of the island. Chad and Tortoise islands are privately owned; Brackman Island is an ecological reserve. *Caution:* Drying and below-water rocks extend a half-mile offshore to the north, east, and south sides of the islands.

⚓ **Princess Margaret Marine Park** has pit toilets; drinking water; camping; swimming; fishing; hiking; open year-round

Royal Cove (Portland Island)

Charts 3476, 3441, 3313; 3.8 mi SE of Fulford Hbr
Entrance (0.06 mi E of Chads I): 48°44.16'N, 123°22.33'W
Anchor: 48°44.07'N, 123°22.26'W

> *Royal Cove is reported to afford anchorage for small craft; a dinghy float is at the head of the cove.* (SD)

Royal Cove is a well-sheltered, all-year anchorage, and a nice base from which to picnic and hike on Portland Island. Moderate ferry-wash enters this cove.

During the busy summer season, many boaters use a stern shore tie, made easier by use of steel rings secured to the rock along shore (7 on the north, 9 on the south).

Royal Cove has a dinghy dock, picnic and toilet facilities, and trails that lead to the other side of the island through the old orchard.

Anchor in 2 to 3 fathoms over sand, mud and small grasses with good holding.

Princess Bay or "Tortoise Bay" (Portland Island)

Charts 3476, 3441, 3313; 4.0 mi NE of Sidney Marina
Entrance: 48°43.03'N, 123°22.00'W
Anchor: 48°43.09'N, 123°22.20'W

> *Princess Bay, entered north of Tortoise Islets, provides anchorage for small craft.* (SD)

Popular Princess Bay, also known as Tortoise Bay, offers fair-weather anchorage in summer for small shallow-draft boats. It is sheltered from northwest winds but exposed to strong southerlies.

Enter the bay via the deep-water route north of Tortoise Islets. Because its depths are shallow, watch tide levels.

Anchor in 1 fathom over soft mud and shells with eel grass; fair-to-good holding.

Pellow Islets

Charts 3476, 3441, 3313; 0.7 mi NE of Princess Bay
Position: 48°43.60'N, 123°21.54'W
Southernmost diving buoy: 48°43.31'N, 123°21.36'W

> *Pellow Islets are on a drying reef extending from the east extremity of Portland Island.* (SD)

Pellow Islets are a popular stop for scuba divers. Small boats with local knowledge can anchor temporarily north of the Pellow Islets. Since the bottom in this area is quite irregular with many rocks, reefs and kelp, caution is required.

The sunken M/V G.B. Church, located 350 yards west of green buoy "U-15," creates an artificial reef that makes diving attractive. The three mooring buoys here are designated exclusively for dive boats. Buoys mark the bow and stern of the sunken vessel. To keep it safe for divers, motor vessels should avoid the vicinity of the artificial reef.

Anne Vipond

Pellow Islets make great scuba diving and kayaking

The area between Pellow Islets and Turnbull Reef is a great place to kayak, and haulout spots can be found on small, sandy beaches.

Brackman Island Ecological Reserve

(Portland Island)

Charts 3476, 3441, 3313; 0.5 mi W of Princess Bay; 1 mi SE of Royal Cove
Entrance (S): 48°43.03'N, 123°22.89'W
Entrance (N): 48°43.34'N, 123°23.27'W
Anchor: 48°43.19'N, 123°23.03'W

Brackman Island, off the SW side of Portland Island, is wooded and cliffy on its east side. Brackman Island and the surrounding area are an Ecological Reserve. (SD)

Small Brackman Island was set aside as a reserve in 1989 to protect the outstanding plant, animal, and bird life representative of the dry Gulf Islands. Old-growth Douglas fir, arbutus trees, Garry oaks, white fawn lily, sea blush, chocolate lily and camas are among the eighty species of plant life found on the island. River otters, mink, and harbor seals can frequently be sighted along the

Portland Island

Portland Island is not only a beautiful marine park, its history is unique. The island's earliest inhabitants were Coast Salish natives, as evidenced by the shell middens. Then, in the mid-1800s, a few hundred Hawaiians were brought to local waters under contract by the Hudson's Bay Company. They were hired to work the Company's land and, because of their facility with the natives' languages, act as interpreters for the fur traders. When their contracts expired, a number of these Hawaiians (known as Kanakas) decided to stay and settle on Portland Island, which had been given to them by the Hudson's Bay Company.

In the 1930s, a colorful character named Major General Frank (One-Arm) Sutton lived on the island. After losing an arm at Gallipoli, for which he received the military cross, Sutton pursued various exploits which included golf championships and gold prospecting in Siberia. After working for a Manchurian warlord during the Chinese civil war, Sutton retired a millionaire in Victoria. Upon buying Portland Island, he stocked it with pheasants and built a stables for his race horses in a pasture near the island's southern anchorage. Nearby is the fruit orchard he planted. The Crash of '29 brought an end to Sutton's lavish lifestyle, but Portland Island remained in private hands until the province acquired it in 1958, then gave it to Britain's Princess Margaret who later returned it so the island could become a marine park in 1967.

A cross-island trail connects the two main anchorages and a shoreside trail loops around the island, taking hikers past shell beaches—perfect for picnics—such as the one overlooking Brackman Island. Most of the islets surrounding Portland are privately owned with the exception of Brackman Island which is a nature reserve created by The Nature Conservancy of Canada.

Sheep once roamed Portland Island and a springtime visit was rewarded with the sight of newborn lambs. The wild sheep were apparently destroying the island's grass land and wild flowers, so they were rounded up in 1989, leaving the island to river otters and other indigenous animals. **—AV**

Anne Vipond

Brackman Island Ecological Reserve

shoreline. Bird life includes songbirds, bald eagles, oystercatchers, great blue herons, and cormorants. The reserve is closed to the public, but on the southwest side of Portland Island, there's a grassy knoll with a picnic table where you can view the animal and bird life without disturbing it.

The narrow channel between Portland and Brackman islands can be used as a fair-weather anchorage, but it is subject to moderate ferry wake and exposed to southeast weather.

Anchor in 1 to 2 fathoms over sand, white shells and grass; fair-to-good holding if your anchor is well set.

Fulford Harbour (Saltspring Island)

Charts 3478, 3441, 3313; 5.5 mi SE of Ganges
Entrance (0.18 mi SW of Jackson Rock): 48°45.10′N, 123°25.88′W
Ferry landing light: 48°46.18′N, 123°27.10′W
Anchor (0.17 mi SW of ferry landing): 48°46.12′N, 123°27.30′W

Fulford Harbour, entered west of Jackson Rock, penetrates the south shore of Saltspring Island for 1.5 miles. It is used mainly by pleasure craft and the B.C. Ferries that run between Saltspring and Vancouver Islands. Fulford Harbour village, at the head of the inlet, has a post office (V0S 1C0), store and restaurant. Numerous private floats and moorings are in Fulford Harbour.

Anchorage can be obtained as convenient, clear of the ferry route, in 18 to 26 m. (SD)

Fulford Harbour is a large bay open to the southeast which offers surprisingly good shelter in summer weather. It has easy access from Satellite Channel and is connected by road to Ganges. There are two small marinas at the head of the bay behind the ferry dock. A small public wharf and float are adjacent to the ferry dock.

Anchorage can be taken anywhere in the center of the bay off the large drying flat, staying clear of the ferry route and public floats.

Anchor in 5 fathoms, over sand and gravel with fair holding.

FULFORD HARBOUR
Use Charts 3478, 3441, 3313 metric
Marina
Ferry Terminal
FULFORD HARBOUR
Public Float
N
0.25 mi
DEPTHS IN FATHOMS AT ZERO TIDE
Fulford Harbour
R
Saltspring Island
Jackson Rock
Satellite Channel

©2009 Don & Réanne Douglass

⚓ **Fulford Harbour Marina**
tel: 250.653.4467; fax: 250.653.4457; monitors VHF Ch 66A; website: www.fulfordmarina.com; email: fulfordmarina@saltspring.com; power; fuel; toilets; showers; tennis courts; open year-round

Anne Vipond
The lovely forest trails on Portland Island

Cowichan Bay (Vancouver Island)

Charts 3478, 3441, 3313; 8.8 mi NW of Swartz Bay; 4.5 mi S of Maple Bay
Entrance (0.29 mi SW of Separation Pt): 48°44.32'N, 123°34.42'W
Public float: 48°44.49'N, 123°37.07'W

Cowichan Bay, entered south of Separation Point, has a large drying mud flat, about 0.8 mile wide, at its west end.

Cowichan Bay settlement, on the south shore, is a resort for sportsmen who take part in the fishing for which the bay has achieved a wide reputation.

A licensed inn, restaurants, post office (V0R 1N0) and garbage disposal facilities are available. (SD)

Fulford Harbour

Fulford Harbour is one of the oldest communities on Saltspring Island, its settlers first arriving in the Burgoyne Valley in 1862. Bob Akerman, a descendant of these early settlers, operates a museum near Fulford at 2501 Fulford-Ganges Road. Housed in a hand-crafted log building, the museum was built as a tribute to Akerman's maternal grandmother who was the daughter of a hereditary chief of the Cowichan. Exhibits include a collection of her woven baskets as well as native arrowheads, fish net weights and canoe anchors. The museum has no set hours but visitors can phone 653-4228 to arrange a viewing or drop by on the chance Akerman is home and free to give a tour.

Also of historical interest are Fulford's St. Paul's Catholic Church, built in 1880, and St. Mary's Anglican Church, built in 1894. The village, clustered around the ferry dock, contains several stores, eateries, galleries and gift shops. Fulford Marina has a grocery store and deli as well as tennis courts. The Fulford Inn, an easy walk from the Fulford Marina, stands on the site of two previous inns. Lunch and dinner can be enjoyed outside on the patio or in the pub with its open fireplace. On summer weekends, an outdoor market is held beside the Fulford Inn.

Inter-island ferry, Fulford Harbour

Drummond Park, on the west side of the harbor, is the site of a Sea Capers festival in June and Fulford Days in August. The park is bordered by a long, partly sandy beach and contains a playground, picnic tables and sheltered cooking area. Further afield, about 5-1/2 miles from the Fulford Harbour ferry dock, is Ruckle Park. Located at Beaver Point, this beautiful park is over a thousand acres in size with plenty of forest and beachside trails. Lying in between Fulford Harbour and Ruckle Park, along Beaver Point Road, are Stowell and Weston lakes, both popular swimming holes. **—AV**

Cowichan Bay, open to southeast winds, is a large, deep-water commercial port fringed with shallow mud flats used for log storage. The attractive village of Cowichan Bay on the south side of the bay is geared to the sportfishing industry, but now has a number of restaurants and shops.

A small and crowded public float (Cowichan Bay Harbour Authority Wharf), lies behind a substantial wooden breakwater. Visiting boats generally raft alongside local boats. West of the public float are several private marinas and the Cowichan Bay Yacht Club. Bluenose Marina offers full facilities and mooring buoys. Cowichan Bay is too deep and exposed for convenient anchorage.

Genoa Bay, on the north shore of Cowichan Bay, offers good anchorage as well as marina facilities.

⚓ **Cowichan Bay Harbour Authority Wharf** tel: 250.746.5911; fax: 250.701.0729; power (20 amp); pumpout; showers; laundry

⚓ **Bluenose Marina** tel: 250.748.2222; fax: 250.748.2380; website: www.bluenosemarina.com; power (15 amp); showers; laundry; restaurant; grocery store nearby

Anne Vipond

Northwest solitude at its best

Cowichan Bay and Genoa Bay

Cowichan Bay was named for a large tribe of natives that once inhabited the sheltered bays of Vancouver Island's east coast. The tribe, which consisted of various small bands such as the Saanich and Chemainus, thrived on the area's abundance of fresh water, wood and seafood. The name "Cowichan" means "between streams" and two rivers form a delta at the head of Cowichan Bay where tidal flats lead to a fertile valley filled with farms and vineyards.

White settlers moved into the area in the mid-1800s and the South Cowichan Lawn Tennis Club was established in 1887, making it the world's oldest lawn tennis club after Wimbledon. The club's early members included Robert Service who would sit in the shade of a maple tree penning his poems. Back then, the seven grass courts were leveled by roller, pulled by a horse wearing leather boots to protect the lawns. Today the club's international tournament, held each summer, attracts seeded players and former champions from across North America. They come not only to play on grass, but to enjoy the club's beautiful setting and genteel atmosphere where traditions include afternoon tea and old fashioned sportsmanship.

The village of Cowichan also features art galleries and restaurants serving local seafood. Several marinas line the bay's south shore and lying opposite is Genoa Bay, named for the Italian birthplace of an early settler who built the first hotel in Cowichan Bay. Genoa Bay is a beautiful inlet with Mount Tzuhalem rising above its shores. The mountain is named for a Cowichan war chief and fierce murderer who lived there in a cave after being banished by his own tribe. From the Genoa Bay Marina, you can hike up Skinner Bluff to Mount Tzuhalem for spectacular views. The marina has a store and licensed restaurant. **—AV**

Genoa Bay (Vancouver Island)

Charts 3478, 3441, 3313; 1.4 mi NE of Cowichan Bay Village; 3.3 mi S of Maple Bay
Entrance: 48°45.42′N, 123°35.72′W
Anchor: 48°45.72′N, 123°35.88′W

> *Genoa Bay ... has a drying reef in the centre of its entrance. The bay affords good anchorage, mud bottom, for small craft. The east side of the bay is a booming ground with private mooring buoys. A marina is on the west side of the bay. Marine farm facilities and a wharf ... are on the west side of Genoa Bay, a short distance inside the entrance.* (SD)

Genoa Bay is a moderately sheltered bay, a popular summer destination for all size boats. It is also a good place to anchor and wait for a change of current in Sansum Narrows or to seek protection from northerly and westerly winds. Small boats can anchor in the snug inner basin at the north end of the bay, avoiding two large derelict barges on the east side of the basin and a boat hull on the west shore. Avoid the private floats and logbooms.

The Genoa Bay Marina, located on the southwest corner of the bay, provides a full range of services on a seasonal basis. A café and art gallery are located in the marina.

Genoa Bay is used as a center for the excellent sportfishing found in the area.

Anchor in 2 to 3 fathoms over sand and mud with reported good holding.

⚓ **Genoa Bay Marina** tel: 800.572.6481 or 250.746.7621; monitors VHF Ch 66A; fuel; moorage; groceries; open seasonally with honor system off-season

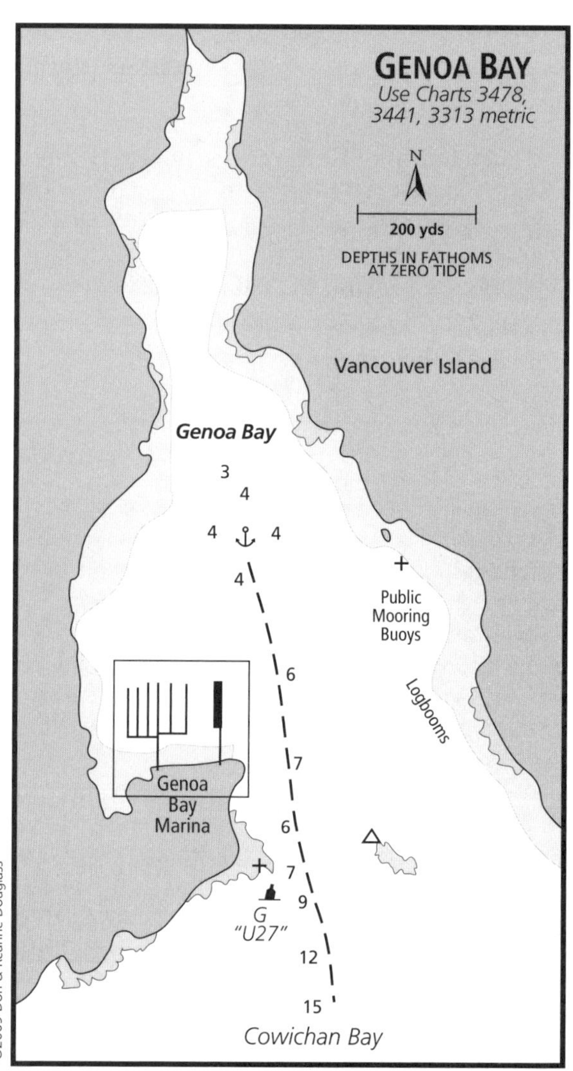

Sansum Narrows

Charts 3478, 3441, 3442, 3313; btwn Vancouver I & W coast Saltspring I
Entrance (S, 0.66 mi SE of Separation Pt): 48°44.46'N, 123°33.15'W
Entrance (N): 48°51.18'N, 123°34.89'W

> *Sansum Narrows leads from Satellite Channel to Stuart Channel; its narrowest part is about 0.3 mile wide. The wind tends to funnel along the axis of the narrows and down the valleys leading into it; for this reason, the wind is inclined to be directionally erratic.*
>
> *Tidal streams flood north and ebb south through Sansum Narrows. In the narrower parts of the fairway, the tidal stream seldom exceeds 3 kn, usually being much less, in the wider portions 1 to 2 kn can be expected.*
>
> *Whirlpools and tide-rips occur around Burial Islet, also between Sansum and Bold Bluff Points. Under some conditions of wind and tide these can be hazardous to small craft.* (SD)

In fair weather, Sansum Narrows seldom presents a problem for cruising boats; on the north-flowing flood current you get a welcome boost. Musgrave Rock, marked by red buoy "U26," can be passed on either side.

Both Maple Bay on Vancouver Island and Burgoyne Bay on Saltspring offer good shelter toward the north end of the narrows.

Classic woody, Birds Eye Cove

Burgoyne Bay (Saltspring Island)

Charts 3478, 3442, 3313; 3.75 mi SE of Maple Bay
Entrance: 48°47.84'N, 123°32.45'W
Public float: 48°47.57'N, 123°31.31'W
Anchor: 48°47.41'N, 123°31.29'W

> *Burgoyne Bay, entered north of Bold Bluff Point, terminates in a mud and sand drying flat. A public wharf, on the north side of the bay, has a float, on its NW side, with a berthing length of 10.5 m.*
>
> *Booming grounds, with log dumps, extend along the north shore of the bay and along the south shore, at the head of the bay. Private mooring buoys are in the bay.* (SD)

Musgrave Landing (Saltspring Island)

Charts 3478, 3441, 3313; S end Sansum Narrows; W side Saltspring I
Public dock: 48°44.95'N, 123°33.00'W

> *Musgrave Landing, on the north side of Musgrave Point, has public floats, 47.3 m long, extending west from an approach ramp; depths alongside range from 1.8 to 6.7 m.* (SD)

Musgrave Landing, the tiny cove immediately north of Musgrave Point, has a small public float; you can find good protection from southeast weather here.

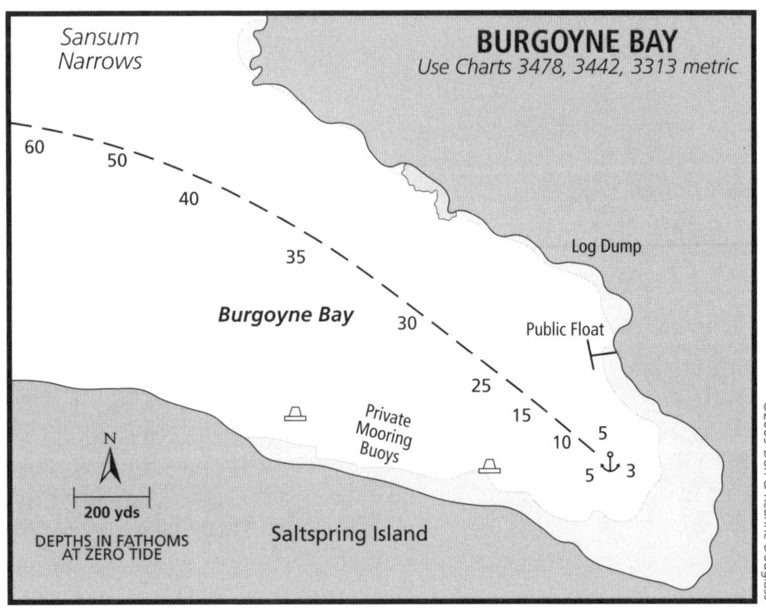

Burgoyne Bay, on the west side of Saltspring Island, provides good shelter in southeast storms, but it is open to northwesterlies. Anchorage can be found deep in the center of the bay off the drying flat, avoiding the private floats. The small public float is used for loading or emergency mooring only.

Anchor in 5 fathoms over mud and sand; fair-to-good holding.

Maple Bay (Vancouver Island)

Charts 3478, 3442, 3313; 3.3 mi N Genoa Bay; 3.5 mi SE Crofton
Entrance (0.33 mi S Arbutus Pt): 48°48.92'N, 123°35.25'W
Public wharf: 48°48.89'N, 123°36.55'W

> *Paddy Mile Stone, 1.2 miles NW of Octopus Point, is the south entrance point of Maple Bay; a conspicuous boulder, 2 m high, lies close north of the point.*
>
> *Maple Bay has the community of Maple Bay on its west side. Two public floats, in the west part of the bay, have depths of 4.6 to 8.2 m alongside.*
>
> *Caution: A rock, with less than 2 m over it, and a shoal with a depth of 2.1 m over it, lie close SE of the public floats.*
>
> *In most parts of Maple Bay, depths are too great for anchorage.* (SD)

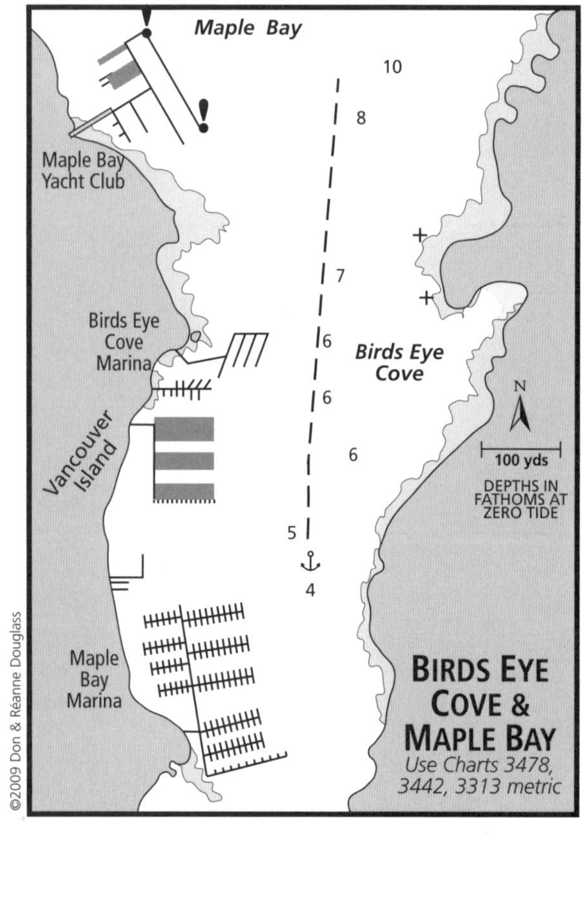

Maple Bay has a public dock with floats which can be used by cruising boats while visiting the community of Maple Bay.

Birds Eye Cove & Maple Bay
Use Charts 3478, 3442, 3313 metric

Birds Eye Cove (Vancouver Island)

Charts 3478, 3442, 3313; 0.9 mi S of Maple Bay public float
Entrance: 48°48.36'N, 123°35.90'W
Anchor: 48°47.92'N, 123°35.98'W

> *Birds Eye Cove, the south arm of Maple Bay, is the site of two marinas and a yacht club.* (SD)

Maple Bay and Birds Eye Cove have facilities for pleasure craft, among which are Maple Bay Marina, Maple Bay Yacht Club, and Birds Eye Cove Marina. Maple Bay Marina has fuel and full amenities for cruising boats, in addition to a store and pub. Birds Eye Cove Marina, in the south end of Maple Bay, has fuel, limited guest moorage and no showers.

Maple Bay

Maple Bay is one of the finest natural harbors found in the Gulf Islands area and contains full-service marinas, a yacht club and government dock. The beach beside the public wharf is popular for swimming; the community of Maple Bay stretches up the hill behind it. Birds Eye Cove at the head of the bay, is where the marina facilities are located, including stores, restaurants and a pub housed in a former shipyard.

The fishing is good both in the bay and in nearby Sansum Narrows, as is the wildlife watching. Maple Bay is also the closest tie-up to Duncan where the Native Heritage Centre is well worth a visit. Situated on the Cowichan River, it features totem poles, a magnificent Big House and a gallery featuring genuine Cowichan sweaters, carvings, masks, prints and jewelry. At the center you can watch totem poles being carved and the traditional weaving, beading, spinning and knitting of native crafts. **—AV**

The western half of the cove is taken up with floats, but well-sheltered anchorage can be found along the east shore. There are reports of a sunken fishing boat 100 feet off the Birds Eye Cove dock.

Anchor in 4 to 6 fathoms over sand and mud with good holding.

⚓ **Maple Bay Marina** tel: 250.746.8482; fax: 250.746.8490; monitors VHF Ch 66A; website: www.maplebay.com; email: info@maplebay.com; full amenities; open year-round with reduced services in the winter

⚓ **Maple Bay Yacht Club** tel: 250.746.5421; reciprocal moorage

⚓ **Birds Eye Cove Marina** tel: 250.746.0679; monitors VHF Ch 66A; limited guest moorage

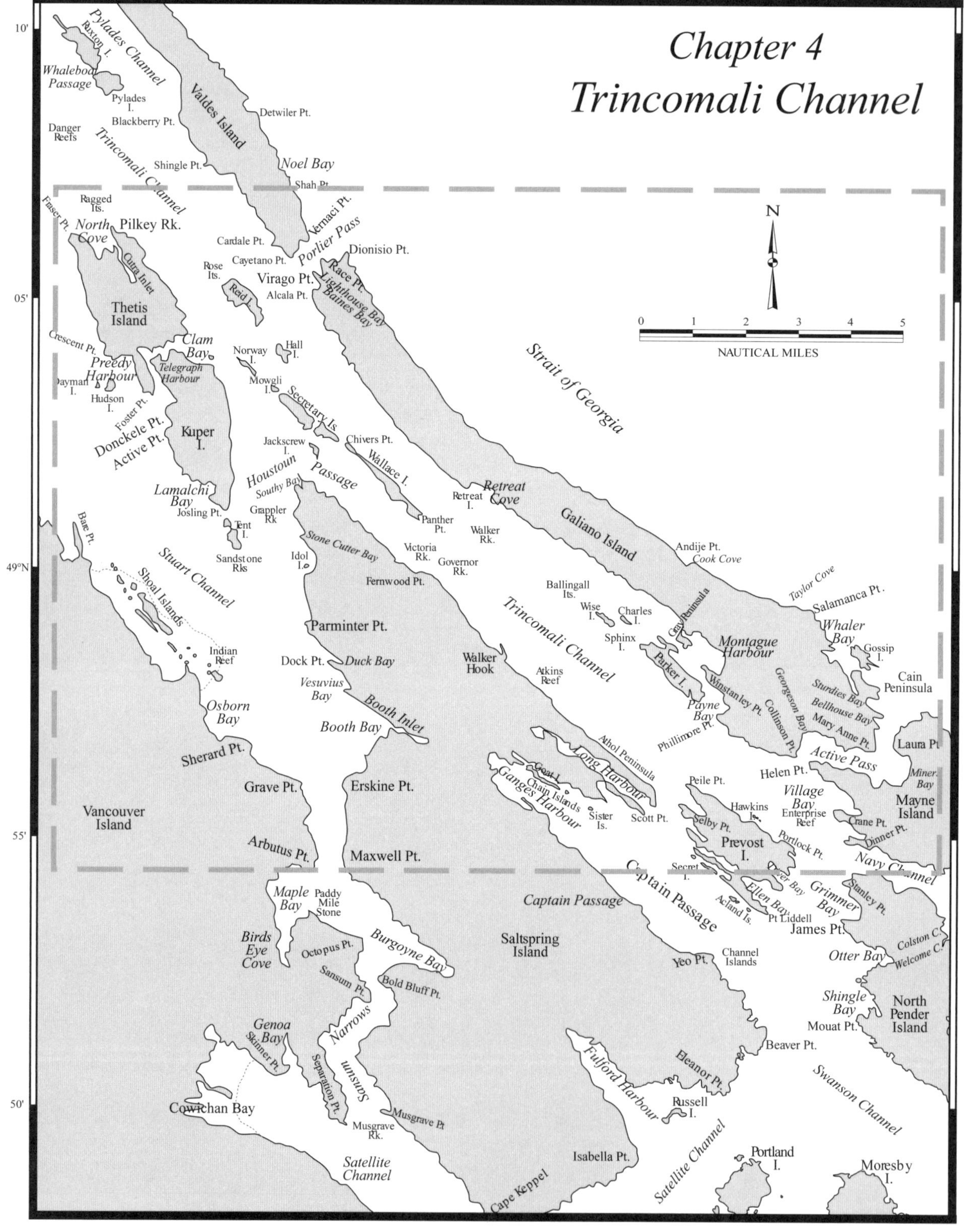
Chapter 4
Trincomali Channel
Pylades Channel
Ruxton I.
Whaleboat Passage
Pylades I.
Blackberry Pt.
Danger Reefs
Trincomali Channel
Valdes Island
Detwiler Pt.
Shingle Pt.
Noel Bay
Shah Pt.
Ragged Its.
Fraser Pt.
North Cove
Pilkey Rk.
Cufra Inlet
Cardale Pt.
Vernaci Pt.
Porlier Pass
Dionisio Pt.
Cayetano Pt.
Rose Its.
Virago Pt.
Race Pt.
Lighthouse Bay
Baines Bay
Alcala Pt.
Reid I.
Thetis Island
Crescent Pt.
Clam Bay
Norway I.
Hall I.
Preedy Harbour
Telegraph Harbour
Hudson I.
Mowgli I.
Secretary Is.
Foster Pt.
Donckele Pt.
Active Pt.
Kuper I.
Jackscrew I.
Chivers Pt.
Wallace I.
Houstoun Passage
Southy Bay
Lamalchi Bay
Josling Pt.
Grappler Rk
Tent I.
Retreat I.
Retreat Cove
Panther Pt.
Walker Rk.
Galiano Island
Bare Pt.
Stone Cutter Bay
Victoria Rk.
Governor Rk.
Stuart Channel
Sandstone Rks
Idol I.
Shoal Islands
Fernwood Pt.
Andije Pt.
Cook Cove
Taylor Cove
Salamanca Pt.
Ballingall Its.
Wise I.
Charles I.
Sphinx I.
Galiano Peninsula
Strait of Georgia
N
0 1 2 3 4 5
NAUTICAL MILES
Parminter Pt.
Trincomali Channel
Whaler Bay
Gossip I.
Indian Reef
Dock Pt.
Duck Bay
Walker Hook
Atkins Reef
Parker I.
Montague Harbour
Cain Peninsula
Vesuvius Bay
Winstanley Pt.
Georgeson Bay
Collinson Pt.
Sturdies Bay
Bellhouse Bay
Mary Anne Pt.
Osborn Bay
Booth Inlet
Booth Bay
Payne Bay
Phillimore Pt.
Athol Peninsula
Long Harbour
Active Pass
Laura Pt.
Sherard Pt.
Helen Pt.
Miners Bay
Grave Pt.
Erskine Pt.
Goat I.
Chain Islands
Ganges Harbour
Peile Pt.
Village Bay
Mayne Island
Hawkins Is.
Enterprise Reef
Vancouver Island
Sister Is.
Scott Pt.
Selby Pt.
Crane Pt.
Dinner Pt.
Prevost I.
Portlock Pt.
Arbutus Pt.
Maxwell Pt.
Navy Channel
Secret I.
Captain Passage
Maple Bay
Paddy Mile Stone
Captain Passage
Ellen Bay
Acland Is.
Grimmer Bay
Stanley Pt.
Pt Liddell
James Pt.
Saltspring Island
Birds Eye Cove
Octopus Pt.
Burgoyne Bay
Yeo Pt.
Channel Islands
Otter Bay
Colston C.
Welcome C.
Sansum Pt.
Bold Bluff Pt.
Shingle Bay
North Pender Island
Mouat Pt.
Genoa Bay
Narrows
Skinner Pt.
Beaver Pt.
Fulford Harbour
Eleanor Pt.
Separation Pt.
Sansum
Swanson Channel
Cowichan Bay
Russell I.
Musgrave Pt.
Musgrave Rk.
Satellite Channel
Portland I.
Isabella Pt.
Satellite Channel
Moresby I.
Cape Keppel
10'
05'
49°N
55'
50'

4

TRINCOMALI CHANNEL: Montague Harbour, Galiano Island, East shore of Saltspring, Kuper and Thetis Islands, Houstoun Passage (Wallace Island), Porlier Pass to Valdes Island

Trincomali Channel lies between Galiano Island to the northeast and Thetis, Kuper, and Saltspring islands to the southwest. Reid, Hall, Secretary, and Wallace islands lie in the channel itself. The Trincomali Channel—a favorite Gulf Islands destination—and Wallace Island Marine Park have excellent anchorages. Numerous small bights and coves along the sides of the channel offer quiet and attractive anchor sites in fair weather.

Long and narrow, Galiano is one of the driest of the Gulf Islands and a good spot for hiking and biking. Bluff Park is a long, hilly hike from beautiful Montague Harbour but its panoramic views make it worthwhile. Montague Harbour Marine Park has a white shell beach, picnic and campsites, and water.

On the northeast side of Saltspring lies Fernwood Point with a public pier and mooring float. There's a store and Salty Springs spa is nearby. A one-mile walk takes you to St. Mary Lake where there is swimming and fishing.

Almost all of Wallace Island is a Provincial Marine Park, well worth a stop on your cruising itinerary. The waters around the various anchorages "Panther Point Cove," Conover Cove, and Princess Bay can be tricky, so keep a sharp lookout.

Kuper Island is an Indian Reserve that is thickly forested and relatively pristine. The Cut is a drying channel between Thetis and Kuper islands, with Telegraph Harbour at its west end and Clam Bay on its east.

Back along the Galiano shoreline, Spotlight and "Flagpole" coves invite exploration, as do Baines and Lighthouse bays. Cruise through Porlier Pass between Galiano and Valdes and around the northernmost tip of Galiano

Fog in Trincomali Channel

An After-Christmas Cruise

After one too many Christmas parties, a cruise in the Gulf Islands starting on New Years Day looked like a dream vacation. The nearest thing to heaven—"far from the madding crowd." Indeed, it was not until the 13th day of our escape that I even thought about our home and began to look forward to picking up the threads of my life again. At that point, we were snugly anchored in Winter Cove, between Saturna and Samuel Islands, from where we could see the lights of Vancouver at night.

On January 2nd, we had crossed the Strait of Georgia from Vancouver and found shelter from southeast winds between the Secretary Islands. This was our first night on the water since the Christmas fever, and it was bliss. To be rocked to sleep on our own modest, though well-found, 25' Northern was at any time a blessing, but then it was absolutely manna from heaven.

Since we'd purchased our first boat, *Wave Dancer,* a 25' Northern 25 three years before, we'd discovered the unbelievable, enchanted Gulf Islands. Experiencing these islands on a boat is far different than in a car, most of the smaller islands not being on the ferry route. It is always a voyage of discovery. Countless protected nooks and crannies in these islands make perfect anchorages, all of enormous beauty. The arbutus tree proliferates in the area, its red bark and gnarly branches framing lofty views of ferries plying blue, blue channels dotted with deep green islands.

We awoke rather late on that first morning to the high, chirping call of a bald eagle. We grabbed our binocs and received our last gift of the Season—the sight of a pair of these majestic creatures high in the branches of a tree, sharing our shelter. We were to see many more during our trip, and each sighting was magical.

The biggest surprise of all was the weather. The Gulf Islands get half the precipitation of the Lower Mainland (Vancouver and its suburbs), approximately 30-35 inches annually. And here we were, accustomed to mild but wet winters, blessed with sunshine on all but two of the 16 days. Added to that was the wonderful solitude of the season. Fact is, most boaters are the proverbial "fair weather sailors" and do not venture beyond hearth and home when they expect wet, cold weather. That was fine with us. We enjoyed each anchorage, walked or ran the trails, and played on the beaches, all the while restoring our inner peace and the harmony between us.

Montague Harbour, at Galiano Island, with its near-perfect circle of protection—white sand beaches formed by ancient middens—has a shoreline trail with wonderful views. The regular blasts of the ferries churning through nearby Active Pass were pleasant background drones, like haunting train whistles. Ganges, on Saltspring Island, an art-lover's paradise, provided a welcome chance to sit and be waited on in a cozy cafe, and to satisfy my shopping compulsion. Princess Margaret Marine Park at Portland Island was truly a jewel bequeathed by a princess, with its well-tended trails, again offering views of the channels beyond.

Sidney felt like Hawaii! Port Sidney Marina offers a no-nonsense breakwater and substantial, well-serviced docks within walking distance to Waikiki-like shops and restaurants, along with a "tropical" view of crescent-shaped Sidney Island. That island is a lovely, thin stretch of sand—a beachcomber's paradise, even in cold weather, with 15-20 mooring buoys to make things easy. At Chatham Islands we tromped the trails, enjoying the arbutus trees and views uncluttered by other boats. Next stop was Victoria for two nights at the Coast Hotel, on the Inner Harbour, which has a convenient marina for visiting boats. Surprisingly, two nights in a hotel just didn't cut it! We enjoyed the quaint, picturesque city but were anxious to get back to our own wee, floating hotel and the freedom from plastic people and their media-driven judgments.

The route back took us to Oak Bay Marina, still in Victoria, and a short walk to Sealand and many quaint shops and teahouses. Leaving Sidney the following day, an ebb tide running in Baynes Channel against a southeast gale made for mountainous waves and a very sick first mate. I worked it off with a walk around Isle de Lis Marine Park on our way to Bedwell Harbour on South Pender Island—an attractive spot when it isn't humming with Customs clearance and resort traffic. The next day a whale surfaced in the strait as we were rounding the south side of Saturna Island en route to Reef Harbour between Tumbo and Cabbage islands, and that night we were entertained with the vigorous smacking of seals working parasites off their pelts. (In my ignorance at the time I thought the whale had followed us into the cove!)

Then it was off to Winter Cove at Saturna Island where we loosened our limbs on another winding trail and were entertained by seals and otters before retiring to play Scrabble. We overnighted at Port Browning on North Pender Island; after a fishburger and a wonderful shower, we discovered another family of cheeky otters under the docks. Doubling back now, we sailed up Trincomali Channel for Wallace Island, where we enjoyed Wallace Island Marine Park, several pairs of bald eagles, and flocks of squawking cormorants whose nesting grounds are on a nearby islet. To clear Gabriola Passage before ebb tide, we left early, making for Silva Bay at Gabriola Island, where we always enjoy a long, hilly run topped off by a luxurious, hot shower.

A vigorous beam reach with 10-15 kn northwest winds across the Strait of Georgia took us to Plumper Cove at Keats Island. A final night in our "stomping grounds"—Snug Cove, Bowen Island, a quick jaunt from Vancouver—eased us back into city living. A Caribbean cruise may be warm but pales in comparison with the serenity and beauty of our Gulf Islands cruise. I'd recommend it any day as a post-Christmas excursion—a great way to start the New Year. **—Tonnae K. Hennigan**

to Dionisio Point Park with its lovely sandy beaches, comfortable swimming waters and tidepools to explore. There are unusual sandstone formations or ledges, and arbutus, oak and juniper can be found upland of the shores.

Cardale Point, on Valdes, has a beautiful beach. Nearby Strawberry Point is the site of native burial grounds. Please honor all such archaeological features and leave them as you found them.

Trincomali Channel

Charts 3442, 3313; northward from Active Pass to Porlier Pass & Stuart & Pylades Channels
Entrance (S, 0.35 mi W of Enterprise Reef): 48°50.71'N, 123°21.42'W
Entrance (NW, at Stuart Ch btwn Danger Reefs & Tree I): 49°03.45'N, 123°42.30'W
Entrance (N, at Pylades Ch): 49°03.60'N, 123°40.20'W
Ben Mohr Rock Light: 48°51.63'N, 123°23.38'W

Trincomali Channel leads NW from Navy Channel, Swanson Channel and Active Pass to Pylades and Stuart Channels. The channel is deep throughout and presents no navigational difficulties; it is 0.8 mile wide at its narrowest part.

At the NW end of Trincomali Channel, Stuart Channel is entered between Thetis Island and Pylades Island.

The NE side of Trincomali Channel is formed by Galiano Island and Valdes Island; Prevost, Saltspring and Thetis Islands form its SW side.

Tidal streams in the SE and wider part of Trincomali Channel attain 1 1/2 kn, but north of Wallace Island there is an increase in velocity and up to 3 kn can be expected. (SD)

Trincomali Channel, the most direct route for boats heading north from the San Juan Islands in the direction of Nanaimo, is well protected by Galiano, Valdes and Saltspring islands. While open to southeast winds, it can be used by small boats in stormy weather when the Strait of Georgia is impassable.

Galiano Island

Charts 3442, 3313; NW of Mayne I & SE of Valdes I

Galiano Island, with Porlier Pass at its north end and Active Pass at its south end, is 14 miles long in a NW/SE direction. (SD)

Sun time, Trincomali Channel

Payne Bay

Galiano Island, one of the chain of islands stretching from Saturna Island to Gabriola Island, provides separation and protection from the Strait of Georgia. The island, with its hills, helps create a smooth-water route in Trincomali Channel.

Montague Harbour is one of the most protected and popular small-craft destinations in the Gulf Islands.

Payne Bay (Galiano Island)

Charts 3442, 3473, 3313; 1 mi SE of the Montague Marine Park float
Entrance (S, 0.1 mi W of Phillimore Pt): 48°52.30'N, 123°23.67'W
Entrance (N, 0.18 mi S of Winstanley Pt): 48°53.07'N, 123°23.97'W
Anchor: 48°52.42'N, 123°23.29'W

> *Payne Bay ... offers temporary anchorage, mud and sand bottom.* (SD)

Payne Bay offers shelter along its south shore east of Phillimore Point. Anchor in its southeast corner where there's good protection from all weather. Avoid the private mooring buoys.

Anchor in 4 to 6 fathoms over mud and sand with good holding.

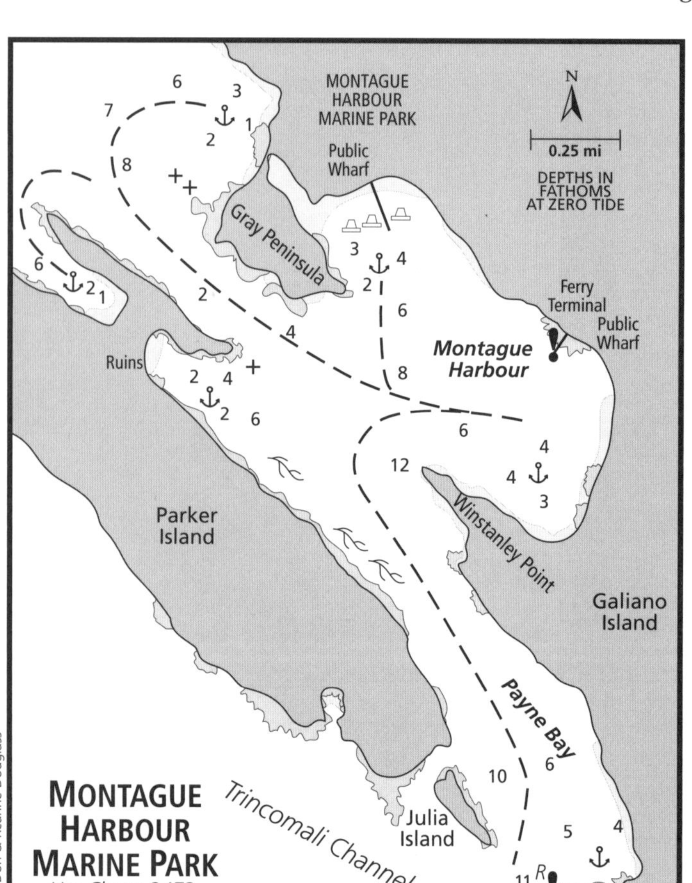

Montague Harbour (Galiano Island)

Charts 3473, 3442, 3313; 2.8 mi NW of the SW entrance to Active Pass
Entrance (S, 0.18 mi S of Winstanley Pt): 48°53.07'N, 123°23.97'W
Entrance (N, 0.23 mi W of Gray Peninsula): 48°53.83'N, 123°24.97'W
Float: 48°53.83'N, 123°24.16'W
Anchor (0.1 mi SE of park float): 48°53.75'N, 123°24.00'W
Anchorage (S, 0.22 mi SW of ferry dock): 48°53.30'N, 123°23.56'W

> *Montague Harbour ... is sheltered by Parker Island and affords a good anchorage for small craft. Its south entrance, between Phillimore Point and Julia Island, is easy of access. The north entrance, between Gray Peninsula and the peninsula on the NE side of Parker Island, has a depth of 5.2 m through the centre of its fairway.*

A ferry occasionally calls into Montague Harbour.

Several public mooring buoys are in the north end of Montague Harbour, to the east of Gray Peninsula; they are part of the facilities provided by Montague Harbour Marine Park.

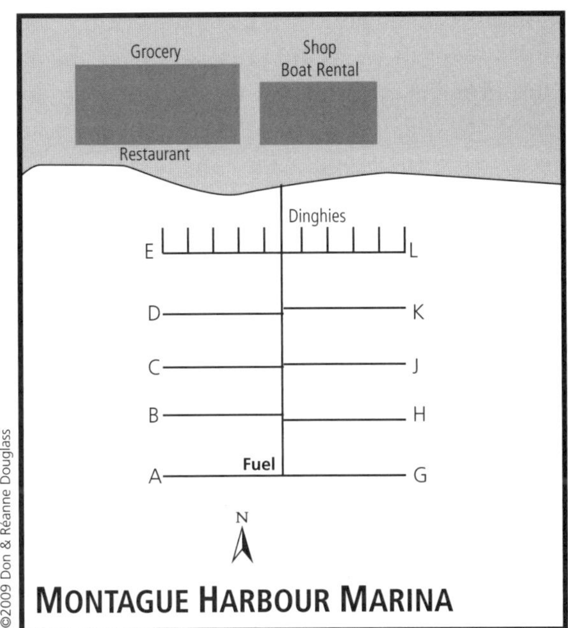

A public wharf and float are at the marine park.

The public floats, on the east side of Montague Harbour 0.4 mile NE of Winstanley Point, have 97.5 m of berthing space. (SD)

Montague Harbour, one of the most protected and well-used shelters in the Gulf Islands, is a primary destination for cruising boats. Montague Harbour Marine Park, the first of the British Columbia marine parks to be established, lies in the northwest corner of the harbor. The park includes a dinghy and mooring dock (length limit 30 feet), 25 mooring buoys (fees collected), picnic tables, toilets and several pay telephones. There are excellent trails and beaches, with swimming off the north beach of Gray Peninsula spit where the water warms to comfortable temperatures in summer due to the shallow depths. Montague Harbour Marine Park is a good place to kayak or sail a dinghy.

Excellent moorage can be found anywhere outside the line of mooring buoys; some shallow-draft boats anchor inside the line of mooring buoys. Boats wishing more isolation can find anchorage in the isthmus coves of Parker Island, as noted on next page. Anchorage can also be found off the beach north of Gray Peninsula.

The southeast corner of the harbor offers very good shelter during southeast gales and provides overflow anchorage for the marine park or for those not interested in using the park facilities.

The north entrance to Montague Harbour is shallow (3 fathoms minimum) but with a clear fairway. In addition to the mooring buoys and public wharf which are frequently filled during the summer, there are other alternatives as indicated on the diagram. In southerly winds, well-sheltered anchorage can be found in the south quadrant of Montague Harbour.

Anchor (southeast) in 4 fathoms over mud and shells with very good holding.

Anchor (southwest) in 3 to 5 fathoms over mud, sand and shells with good holding.

⚓ **Montague Harbour Marina** tel: 250.539.5733; monitors VHF Ch 66A; fuel; power; moorage; groceries

⚓ **Montague Harbour Marine Park** toilets; water; camping; picnic area; pay telephones; hiking trails; beaches

Isthmus Coves (Parker Island)

Charts 3473, 3442, 3313; 0.6 mi SW of the Montague Marine Park float
Anchor (S, Isthmus Cove): 48°53.42′N, 123°24.72′W
Anchor (N, Isthmus Cove): 48°53.70′N, 123°25.21′W

Parker Island, across the entrance of Montague Harbour, has steep cliffs on its SW side. Julia Island lies close-off its SE extremity and Wilmot Head is the NW extremity of Parker Island. The channel between Wilmot Head and Sphinx Island has a depth of 7.3 m through its fairway. (SD)

Isthmus Coves are the two coves—one on each side of the isthmus—formed by the mushroom-shaped peninsula on the northeast side of Parker Island. Avoid private mooring buoys in both coves.

Anchor in 3 to 5 fathoms over sand and gravel with fair-to-good holding.

Gray Peninsula Anchorage (Galiano I)

Charts 3473, 3442, 3313; 0.35 mi NW of the Montague Hbr Marine Park float
Entrance (W, btwn Parker & Sphinx Is): 48°43.66'N, 123°25.77'W
Anchor: 48°53.96'N, 123°24.64'W

The tower on Gray Peninsula is a useful landmark. (SD)

Gray Peninsula can be entered from Trincomali Channel on either side of Sphinx Island. A pleasant anchorage—with good beach access to marine park facilities, beautiful sunsets and less commotion—can be found on the west side of the peninsula. Avoid the rocks off the northwest corner of Gray Peninsula that are marked by kelp in the summer; anchor in front of the long sandy beach. Although this site is open to westerly chop, it is otherwise well sheltered.

Anchor in 3 to 4 fathoms over mud, sand and gravel with fair-to-good holding.

Learning About the Venturi Effect

I learned firsthand about the Venturi effect when I was a student biologist conducting research in the Gulf Islands. It happened many years ago during a wonderful summer I spent aboard a 22-foot Lynwood. My work involved towing an underwater video camera with a lure attached. I watched the video monitor on top of the small galley table and was fascinated by the fish that appeared on the flickering screen. I marveled at the power and precision of coho as they torpedoed unerringly toward the bait. I watched dogfish make awkward attempts at capturing my slow-moving lure and wondered how they could make a living trying to catch live prey. These observations, along with a paper printout from the echo sounder, told me how many and what kinds of fish lurked beneath as I weaved my little boat through a fleet of anglers. My research involved correlating the fish population with the fishermen's catch and to do this I also needed a catch survey.

The survey was simple enough—just a few questions on a sheet of paper asking how long the fishermen had been fishing and how many fish they had caught. The difficult part was to get the questionnaire to the anglers and recover it without bumping into their boat or making them reel in their lines.

I devised a long pole made from a 14-foot length of 2-inch doweling and affixed a clip to the end. To prevent damage when I stretched the pole between my boat and the fishermen's, I added a soft rubber ball to the end.

Things went well on the first field trial. After a few careful maneuvers I was able to hold the pole under one arm while I steered with the other. The fishermen would unclip the envelope containing the form and, later when I returned, they would reclip the completed form to the pole.

I had just completed the survey, but there was one last boat. He was fishing in the swift current of Porlier Pass. Eager to get every last data point, and having gained confidence in the form-transfer maneuver, I sped toward him with the pole tucked under my arm, like a knight in a jousting tournament. I smiled inwardly at his look of concern as I approached.

Then the Venturi effect came into play. A fluid flowing between two objects produces a force that pulls the objects together. The Venturi effect can occur with surprising suddenness, and our boats were sucked together by the fast-moving current. The pole found the centre of the fisherman's chest as he reached for the form, knocking him to the deck of his boat. Thinking my steering or his was at fault, I pulled away and reined my boat into a 360-degree turn to make ready for the second pass. If he had looked concerned on my first approach, he now looked downright alarmed as he ducked to avoid being impaled a second time. He had, however, managed to get possession of the envelope. Deciding against a third attempt, I shouted that he could post the self-addressed stamped envelope when he got to shore. His hand gestures, however, left no doubt that this was one data point science was going to have to do without.

—Tom Shardlow

[*Editor's note:* Tom is an author and marine biologist who also holds a 40-ton vessel masters ticket. He has cruised extensively on the coast of B.C.]

Cook Cove & Taylor Cove (Galiano Island, Strait of Georgia)

Charts 3442, 3473, 3313; (Cook Cove) 1.4 mi N of Montague Hbr; (Taylor Cove) 1.7 mi NE of Montague Hbr
Position (Cook Cove): 48°55.23'N, 123°24.35'W
Position (Taylor Cove): 48°54.43'N, 123°21.68'W

Cook and Taylor coves, on the north side of Galiano Island, are the only named coves on the Strait of Georgia side of the island. They may provide temporary emergency shelter for small craft in southerly weather.

Ballingall Islets Park (Trincomali Channel)

Charts 3473, 3442, 3313; 2.3 mi NW of Montague Hbr
Position: 48°54.40'N, 123°27.48'W

> *Ballingall Islets, NW of Wise Island, are low and covered with stunted shrubs. Ballingall Islets Park is a nature reserve.* (SD)

Strangely-shaped trees and abundant wildlife make this islet park a good place for some great nature shots with a telephoto lens.

Retreat Cove (Galiano Island)

Charts 3473, 3442, 3313; 4.7 mi NW of Montague Hbr; 5.5 mi SE of Porlier Pass
Entrance: 48°56.33'N, 123°30.13'W
Anchor: 48°56.41'N, 123°30.10'W

> *Retreat Cove has depths of 1.8 to 8.2 m in its SE corner and affords good shelter for small craft. Retreat Island, in the middle of the cove, is connected to shore by a drying flat. Scarrow Reef dries 2.7 m.*
>
> *The public wharf, with a float attached to its outer end, is in the SE part of Retreat Cove; the float is 30.5 m long with a depth of 4 m alongside.* (SD)

Retreat Cove, a small nook with temporary shelter available at the public float or immediately north, should be entered on the southeast side of Retreat Island.

Anchor in 1 fathom over mud with good holding and limited swinging room.

Fernwood Point (Saltspring Island)

Charts 3442, 3313; 1.87 mi SW of Retreat Cove; 3.1 mi SE of Southey Pt
Public float: 48°54.98'N, 123°31.94'W

> *Fernwood Point is the SE entrance point to Houstoun Passage.*
>
> *A public pier, with a float attached to its outer end, extends over the tidal flats at Fernwood Point; the float has 24.4 m of berthing space with 3 m alongside.* (SD)

The public dock on the north side of Fernwood Point is used as a dinghy dock for commuters going to Galiano Island. A small store, located 50 yards above the dock on the left side of Fernwood Road, has a deli with produce, dairy, some staples, gasoline and very good homemade pizza. Boats from Wallace Island Marine Park can place their orders by cell phone and make a dinghy run for pickup!

Anne Vipond

Montague Harbour Marine Park in autumn

Houstoun Passage

[Note: Houstoun is spelled "Houston" on Chart 3313 but "Houstoun" elsewhere.]

Charts 3442, 3313; wraps around the N tip of Salt Spring I
Entrance (E, 0.44 mi S of Panther Pt Lt): 48°55.39'N, 123°31.96'W
Entrance (W, 0.98 mi SE of North Reef; 0.66 mi NW of Parminter Pt): 48°54.30'N, 123°36.40'W

> *Houstoun Passage connects Stuart Channel to Trincomali Channel.*

Tidal streams within Houstoun Passage are generally weak. The flood sets NW and the ebb SE. (SD)

Houstoun Passage affords convenient passage to Wallace Island Marine Park and to Telegraph Harbour and Chemainus. Avoid North Reef at the west entrance, the reefs on the south side of Wallace Island, and the rocks in Trincomali Channel east of Fernwood Point.

Retreat Cove public floats

Wallace Island Marine Park

(Wallace Island)

Charts 3442, 3313; 1.5 mi E of the N tip of Saltspring I
SW end (Panther Pt Light): 48°55.82'N, 123°31.98'W
NW end (Chivers Pt): 48°57.40'N, 123°34.46'W

Wallace Island, SE of Secretary Islands, is separated from them by a narrow channel that has a drying reef and below-water rocks in the centre of its fairway. A narrow chain of rocky islets, drying rocks and shoals lie parallel with and 0.2 mile from the SW shore of Wallace Island. (SD)

Wallace Island Marine Park, open all year, is one our favorite off-season anchorages. It is tree-covered and has toilets, campsites, picnic areas and hiking trails. While the most popular anchorages are Conover and Princess coves, anchor sites can be found in many nooks and crannies, including the window between the Secretary Islands. The Chuckanut sandstone formations of the San Juan and Gulf islands are clearly visible as narrow seams in a northwest-southeast orientation. When these seams reach the surface, they create many reefs and rocks which, in Houstoun Passage, are not marked by navigation aids and must be carefully avoided, particularly on the southeast side of Wallace Island.

⚓ **Wallace Island Marine Park** pit toilets; water; camping; picnic areas; hiking trails; no fires; open year-round

Horizontal Datum Makes a Difference!

Compare the two charts that show Retreat Cove on Galiano Island; this is a good place to note the graphic differences in chart horizontal datum.

On Chart 3442 (NAD 27), the longitude line for 123°30.00' W runs through the very tip of the south entrance to Retreat Cove—west of the public wharf. On Chart 3313, p. 17 (NAD 83), the same longitude line (123°30.00' W) lies entirely over land—east of the public wharf on the south side of Retreat Cove!

Panther Point Cove (Wallace Island)

Charts 3442, 3313; 1.0 mi N of Fernwood Pt
Entrance: 48°55.88'N, 123°31.81'W
Anchor: 48°55.96'N, 123°32.13'W

Panther Point has a drying ledge extending 0.2 mile SE from it. (SD)

Panther Point Cove, our favorite small nook on the south end of Wallace Island, is scenic and well sheltered from all winds but those

Fernwood Point public float

which blow up Trincomali Channel from the southeast. It makes a wonderful lunch stop or overnighter in fair weather. The bottom shoals gradually to the drying flat so keep a lookout over your bow while you choose your spot.

Avoid crossing the reef that extends from Panther Point to the daymark. The waters around this reef and the submerged rocks a quarter-mile north are good for snorkeling or kayaking. Starfish and other sea life are clearly visible in these waters.

Anchor in 1 to 2 fathoms midchannel over sand and mud with good holding.

Conover Cove (Wallace Island)

Charts 3442, 3313; 1.3 mi NW of Fernwood Pt
Entrance: 48°56.11'N, 123°32.71'W
Anchor: 48°56.18'N, 123°32.64'W

> *Conover Cove within Wallace Island Marine Park affords good shelter for small craft and has a small float.* (SD)

Conover Cove, the focal point of the popular Wallace Island Marine Park, is a small, well-sheltered cove.

The entrance bar is quite shallow (less than a fathom at zero tide) and should be approached cautiously. The deepest water appears to favor the south shore. Conover Cove largely dries, but several small craft can find room to anchor with limited swinging room on either side of the public float. Avoid impeding access to the float. Any anchoring here should be done in concert with prior arrivals who sometimes use a stern shore tie or a very short scope. Nice hiking and nature trails lead from the head of the float gangway.

Anchor in 1 fathom south of the float and off two pilings; sand and mud with fair holding.

Princess Bay (Wallace Island)

Charts 3442, 3313; 1.8 mi NW of Fernwood Pt
Entrance: 48°56.64'N, 123°33.58'W
Anchor: 48°56.56'N, 123°33.28'W

Princess Bay offers good anchorage with more swinging room than Conover Cove. Shore ties are helpful onshore rings at the head of the cove facilitate tying. Dinghies can be landed at the head of the bay, avoiding the private inholdings on the north shore. Princess Bay provides snug protection from southeast winds and very pleasant anchorage in anything but a strong northwester.

On low tides, it's fun to watch the mud flats at "South Window" erupt with clams squirting water 2 to 3 feet in the air like a programmed fountain.

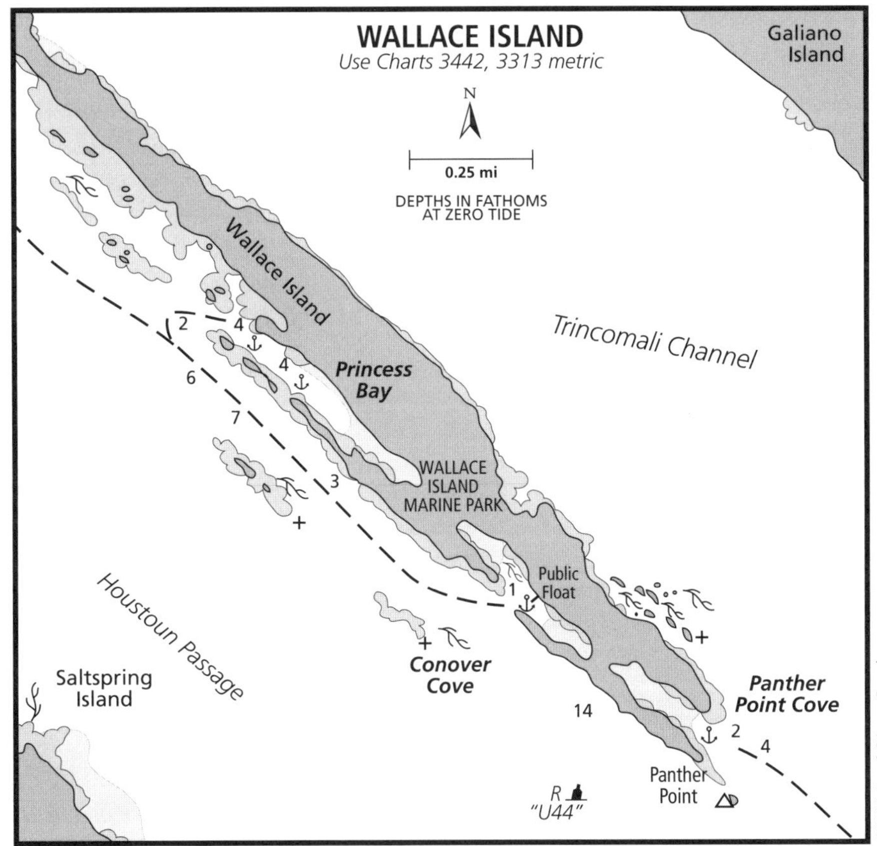

Caution: The submerged ridges on the south side of the bay and farther offshore are hazardous and should be avoided.

Anchor in 4 fathoms deep in the bay opposite South Window over mud with good holding.

Secretary Islands Window (Secretary Is)

Charts 3442, 3313; 1.6 mi NW of Princess Bay
Anchor: 48°57.68'N, 123°35.23'W

> *Secretary Islands, north of Jackscrew Island, are connected to one another by a drying sand and gravel ridge.*
>
> *Mowgli Island, NW of Secretary Islands, is known locally as Spike Island. A narrow chain of wooded islets and drying reefs, 0.4 mile long, lies 0.2 mile south of Mowgli Island.* (SD)

In fair weather, small craft can find temporary anchorage in the window between the Secretary Islands or in the shoals between Secretary and Mowgli islands. Use care in navigating these waters since a number of parallel ridges just below the surface or awash in this area make travel hazardous. Secretary Islands Window, entered from Trincomali Channel, has room for two or three boats.

There is room for just one boat between Mowgli Island and north Secretary Island. We have also seen a boat anchored between south Secretary Island and Chivers Point on Wallace Island, but this area may be foul and careful reconnoitering is advised. From Secretary Islands, the closest protection in southeast weather is Princess Bay (Wallace Island) to the southeast or Clam Bay to the northwest.

Réanne at work in Conover Cove

Anchor in about 2 fathoms over sand and gravel with fair holding.

Clam Bay (Kuper and Thetis Islands)

Charts 3477, 3442, 3443, 3313; 1 mi E of Telegraph Hbr; 2.5 mi SW of Porlier Pass
Entrance (E, 0.13 mi W of Centre Reef Buoy): 48°59.17'N, 123°38.01'W
Entrance (N, 0.18 mi SE of Leech I): 48°59.41'N, 123°38.61'W
Anchor (W of Penelakut Spit & Island 27): 48°58.90'N, 123°38.55'W
Anchor (off The Cut): 48°59.10'N, 123°39.08'W

Wallace Island

In the early 1980s, when Wallace Island belonged to a consortium of property owners, Princess Cove offered good shelter from winter winds but little in the form of shoreside activity. The island is now a marine park (except for two private properties at the mouth of Princess Cove) and a trail runs the length of the island, joining its two anchorages. Originally called "Narrow Island," Wallace was the site of a boys camp when it first attracted the attention of David Conover, a young man living in Los Angeles who spotted a newspaper ad seeking youth counselors for an island retreat in the Canadian wilderness.

Conover and his wife Jeanne eventually purchased the island in 1946 and, with little experience but plenty of enthusiasm for the pioneering life, packed up a trailer and moved from Los Angeles to Wallace Island. After a series of setbacks and hardships, they developed a summer resort at Conover Cove which they operated for 20 years before selling most of the island to a group of private investors and moving into a house they had built at Princess Cove. David also wrote two books—*Once Upon an Island and One Man's Island*—about their life on Wallace Island.

Three of the island resort's cabins remain and are part of a tour offered on summer long weekends by Cees and Ellen den Holder, the park's first facility operators. Semi-retired residents of Galiano Island, the den Holders spend over a hundred hours each month maintaining the park. They also taxi Galiano residents—seniors and those with disabilities—to Wallace Island for afternoons of picnicking and exploring the island's trails. **—AV**

Clam Bay, between the north end of Kuper Island and the SE part of Thetis Island, is entered between Penelakut Spit and Leech Island. Centre Reef, in the entrance to Clam Bay, dries 0.6 m and is marked at its SE end by starboard hand buoy "U42." Rocket Shoal, 0.2 mile south of Leech Island, consists of several rocks, with less than 2 m over them.

Anchorage for small craft can be obtained south of Rocket Shoal in about 9 m, mud bottom.

The Cut, at the west end of Clam Bay, is a very narrow dredged channel leading to Telegraph Harbour; it is usable by small craft at or near HW.

Caution.— The Cut is not recommended without the aid of local knowledge. (SD)

Clam Bay offers calm anchorage behind the spit just west of Island (27). In northwest weather, you can anchor in 4 fathoms in the cove west of Leech Island, or west of Rocket Shoal in 5 fathoms near the entrance to "The Cut." We prefer the south anchorage west of Island (27), particularly when the wind howls from the southeast. From this site you can comfortably watch all the action since Penelakut Spit breaks the seas.

Clam Bay, however, is open to the north and only partially protected by Centre Reef and Rocket Shoal. Depths along its flat bottom are 5 to 8 fathoms.

Anne Vipond

Princess Bay, Wallace Island Marine Park

Anchor (west of Penelakut Spit and Island 27) in 4 to 6 fathoms over sand, mud and shells with very good holding.

Hall Island (Trincomali Channel)

Charts 3442, 3443, 3313; 1.6 mi S of Porlier Pass; 1.4 mi E of Penelakut Spit
Entrance: 48°58.94'N, 123°35.82'W
Anchor: 48°58.90'N, 123°36.01'W

Hall Island, Reid Island and Rose Islets front Clam Bay and form a chain south and west of Porlier Pass. Rose Islets are an Ecological Reserve; landing is not permitted without a permit. (SD)

Good shelter from prevailing northwesterlies can be found on the southeast corner of Hall Island. Anchor off the small gravel beach, avoiding the rock in the inner bay to the west.

Anchor in about 3 fathoms.

Reid Island (Trincomali Channel)

Charts 3442, 3443, 3313; 1.6 mi W of Porlier Pass; 1.4 mi N of Penelakut Spit
Position (S end): 48°59.45'N, 123°36.85'W
Position (N end): 49°00.42'N, 123°37.98'W

Temporary anchorage can be found along the perimeter of Reid Island in fair weather avoiding private mooring buoys along shore and the reefs and rocks associated with Rose Islets. There is limited swinging room since the water is largely steep-to with the exception of the south and north ends of Reid Island. Local boats anchor off the northwest side of Reid Island with fair protection from southerly chop, but the area is entirely exposed to the northwest.

Spotlight Cove (Galiano I)

Charts 3442, 3473, 3313; 3.6 mi NW of Retreat Cove; 2 mi S of Porlier Pass
Entrance: 48°58.71'N, 123°34.16'W

Spotlight Cove ... has a booming ground and private moorings. (SD)

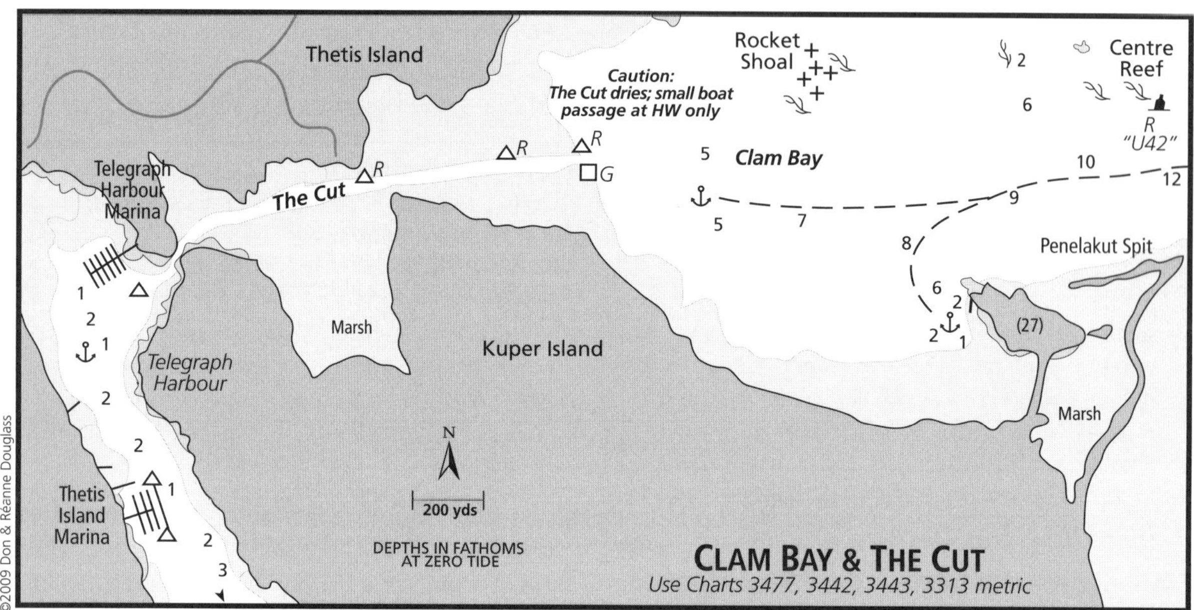

Spotlight Cove, a tiny, shallow, and largely foul cove, has an irregular bottom and large amounts of kelp. Some private residents find shelter in the narrow channels in the north end, but expert local knowledge is required.

Flagpole Cove (Galiano Island)

Charts 3442, 3473, 3313; 1.6 mi SE of Porlier Pass
Entrance: 48°59.12'N, 123°34.61'W

We call this Flagpole Cove because of the conspicuous flagpole on the south peninsula. Temporary shelter from southeast winds can be found just east of the flagpole.

North Galiano (Galiano Island)

Charts 3442, 3313; 0.96 mi S of Porlier Pass
Public float: 48°59.69'N, 123°35.09'W

North Galiano, 1 mile north of Spotlight Cove, has a general store.

Clam Bay

A striking natural feature of Clam Bay is Penelakut Spit—a natural jetty of clamshell beach that was named for the natives whose original village stood nearby. They were members of the powerful Cowichan tribe which once thrived along the east coast of Vancouver Island and in the Gulf Islands. When white colonists began settling the area, clashes ensued between the Cowichans and the newcomers. Disease killed many of these natives, and today their reserves are located on several of the Gulf Islands, including Kuper Island. Reserve land is private but the foreshore, up to the high tide mark, is public.

Kuper Island originally was joined by a narrow strip of land to Thetis until a canal was dug in 1905 to allow the passage of small boats. A bridge was built, only to be knocked down in 1946. However, livestock owned by the natives on Kuper Island continued to cross over to Thetis at low tide and help themselves to the farmers' crops—a source of grievance on both sides whenever an animal got shot.

The first white settler arrived on Kuper in 1870, before the island was designated a reserve. Two bands of Cowichan natives —the Penelakut and Lamalchi—lived on the island at the time. In 1882, an Anglican missionary named Reverend Roberts moved his family to Kuper Island where he ran a mission and residential school at Lamalchi Bay. In summer, the native students would join their parents fishing or working in canneries on the Fraser River. In 1890, the government built a school on the west side of the island which was administered by the Roman Catholic Church until it was closed in 1975 and students commuted by ferry to the school in Chemainus. **—AV**

The public wharf in North Galiano has a depth of 3 m alongside the wharf face; a float on the north side of the wharf has a depth of 2.4 m alongside. (SD)

North Galiano, a shallow bight, offers limited protection in fair weather only. It is exposed to westerlies and the traffic in Trincomali Channel. The public float is used by sportfishing boats and dinghies. The small community is on the road to Porlier Pass.

Colin Jackson

The Cut, looking east toward Clam Bay

Porlier Pass ("Cowichan Gap")

Charts 3473, 3442, 3313; 11 mi SE of Dodd Narrows; 10 mi NW of Montague Hbr
Entrance (S): 49°00.31'N, 123°35.48'W
Entrance (N): 49°01.55'N, 123°34.79'W
Mid-pass position (0.15 mi NW of Race Pt): 49°00.91'N, 123°35.26'W

Porlier Pass ... is known locally as Cowichan Gap. ... It is not less than 0.4 mile wide but the navigable channel is narrow and the tidal streams run with considerable strength.

The maximum flood is 9 kn and the ebb is 8 kn; it sets from Trincomali Channel into the

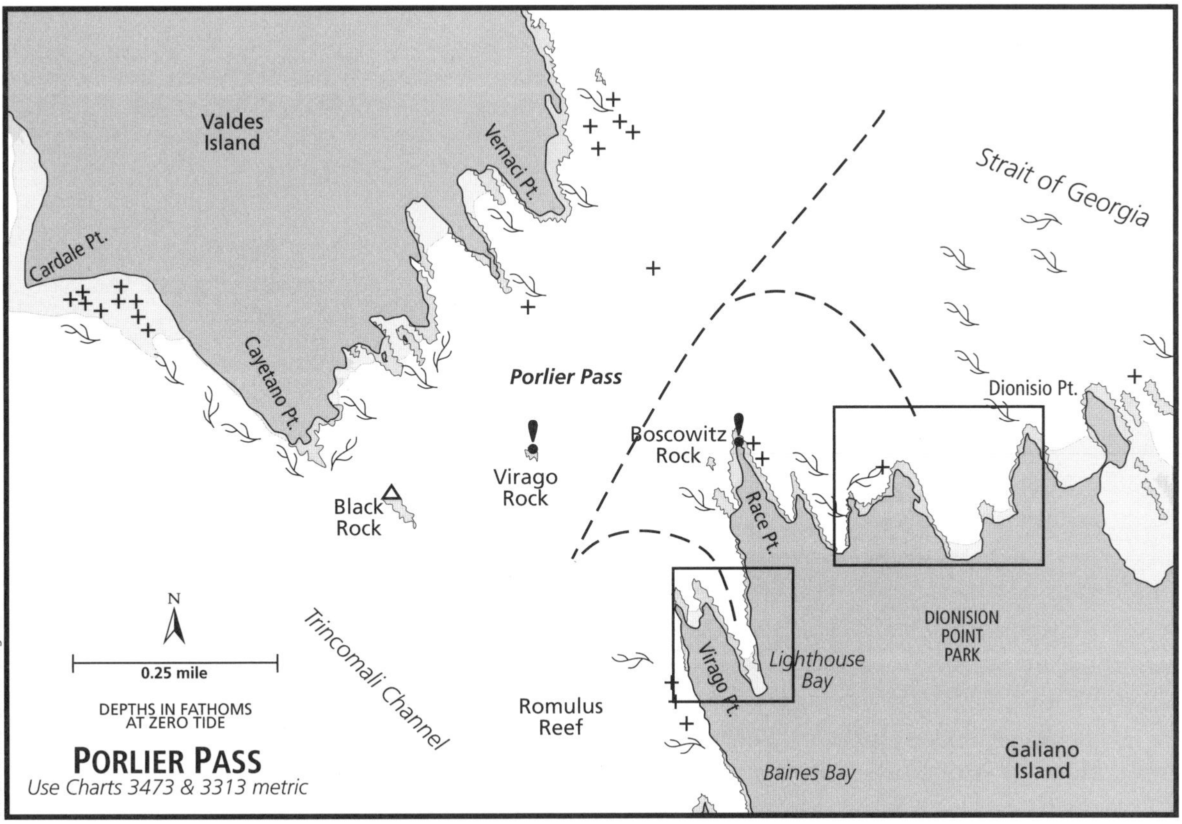

Valdes Island
Vernaci Pt.
Strait of Georgia
Cardale Pt.
Cayetano Pt.
Porlier Pass
Dionisio Pt.
Boscowitz Rock
Virago Rock
Black Rock
Race Pt.
N
0.25 mile
DEPTHS IN FATHOMS AT ZERO TIDE
Trincomali Channel
Virago Pt.
Lighthouse Bay
DIONISION POINT PARK
Romulus Reef
Baines Bay
Galiano Island

PORLIER PASS
Use Charts 3473 & 3313 metric

Sunset at Mowgli Island near Porlier Pass

Strait of Georgia on the flood and in the reverse direction on the ebb.

During the summer months the effects of the freshet from the Fraser River and NW winds that blow strongly nearly every afternoon cause rough conditions, for small craft, along the west portion of the Strait of Georgia. Crossings to the mainland or travel along the east shores of the Gulf Islands should be carried out early in the morning, but the most preferred time is late afternoon or early evening when the winds die away. (SD)

Porlier Pass is known for excellent fishing due to upwellings caused by its highly irregular bottom. This irregular bottom and the numerous rocks on both sides of the pass create turbulence and hazardous eddies, especially at spring tides when current in the pass can reach 9 knots. It is best to transit Porlier Pass at slack water.

The safest passage through Porlier Pass favors the Galiano Island shore. Remain about 200 yards west of both Virago and Race points, avoiding Boscowitz Rock, Virago Rock, Black Rock and the shoals northwest of Dionisio Point. When you approach from the Strait of Georgia, the two lights—one on Race Point and one on Virago Point—make a range bearing 196° true or the reciprocal, 016° true. This course will take you 175 yards east of bell buoy "U41" on the east side of Canoe Islets, and you can guide west as you cross midchannel in order to remain about 200 yards west of both lights.

Baines Bay (Galiano Island)

Charts 3473, 3442, 3313; 0.23 mi SE of Virago Pt
Entrance: 49°00.35'N, 123°35.23'W
Anchor: 49°00.33'N, 123°35.17'W

Baines Bay offers temporary shelter with limited swinging room in southeast weather or from the strong currents of Porlier Pass. Avoid

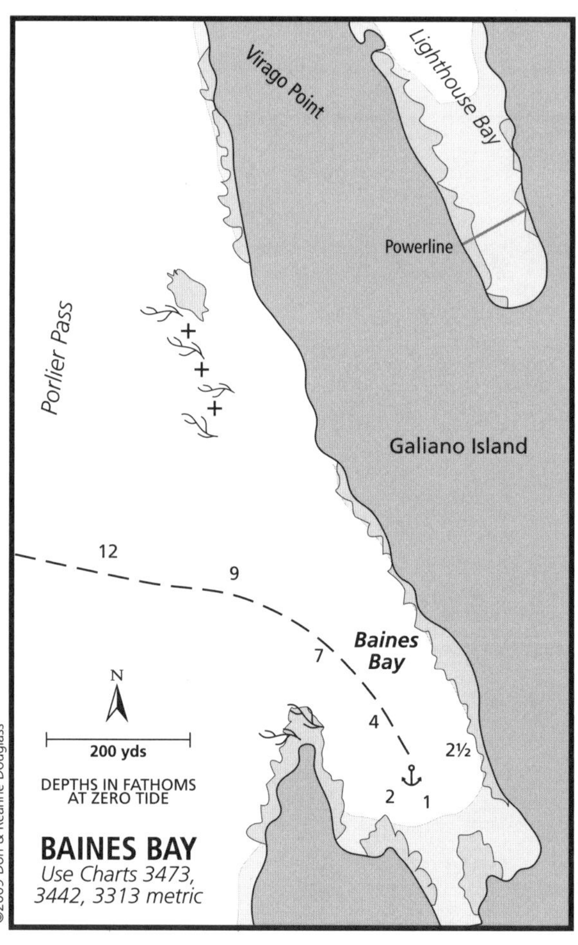

the rocks and kelp patches along the east shore of Baines Bay and the kelp patches off the west entrance. There is a deadhead on the east side of the bay and an old mooring on the west side. The bay is a favorite area for dive boats.

Anchor in 4 to 5 fathoms over sand and mud with good holding.

Lighthouse Bay (Galiano Island)

Charts 3473, 3442, 3313; 0.24 mi N of Baines Bay
Entrance: 49°00.68′N, 123°35.21′W
Anchor: 49°00.56′N, 123°35.15′W

> *Lighthouse Bay, between Virago and Race Points, affords shelter for small craft. ... A fish buyers float is in the bay.*
>
> *Anchorage for small craft can be obtained in Lighthouse Bay, south of the submarine cable.* (SD)

Lighthouse Bay, which is out of the main current, provides good protection in most weather. The inner bay does not get much sunlight and is rather dark and dank.

Anchorage can be taken anywhere south of the submarine cable that crosses the entrance to Lighthouse Bay. Swinging room is limited. Avoid the derelict float in the middle of the bay off the old cannery ruins. *Caution:* The bottom may contain old cables.

Anchor in about 4 fathoms over mud and sand with rocks; fair holding.

Cove 0.25 Mile NW of Virago Rock (Valdes Island)

Charts 3473, 3442, 3313; half-way btwn Cayetano Pt & Vernaci Pt on N side Porlier Pass
Anchor: 49°01.00′N, 123°35.73′W

> *Virago Rock, 0.2 mile NE of Black Rock, dries 0.6 m and lies on a shoal with depths of 1.8 to 2.1 m.* (SD)

Cove 0.25 Mile NW of Virago Rock—the unimaginative name we have given to this small unnamed cove—offers good temporary shelter from strong currents and from west through northeast winds. On the north shore of the cove is a small, private float. Temporary anchorage can be taken due south of this float. A house on the beach with the letters RUS on its roof serves as a landmark.

When transiting Porlier Pass to reach this cove during a south-flowing ebb current, low-powered boats should stay north of Black and Virago rocks and favor the Valdes Island shore. When conditions are favorable, you can power across Porlier Pass, passing 200 yards off Race Point. Avoid the unmarked rocks off the cove.

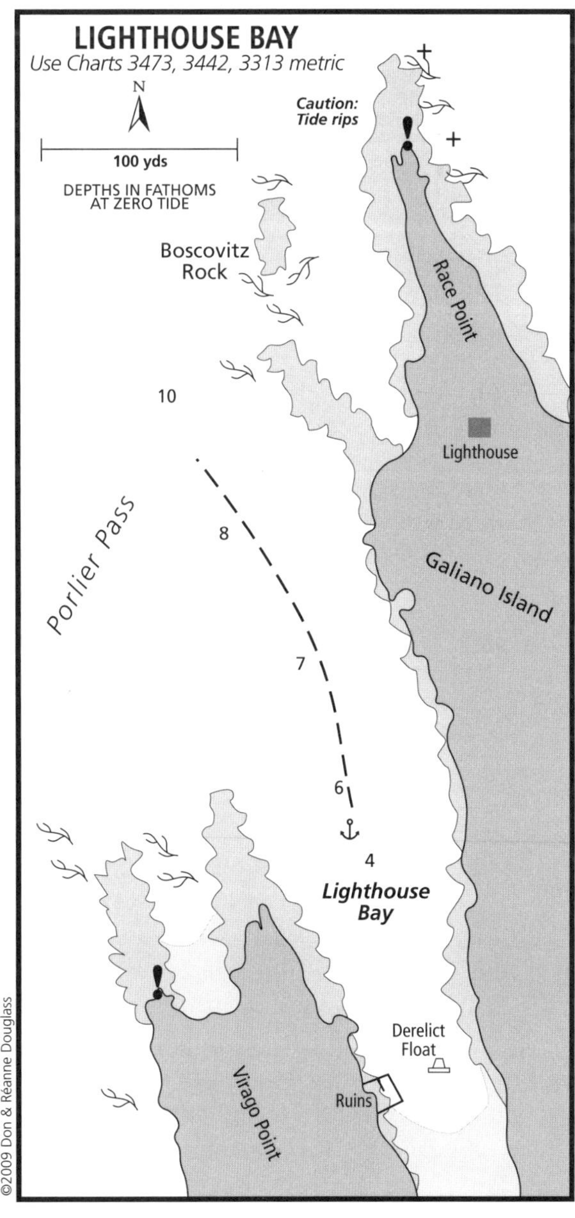

Peter Fromm

Catching the wind in Cowichan Gap

Anchor in 3 to 4 fathoms south of the pilings over grey mud with shells, isolated gravel and kelp with fair-to-good holding.

Dionisio Point Park (Galiano Island)

Charts 3473, 3442, 3313; 0.44 mi E of Race Pt Lt
Entrance: 49°00.88'N, 123°34.89'W
Anchor: 49°00.73'N, 123°34.68'W

> *Dionisio Point is connected to Galiano Island by a narrow ridge of sand.* (SD)

Dionisio Point, one of the more recently designated provincial parks, becomes an island at high tide. The lovely bay immediately west of the point has a nice sandy beach with weathered drift logs. Although open to the Strait of Georgia, the bay is fine as a temporary anchorage in fair weather; it does, however, receive sizable chop during strong northwesterlies. The next bay to the west, 0.3 mile southeast of Race Point, offers somewhat better shelter.

The eroded sandstone formations on shore are the largest examples of such rocks in the Gulf Islands. Some of the hollows make wonderful tidepools, and cormorants have even been known to use them for nesting. In summer, the shallow waters of the bay heat up enough for pleasant swimming. Scuba diving is also reported to be good in this area.

Small boats can pass carefully between the two coves at the north end of Galiano Island by staying south of the large kelp bed.

Anchor immediately west of Dionisio Point in 1.5 fathoms over sand and kelp with poor-to fair-holding.

⚓ **Dionisio Point Park** pit toilets; water from hand pump; camping; picnic area; hiking; swimming; kayaking; fishing, scuba diving

Second Bay West of Dionisio Point

(Galiano Island)
Charts 3473, 3442, 3313; 0.3 mi SE of Race Pt
Entrance: 49°00.91'N, 123°34.85'W
Anchor: 49°00.70'N, 123°34.70'W

The Second Bay West of Dionisio Point offers better protection under most conditions than the bay directly off the park's sandy beach. It is a good place to wait for slack water in Porlier Pass.

Anchor in about 3 fathoms over a sandy, rocky bottom with shells; poor-to-fair holding.

Cardale Point (Valdes Island)

Charts 3473, 3442, 3313; 0.7 mi NW of Porlier Pass
Position: 49°00.92'N, 123°36.65'W

> *Cardale Point is a low, sandy projection at the SW end of Valdes Island.* (SD)

On the south side of Cardale Point is a particularly beautiful white shell beach with a warm southern exposure. The drying flat off the beach is foul with rocks. However, temporary anchorage in fair weather can be obtained just off the drying flat, allowing exploration on shore. Nice beaches and temporary anchorage can also be found at Shingle Point, 2.0

mile northwest of Porlier Pass, and Blackberry Point, 3.0 mile northwest of Porlier Pass.

Caution: You should always leave a responsible crew member aboard your vessel here, because wind or current off the point can easily cause an anchor to drag.

Noel Bay (Valdes Island)

Charts 3473, 3442, 3313; 1 mi SE of Detwiller Pt; 1.5 mi N of Cardale Pt
Position: 49°02.49'N, 123°36.45'W

Although Noel Bay is found on the charts, it is not mentioned in the *Sailing Directions* and we have no local knowledge to add.

Canoe Islet (Valdes Island)

Charts 3473, 3442, 3313; 0.9 mi N of Race Pt
Position (diver information buoy, 0.95 mi NW of Dionisio Pt): 49°01.60'N, 123°35.30'W

> *Canoe Islet, 0.3 mile east of Shah Point, is 3 m high with drying reefs extending 0.2 mile SSE from it.*
>
> *An information/mooring buoy, close west of the reef SSE of Canoe Islet, has been installed to prevent dive vessels visiting the site of the wrecked sidewheel steamer Del Norte from damaging the remains by anchoring in its vicinity.* (SD)

Canoe Islet Ecological Reserve is known to scuba divers because of the nearby wreckage of the sidewheel steamer Del Norte. Located on the Strait of Georgia, the islet is exposed to the wind and currents found off the entrance to Porlier Pass.

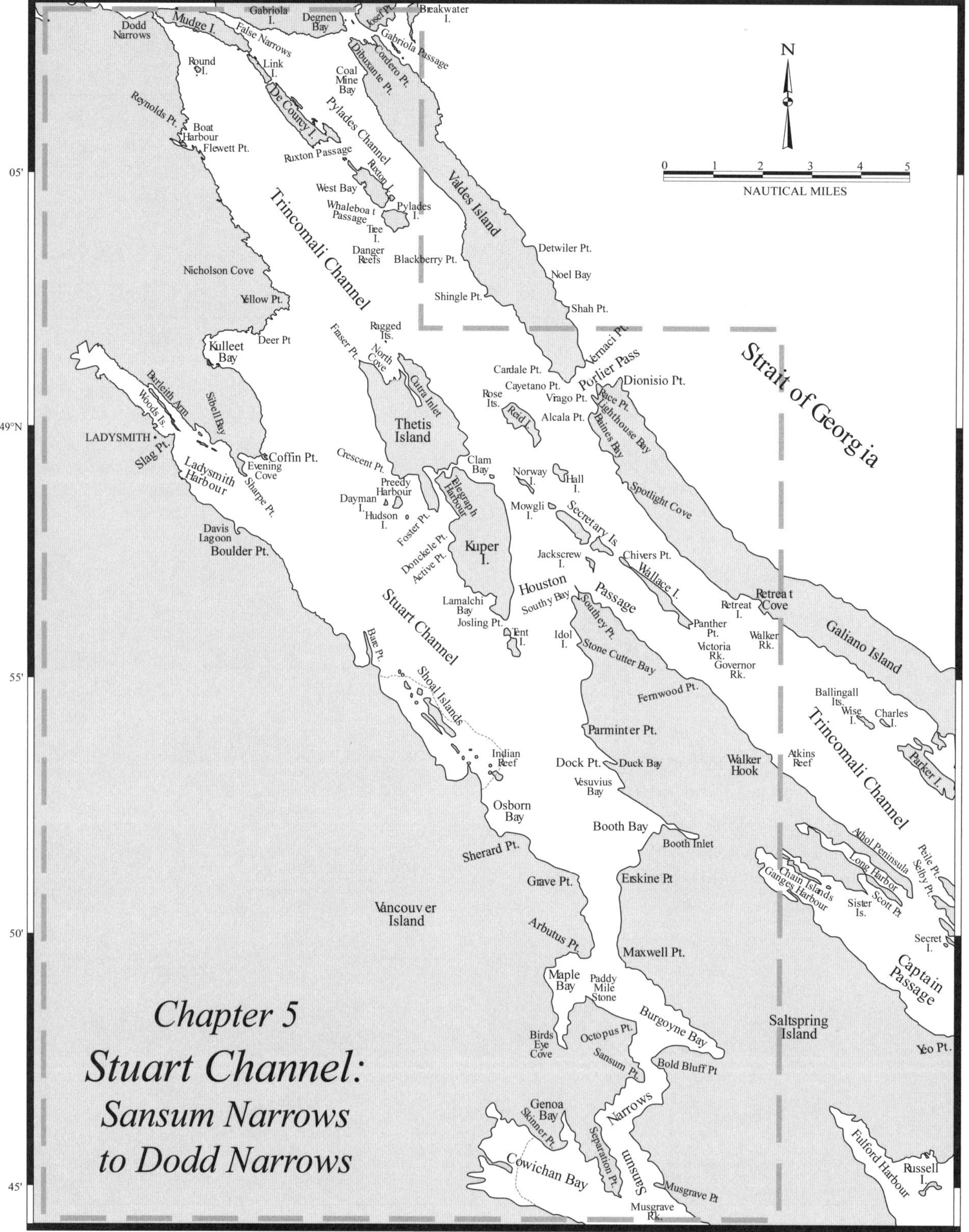

Chapter 5

Stuart Channel:

Sansum Narrows to Dodd Narrows

5

STUART CHANNEL FROM SANSUM NARROWS TO DODD NARROWS

From Sansum Narrows, head north into Stuart Channel, the "pathway" to Dodd Narrows, passing Booth and Vesuvius bays on the northwest end of Saltspring Island. Booth is an open roadstead that has little appeal for pleasure boaters. Vesuvius Bay has a small public dock with a pub at its head. In nearby Duck Bay, north of Vesuvius, cruising boats can find good anchorage and enjoy lovely sunsets. Osborn Bay, on the Vancouver Island shore across from Booth Bay, is a commercial center with little interest for cruising boats. Tent Island, off the south entrance to Houstoun Passage, is an Indian Reserve with no public access.

Well-protected Stuart Channel has generally light winds, gentle currents and warm waters. Cruising boats can find a number of rarely-visited small coves that provide quiet anchorage. Telegraph Harbour, one of the major attractions for yachts, has two marinas, both of which offer just about everything you need in the way of food, supplies, showers, laundry, and more. Thetis Island Marina has a restaurant and pub, Telegraph Harbour Marina has a coffee shop and great ice cream concoctions.

Chemainus and Ladysmith, on the Vancouver Island side of the channel, are commercial centers. The lovely town of Chemainus—one of the oldest European settlements—is renowned for its numerous murals. In June, the Festival of Murals begins and continues throughout the summer; there are parades, entertainment, artists in action, and much more.

Ladysmith is a charming place with historic buildings, shops, restaurants, and services of every kind. The Black Nugget Museum, Community Center Pool, and Transfer Beach Park are some of the attractions. Ladysmith Celebration Days are held in August, and there are fireworks, parades, and a soap box derby.

Following the Vancouver Island shore,

Rocky shores abound along the coast

Native arbutus

you transit Dodd Narrows in the direction of Nanaimo. The current in the narrows is swift and there is strong turbulence on spring tides so passage should be timed near slack water.

Stuart Channel

Charts 3442, 3443, 3475 inset, 3313; runs N of Maple Bay to Northumberland Channel
Entrance (S, 0.42 mi E of Grave Pt Light): 48°50.90'N, 123°34.92'W
Entrance (N, 0.34 mi N of Round I): 49°07.40'N, 123°47.75'W

Stuart Channel leads from the north end of Sansum Narrows to Dodd Narrows and is bounded on its east side by Saltspring, Kuper, Thetis, Ruxton and De Courcy Islands. The harbour facilities of Crofton, Chemainus and Ladysmith are on the west side of the channel.

Tidal streams in Stuart Channel ebb in a general south direction, following the contour of the channel; a velocity of 1 kn can be expected. The flood stream is weak and variable. At the north end of Stuart Channel, in the approach to Dodd Narrows, both the flood and ebb attain 3 kn. (SD)

Stuart Channel, a major north-south route along the western edge of the Gulf Islands, is the direct route from Saanich Inlet to Nanaimo. The channel is well sheltered and a smooth-water route in most weather.

Osborn Bay, Crofton (Vancouver Island)

Charts 3475 inset, 3442, 3313; 3.3 mi NW of Maple Bay
Entrance: 48°52.27'N, 123°37.16'W
Entrance (small-craft basin): 48°51.91'N, 123°38.23'W

The south and SW shores of [Osborn Bay] are fronted by a mud and sand drying bank extending 0.1 mile offshore.

Crofton, in the SW part of Osborn Bay, is a community and port engaged almost exclusively in processing and shipping forest products; it has a post office (V0R 1R0), bank, hotel and motel accommodation.

A small craft basin, close south of the public wharf, has approximately 137 m of berthing. The basin, sheltered by a breakwater, was dredged to a depth of 2 m (1976).

Fuel and provisions are available in small quantities only. Fresh water is available at Berths No. 1 and 2. (SD)

Osborn Bay, with the town of Crofton on its south quarter, is a giant logging complex with limited facilities and little appeal for cruising boats. A small public wharf and float and a small-craft basin principally serving locals can be used in case of emergency.

Booth Bay (Saltspring Island)

Charts 3442, 3313; 3.8 mi NE of Maple Bay
Position: 48°52.00'N, 123°33.26'W

Booth Bay has shoals near its head that extend 0.1 mile offshore. Marine farm facilities are in the bay. Temporary anchorage can be obtained, 0.3 mile from the head of the bay, in a depth of 22 m, mud, but being exposed to the prevailing wind is not recommended. (SD)

Booth Bay is suitable for anchorage only in fair weather.

Vesuvius Bay (Saltspring Island)

Charts 3442, 3313; 4.3 mi NE of Maple Bay
Entrance: 48°52.89'N, 123°34.63'W
Public dock in Vesuvius: 48°52.85'N, 123°34.40'W

> *Vesuvius Bay, close north of Booth Bay, has a public wharf with a depth of 2.4 m alongside. Regular ferry service is maintained between Vesuvius Bay and Crofton on Vancouver Island. The settlement has a hotel, stores and is on the main Saltspring Island road system.* (SD)

Vesuvius Bay, a tiny bay with a small public dock and a few facilities, has ferry service to Crofton on Vancouver Island. Between Vesuvius Bay and Houstoun Passage, you can find several small coves that offer limited anchorage and shelter from southeast weather. The first of these is Duck Bay.

Duck Bay (Saltspring Island)

Charts 3442, 3313; 0.5 mi NW of Vesuvius Bay
Entrance: 48°53.43'N, 123°35.09'W
Anchor: 48°53.29'N, 123°34.70'W

> *Dock Point has a drying ridge extending 0.1 mile NW from it.* (SD)

Duck Bay, a half-mile northwest of Vesuvius Bay, is reported to offer emergency protection from southerlies. Anchor well inside the bay, close to the drying flat which is steep-to; avoid Duck Point Reef.

Anchor in 6 to 7 fathoms.

Idol Island (Houstoun Passage)

Charts 3442, 3313; 1.6 mi S of Southey Pt
Entrance (S): 48°54.93'N, 123°35.67'W
Entrance (N): 48°55.26'N, 123°35.74'W
Anchor: 48°55.19'N, 123°35.39'W

> *Idol Island lies 1 mile east of Sandstone Rocks.* (SD)

Idol Island, once an Indian ceremonial burial ground, is now a park reserve. Protection from easterly weather may be found 0.2 mile east of the island.

Anchor in 6 to 10 fathoms.

Light winds! Time for the spinnaker

Stone Cutters Bay (Saltspring Island, Houstoun Passage)

Charts 3442, 3313; 1.1 mi S of Southey Pt
Entrance: 48°55.76'N, 123°35.84'W
Anchor: 48°55.68'N, 123°35.64'W

> *Stone Cutters Bay is the site of a log dump. Houses surround the bay.* (SD)

Stone Cutters Bay, a small indentation in Saltspring Island, provides some protection from easterly and southerly weather. Anchor off the private breakwater extending from the west point, but be careful to avoid the private buoys along the stone bluff. In 1998, there were no longer logbooms stored in the bay. Swinging room is limited and larger boats will find more acceptable anchorage east of Idol Island.

Anchor in about 7 fathoms.

Far from the madding crowd

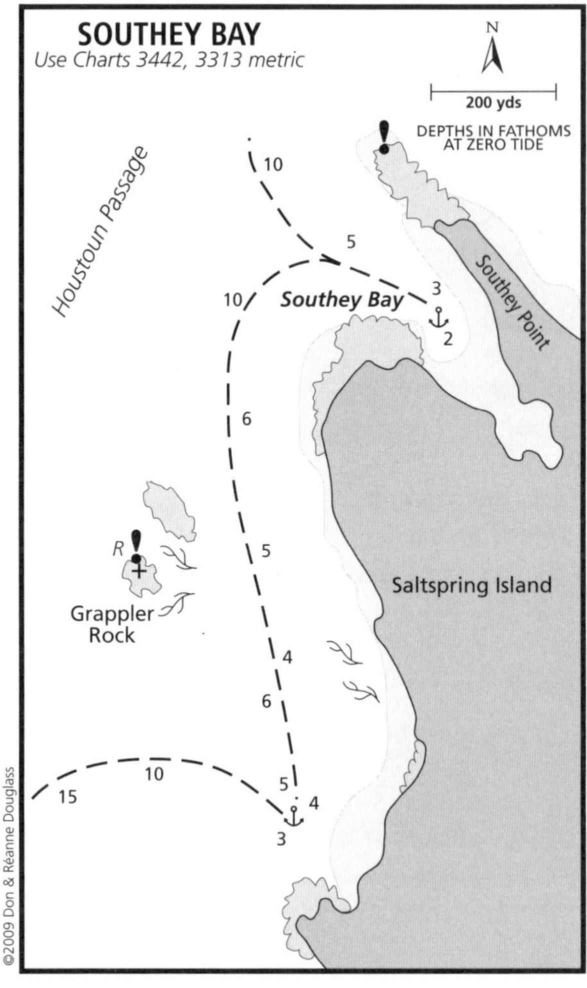

Southey Bay (Saltspring Island, Houstoun Passage)

Charts 3442, 3313; 2.1 mi NW of Conover Cove; 4.8 mi E of Chemainus
Entrance: 48°56.69′N, 123°35.85′W
Anchor: 48°56.61′N, 123°35.71′W

> *Southey Point is the north extremity of Saltspring Island.*
>
> *Grappler Rock has three drying heads.* (SD)

Southey Bay, the tiny indentation on the south side of Southey Point, affords good protection from southeast storms when anchored close to the beach behind the shoal projecting out from the north shore. Avoid the private mooring buoys.

Another anchorage with more swinging room can also be found off a sandy beach, 0.28 mile southeast of Grappler Rock in about 5 fathoms.

Anchor in 4 to 5 fathoms.

Tent Island (Stuart Channel)

Charts 3442, 3313; 3.3 mi E of Chemainus; 3.3 mi SE of Telegraph Hbr
Position: 48°55.66′N, 123°37.88′W

> *Tent Island is connected to Josling Point by a drying ridge. North Reef ... lies 0.5 mile south of the island. Sandstone Rocks lie close SE of Tent Island.*
>
> *Tent Island Reef daybeacon, on a drying rock 0.1 mile NE of Sandstone Rocks, is a white tower with a green band around the top.* (SD)

Temporary anchorage can be found off the drying flat in the west indentation of Tent Island in fair weather only or sometimes off the northern tip of the island. Both locations are completely exposed to westerlies. Camping is not allowed on shore without prior permission from the Indian Reserve. Interesting sandstone formations are found at the south end of Tent Island, including a formation that resembles a large throne.

Anchor in about 2 fathoms off the drying mud flat in sand and mud with fair holding.

Lamalchi Bay (Kuper Island)

Charts 3442, 3313; 2.3 mi SE of Telegraph Hbr
Anchor: 48°56.42'N, 123°38.44'W

Kuper Island is an Indian Reserve. (SD)

The entire Kuper Island is an Indian Reserve and permission is required to go ashore. (The painted sign on a building warns Salish Nation Penelakut Band, Stay Off.)

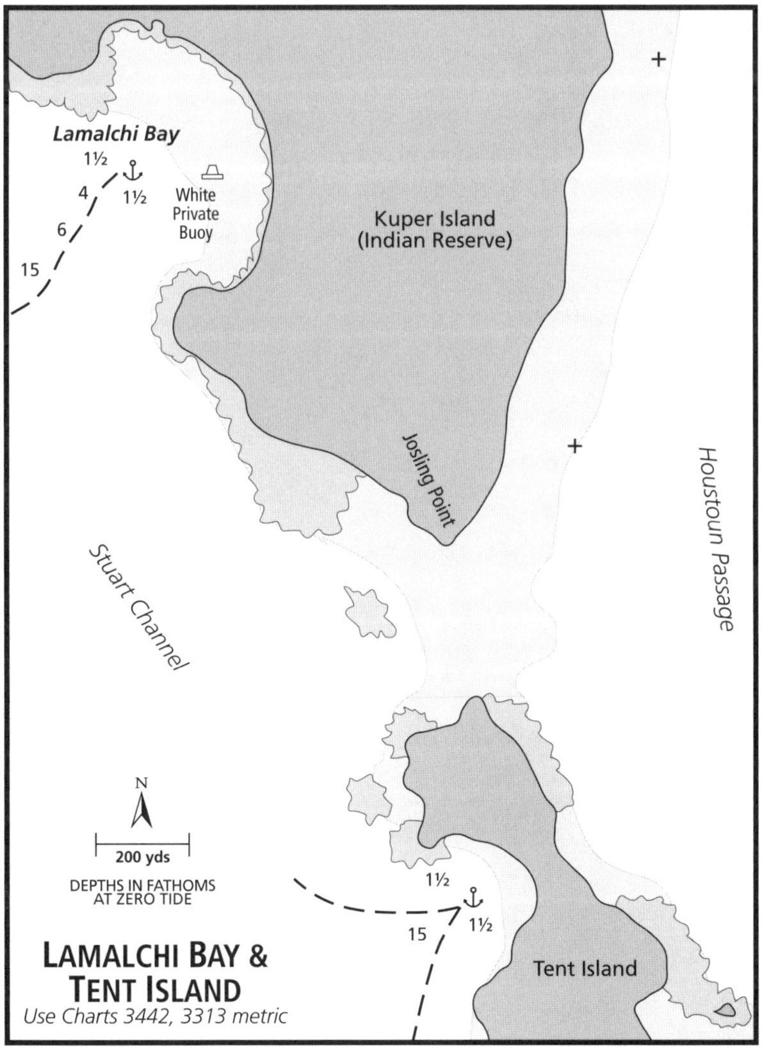

Anchorage is available in fair weather only. The inner bay, which is quite shallow, should be used only when tide tables indicate adequate depth.

Anchor in 1.5 fathoms, sandy bottom with some grass; fair holding.

Telegraph Harbour (Kuper/Thetis Islands)

Charts 3477, 3442, 3443, 3313; 3.7 mi NE of Chemainus; 3.4 mi SW of Porlier Pass
Entrance (outer): 48°57.76'N, 123°40.02'W
Entrance (inner): 48°58.13'N, 123°39.75'W
Anchor: 48°58.91'N, 123°40.26'W
Public dock (Kuper Island): 48°58.19'N, 123°39.58'W
Thetis Island Marina: 48°58.61'N, 123°40.09'W
Telegraph Hbr Marina: 48°58.94'N, 123°40.20'W

Telegraph Harbour ... lies between the NW side of Kuper Island and the SE extremity of Thetis Island. Pleasure craft congregate in the harbour and a ferry that plies between Kuper Island and Chemainus makes frequent calls. The post office (V0R 2Y0) is near the head of Telegraph Harbour.

Anchorage can be obtained in Telegraph Harbour, for vessels of moderate size, in a depth of 13 m, mud, NW of the public wharf and submarine cable. (SD)

Telegraph Harbour, a major cruising destination for pleasure craft, contains two popular marinas. The marinas lie at the north end of the harbor in the narrow channel between Kuper and Thetis islands, 0.75 mile northwest of the B.C. ferry dock with service to Chemainus. Shallow water between the two marinas offers anchorage for several small- to medium-sized boats among the many private mooring buoys found there. Large vessels can anchor in deeper water off Foster

LAMALCHI BAY & TENT ISLAND
Use Charts 3442, 3313 metric

Point and have more swinging room. A small, drying canal known as "The Cut" leads through the mud flats to the east, allowing small boats to enter Clam Bay at high water.

Both Thetis Island Marina on the west shore, and Telegraph Harbour Marina at the northeast head of the bay are popular stops that offer warm, friendly facilities for cruising boats. From the marinas, it's just a half-mile walk to the ferry in Preedy Harbour on Thetis Island.

Please respect the no-wake speed limit in the upper reaches of Telegraph Harbour, and watch for small float planes which use the channel.

Anchor in 1 to 2 fathoms over mud and sand with good holding.

⚓ **Thetis Island Marina** tel: 250.246.3464; monitors VHF Ch 66A; website: www.thetisisland.com; email: marina@thetisisland.com; full service marina; showers; laundry; groceries; restaurant and pub; reservations recommended

⚓ **Telegraph Harbour Marina** tel: 250.246.9511 or 800.246.6011; fax: 250.246.2668; monitors VHF Ch 66A; website: www.telegraphharbour.com; fuel; power; showers; laundry; coffee shop; farmers market on Saturdays; open seasonally; reservations recommended

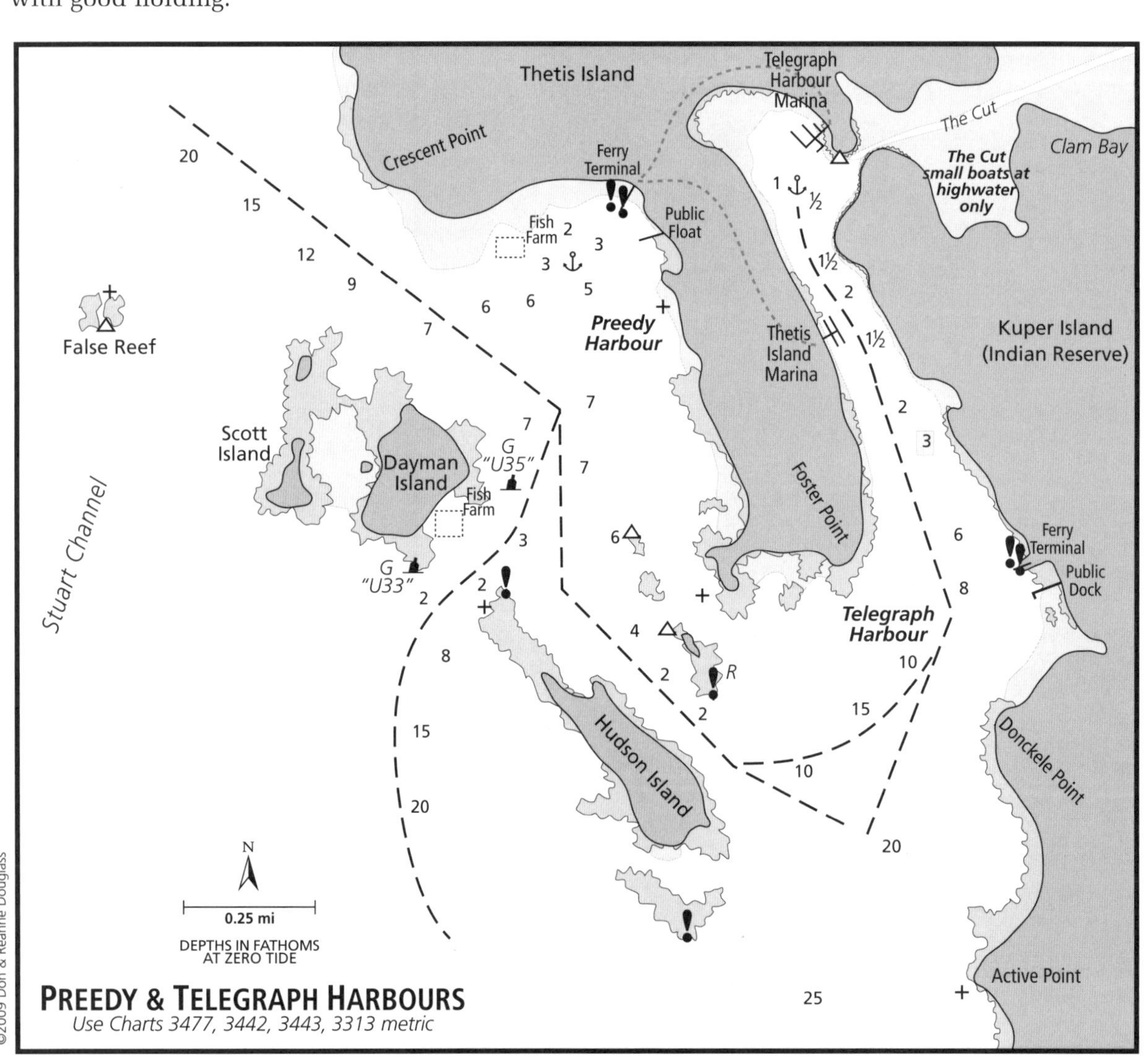

PREEDY & TELEGRAPH HARBOURS

Use Charts 3477, 3442, 3443, 3313 metric

Preedy Harbour (Thetis Island)

Charts 3477, 3442, 3443, 3313; 0.5 mi W of Telegraph Hbr
Entrance (SW, 0.17 mi S of Dayman I): 48°58.11'N, 123°41.26'W
Entrance (NW, 0.5 mi W of Crescent Pt): 48°59.05'N, 123°42.17'W
Public float: 48°58.79'N, 123°40.70'W
Anchor: 48°58.76'N, 123°40.87'W

Preedy Harbour, fronted by Hudson Island and Dayman Island, has three entrances. The entrance from Telegraph Harbour, between Hudson Island and Foster Point, has drying reefs along its centre line; the fairway, which lies between the drying reefs and Hudson Island, has a least depth of 3 m.

Hudson Island North light (294.5) is on

Thetis Island Marina

Telegraph Harbour

This popular harbor offers plenty of shoreside diversions with two full-service marinas and numerous crafts shops and studios within walking distance of the waterfront. Thetis Island Marina offers patio dining at its fully licensed restaurant and pub. Telegraph Harbour Marina is ideal for families with its spacious grounds and freshly baked homemade pies. Both marinas are a 10-minute walk to the ferry terminal at Preedy Harbour where the Chemainus ferry docks ten times a day.

A pleasant day excursion from Telegraph Harbour is the 30-minute ferry trip across Stuart Channel to Chemainus, a former logging town now famous for its colorful street murals which depict local history and have transformed a small mill town into the world's largest outdoor art gallery. Sidewalk cafes, ice cream parlors and tea rooms line the charming streets as do art galleries, antique shops and a museum. A pleasant stroll can be enjoyed in Waterwheel Park, taking the Gateway to Old Town where Heritage Path leads to more murals and shops.

Telegraph Harbour has its own share of artisans and a walk along the road that joins the two marinas will take you past a few crafts shops and studios. The island's three bible camps attract student visitors, a tradition that began back in 1904 when a retired British major and his spinster sister established an Anglican retreat on Thetis. The island had already become known as an English colony through the efforts of Mr. and Mrs. Henry Burchell who trained young bachelors from England the

Float plane mooring at Telegraph Harbour

rudiments of farming. These men lived in a dormitory building behind Preedy Hall, a spacious home that the energetic Burchells built using lumber they cut at their own sawmill.

The Burchells had lost most of their life savings in a business venture when they settled at Preedy Harbour in 1892, working diligently to establish a new life on Thetis where they operated a store, farm and orchard. Each Christmas they held a children's party and in the fall, on the night of the first full moon after haying, a dance complete with oysters and sparkling white wine was attended by guests who would sail or row from the other Gulf Islands. The original Preedy Hall burned down in the 1920s after a widowed Mrs. Burchell sold it, and a new Preedy Hall was built around 1930. **—AV**

Preedy Harbour public float

the south extremity of the drying reefs between Hudson Island and Foster Point.

Two daybeacons with starboard hand daymarks are on the drying reefs.

The entrance channel between Hudson and Dayman Islands has a least depth of 4.3 m between the drying ledges extending from both islands.

Preedy Harbour affords good anchorage, mud bottom, in its north part avoiding the submarine cables.

The public wharf, in the NE corner of Preedy Harbour, is 18.3 m long with a depth of 5.5 m alongside. A float attached to the west corner of the wharf is 11 m long with a depth of 2.4 m alongside.

Caution.—A rock, with 0.3 m over it, lies about 45 m due south of the head of the public wharf. (SD)

Preedy Harbour is less protected than Telegraph Harbour, but pleasant anchorage in fair weather can be found in either its extreme northern or southern end. It is far less crowded than Telegraph Harbour and provides more swinging room. Good anchorage can be found about 250 yards west of the public float.

Anchor in 3 fathoms over mud and sand with good holding.

Chemainus Bay (Vancouver Island)

Charts 3475 inset, 3442, 3313; 8.42 mi NW of Maple Bay; 3.7 mi SW of Telegraph Hbr
Entrance: 48°55.78′N, 123°42.54′W
Entrance (Marina): 48°55.51′N, 123°42.80′W
Anchor (W of Bird Rock Light): 48°55.87′N, 123°43.23′W

Anchorage in Chemainus Bay is not advisable because of extensive booming grounds and congestion inside the bay. Vessels awaiting a berth usually anchor in Houstoun Passage.

The community of Chemainus, on the west side of Chemainus Bay, has a hospital, post office (V0R 1K0), stores and motels. (SD)

Chemainus has undergone a metamorphosis from a logging and mill town to an attractive town that lures tourists to its many shops and galleries. Since anchoring is not convenient in the bay, you may wish to anchor in Telegraph Harbour and take the Thetis Island ferry to Chemainus for a day of shopping and eating.

A small public boat harbor, lies immediately south of the Chemainus ferry terminal offering day moorage for nominal fee for those who want to just visit the town, or overnight moorage.

Classic "old world" style architecture at Preedy Harbour

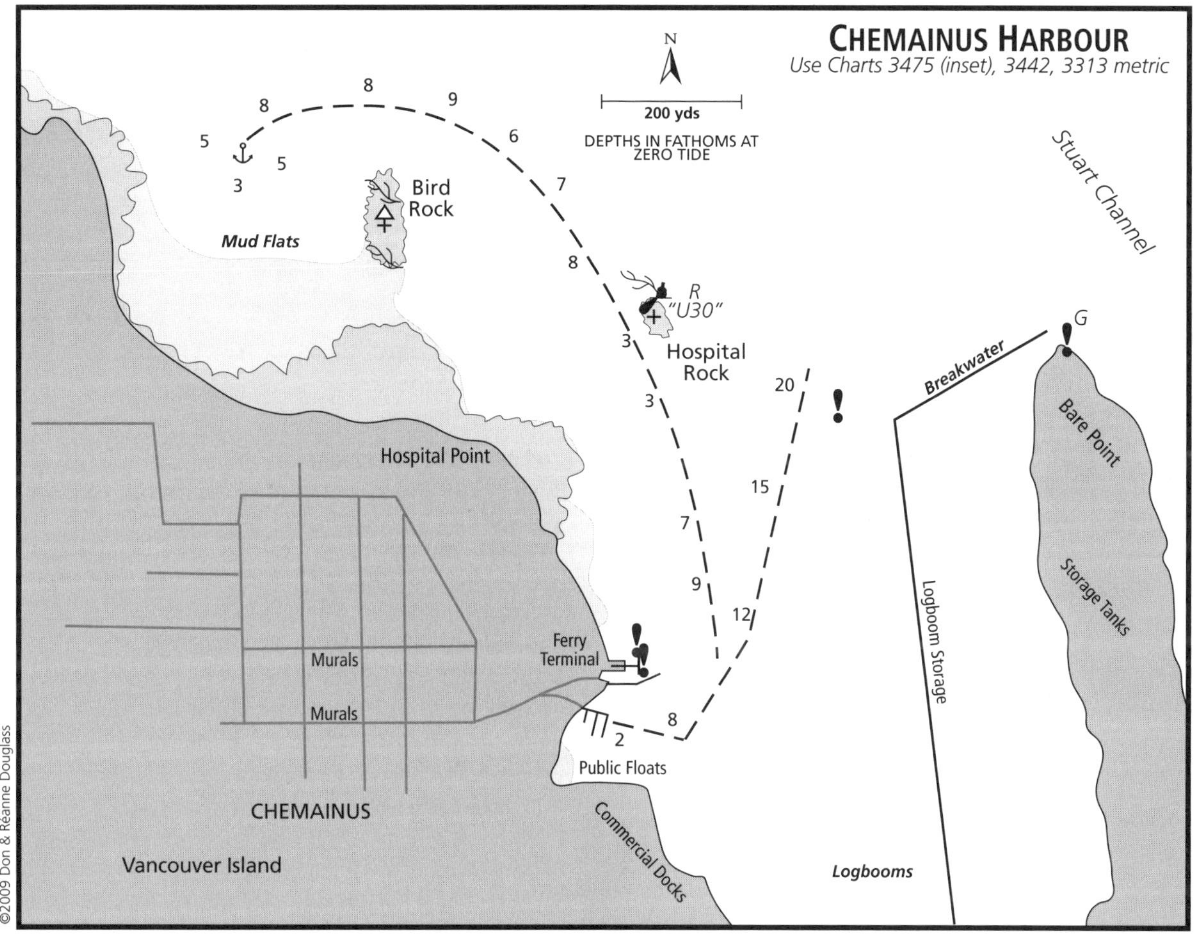

Chemainus

Only 4,500 people live here, but nearly half a million people visit each year. They come to see a town adorned with public artwork. Starting in 1982 when five murals were painted on downtown walls, the revitalization project has expanded to thirty-six large murals and several sculptures. New murals are still being added and the older ones are refurbished periodically and kept graffiti-free. Yellow footprints painted on sidewalks lead past the murals, or you can view them from a horse-drawn carriage.

The artworks depict the history of native inhabitants and immigrants. With vivid images of ships, trains and stores, the murals show how loggers, miners and stevedores eked out a living. Some of the paintings are abstract and others, like the depiction of the Hong Hing Waterfront Store, so realistic you might be tempted to climb the steps and go inside.

Waterwheel Park has a replica of the wheel that powered the town's sawmill, and a museum open in summer. Evenings you can dine and take in a play at the Chemainus Theatre (tel. 250.246.9820).

Chemainus's newest tourist attraction rests 100 feet under the waters of Chemainus Bay. In January of 2006, a retired Boeing 737 was sunk in the bay as a diving destination and haven for marine life. It's named the Xihwu Reef (pronounced kee-quat) after the red sea urchin, and divers hope the urchin and other marine life will become re-established there. Originally part of the Air Canada fleet, the plane is 100 feet long. Xihwu Reef's coordinates are 48°56.14'N and 123°43.13'W.

The municipal dock is busy in summer, so plan ahead. For docking reservations, call 250.715.8186 or email hbootsma@island.net.

The Chemainus Visitor Centre has maps and information. It's located at 9758 Chemainus Rd., tel. 250.246.3944.

One of the many Chemainus murals

A temporary and somewhat exposed anchorage can be found on the northwest side of Chemainus Bay 0.1 mile west of Bird Rock Light. The head of this small bay has a park and launching ramp, but it largely dries at low water.

Anchor in 3 to 5 fathoms off the drying mud flat, over sand and mud with fair-to-good holding.

⚓ **Chemainus Municipal Dock** tel: 250.715.8186; fax: 250.246.1398; monitors VHF Ch 66A; email: harmen.chemainus.munimarina@gmail.com; power; water; showers

Chemainus Ferry

Ladysmith Harbour (Vancouver Island)

Charts 3475 inset, 3442, 3443, 3313; 6 mi NW of Chemainus; 5.5 mi W of Preedy Hbr
Entrance: 48°58.50'N, 123°46.25'W
Ladysmith Maritime Society floats: 48°59.72'N, 123°48.70'W
Public docks: 48°59.98'N, 123°48.86'W
Ladysmith Yacht Club: 49°00.39'N, 123°49.61'W
Anchor (deep in hbr): 49°00.74'N, 123°49.78'W
Mañana Lodge mooring: 49°00.68'N, 123°49.37'W

Ladysmith Harbour, also known as Oyster Harbour, is entered between Boulder Point and Sharpe Point, 1.5 miles NNW.

The public wharf, 0.35 mile NW of Slag Point, consists of a pier with three floats attached to it. ...The area around the floats has been dredged to 3 m. Power is laid on the float; water, garbage and used oil disposal facilities are available on the wharfhead. (SD)

Chemainus Bay public floats

Although the town of Ladysmith has undergone extensive renovations, the waterfront is still largely industrial and offers little in the way of facilities for cruising vessels; local and commercial fishing boats have priority. Temporary anchorage can be taken beyond the log-boom areas, deep in Ladysmith Harbour, 0.3 mile west of Page Point, or preferably in Sibell Bay between Dunsmuir Islands and Hunter Point on the north side of Ovens Island (the southernmost

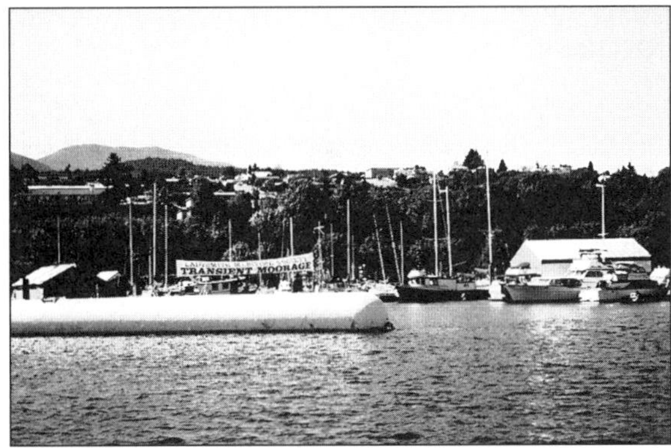

TRANSIENT MOORAGE
Ladysmith Harbour entrance breakwater

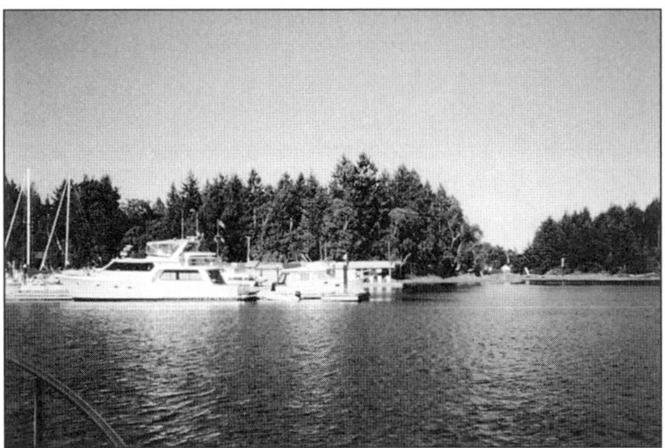

Ladysmith Harbour

Dunsmuir island). Temporary moorage may be available at the Ladysmith Marine Society floats, the first float complex located approximately 0.4 mile northwest of Slag Point.

⚓ **Page Point Inn** tel: 250.245.2312 or 877.860.6866; power; water; pumpout; toilets; showers; laundry; hot tubs; restaurant

⚓ Ladysmith Fisherman's Wharf tel: 250.245.7511; monitors VHF Ch 66A; website: www.ladysmithfishermanswharf.com; e-mail: ladysmithfishermanswharf@gmail.com; power; garbage collection; public telephone; open year-round

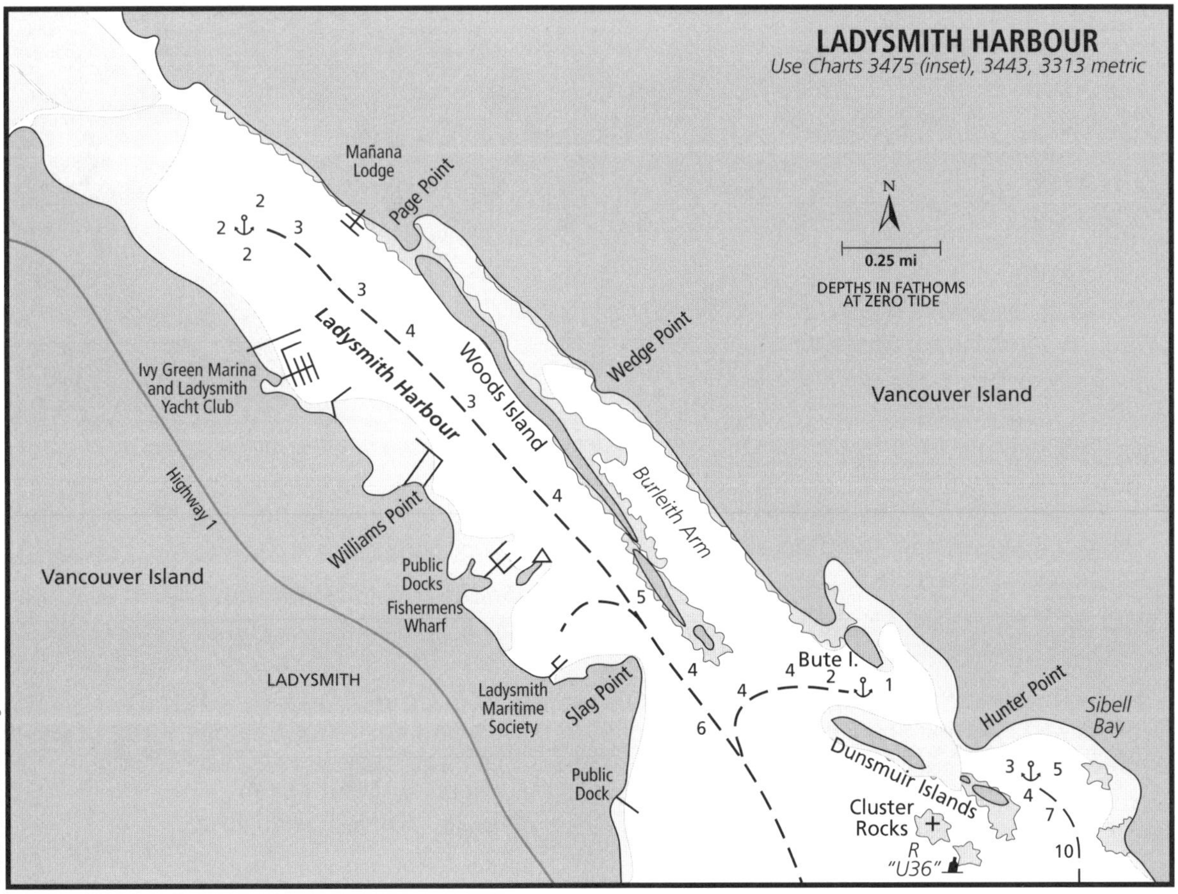
LADYSMITH HARBOUR
Use Charts 3475 (inset), 3443, 3313 metric
N
0.25 mi
DEPTHS IN FATHOMS AT ZERO TIDE
Mañana Lodge
Page Point
Wedge Point
Woods Island
Burleith Arm
Ladysmith Harbour
Ivy Green Marina and Ladysmith Yacht Club
Highway 1
Williams Point
Public Docks
Fishermens Wharf
Vancouver Island
Vancouver Island
LADYSMITH
Ladysmith Maritime Society
Slag Point
Public Dock
Bute I.
Hunter Point
Sibell Bay
Dunsmuir Islands
Cluster Rocks
R "U36"

Ladysmith Harbour

Ladysmith Harbour was first called Oyster Bay in 1859 when extensive oyster beds were found along the south shore. The town of Ladysmith was founded in 1900 as a shipping port by the powerful coal baron James Dunsmuir. He chose the name upon receiving news that Ladysmith in South Africa, under siege by the Boers, had been relieved by British troops. The woman who originally inspired this place name was a descendant of a noble Spanish family. A beautiful 14-year-old maiden in 1812, she was brought by her older sister to a British military camp for protection. There she met Sir Harry Smith, a young captain who soon became her husband. He pursued a successful military career, accompanied by Lady Smith, and eventually retired a major general.

The town of Ladysmith is pleasant for strolling with its award-winning collection of restored heritage buildings, such as those lining First Avenue. Shoppers can browse the antique shops and craft stores, and those seeking outdoor recreation can visit Transfer Beach Park where you'll find a playground, picnic shelters and horseshoe pitch. The town holds a Maritime Festival the first weekend in June and Ladysmith Days are held on the August long weekend.

Times were once a lot tougher for the town that recently won a provincial award as the most beautiful community on Vancouver Island. When James Dunsmuir operated mines in the area, conditions were less than ideal for the men working in them. On October 5th, 1901—the "Day of Horror"—an underground explosion killed 32 miners at the Extension Mine, which continued operations until the 1930s. Dunsmuir, who was appointed lieutenant governor of British Columbia in 1906, was the eldest son of Robert Dunsmuir who immigrated from Scotland in 1851 and built a family fortune in coal mining on Vancouver Island. James was born at Fort Vancouver on the Columbia River while his parents were en route to their new country, arriving at Victoria a few months later on board a brigantine. **—AV**

Sibell Bay and Dunsmuir Islands (Vancouver Island)

Charts 3475 inset, 3443, 3313; 0.8 mi NW of Sharpe Pt; 1.0 mi SE of Slag Pt
Entrance: 48°59.32'N, 123°46.90'W
Anchor (Sibell Bay): 48°59.47'N, 123°47.09'W
Anchor (N side Dunsmuir I, 0.17 mi NW of Hunter Pt): 48°59.64'N, 123°47.42'W

Dunsmuir Islands, 0.6 mile NE of Holland Bank, are wooded. Cluster Rocks, 0.1 mile south of Dunsmuir Islands, dry 1.2 m at their highest point; they are marked by starboard hand buoy "U36."

Sibell Bay, east of Dunsmuir Islands, and the bay to the north with Bute Island in it, have marine farm facilities in them. (SD)

Seattle Yacht Club Outstation in Sibell Bay

Sibell Bay provides shelter from prevailing northwest winds in a quiet setting. Shallow-draft boats can find good shelter north of Dunsmuir Islands and southeast of Bute Island, avoiding the shoal areas and mud flats. Deeper-draft boats can anchor 100 yards northeast of the Seattle Yacht Club outstation located on Ovens Island (the southernmost Dunsmuir Island).

Anchor (Sibell Bay) in 2 to 3 fathoms over mud with good holding.

Anchor (north side Dunsmuir Island) in 2 fathoms over mud with good holding.

Evening Cove (Vancouver Island)

Charts 3475 inset, 3443, 3313; 0.6 mi SE of Sibell Bay; 3.5 mi W of Preedy Hbr
Entrance: 48°58.93'N, 123°45.08'W
Anchor: 48°59.25'N, 123°46.20'W

Evening Cove, between Sharpe Point and Coffin

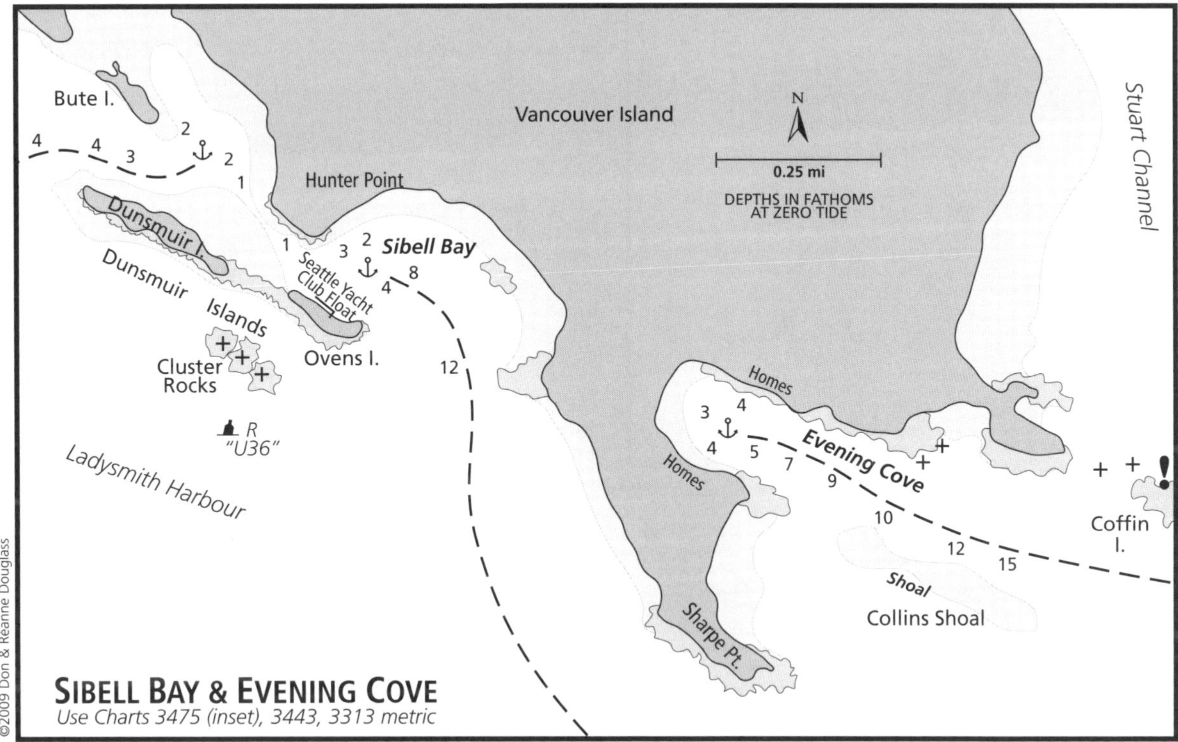

Entering Evening Cove in the morning

Point, has Collins Shoal in the centre of its entrance. (SD)

Evening Cove offers easy access and good protection from northwest winds with moderate exposure to southeast winds. Avoid the private buoys off the homes along shore. When transiting Stuart Channel, avoid Collins Shoal in the center of the entrance south of Coffin Point.

Anchor in 4 fathoms over mud and gravel with fair-to-good holding.

Kulleet Bay (Vancouver Island)

Charts 3443, 3313; 2.2 mi NE of Evening Cove
Entrance: 49°01.31'N, 123°45.83'W
Anchor: 49°01.23'N, 123°47.15'W

Kulleet Bay is entered south of Deer Point. It is a good anchorage in fine weather only as it is exposed to east winds. (SD)

Kulleet Bay, a large bay fringed with rocks and reefs, provides temporary anchorage in the southwest corner, to the east and off the front of a muddy lagoon.

Anchor in 5 to 6 fathoms over sand and shells with fair holding.

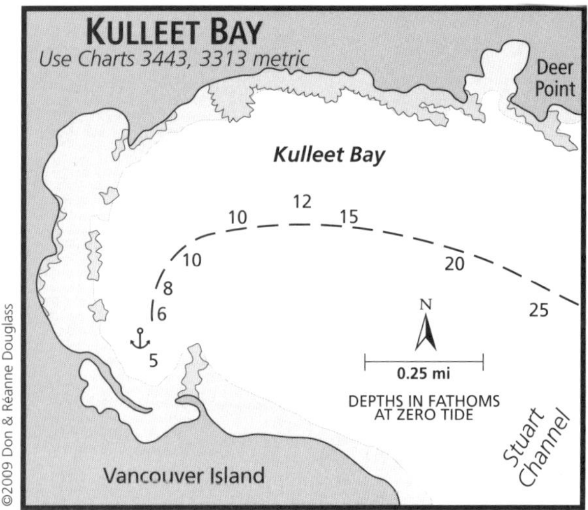

North Cove (Thetis Island)

Charts 3442, 3443, 3313; 2.5 mi N of Preedy Hbr; 3.9 mi W of Porlier Pass
Entrance: 49°01.53'N, 123°42.08'W
Anchor: 49°00.88'N, 123°41.72'W

Anchor check—good mud bottom

> *North Cove, at the north end of Thetis Island, lies between Fraser Point and Pilkey Point. A rock breakwater and a private float lie in the SW part of the cove.*
>
> *Anchorage in a depth of 13 m, mud, can be obtained in the middle of North Cove; the cove affords shelter from south winds.* (SD)

North Cove offers two anchor sites: North Cove, the broader of the two anchorages, is the more accessible, but it is open to northwest winds; a smaller and more protected anchorage can be found in Cufra Inlet, but with space limited to about two boats.

Anchor in about 4 fathoms (off the small sandy beach in the southwest corner of North Cove) over sand and mud with good holding.

Cufra Inlet (Thetis Island)

Charts 3442, 3443, 3313; a narrow & shallow indentation at the SE end of North Cove
Entrance (0.61 mi N of Pilkey Pt): 49°01.46'N, 123°41.42'W
Anchor: 49°01.01'N, 123°41.22'W

> *Cufra Inlet ... has a breakwater near its entrance that extends out from its east shore; the breakwater affords good shelter to small craft, but the major portion of Cufra Inlet dries.* (SD)

You can explore Cufra Inlet by dinghy for quite a distance at high water by carefully watching your echo sounder or by watching the bottom. Be sure to consult the tide tables ahead of time.

When entering North Cove, avoid the rocks off the northwest entrance, and the rocks and shoals northwest of Pilkey Point and Ragged Islets. Anchor in Cufra Inlet just inside the old stone breakwater (space permitting) near the drying flat, with limited swinging room.

Anchor in about 1 fathom over sand and grass with fair holding.

Nicholson Cove (Vancouver Island)

Charts 3443, 3313; 0.7 mi NW of Yellow Pt; 1.8 mi NE of Kulleet Bay
Entrance: 49°02.72'N, 123°44.94'W
Anchor: 49°02.87'N, 123°45.40'W
Inn of the Sea dock: 49°02.77'N, 123°45.28'W

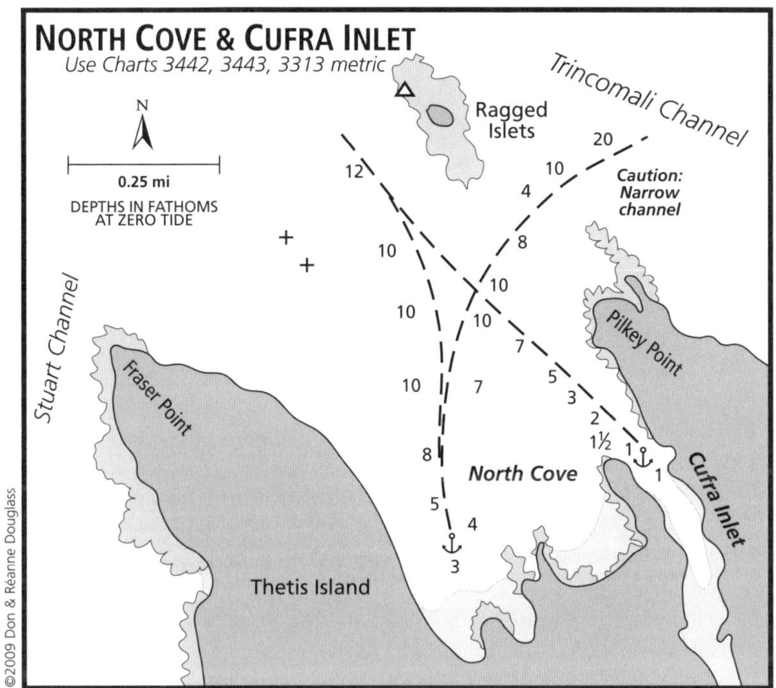

A resort on [Yellow Point] and another in Nicholson Cove have floats and private mooring buoys.

A daybeacon on a drying rock, in the entrance to Nicholson Cove, has a starboard hand daymark. (SD)

Nicholson Cove can be used as a temporary anchorage with shelter from westerly winds. There are rocks along both shores which must be avoided and the inner bay is full of private mooring floats. A starboard daymark is located on one of the drying rocks and caution is advised upon entering the small cove. Anchor just outside the line of mooring buoys.

Inn of the Sea has a restaurant and a private dock with moorage for guests only. For information, telephone 250.245.01011.

Anchor in 1 to 2 fathoms over sand and gravel and some rocks with fair holding.

Boat Harbour/"Kenary Cove" (Vancouver Island)

Charts 3443, 3313; 4.4 mi N of Kulleet Bay; 2.6 mi S of Dodd Narrows
Entrance: 49°05.70'N, 123°47.69'W
Anchor: 49°05.65'N, 123°48.00'W

Boat Harbour ... is often used as a temporary anchorage for vessels awaiting slack water in Dodd Narrows. The cove in the south part of Boat Harbour, west of Flewett Point, is known locally as Kenary Cove. The floats in Boat Harbour are private.

Anchorage can be obtained in the entrance of Boat Harbour, in 15 m, mud bottom. Small craft can obtain well-sheltered anchorage in Kenary Cove, in 3 to 5 m, mud bottom. (SD)

Boat Harbour

A visit to Boat Harbour is an opportunity to hike into beautiful Hemer Provincial Park where wide groomed trails lead past the pristine shores of Holden Lake. The park, a gift to the province from John and Violet Hemer, can be reached by a trail that starts on the peninsula near the head of Boat Harbour. This peninsula is where a marine engineer named Flewett used to load coal onto a steam launch in the 1870s, and the narrow neck of land was once a rail embankment. The foreshore is also fascinating to explore; here low banks of sandstone have been eroded over time into smooth and unusual shapes. **—AV**

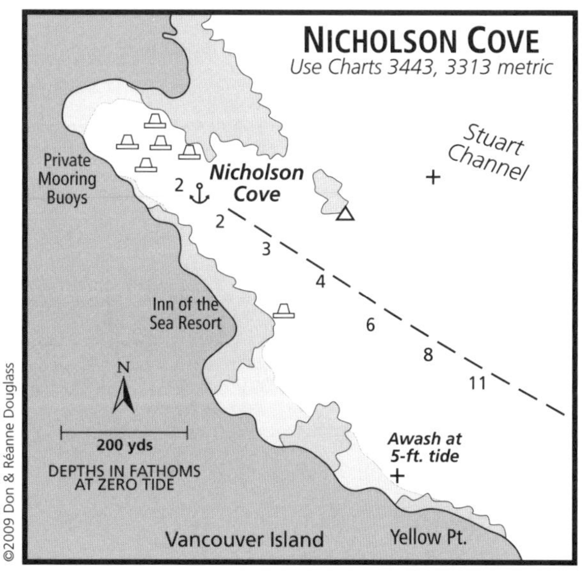

Boat Harbour, another lovely anchor site

Boat Harbour (Kenary Cove) offers temporary anchorage for boats awaiting slack water at Dodd Narrows.

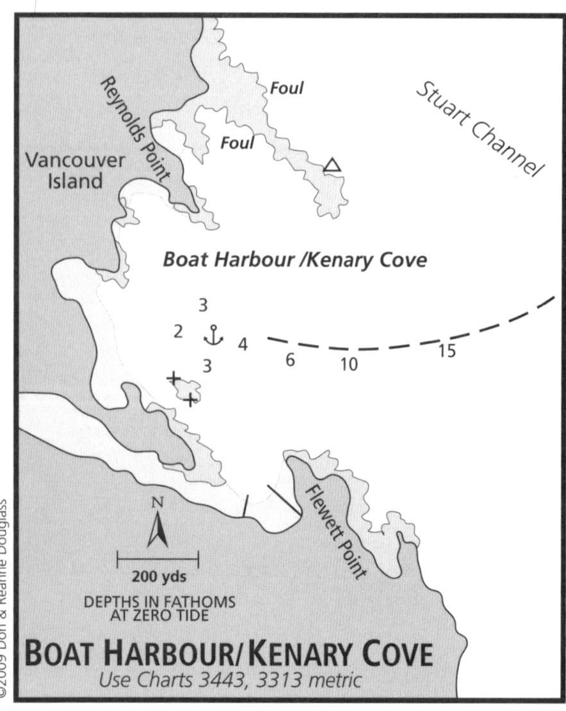

Boat Harbour

The marina at the south end of Boat Harbour has private moorage only. Temporary anchorage may be found on the west side of the bay.

Anchor in about 3 fathoms over mud and gravel with fair holding.

Dodd Narrows

Charts 3443, 3313; 21 mi N of Maple Bay; 5 mi SE of Nanaimo Hbr
Entrance (S): 49°07.96′N, 123°48.85′W
Entrance (N): 49°08.04′N, 123°49.01′W

Dodd Narrows, separated from False Narrows by Mudge Island, connects Stuart Channel with Northumberland Channel. It is used mainly by tugs, barges and logbooms. Because of the narrowness of the channel and the velocity of the tidal streams, it is not a recommended passage for much larger craft. However, vessels up to 70 m have passed through without undue difficulty at slack water.

Private moorage in Kenary Cove Marina

Turbulence at flood, Dodd Narrows

Predictions for the times and rates of maximum current, and the time of slack water when the direction of the current turns, are given for Dodd Narrows (Index No. 3500) in the Tide Tables, Volume 5. The maximum flood is 9 kn and the ebb is 8 kn; it floods north and ebbs south.

When the tidal stream is running at strength, tide-rips, formed by the stream and its counterflow, occur off the north entrance on the flood and in the vicinity of the overhead cable on the ebb. No attempt should be made to alter course out of the main stream until clear of this turbulence. The gradual disappearance of these tide-rips is an indication of the slackening in the tidal stream.

Dodd Narrows is more difficult to pass through when entering from north than from south, for in the former case, the slight alteration of course, necessary when passing through, has to be made immediately on entering the narrow part; in addition the entrance to Dodd Narrows is difficult to see when approaching from Northumberland Channel.

It is recommended that passage through Dodd Narrows be made at slack water. Before passing through Dodd Narrows other than at slack water be sure the vessel is able to proceed against the tidal stream; if there is any doubt, passage should be delayed until slack water.

Care should be taken not to hinder tugs with barges passing through and attention should be given to the sound and radio signals for narrow channels. (SD)

Dodd Narrows is one of the many fast-moving saltwater rapids along the south coast of British Columbia. Transiting is not particularly difficult at or near slack water, especially during neap tides—the window of passable times is usually quite wide. Consult the Current Tables in Volume 5; if you're in doubt about entering the Narrows, follow the lead of experienced boats your size. Boats passing through Dodd Narrows against the current should be especially careful with their wake to avoid swamping small boats heading in the opposite direction.

If you wish to avoid Dodd Narrows on your way to Nanaimo, you can use Gabriola Passage (moderate rapids and tide rips), passing north of Gabriola Island. Or you can transit False Narrows on the north side of Mudge Island, an alternative route for intrepid skippers that is very narrow and encumbered with reefs. False Narrows has less current than Dodd, but the fairway is very shallow and choked with kelp.

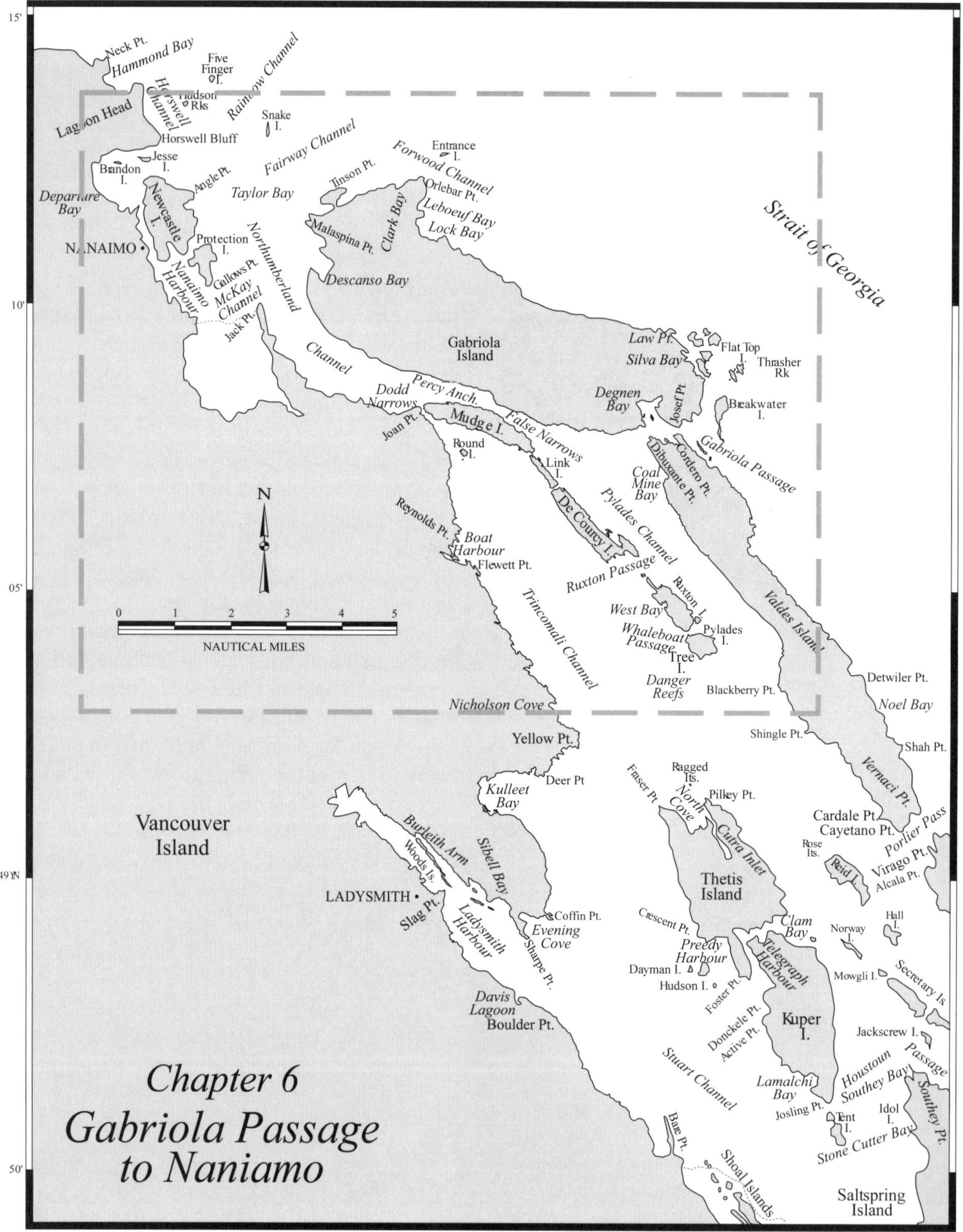

Chapter 6
Gabriola Passage to Naniamo

6

GABRIOLA PASSAGE TO NANAIMO

The northwestern section of the Gulf Islands, centered around Pylades Channel and Gabriola Passage, has a charm of its own with well-sheltered nooks and crannies that allow explorers to get off by themselves, particularly during off-season. Pirates Cove and Whaleboat Island—both small Marine Parks in the De Courcy Group—are popular cruising destinations. Pirates Cove Marine Park has a lovely hiking trail, picnic tables, well water, and walk-in campsites. Throughout this area, there are striking examples of the wind- and wave-sculpted sandstone for which the Gulf and San Juan islands are so well known.

If you are heading for Dodd Narrows from Pylades Channel, Ruxton Passage—which dissects the De Courcy Group—provides easy access to Stuart Channel.

False Narrows, a difficult passage that leads northwest from Pylades Channel to Northumberland Channel is used by small, shallow-draft boats should be used only by experienced boaters with local knowledge. Before transiting this area, consult a detailed chart, noting the serious cautions.

Valdes Island is notable for its steep cliffs which can be seen from Trincomali Channel. As you approach the island, you may imagine that you see "carvings" of people's faces in the unusual rock formations.

Gabriola Passage is a major route to the Strait of Georgia, as well as to Degnen and Silva bays on Gabriola Island and Dogfish Bay at the north end of Valdes Island. Be sure to note the listed cautions on the charts before transiting Gabriola Passage. Degnen Bay has a public wharf; from there you can walk southeast to Drumberg Provincial Park for swimming, fishing or hiking. At the head of the bay is a petroglyph of a killer whale. Silva Bay, surrounded by the Flat Top Islands off the east side of Gabriola Island, is a favorite stop for pleasure boats wishing a few more amenities. It has marinas, stores, laundry facilities and a pub.

Pylades Channel

Charts 3443, 3475, 3313; Trincomali Ch to Gabriola Passage (NE end); to False Narrows (NW end)
Entrance (S, 0.65 mi SE of Pylades I): 49°03.60'N, 123°40.20'W
Entrance (NW, False Narrows): 49°07.43'N, 123°45.58'W
Entrance (NW, Gabriola Passage): 49°07.60'N, 123°43.22'W

Pylades Channel leads NW from Trincomali Channel, between the west side of Valdes Island and the De Courcy Group to the SE. From the NW end of Pylades Channel, Gabriola Passage leads east into the Strait of Georgia and False Narrows leads NW into Northumberland Channel.

Whaleboat Passage and Ruxton Passage lead west through the De Courcy Group to Stuart Channel.

Tidal streams in Pylades Channel attain 2 kn at times; the flood sets NW and the ebb SE. (SD)

Pylades Channel

Pylades Channel is sheltered by Gabriola Island on the north, Valdes Island on the east, and the De Courcy Group on the west. False Narrows, described further in the text, is a shallow, kelp-infested channel that lead northwest from Pylades Channel into Northumberland Channel.

Pylades Island (Pylades Channel)

Charts 3443, 3313; 3.7 mi SE of Gabriola Passage; 6.4 mi SE of Dodd Narrows
Anchor (S side): 49°03.78'N, 123°41.27'W

> *Pylades Island has some broken cliffs about 24 m high on its west side.* (SD)

Small craft can find anchorage in calm weather along the south and east shores of Pylades Island. Avoid the rocks and shoal areas on the east side of Pylades Island. This area, exposed to southerly weather up Trincomali Channel, should be used in stable conditions only.

Whaleboat Passage

Charts 3443, 3313; btwn Pylades I on the S & Ruxton & Whaleboat Is on the N
Entrance (W): 49°04.20'N, 123°42.04'W
Entrance (E): 49°04.35'N, 123°41.34'W

> *Whaleboat Passage ... has a least depth of 2.1 m in mid-channel and is only suitable for small craft. Several private mooring buoys lie close to shore.* (SD)

Whaleboat Passage leads from Stuart Channel to Whaleboat Island Marine Park on the east side of Ruxton Island. Avoid the rock and shoal off the north end of Pylades Island.

Whaleboat Island Marine Park

Charts 3443, 3313; 2.0 mi SE of Pirates Cove Marine Park
Position: 49°04.50'N, 123°41.60'W

> *Whaleboat Island lies in the NE approach to Whaleboat Passage; Whaleboat Island Marine Park is undeveloped.* (SD)

Whaleboat Island Marine Park is a small, undeveloped area. Anchorage can be found on the north side of the 5-foot rock between Ruxton and Whaleboat islands. We have also seen boats anchored on the south side of Whaleboat Island; however, the bottom along this south shore of the De Courcy Group is irregular and likely to be rocky or foul. Avoid the rocks and shoals off the east side of Pylades Island north to Ruxton Passage. The small passage between Whaleboat and Ruxton islands is primarily a dinghy passage and choked with kelp. This is a fair-weather anchorage only with limited swinging room.

Anchor between 3 and 6 fathoms over rock and sand with poor-to-fair holding.

⚓ **Whaleboat Island Marine Park** popular with kayakers; no facilities

West Bay (Ruxton Island)

Charts 3343, 3313; 1.4 mi S of Pirates Cove Marine Park
Entrance: 49°04.65′N, 123°42.56′W
Anchor: 49°04.70′N, 123°42.48′W

> *Private mooring buoys lie close offshore from Ruxton Island.* (SD)

Good News *on moorings*

Gillcrest *in Herring Bay*

West Bay is full of mooring buoys; the shore is lined with homes. The tiny bay, open to southwest weather, is useful mainly for sportfishing skiffs.

Herring Bay (Ruxton Island)

Charts 3475, 3443, 3343, 3313; 1.0 mi SE of Pirates Cove Marine Park
Entrance (N): 49°05.28′N, 123°43.20′W
Entrance (W): 49°05.06′N, 123°43.13′W
Anchor: 49°05.00′N, 123°42.88′W

> *Herring Bay, at the NW end of Ruxton Island, offers good anchorage for small craft. Caution is advised because of the drying reefs. The mooring buoys in the bay are private.* (SD)

Herring Bay, on the south side of Ruxton Passage, is a lovely cove with white shell beaches and interesting sandstone formations. It has become an alternative to popular Pirates Cove. A daymark identifies the tip of the reef off the north entrance—the preferred way to enter is by taking the daymark to starboard. Entrance can be made from the west through a break in the reef and the peninsula. However, the reef is unmarked at its south end and the fairway difficult to locate at high water.

Swinging room is limited and the cove is unsafe in strong northerly winds, but in fair weather or moderate southerlies this can be a delightful anchor site. The sandstone islets and reefs of Herring Bay are fun to explore by dinghy.

Anchor northwest of the private mooring buoys at the south end of Herring Bay with good protection from the southeast.

Anchor in 3 to 4 fathoms over sand and shells with fair-to-good holding.

Ruxton Passage

Charts 3475, 3443, 3313; joins Pylades & Stuart Channels at the N end of Ruxton I
Entrance (W): 49°05.26'N, 123°43.66'W
Entrance (E): 49°05.43'N, 123°42.88'W

> *Ruxton Passage, between Ruxton Island and De Courcy Island, connects Stuart Channel to Pylades Channel. A shoal, with 7.6 m over it, lies in the east entrance, otherwise the fairway is deep.* (SD)

Ruxton Passage connects Stuart Channel to Pylades Channel south of De Courcy Island and north of Ruxton Island. The center of the passage is deep, presenting little difficulty. Avoid the shoal off the southeast point of De Courcy Island.

Anchored off the driftwood-covered beach, Ruxton Passage Cove

Ruxton Passage Cove (De Courcy Island)

Charts 3475, 3343, 3313; 0.75 mi NW of Herring Bay
Entrance: 49°05.48'N, 123°43.37'W
Anchor: 49°05.56'N, 123°43.43'W

Ruxton Passage Cove is the cove off the small driftwood-choked beach along Ruxton Passage; it is just a short walk across the spit from Pirates Cove. The amount of driftwood on the beach is evidence of exposure to southeast gales, meaning that the site should be used only in fair weather.

The north end of De Courcy Island can also be used as temporary anchorage when Pirates Cove is too crowded. (See Link Island Cove on page 142.)

Anchor in 2 to 3 fathoms over sand and gravel with fair holding.

Pirates Cove Marine Provincial Park (De Courcy Island)

Charts 3475, 3443, 3343, 3313; 4.1 mi SE of Dodd Narrows; 1.85 mi SW of Gabriola Passage
Entrance: 49°06.08'N, 123°43.91'W
Anchor: 49°05.87'N, 123°43.83'W

> *Pirates Cove Marine Park is on the SE side of De Courcy Island. A drying reef in the entrance of Pirates Cove extends NW from the north end of this peninsula; it is marked by a daybeacon with a port hand daymark. Starboard hand buoy "U38" is west of the daybeacon. Pass between the beacon and buoy when entering. A white line painted on a rock, with a white cross on a pole above it, serves as a range to clear the north end of the drying reef.*
>
> *Public dinghy floats are in the cove.*
>
> *Anchorage for small craft can be obtained in Pirates Cove; it is sheltered from all but north winds. Ring bolts for stern mooring are located along the shore of the peninsula, on the east side of the cove.*
>
> *Port hand buoy "U37" marks the outer edge of*

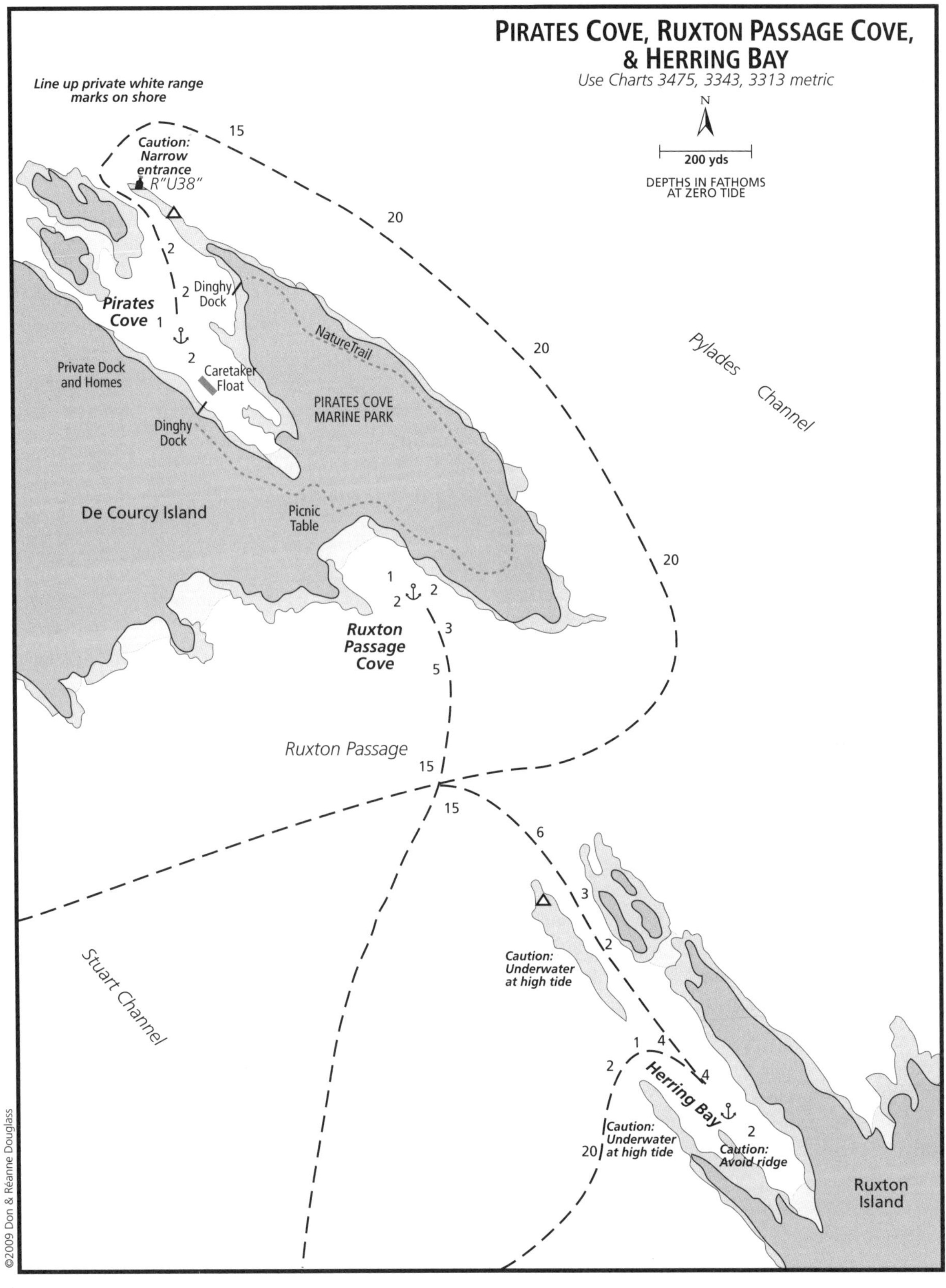
PIRATES COVE, RUXTON PASSAGE COVE, & HERRING BAY
Use Charts 3475, 3343, 3313 metric
N
200 yds
DEPTHS IN FATHOMS AT ZERO TIDE
Line up private white range marks on shore
Caution: Narrow entrance
R"U38"
Dinghy Dock
Pirates Cove
Private Dock and Homes
Caretaker Float
Dinghy Dock
NatureTrail
PIRATES COVE MARINE PARK
Pylades Channel
De Courcy Island
Picnic Table
Ruxton Passage Cove
Ruxton Passage
Stuart Channel
Caution: Underwater at high tide
Herring Bay
Caution: Underwater at high tide
Caution: Avoid ridge
Ruxton Island

Anne Vipond

Entrance to Pirates Cove

the drying reefs extending from the NE extremity of De Courcy Island. (SD)

Pirates Cove is one of the most popular marine parks in the Gulf Islands, and in summer it frequently has "wall-to-wall" boats. A seasonal host ranger stationed here can direct you to a space. However, if you show up in off-season, you'll probably have the cove to yourself. Shore ties to rings in the rock along the eastern shore are often used in high season or conditions of high north winds.

To enter Pirates Cove, stay well to the north until directly off the white "range mark" found on a tree on shore, then head in close to the range mark before turning carefully south across the shallow bar into the cove proper. Avoid the reef extending northwest from the daymark and pass between the daymark and red buoy "U38."

There are two dinghy docks in Pirates Cove; a nice trail system takes off above one of these docks, passes through lovely stands of arbutus, and leads to the tip of the eastern peninsula. A picnic area is located on the spit between Pirates Cove and Ruxton Pass Cove. The dock and islands at the northwest end of Pirates Cove are private.

Anchor in the center of the cove—or as directed by the park host—in 2 fathoms over mud with good holding.

⚓ **Pirates Cove Marine Provincial Park** has pit toilets; drinking water; hiking trails; picnic area; camping; canoeing; kayaking; fishing; swimming; moorage; 2 dinghy floats; open year-round

Link Island Cove (Link and De Courcy Islands)

Charts 3475, 3343, 3313; 1.3 mi NW of Pirates Cove Marine Park
Entrance: 49°06.83'N, 123°45.28'W
Anchor: 49°06.77'N, 123°45.38'W

Link Island is connected to the north end of De Courcy Island and the south end of Mudge Island by drying ridges. (SD)

Quiet anchorage can be found in the small bight between Link and De Courcy islands. From this site, it is fun to explore the east side of De Courcy by dinghy or kayak. A number of private homes are in the area.
Anchor in about 1 fathom over sand with fair holding.

Coal Mine Bay (Valdes Island)

Charts 3475, 3343, 3313; 0.83 mi SE of Gabriola Passage
Position: 49°06.94'N, 123°42.50'W

Coal Mine Bay, 0.7 mile SE of Dibuxante Point, is a booming ground and has mooring buoys in it. (SD)

You may be able to find temporary shelter from southeast gales tucked up close to shore in Coal Mine Bay. However, Degnen Bay and Wakes Cove in Gabriola Passage offer superior shelter and more swinging room.

Anne Vipond

Thar she blows!

False Narrows

Charts 3475, 3443, 3343, 3313; joins Pylades Ch to Percy Anchorage
Entrance (E): 49°07.43'N, 123°45.58'W
Entrance (W): 49°08.21'N, 123°47.61'W

> *[False Narrows] is suitable only for boats and small craft; local knowledge is advised. The navigable channel, with depths of 0.9 to 1.5 m, leads north of a long narrow drying ledge near the middle of the passage. Kelp grows profusely in the narrows, during summer and autumn, and is an additional source of danger.*
>
> *Tidal streams through False Narrows, in the vicinity of the drying reef, run parallel with shore on both the flood and ebb. The flood sets NW and the ebb SE. At the east end of the narrows, at LW, the stream runs smoothly along the north shore of Mudge Island, and gradually extends over the whole narrows as the tide rises; on a falling tide the effect is reversed.*
>
> *Logbooms are often towed through False Narrows, usually southbound with the first of the ebb; mariners intending to navigate the passage should therefore be prepared to give them adequate clearance. Approaching False Narrows from Pylades Channel hold to the Mudge Island shore to avoid the drying area to the north that has a number of large boulders on it. At the west end keep on the West Range until close to the Mudge Island shore to avoid the drying spit extending west of the West Range.* (SD)

False Narrows leads northwest along the north shore of Mudge Island from Pylades Channel to Percy Anchorage and Northumberland

---

Pirates Cove

De Courcy Island was named for Captain Michael De Courcy of Britain's Royal Navy who was stationed in local waters from 1859-61, in command of HMS *Pylades*. However, the Englishman who gave De Courcy Island its fascinating history was Edward Arthur Wilson, who eventually became known as the notorious Brother Twelve—one of the 20th century's most fascinating cult leaders. A former sea captain, Wilson was a mysterious and charismatic man who could convince seemingly sensible people to donate large sums of money to his religious organization, called the Aquarian Foundation, and work like slaves at one of his colonies.

In 1927, he built his headquarters at Cedar, north of Boat Harbour on Vancouver Island, before establishing a colony on De Courcy Island. With the help of his whip-wielding mistress named Madame Zee, he turned the southern end of De Courcy into a secluded retreat. If any outsiders entered the harbor, they were driven out by Brother Twelve's curses and threats to ram them with his tugboat. After seven years of tyranny, his profitable cult collapsed as disgruntled disciples eventually rebelled and notified authorities of his activities. As the police closed in, Brother Twelve disappeared and died a few years later in Switzerland. Mystery still surrounds his life and death and the fate of his accumulated treasure, said to be 43 boxes of gold coins weighing close to half a ton, of which no trace was ever found. **—AV**

An off-season pirate ready to load his sea-chest

Channel. This shallow, intricate channel is entirely choked with kelp in late summer and should be attempted only by boaters who want a navigational challenge since it may take longer than the "straight-forward" transit of Dodd Narrows.

From west to east (southbound): Start from Percy Anchorage on the Mudge Island side, in line with the range markers (white with red center marks) located east of a housing complex on Gabriola Island. Do not let the ebb current carry you onto the midchannel reef. The recommended route follows quite close to the north shore between the two ranges until the eastern range is directly behind.

We have found shallow spots of 1 or 2 feet at zero tide just west of the easternmost range and again at the east entrance, north of Link Island. There are large patches of bull kelp throughout the narrows, but the north-shore route is sometimes clear of kelp—except within the vicinity of the eastern ranges.

The strength of the current in False Narrows is about half that of Dodd Narrows. Although False Narrows is used as a shortcut by local boats heading from Gabriola Passage to Nanaimo, such a slow, careful transit—with the additional anxieties involved—may not save much time or energy for visiting pleasure craft. In southeast gales, we have found False Narrows less choppy than Dodd Narrows.

Skippers of the small, shallow-draft logging boats that draw less than 3 feet have told us they regularly traverse False Narrows at low water. However, since the narrows are a challenge of navigational skills and suited only to the intrepid, Dodd Narrows is the preferred passage to Northumberland Channel.

Gabriola Passage

Charts 3475, 3443, 3343, 3313; 8.3 mi NW of Porlier Pass

Entrance (W, Gabriola Passage): 49°07.60'N, 123°43.22'W

Entrance (SE, 0.39 mi SE of Breakwater I): 49°07.20'N, 123°40.62'W

Entrance (NE, 0.5 mi E of Acorn I): 49°09.37'N, 123°40.10'W

Gabriola Passage ... is narrow, intricate and has numerous dangers in its east approach. This combined with the velocity of the tidal streams

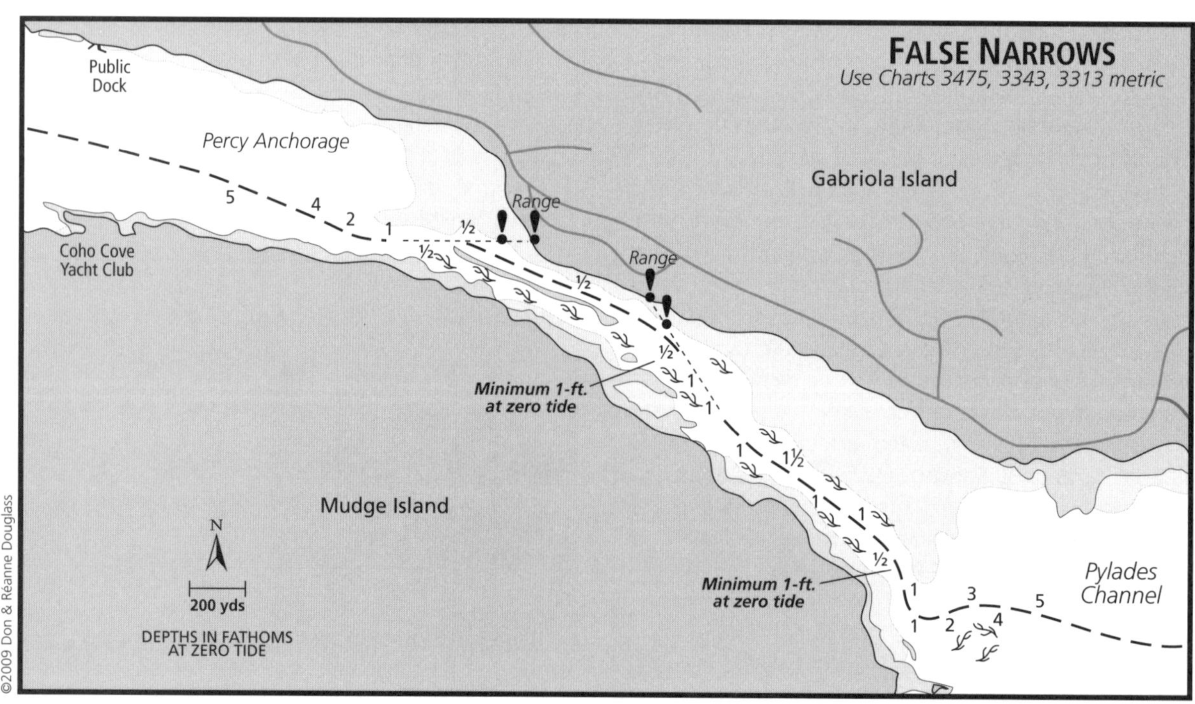

does not recommend it for general navigation. It should only be navigated at slack water, by those familiar with local conditions.

Predictions of the times and rates of maximum current and the times of slack water are given for Gabriola Passage (Index No. 3300) in the Tide Tables, Volume 5. The flood sets east and the ebb west through Gabriola Passage; the maximum on the flood is 8 1/2 kn and on the ebb 9 kn.

Breakwater Island, 0.7 mile east of Cordero Point, lies across the east approach to Gabriola Passage. Rogers Reef, on the north side, at the east entrance to Gabriola Passage consists of a group of drying and sunken rocks.

Caution for Small Craft.—During summer months, the effects of the freshet from the Fraser River and NW winds that blow strongly nearly every afternoon cause rough conditions, for small craft, along the west portion of the Strait of Georgia. Crossing to the mainland or travel along the east shores of Gulf Islands should be carried out early in the morning, but the most preferred time is late afternoon or early evening when the winds die away. (SD)

Gabriola Passage is the northeasternmost entrance from the Strait of Georgia to the protected waters of the Gulf Islands. It is best transited at or near slack water; even then turbulence can be significant during spring tides or southeast gales. It can be entered from or exited directly into the Strait of Georgia southeast of Breakwater Island or from the northeast through the Flat Top Islands. Thrasher Rock and Gabriola Reefs, east of Flat Top Islands, usually marked by kelp, have caused many groundings.

On spring tides there is a short section of highly turbulent and dangerous water at the east entrance of Gabriola Passage just north of Kendrick Island. When a stiff east wind is blowing on a spring flood tide, standing waves in the turbulent water can reach 2 meters in height and swamp a small boat. Degnen Bay and Wakes Cove provide good shelter to wait for optimum conditions when eastbound. Silva Bay and, to a lesser extent, Dogfish Bay provide shelter when westbound. Drumbeg Provincial Park is on the north shore of Gabriola Passage at the east end of Gabriola Passage.

⚓ **Drumbeg Provincial Park** has pit toilets; picnic area; hiking trails; swimming; fishing; open year-round

Degnen Bay (Gabriola Island)

Charts 3475, 3443, 3343, 3313; 2.3 mi NW of Pirates Cove Marine Park
Entrance: 49°07.85'N, 123°42.61'W
Anchor: 49°08.24'N, 123°42.66'W

Degnen Bay, on the north side of Gabriola Passage, affords excellent shelter for small craft. ... Several public floats, close west of the public wharf, are protected by a floating breakwater. (SD)

Degnen Bay, while beautifully protected, is crowded nearly year-round due to private floats (No Trespassing!), moored boats and float planes that come and go regularly. A small L-shaped public float that lies to port as you enter, has room for about 30 boats, but you may have to raft. There is a public telephone and garbage disposal (for paying guests only).

Anne Vipond

Public floats in Degnen Bay, Gabriola Island

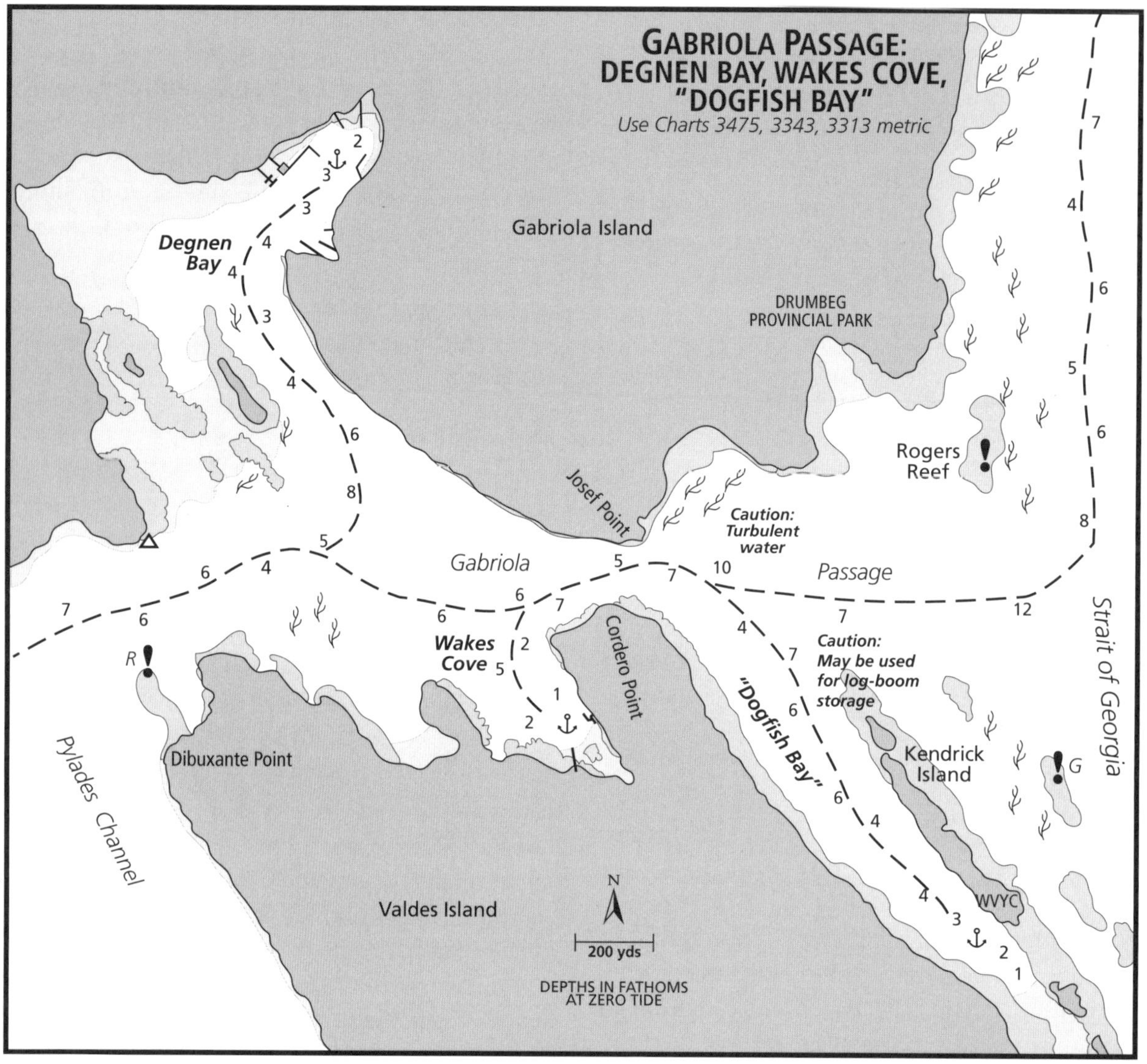
GABRIOLA PASSAGE:
DEGNEN BAY, WAKES COVE, "DOGFISH BAY"
Use Charts 3475, 3343, 3313 metric
Gabriola Island
Degnen Bay
DRUMBEG PROVINCIAL PARK
Rogers Reef
Josef Point
Caution: Turbulent water
Gabriola
Passage
Wakes Cove
Cordero Point
Caution: May be used for log-boom storage
"Dogfish Bay"
Kendrick Island
Strait of Georgia
Dibuxante Point
Pylades Channel
Valdes Island
WVYC
200 yds
DEPTHS IN FATHOMS AT ZERO TIDE
©2009 Don & Réanne Douglass

When entering the bay, favor the east shore; the low islet to port has a reef that extends quite a distance. This islet is a draw for birds and seals.

Anchorage, with very limited swinging room, may be possible in shoal water on the west side of the bay, but beware that the upper part dries. The petroglyph of a killer whale can be viewed at low tide near the head of the bay. From Degnen Bay, it's about a half-hour walk to Silva Bay.

Anchor in 2 fathoms over mud with good holding.

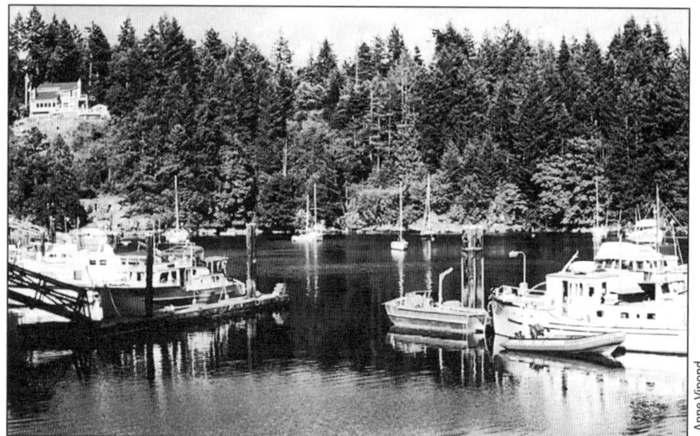

Anne Vipond

Degnen Bay, Gabriola Island

Wakes Cove (Valdes Island)

Charts 3475, 3443, 3343, 3313; 0.7 mi SE of Degnen Bay; 1.5 mi SW of Silva Bay
Entrance: 49°07.65'N, 123°42.35'W
Anchor: 49°07.56'N, 123°42.21'W

Wakes Cove offers anchorage for small craft but is exposed to the NW. (SD)

Wakes Cove offers very good protection from east to southeast gales. It is open to the northwest but fetch is small. A 5-fathom shelf is located just west of the private float on the east shore.

Wakes Cove is out of the current stream and receives only slight eddy currents. It is, however, subject to the wake of larger traffic transiting Gabriola Passage.

Anchor in 1 to 2 fathoms over sand with fair-to-good holding.

Dogfish Bay (Kendrick Island)

Charts 3475, 3443, 3343, 3313; 1.7 mi S of Silva Bay
Entrance: 49°07.65'N, 123°41.79'W
Anchor: 49°07.29'N, 123°41.42'W

The three small islets SE of Cordero Point are wooded; the largest of these islets is Kendrick Island. The bay formed between these three islets and the east shore of Valdes Island, known locally as Dogfish Bay, offers good sheltered anchorage and is used regularly by towboats with rafts when awaiting tides or are weather-bound. Floats and mooring buoys of a yacht club are on the west side of Kendrick Island. (SD)

Dogfish Bay, the local name for the anchorage on the south shore of Gabriola Passage, lies in the lee of Kendrick Island, 0.5 mile southeast of Cordero Point. It is a good place to await slack water in Gabriola Passage. Use caution on entering Dogfish Bay during spring tides or southeast gales since turbulent water and large standing waves northeast of Cordero Point are dangerous for small craft.

Enter Dogfish Bay from the north and anchor between Valdes and Kendrick islands, south of the West Vancouver Yacht Club floats and mooring buoys. In fair weather this is a good spot, but in a storm you should head for Degnen Bay or Wakes Cove. At high water, small, shallow-draft boats may be able to use the southern exit of Dogfish Bay. Local knowledge is advised. The bay has been used for log boom storage in recent years, so beware.

The rock face, north of the yacht club, has names of boats that have anchored there.

Anchor in 3 to 4 fathoms over sand and small seaweed with very good holding.

Degnen Bay

Degnen Bay was a one-man show back in 1862 when a 30-year-old Irish immigrant named Robert Degnen pre-empted 160 acres of waterfront property. He and his wife Jane, the daughter of a local chief, began farming the land and raising a family. To support their nine children, all of whom were born on the island, they worked hard plowing the fields with oxen, shooting the local deer and pheasant, planting an apple orchard and keeping various farm animals which included sheep, pigs, chickens and a dairy cow. Degnen ferried their produce to the market in Nanaimo using a large dugout canoe which he loaded at a small wharf he had built in Degnen Bay. As his freight business increased, Degnen replaced the canoe with a steam launch, followed by a gas launch.

Descanso Bay is now Gabriola's freight transportation hub with the car ferry from Nanaimo docking there, and today Degnen Bay is busy instead with pleasure craft. A short walk from the government dock is one of the most accessible petroglyph sites in the Gulf Islands, located behind the United Church on South Road. These ancient rock carvings are a legacy of the complex and artistically accomplished civilizations that once thrived throughout the Pacific Northwest. The Gulf Islands lie within the territory of the Coast Salish, the southernmost group of natives inhabiting the Inside Passage when European explorers first ventured into these waters. **—AV**

Silva Bay (Gabriola Island)

Charts 3475, 3443, 3343, 3313; 1.3 mi N of Gabriola Passage; 9.5 mi E of Nanaimo Hbr
Entrance (E, 0.1 mi W of Shipyard Rock): 49°09.20′N, 123°41.34′W
Dinghy entrance (SE, S side of Sear I): 49°08.58′, 123°41.29′W
Dinghy entrance (N, W of Carlos I): 49°09.59′N, 123°41.95′W
Anchor: 49°09.05′N, 123°41.78′W

> *Silva Bay has three passages leading into it and is frequently used by small craft. It is sheltered by Vance, Tugboat and Sear Islands.*
>
> *The main entrance to Silva Bay is between Tugboat and Vance Islands; it is encumbered with a drying reef projecting north from Tugboat Island and Shipyard Rock in mid-channel. The least depth, in the channel north of Shipyard Rock, is 5.9 m.*
>
> *Silva Bay light (434.3), on Shipyard Rock, has a port hand daymark.*
>
> *The south entrance to Silva Bay leads between Sear and Gabriola Islands; it is about 30.5 m wide and has a least depth of 1 m.*
>
> *The north entrance to Silva Bay, between Lily and Vance Islands, is entered at its north end between Carlos Island and the shoals north of Lily Island. The least depth through this channel is 3.6 m.* (SD)

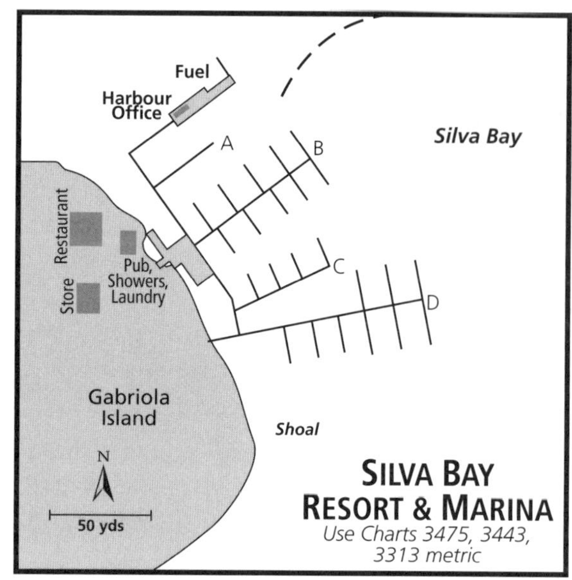

SILVA BAY RESORT & MARINA
Use Charts 3475, 3443, 3313 metric

Silva Bay, set in a maze of small, wooded islands, is protected from almost all weather. The bay is a popular destination spot for cruising boats not only for its calm waters, but also because it is home to several excellent marinas. From north to south, upon entering the bay, you find Silva Bay Inn (formerly Silva Bay Boatel), Silva Bay Resort and Marina and Page's Marina. All three are open year-round and each offers different amenities or activities. Silva Bay Inn, recently renovated under new owners, has new docks, a new store with ample choice of provisions (including fresh meat), limited guest moorage with power (15 amp), washrooms and laundromat.

Silva Bay Resort and Marina, the largest of the three marinas, has upgraded docks, fuel, power (30 amp), showers, laundry, public telephone, liquor store and a café and a restaurant, wireless internet service and facilities for children. Pacific Spirit (tel: 800.665.2359 or 250.247.9992) offers daily seaplane service to the marina if you have crew that wants to join you here.

The Silva Bay Shipyard School, next door to the Resort, is fun for amateurs of wooden boats. (On our most recent visit, Blithe Spirit, a Monk design sailboat was being restored.)

Page's Resort, at the south end of the bay, is the quietest of the three and, certainly interesting, from our point of view. In addition to fuel, power (15 amp), showers, laundry and cottages, the resort features small concerts during the summer season. (Unfortunately, our visits tend to occur off-season.)

Reservations are advised at any of the marinas. The Royal Vancouver Yacht Club has an outstation across the bay on Tugboat Island.

Vessels headed south in the Strait of Georgia that want to avoid Nanaimo and Dodd Narrows often enter sheltered waters via Silva Bay and Gabriola Passage.

To enter Silva Bay, the easiest route is to use Commodore Passage. Give Shipyard Rock due respect when passing through the entrance. Favor the north side of the entrance channel

Anne Vipond

Main entrance to Silva Bay

until you pass west of can-buoy "U39," then turn south.

Small craft can enter from the north between Lily and Vance islands. This passage, marked by buoy "PA," can be used at all stages of the tide. However, it is very narrow with little turning room and reefs that extend from both islands. A small-boat entrance to the south of Silva Bay carries about 3 feet of water, and the fairway favors the Sear Island shore.

Anchorage can be found in the center of Silva Bay.

Anchor in 2 fathoms over mud with good holding.

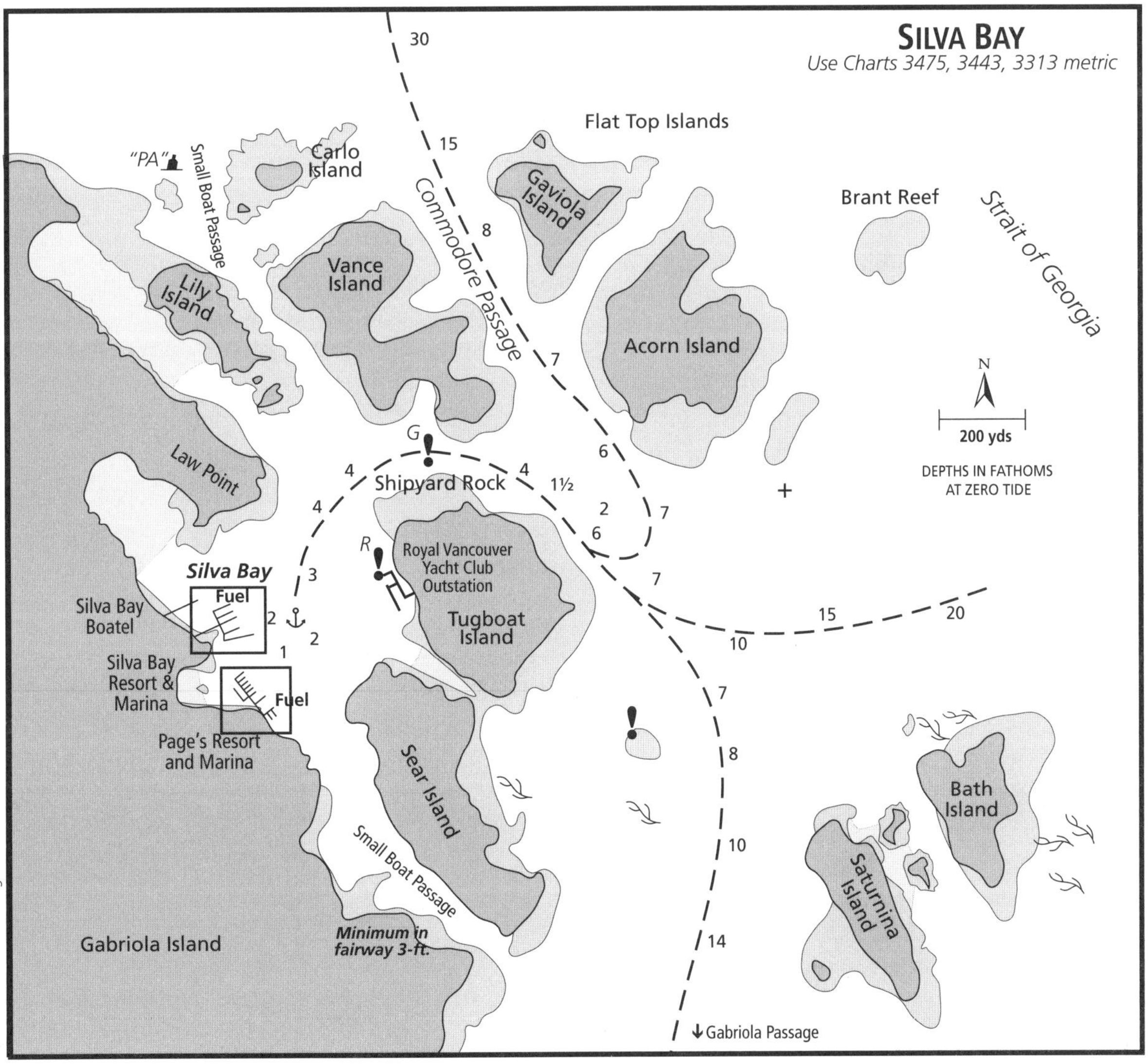

Anne Vipond

Silva Bay

⚓ **Silva Bay Inn** tel: 250.247.9351; power; groceries; open year-round

⚓ **Silva Bay Resort and Marina** tel: 250.247.8662; fax: 250.247.8663; monitors VHF Ch 66A; website: www.silvabay.com; email: info@silvabay.com; swimming pool; tennis courts; complete facilities for pleasure boats; dive shop; reservations recommended; open year-round

⚓ **Page's Resort and Marina** tel: 250.247.8931; monitors VHF Ch 66A; website: www.pagesresort.com; email: mail@pagesresort.com; full facilities; dive shop; store; open year-round

Flat Top Islands

Charts 3475, 3343, 3313; 1.5 mi N of Gabriola Passage
Position: 49°09.25'N, 123°41.25'W

> *Flat Top Islands, north of Breakwater Island, consist of Bath Island, Saturnina Island, Sear Island, Tugboat Island, Vance Island, Lily Island, Carlos Island, Gaviola Island and Acorn Island. Brant Reef, 0.2 mile NE of Acorn Island, is 1 m high. (S)*

The Flat Top Islands are fun to explore by dinghy or kayak in fair weather when you are safely anchored in Silva Bay. This is a popular sportfishing area. Use caution around the reefs surrounding the islands and rocks.

Commodore Passage

Charts 3475, 3343, 3313; E of Vance & Tugboat Is; W of Gaviola & Acorn Is
Entrance (N, 0.13 mi NW of Rowboat Pt on Gaviola I): 49°09.63'N, 123°41.52'W
Entrance (S, 0.17 mi S of Acorn I): 49°09.12'N, 123°41.02'W

> *Commodore Passage is formed by Tugboat and Vance Islands on its SW side; Acorn and Gaviola Islands form its NW side. A reef, which dries 4.8 m, lies 0.1 mile SE of Acorn Island; a rock awash lies close south of this reef.* (SD)

Commodore Passage is a shortcut for entering or exiting Gabriola Passage and for heading north to the Strait of Georgia.

Gabriola Reefs

Charts 3475, 3343, 3313; E of Flat Top & Breakwater Is

> *Gabriola Reefs, extending 1.5 miles SSW from Thrasher Rock, consist of drying and below-water rocks.* (SD)

Gabriola Reefs are a long, curving series of reefs and rocks surrounded by kelp. The northeast and south ends are marked by buoys. The reefs have been the scene of many pleasure-craft disasters and must be avoided when entering and exiting Gabriola Passage.

Percy Anchorage (Gabriola & Mudge Is)

Charts 3475, 3458, 3443, 3313; 5.8 mi SE of Nanaimo Hbr; 0.9 mi E of Dodd Narrows
Entrance (W): 49°08.37'N, 123°48.29'W
Entrance (E, False Narrows): 49°08.21'N, 123°47.61'W
Float (Gabriola I shore): 49°08.53'N, 123°48.29'W
Anchor: 49°08.32'N, 123°47.70'W

> *Percy Anchorage, at the west end of False Narrows, is a convenient place to anchor to await slack water in Dodd and False Narrows. ... The public float, on the north side of Percy Anchorage, has been damaged and is closed to the public (1996).* (SD)

Open and somewhat exposed, Percy Anchorage is used principally by large or commercial boats, but quiet shelter can be found close to shore at the head of the anchorage.

The small public float on Gabriola Island near Hoggan Lake is usually filled with local commercial and commuter boats.

Anchor in 3 to 5 fathoms over sand and gravel with fair-to-good holding and unlimited swinging room.

Coho Cove (Mudge Island)

Charts 3458, 3443, 3313; 0.4 mi E of Dodd Narrows
Position: 49°08.25'N, 123°48.45'W

> *On the north shore of Mudge Island, close east of the power line, is a small cove occupied by a yacht club.* (SD)

The Coho Cove Yacht Club maintains a small float between a natural breakwater on the north side of Coho Cove and a small rock breakwater on the west side. *Caution:* A submerged reef extends west of the point.

Peter Fromm

Island silhouettes

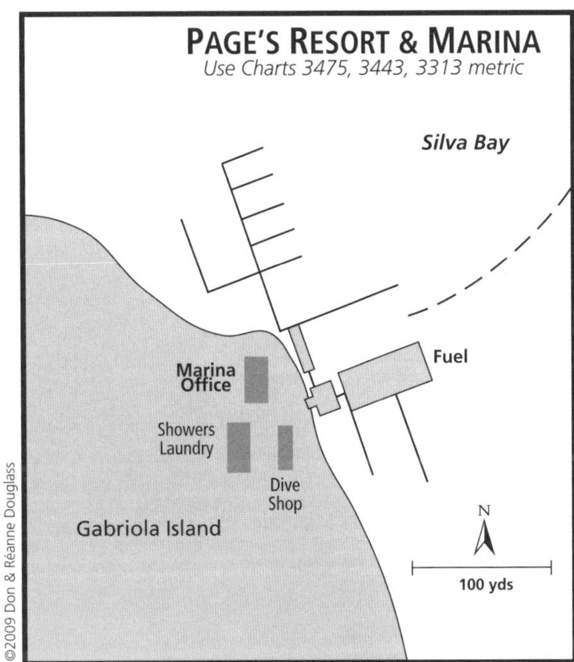

©2009 Don & Réanne Douglass

This tiny cove, which is too small for anchoring, is used by busy workboats. However, it's a good place to get up-to-date local information on False Narrows.

Northumberland Channel

Charts 3475, 3458, 3443, 3313; btwn Gabriola & Vancouver Is
Entrance (S, Dodd Narrows): 49°08.28'N, 123°49.09'W
Entrance (E, False Narrows): 49°08.21'N, 123°47.61'W
Entrance (N): 49°10.23'N, 123°53.13'W

> *Northumberland Channel leads NW from Dodd and False Narrows ... toward Nanaimo Harbour and the Strait of Georgia.*
>
> *Tidal streams in Northumberland Channel are unusual as the set is continually to the east, due to the more rapid progression of the tide in the Strait of Georgia than in the channels south of Dodd Narrows; the maximum of this east-going stream is 1 to 2 kn at springs.* (SD)

Once you pass through Dodd Narrows and enter Northumberland Channel, signs of urban civilization increase. There are log rafts nestled along the steep cliffs of Gabriola's west shore, the large MacMillan Bloedel Industrial complex along Vancouver Island, and the new ferry dock just south of Jack Point. Northumberland Channel receives the bulk of vessel traffic bound for Nanaimo and small craft heading for the north coast of Vancouver Island, and the concentration of commercial and pleasure traffic requires alert helmsmanship. Both the wake of passing vessels and low visibility in foggy weather can be problems.

Headed for town, Northumberland Channel

The channel has a large lumber mill operation on its south shore and a logboom storage area off its Gabriola Island shore. Be on the lookout for logging tugs that shuttle back and forth across the channel. Boats entering Nanaimo Harbour at Jack Point should avoid submerged rocks near the point, as well as ferries and other traffic approaching from Gabriola Island. The high-speed ferry dock, 0.75 mile south of Jack Point, began operation in 1997.

Percy Anchorage, at the east end of Northumberland Channel, provides anchorage for boats waiting to transit Dodd or False narrows.

If you prefer to anchor rather than head directly into Nanaimo Harbour, you can tuck into Descanso Bay on the northwest side of Gabriola Island; however, the anchorage is subject to wake. Noted for it many petroglyphs, Gabriola has striking formations of wave-carved sandstone. The Galiano (or Malaspina) Galleries just south of Malaspina Point are one of many fine examples.

The B.C. ferry dock in Descanso connects the island to Nanaimo. Taylor and Pilot bays, part of Gabriola Sands Park, are closed to boat entry because of their bathing beaches.

Descanso Bay (Gabriola Island)

Charts 3458, 3443, 3313; 2.7 mi E of Nanaimo Hbr
Entrance: 49°10.74'N, 123°52.16'W
Anchor: 49°10.48'N, 123°51.85'W

> *Descanso Bay, south of Malaspina Point, has a ferry landing in its NE part; frequent ferry service to and from Nanaimo is maintained.* (SD)

Good shelter from southeast weather can be found deep in the southern end of Descanso Bay. Due to frequent ferries and exposure to channel traffic, wakes are noticeable.

Anchor in 5 to 10 fathoms over an irregular bottom.

Taylor Bay (Gabriola Island)

Charts 3458, 3443, 3313; 2.9 mi NE of Nanaimo Hbr
Position: 49°11.61'N, 123°51.84'W

Gabriola Sands Park, between Taylor and Pilot bays, has lovely swimming beaches for day-use only; facilities include toilets. During the summer, when water temperatures rise, you will often see a dozen boats or more anchored in one to three fathoms, sand and mud bottom, avoiding the large shoal areas off the beach.

⚓ **Gabriola Sands Park** has pit toilets; drinking water from hand pump; picnic area; kayaking; swimming; fishing; day-use only; open year-round

Clark Bay (Gabriola Island)

Charts 3458, 3443, 3313; 0.9 mi E of Pilot Bay
Position: 49°12.07′N, 123°49.75′W

> *The north coast of Gabriola Island between Law Point and Orlebar Point, 5.5 miles NW, is bold and thickly wooded.* (SD)

Small craft can find temporary anchorage in Clark Bay, with some shelter from southerly winds but subject to wake from passing vessels.

Leboeuf Bay (Gabriola Island)

Charts 3458, 3443, 3313; 0.9 mi SW of Entrance I
Position: 49°11.66′N, 123°48.96′W

Leboeuf Bay may provide anchorage from westerly winds; however, it is exposed to southeast winds. *Caution:* Avoid the reef and rock 0.3 mile southeast of Orlebar Point.

Lock Bay (Gabriola Island)

Charts 3458, 3443, 3313; 1.25 mi SW of Entrance I
Position: 49°11.27′N, 123°49.00′W

> *Lock Bay is exposed and not recommended as an anchorage.* (SD)

Lock Bay is encompassed by Sandwell Provincial Park. The bay is open to the east and southeast.

⚓ **Sandwell Provincial Park** has pit toilets; picnic area; hiking trails; swimming; day-use only; open year-round

Approaches to Nanaimo Harbour

> *The NE approach to Nanaimo Harbour lies between Entrance Island, 0.5 mile NE of Orlebar Point, and Neck Point.*
>
> *The approach to Nanaimo Harbour from the Strait of Georgia is between Entrance Island and Lagoon Head, 5.5 miles WNW. The navigable channels in this approach, from east to west, are Fairway Channel, Rainbow Channel and Horswell Channel. These channels, divided by islands and shoals, are deep and well lighted.*
>
> *Vessels bound to and from Nanaimo, or passing through the Strait of Georgia, should pass north of [Entrance Island].* (SD)

Fairway Channel

Charts 3458, 3443, 3313; btwn Gabriola I on the S & Snake I on the N
Position (mid-ch, 0.75 mi NW of Malaspina Pt; 0.74 mi SE of Snake I): 49°12.20′N, 123°52.92′W

> *Fairway Channel, between the NW end of Gabriola Island and Snake Island, has a navigable width of about 0.7 mile.* (SD)

Fairway Channel is used by boats exiting Nanaimo Harbour or Departure Bay and heading for Vancouver.

Rainbow Channel

Charts 3458, 3443, 3313; btwn Snake I on the SE & Five Fingers I on the NW
Position (0.52 mi NE of Snake I, 1.1 mi E of Hudson Rock, 0.9 mi SE of Five Finger I): 49°13.55′N, 123°53.64′W

> *Hudson Rocks consist of five islets and rocks,*

A sea dog

from 1 to 10 m high, encircled by reefs. (SD)

Rainbow Channel is used by vessels leaving Nanaimo Harbour or Departure Bay bound for the Sunshine Coast on the north shore of the Strait of Georgia.

Float plane taxi service

Horswell Channel

Charts 3458, 3443, 3313; btwn Hudson & Clarke Rocks; N of Horswell Rock
Position (mid-ch, 0.21 mi E of Clarke Rock): 49°13.52'N, 123°56.15'W

> *Horswell Channel lies between Hudson Rocks and the coast of Vancouver Island. Clarke Rock, on the west side of Horswell Channel, is separated from Vancouver Island by a narrow channel in which there is foul ground.* (SD)

Horswell Channel is used by vessels leaving Nanaimo Harbour or Departure Bay bound for the north coast of Vancouver Island.

Peter Fromm

Heading up-channel close-hauled

Nanaimo Harbour Entrance

Charts 3457, 3447, 3443, 3458, 3313

> *The inner portion of Nanaimo Harbour, entered 1 mile west of Jack Point, has a large mud flat on its south side and is protected on its north and east sides by Newcastle Island and Protection Island.*
>
> *Entry into the inner portion of Nanaimo Harbour is through McKay and Meakin Channels using the Colliery range beacons.*
>
> *A ferry wharf, close NW of Gallows Point, is protected by a rock breakwater.*
>
> *A public float, alongside the ferry wharf NW of Gallows Point, is for loading and unloading.*
>
> *A public float and ferry landing are at Good Point.* (SD)

Nanaimo is the transportation, supply, and repair center for the northern part of the Gulf Islands and home of the famous Nanaimo bars. Nanaimo Harbour, a major supply center for Gulf Island boats, offers complete yacht facilities. Yachts can tie up at the public floats in Commercial Inlet for two hours at no cost, and moorage can be found here or at the several private facilities in Newcastle Island Passage. Nanaimo is a good place to drop off or pick up crew or to leave your boat if you need to.

The harbor is entered through McKay Channel on the south or Departure Bay on the north. Entry to the harbor should not be attempted between Newcastle and Protection islands.

West of Jack Point, Nanaimo Harbour is well protected by the shallow bay off Nanaimo River to the south and by Protection Island on its east. Narrow McKay Channel leads directly into the harbor past the south end of Protection Island. Much of the bay south of a line west of Jack Point (49°10.00'N) dries at low water and many visiting boats have grounded here. You can avoid this area by favoring the Protection Island side of the channel.

McKay Channel

Charts 3457, 3458, 3313; S of Protection I
Entrance (E): 49°10.19′N, 123°54.49′W
Entrance (W): 49°10.16′N, 123°55.42′W

> *McKay Channel, between Protection Island and Middle Bank, is deep and without dangers.* (SD)

McKay Channel, the busy south entrance to Nanaimo Harbour, has heavy traffic converging on the south side of Gallow Point off Protection Island. Avoid the large drying mud flat off the Nanaimo River outflow south of a line running through Jack Point.

Nanaimo fishing float, Newcastle Island far left

Nanaimo Harbour (Vancouver Island)

Charts 3457, 3458, 3447, 3313; 2.5 mi W of Gabriola I; 33 mi SW of Vancouver Hbr, 38 mi NW of Sidney; 63 mi NW of Anacortes
Floating breakwater: 49°10.25′N, 123°55.82′W
Entrance (Commercial Inlet): 49°10.21′N, 123°55.97′W
Fuel dock: 49°10.10′N, 123°56.04′W

> *Anchorage berths in Nanaimo are assigned by the Harbour Master. ... Small vessels are assigned anchorage berths in Mark Bay.*
>
> *The city of Nanaimo [is] along the west side of the harbour. ... The main industries are lumber, pulp, newsprint and fisheries. The city has a full range of municipal services which include a post office (V9R 5J9), hospital with a heliport, shopping centres and recreational facilities. Radio station CHUB broadcasts on a frequency of 1570 kHz....*
>
> *Commercial Inlet, entered between the breakwater and the small vessels pier, is a small craft basin, with 2,800 m of berthing at the public floats. Power and water are laid on the floats; toilets, showers, public telephones, garbage and used oil disposal facilities and sewage pumpout are available. A fuel barge is at the floats. A wharfinger is in charge of these floats.* (SD)

From its origins as a coal supply center to recent years, Nanaimo has undergone a dramatic transformation. In the past 10 years, its waterfront and harbour have seen extensive redevelopment with attractive condominiums, small shops, restaurants, green spaces, a 4-kilometer walking-bicycle path (Harbourside Walkway), a man-made saltwater lagoon and Maffeo Sutton Park which features a children's sandlot playground, picnic tables and benches. The city and harbor officials can be commended for their foresight and planning in making Nanaimo a destination for tourists whether they come by land and by water. The city publishes a substantial Visitor's Guide each year that details all the activities and businesses. (See their website: www.tourism-nanaimo.com)

The facilities of Nanaimo Port Authority Marina are excellent. The wharfinger's office, whose shape calls to mind that of a ship, was completed in 2003, along with new restrooms, showers, laundry, and improved docks and gangways. Both the inner boat basin and Cameron Island accommodate pleasure craft—with larger vessels usually being allocated to Cameron Island and the Visiting Vessel Pier. Water and power (15, 20 and 30 amp; limited 50 and 100), garbage and oil disposal, are available, as are email, fax and photocopying services (at the wharfinger's office). Pump-out can be made at the Eco-Barge stationed at the central breakwater at the harbor entrance.

Penny's Palapa, on H dock, is a favorite of ours for breakfast or lunch (or carry out--tel: 250.753.6300); they are open from May to mid-September (closed on rainy days).

Advance reservations for both Cameron Island and the inner basin are advised in high season; telephone at least 24 hours in advance of your arrival. For free short-term transient moorage, call the wharfinger on Channel 67 before entering the harbor for instructions.

During the high season, docking in the inner basin can sometimes be a squeeze (depending on the size of your vessel), but harbor personnel are happy to give you a hand at your assigned moorage. Docking at Cameron Island can present a challenge when strong currents are running.

Nanaimo is a designated Customs Port of Entry; phone ahead to arrange for clearance if this is your first port of call in Canada (tel: 888.226.7277). Convenient shopping and outfitting facilities are located within easy walking distance of the public floats. Port Place Shopping Centre (formerly Harbour Park Mall), just south of the Port Authority Marina, has a Thrifty Foods supermarket, bakery, London Drugs, Liquor Store, Post Office, a variety of shops and fast food services, as well as a laundromat (wash and fold service available). Charts and books can be purchased at the Dock Shoppe in the harbor or at their main store, the Harbour Chandler (52 Esplanade) and at Nanaimo Maps and Charts (8 Church Street). Repairs can be arranged at Nanaimo Shipyard and Marine Center and Nanaimo Harbour City Marina (see telephone numbers below).

Families with children will certainly want to spend some time at the Nanaimo Aquatic Centre at 741 Third Street. From the marina, it's about a 20-minute walk uphill—a bit of a stretch for small children, but you can call a taxi for a short ride. In addition to the three creative water slides and a play lagoon for kids, the centre features a 50-metre pool, a leisure pool, steam room, hot tub, a weight room, a Pro Shop and—a special for families—changing rooms for parent with kids. For more information, tel: 250.756.5200 or check out their website: www.city.nanimo.bc.ca.

Other areas of interest to visitors include The Bastion, whose white, octagonal tower sits just above the harbor. Built in 1853 by the Hudson's Bay, it is the oldest build-

Anne Vipond

Fishing fleet in Nanaimo Harbour

ing in Nanaimo. During summer, firings from its cannon take place at noon. Petroglyph Park, south of Nanaimo, gives children and adults, alike, a view of the region's ancient history carved in rock.

A small passenger ferry runs hourly from the south end of the inner basin to the popular pub, Dinghy Dock, on Protection Island. You can also take your own tender or kayak, but space is often at a premium in high season.

Nanaimo Inner Harbour, Commercial Inlet and waterfront

If you feel the call of the big city, the fast ferry, Harbour Lynx (passenger-only), runs daily from the harbor to Granville Island in Vancouver. (See their website for schedules: www.harbourlynx.com)

Listed from south to north:

⚓ **Naniamo Port Authority** tel: 250.755.1216 (July–August) or 250.754.5053; monitors VHF Ch 67; transient dock space (free for 2 to 3 hours); reservations recommended

⚓ **Nanaimo Yacht Club** tel: 250.754.7011; power; toilets; showers; laundry; moorage is for members of reciprocal yacht clubs only

⚓ **Townsite Marina** tel: 250.716.8801 or 877.616.8801; fax: 250.716.7288; monitors VHF Ch 66A; website: www.townsitemarina.com; power; toilets; showers; laundry; water; 24-hour security; open year-round

⚓ **Channel View Marina** tel: 250.741.0848

⚓ **Moby Dick Oceanfront Lodge & Marina** tel: 250.753.7111 or 800.663.2116; power; toilets; showers; open year-round

⚓ **Nanaimo Harbour City Marina** tel: 250.754.2732; fax: 250.754.7140; email: nanaimohcm@telus.net; power; toilets; showers; full-service boatyard; emergency services & towing; 30-ton Travelift; reservations recommended; open year-round

⚓ **Newcastle Marina** tel: 250.753.1431; fax: 250.753.2974; email: newcastle@shaw.ca; power; toilets; showers; laundry; 60-ton Travelift; limited guest moorage; reservations recommended; open year-round

⚓ **Anchorage Marina** tel: 250.754.5585; power; toilets; limited guest moorage; open year-round

⚓ **Gabe's Petro-Canada Marine** tel: 250.754.7828; fuel dock; open year-round

⚓ **Naniamo Shipyard** tel: 250.753.1151

Ultra-light float plane at Newcastle Park

Mark Bay (Newcastle Island)

Charts 3457, 3458, 3313; 0.75 mi N of Commercial Inlet
Entrance: 49°10.75′N, 123°55.85′W
Anchor: 49°10.82′N, 123°55.89′W

> *Newcastle Island Marine Park has public floats and mooring buoys in Mark Bay. The head of Mark Bay is a booming ground.*
>
> *Anchorage for small craft can be obtained in Mark Bay in about 7 m, mud bottom, north of a line drawn between the yellow spar buoys 0.1 mile SE of Good Point and 0.2 mile SW of Bate Point.* (SD)

Mark Bay, off the entrance to Newcastle Island Provincial Park, offers good protection in all weather and is a major yacht destination as well as a stop-over for boats heading north. From Nanaimo Harbour you can easily dinghy across to the Marine Park.

Anchor west of the public floats, or where room allows, in 2 to 4 fathoms over sticky mud with very good holding.

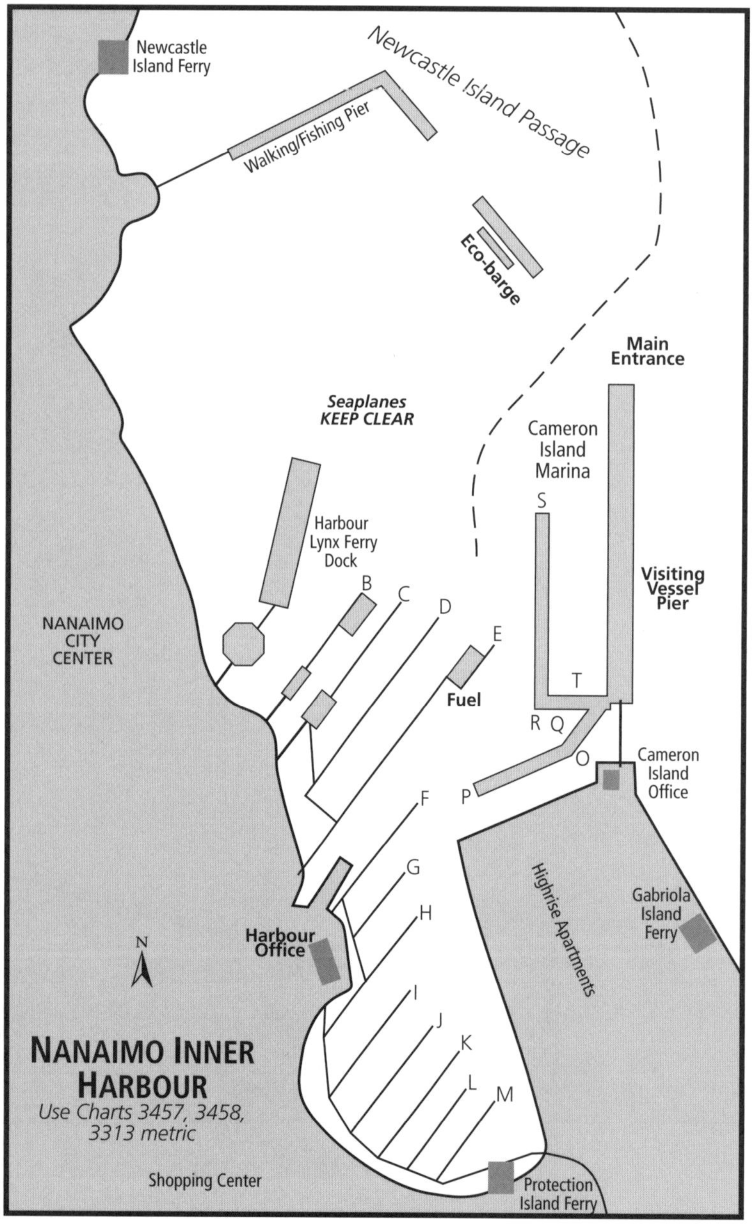

NANAIMO INNER HARBOUR
Use Charts 3457, 3458, 3313 metric

Newcastle Island Marine Park (Newcastle Island)

Charts 3457, 3458, 3313; Marine Park comprises all of Newcastle I
Dinghy Dock & Park Floats:: 49°10.80′N, 123°55.75′W
Dinghy Dock Pub floats (Good Pt): 49°10.60′N, 123°55.62′W

Popular Newcastle Island Marine Park is located at the north end of Nanaimo Harbour in Mark Bay. In addition to excellent anchorage, the park facilities are readily accessible from the dinghy docks (limited moorage available) or by foot passenger ferry service; there are no cars on the island. Newcastle Island Marine Park public floats are reserved for small boats and have a time limit; overnight moorage is available for a fee. In summer when space is at a premium, it's best to anchor offshore and take your dinghy to the floats.

Twelve miles of wooded trails, lovely swimming beaches and campsites, and picnic grounds are included in the Park. The interesting grinding-stone quarry site is just north of the floats. Mallard Lake is a man-made lake, home to wood ducks, great blue herons, and beavers. The shallow, rocky slabs along the south and east sides of the island provide some of the warmest and most pleasant swimming in the Gulf Islands; to get away from the city drone, just hike around to the east side of Newcastle Island and sit looking out toward the Strait of Georgia—you'll forget all your worries!

During summer months, a small passenger ferry makes hourly runs between Newcastle Island and Nanaimo. Across (south) from Newcastle Island dock, Protection Island's popular floating pub—Dinghy Dock—is open from 1100 hours to 2300 hours in summer season. A small ferry runs hourly from Nanaimo Harbour directly to the pub.

We prefer to anchor in Mark Bay

⚓ **Newcastle Island Provincial Marine Park** has water; toilets; showers; picnic area; hiking trails; individual and group campsites; open year-round

The Bastion overlooks Nanaimo Harbour

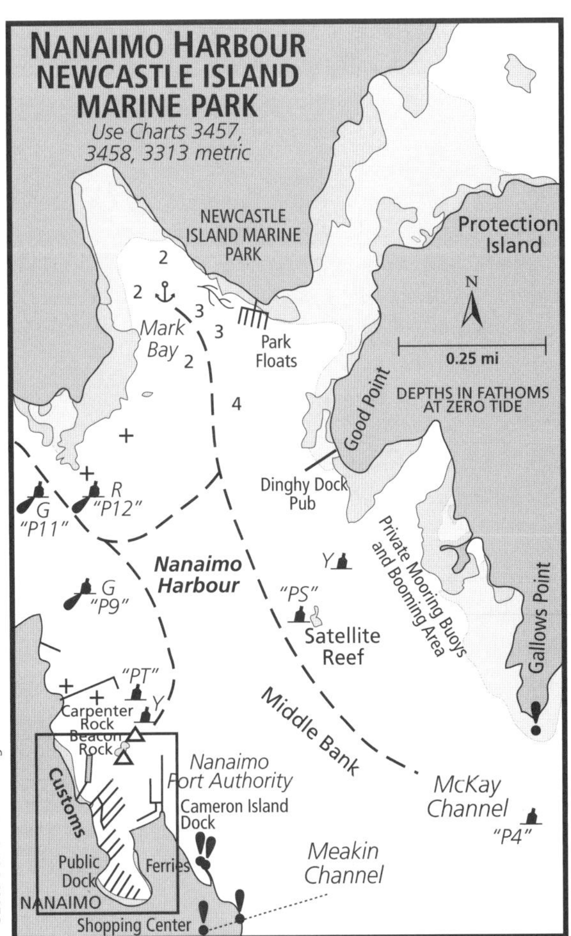

Newcastle Island Passage

Charts 3457, 3458, 3443, 3313; leads from Nanaimo Hbr to Departure Bay
Entrance (S): 49°10.52'N, 123°56.17'W
Entrance (N): 49°11.64'N, 123°56.92'W

Newcastle Island Passage ... leads north from the inner portion of Nanaimo Harbour to Departure Bay; it is narrow, shallow and suitable only for small vessels. The west shore of the passage has numerous wharves, marinas and fuel jetties.

No vessel shall proceed at a speed greater than 5 kn in Newcastle Island Passage between Bate Point and Pimbury Point. A buoy, 0.1 mile SE of Bate Point, has a speed caution sign.

Oregon Rock, 0.2 mile NNW of Bate Point, dries 0.3 m and is marked by port hand buoy "P13." Passage Rock, close north of Oregon Rock, has 0.1 m over it and is marked by a daybeacon with a port hand daymark. Vessels should not pass between these markers as the channel lies on the east side, off the Newcastle Island shore.

Numerous marinas line the west shore of Newcastle Island Passage.

A small foot passenger ferry operates between Nanaimo and Newcastle and Protection Islands. (SD)

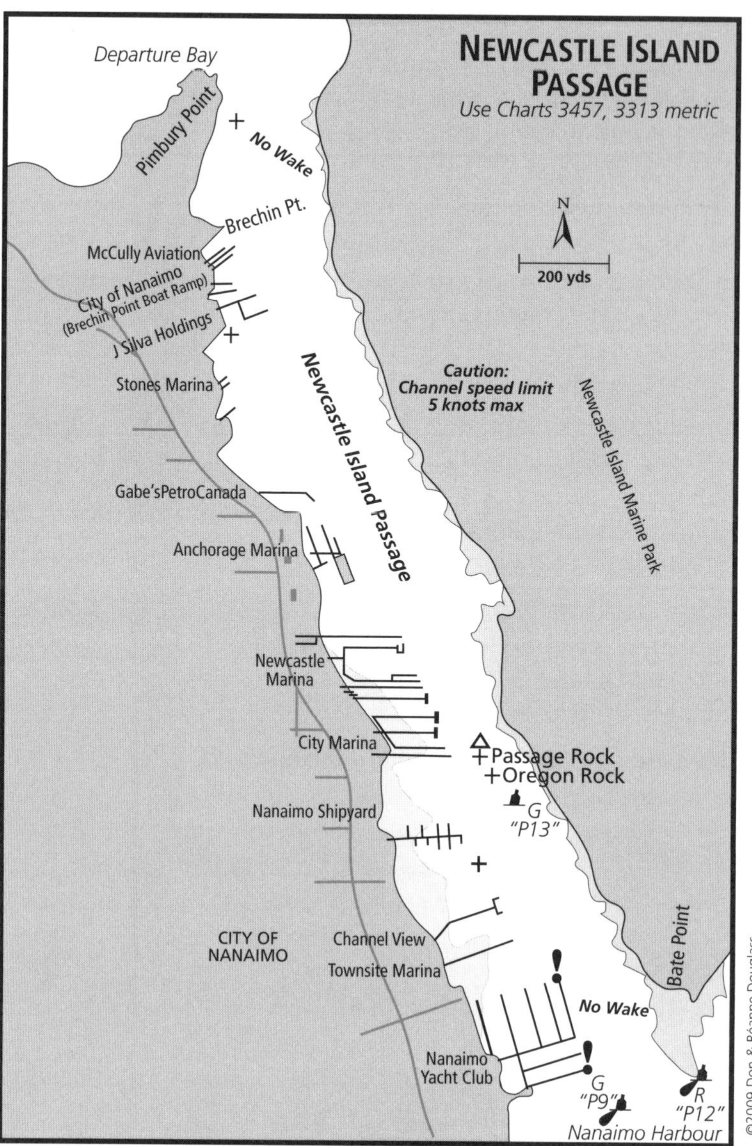

Newcastle Island Passage is narrow, shallow, and heavily used by local traffic and northbound pleasure craft. The channel skirts the city of Nanaimo and the many yacht facilities along its shore. Brechin Point Marina, at the north end of Newcastle Passage, has gasoline and diesel fuel. A strict no-wake speed limit is enforced in Newcastle Passage to protect the numerous marinas and boat docks along the Vancouver Island shore. Avoid Passage Rock and Oregon Rock in midchannel.

⚓ **Brechin Point Marina** tel:250.753.6122; fax: 250.753.2974; email: dasmith@island.net; fuel; toilets; no showers

Departure Bay (Vancouver Island)

Charts 3457, 3458, 3443, 3313; NW of Newcastle I
Entrance (E): 49°12.40'N, 123°56.00'W
Entrance (S, Newcastle I Passage): 49°11.64'N, 123°56.92'W

Departure Bay ... is entered between Horswell Bluff and Nares Point 0.6 mile south. ... It is well-sheltered, however, a constant passage of ferries to and from the mainland causes large swells, which can be a problem to small craft.

Anchorage is prohibited in the area north of Brandon Islands.

Swimming area marker floats, diving rafts, and a water-ski raft are moored off the west shore of Departure Bay. (SD)

Although Departure Bay is well sheltered, no anchoring is permitted due to heavy ferry traffic and the public bathing beach. The large ferry terminal is located 0.25 mile west of Pimbury Point; small craft should avoid this busy area. The Pacific Biological Station, which monitors fish and shellfish, is located on the north shore. The east entrance to Departure Bay leads to Horswell, Rainbow and Fairway channels. Boats headed to the north coast usually exit through Horswell; those heading to the Sunshine Coast use Rainbow Channel; those heading to Vancouver use Fairway Channel.

Newcastle float

Newcastle Island

Summer visitors to Newcastle Island used to arrive by steamship when the island was owned and operated as a resort by the Canadian Pacific Steamship Company. Today they arrive by passenger ferry from Nanaimo, and it's the island's absence of vehicle access that makes it an ideal destination for pleasure boaters who tie up at the public floats or anchor nearby in Mark Bay. The entire island is park land and is home to blacktail deer, beavers, river otters, rabbits and raccoons, including some rare champagne-colored ones.

Groomed trails crisscross the island and it takes about two-and-a-half hours to hike right around the island. Maps are available at the Visitor Centre, a short walk from the floats where boaters who anchor out can tie their dinghies. Kanaka Bay, on the island's west side, offers good swimming with its sandy bottom and warm, shallow water. At the north end of the island, Giovando Lookout provides superb views overlooking the Strait of Georgia.

An exceptionally strong sandstone, used in many buildings on the west coast, was quarried on Newcastle Island from 1869 to 1932. Coal was also mined on the island, its name bestowed by British miners in honor of the famous coal town of northern England. Japanese settlers moved to the island in the early 1900s where they established a herring saltery and shipyard.

In 1931 the Canadian Pacific Steamship Company purchased the island and developed it as a resort for company picnics and Sunday outings. A dance pavilion (now the park's Visitor Centre) was built along with a tea house, picnic areas, change houses and a soccer field. An old ship was docked in Mark Bay to serve as a floating hotel and, until World War II, the ships arriving from Vancouver would bring as many as 1,500 people at a time. The City of Nanaimo acquired the island in 1955 and six years later it became a provincial marine park. **—AV**

Anne Vipond

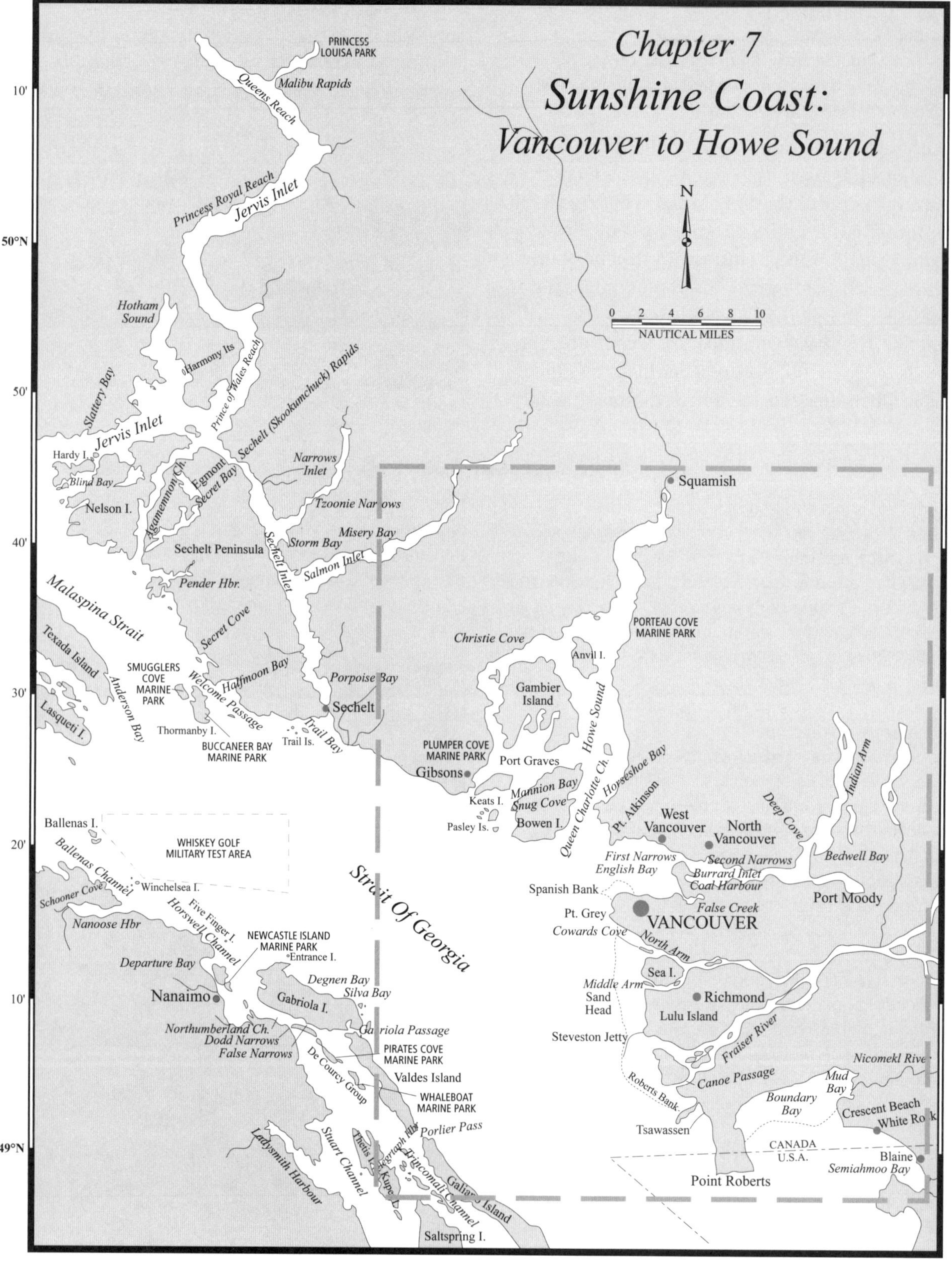
Chapter 7
Sunshine Coast:
Vancouver to Howe Sound
N
0 2 4 6 8 10
NAUTICAL MILES
10'
50°N
50'
40'
30'
20'
10'
49°N
PRINCESS LOUISA PARK
Malibu Rapids
Queens Reach
Princess Royal Reach
Jervis Inlet
Hotham Sound
Harmony Its
Prince of Wales Reach
Sechelt (Skookumchuck) Rapids
Slattery Bay
Jervis Inlet
Hardy I.
Blind Bay
Nelson I.
Agamemnon Ch.
Egmont
Secret Bay
Narrows Inlet
Tzoonie Narrows
Misery Bay
Storm Bay
Sechelt Peninsula
Sechelt Inlet
Salmon Inlet
Pender Hbr.
Malaspina Strait
Secret Cove
Texada Island
SMUGGLERS COVE MARINE PARK
Welcome Passage
Halfmoon Bay
Porpoise Bay
Sechelt
Anderson Bay
Lasqueti I.
Thormanby I.
BUCCANEER BAY MARINE PARK
Trail Is.
Trail Bay
Squamish
PORTEAU COVE MARINE PARK
Christie Cove
Anvil I.
Gambier Island
Howe Sound
PLUMPER COVE MARINE PARK
Gibsons
Port Graves
Keats I.
Mannion Bay
Snug Cove
Bowen I.
Pasley Is.
Queen Charlotte Ch.
Horseshoe Bay
Pt. Atkinson
West Vancouver
North Vancouver
Deep Cove
Indian Arm
Bedwell Bay
First Narrows
English Bay
Second Narrows
Burrard Inlet
Coal Harbour
Spanish Bank
Port Moody
Pt. Grey
False Creek
VANCOUVER
Cowards Cove
North Arm
Sea I.
Middle Arm
Sand Head
Richmond
Lulu Island
Steveston Jetty
Fraiser River
Canoe Passage
Roberts Bank
Nicomekl River
Mud Bay
Boundary Bay
Crescent Beach
White Rock
Tsawassen
CANADA
U.S.A.
Blaine
Semiahmoo Bay
Point Roberts
Ballenas I.
WHISKEY GOLF MILITARY TEST AREA
Ballenas Channel
Winchelsea I.
Schooner Cove
Five Finger I.
Horswell Channel
Nanoose Hbr
Strait Of Georgia
NEWCASTLE ISLAND MARINE PARK
Entrance I.
Departure Bay
Degnen Bay
Silva Bay
Nanaimo
Gabriola I.
Gabriola Passage
Northumberland Ch.
Dodd Narrows
False Narrows
PIRATES COVE MARINE PARK
De Courcy Group
Valdes Island
WHALEBOAT MARINE PARK
Porlier Pass
Ladysmith Harbour
Stuart Channel
Thetis I.
Kuper
Trincomali Channel
Galiano Island
Saltspring I.

7

SUNSHINE COAST: Vancouver to Howe Sound

The Fraser River arms and deltas dominate the mainland coast between Boundary Bay and the Canadian border to Vancouver. Sediment carried down the river's three arms has created shoals offshore, while close to the deltas are found marshy areas and shifting sand bars. Prevailing winds and the river currents can combine to produce steep seas, so diligent navigating is required. The Arctic outflow winds in the delta areas can be severe in the winter months.

Canadian Navy training ship on maneuvers

The area from Point Roberts to Point Grey is considered by some to be uninteresting. However, there are some places worth visiting. Steveston's streets are quaint and movies are often filmed there and Tsawwasen has a ferry terminal. The marshlands are filled with wildlife, mammals and birds, especially bald eagles.

Vancouver is a beautiful, cosmopolitan city, with museums, shops, parks, and good dining, so be sure to allow time to visit. The new Coal Harbour Marina, in the heart of downtown, makes it possible to sail right into the city.

Burrard Inlet, cutting into the mainland just north of the city, has numerous bays and coves, many of which—like English Bay and False Creek—are popular cruising destinations. Indian Arm gives you a taste of the steep-sided fjords you'll find farther north. Here you can feast your eyes on mountain peaks and ridges, with streams and waterfalls. Indian Arm Marine Park and Fairy Falls are major attractions.

Northwest of Burrard Inlet, Queen Charlotte Channel leads into Howe Sound, a lovely, well-sheltered sound. Popular destinations include Snug Cove, Mannion Bay, and Plumper Cove Marine Park. There are beautiful beaches and great opportunities for exploring by dinghy or kayak.

Note: Charts 3312 and 3313 are chart books in atlas format. They are designed for use by small craft, and include additional information and aerial photographs. However, these charts are not available as NDI digital charts, nor do they lend themselves easily to measurement of latitude and longitude.

Semiahmoo Bay

Chart 3463; straddles the U.S./Canadian border btwn Blaine & Boundary Bay
Entrance (U.S./Canadian border, 1.4 mi SW of White Rock pier): 49°00.12'N, 122°50.09'W

Canadian boats heading south can enter Customs in Blaine, 0.5 mile south of the border, and U.S. boats can enter Customs at White Rock 0.9 mile north of the border.

White Rock

Chart 3463; NE side of Semiahmoo Bay; N of Blaine
Breakwater Light: 49°01.01'N, 122°48.48'W

> *White Rock, 3.5 miles SE of Crescent Beach, is on the north side of Semiahmoo Bay ... The community takes its name from a conspicuous white boulder on the beach close east of the shore end of the jetty.* (SD)
>
> *The float on the east side of the jetty is used by seaplanes and small craft making Customs entry....* (SD)

White Rock is a convenient Customs entry point for U.S. boats that enter Canada by following the mainland coast. It is essentially an open roadstead, but some protection can be found behind the "T"-shaped pier for a temporary stop.

A sunny day on the Sunshine Coast

⚓ **Canadian Customs** tel: 888.226.7277

Boundary Bay

Chart 3463; btwn Pt Roberts & the entrance to the Nicomekl River
Entrance (Nicomekl River, flashing red light): 49°00.76'N, 122°56.30'W

> *Caution. —It is advisable for those without local knowledge to use the river channel at not less than half tide and only on a rising tide.* (SD)

Boundary Bay is one of the richest biological tidal flats on the west coast. The bay and its freshwater streams provide a natural environment for all kinds of birds, fish, and creatures that live on and in the mud flats.

White Rock

White Rock may be your first stop in Canadian waters for clearing Customs and spending a pleasant afternoon. It's located on Semiahmoo Bay, just three miles north of the Peace Arch marking the U.S.-Canada border. In fact, you can see the arch from the pier.

After docking at the end of the 1,500-foot pier, walk along its wooden planks to shore. Looking up, you'll see pastel houses that seem to cascade down to the wide, sandy beaches. You won't find much in the way of historical atmosphere in this affluent, bustling seaside resort, but you'll find plenty of shops and restaurants.

And, check it out—there really is a white rock at White Rock. A glacier deposited the massive boulder on the beach eons ago and the Semiahmoo First Nation people incorporated it into their lore. According to legend, the love-struck son of the Sea God hurled the rock from Vancouver Island, and then brought his bride to its landing place to begin their new life.

Even if you don't have time for anything else, stretch your legs along the attractive waterfront promenade. Mix with the locals as they jog along the brick path highlighted with blue railings and yellow benches. At the east end of the promenade there is a footbridge to the Semiahmoo Indian Reserve.

Watch out for trains on the tracks that parallel the path.Visit the Great Northern Railway Station built in 1912. It's now the White Rock Museum and Archives, housing photographs and artifacts pertaining to the area's First Nation, settlement and railway history.

Restaurants along Marine Drive offer everything from fish 'n' chips to more exotic fare. Walk uphill along Johnston Road for shopping, or visit the Farmers' Market at the Upper Town Centre.

You can ask questions at the tourist center at base of pier, or go to www.whiterockonline.com for information before you arrive.

Mud Bay (Boundary Bay)

Chart 3463; NE corner of Boundary Bay
Entrance (confluence of Nicomekl & Serpentine rivers, N of Blackie Spit): 49°03.79'N, 122°52.66'W

Mud Bay, in the NE part of Boundary Bay, has several narrow, shallow channels leading across its drying flats through which the Nicomekl River and Serpentine River discharge. These channels converge at Blackie Spit. (SD)

Mud Bay is the large drying mud flat at the confluence of Nicomekl and Serpentine rivers.

Crescent Beach (Mud Bay)

Chart 3463; on the SE side of Mud Bay
Position (railway bridge): 49°03.45'N, 122°52.20'W

Crescent Beach is a summer resort at Blackie Spit. A store and restaurant are close to the public wharf. (SD)

A marina is in a dredged basin close east of the Burlington Northern Railway Bridge. (SD)

You can observe the fascinating changes from ocean to estuary to fresh-water environment by visiting this delta region. Small boats can find shelter east of the railway bridge.

Nicomekl River

Chart 3463; on the N side of Crescent Beach
Position (railway bridge): 49°03.45'N, 122°52.20'W

The Burlington Northern Railway Bridge which crosses the Nicomekl River, is a swing bridge. The swing span has a vertical clearance of 2.7 m (9 ft) when closed; the trestle has a vertical clearance of 3.7 m (12 ft). A height clearance gauge is on the NW end of the bridge … (SD)

The latest information on the railway bridge is that the swing span is manned from 6:30 a.m. to 10:30 p.m., seven days a week. Sound your horn three times to have it opened. (Information in the Small Craft Guide is obsolete.) The phone number for the Crescent Beach Marina is 604.538.9666.

With farmland along the edges of the river, it's easy to imagine that you are on a French canal. Anchorage is reported to be found in a wide bend in the river upstream from Crescent Beach. The river bottom here was dredged to provide sand and gravel for construction of the freeway to the east.

Anchor adjacent to the farming complex located on the north shore in reportedly deep water. The approach to this bend is by midchannel at or near high water.

⚓ **Bridge tender** tel: 604.538.3233

⚓ **Crescent Beach Marina** tel: 604.538.9666; monitors VHF Ch 66A; website: www.crescentbeachmarina.com; email: info@crescentbeachmarina.com; fuel; power; restrooms; showers

Point Roberts to Point Grey

Chart 3463

From a distance, particularly from the south, Point Roberts has the appearance of an island.

The coast between Point Roberts and English Bluff, 3 miles north, consists of bluffs of moderate elevation; farther north it merges into the swampy Fraser River delta and is low, featureless and barely discernible from a vessel in the strait. Fronting this portion of the coast are Roberts Bank, south of the main channel of the Fraser River, and Sturgeon Bank, north of it. These banks, dry in patches, are steep-to and extend up to 5 miles offshore. (SD)

The University of British Columbia buildings,

Observer *heading out*

on the high ground above (Point Grey), are conspicuous landmarks. (SD)

Point Roberts

Chart 3463; 3.3 mi SE of the Tsawwassen ferry terminal & 11.8 mi W of Blaine
Pt Roberts Light (SW corner of Pt Roberts): 48°58.29'N, 123°05.04'W
Entrance (Marina): 48°58.33'N, 123°03.94'W

Point Roberts is the termination of a remarkable promontory extending south from the Fraser River delta.... A rocky ledge, which dries in places, extends 1 mile SE of the SE extremity of the promontory.

A large marina, on Point Roberts about 1 mile east of Point Roberts light structure, is entered to the west of and protected by a detached rock breakwater. (SD)

Point Roberts is convenient to the Gulf Islands and offers unique shelter for those boats traversing the Strait of Georgia along the mainland shore.

⚓ **Point Roberts Marina** tel: 260.945.2255; fax: 360.945.0927; monitors VHF Ch 66A; website: www.pointrobertsmarina.com; fuel; power; restrooms; showers; laundry; pumpout

Roberts Bank

Chart 3463; extends from Pt Roberts on the S to the Steveston Jetty on the N
Canoe Passage Light & bell buoy "T14": 49°02.28'N, 123°15.39'W
Racon fog signal No. 309 (1.1 mi SW of Sand Heads): 49°05.26'N, 123°18.61'W

Caution: When proceeding toward the Fraser River or cruising off Roberts Bank it should be kept in mind that water conditions near the bank can be hazardous under certain conditions. When the wind opposes the tide; e.g., a NW wind and a flood tide, short steep waves can develop. This situation is worsened off the main entrance to the Fraser River by the addition of the flow from the river during the freshet period (May-August). Under these conditions the buoys are difficult to sight. An additional hazard during freshets is the quantity of logs and floating debris which come out of the river.

All set for a quiet weekend retreat

Mariners navigating along or close to Roberts and Sturgeon Banks on the flood tide are warned to avoid being set toward the banks by the onflow of water onto the banks. (SD)

Roberts Bank is a large, flat shoal area which extends 5 miles or more west of Westham Island and Tsawwassen Peninsula. The bank rises with little warning and caution is advised when transiting this area.

Tsawwassen Beach

Charts 3499, 3463; 1.4 mi NE of the Tsawwassen ferry terminal; 3.2 mi NW of Pt Roberts Marina
S bkw light (W end): 49°00.13'N, 123°07.72'W
Anchor: 49°01.12'N, 123°06.30'W

Port and starboard hand buoys mark the dredged channel leading to the yacht club. From April to October mooring buoys are at the head of this channel.

Note. Small craft operating in this vicinity should keep well clear of the ferries, they generate bow waves and wash which can be hazardous in some conditions of tide and weather. (SD)

Just south of the large ferry complex is a narrow channel leading to a small turning basin where surprising protection from prevailing summer winds can be found. This is recommended only for small boats needing a respite from the Strait of Georgia. The channel and turning basin have a least depth of about 1 fathom. *Caution:* The channel is as narrow as 60 feet in places, and its south side is irregular.

Anchor in about 1 fathom, as the tide allows, avoiding the mooring buoys.

Fraser River

Charts 3463, 3490, 3491; S of Vancouver & N of Tsawwassen

The Fraser River in size and commercial importance is exceeded in the Pacific NW only by the Columbia River. Its estuary empties into the Strait of Georgia and is protected from the open ocean by Vancouver Island.

Caution.—A NW wind opposing the flood tide or a SW wind blowing against the freshet cause short steep seas; under these conditions numerous small vessels have been swamped.

The Fraser River delta consists of several channels, namely, North Arm, Middle Arm, Canoe Passage and the Main Channel. (SD)

Photo courtesy CHS, Pacific Region

Steveston and Cannery Channel

Wake from heavy commercial traffic and numerous ferries crossing in summer, and the prevailing northwest winds off the Fraser River, are reasons most pleasure craft avoid this area and use the protected waters of the Gulf Islands on north- and southbound trips. During winter, Arctic outflow winds—sometimes attaining storm force—blast down the Fraser River delta and Howe Sound bringing subfreezing weather. During these conditions, the north to easterly winds can blow saltwater spray causing icing on deck that is dangerous to small craft transiting this area.

Canoe Passage

Chart 3463; 5.0 mi NW of Tsawwassen ferry terminal; 4.5 mi SE of Sand Heads Light
Canoe Passage light & bell buoy "T14": 49°02.28'N, 123°15.39'W

The only portion of Canoe Passage navigable with certainty at all stages of the tide is between Westham Island and the mainland. A channel across Roberts Bank, regularly used by local fishermen, is marked by private dolphins. Local knowledge is required for navigating this channel. It is very shallow and winding and the depths, like those elsewhere on Roberts Bank, are constantly changing. (SD)

Unless you can follow a larger fishing vessel or local boat through Canoe Passage, it is advisable to use the main Fraser River channel entrance 4 miles north at Sand Heads.

Fraser River, Main Channel

Chart 3490; S of Lulu I & N of Westham I
Sand Heads Light (outer Steveston Jetty): 49°06.36'N, 123°18.20'W

Main Channel, entered at Sand Heads, is used by deep-sea vessels, tugs, barges, logbooms and fish boats.

The river is navigable by deep-sea vessels as far as Douglas Island, 24 miles from the entrance. Upstream from Douglas Island the river is uncharted but navigable by small vessels as far as Hope, 73 miles from the entrance; local knowledge is required. Pitt River leads NE from Douglas Island to Pitt Lake and is navigable by small vessels.

September, October and November are favourable months for river navigation, as the water is then sufficiently high for small vessels to reach

Classic yachts buddy up

Hope, and the strength of the current considerably abated.

During freshets the greatest rate of the outgoing stream occurs 40 minutes before LW, when it can amount to 6 kn. After the freshet is over it reduces to 3 or 4 kn. (SD)

The main channel of the Fraser River is entered on the south side of the Steveston Jetty at Sand Heads Light. If you're interested in exploring part or all of the navigable portion of Fraser River (73 miles to Hope), or if you want visit Pitt Lake (Chart 3062), consider contacting local yacht clubs about joining one of their annual outings up the river. Currents and depths are changeable from year to year and local knowledge or a helping hand are important.

Fine weather for crossing the Strait of Georgia

The entrance is well marked with navigation aids (see chart), and midchannel depths are from 4 to 5 fathoms minimum.

Steveston Jetty

Chart 3490; extends 4.3 mi SW from the town of Steveston
Sand Heads Light (outer Steveston Jetty): 49°06.36′N, 123°18.20′W

Steveston Jetty, a stone training wall, forms the north side of the entrance channel between Sand Heads and Garry Point 4.3 miles ENE.

Caution.—The jetty has several gaps in it through which a cross current flows; it is advisable to give these a wide berth. (SD)

Cannery Channel (Steveston Harbour)

Chart 3490; on the Fraser River main branch N of Steveston Island
Entrance (W, 0.14 mi SE of Garry Pt): 49°07.43′N, 123°11.63′W
Anchor (Cannery Ch): 49°06.95′N, 123°09.56′W

Cannery Channel, known locally as Cannery Basin, is entered close east of Garry Point and separated from the main river channel by Steveston Island, known locally as Shady Island, and the rock breakwater extending NW from it. This channel, closed by a rock dam at

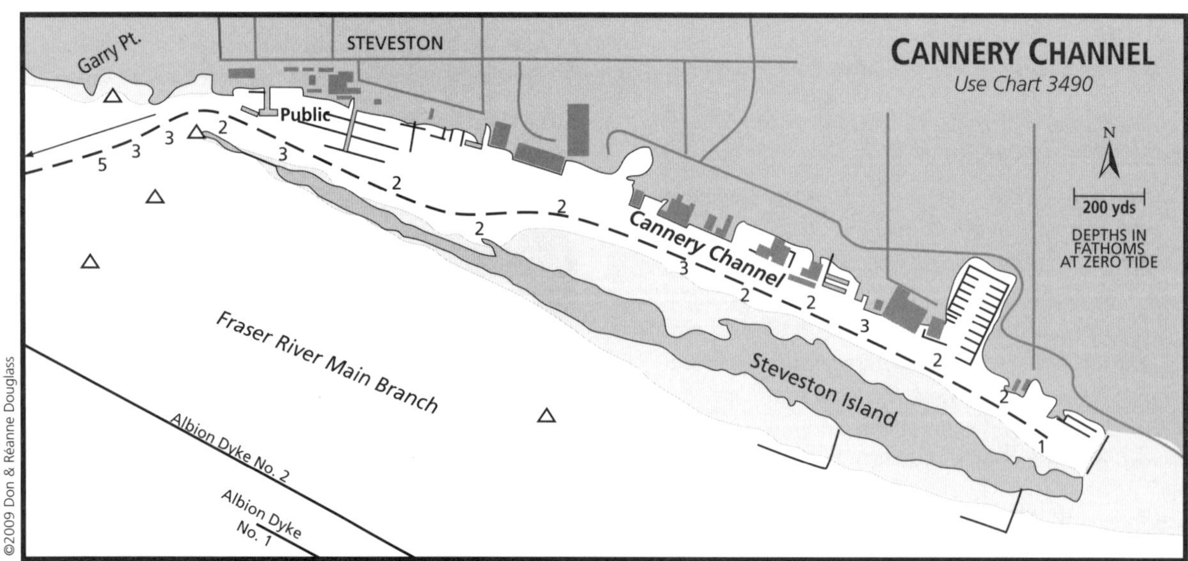

its east end, is used extensively by commercial fishermen.

A public wharf complex, with a pier and several floats, is in the NW part of Cannery Channel; power and water are available on the floats. The other wharves and floats are used by the fishing fleet, but may also provide mooring for pleasure craft while the fleet is at sea. (SD)

Cannery Channel (Steveston Harbour) serves a large commercial fishing fleet, and you may be able to buy salmon, tuna, shrimp or assorted bottom fish directly from the fishing boats here. You may find temporary anchorage at the end of Cannery Channel just short of the rock dam which forces the bulk of the river current to the south of Steveston Island. *Caution:* This dam is awash at high water.

Anchor in 1 to 2 fathoms over an unrecorded bottom.

⚓ **Steveson Harbour Authority**
tel: 604.272.5539

Fraser River (North Arm)

Chart 3491; S of Vancouver & N of Sea & Lulu Is
Entrance (0.34 mi NW of jetty light): 49°15.68'N, 123°17.14'W
North Arm (jetty light): 49°15.44'N, 123°16.78'W

North Arm, known to coastal shipping as The Ditch, is entered close SW of Point Grey and used mainly by tugs towing barges and logbooms. (SD)

When approaching the entrance to North Arm from northward care must be taken not to cut across the drying flats SW of Point Grey. During freshets the water in this entrance can become very rough with an opposing wind. (SD)

There is a small sheltered spot for temporary shelter located 1.5 miles south of Point Grey.

Urban cruising

This strategic place has a name which says it all—Cowards Cove!

Cowards Cove (North Arm, Fraser River)

Chart 3491; immediately E of the bkw; is 0.6 mi S of Grey Pt
Entrance: 49°15.23'N, 123°15.99'W
Anchor: 49°15.34'N, 123°15.90'W

Cowards Cove, the dredged area within the outer end of the breakwater, is a mooring ground for fishing vessels. (SD)

Tiny Cowards Cove, the first anchor site if you're entering Fraser River, offers protec-

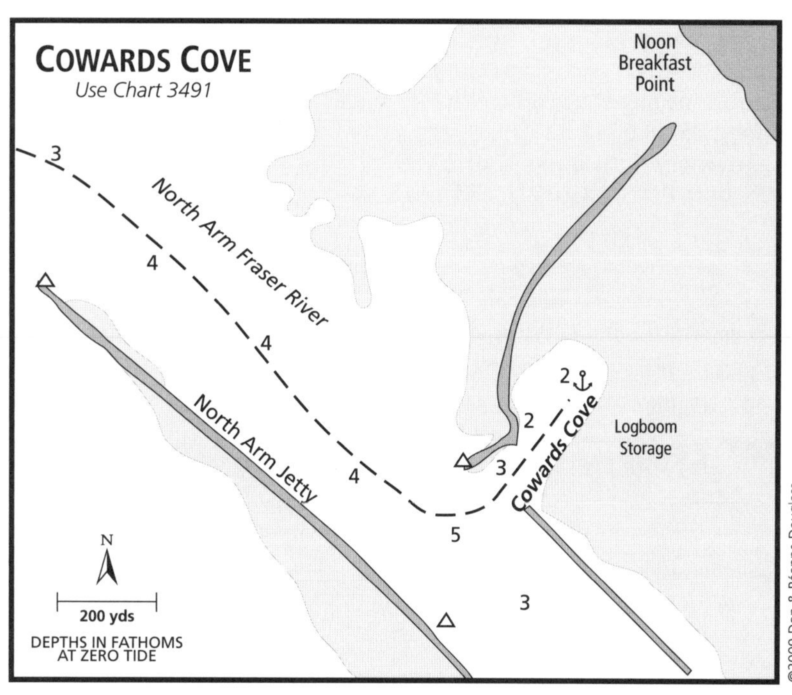

tion behind the breakwater, but there are frequently logbooms stored there.

Anchor in 2 fathoms over an unrecorded bottom.

Fraser River, Middle Arm

Chart 3491; S of Vancouver btwn Sea & Lulu Is
Junction of North Arm with Middle Arm: 49°11.90'N, 123°08.00'W
Position (Middle Arm swing bridge): 49°11.52'N, 123°08.25'W

> *Middle Arm, entered south of Sea Island, is used mainly by pleasure craft.*
>
> *... It is reported that these marinas become very congested during summer months. In an emergency it may be possible to tie up to the logbooms lying along the Dinsmore Island shore in Morey Channel.*
>
> *Middle Arm ... is part of North Fraser Harbour. It is entered from North Arm. Sturgeon Bank obstructs its west end and has no marked channel across it.* (SD)

Note: The Middle Arm is not reachable directly from the Strait of Georgia but from the east side of Sea Island in the North Arm of the Fraser River.

Burrard Inlet

Charts 3481, 3463; on the N side of downtown Vancouver, extends from Grey Pt to Indian Arm
Cautionary light buoy "QA" (2.35 mi NW of Pt Grey): 49°16.57'N, 123°19.31'W
Cautionary light buoy "QB" (2.35 mi W of Prospect Pt): 49°19.04'N, 123°12.08'W

> *Burrard Inlet, close north of the mouth of the Fraser River, is entered between Point Grey and Point Atkinson 4 miles north.*
>
> *In 1792, Captain George Vancouver, R.N., when on a voyage of exploration in HMS Discovery, sailed into the Strait of Georgia, and, leaving his vessel and her consort, HMS Chatham, proceeded with his ship's boats through the channel now known as First Narrows and entered the sheltered waters of Burrard Inlet. The inlet penetrates 12.5 miles east where it divides into Indian Arm and Port Moody. Vancouver Harbour is the portion of Burrard Inlet east of First Narrows.* (SD)

Future sailor learns the ropes from the bottom up

Burrard Inlet is a large inlet which includes English Bay at its entrance, the Port of Vancouver in its center, Port Moody at its head, and Indian Arm, a sizable offshoot to the north. This is a colorful and busy place with a number of special safety considerations. (See Port of Vancouver information on following page.)

English Bay

Chart 3481; on the S side of the entrance to Burrard Inlet, W of False Creek
Entrance (0.12 mi N of RVYC floats): 49°17.71'N, 123°11.28'W
Jericho public pier: 49°16.64'N, 123°12.09'W
Royal Vancouver Yacht Club (bkw light): 49°16.52'N, 123°11.29'W
Anchor (Jericho Beach): 49°16.53'N, 123°11.79'W

> *English Bay, between Spanish Bank and Stanley Park 3 miles NE, is a very popular yachting area. Yacht races, some of them international, take place in the Jericho-Kitsilano Beach area of English Bay between April and October.*

Photo courtesy CHS, Pacific Region

False Creek

English Bay is also an anchorage for merchant ships awaiting berths in Vancouver. Sixteen anchorage berths lie between the measured distance beacons and the approach to False Creek; it is not unusual to find most of them occupied. (SD)

The south shore of English Bay is at the east end of the Spanish Bank sand flats. Temporary anchorage may be found 0.23 mile southeast of the Jericho public pier and west of the Royal Vancouver Yacht Club facility.

False Creek

Chart 3493; in the SE part of English Bay
Entrance (0.12 mi N of buoy "Q52"): 49°17.01'N, 123°08.98'W
Burrard Bridge (center): 49°16.53'N, 123°08.20'W

The approach to False Creek is relatively shallow and no attempt to enter should be made except in the white sector of the light on the north pier of Burrard Bridge.

There is no anchorage in False Creek. (SD)

Photo courtesy CHS, Pacific Region

First Narrows from seaward

False Creek, the easiest approach to the downtown part of Vancouver, has a host of marinas and small-craft facilities.

Brokers Bay (Fishermans Terminal)

Chart 3493; S of Burrard Bridge & W of Granville Island
Entrance: 49°16.43'N, 123°08.16'W

Floats for fishing vessels ... are close south of Burrard Bridge, on the west shore of False Creek in Brokers Bay. They vary in length between 67 and 127 m (220 and 417 ft) and depths alongside are between 2.6 and 3.2 m (9 and 10 ft).

Berthing for pleasure craft may also be obtained, but only if the space is not required for fish boats. (SD)

Vancouver Harbour (Port of Vancouver)

Chart 3493; lies E of First Narrows (Lions Gate Bridge)
Entrance (small craft, inbound; 0.06 mi N of Prospect Pt Light): 49°18.90'N, 123°08.48'W
Exit (small craft, outbound; 0.2 mi NE of Prospect Pt Light): 49°19.02'N, 123°08.36'W

As Burrard Inlet is the entrance to Vancouver Harbour, one of the busiest seaports on the Pacific coast, a considerable amount of merchant shipping as well as ferries, tugs, barges and logbooms will be encountered. Because of this it should be kept in mind that the Collision Regulations, Rule 9(b) states "A vessel of less than 20 meters in length or a sailing vessel shall not impede the passage of a vessel which can safely navigate only within a narrow channel or fairway." (SD)

A cruise in Burrard Inlet can provide an adrenaline rush to anyone used to cruising in quieter, non-developed areas.

Vancouver Harbour is regulated by the Port of Vancouver Corporation and controlled by the Vancouver Harbourmaster. Please note carefully the adjacent diagram which illustrates important safety and traffic requirements. Telephone numbers are listed for reporting marine accidents, navigational hazards, or for obtaining up-to-date information.

Small craft must remain well clear of com-

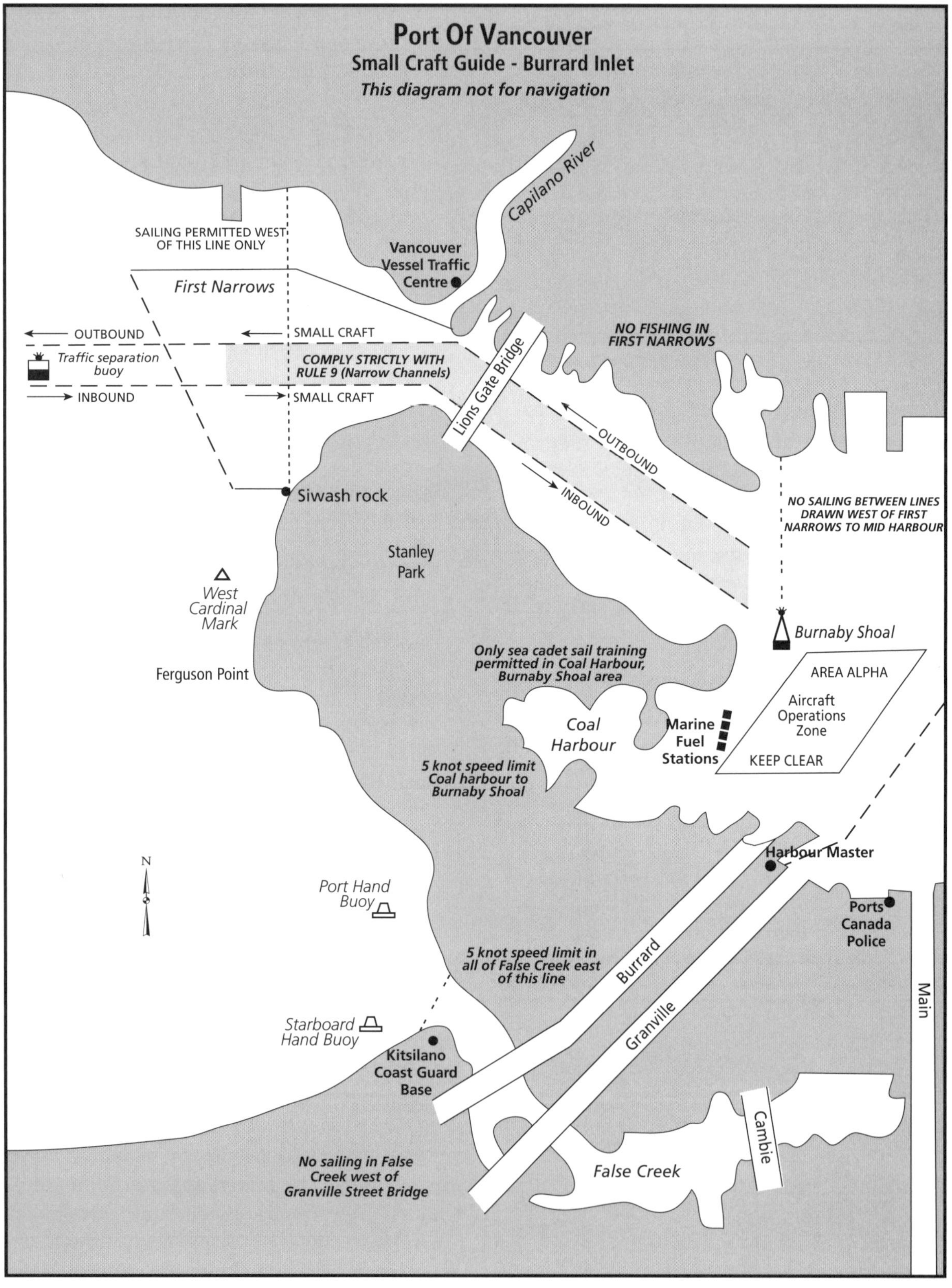
Port Of Vancouver
Small Craft Guide - Burrard Inlet
This diagram not for navigation
Capilano River
SAILING PERMITTED WEST OF THIS LINE ONLY
Vancouver Vessel Traffic Centre
First Narrows
OUTBOUND
SMALL CRAFT
Traffic separation buoy
COMPLY STRICTLY WITH RULE 9 (Narrow Channels)
INBOUND
SMALL CRAFT
Lions Gate Bridge
NO FISHING IN FIRST NARROWS
OUTBOUND
INBOUND
Siwash rock
NO SAILING BETWEEN LINES DRAWN WEST OF FIRST NARROWS TO MID HARBOUR
Stanley Park
West Cardinal Mark
Burnaby Shoal
Only sea cadet sail training permitted in Coal Harbour, Burnaby Shoal area
AREA ALPHA
Aircraft Operations Zone
KEEP CLEAR
Ferguson Point
Coal Harbour
Marine Fuel Stations
5 knot speed limit Coal harbour to Burnaby Shoal
Harbour Master
N
Port Hand Buoy
Ports Canada Police
5 knot speed limit in all of False Creek east of this line
Burrard
Granville
Main
Starboard Hand Buoy
Kitsilano Coast Guard Base
Cambie
No sailing in False Creek west of Granville Street Bridge
False Creek

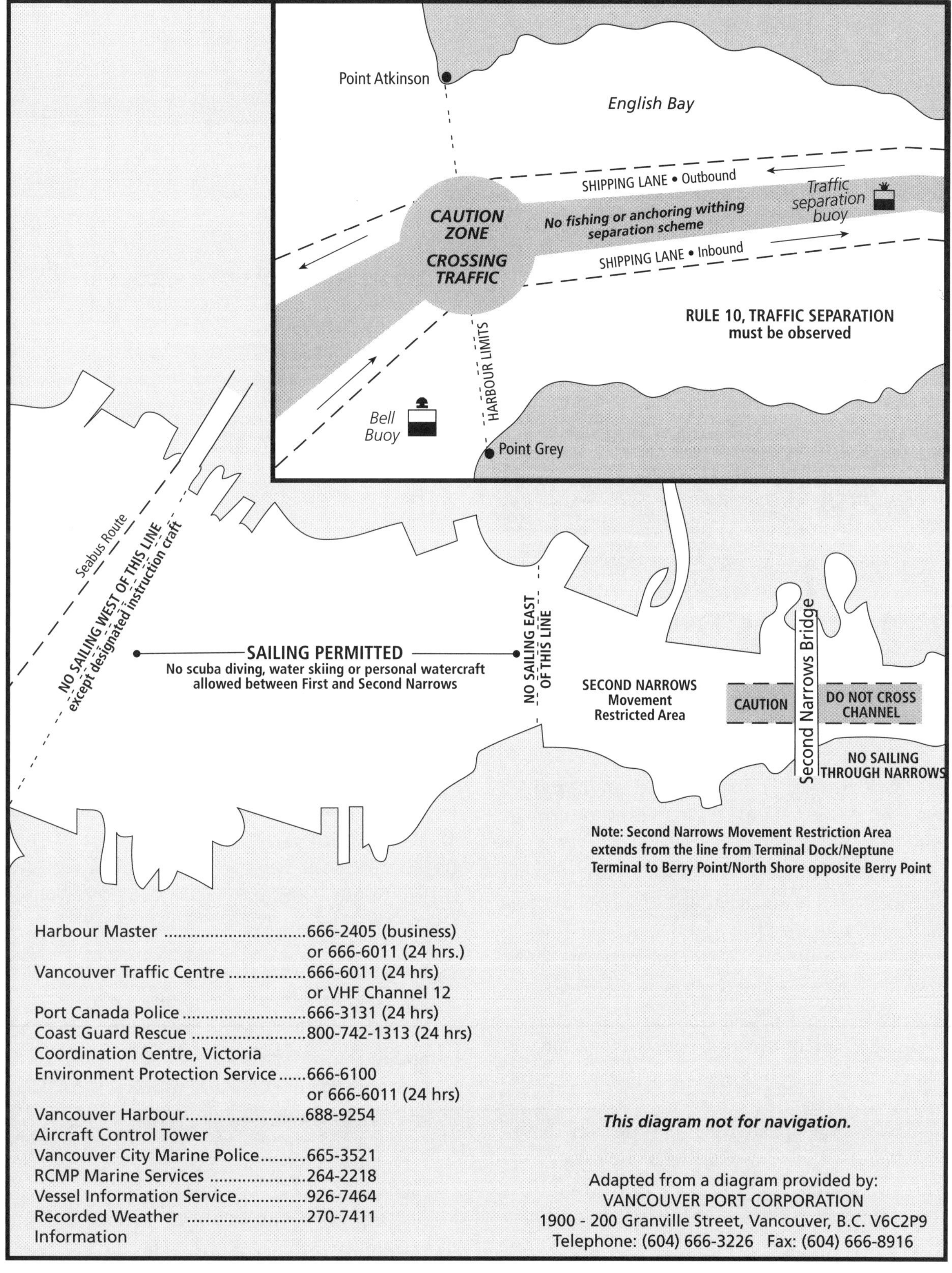
Point Atkinson
English Bay
SHIPPING LANE • Outbound
Traffic separation buoy
CAUTION ZONE
CROSSING TRAFFIC
No fishing or anchoring withing separation scheme
SHIPPING LANE • Inbound
RULE 10, TRAFFIC SEPARATION must be observed
HARBOUR LIMITS
Bell Buoy
Point Grey
Seabus Route
NO SAILING WEST OF THIS LINE except designated instruction craft
SAILING PERMITTED
No scuba diving, water skiing or personal watercraft allowed between First and Second Narrows
NO SAILING EAST OF THIS LINE
SECOND NARROWS Movement Restricted Area
CAUTION
Second Narrows Bridge
DO NOT CROSS CHANNEL
NO SAILING THROUGH NARROWS
Note: Second Narrows Movement Restriction Area extends from the line from Terminal Dock/Neptune Terminal to Berry Point/North Shore opposite Berry Point
Harbour Master ....666-2405 (business)
or 666-6011 (24 hrs.)
Vancouver Traffic Centre ....666-6011 (24 hrs)
or VHF Channel 12
Port Canada Police ....666-3131 (24 hrs)
Coast Guard Rescue ....800-742-1313 (24 hrs)
Coordination Centre, Victoria
Environment Protection Service......666-6100
or 666-6011 (24 hrs)
Vancouver Harbour.........................688-9254
Aircraft Control Tower
Vancouver City Marine Police..........665-3521
RCMP Marine Services 264-2218
Vessel Information Service..............926-7464
Recorded Weather 270-7411
Information
This diagram not for navigation.
Adapted from a diagram provided by:
VANCOUVER PORT CORPORATION
1900 - 200 Granville Street, Vancouver, B.C. V6C2P9
Telephone: (604) 666-3226 Fax: (604) 666-8916

Ian Douglas

Weekend fun

mercial vessels underway, and anchored or berthed vessels should be expected to move at any time.

Caution: Note the no-sailing areas on the diagram, and be aware that turbulent seas can be found in both First and Second Narrows.

Tugs should not be passed between their tow or close astern of the tow as there may be a lengthy floating line.

Keep clear of aircraft operations zones as they can be very busy with float planes landing and taking off.

The 5-knot speed limit is enforced in the restricted areas of the Port of Vancouver.

The easiest approach to downtown Vancouver for visiting yachts is to enter False Creek at the head of English Bay. Those wishing to enter Vancouver Harbour proper may want to use the berthing and fuel facilities at Coal Harbour. When you enter First Narrows, downtown Vancouver and Coal Harbour are found on the south shore, while North Vancouver is on the north shore. The north shore west of First Narrows, called West Vancouver, leads to the ferry complex at Horseshoe Bay.

Coal Harbour, Port of Vancouver

Chart 3493; 1.2 mi SE of Lions Gate Bridge; 1.1 mi NE of False Creek
Entrance: 49°17.56′N, 123°07.03′W

Coal Harbour, which leads NW from the south end of Deadman Island, has a channel about 120 m (394 ft) wide with a least depth of 3 m (10 ft); it affords excellent shelter for small craft alongside any of the numerous floats. On the south side of the harbour there are several boatyards and marinas. The Vancouver Rowing Club headquarters and floats are at the head of the harbour, and the Royal Vancouver Yacht Club floats are on the north side. (SD)

Coal Harbour affords entry to the north side of downtown Vancouver. From here, it is just a short walk to beautiful Stanley Park north of Lost Lagoon. There is no sailing or anchoring allowed in Coal Harbour. Moorage may be possible at Coal Harbour Marina, or at Bayshore West Marina in front of the Bayshore Hotel. Several large fuel barges in the entrance afford easy access to fuel, water, ice and bait.

⚓ **Coal Harbour Marina**
tel: 604.681.2628; fax: 604.681.4666; monitors VHF Ch 66A; website: www.coalharbourmarina.com; email: info@coalharbourmarina.com; power; restrooms; showers; laundry

⚓ **Bayshore West Marina**
tel: 604.689.5331; fax: 604.689.5332; website: www.thunderbirdmarine.com; power; restrooms; showers; laundry; pumpout

Port Moody

Chart 3495; 9 mi E of Lions Gate Bridge
Entrance (0.1 mi NE of Gosse Pt): 49°17.61'N, 122°55.39'W
Anchor: 49°17.34'N, 122°51.28'W

Port Moody, the eastern extremity of Burrard Inlet, is entered between Admiralty Point on the north and Gosse Point 0.3 mile south.

Anchorage is possible along the northern shore of Port Moody. The bottom in Port Moody

Vancouver

It isn't often you sail into a port surrounded by towering skyscrapers and half a million residents. Vancouver, British Columbia's financial and shipping hub, has endless recreational, cultural and shopping opportunities. It's also among the most photogenic of cities, so whichever part of the city you decide to explore, keep your camera at the ready.

In a city of waterways, False Creek provides the best access to downtown Vancouver. Call the False Creek Welcome Centre (866.677.2628 or 604.648.2628) for available marina space.

You can get to many places on foot, but taxis (Yellow Cab 604.681.1111; Black Top 604.731.1111) and the Translink system (604.521.0400) will take you everywhere else. To make transportation fun, rent bikes or in-line skates near Stanley Park along Robson and Denman Streets.

Vancouver's multicultural ambience is evident in its neighborhoods. In Chinatown see the Dr. Sun Yat-sen Classical Chinese Garden (578 Carrall St.). The Punjabi Market area is a good place to buy jewelry, spices and fabric. Other distinctive districts are Gastown, the old section with a Victorian atmosphere; Yaletown with its nightclubs, galleries and lofts; and Kitsilano, former hippie haven and now a place of trendy shops and coffeehouses.

On Granville Island (take the False Creek Ferry or Aquabus) you'll find the huge Granville Public Market brimming with fresh produce, fish, meats, exotic food stalls and artists' studios. At many places you can watch the artists and craftsmen at work. Photo opportunities abound.

Stanley Park, a thousand acres of woods jutting up between English Bay and Burrard Inlet, provides a home for wildlife and attractions for visitors. A walk around the 5.5-mile seawall promenade is de rigueur. There are totem poles, a water park, beaches, swimming pools, tennis courts and trails, as well as the Vancouver Aquarium Marine Science Center (845 Avison Way; 604.659.3474; www.vanaqua.com).

Other important museums in Vancouver:

H.R. MacMillan Space Centre (1100 Chestnut St.; 604.738.7827; www.hrmacmillanspacecentre.com).

Science World, British Columbia (1455 Quebec St.; 604.443.7443; www.scienceworld.bc.ca).

U.B.C. Museum of Anthropology and Haida Village (6393 N. W. Marine Dr.; 604.822.5950; www.moa.ubc.ca).

Vancouver Art Gallery (750 Hornby St.; 604.662.4719; www.vanartgallery.bc.ca).

Vancouver Maritime Museum (1905 Ogden Ave.; 604.257.8300; www.vancouvermaritimemuseum.com)

Vancouver Museum (1100 Chestnut St.; 604.736.4431; www.vanmuseum.bc.ca).

For a unique 70-minute tour, go to Storyeum where you'll see dramatizations of British Columbia history performed underground (142 Water St.; 604.687.8142; www.storyeum.com). There's a musical steam-powered clock at the corner of Cambie and Water. And you can get an eagle's-eye view of the city from the Vancouver Lookout deck atop Harbour Centre.

In North Vancouver, the Capilano Suspension Bridge and Treetops Adventure (3735 Capilano Road; 604.985.7474; www.capbridge.com) lets you experience a footbridge over a deep gorge and life in a coastal forest. Nearby Lynn Canyon also has a swinging bridge and hiking trails. At Grouse Mountain you can catch the Skyride gondola for mountaintop sports and attractions (6400 Nancy Greene Way; 604.984.0661; www.grousemountain.com).

Before heading into less inhabited reaches of British Columbia, you might want to take advantage of Vancouver's vibrant nightlife. The Vancouver Alliance for Arts & Culture at 938 Howe St. (604.681.3535) can tell you what is playing and how to get tickets. Or pick up a copy of the weekly Georgia Straight.

For more information, visit or contact Tourism Vancouver, 200 Burrard St.; 604.683.2000; www.tourismvancouver.com.

consists of soft mud and organic silt and the charted depths are to the top of the silt layer. (SD)

Port Moody has decent anchorage northeast of Caraholly Point in 4-5 fathoms, or 0.25 mile south of the range light at the east end of the bay in 2 fathoms. Reed Point Marina offers guest moorage with facilities that include power (20 amp), washrooms, pumpout and marine supplies and services. Best to call ahead. If you anchor out, you can dinghy in to the marina and catch public transportation along Barnett Highway into downtown Vancouver.

Photo courtesy CHS, Pacific Region

Indian Arm and Twin Islands

Anchor (Carholly Pt) in 4-5 fathoms over mud and silt with good holding.

Anchor (0.25 mi S of the range light) in 2 fathoms over mud and silt with good holding.

⚓ **Reed Point Marina** tel: 604.937.1600; website; www.reedpoint.com; email: office@reedpoint.com; fuel; restrooms

Indian Arm

Chart 3495; 8 mi E of Lions Gate Bridge
Entrance (0.45 mi E of Roche Pt): 49°17.97'N, 122°56.69'W

Indian Arm, entered between Roche Point and Admiralty Point, 1.2 miles east, extends 11 miles north. It is deep and underwater hazards are few.

Indian Arm is entirely different in its character from other portions of Burrard Inlet. It is enclosed on both sides by rugged mountains rising to elevations of 600 to 1,500 m (2,000 to 5,000 ft). During spring and summer months melting snow falls in foaming cascades down the mountain sides rendering the surface water in the arm nearly fresh.

The area south of Boulder Islands is a designated anchorage for merchant ships waiting for a berth in Vancouver or Port Moody. (SD)

Indian Arm is a gem that offers Vancouver boaters a retreat reminiscent of the steep-sided fjords found farther north. Here, visiting skippers can focus on high peaks and long ridges with waterfalls and cascades instead of worrying about the busy port traffic of downtown Vancouver.

Deep Cove (Indian Arm)

Chart 3495; 1.8 mi N of the Indian Arm entrance
Entrance: 49°19.74'N, 122°56.19'W
Yacht Club floats: 49°19.67'N, 122°56.78'W

Several stores, restaurants and a laundromat are available and there is a direct highway connection with Vancouver.

The public wharf and float, at the head of the cove, are for loading and unloading only ... The Deep Cove Yacht Club floats are close north of the public wharf.

Marina facilities are located in Deep Cove. (SD)

Deep Cove was a popular cruising destination but, alas, the place has been over-loved and a number of restrictions on speed, mooring, etc. are presently in effect.

Belcarra (Indian Arm)

Chart 3495; at the S end of Belcarra Bay; 0.3 mi NE of Boulder I
Entrance: 49°18.84'N, 122°55.88'W
Public pier: 49°18.79'N, 122°55.73'W

[Belcarra] *has a pier and floats with a depth of 2.4 m (8 ft) alongside leading off a park.*

Belcarra National Park has picnic facilities and a public telephone. (SD)

Cozy Cove (Indian Arm)

Chart 3495; 0.8 mi NE of Turtle Head
Position: 49°19.70'N, 122°55.13'W

Cozy Cove is a tiny bight with private piers and offers little shelter for cruising boats.

Bedwell Bay, 0.7 miles southeast, provides well-sheltered anchorage.

Bedwell Bay (Indian Arm)

Chart 3495; on the E side of Indian Arm; 0.6 mi E of Turtle Head
Entrance (0.43 mi SE of Jug I): 49°19.76'N, 122°54.26'W
Anchor: 49°18.98'N, 122°55.06'W

Bedwell Bay is entered east of Jug Island. A drying reef extends NE from its west entrance point. The bay provides one of the few good anchorages in Indian Arm. In winter months the anchorage is exposed to the occasional strong NE winds. (SD)

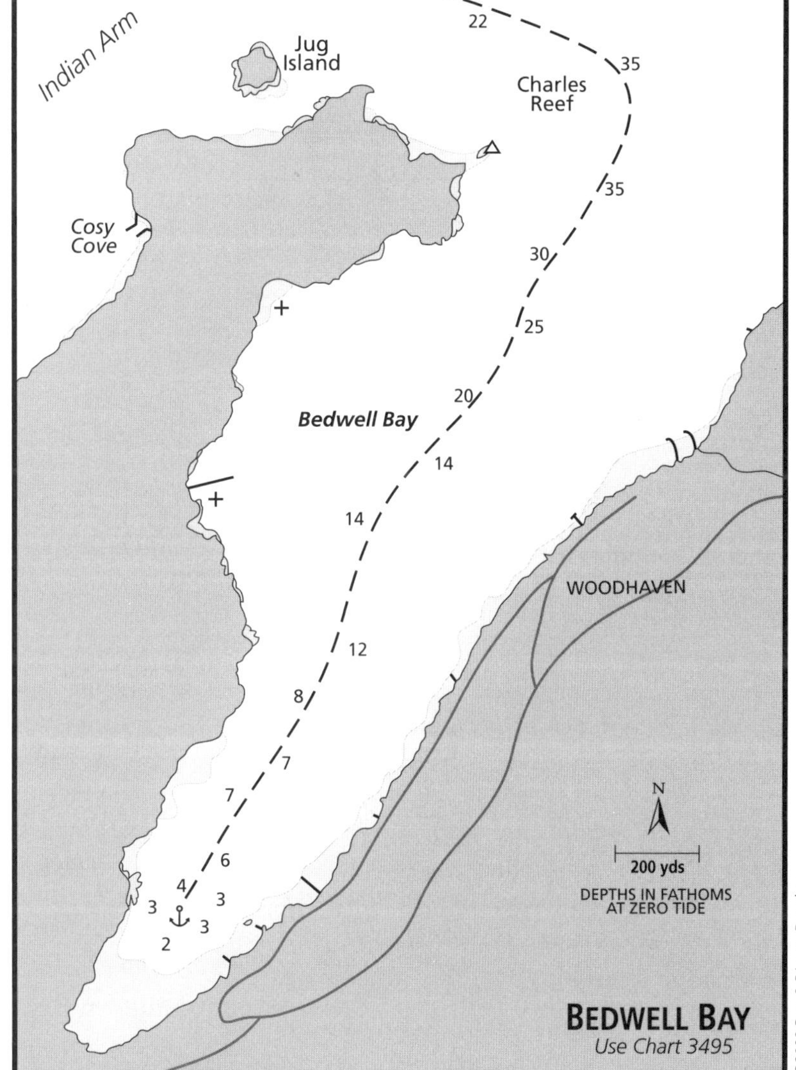

Caught in irons

Because Bedwell Bay is the most protected anchorage in Indian Arm and has easy access, it is a popular cruising anchorage.

Good protection from southeast winds can be found in the head of the cove. For protection from northeast winds, you can use Farrer Cove one mile north.

Anchor in 3 to 5 fathoms over a mud bottom with good holding.

Vancouver traffic calls for careful navigation

Farrer Cove (Indian Arm)

Chart 3495; 0.9 mi NE of Bedwell Bay
Entrance (0.06 mi S of Belvedere Rock): 49°20.13′N, 122°53.52′W
Anchor: 49°20.14′N, 122°53.33′W

> *Farrer Cove, NE of Bedwell Bay, is fronted by Belvedere Rock, a shoal area with less than 2 m (6 ft) over it.*
>
> *Anchorage can be obtained at the south end of Farrer Cove.* (SD)

Farrer Cove is a shallow bight in the east side of Indian Arm. Steep bluffs on its north side provide fair-to-good protection from downslope winds.

Anchor in 4 fathoms off the sand and gravel beach; holding is unknown.

Racoon Island (Indian Arm Marine Park)

Chart 3495; is 0.7 mi N of Bedwell Bay
Anchor (Racoon Island): 49°20.53′N, 122°54.24′W

> *Indian Arm Marine Park comprises Racoon Island and Twin Islands. Information shelters are on the south shores of the south Twin Island and Racoon Island. The largest Twin Island, with a dinghy float on its east side, has picnic and sanitary facilities.* (SD)

Indian Arm Marine Park, in the center of the inlet, is a favorite picnic site and a good place to explore by dinghy or kayak. Temporary anchorage can be taken off the north end of Racoon Island, but avoid the two drying rocks close off the northwest shore. The island is steep-to with a small shoal on its north side.

Anchor in about 1 fathom over an unrecorded bottom.

Twin Islands (Indian Arm Marine Park)

Chart 3495; 0.5 mi NE of Racoon Island
Position: 49°20.88′N, 122°53.48′W

> *Twin Islands close off the east shore ... are joined by a drying isthmus. The channel east of the islands can be used by small craft. A rock, which dries 1.5 m (5 ft), lies close inshore at the north end of the channel.* (SD)

White shell beaches and numerous tidepools make this a favorite place to explore by kayak or canoe.

Buntzen Bay (Indian Arm)

Chart 3495; on the E side of Indian Arm; 0.6 mi E of Best Pt
Entrance: 49°22.93′N, 122°51.92′W

> *Buntzen Bay ... is about 2.3 miles NNE of Twin Islands and has several private floats.*
>
> *Caution should be exercised when approaching the power houses as the gates may be opened, without warning, to discharge huge volumes of water.* (SD)

Buntzen Bay, a shallow bight on the east side of Indian Arm, is too deep for convenient anchorage.

Granite Falls, Fairy Falls (Indian Arm)

Chart 3495 inset; 9.9 mi NE of the entrance to Indian Arm; 0.35 mi NW of Croker Island
Granite Falls Light: 49°26.95′N, 122°51.79′W

> *Granite Falls, on the east side of the arm abreast the north end of Croker Island, is the site of Fairy Falls, a conspicuous waterfall.* (SD)

Fairy Falls is a major attraction of Indian Arm. Its location on the east side of the arm means that it enjoys sunny afternoons. Temporary anchorage in fair weather only can be taken on the Grand Creek delta off the grassy flat, as close in as tide and weather allow.

West Bay (Burrard Inlet)

Chart 3481; 2.3 mi E of Pt Atkinson
Entrance (launch ramp): 49°20.36'N, 123°12.40'W

West Bay has a launching ramp. (SD)

Sandy Cove (Burrard Inlet)

Chart 3481; 1.5 mi NE of Pt Atkinson
Entrance: 49°20.43'N, 123°13.86'W

The two shallow bights immediately east of Point Atkinson—Pilot and Sandy coves—afford some protection close to shore from strong northerlies. The Pacific Environment Institute, located in Sandy Cove, owns the berthing facilities.

Pilot Cove (Burrard Inlet)

Chart 3481; 0.8 mi NE of Pt Atkinson
Entrance: 49°20.52'N, 123°14.43'W

Pilot Cove has a drying sand bank extending 0.1 mile offshore. (SD)

Pilot Cove is used by sportfishing boats for temporary anchorage in fair weather.

Caulfeild Cove (Burrard Inlet)

Chart 3481; 0.6 mi NE of Pt Atkinson
Entrance: 49°20.20'N, 123°15.21'W
Anchor: 49°20.25'N, 123°15.25'W

Caulfeild Cove has a public float, 12 m (40 ft) long with a depth of about 1.8 m (6 ft) alongside, on its east shore. Numerous private mooring buoys lie in the cove. (SD)

Caulfeild Cove is a small indentation east of Point Atkinson. If you need a place to catch your breath after having survived Vancouver Harbour, this is a good place to stop temporarily.

A quiet anchorage

Starboat Cove (Burrard Inlet)

Chart 3481; 0.2 mi NE of Pt Atkinson
Entrance: 49°19.89'N, 123°15.64'W

Starboat Cove has a rock, with 0.3 m (1 ft) over it, in its entrance. A rock, which dries 1.2 m (4 ft), lies close inshore off the east entrance point to the cove. (SD)

Point Atkinson

Chart 3481; 3.9 mi N of Pt Grey & 6.2 mi W of Lions Gate Bridge
Pt Atkinson Light: 49°19.82'N, 123°15.88'W

Point Atkinson, the north entrance point of Burrard Inlet, is moderately steep-to. Caution.—Strong tide-rips, caused by the meeting of the tidal streams from Burrard Inlet and Howe Sound, frequently occur off the point. When a strong ebb tide is running against a westerly wind a nasty short chop can be experienced along the north shore between Point Atkinson and First Narrows. (SD)

Point Atkinson features a classic and picturesque lighthouse on its rocky point. The 185-acre lighthouse park extends to both sides of the point. It is well known for its stand of large Douglas fir and its 8 miles of hiking trails.

Howe Sound

Chart 3526; immediately NW of Burrard Inlet; lies in a SW/NE direction; extends 23 mi from Bowen I to Squamish
Pt Atkinson Light: 49°19.82'N, 123°15.88'W

Howe Sound is entered between Point Atkinson and Gower Point, 11 miles WNW. Several Islands divide the entrance to Howe Sound into four main channels, named from east to west, Queen Charlotte Channel, Collingwood Channel, Barfleur Passage and Shoal Channel.

The sound is almost entirely hemmed in by rugged, precipitous mountains rising abruptly from the water's edge. There are few anchorages in Howe Sound due to great depths and lack of protected bays. (SD)

Haida Brave, *with load of logs, dominates shipping lanes*

Beautiful Howe Sound is much like the fjords and inlets found farther to the north; because it is well-sheltered, you can practice the cruising skills you need for exploring the more remote inlets of northern British Columbia.

Town facilities are readily available along the West Vancouver shore, and Bowen Island is ringed with small coves and bays where you can try out your anchoring skills close to a friendly shore. Be watchful of fast-moving ferryboats leaving and entering Horseshoe Bay and other local traffic that comes in all sizes.

Many of the coves in Howe Sound are filled with private floats and mooring buoys and are crowded in the summer. The lovely beaches in the sound are a draw for exploration by dinghy or kayak. The area north of Gambier and Anvil islands has less traffic and can provide excellent and leisurely sailing.

In winter, Howe Sound is often the "home" of strong, cold north winds and williwaws.

Queen Charlotte Channel

Chart 3526; immediately NW of Burrard Inlet, entered btwn Atkinson & Cowan Pts
Entrance (SE, 0.8 mi NW of Pt Atkinson): 49°20.00′N, 123°17.10′W
Entrance (SW, 0.8 mi SE of Pt Cowan): 49°20.00′N, 123°20.50′W
Entrance (N mid-ch btwn Finisterre Island Light & Bowyer Island): 49°25.25′N, 123°17.55′W

Queen Charlotte Channel separates Bowen Island from the mainland to the east ... the channel extends north to Bowyer Island.

Caution. Strong tide-rips frequently occur off Point Atkinson; they are caused by the meeting of the tidal streams from Burrard Inlet and Howe Sound. (SD)

Eagle Harbour (Queen Charlotte Channel)

Chart 3534 inset; 1.3 mi N of Pt Atkinson
Entrance (0.03 mi S of bkw light): 49°21.12′N, 123°16.19′W

Eagle Harbour has a floating breakwater with a private light on its south extremity. The breakwater extends from the NW entrance point. A yacht club with small craft floats lies on the north side of the harbour and numerous private mooring buoys are in the harbour. (SD)

Fishermans Cove (Queen Charlotte Ch)

Chart 3534 inset; on the N side of Eagle Island, 0.25 mi NW of Eagle Hbr
Entrance: 49°21.23′N, 123°16.70′W

Fishermans Cove, north of Eagle Harbour, can be entered east or NW of Eagle Island. The entrance channel NW of Eagle Island is 20 m (66 ft) wide and has a least depth of 1.2 m (4 ft). The entrance east of Eagle Island has a least depth of 0.6 m (2 ft). (SD)

Fishermans Cove is the site of West Vancouver Yacht Club.

Larsen Bay (Queen Charlotte Channel)

Chart 3481; 0.6 NW of Eagle Island
Entrance: 49°21.66'N, 123°17.14'W

Larsen Bay ... is entered between Batchelor Point and Kettle Point. (SD)

Submarine cables cross Queen Charlotte Sound commencing on the east shore from Larsen Bay, Batchelor Cove, Cliff Cove, and Copper Cove. (SD)

Larsen Bay is the home of the Gleneagles Golf and Country Club with its many amenities. The bay is exposed to southwest winds and chop. Temporary anchorage can be found avoiding the cable area in the center of the bay.

Batchelor Cove (Queen Charlotte Channel)

Chart 3481; 0.4 mi SE of Lookout Pt Light
Entrance: 49°22.07'N, 123°17.39'W
Anchor: 49°22.25'N, 123°17.18'W

Travelling companions, securely rafted

Batchelor Cove is entered between Bird Islet and Whyte Islet, 0.4 mile north ... Temporary anchorage can be obtained at the head of Batchelor Cove. (SD)

Anchor in about 4 fathoms.

Whyte Cove (Queen Charlotte Channel)

Chart 3481; 0.35 mi SW of Lookout Pt Light
Entrance: 49°22.25'N, 123°17.62'W

Whyte Cove lies between Whyte Islet and White Cliff Point. Whytecliff Park, at the head of the cove, has picnic and sanitary facilities. Numerous private mooring buoys lie in the cove.

Whyte Cove has a municipal park with a trail which goes to a lookout atop Whyte Cliff Point and on to Cliff Cove. The Whytecliff Marina is located at the northwest corner of the cove and the five rows of mooring buoys are private. Temporary anchorage may be found on the south side of the mooring buoys, avoiding the steep-to channel west of Whyte Islet.

Cliff Cove (Queen Charlotte Channel)

Chart 3481; 0.4 mi NE of Whyte Cove
Entrance (immediately E of Lookout Pt): 49°22.60'N, 123°17.29'W

An underwater reserve extends from Whyte Islet to Cliff Cove. Spearfishing and removal of specimens are prohibited in this area. (SD)

Disturbing or removing specimens from this underwater reserve is forbidden. Some temporary protection may be available in southeast conditions.

Copper Cove (Queen Charlotte Channel)

Chart 3481; immediately W of Horseshoe Bay
Entrance (0.24 mi SW of Tyee Pt Light): 49°22.77'N, 123°16.76'W

Copper Cove lies 0.4 mile ENE of Lookout Point. (SD)

Copper Cove, a shallow bight, affords some temporary shelter from southeast winds in about 1 fathom or you can seek temporary moorage or anchorage in Horseshoe Bay immediately east of Tyee Point.

A lovely South Coast anchorage

Horseshoe Bay (Queen Charlotte Ch)

Chart 3534 inset; 2.8 mi N of Pt Atkinson
Entrance (0.08 mi E of Tyee Pt Light):
49°22.83'N, 123°16.28'W

> *The public wharf, with floats attached to its end and west sides, is at the head of the bay.*
>
> *Close NW of the public wharf is a marina protected by two barge breakwaters.* (SD)

Horseshoe Bay, in West Vancouver, houses the terminal of the Nanaimo ferry and the ferries that service the Sunshine Coast. Limited moorage is available at Sewell's Marina, southeast of the small public dock. Anchoring is not recommended in the bay due to all the traffic.

⚓ **Sewell's Marina Ltd** tel: 604.921.3474; fax: 604.921.7027; website: www.sewellsmarina.com; fuel; power

Bowen Island, South Coast

Chart 3526; Five small coves lie immediately W of Pt Cowan on the S coast of Bowen Island—Alder Cove, Konishi Bay, Arbutus Bay, Echo Cove & Fairweather Bay
Position (Alder Cove, 0.3 mi W of Pt Cowan):
49°29.16'N, 123°21.90'W
Entrance (Konishi Bay, 0.19 mi W of Pt Cowan):
49°20.13'N, 123°21.97'W
Entrance (Arbutus Bay, 0.37 mi W of Pt Cowan):
49°20.10'N, 123°22.19'W
Entrance (Echo Cove,0.63 mi W of Pt Cowan):
49°20.05'N, 123°22.60'W
Entrance (Fairweather Bay, 0.82 mi W of Pt Cowan): 49°20.04'N, 123°22.91'W

> *The south coast of Bowen Island is steep-to and cliffy. It is indented by several small coves and bays named, from east to west, Alder Cove, Konishi Bay, Arbutus Bay, Echo Cove and Fairweather Bay. Drying and sunken rocks lie in the above-mentioned coves and bays.* (SD)

The rugged coastline 1 mile west of Point Cowan has five tiny coves that can provide a temporary stopping place for small craft in fair weather only.

Bowen Island, Southeast Coast

Chart 3526
Entrance (Union Cove, 0.09 mi NE of Pt Cowan): 49°20.21'N, 123°21.58'W
Entrance (Trinity Bay, 0.19 mi NE of Pt Cowan):
49°20.28'N, 123°21.48'W
Entrance (Seymour Bay, 0.50 mi NE of Pt Cowan): 49°20.56'N, 123°21.23'W
Entrance (Apodaca Cove, 1.3 mi NE of Pt Cowan): 49°21.14'N, 123°20.36'W

> *Union Cove and Trinity Bay lie close NE of Point Cowan.*
>
> *Seymour Bay, the most protected bay at this end of* [Bowen Island], *is exposed to ferry wash.*
>
> *Apodaca Cove, 1.3 miles NE of Point Cowan, offers anchorage and shelter from westerly weather. Apodaca Provincial Park, on the north side of the cove, is a nature reserve.* (SD)

Small craft can find temporary shelter from westerlies in Union Cove and Trinity Bay, but both are open to easterlies and ferry wake. Apodaca Cove is a small, shallow bight, exposed to southerly winds and channel wake. You can walk from the 20-acre Apodaca Provincial Park to Snug Cove, 2 miles to the north. If you want to wait out an ebb tide against the northwesterly or make a lunch stop, you can find temporary anchorage in Seymour Bay, tucked behind the rocky point.

Dorman Bay (Bowen Island)

Chart 3534 inset; 0.3 mi SE of Snug Cove
Entrance: 49°22.50'N, 123°19.50'W

> *Dorman Bay, 1.5 miles NNE of Apodaca Cove, offers anchorage and shelter from westerly weather.* (SD)

Photo courtesy CHS, Pacific Region

Snug Cove

Although it is deep, steep-to, and open to southerlies and channel wake, Dorman Bay can provide temporary anchorage in fair weather if you tuck in close to shore. Under these conditions, it can be used as an alternative to busy and crowded Snug Cove or Mannion Bay.

Snug Cove (Bowen Island)
Chart 3534 inset; 2.2 mi W of Horseshoe Bay
Entrance: 49°22.87'N, 123°19.46'W

Bowen Island

Bowen Island, eight nautical miles northwest of Vancouver, has been welcoming visitors for more than a century. In 1900, Captain John Cates developed the area around Snug Cove with amusements to tempt mainlanders, and they've been coming ever since.

The island was named in 1860 for James Bowen, master of the HMS *Queen Charlotte* (replacing an earlier Spanish name, the Isles of Apodaca). But long before Europeans arrived, the island had been used for hunting and fishing by the Squamish First Nations.

Now the forested island has about 3,000 year-round residents, many of whom commute to work on the mainland. In summer, another 1,500 people move in. And since it's only a 20-minute ferry ride from Horseshoe Bay, daytrippers come over to enjoy the relaxed atmosphere.

Boaters can tie up to a busy dock or anchor in one of its many coves and bights and go ashore by dinghy. Be on the lookout for deer, seals, grouse, bald eagles, blue herons and other island wildlife.

Most of Bowen's commerce is near Snug Cove, dominated by the Union Steamship Company Marina. There's no fuel here, but there are showers, laundry facilities and chandlery. Roam around the complex's lawns and orchards and the restored Union Steamship Company Store.

You can pick up a map to help plan your activities at the Chamber of Commerce Visitor Info Centre on Cardena Drive, the first right as you leave the ferry dock. Then walk up Government Street to cafés and shops.

Artisan Square is a 15-minute walk from the ferry dock, or you can hop on a shuttle bus for a quick ride. See Arts and Crafts-style architecture, gardens and artists' studios. There's an eclectic mix of services here, including a yoga studio and veterinarian.

If you have more time to spend, you can rent a kayak at the Bowen Island Sea Kayaking shop at the Bowen Island Marina, also tucked into Snug Cove. Choose a guided tour, or strike out on your own. Rent tandem or mountain bikes to explore the wooded island. Some of them have small motors to help you navigate the hilly roads.

An easy hike goes from the 600-acre Crippen Regional Park through rainforest to Bridal Veil Falls and on to Killarney Lake. Another trail leads from the picnic grounds at the head of Snug Cove to Dorman Point. More strenuous is the 7-mile Mt. Gardner Trail which climbs to the 2,480-foot summit where you're rewarded with spectacular views of Vancouver and the Strait of Georgia.

Learn about Bowen's history at two museums, the Cottage Museum in Davies Orchard, or the Bowen Island Historians Community Museum and Archives at the corner of Government and Miller. Summer hours are 10 to 4.

Have dinner at the Tuscany Café, Doc Morgan's Inn or Blue Eyed Mary's Bistro. You can spend a night ashore in a cottage at the marina, or in a bed-and-breakfast. There are no hotels or campgrounds.

See www.bowenisland.org for more information and a downloadable guide.

Although narrow, Snug Cove offers excellent shelter and anchorage to small craft, in a depth of about 17 m (56 ft). Care must be taken to keep clear of the submarine cables and the ferry route. (SD)

Snug Cove, small and well-protected from all weather, is a good place to head if a blow develops in Howe Sound. It can also offer pleasant anchoring during the off-season.

The dredged inner bay of Snug Cove is occupied by Bowen Island Marina, the government wharf, and the popular Union Steamship Marina, so the entire cove is a busy place. If you're looking for some urban entertainment, this is the place to stop. There are restaurants and shops, a nearby park with hiking and bicycling trails, and full amenities at the old Union Steamship Company landing.

⚓ **Bowen Island Marina** tel: 604.947.9710; website: www.bowen-island.com; power

⚓ **Union Steamship Company Marina** tel: 604.947.0707; fax: 604.947.0708; monitors VHF Ch 66A; website: www.ussc.ca; email: marina@ussc.ca; power; restrooms; showers; pumpout

Mannion Bay (Deep Bay) (Bowen Island)

Chart 3534 inset; immediately N of Snug Cove
Entrance: 49°23.02'N, 123°19.46'W
Anchor (S side): 49°23.00'N, 123°19.74'W
Anchor (N side): 49°23.14'N, 123°19.82'W

Mannion Bay, formerly known as Deep Bay, is north of Snug Cove. The bay is exposed and during SE weather a heavy swell rolls into it. Drying and sunken rocks lie on the south side of the bay. (SD)

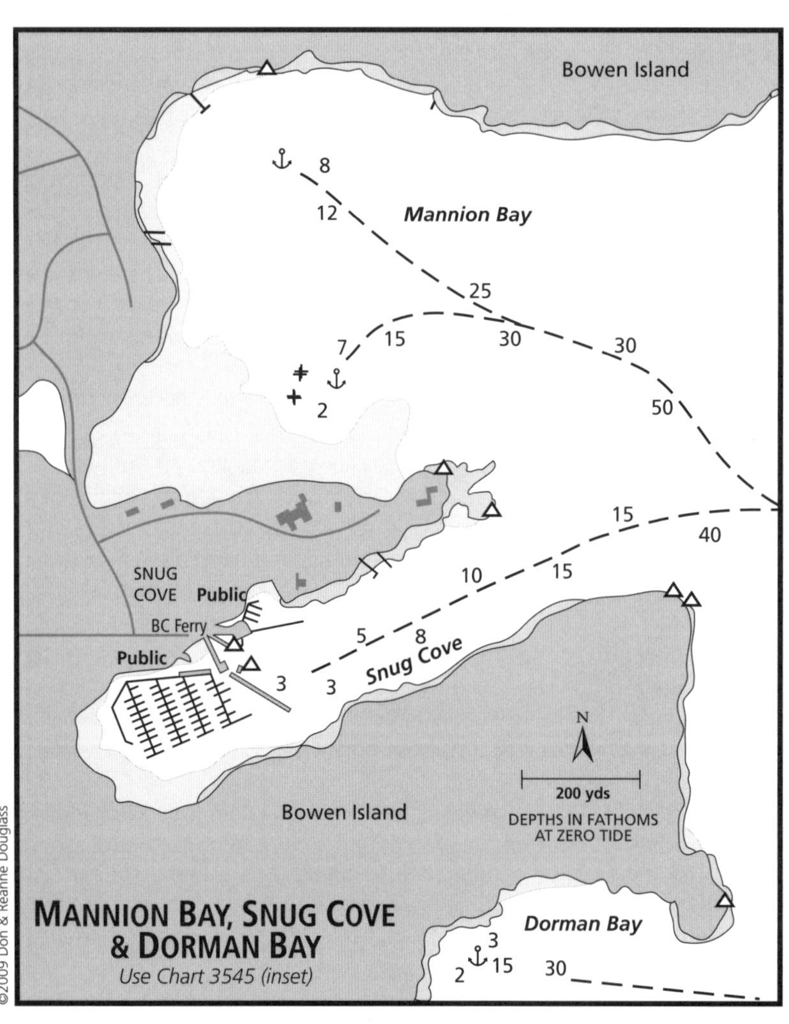

Mannion Bay is also known as Deep Bay, Hotel Bay, or simply Bowen Island. In the northern part of the bay there are a number of private buoys or boats at anchor. However, it is reported that you can find reasonable protection from southeast storms near the shallow southwestern part of the bay. The southern part is shallow and has rocks and shoals. Watch your echo sounder carefully and consult the tide tables if you approach the outlet to the creek. The beach here is one of the best on Bowen Island.

Avoid two rocks west of the principal reef at the outflow of Killarney Creek. Both anchor sites are rolly from ferry traffic and when the inflow or outflow winds are strong in the channel.

Anchor (S side) in 2 to 4 fathoms over a sandy bottom with excellent holding.

Anchor (N side) outside the mooring buoys in 8 to 12 fathoms over sand and mud with good holding.

Hood Point (Bowen Island)

Chart 3526; W of Finisterre Light, on the NE corner of Bowen Island
Entrance (Cates Bay): 49°24.87'N, 123°18.52'W
Entrance (Safety Cove): 49°24.92'N, 123°18.75'W
Entrance (Poca Cove): 49°24.98'N, 123°18.61'W
Entrance (Montevista Bay): 49°25.10'N, 123°18.64'W
Entrance (Enchanta Bay): 49°25.15'N, 123°18.78'W
Entrance (Columbine Bay): 49°25.17'N, 123°19.06'W
Entrance (Smugglers Cove): 49°24.99'N, 123°19.41'W

A peaceful sail at the end of the day

Cates Bay, Enchanta Bay, Columbine Bay and Smugglers Cove, east and west of Hood Point, provide shelter and anchorage for small craft.

A rock, which dries 3.7 m (12 ft), lies in the middle of Enchanta Bay. (SD)

Hood Point has several small and picturesque coves with curving sandy beaches. These coves offer temporary anchorage in fair weather; however, since they are subject to frequent ferry wash, you may want to anchor with your bow facing out. Anchor as close to shore as depths allow and consider using a stern anchor.

"Bowyer Island Cove" (Bowyer Island)

Chart 3526; 1.8 mi E of Hood Pt; 2.5 mi N of Horseshoe Bay
Entrance (0.1 mi N of 5-meter): 49°25.06'N, 123°16.13'W
Anchor: 49°25.17'N, 123°16.11'W

Bowyer Island, 1.5 miles ENE of Finisterre Island, has a 5.5 m (18 ft) shoal off its south end and a 2.4 m (8 ft) shoal 0.1 mile off its NW part.

The floats and moorings on the island are private. (SD)

Anchor in about 10 fathoms avoiding private mooring buoys.

Collingwood Channel

Chart 3526; W side of Bowen Is & E of Worlcombe, Pasley, & Keats Is
Entrance (S, mid-ch btwn Worlcombe I & Cape Roger Curtis): 49°20.68'N, 123°26.70'W
Entrance (N, 0.5 mi W of Hutt Island): 49°24.62'N, 123°23.87'W

Collingwood Channel ... is entered from the south between Cape Roger Curtis and Worlcombe Island 1 mile WNW; it extends north to Hutt Island. (SD)

Tunstall Bay (Bowen Island)

Chart 3526; 0.5 mi S of Bowen Bay; 1 mi NE of Cape Roger Curtis
Entrance: 49°21.17'N, 123°25.70'W

Tunstall Bay, 0.8 mile NNE of Cape Roger Curtis, has several drying rocks and an islet in its north part; the bay is too deep for anchorage. (SD)

The many mooring buoys in Tunstall Bay are private. Temporary anchorage may be found close to shore over a mud bottom avoiding these buoys.

Explosive Creek, which flows into Tunstall Bay, commemorates a dynamite plant disaster in the early part of the 20th century during which 12 men were killed in four separate explosions. The last blast was strong enough to be felt in Nanaimo.

Shelter can be found in both Tunstall and Bowen bays in strong, northerly "Squamish" weather.

Bowen Bay (Bowen Island)

Chart 3526; 1.5 mi N of Cape Roger Curtis
Entrance: 49°21.76'N, 123°25.69'W

Bowen Bay, north of Tunstall Bay, has drying rocks in its south part. A private float is in the south part of the bay. (SD)

King Edward Bay (Bowen Island)

Chart 3526; King Edward Bay is 0.4 mi N of Bowen Bay
Entrance: 49°22.21'N, 123°25.72'W

King Edward Bay is a tiny bay with private mooring buoys.

Galbraith Bay (Bowen Island)

Chart 3526; 2.7 mi SW of Hood Pt
Entrance (S, 0.18 mi NE of Hutt Rock): 49°24.25'N, 123°23.11'W
Entrance (N, 0.18 mi E of Hutt I): 49°24.62'N, 123°22.47'W

Galbraith Bay, east of Hutt Rock, has a public float, 18 m (59 ft) long with a depth of 4.6 m (15 ft) alongside. Mount Gardner locality, in the south part of the bay, is connected by road to Snug Cove, on the east side of Bowen Island. (SD)

Temporary anchorage in fair weather can be found in the nooks and behind the rocks of Galbraith Bay and the east shore of Hutt Island. Afternoon westerlies are common along this part of the coast.

The bay is at the base of 2,500-foot Mt. Gardner. Temporary moorage may be found at the small public float. Galbraith and Grafton bays are open to Squamish winds common during the winter.

Grafton Bay (Bowen Island)

Chart 3526; 2.1 mi SW of Hood Pt
Entrance: 49°24.61'N, 123°22.10'W

Grafton Bay, east of the north end of Hutt Island, is too deep for satisfactory anchorage. The floats and mooring buoys in the bay are private. (SD)

Barfleur Passage

Chart 3526; leads E & W on the S side of Keats I & N of Pasley I
Entrance (W, mid-ch btwn Popham & Home Is): 49°22.39'N, 123°29.70'W
Entrance (E, 0.4 mi SE of Keats I & 0.95 mi NE of Ragged I): 49°23.23'N, 123°25.80'W

Barfleur Passage ... is entered from the west between Popham Island and Home Island, 1.1 miles NNW. (SD)

Barfleur Passage is on the main ferry route from Horseshoe Bay to Departure Bay. Afternoon westerlies flow through Barfleur Passage into Howe Sound.

Pasley Island

Chart 3526; btwn Barfleur Passage & Collingwood Channel
Entrance (0.2 mi SE of Mickey I): 49°22.03'N, 123°27.34'W
Anchor: 49°22.18'N, 123°27.30'W

Pasley Island and the rugged, picturesque islets and rocks nearby make for some intimate exploring. Small indentations along the rocky shores can provide temporary anchorage in fair weather. The rocks and shoals are somewhat hazardous and are best seen up close from a dinghy or kayak. The notch in the northeast end of Pasley Island provides fair-weather protection, and temporary anchorage can be found among the many private mooring buoys.

Anchor in 3 to 5 fathoms over sand and mud with good holding.

Shoal Channel

Chart 3534 inset; btwn Keats I & the mainland
Entrance (S, 0.36 mi NE of Home I): 49°23.18'N, 123°30.20'W
Entrance (N, mid-ch btwn Observatory & Somas Pts): 49°24.69'N, 123°28.63'W

[Shoal Channel's] south entrance is obstructed by a bar of sand and rock with 2.1 m (7 ft) over it. The bar has depths of 1.5 m (5 ft) over a rock bottom near mid-channel with drying and sunken rocks closer inshore. The sea breaks over the bar when the wind opposes the tide. This entrance to Shoal Channel should only be used by those familiar with local conditions. (SD)

The south entrance fairway carries 1 fathom at zero tide and should be avoided during times of strong winds or currents or spring tides.

Gibsons

Chart 3534 inset; W side of Shoal Channel; 1.3 mi SW of Plumper Cove Marine Park
Entrance (0.15 mi N of Gibsons Landing Rock Light): 49°24.07'N, 123°29.92'W
Entrance (0.025 mi NE of Gibsons Landing Breakwater South Light): 49°23.97'N, 123°30.24'W
Anchor (0.125 mi NE of wharf): 49°24.12'N, 123°30.07'W

Anchorage, with good holding, can be obtained off the wharf in a depth of about 17 m (56 ft). Anchor clear of the submarine cable which lands close north of the wharf. (SD)

Gibsons is a town, on the west side of a bight, on the north side of Steep Bluff. It is a tourist resort and distributing centre for towns on the north side of the Strait of Georgia. A variety of stores, restaurants, lodging, businesses, services and postal office are available. The Sunshine Coast Museum and Archives is located in Gibsons. ...

The public wharf has floats, from 40 to 90 m long attached to it; 14 m of the sourth finger float is reserved for aircraft. Depths alongside the wharfhead are 2.4 to 6 m at the NE face, and 4.2 to 4.8 m at the SE face. Power is laid on the floats. Water, garbage and used oil disposal facilities and a 3 tonne crane are on the wharfhead. ...

Anchorage, with good holding, can be obtained off the wharf, in a depth of about 17 m, but care should be taken to keep clear of the submarine cable that lands close north of the wharf. (SD)

Gibsons, once just a village where people on their way north or south Highway 101 hardly give it a nod, has become a tourist destination in itself. The town is now lined with smart boutiques, cafés, a new park above the strait and possibilities for pleasure-croft moorage–GIbsons Marina, behind the breakwater, and Gibsons Landing Harbour Authority.

Anchorage may be available 300 yards northeast of the Harbour Authority pier, but we would recommend tying up at one of the marina. Both marinas advise calling ahead for space availability.

Anchor in 5 fathoms with fair-to-good holding.

⚓ **Gibsons Marina** tel: 604.886.8686; monitors VHF Ch 66A; power; restrooms; showers; laundry; pumpout

⚓ **Gibsons Landing Harbour Authority** tel: 604.887.8017; monitors VHF Ch 66A; email: GLHA@telus.net; power; restrooms; showers; laundry; pumpout

Settlement of Keats Island (Shoal Ch)

Charts 3534, 3536; on the W side of Keats I
Public wharf: 49°23.68'N, 123°29.03'W

Keats Island settlement ... consists mainly of summer homes with private floats. A public wharf and float, with a depth of 4 m (13 ft) alongside, and a launching ramp are at the settlement. Water taxi service is available to Gibsons. (SD)

Plumper Cove & Plumper Cove Marine Park

Chart 3534 inset; 1.3 mi NE of Gibsons
Entrance (N, mid-ch btwn Shelter Islets & Observatory Pt): 49°24.30'N, 123°28.51'W
Entrance (S, 0.08 mi S of Shelter Islets): 49°23.97'N, 123°28.70'W
Anchor: 49°24.11'N, 123°28.50'W

Plumper Cove, entered north of Shelter Islets, is a snug anchorage; however hard it may be blowing in the Strait of Georgia it is usually calm in the cove.

Anchorage can be obtained in the middle of Plumper Cove, in a depth of 13 to 15 m (43 to 49 ft), and though small vessels could lie at single anchor it is recommended to moor with two anchors.

Plumper Cove Marine Park, in the NE part of Plumper cove, has public floats, mooring buoys, drinking water, camping and picnic facilities and garbage disposal. (SD)

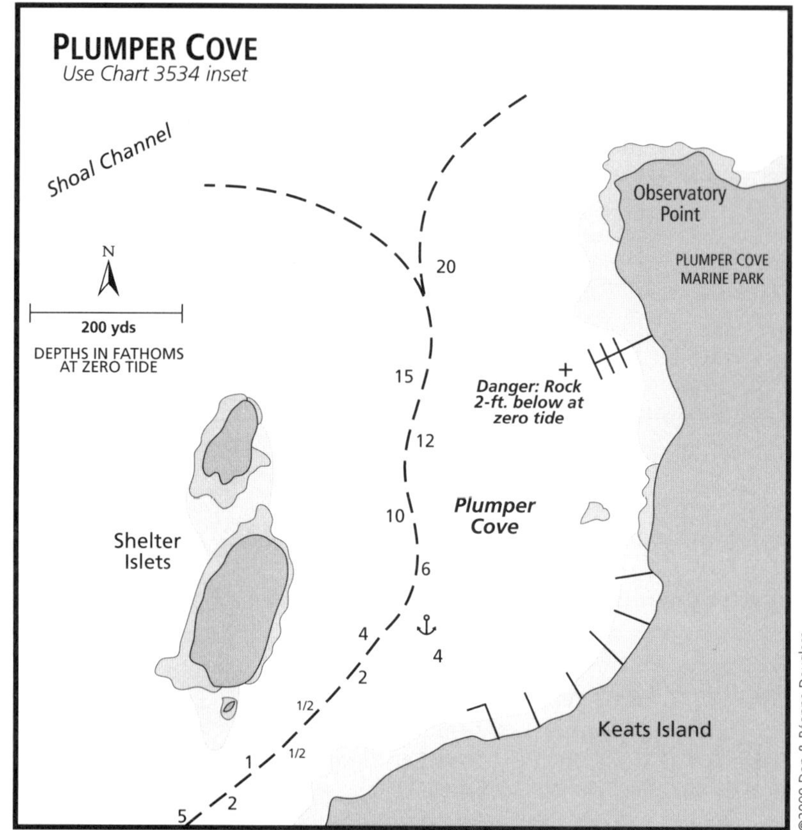

Due to its scenic qualities and good protection, Plumper Cove is a popular summer cruising destination. In the northeast corner of the cove is Plumper Cove Marine Park which offers public floats and a grassy picnic area; trails lead to a camping area and through woods that were formerly an apple orchard. Hike to the top of Lookout Mountain (795 ft.) or Stony Hill (710 ft.) for a view of the area.

Public floats in the park offer moorage for a dozen or so small boats and they are used primarily in summer for boats that don't carry a dinghy. There is a dangerous charted rock with only 2 feet of water over it at zero tide about 25 yards directly off the public float, as well as a reef awash about 200 yards to the south-southeast. The spit to Shelter Islets that carries about 3 feet of water at zero tide can be crossed by dinghies and kayaks at all tides and by small craft at adequate tide levels.

The entire bay is relatively shallow and makes for good anchoring. Shelter Islets sometimes have logbooms moored on their east side. The islets reduce the southwest swell and make Plumper Cove one of the most comfortable anchorages in Howe Sound. Anchorage can be taken anywhere north of the shallow spit that leads to Shelter Islets in a depth which pleases the skipper.

Anchor in 4 fathoms over a sand and mud bottom with very good holding.

Halkett Bay (Gambier Island)

Chart 3526; on the E side of Gambier I; 5 mi NW of Horseshoe Bay
Entrance: 49°26.71′N, 123°19.71′W
Anchor: 49°27.22′N, 123°19.50′W

Halkett Bay ... is the east and smallest of the four indentations on the south side of Gambier Island.

A public wharf and float are in the small cove close west of Halkett Bay. (SD)

Halkett Bay offers well-protected anchorage deep in the bay; avoid the numerous rocks and shoals on the west shore. There are two submerged rocks mid-bay at center left (shown as a single rock on the chart) with less than 6 feet of water over them. Halkett Bay, except for the east shore, is part of undeveloped Halkett Bay Marine Park.

Anchor in 2 to 5 fathoms at the head of the bay.

Port Graves (Gambier Island)

Chart 3526; 1.6 mi NW of Halkett Bay
Entrance (0.28 mi S of Gambier Pt): 49°27.00'N, 123°22.40'W
Position (East Bay): 49°27.41'N, 123°22.32'W
Position (Mitchell Cove): 49°27.62'N, 123°22.01'W
Anchor: 49°28.33'N, 123°21.25'W

> *Port Graves is the principal anchorage in Howe Sound. ...*
>
> *Anchorage can be obtained north of Potts Point ... ; a good position is between 0.5 and 0.7 mile north of Potts Point in a depth of 13 m (43 ft). It has been reported that the bottom is littered with sunken logs, cables and chains which have a tendency to snag anchors.* (SD)

An undesirable bottom notwithstanding, Port Graves offers good shelter with easy access under all conditions. A good small-boat anchorage can be found near the head of the bay; avoid the numerous logbooms. However, some boats prefer to tie to the logbooms rather than anchoring.

East Bay, also known locally as Daisy Bay, is 0.24 mile northeast of Gambier Point and Mitchell Cove is 0.52 mile northeast of Gambier Point.

Along with Port Graves, Centre Bay and West Bay offer well-sheltered anchorage and are easily accessible as cruising destinations from Vancouver.

Anchor in 4 fathoms, sand bottom, with caution noted above.

Centre Bay (Gambier Island)

Chart 3526; 0.9 mi W of Port Graves
Entrance (0.35 mi W of Gambier Pt): 49°27.25'N, 123°23.10'W

> *Centre Bay ... is entered between Gambier Point and Carmelo Point. Alexandra Island lies on the west side of the bay 0.8 mile within the entrance. An above-water rock and a rock, which dries 2.1 m (7 ft), lie close off the east shore of Alexandra Island.*
>
> *Yacht clubs have floats on the west side of Alexandra Island, on the east shore opposite Alexandra Island, and at the head of the bay. All facilities are private, for members only.* (SD)

Centre Bay is well sheltered from all weather; however, the bay is deep and anchorage can be found close to shore only.

Readers respond that the nook on the west shore, south of Alexandra Island, offers good shelter in an inflow wind with room for three or four boats using stern ties, or food swinging room for one boat.

West Bay (Gambier Island)

Chart 3526; entered W of Carmelo Pt
Entrance (0.6 mi NW of Carmelo Pt): 49°27.40'N, 123°24.79'W
Public float (Whispering Creek): 49°27.58'N, 123°25.06'W

> [West Bay] *is partially obstructed by above-water and drying rocks a short distance within the entrance but a clear channel, 0.1 mile wide, lies along the west shore. Both sides of the bay are booming grounds and the entrance may be blocked off by logbooms.*
>
> *A summer resort is on the west side of the entrance to West Bay. A public float, 6 by 15 m (20 by 50 ft) with a shed on it, is attached to a long approach gangway.* (SD)

West Bay is another of the well-sheltered bays on the south end of Gambier Island. It is steep-to and, as logbooms diminish, good anchorage can be found in deep waters by using a stern shore tie.

Gambier Harbour (Gambier Island)

Chart 3526; 2.8 mi NE of Plumper Cove & 3.5 mi SW of Port Graves
Public floats: 49°26.36'N, 123°25.92'W

> *Gambier Harbour, near the SW point of Gambier Island, is very exposed and bad weather conditions can develop quickly in this area. A public wharf, with depths of 3 to 4.6 m (10 to 15 ft)*

alongside, has two floats, each 18 m (60 ft) long, attached to its west side. A store is near the wharf. (SD)

Gambier Harbour is a small exposed bight with no protection from southeast weather. Avalon Bay, 0.5 mile to the southwest, affords the closest lee in case of southeasterlies. Plumper Cove or Port Graves offer better shelter in southeast storms.

The security of a safe anchorage

Thornbrough Channel

Chart 3526; on the W side of Gambier Island
Entrance (S, 0.44 mi W of Grace Is Lt): 49°25.84′N, 123°27.57′W
Entrance (N, 1.1 mi NW of Ekins Pt Lt): 49°32.60′N, 123°21.30′W

Thornbrough Channel, on the west side of Howe Sound, leads west and north of Gambier Island.

Grace Islands, the SE entrance point of Thornbrough Channel, are connected to one another by a drying ledge and fringed by drying and sunken rocks. (SD)

Langdale

Chart 3526; 2.4 mi NE of Gibsons
Ferry terminal: 49°26.03′N, 123°28.31′W

Langdale ... is the site of the B.C. Ferries terminal for the ferry from Horseshoe Bay. A large Salvation Army summer camp is in this vicinity. (SD)

Thornbrough Bay (New Brighton floats) (Gambier Island)

Chart 3526; 1.2 mi N of Grace Is Lt
Entrance: 49°26.90′N, 123°26.70′W
Eharf (public): 49°26.99′N, 123°26.45′W
Position (Burgess Cove, 0.6 mi N of Grace Is Lt): 49°26.44′N, 123°26.77′W

Thornbrough Bay ... has several private floats and small mooring buoys in it. A rock, which dries 2.4 m (8 ft), lies close inshore at the head of the bay.

New Brighton, a settlement at the head of Thornbrough Bay, has a public wharf, with a depth of 8.2m (27 ft.) alongside, to which are attached two floats for the use of small craft. (SD)

The New Brighton government floats are used for water taxis and local residents.

Burgess Cove, a small shallow bight, is found 0.6 mile to the southwest of New Brighton floats. It has a submarine cable and is of little interest.

⚓ **New Brighton Public Wharf**
groceries; restaurant

Andys Bay (Gambier Island)

Chart 3526; 3.35 mi N of Grace Is Lt
Float: 49°29.20′N, 123°26.61′W

Andys Bay, NE of Mariners Rest, has a float; diesel fuel, gasoline and fresh water are obtainable.

Booming grounds with mooring buoys are in Andys Bay. (SD)

"Christie Cove" (Christie Creek, Plowden Bay)

Chart 3526; 1 mi N of Woolridge Island on the W shore of Thornbrough Channel
Entrance: 49°32.13′N, 123°27.22′W
Anchor: 49°32.12′N, 123°27.30′W
Position (Plowden Bay): 49°31.91′N, 123°27.85′W

The small bight 0.4 mile ENE of Plowden Bay is known locally as Christie Creek. (SD)

Although Christie Cove is sometimes used for

logboom storage, when it's vacant this picturesque spot can be used to advantage by a couple of boats using shore ties. Open to northerly winds, Christie Cove can be hazardous in winter williwaws or Squamish winds. Swinging room is limited and a shore tie (ties) may be useful. Anchor near the center of the cove.

Plowden Bay, a booming ground, is part of the Port Mellon industrial complex, 1 mile to the southwest.

A shallow-water anchorage

Ekins Point (landing)

Chart 3526; 0.33 mi SW of Ekins Pt Light
Entrance: 49°31.97'N, 123°23.26'W

> *Ekins Point (landing) ... is the site of a yacht club which has two sets of floats. These floats are for members only.* (SD)

A Provincial Recreation Reserve extends along the shore on either side of Ekins Point, offering hiking and picnicking opportunities.

Douglas Bay (Gambier Island)

Chart 3526; on the NW side of Gambier I; 1.3 mi SE of Ekins Pt Light
Position: 49°31.14'N, 123°21.34'W

> *Douglas Bay is 2 miles NW of Brigade Bay ... Care should be taken in Douglas Bay to avoid the drying rock and shallows extending from the mouth of Gambier Creek.* (SD)

Temporary anchorage can be found in a small bight just off the Gambier Creek shoal.

Brigade Bay (Gambier Island)

Chart 3526; on the W side of Gambier I; 2.3 mi N of Halkett Bay; 3.2 mi SE of Ekins Pt Light
Entrance: 49°29.34'N, 123°19.92'W

> *Brigade Bay, on the west side of [Ramillies Channel], is 1.3 miles west of Pam Rock ... Temporary anchorage is possible in the south part of Brigade Bay and in Douglas Bay.* (SD)

Other than mild outflow conditions, Brigade Bay is not advised for adequate protection. During a "Squamish", the wind funnels through Montagu Channel, swings along the southeast shore of Anvil Island and across Christie Islet, pinning boats on a lee shore.

Anvil Island

Chart 3526; btwn Ramillies & Montague Chs; 8.5 mi N of Horseshoe Bay
Entrance (N bight): 49°31.59'N, 123°17.28'W
Entrance (S bight, Fern Bay): 49°31.19'N, 123°17.42'W

> *Reasonable small craft anchorage can be obtained in about 10 m (33 ft), sand and mud bottom, on the north and south sides of a small peninsula extending from the SE side of Anvil Island.* (SD)

For city-dwellers desiring to get away, Anvil Island offers fair-weather anchorage north and south of the anvil-shaped peninsula on the east side. The peninsula offers shelter from south winds in the north bight, while the south bight (called Fern Bay) offers shelter from north outflow or Squamish winds.

Skippers with imagination can also find temporary anchorage close along the pebble shore around Irby Point on either side of Daybreak Point. Pay attention to local wind and tide conditions and use the rocks and islets to your advantage.

Cruising the quiet waters

Porteau Cove Marine Park

Chart 3526; 10.6 mi N of Horseshoe Bay
Entrance: 49°33.19'N, 123°14.58'W
Anchor: 49°33.03'N, 123°14.33'W
Dive wrecks: 49°33.68'N, 123°14.12'W

Porteau Cove Marine Park has launching ramps, picnic and camping facilities, showers, garbage disposal and a car park. Three wrecks and a man-made reef, in about 9 m (30 ft) of water, are for the use of scuba divers. The wrecks are marked by buoys. Mariners should exercise great caution in the vicinity of the wrecks because scuba divers may be operating in the vicinity. (SD)

Porteau Cove is one of the few relatively well-protected anchorages in upper Howe Sound. Although it is listed as a Marine Park, most of its facilities are used by campers who drive in from greater Vancouver or by small runabouts. However, cruising boaters do use and appreciate many of the facilities.

Protection from northerlies can be found by tucking at the south side of the wooded rocky peninsula 0.7 mile south of the dive wrecks. Swinging room is limited in this tiny cove.

"Zorro Bay"

Chart 3526; 2 mi N of the Defence Islands
Position: 49°36.00'N, 123°15.49'W

As noted in Bill Wolferstan's Cruising Guide to British Columbia, Vol. 3 Sunshine Coast, page 122: "On the west shore of Howe Sound is a small peninsula similar to the 'Anvil.' "

Temporary anchorage is reported available on either the north or south side of the peninsula in the areas known locally as "Five Coves" or "Zorro Bay."

Squamish

Chart 3534 inset; 18.8 mi N of Horseshoe Bay
Entrance (0.14 mi NE of Mamquam Blind Ch entr lt): 49°40.91'N, 123°09.82'W
Yacht Club floats (N end of Mamquam Blind Ch): 49°41.67'N, 123°09.26'W

Squamish, at the head of Howe Sound, is in the entrance to the east arm of the Squamish River.

The municipality has a population of 10,157 (1986). (SD)

An industrial town devoted largely to shipping chemicals, aluminum, and forest products, Squamish is not usually a favorite destination of cruising boats; its noise, congestion, and effluence reduce its attractiveness. Approach to the town is through Mamquam Blind Channel at the far eastern arm of the Squamish River. There is a public dock with five floats and, just south on the west shore of the east arm, is the Squamish Yacht Club. The dredged channel is marked with range markers; log-booms frequently choke the narrow passage.

⚓ **Harbour Authority of Squamish**
tel: 604.892.3725 or 604.898.4101 (Squamish Yacht Club); restrooms; showers; pumpout

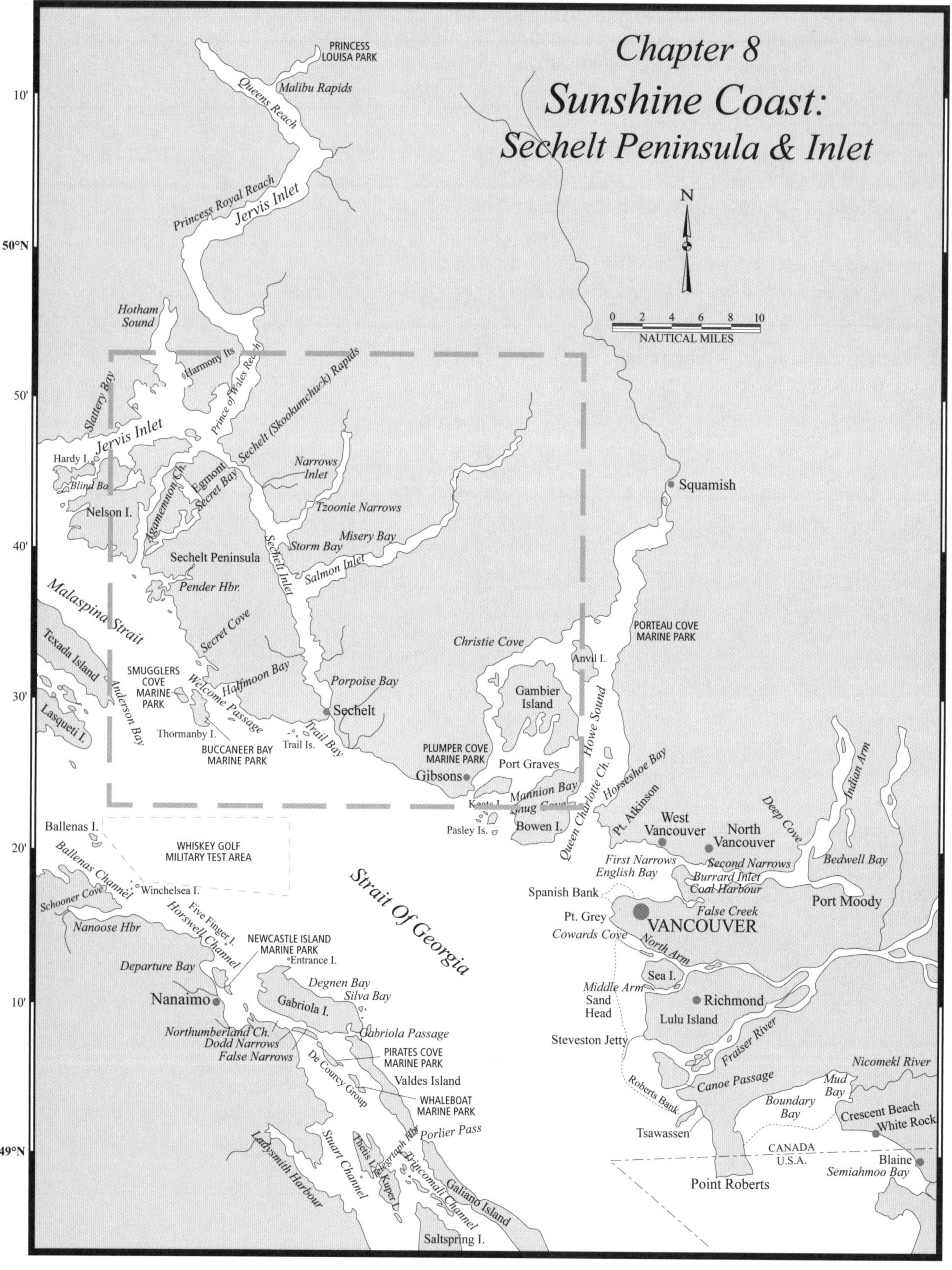
Chapter 8
Sunshine Coast:
Sechelt Peninsula & Inlet
N
0 2 4 6 8 10
NAUTICAL MILES
10'
50°N
50'
40'
30'
20'
10'
49°N
PRINCESS LOUISA PARK
Malibu Rapids
Queens Reach
Princess Royal Reach
Jervis Inlet
Hotham Sound
Harmony Its
Prince of Wales Reach
Sechelt (Skookumchuck) Rapids
Slattery Bay
Jervis Inlet
Hardy I.
Blind Ba
Nelson I.
Agamemnon Ch.
Egmont
Secret Bay
Narrows Inlet
Tzoonie Narrows
Misery Bay
Storm Bay
Sechelt Inlet
Salmon Inlet
Sechelt Peninsula
Pender Hbr.
Malaspina Strait
Secret Cove
Texada Island
SMUGGLERS COVE MARINE PARK
Anderson Bay
Welcome Passage
Halfmoon Bay
Lasqueti I.
Thormanby I.
BUCCANEER BAY MARINE PARK
Trail Is.
Trail Bay
Porpoise Bay
Sechelt
Christie Cove
Gambier Island
Anvil I.
PORTEAU COVE MARINE PARK
Squamish
PLUMPER COVE MARINE PARK
Gibsons
Port Graves
Howe Sound
Mannion Bay
Snug Cove
Bowen I.
Pasley Is.
Queen Charlotte Ch.
Horseshoe Bay
Pt. Atkinson
West Vancouver
North Vancouver
Deep Cove
Indian Arm
Bedwell Bay
Ballenas I.
Ballenas Channel
WHISKEY GOLF MILITARY TEST AREA
Winchelsea I.
Schooner Cove
Nanoose Hbr
Five Finger I.
Horswell Channel
Strait Of Georgia
First Narrows
English Bay
Second Narrows
Burrard Inlet
Coal Harbour
Port Moody
Spanish Bank
Pt. Grey
False Creek
VANCOUVER
Cowards Cove
North Arm
NEWCASTLE ISLAND MARINE PARK
Entrance I.
Departure Bay
Degnen Bay
Silva Bay
Gabriola I.
Nanaimo
Sea I.
Middle Arm
Sand Head
Richmond
Lulu Island
Northumberland Ch.
Dodd Narrows
False Narrows
Gabriola Passage
PIRATES COVE MARINE PARK
De Courcy Group
Valdes Island
WHALEBOAT MARINE PARK
Steveston Jetty
Fraiser River
Roberts Bank
Canoe Passage
Nicomekl River
Mud Bay
Boundary Bay
Crescent Beach
White Rock
Tsawassen
CANADA
U.S.A.
Blaine
Semiahmoo Bay
Point Roberts
Porlier Pass
Ladysmith Harbour
Stuart Channel
Thetis I.
Kuper I.
Trincomali Channel
Galiano Island
Saltspring I.

8

SUNSHINE COAST: Sechelt Peninsula and Inlet

One hundred and fifty kilometers long, the Sunshine Coast stretches along the mainland from Howe Sound on the south to Desolation Sound on the north. This area of broad, sandy beaches, rugged, rocky headlands, quiet lagoons and inlets, and numerous waterfalls beckons the sailor, promising sunshine, warm weather, and calm waters. Lying in the rain shadow of mountainous Vancouver Island, the Sunshine Coast has one of the highest totals of sunshine in Canada and relatively little rain or fog, especially in the summer months. High temperatures average 70°F, although the mercury can climb to 100°F in a few spots.

Ian Douglas

Safe anchorage off B.C. beach

The mainland coastal mountains, covered with thick green forests of arbutus and fir, provide a stunningly beautiful backdrop to the coastline. These mountains were once ancient volcanic islands and there has been volcanic activity in some places as recently as a few thousand years ago. Parts of the range have been repeatedly scoured by glaciers, leaving vivid marks on the land. There are sandstone cliffs, volcanic rock outcrops, and granite cliffs. Siwash Rock is a remnant volcanic vent. Prospect Point features a spectacular ledge of black volcanic rock.

Note: Charts 3312 and 3313 are chart books in atlas format. They are designed for use by small craft, and include additional information and aerial photographs. However, these charts are not available as NDI digital charts, nor do they lend themselves easily to measurement of latitude and longitude.

Trail Bay, Sechelt

Charts 3512, 3311; S of the isthmus at Sechelt; 10.5 mi NW of Gibsons
Entrance: 49°27.07'N, 123°45.58'W

Trail Bay is an indentation between Mission Point and a point 3 miles NW. Its head is formed by a low isthmus which joins Sechelt Peninsula to the mainland and separates the Strait of Georgia from Sechelt Inlet. Numerous private mooring buoys are located throughout Trail Bay.

Anchorage can be obtained in a depth of about 27 m (90 ft) off the village abreast a bluff in the NE corner of Trail Bay. (SD)

Trail Bay, between Trail Islands on the west and Selma Park on the east, is an open roadstead subject to wind changes. The village of Sechelt is situated on a low, flat isthmus and is subject to winds that blow across from Sechelt Inlet less than a mile to the north. Temporary anchorage can be found off the village; however, the site is useful in fair weather only and boats should not be left unattended.

Selma Park, at the northeast corner of Trail Bay, offers limited shelter.

Selma Park

Charts 3512, 3311; 1.8 mi NW of Mission Pt
Breakwater light: 49°28.00'N, 123°44.72'W

Selma Park, 1 mile north of Davis Bay, is a summer resort with a boat harbour, about 53 m (175 ft) wide, protected by a breakwater. A float, belonging to the Sechelt Indian Band, is behind the breakwater. (SD)

Selma Park offers the only shelter between Gibsons to the south and Welcome Passage to the north. The small rock breakwater cuts southerly seas, but the float is generally crowded. Temporary anchorage may be found in the lee of the breakwater.

Trail Islands

Chart 3311; immediately W of Trail Bay
Position: 49°27.56'N, 123°48.66'W

Small craft can find anchorage to the north of Trail Islands. This anchorage is frequently used by tugs with tows of logbooms. (SD)

Trail Islands and Welcome Passage are popular fishing spots for local day-boats. Temporary anchorage is reported to be found in about 5 fathoms just north of island (58).

Sargeant Bay (Sechelt Peninsula)

Chart 3311; 2.2 mi NW of Trail Islands
Entrance: 49°28.10'N, 123°50.68'W
Anchor: 49°28.53'N, 123°51.58'W

Sargeant Bay, 2 miles NW of the Trail Islands, is deep but offers shelter and anchorage for small vessels close to shore on either side. Drying and below-water rocks lie within 0.2 mile of the west entrance point to the bay. (SD)

Sargeant Bay offers shelter from the prevailing northwest winds in fair weather, deep in the bay on the west side. The number of drift logs on shore indicates that southeasterlies blow into the bay with great force.

Anchor in 4 fathoms over sand and gravel.

Welcome Passage

Charts 3535 inset, 3512; 7 mi NW of Sechelt; 8 mi SE of Pender Hbr
Entrance (S, W of Merry Island): 49°27.87'N, 123°56.10'W
Entrance (S, E of Merry Island): 49°27.85'N, 123°53.88'W
Entrance (N, 0.19 mi E of Tattenham Ledge buoy "Q51"): 49°31.13' N, 123°58.81' W

Welcome Passage separates Thormanby Islands from the British Columbia mainland. The fairway is deep but has several rocks on either side; it has a minimum width of 0.2 mile. The channel east of Merry Island is free of off-lying dangers, with the exception of a 9.1 m (30 ft) shoal in mid-channel off Reception Point, and a 10.1 m (33 ft) shoal lying 0.2 mile north of Merry Island. The channel west of Merry Island is deep. (SD)

Halfmoon Bay (Sechelt Peninsula)

Charts 3535 inset, 3512; on the NE side of Welcome Passage
Entrance: 49°29.94'N, 123°55.81'W

Halfmoon Bay, 2 miles NNW of Reception Point, is deep throughout, but exposed to the south; during strong SE weather a heavy swell sets into the bay.

Anchorage in Halfmoon Bay is not recommended. In fine weather small craft can obtain anchorage in Priestland Cove.

Jeddah Point is the west entrance point to Halfmoon Bay; islets and rocks extend SE from the point. A rock, with less than 2 m (6 ft) over it, lies 0.4 mile SE of Jeddah Point. (SD)

Halfmoon Bay has an irregular shoreline which offers limited shelter in fair weather in Priestland Cove, Square Bay, Brooks Bay, and Frenchmans Cove.

Priestland Cove (Halfmoon Bay)

Charts 3535 inset, 3512; in the NE corner of Halfmoon Bay
Public wharf: 49°30.59'N, 123°54.78'W

Priestland Cove, in which there are numerous above-water and drying rocks, is at the head of Halfmoon Bay. (SD)

Priestland Cove has a small public float, usually crowded with small runabouts. There are many private mooring buoys along the eastern shore of Halfmoon Bay. Anchorage can be taken south of the wharf, with some protection provided by the islets. While shelter from prevailing northwest winds is afforded, this is considered a fair-weather anchorage only.

Square Bay (Halfmoon Bay)

Charts 3535 inset, 3512; 1 mi W of Priestland Cove
Entrance: 49°30.54'N, 123°56.25'W

Square Bay ... has above-water and drying rocks close offshore at the head of the bay. Numerous private moorings are in the bay. (SD)

Brooks Cove (Halfmoon Bay)

Charts 3535 inset, 3512; 0.3 mi NE of Jeddah Pt
Entrance: 49°30.32'N, 123°56.54'W
Anchor: 49°30.50'N, 123°56.77'W

Brooks Cove, close SW of Square Bay, offers limited anchorage for small craft. (SD)

Brooks Cove is encumbered with rocks and reefs (some may not be charted on the new large-scale Chart 3535 since the surveys date up to 60 years). This place, and Frenchmans Cove to the immediate south, are fun to explore. Cautious sailors who can locate the 1- to 2-fathom holes at the head of either cove will enjoy an intimate scenic spot.

This area provides good shelter in summer weather. One or two well-positioned shore ties can be used to advantage since swinging room is tight.

Anchor in 1 fathom; reported mixed bottom with fair-to-good holding.

Frenchmans Cove (Halfmoon Bay)

Charts 3535 inset, 3512; 0.2 mi NE of Jeddah Pt
Entrance: 49°30.19'N, 123°56.58'W
Anchor: 49°30.45'N, 123°56.91'W

It is reported that the entrance is very narrow and difficult to locate. (SD)

Frenchmans Cove is the passageway between the islets and rocks east of Jeddah Point. If you choose to enter the cove, you'll get a taste of the exploring opportunities that are found all along northern British Columbia coastlines. The rocks and reefs here are not well charted; while the large-scale inset on Chart 3535 is helpful, you should not rely on it for the vicinity of Jeddah Point.

It is relatively easy to explore this area in calm weather (proceed very slowly and use alert bow lookouts), but difficult and dangerous in a southeasterly when waves ricochet off the steep, rocky bluffs a few yards to either side of your boat.

Find the 10-foot hole to port just before the drying inner lagoon. A shore tie is helpful in the tight swinging room.

Anchor in 2 fathoms over mixed bottom with fair-to-good holding.

South Thormanby Island (Welcome Passage)

Charts 3535 inset, 3512; 8 mi S of Pender Hbr, on the SE side of Welcome Passage

Loaded for fun, Buccaneer Bay

Thormanby Islands form the west side of Welcome Passage and when viewed from some directions are difficult to distinguish from the mainland.

Several bays along the east shore of South Thormanby Island offer sheltered anchorage from south and west winds. (SD)

Between Dennis Head and Lemberg Point, South Thormanby Island's east side has a rugged volcanic shore with steep headlands. A number of small coves facing Welcome Passage offer good shelter in prevailing northwest winds. These coves are also in close proximity to popular fishing grounds between Thormanby and Merry islands. The well-worn headlands suggest that these coves are exposed during southeast storms. Buccaneer Bay, Smugglers Cove or Secret Cove would be the closest secure protection.

Mt. Seafield Cove (South Thormanby I)

Chart 3535 inset; 1.0 mi N of Dennis Head
Entrance: 49°28.99'N, 123°57.04'W
Anchor: 49°29.04'N, 123°57.52'W

Mt. Seafield Cove, our name for the tiny cove at the base of 400-foot Mt. Seafield, can be a comfortable cove in fair weather. It is out of the current of Welcome Passage, but is exposed to southeasterlies and has limited swinging room.

Anchor in the head of the bay over an unrecorded bottom.

Derby Point East (South Thormanby I)

Charts 3535 inset, 3512; immediately E of Derby Pt
Entrance: 49°30.66'N, 123°58.81'W
Anchor: 49°30.52'N, 123°58.78'W

Derby Point East is what we call the short inlet-like cove east of the islets located northeast of Derby Point. This cove is out of the strong currents that run in Welcome Passage during spring tides or storm winds. The islets, reef and rocks give fairly good protection from northwest winds and very good protection in southeasterlies.

Caution: Tattenham Ledge, which has isolated rocks and reefs, is the shoal extending a half-mile north of Derby Point. The tidal stream which is reported to run diagonally across the ledge can easily set a boat aground.

Temporary anchorage can be found near the head of the bay over an unknown bottom.

Buccaneer Bay and Buccaneer Bay Marine Park

Charts 3535 inset, 3512; 1 mi W of Welcome Passage, btwn N & S Thormanby Islands
Entrance (mid-ch btwn Oaks & Derby Pts): 49°30.51'N, 123°59.37'W
Anchor (Vaucroft Beach): 49°30.30'N, 123°59.66'W
Anchor (0.12 mi E of Grassy Pt): 49°29.73'N, 123°59.29'W

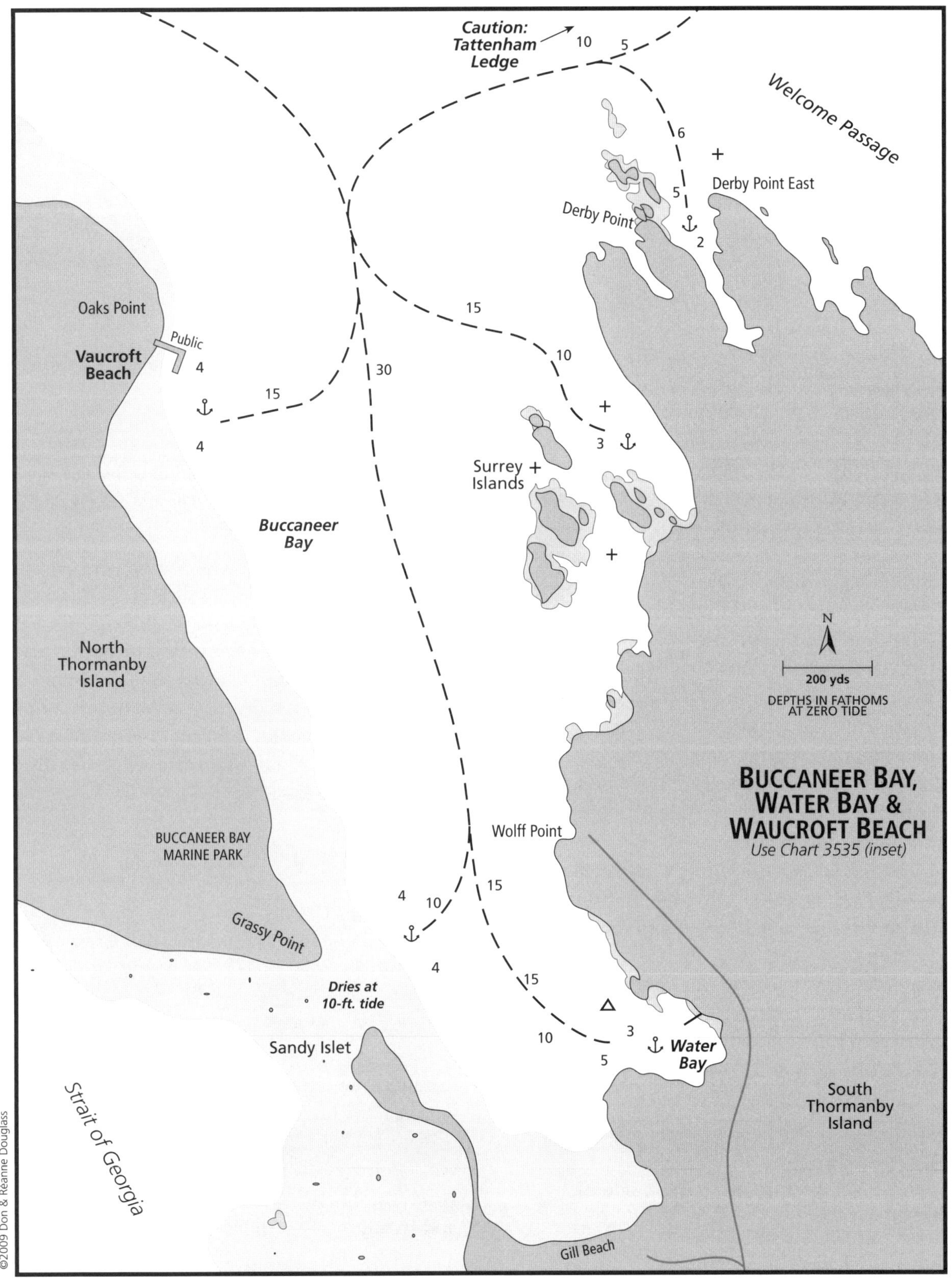
Caution: Tattenham Ledge
Welcome Passage
Derby Point East
Derby Point
Oaks Point
Public
Vaucroft Beach
Surrey Islands
Buccaneer Bay
North Thormanby Island
BUCCANEER BAY MARINE PARK
Grassy Point
Wolff Point
Dries at 10-ft. tide
Sandy Islet
Water Bay
Strait of Georgia
Gill Beach
South Thormanby Island
N
200 yds
DEPTHS IN FATHOMS AT ZERO TIDE
BUCCANEER BAY, WATER BAY & WAUCROFT BEACH
Use Chart 3535 (inset)

Caution must be exercised when entering Buccaneer Bay because of Tattenham Ledge and the shoal water extending north from the north end of North Thormanby Island. The middle of Gill Beach, at the head of the bay, bearing 165°, leads in the fairway between these dangers.

Anchorage can be obtained between Wolf and Grassy Points, in a depth of about 30m (98-ft), sand bottom. It is exposed to north winds. (SD)

A quiet day in port

Buccaneer Bay is an expansive bay offering access to some of the most beautiful sandy beaches found in the Northwest. The conglomerate rock of North Thormanby Island, as contrasted with the volcanic rock of South Thormanby Island, has eroded to create a wonderful sandspit complete with sand dunes.

Buccaneer Bay Marine Park has been created on the southern tip of North Thormanby Island. Its development is presently limited to toilets and picnic facilities.

Anchorage in Buccaneer Bay is usually taken between "Sandy Islet" and Grassy Point on the east side of the drying bar separating the two islands. The bar is awash on about a 10-foot tide. Driftwood and flotsam wash up on the beaches on either side of the bar making beachcombing enjoyable.

There is fair-to-good protection in Buccaneer Bay in most weather but, on occasions, some uncomfortable northerly chop may be felt. (For the best protection, tuck in near the private float in Water Bay. Anchorage can also be found just south of Vaucroft Beach float or, for more seclusion, among the Surrey Islands.)

Anchor in 4 fathoms off the bar over a sandy bottom with fair holding

Surrey Islands

Charts 3535 inset, 3512; on the E side of Buccaneer Bay
Entrance: 49°30.36′N, 123°59.02′W
Anchor: 49°30.27′N, 123°58.91′W

Surrey Islands, on the east side of the north part of Buccaneer Bay, are wooded and steep-to on their west sides. The channel east of the islands is foul. (SD)

The Surrey Islands have shallow water on their east side and a modicum of privacy. Some rocks and reefs are reported to be uncharted, so enter carefully and personally survey your swinging area. Avoid the mid-channel rock in the bay east of Surrey Islands. Protection is considered fair-to-good in most weather with some exposure to prevailing northwest winds.

Anchor as desired over a bottom reported to be sand and mud with fair holding.

Water Bay (South Thormanby Island)

Charts 3535 inset, 3512; 0.4 mi SE of Grassy Pt
Entrance: 49°29.56′N, 123°58.98′W
Anchor: 49°29.59′N, 123°58.88′W

Wolf Point, 0.3 mile south of Surrey Islands, is the north point of Water Bay. (SD)

In Buccaneer Bay, the best protection from southeasterlies can be found just off the private float in Water Bay. The reef south of Wolf Point affords moderate protection from annoying northerly chop; fetch here is minimal in southerly winds.

Anchor in 1.5 fathoms over sand with fair-to-good holding.

Smuggler Cove & Smuggler Cove Marine Park

Charts 3535 inset, 3311, 3512;
1.5 mi NE of Buccaneer Bay;
1 mi S of Secret Cove
Entrance: 49°30.90'N, 123°58.19'W
Anchor (third basin): 49°30.80'N, 123°57.72'W

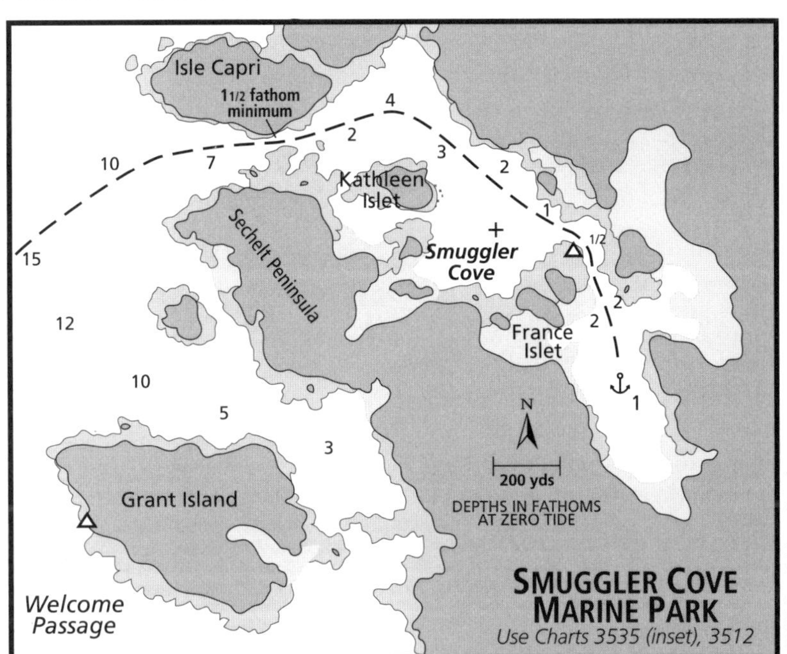

Smuggler Cove is a popular small craft stopover; caution is required when entering the cove. It is entered by passing close south of Isle Capri. Two islets, 0.2 mile within the entrance, are connected to the south shore by drying ledges. France Islet, the higher of these two islets, has drying reefs extending north and east from it. A rock, with 0.9 m (3 ft) over it, lies in the middle of the cove, about 90 m (295 ft) NW of France Islet. The inner anchorage is entered through the narrow channel between France Islet and Kathleen Islet (a local name) to the east.

Smuggler Cove Marine Park encompasses the area around Smuggler Cove; it is undeveloped.

Anchorage in Smuggler Cove affords good protection, with fairly good holding ground. (SD)

Tied up on the beach

Smuggler Cove resembles an alpine lake with its granite outcroppings and evergreen trees to the water's edge. If you happen to arrive during an uncongested period, this is a beautiful and secluded spot. Don't miss the fun of rowing along the convoluted shore.

Smuggler Cove, once the home of "King of the Smugglers," derives its name from a time when "assisting" Chinese laborers across the border into the United States was profitable. (For a short description of these smuggling "services," see Bill Wolferstan's book listed in the Bibliography.)

When entering and anchoring in Smuggler Cove, be aware of the small rocks, reefs and shoals. The large-scale inset in Chart 3535 is particularly helpful. Since the entrance to Smuggler Cove can easily be missed, the Marine Park sign on the headland gives you confidence that this is the right place. Hug the Isle Capri shore on the port side, watching for and avoiding the underwater obstacles in order to miss the reef that extends well over three-quarters of the way from the starboard peninsula. Proceed at dead-slow and post alert bow lookouts.

South Coast lighthouses help to ensure safe sailing for small craft

You can find very good protection from all weather in any of the three basins of Smuggler Cove. However, the most sheltered of the three is the inner basin, entered close to the starboard daymark. This passage has only a foot or two of water at zero tide. (The first anchorage has depths of 2 to 3 fathoms.)

Anchor in the third basin in an 8- to 10-foot hole over sand, mud and shell with good holding.

Secret Cove (Malaspina Strait)

Charts 3535 inset, 3512; 1.5 mi N of Welcome Passage; 7 mi S of Pender Hbr
Entrance: 49°31.64'N, 123°58.12'W
Anchor (Turnagain I): 49°32.05'N, 123°58.07'W
Anchor (E of reefs): 49°32.01'N, 123°57.74'W
Anchor (S inlet): 49°31.70'N, 123°57.20'W

Secret Cove lies between Turnagain Island and the mainland to the east. It is entered between the south end of Turnagain Island and Jack Tolmie Island, about 91m (300-ft) SE.

Secret Cove consists of three arms which extend south, east and north from the entrance. Numerous private floats and moorings lie within the cove.

Dangers.—A rock, which dries 3.7 m (12 ft), lies south of Turnagain Island in the entrance to Secret Cove.

Anchorage can be obtained near the head of the north arm. (SD)

Secret Cove is hidden from Malaspina Strait, and while not as small and intimate as Smuggler Cove, it is well protected and a popular destination for cruising boats. Secret Cove has a number of commercial developments (marinas and inns), private property, and private floats. The public float in the north arm, east of Turnagain Island, is generally crowded.

The entrance to the cove can be made easily in most weather. Keep the triangular, red entrance daymark (flashing red at night) to starboard in the narrow channel. Minimum depth is about 6 fathoms.

Anchorage can be taken in either of the two main inlets; most popular is just south of the islet close to the east side of Turnagain Island or in the shallows behind the reefs southeast of the public floats. The southernmost inlet also offers very good shelter off the Royal Vancouver Island Yacht outstation. The eastern inlet contains four major marinas and several private floats.

Anchor (Turnagain I) in 3 fathoms, sand and mud bottom with good holding.

Anchor (E of reefs) in 1 to 2 fathoms over a mud bottom with very good holding.

Anchor (S inlet) in 1-1/2 fathoms over mud with very good holding.

⚓ **Buccaneer Marina & Resort Ltd.** tel: 604.885.7888; fax: 604.885.7824; website: www.buccaneermarina.com; email: bucaneermarina@telus.net; fuel; power; restrooms

⚓ **Secret Cove Marina** tel: 604.885.3533; fax: 604.885.6037; monitors VHF Ch 66A; website: www.secretcovemarina.com; fuel; power; restrooms; showers; groceries

⚓ **Secret Cove Public Wharf**

Wood Bay, Ole's Cove (Malaspina Strait)

Charts 3311, 3512; 1.0 mi N of northern tip of Turnagain I; 0.2 mi NW of Turnagain I
Entrance (Wood Bay): 49°32.92'N, 123°59.51'W

Wood Bay, 0.6 mile ESE of McNaughton Point affords temporary anchorage. Marine farm

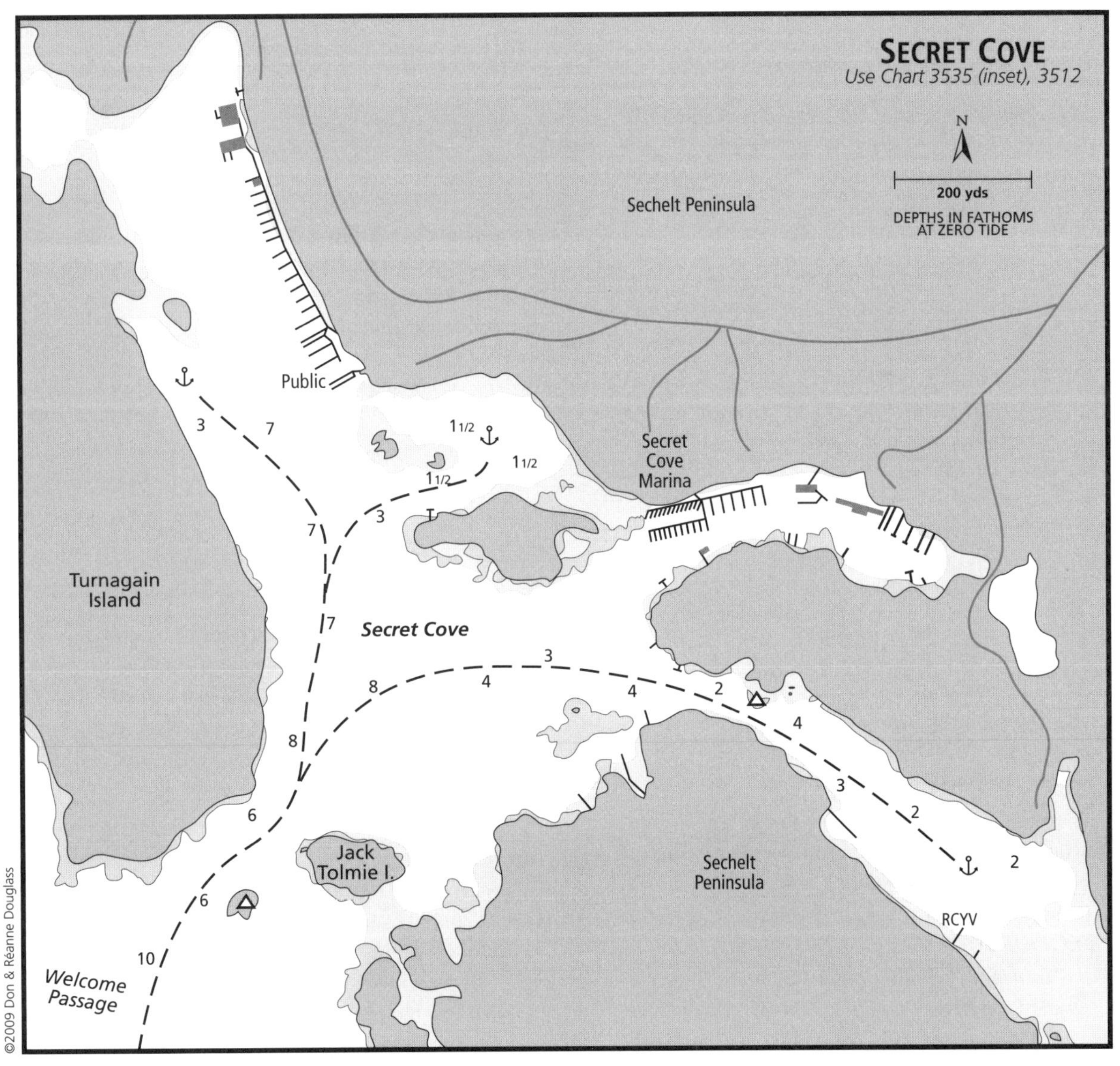

facilities, protected by a logboom and marked by cautionary light buoys, are in the bay.

Ole's Cove [is] a local name ... A drying rock ledge, with a 1 m (3 ft) high islet on it, extends from the east shore into the entrance of the cove and the head is filled with drying sand flats. (SD)

Wood Bay is a small nook suitable for temporary anchorage. Ole's Cove is a tiny cove with a private float and resort.

Harness Island Anchorage (Malaspina Strait)

Charts 3311, 3512; 2.5 mi SE of Pender Hbr
Entrance (S, 0.9 mi SW of Harness I): 49°35.40'N, 1234°01.33'W
Anchor: 49°35.48'N, 124°01.01'W

Anchorage, with fair shelter, can be obtained by small craft inside Harness Island. Several mooring buoys lie between Harness Island and the mainland. (SD)

Anchorage in fair weather can be found in the lee of Harness Island off the Silver Sands Resort, or close to the northeast corner of the island.

If you enter from the south, pass between the island and the bare islets, avoiding rocks which may be marked with kelp.

Anchor in 4 to 5 fathoms between the resort and Harness Island, or close to the northeast side of the island, unrecorded holding.

Bargain Bay (Pender Harbour)

Charts 3535 inset, 3311; 0.2 mi SW of Bargain Narrows; 1.1 mi NE of Francis Pt
Entrance (W of Edgecombe Island): 49°36.16'N, 124°02.23'N
Anchor: 49°36.89'N, 124°02.19'W

Bargain Bay, within the limits of Pender Harbour, is small, narrow and best approached west of Edgecombe Island; extra caution is necessary. Numerous private floats line the shores of the bay.

Dangers.—A shoal, with 2.2 m (7 ft) over it, lies on the east side of the fairway, 0.1 mile west of Edgecombe Island. Two rocks, 0.25 mile NW of Edgecombe Island, have less than 2 m (6 ft) over them; the fairway between these two rocks is about 100 m (328 ft) wide.

The head of Bargain Bay affords sheltered anchorage for small craft in a depth of about 7 m (23 ft.). (SD)

Bargain Bay, on the south side of the Pender Harbour complex, offers good shelter at the head of the bay. Avoid the midchannel rocks by slightly favoring the starboard shore once you've passed Edgecombe Island, following the 5-fathom curve.

Bargain Bay connects with Gerrans Bay via Bargain Narrows ("Canoe Pass"), a drying and narrow small-boat passage which has a bridge with a 13-foot clearance.

Anchor in 3 to 4 fathoms over mixed bottom of mud, sand, rock and shells, fair-to-good holding.

Martin Cove and Francis Cove

Charts 3535 inset, 3311, 3512; on the W side of Francis Peninsula
Entrance (Francis Cove): 49°36.63'N, 124°03.65'W
Entrance (Martin Cove): 49°37.14'N, 124°03.91'W
Anchor (Martin Cove): 49°37.06'N, 124°03.82'W

Francis Bay, south of Moore Point, and Martin Cove, north of Moore Point, are open to the west but can provide shelter and anchorage from SE weather. (SD)

Pender Harbour

Charts 3535 inset, 3311, 3512; of the W side of Sechelt Peninsula; 1.5 mi S of Agamemnon Ch
Entrance (0.08 mi N of Pender Hbr Light): 49°37.85'N, 124°03.65'W

The main entrance is between Henry Point and Williams Island, 0.1 mile SSW. The channel between Williams Island and Charles Island has a drying reef in the centre of its fairway at the east end. The Gap, south of Charles Island, is obstructed by an islet and drying reefs; it should not be attempted.

Several islets and shoals lie within the entrance but they are well marked by buoys and beacons. (SD)

Water taxi, anyone?

Pender Harbour is entered east of Pearson Island and offers the only completely sheltered anchorage on this part of the coast. Pender Harbour is a major destination for cruising boats as well as a stop for those heading north or south.

Marinas and floats are located in Irvines Landing, Duncan Cove, Hospital Bay, Garden Bay, Gerrans Bay, Madeira Park and in the cove .3 miles east of Madeira Park. A pier with a fuel float at its outer end is at Pope Landing. Garden Bay Marine Park, on the north shore of Garden Bay, is a full service marina and has a dinghy float, picnic and sanitary facilities. Public floats connected to shore on the east side of Hospital Bay have power, garbage and oil disposal facilities. The public wharf in Madeira Park at the head of Welbour Cove has power on the float, water, garbage and used-oil disposal facilities at the wharf head.

At the entrance, Irvines Landing Marina is good for rest and refreshment. They have 700' of guest moorage, unlimited fresh water, showers, laundry and complimentary garbage dump, plus a pub. For a longer visit, the Pender Habour Authority facilities at Madeira Park have excellent amenities and visiting vessels receive a warm welcome. Madeira Park is a great place to walk around and has a great variety of stores. Malaspina Coachlines also picks up here if any crew needs to get back to Vancouver.

Fisherman's Marina located in Hospital Bay, has 2300 feet of docks for moorage, with 20 & 30 amp power and fresh potable drinking water. Float plane service is available for transportation to Vancouver. There are showers, laundry and mechanics and divers on call for any marine repairs you may need.

The Pender Harbour Hotel and Marina is a short walk to the main hotel building. You can sail your boat right into the marina and spend the night in the newly remodeled 1 or 2 bedroom or 2 bedroom cabins. The marina offers short-term and long-term moorage. Amenities include a liquor store, moorage and a pub.

⚓ **Pender Harbour Resort** tel: 604.883.2424; fax 604.883.2414; monitors VHF Ch 66A; website: www.penderharbourresort.com; email: info@penderharbourresort.com; power; restrooms; showers; laundry

Joe Bay (Pender Harbour)

Charts 3535 inset, 3311, 3512; at the entrance of Pender Hbr; E of Henry Pt
Position (Joe Bay): 49°37.91'N, 124°03.38'W
Public wharf (Irvines Landing): 49°37.92'N, 124°03.42'W
Position (Bill Bay): 49°37.92'N, 124°03.16'W
Position (Dingman Bay): 49°37.94'N, 124°02.93'W
Position (Farrington Cove): 49°37.92'N, 124°02.75'W
Position (Duncan Cove): 49°37.99'N, 124°02.58'W

Joe Bay is on the north side of the entrance to Pender Harbour. Irvines Landing, on the east

side of Joe Bay, has a public wharf and float providing about 30m (99-ft) of berthing space.

Bill Bay, Dingman Bay, Farrington Cove and Duncan Cove are east of Irvines Landing and have private floats and moorings. (SD)

Hospital Bay (Pender Harbour)

Charts 3535 inset, 3311, 3512; 1.0 mi E of Williams Island
Entrance (NW of entrance rock): 49°37.90'N, 124°02.22'W
Public floats: 49°37.93'N, 124°01.94'W

Hospital Bay, close east of Duncan Cove, has a drying rock in the middle of its entrance.

In the east part of Hospital Bay, there are three public floats each 37m (120-ft) long, with a common connection to shore; depths alongside are 3 to 6m (10 to 20 ft). Garbage and used oil disposal facilities are available and power is laid on the floats. A fuel barge, store, liquor store and marinas are in Hospital Bay; marina facilities are listed in an Appendix. (SD)

⚓ **John Henry's Marinas, Inc.** tel: 604.883.2253; fuel; propane; groceries

⚓ **Fisherman's Marina** tel: 604.883.2336; monitors VHF Ch 66A; website: www.fishermansresort.com; showers; laundry

Garden Bay (Pender Harbour)

Charts 3535 inset, 3311, 3512; 0.4 mi SE of Hospital Bay
Entrance: 49°37.70'N, 124°01.36'W
Anchor: 49°37.84'N, 124°01.38'W

Garden Bay, east of Hospital Bay and separated from it by Garden Peninsula, is clear of obstructions. A post office (V0N 1S0), hotel and a marina are available in Garden Bay. A boat building shop is on the east side of the bay. Repair facilities are available.

Garden Bay Marine Park, on the north shore of Garden Bay, is undeveloped. (SD)

Garden Bay has moorage which provides convenient access to stores and shops in the area. You can also find anchorage off the undeveloped Garden Bay Marine Park.

Anchor in 4 fathoms over mud and shells with good holding.

⚓ **Garden Bay Hotel Marina & Pub**
tel: 604.883.2675; monitors VHF Ch 66A; website: www.gardenbaypub.com; email: gbhm@decnet.com; power; restrooms

⚓ **Sportsman's Marina & Resort**
tel: 604.970.1563; website: www.sportsman-marina.com; email: office@sportsman-marina.com; power; showers; laundry

Gunboat Bay and Oyster Bay (Pender Harbour)

Charts 3535 inset, 3311, 3512; E end of Pender Hbr
Entrance: 49°37.57'N, 124°01.16'W
Anchor (Gunboat Bay, 0.18 mi E of Goat Islet): 49°37.64'N, 124°00.07'W
Anchor (Oyster Bay): 49°37.85'N, 123°59.76'W

Gunboat Bay, at the head of Pender Harbour, is entered through a narrow channel with a least depth of 0.7m (2 ft). A rock, which dries 1.1m (4 ft), lies close to the north shore 0.1 mile from the entrance.

Good anchorage, mud bottom, can be obtained in Gunboat Bay. (SD)

Gunboat Bay, which has a narrow and shallow entrance as noted above, is less busy and noisy than the resort areas to the west.

Well-sheltered and excellent anchorage can be found 0.18 mile east of Goat Islet at the entrance to the north arm known as Oyster Bay.

Anchor (0.18 mile east of Goat Islet) in 3 fathoms over gray mud with very good holding.

Anchor (Oyster Bay) in 2 fathoms off the mud flat with very good holding.

⚓ **Pender Harbour Hotel & Marina**
tel: 604.883.9013; fax: 604.883.9014; website: www.penderharbourhotel.com; power; open year-round

Welbourn Cove, Madeira Park (Pender Harbour)

Charts 3535 inset, 3311, 3512; 0.25 mi SE of Garden Peninsula
Entrance: 49°37.46'N, 124°01.56'W
Public float: 49°37.41'N, 124°01.53'W

Madeira Park, at the head of Welbourn Cove, is the main community of Pender Harbour. Among its amenities are a post office (V0N 2H0), pharmacy, grocery store, bank and liquor store. A medical clinic is held here on weekdays.

A public wharf, at the head of the cove, has a depth of about 4.8 m (16 ft) alongside ... Three floats, attached to the west side of the wharf, have a combined length of 104 m (340 ft) with depths of 4 to 8.4 m (12 to 28 ft) alongside. Power is laid on the floats; water, garbage and used oil disposal facilities are available on the wharfhead.

Anchorage can be obtained west of Garden Peninsula in 15 to 20 m (49 to 66 ft), mud bottom or off Welbourn Cove in 11 to 15 m (36 to 49 ft), mud bottom. Small craft can obtain anchorage in 6 to 11 m (20 to 35 ft) in Gerrans Bay, or in about 9 m (30 ft) in Garden Bay; in the latter swinging space is limited.

Caution.—During strong SE gales the various passages in Pender Harbour are subject to heavy squalls. (SD)

⚓ **Sunshine Coast Resort & Marina Ltd.** tel: 604.883.9177; fax: 604.883.9171; website: www.sunshinecoastresort.com; power; restrooms; showers; laundry

Photo courtesy CHS, Pacific Region

Green Bay, Agamemnon Channel

⚓ **Maderia Park Public Wharf** (Pender Harbour Authority) tel: 604.883.2234; monitors VHF Ch 66A; email: penderauthority@telus.net; power; restrooms; showers; pumpout

Gerrans Bay ("Whiskey Slough") (Pender Harbour)

Charts 3535 inset, 3311, 3512; S arm of Pender Hbr
Entrance (0.1 mi SW of Garden Peninsula & 0.1 mi NW of Mary Islet): 49°37.73'N, 124°02.16'W
Anchor (0.13 mi SW of Dusenbury I): 49°37.19'N, 124°02.52'W

Gerrans Bay, the south arm of Pender Harbour, has several rocks within it, but most of them are marked.

The SW arm of Gerrans Bay, known locally as Whiskey Slough, has a public float with a berthing length of 93 m (305 ft). Power is laid on the float and garbage and used oil disposal facilities are available. (SD)

Anchorage can be found in 3 to 4 fathoms in the bay southwest of Dusenbury Island or behind Dusenbury and Calder islands.

Lee Bay (Malaspina Strait)

Charts 3535 inset, 3311, 3512; 0.5 mi NE of Pearson I
Entrance: 49°38.16'N, 124°04.06'W

Lee Bay lies between Daniel Point and Fisher Island, 0.4 mile SE. (SD)

Lee Bay is exposed to all southerly weather; however, temporary shelter may be found in the narrow and shallow channel on the east side of Fisher Island.

Green Bay (Agamemnon Channel)

Charts 3312, 3512; on Nelson I at the midway pt of Agamemnon Ch
Entrance: 49°42.14'N, 124°04.52'W
Anchor: 49°42.61'N, 124°04.85'W

Green Bay, on the west side of the channel, has rocks close off its east shore and a drying rock near the head of the bay.

Anchorage with limited swinging room for

small craft can be obtained in 9 to 13 m (30 to 43 ft) in Green Bay. (SD)

Agamemnon Channel is a shortcut for northbound boats heading to upper Jervis Inlet. Egmont is the only fuel supply center in this channel. Well-protected anchorage can be found in Green Bay in the westernmost nook among the logbooms. Avoid the drying and submerged rocks in the head of the bay.

Anchor in 5 fathoms over an unreported bottom.

Photo courtesy CHS, Pacific Region

Skookumchuck Rapids, Sechelt Inlet

Agamemnon Bay & Earls Cove
(Agamemnon Channel)
Charts 3312, 3512, 3514; at the NE end of Agamemnon Ch
Position (Agamemnon Bay): 49°45.25'N, 123°59.49'W
Position (Earls Cove): 49°45.26'N, 124°00.75'W

Earls Cove, 1.9 miles NW of Caldwell Island, is a small indentation on the west entrance point of Agamemnon Bay. It is the site of a ferry landing from which regular service for passengers and automobiles is maintained to and from Saltery Bay on the north shore of Jervis Inlet. The landing is connected by road to Pender Harbour and Howe Sound.

A marina, in the SE part of Agamemnon Bay, is protected by a floating log breakwater. (SD)

Annis Bay (Agamemnon Channel)
Charts 3312, 3512, 3514; 0.65 mi NW of Earls Cove
Position: 49°45.75'N, 124°01.04'W

Annis Bay, on the north side of Agamemnon Channel opposite Earls Cove, has marine farm facilities and mooring buoys in its SW part. (SD)

Sechelt Inlet
Charts 3312, 3512, 3514; extends 20 mi btwn Sechelt Peninsula & the mainland; terminates in Porpoise Bay; 0.4 mi N of the town of Sechelt
Entrance (0.52 mi SW of Egmont Pt): 49°46.36 N, 123°57.59'W

Sechelt Inlet commences at the junction of Agamemnon Channel and Jervis Inlet. Narrows Inlet and Salmon Inlet lead NE from its east side. Apart from Skookumchuck Narrows and Sechelt Rapids, in the entrance, the inlet and its branches are deep.

Entry to Sechelt Inlet is governed entirely by tidal conditions at Sechelt Rapids and, in general, can be effected only at slack water.

Because of the tortuous nature of the fairway and strong tidal streams in Sechelt Rapids it is recommended that no vessel in excess of 40 m (130 ft) long and 3.4 m (11 ft) in draught should attempt to enter the inlet.

Sechelt Inlets Marine Park consists of eight sites; Tzoonie Narrows, Kunechin Point, Thornhill Creek, Nine Mile Point, Tuwanek Point, Piper Point, Skaiakos Point and Halfway Islet. Most of the sites are marked by park signs with a dogwood emblem and have primitive camping and sanitary facilities. (SD)

Sechelt Inlet, which is one of our favorite areas, is visited less frequently by cruising boats than other inlets. This is probably because Skookumchuck Rapids screens out the casual visitors and because easy or convenient anchorages are not readily available. We have visited Sechelt Inlet, both by kayak—launching from the head of the inlet—and by motor vessel via the Skookumchuck. We appreciate its quiet and solitude.

About 15 miles long, the inlet ends at Porpoise Bay, the "harbor" for the town of Sechelt. Two arms—Narrows Inlet and Salmon Inlet—stretch east from Sechelt

Photo courtesy CHS, Pacific Region

Egmont, Secret Bay

Inlet. Depths in these two arms are considerable, but Storm Bay at the mouth of Narrows Inlet, and Tzoonie Narrows, about a third of the way in, both offer good anchorage. It is also possible to anchor in Misery Bay deep in Salmon Inlet. There are several places in Sechelt Inlet where temporary anchorage can be found. Most of the marine park sites are shallow bights or open roadsteads; in fair weather they can be visited during the day for their beaches, trails, picnic or camping facilities, but overnight anchoring is not recommended.

The tidal range in Sechelt Inlet is considerably less than that of outside waters, seldom exceeding 10 feet.

Sutton Islets (Sechelt Inlet)

Charts 3312, 3512, 3514; 0.8 mi SE of Egmont Pt
Position: 49°45.75'N, 123°56.39'W

Sutton Islets, a mile and a half northwest of Skookumchuck Rapids, provide a good temporary anchorage in which to rest, reconnoiter the rapids by fast inflatables or wait for proper tidal conditions.

We have anchored in the lee of the larger islet, avoiding the submerged rocks, and found the current minimal and the stay pleasant. The bottom has marginal holding, however, so you should not leave your boat unattended.

Secret Bay (Egmont) (Sechelt Inlet)

Charts 3312, 3512, 3514; 1.6 mi SE of Egmont Pt
Entrance: 49°45.19'N, 123°55.61'W
Public float: 49°45.01'N, 123°55.78'W

Secret Bay has a 2 m (7 ft) high islet in the centre of its entrance and offers very limited anchorage, for small craft, out of the tidal stream.

Egmont, the village at Secret Bay ... Gasoline and diesel fuel are obtainable, but there are no repair facilities.

The public wharf has a wharfhead width of 15 m (50 ft) and a depth of 5.5 m (18 ft) alongside its north face... . Two floats, attached to the south side of the wharfhead, are 62 and 49 m (204 and 160 ft) long; the south float is reserved for seaplanes. (SD)

Secret Bay, known more commonly as Egmont, is another good temporary stop—the last place to fuel and supply before heading to Princess Louisa Inlet. Its inner bay is very shallow, and you must take care to avoid the shoal between the red buoy "Q32" and the daymark to the west. Refer to the large-scale chart inset on page 4 of Chart 3312. This is a busy place as well as a source for local knowledge. If you're looking for a buddy boat to transit the rapids and/or head up Jervis Inlet, you're likely to find one here.

To view the Skookumchuck in all its glory, take the 3-mile trail that starts a quarter-mile uphill from Egmont on the main road. The park sign at the trailhead lists the best updated viewing times. Public toilets are located along the trail. North Point has the best viewing for ebb tides, while Roland Point is best for flood tides.

⚓ **Egmont Public Wharf**

⚓ **Backeddy Resort & Marina** tel: 604.883.2298; fax: 604.883-2239; monitors VHF Ch 66A; website: www.backeddy.ca; email: info@backeddy,ca; fuel; power; restrooms; showers; laundry

⚓ **Bathgate General Store, Resort & Marina** tel: 604.883.222; fax: 604.883.2750; monitors VHF Ch 66A; website:

www.bathgate.com; email: info@bathgate.com; fuel; power; showers; laundry

Sechelt Rapids ("Skookumchuck Rapids")

Charts 3312, 3512, 3514; 1.5 mi E of Egmont
Entrance (NW): 49°44.90'N, 123°54.10'W
Entrance (SW, 0.23 mi NW of Skookum I Light): 49°43.73'N, 123°52.98'W

Sechelt Rapids, known locally as Skookumchuck Rapids, is at the south end of Skookumchuck Narrows. It is formed by Boom Islet, Sechelt Islets and numerous rocks and shoals. The roar from the rapids can be heard for several miles.

It is hazardous for any vessel to attempt to navigate Sechelt Rapids except at or near slack water.

Tidal streams attain 15 kn on the flood and 16 kn on the ebb during large tides. The turn to flood occurs earliest off Roland Point, approximately 0.15 mile south of Sechelt Islets light. Flood streams of 5 kn can be experienced as little as 15 minutes after LW slack off Roland Point.

The strongest flow occurs off Roland Point and to the SE where an extremely hazardous rip forms shortly after slack water. West of Sechelt Islets light the flood stream attains a maximum rate of approximately 8 kn. A backeddy forms east of the light which might be used as a haven in an extreme emergency.

The strongest ebb stream occurs just west of Sechelt Islets light with a strong cross-channel set toward the WNW. A large backeddy occurs to the north of the light and whirlpools form close to the light; they break away and are carried downstream. During large tides, ebb streams of 5 kn can be encountered as far as 0.4 mile SE of Sechelt Islets light.

The preferred time for transit of Sechelt Rapids is at HW slack. The best route through is west of Boom Islet and Sechelt Islets light; give Roland Point a wide berth on the flood to avoid the dangerous rips and heavy overfalls in its vicinity.

When the ebb is running it is recommended that larger vessels avoid the passage between Sechelt Islets light and the small island 0.2 mile NW. The main ebb stream runs approximately WNW from the light toward the opposite shore; low powered vessels, or those that tend to answer the helm sluggishly, may find themselves being spun about or set upon the west shore if attempting to abort passage through the rapids. (SD)

Skookumchuck Rapids deserve a skipper's respect. After all, these rapids are world class, right up there in speed and turbulence with the granddaddy of them all—Nakwakto Rapids—or with famous Seymour Narrows.

If you haven't thoroughly reconnoitered the rapids and you're a first-time user, it's best to relax and wait for ideal conditions before transiting. *Caution:* It is extremely hazardous to navigate Skookumchuck Rapids except at or near slack water.

Predictions of the time for slack water and maximum current velocities are given directly for the Sechelt Rapids in the Tide Tables, Vol. 5. Arrive ahead of the predicted slack time, stop short of the rapids, and watch carefully for the precise time of slack water; this will make your transit quite safe. If you do this during moderate neap tides, you may wonder what all the fuss is about.

Narrows Inlet

Charts 3312, 3512; enter 4.2 mi SE of Sechelt Rapids

Entrance (midchannel between Sockeye and Highland points): 49°40.83'N, 123°50.01'W

Narrows Inlet ... extends 8 miles NE from Sechelt Inlet. Depths in the inlet are too great for anchorage. (SD)

Tzoonie Narrows (Narrows Inlet)

Charts 3312, 3512; 3 mi E of the Narrows Inlet entrance
Entrance (SW): 49°42.51'N, 123°47.02'W
Entrance (NE): 49°42.91'N, 123°46.32'W
Anchor: 49°42.30'N, 123°46.90'W

Tzoonie Narrows, 0.7 mile NE of Tzoonie Point, is about 90 m (295 ft) wide and free of turbulence. A depth of 11 m (36 ft) can be carried through the narrows, but it is so constricted it is only suitable for small vessels.

Photo courtesy CHS, Pacific Region

Tzoonie Narrows

Tidal streams in Tzoonie Narrows attain 3 to 4 kn. (SD)

Tzoonie Narrows is charming and quiet. You can find good temporary anchorage at the Marine Park site on the south shore, one-half mile west of the narrows avoiding a flat rock-and-reef system and anchoring in a large shoal area to the east; find a good hole in 1 to 2 fathoms. This anchor site is out of the main current. Since this is a mixed bottom of sand and rocks with marginal holding, make sure your anchor is well set.

There are logging camp buildings below the waterfalls at Ramona Creek and a 40-foot float used by loggers off the drying mud flats at the Tzoonie River outlet.

Anchor in about 1 fathom over a sand and rock bottom with marginal holding.

Storm Bay (Sechelt Inlet)

Charts 3312, 3512; 5 mi SE of Sechelt Rapids
Entrance (midway btwn Cawley & Sockeye Pts): 49°40.23'N, 123°49.85'W
Anchor (head of bay): 49°39.58'N, 123°49.27'W
Anchor (inside small islet): 49°39.81'N, 123°49.75'W

Storm Bay is entered between Sockeye Point and Cawley Point. The bay provides good anchorage for small vessels near its head and for small craft in the bay south of the islets on the west side of the entrance. (SD)

Storm Bay is both centrally located and has the best all-weather protection in Sechelt Inlet. Now that aquaculture has come to Sechelt Inlet, the great blue herons have easier pickings. Their numbers, and the squawks vibrating off the high ridges above, seem to have increased dramatically.

Anchorage can be found at the head of the broad beach or, for a more intimate setting, in the cove inside and next to the islet a quarter-mile east of Cawley Point.

Anchor (inside the small islet) in 2 to 3 fathoms over sand and mud with good holding.

Salmon Inlet

Charts 3312, 3512; 8.5 mi S of Sechelt Rapids; 8 mi N of Porpoise Bay
Entrance (mid-ch btwn Nine Mile Pt & Kunechin Islets Light:) 49°36.70'N, 123°47.87'W

Sechelt Creek enters Salmon Inlet 1.5 miles NE of Thornhill Point. The drying spit off Sechelt Creek should be given a wide berth as the limits of the shoal water are difficult to see at HW.

Clowhom River flows into the head of Salmon Inlet.

Anchorage can be obtained in depths of 20 to 40 m (66 to 131 ft) near the head of Salmon Inlet. (SD)

Salmon Inlet is reported to be a great fishing spot. Its upper reaches are high and steep like Narrow Inlet. The transmission lines from the generating plant at the dam on Clowhom River are a man-made annoyance; care must be taken in the vicinity of Sechelt Creek, especially the south shore, to avoid contact—one line is as low as 25 feet above high water.

Kunechin Islets, North Cove (Salmon Inlet)

Charts 3312, 3512; N side of entr to Salmon Inlet
Entrance: 49°37.87'N, 123°47.90'W
Kunechin Islets Light: 49°37.26'N, 123°48.28'W

The Kunechin Islets offer an out-of-the-way place to explore. Temporary shelter from both upslope and downslope winds is available here since you can drop your anchor close to shore on either side of the peninsula.

Summer nights are usually still and calm, so the small cove 0.7 mile north of the islets on the east side of the peninsula offers good protection in stable weather. The west end of the cove dries, and you must avoid the charted rock mid-bay as well as those rocks near shore. In strong down-inlet winds, consider the small coves just north of Kunechin Point on the west side of the peninsula.

Anchor in about 4 fathoms, avoiding the mid-bay rock, over a mixed bottom of unrecorded holding.

Gustafson Bay (Salmon Inlet)

Charts 3312, 3512; 6.4 mi NE of Salmon Inlet entrance
Entrance: 49°39.60′N, 123°39.08′W

> *Gustafson Bay … lies between Mid Point and Steelhead Point.* (SD)

Gustafson Bay is a shallow bight on the north shore of Salmon Inlet. It is too deep for convenient anchorage.

Misery Bay (Salmon Inlet)

Charts 3312, 3512; 0.7 mi W of Sechelt Creek; 9.7 mi NE of Salmon Inlet entrance
Entrance: 49°40.83′N, 123°34.23′W
Anchor: 49°40.84′N, 123°34.45′W

> *Misery Bay, 1 mile NE of Thornhill Point, affords good anchorage in depths of 10 to 20 m (33 to 66 ft). The bay is a booming ground.* (SD)

Photo courtesy CHS, Pacific Region

Misery Bay

Misery Bay is the indented bay on the north shore of Salmon Inlet, about 10 miles up from Kunechin Islets. It is well protected, affording good anchorage now that it is no longer filled with logbooms. Look for primitive rock art in Misery Bay and other sites in Salmon Inlet, indicating a long and interesting native history.

Anchor in about 8 fathoms over an unreported bottom.

Tillicum Bay (Sechelt Inlet)

Charts 3312, 3512; 3.2 mi N of the public wharf in Porpoise Bay
Position: 49°32.22′N, 123°46.04′W

> *Tillicum Bay, close south of Gray Creek, is the site of a marina protected by a rock breakwater. Fuel and repairs are obtainable.*
>
> *Four Mile Point lies 1 mile SW of Tillicum Bay. A launching ramp is on the north side of the point.* (SD)

Lamb Islets (Sechelt Inlet)

Charts 3312, 3512; 0.8 mi N of Tillicum Bay
Lamb Islets (N side): 49°33.01′N, 123°45.98′W

> *Lamb Islets, 0.7 mile SE of Tuwanek Point, lie close north of Gray Creek. A rock, which dries 1.2 m (4 ft), lies close off the north islet. A submarine cable connects the islets to the mainland; it is marked by signs onshore.*
>
> *Booming grounds and a log dump are in the bay 0.25 mile SE of Lamb Islets.* (SD)

Lamb Islets provide temporary anchorage.

Snake Bay (Sechelt Inlet)

Charts 3312, 3512; at entrance to Porpoise Bay
Position: 49°30.68′N, 123°47.51′W

> *Snake Bay, 1.2 miles south of Carlson Point, is an indentation on the west shore …* (SD)

Porpoise Bay (Sechelt Inlet)

Charts 3312, 3512; N edge of Sechelt town
Entrance (0.6 mi S of Four Mile Pt): 49°30.81′N, 123°46.76′W
Anchor (W of Poise I): 49°29.83′N, 123°46.00′W
Public floats: 49°29.04′N, 123°45.52′W

A great way to explore is by canoe

> *Porpoise Bay is the head of Sechelt Inlet. A narrow isthmus, connecting Sechelt Peninsula to the mainland, separates the bay from the Strait of Georgia.*
>
> *Anchorage can be obtained west of Poise Island in about 15 m (49 ft) and off the public wharf in 12 m (39 ft); the holding ground is good.* (SD)

Porpoise Bay has several marine parks and commercial operations. The public floats offer easy access to telephones, restaurants, and the center of town, a half-mile south.

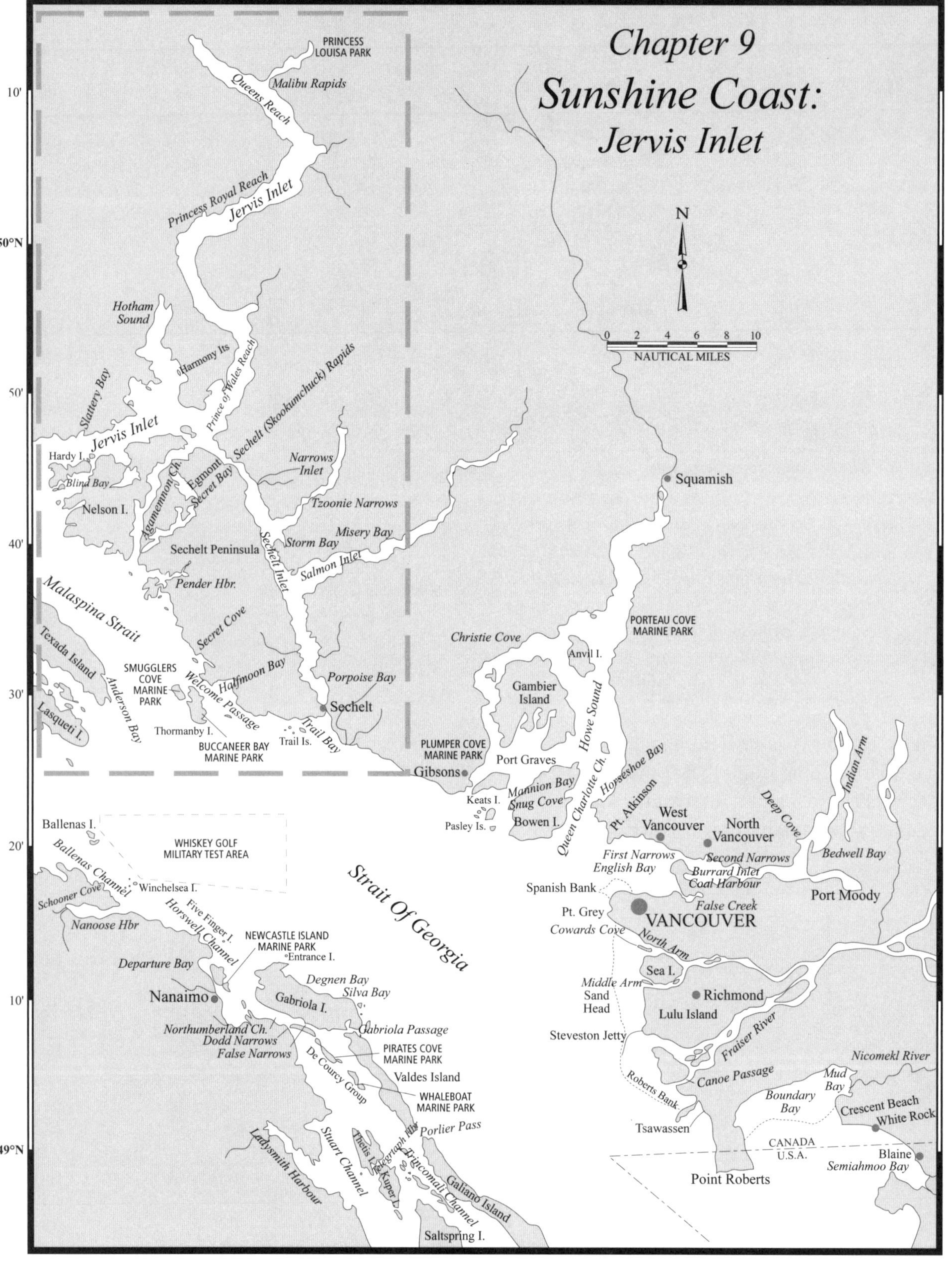
Chapter 9
Sunshine Coast:
Jervis Inlet
N
0 2 4 6 8 10
NAUTICAL MILES
PRINCESS LOUISA PARK
Malibu Rapids
Queens Reach
Princess Royal Reach
Jervis Inlet
Hotham Sound
Harmony Its
Prince of Wales Reach
Sechelt (Skookumchuck) Rapids
Slattery Bay
Jervis Inlet
Hardy I.
Blind Bay
Nelson I.
Agamemnon Ch.
Egmont
Secret Bay
Narrows Inlet
Tzoonie Narrows
Misery Bay
Storm Bay
Sechelt Peninsula
Sechelt Inlet
Salmon Inlet
Pender Hbr.
Malaspina Strait
Texada Island
Secret Cove
SMUGGLERS COVE MARINE PARK
Welcome Passage
Halfmoon Bay
Porpoise Bay
Sechelt
Anderson Bay
Lasqueti I.
Thormanby I.
BUCCANEER BAY MARINE PARK
Trail Is.
Trail Bay
Squamish
PORTEAU COVE MARINE PARK
Christie Cove
Anvil I.
Gambier Island
Howe Sound
PLUMPER COVE MARINE PARK
Port Graves
Gibsons
Keats I.
Pasley Is.
Mannion Bay
Snug Cove
Bowen I.
Queen Charlotte Ch.
Horseshoe Bay
Pt. Atkinson
West Vancouver
North Vancouver
Deep Cove
Indian Arm
Bedwell Bay
First Narrows
English Bay
Second Narrows
Burrard Inlet
Coal Harbour
Port Moody
Spanish Bank
Pt. Grey
False Creek
VANCOUVER
Cowards Cove
North Arm
Sea I.
Middle Arm
Sand Head
Richmond
Lulu Island
Steveston Jetty
Fraiser River
Canoe Passage
Roberts Bank
Boundary Bay
Mud Bay
Nicomekl River
Crescent Beach
White Rock
Tsawassen
CANADA
U.S.A.
Blaine
Semiahmoo Bay
Point Roberts
Ballenas I.
WHISKEY GOLF MILITARY TEST AREA
Ballenas Channel
Schooner Cove
Winchelsea I.
Nanoose Hbr
Five Finger I.
Horswell Channel
Strait Of Georgia
NEWCASTLE ISLAND MARINE PARK
Entrance I.
Departure Bay
Degnen Bay
Silva Bay
Nanaimo
Gabriola I.
Gabriola Passage
Northumberland Ch.
Dodd Narrows
False Narrows
PIRATES COVE MARINE PARK
De Courcy Group
Valdes Island
WHALEBOAT MARINE PARK
Porlier Pass
Ladysmith Harbour
Stuart Channel
Thetis I.
Telegraph Hbr
Kuper I.
Trincomali Channel
Galiano Island
Saltspring I.
10'
50°N
50'
40'
30'
20'
10'
49°N

9

SUNSHINE COAST: Jervis Inlet

If you are seeking solitude and great natural beauty, Jervis Inlet is the place for you. From Malaspina Strait you can access this long fjord using either Agamemnon Channel along the northwest side of Sechelt Peninsula, Telescope Passage between Nelson and Hardy islands, or directly from the Strait farther north. Sechelt Inlet leads directly into Jervis Inlet via Skookumchuck Narrows.

As you make your way north toward lovely Princess Louisa Inlet and Marine Park, there are few bays and coves in Jervis Inlet where you can find anchorage; the best are at the south end in the Harmony Islands, Hotham Sound.

There are no facilities in Jervis Inlet, so you must be self-sufficient when you set off to explore Princess Louisa Marine Park. Egmont, in Secret Bay, is the final supply point for fueling and provisioning before you head north.

Jervis Inlet

Charts 3312, 3512, 3514; enter from Malaspina Strait; 10 mi NW of Pender Hbr
Entrance (mid-ch btwn Scotch Fir & Alexander Pts): 49°44.06′N, 124°14.74′W

> *Jervis Inlet ... is 46 miles long with a general width of 1 to 1.5 miles. The main entrance is between Alexander Point and Scotch Fir Point, 2 miles NW. The inlet can also be entered by way of Telescope Passage, which separates the east end of Hardy Island from Nelson Island, or by way of Agamemnon Channel, along the east side of Nelson Island.*
>
> *Jervis Inlet is hemmed in by high rugged mountains rising steeply from steep-to shores. The slopes in most places are thickly wooded, but there are bare strips caused by logging, winter storms, or avalanches during spring thaws. Several rivers entering the inlet have flat deltas at their mouths; other rivers or creeks plunge as waterfalls off the mountain sides.*
>
> *Numerous logging camps are in the inlet, many of them on floats moored to shore, which are moved according to requirements ...*
>
> *Tidal streams in Jervis Inlet are weak and irregular and influenced by winds. In the entrances to Princess Louisa and Sechelt Inlets tidal streams are strong and are described with the inlets.* (SD)

Jervis Inlet is one of the longer fjords indenting the British Columbia mainland. At its head is one of the world's great jewels—Princess Louisa Inlet and its famous Chatterbox Falls.

Note: Charts 3312 and 3313 are chart books in atlas format. They are designed for use by small craft, and include additional information and aerial photographs. However, these charts are not available as NDI digital charts, nor do they lend themselves easily to measurement of latitude and longitude.

Quarry Bay

Quarry Bay (Nelson Island)

Charts 3311, 3312, 3512; 3.5 mi NW of Pender Hbr
Entrance: 49°39.34'N, 124°08.28'W
Anchor: 49°39.69'N, 124°07.26'W

> *Quarry Bay has submarine cables laid down its centre. Private floats, a floating log breakwater and private mooring buoys are near the head of the bay. Numerous above- and below-water rocks lie at the head of the bay. Anchorage for small craft can be obtained close to shore.* (SD)

The best anchorage in Quarry Bay is reported to be in the southern portion of the easternmost arm. This site is just south of the old granite quarry which furnished much of the fine stone used in Vancouver and Victoria buildings. The ramparts of the quarry are visible from the bay and make interesting exploration.

The bay has a number of above- and below-water rocks that require careful piloting. One rock is in the fairway 200 yards north of the southern shore; another is 20 yards north of the rock ledge that forms a natural breakwater for the inner cove. A careful reading of Chart 3312 and a slow approach is advised.

Anchor in 6 fathoms over an unrecorded bottom.

Cockburn Bay

Cockburn Bay (Nelson Island)

Charts 3311, 3312, 3512; 2.9 mi NW of Quarry Bay
Entrance: 49°40.86'N, 124°12.18'W

> *It can be entered by small craft at or near HW; local knowledge is required.* (SD)

Cockburn Bay is actually a narrow inlet with a foul entrance that can be navigated only near high water. There is about 2 feet of water at zero tide at the narrowest point just southwest of the midchannel rock.

Avoid anchoring near the B.C. Tel submerged cable which is laid through the entrance and terminates near the B.C. Hydro facility. Cockburn Bay is reported to be a good place if you're looking for solitude.

Billings Bay (Nelson Island)

Charts 3311, 3312, 3512; 1.4 mi SE of Blind Bay; 3.6 mi NW of Quarry Bay
Entrance: 49°41.88'N, 124°12.19'W

> *Billings Bay, 1.75 miles north of Cape Cockburn, is close east of Maynard Head. A rock, which dries 2.4 m (8 ft), lies 30 m (98 ft) off the NE shore of Billings Bay. A submarine cable passes down the centre of the bay.* (SD)

Hidden Basin (Nelson Island)

Charts 3311, 3312, 3512; immediately E of Billings Bay
Entrance: 49°41.97'N, 124°11.70'W

> *Hidden Basin, east of Billings Bay, has an islet, 30 m (98 ft) high, in the centre of its entrance. The channel north of the islet dries and is encumbered with boulders which dry 3.4 m (11 ft). The entrance channel south of the islet has boulders in it which dry 3 m (10 ft). Tidal streams are strong in the entrance and the*

Entrance to Hidden Basin

south passage is preferred; it should be entered only at or near HW slack and local knowledge is required. A drying spit, 0.2 mile east of the above-mentioned islet, extends from the north shore and considerably narrows the entrance channel. Several drying rocks lie close off the south and east shores of the basin, inside the 10 m (33 ft) contour line. Several private floats and marine farm facilities are located in Hidden Basin.

Anchorage can be obtained in 10 to 15 m (33 to 49 ft) at the NE end of Hidden Basin. The maximum recorded depth in the basin is 38 m (125 ft). (SD)

Due to its foul entrance, Hidden Basin is another seldom-visited inlet. A tree-covered islet plugs the entrance of the mile-and-a-half-long basin.

During spring ebb tides, the channels on either side of the islet become raging waterfalls. Boats can negotiate the south channel at high water slack only—it dries at 10 feet!

Temporary anchorage can be found at the head of Billings Bay, allowing you to reconnoiter the entrance to Hidden Basin and wait for high water. Avoid the uncharted rock in the northeast shore which is reported to dry at 8 feet.

Blind Bay (Nelson Island)

Charts 3312, 3512; 1.3 mi SE of Jervis Inlet entrance
Entrance (0.45 mi S of Alexander Pt): 49°43.07'N, 124°13.26'W

Blind Bay lies between the NW side of Nelson Island and the SE side of Hardy Island. Numerous islands and islets lie on either side of the entrance, with a deep channel between them. Fox Island, Kelly Island, Nocturne Island and Clio Island are named islands in the bay. Marine farm facilities are located in Blind Bay and numerous private floats line the shores. (SD)

Blind Bay, situated between Nelson and Hardy islands, offers a number of islands, islets and coves to explore. Opportunities for small-boat anchoring are limited only by one's imagination. The bay is ringed with rocks and reefs and requires slow and careful piloting; depths can rise precipitously. Stern ties can be used to good advantage in Blind Bay.

Ballet Bay (Nelson Island)

Charts 3312, 3512; on S side of Blind Bay
Entrance: 49°43.02'N, 124°11.83'W
Anchor (SE shore): 49°43.13'N, 124°10.85'W

Ballet Bay ... is a popular small craft anchorage. Numerous islands, rocks and shoals lie in its approach and local knowledge is recommended. Mariners without local knowledge are advised to approach with caution, and at LW when reefs are more likely to be visible.

Anchorage in Blind Bay is reported to be good north of Fox Island, or in Ballet Bay clear of the submarine cables. (SD)

Ballet Bay is a small, well-sheltered and popular anchorage, entered east of Nocturne and Clio islands through a narrow shallow passage of 1 fathom or less. An alert bow watch and slow speed are required to identify and avoid the many uncharted rocks and reefs in this fasci-

Ballet Bay, facing southwest

nating and beautiful area. Avoid the poles that stick up out of the water; this is the way locals identify major hazards. The bottom may be rocky, so be sure your anchor is well set.

Anchor close to the southeast shore in about 2 to 3 fathoms, or in the outer bay in 5 to 6 fathoms, unrecorded holding.

Loaded for adventure

Dol Cove (Hardy Island)

Charts 3312, 3512, 3514; 4.7 mi N of W tip of Fox Island
Entrance: 49°43.31′N, 124°12.85′W
Anchor: 49°43.85′N, 124°12.73′W

Dol Cove, the local name for the cove northwest of Fox Island, indents Hardy Island in a T-shape. It is entered west of Fox Island. Dol refers to the old pilings at the head of the cove which can sometimes be used as stern-tie posts. The chart indicates that a trail leads across Hardy Island to a small cove with a view of the entrance to Jervis Inlet.

Anchor in about 2 fathoms over mud with good holding.

9 Fathom Cove (Hardy Island)

Charts 3312, 3512, 3514; 0.64 mi NE of W tip of Fox Island
Entrance: 49°43.31′N, 124°12.85′W
Anchor: 49°43.97′N, 124°12.43′W

9 Fathom Cove is the local name for the small, northeast-trending inlet 0.2 mile east of Dol Cove. This is a steep-sided cove with a dark aspect and limited swinging room. Not many boats use this slender cove because the charts indicate the bar across its entrance has only 2 feet of water at zero tide. However, if you favor the eastern shore, there is plenty of water and you can enter and exit at any time. The name of the cove comes from the depth of the hole shown on the chart.

A quiet and secluded anchorage can be had at the far end of the 9-fathom hole. Place your bow anchor midchannel and run a stern line to the steep, rocky shore on the south side of the cove. (Some of the old stern lines have been hanging in place here for nearly 20 years.)

Anchor in 8 fathoms or less with a stern tie ashore, mixed bottom, fair holding.

Telescope Passage

Charts 3312, 3512, 3514; E end of Hardy Island; N end of Nelson Island
Entrance (S): 49°45.01′N, 124°09.37′W
Entrance (N): 49°45.57′N, 124°08.82′W

> *Telescope Passage is a very narrow channel separating the islands NE of Hardy Island from Nelson Island and connects the head of Blind Bay ... with Jervis Inlet... . Drying rocks lie in mid-channel and on the west side of the channel; the Nelson Island side of the channel should be favoured. The least depth through the fairway is 7.2 m (24 ft). Mariners not familiar with Telescope Passage are advised to navigate it at LW when dangers are visible.* (SD)

Telescope Passage, a picturesque narrows, can be navigated by small craft with little difficulty, avoiding the rocks described above. The fairway favoring the Nelson Island shore, abeam the unnamed 70-meter island, has 4 fathoms at zero tide. The two rocks at the entrance to Jervis Inlet can be seen at low water and should be passed on their south side.

Telescope Passage

Temporary anchorage is sometimes taken near the small bight between the east end of Hardy Island and the 70-meter island.

Vanguard Bay (Nelson Island)

Charts 3312, 3512, 3514; N side of Nelson Island; 2 mi E of Telescope Passage
Entrance: 49°45.86'N, 124°06.45'W
Anchor: 49°45.60'N, 124°05.48'W

> *Two islets lie close off the east shore of the bay and a rock, which dries 2.1 m (7 ft), lies close off the south shore. The bay is deep, but small craft can find limited anchorage close inshore north of the islets.* (SD)

Thunder Bay, Maude Bay (Jervis Inlet)

Charts 3312, 3512, 3514; Thunder Bay is 1.7 mi N of Scotch Fir Pt; Maude Bay is 0.36 mi NW of Thunder Pt, in S part of Thunder Bay
Entrance: 49°46.10'N, 124°15.64'W
Anchor (Maude Bay): 49°45.80'N, 124°16.14'W

> *Thunder Bay is one of the few places where anchorage can be obtained in Jervis Inlet. Small craft can anchor near the sandy beach at the head of the bay.* (SD)

Thunder Bay, a good place from which to launch the final leg of a trip to Princess Louisa, provides easily-accessible shelter when a southerly kicks up in Malaspina Strait. The main part of the bay is fairly deep, but anchorage can be found close to the wide beach. The small peninsula northwest of Thunder Point provides very good protection. In a southeasterly, you can tuck into the south nook, known locally as Maude Bay, and anchor close to shore avoiding the rock. If you anchor in Maude Bay, avoid the rock on the west side of the nook that dries at 8 feet.

Anchor (Maude Bay) in about 4 fathoms over sand and gravel with fair holding.

Saltery Bay (Jervis Inlet)

Charts 3312, 3512, 3514; 4 mi E of Thunder Bay
Entrance: 49°46.70'N, 124°10.50'W
Public floats: 49°46.90'N, 124°10.48'W

> *Saltery Bay ... has depths of 14 m (46 ft) and provides limited anchorage to small craft.*
>
> *Saltery Bay Provincial Park, with two beach-fronting areas, has camping and picnic facilities.* (SD)

Saltery Bay is the British Columbia ferry terminal that connects to Earl Cove and serves the northernmost section of Highway 1. A public float with limited room is located between the ferry docks and a logboom area to the east. The floats are used principally by the logging community. The nearest fuel and supplies available can be found in Powell River by road, or at Egmont (Secret Cove) in Sechelt Inlet by boat.

Fairview Bay (Jervis Inlet)

Charts 3312, 3514; 1.6 mi NE of Vanguard Bay
Position: 49°47.42'N, 124°07.05'W

Fairview Bay appears to offer shelter from prevailing northwest winds but it is exposed to downslope winds. We have no local knowledge.

St. Vincent Bay (Sykes Island), Junction Island

Charts 3312, 3514; N side of Jervis Inlet btwn Culloden & Elephand Pts
Entrance (0.3 mi NE of Culloden Pt): 49°48.26'N, 124°04.35'W
Anchor (S cove): 49°48.69'N, 124°04.93'W
Anchor (N side, Junction I): 49°49.92'N, 124°03.17'W

> *Caution. Military exercise area. The area between St. Vincent Bay, Captain Island, and the entrance to Hotham Sound is used as an exercise area by the Canadian Armed Forces for air to surface*

Photo courtesy CHS, Pacific Region

Sykes Island, St. Vincent Bay

and torpedo firing. For details concerning this area the Annual Edition to Mariners should be consulted. (SD)

St. Vincent Bay has been a logboom storage and oyster spat collection area for a few entrepreneurs. From here north to the head of Hotham Sound, the south-facing rocks and lack of strong tidal currents cause the waters to warm up to temperatures not found elsewhere until deep in Desolation Sound.

Sykes Island, in the southwest corner of St. Vincent Bay, gives moderately good shelter either deep in the cove indenting the south side, along the shore, or in the nook on the northwest corner.

The south cove of Sykes Island is reported to have a small reef—that dries at 12 feet—attached to its eastern entrance point.

The military exercise area is identified on the charts as "WN" (Whiskey November).

Anchor (S cove, Sykes I) in 5 fathoms over an unrecorded bottom.

Junction Island, on the north end of St. Vincent Bay, has a number of interesting islets with water shallow enough for good anchoring. Due to its warm waters, the area is filled with private oyster farms. Good anchorage can be found on the north side of Junction Island. Small craft may also find anchorage in the hidden cove 0.4 mile northwest of Junction Island and 0.25 mile northeast of Junction Island by carefully avoiding the numerous rocks in the entrance to the unnamed cove.

Hotham Sound

Charts 3312, 3514; 10.5 mi NE of Jervis Inlet entrance
Entrance (0.64 mi SE of Elephant Pt): 49°49.84'N, 124°01.43'W

Hotham Sound, entered east of Elephant Point, extends 6 miles north and is too deep for anchorage except for small craft. Mountains rise steeply from its steep-to shores. (SD)

Hotham Sound is generally deep, but the Harmony Islands offer a welcome shallow anchorage.

Granville Bay (Hotham Sound)

Charts 3312, 3514; 1.5 mi E of Elephand Pt
Position: 49°50.27'N, 123°59.87'W

Granville Bay, on the east side of the entrance to the sound, is deep. A conspicuous waterfall is at the north end of the bay and a logging camp and marine farm facilities are at the head of the bay. (SD)

Granville Bay, a shallow bight on the east side of Hotham Sound, is too deep for convenient anchorage.

Harmony Islands (Hotham Sound)

Charts 3312, 3514; 1.9 mi NE of Elephant Pt
Entrance: (S passage) 49°51.58'N, 124°00.67'W
Entrance: (N passage) 49°52.12'N, 124°01.07'W
Anchor: 49°51.80'N, 124°00.88'W

The channel east of Harmony Islands and the basin inside the three north islands are popular small craft anchorages; most craft anchor with a stern line to shore. A rock, with less than 2 m (6 ft) over it, lies in the entrance to the basin.

Two islets lie 0.2 mile SE of Syren Point. A rock, with 2.1 m (7 ft) over it, lies 0.2 mile southwest of the last-mentioned islets. (SD)

Harmony Islands are just that—a wonderful, quiet place, out of the main track, good for re-establishing domestic tranquility if you've just come in from a stormy Malaspina Strait. Anchorage for all vessels can be found in the passage east of the Harmony Islands on either shore using stern ties.

One mile to the south, a 1,400-foot cascade draining hidden Freil Lake drops vertically into Hotham Sound.

Small craft can find anchorage in the passage between the southern and middle Harmony Islands and the mainland—watch depths in the shoal—at the narrowest part they are about one foot!

Kipling Cove (Harmony Islands)

Charts 3312, 3514; btwn three N island in Harmony group
Anchor: 49°51.97′N, 124°01.06′W

Kipling Cove is the local name for the very small shallow nook east of the large north island. The cove provides good shelter for two or three small boats if all boats use a stern tie to shore. In spring and autumn, you may be fortunate enough to have the place to yourself with the cascade as your only neighbor.

Anchor in 1 to 2 fathoms using a stern tie.

Lena and Baker Bays (Hotham Sound)

Charts 3312, 3514; at the head of Hotham Sound
Entrance (Lena Bay): 49°54.94′N, 124°01.47′W
Entrance (Baker Bay): 49°54.92′N, 124°02.27′W

> *Marine farm facilities lie along the west shore north of Elephant Point and at the head of the sound in Lena Bay.*
>
> *Baker Bay, at the head of Hotham Sound, has a conspicuous peak on its west side.* (SD)

Photo courtesy CHS, Pacific Region

Harmony Islands

Both Lena and Baker bays are considered too deep for anchorage; however, Lena Bay has a shoal on its east side which may be useful for small craft and those interested in visiting the lagoon on the peninsula to the west.

Prince of Wales Reach (Jervis Inlet)

Charts 3312, 3514; 3.1 mi NW of Egmont
Entrance (S, 0.5 mi SE of Foley Head): 49°47.84′N, 123°57.84′W
Entrance (N, 0.68 mi E of McMurray Bay): 49°58.07′N, 123°59.45′W

> *Prince of Wales Reach, entered between Egmont Point and Foley Head, trends 6 miles NNE to Saumarez Bluff then 6.4 miles NW to Moorsam Bluff. It is deep and steep-to on both sides.* (SD)

Killam Bay (Prince of Wales Reach)

Charts 3312, 3514; 1.1 mi NE of Egmont Pt
Position: 49°47.13′N, 123°55.34′W

> *Killam Bay, about 1 mile east of Miller Islet, is deep but can afford anchorage to small craft close inshore. A small breakwater is at the head of the bay.* (SD)

Killam Bay, a bight in the east shore of Prince of Wales Reach just north of Sechelt Inlet, is reported to provide fair protection from up- and downslope winds. Anchorage is off the sand beach.

Dark Cove (Prince of Wales Reach)

Charts 3312, 3514; 0.65 mi N of Foley Head
Entrance (S, 0.2 mi S of Sydney I): 49°48.64′N, 123°57.39′W
Entrance (N, 0.34 mi NE of Sydney I): 49°49.20′N, 123°57.02′W

> *Dark Cove … at the base of Mount Foley, affords anchorage to small vessels west of Sydney Island in 30 m (98 ft) but the holding ground is reported to be poor.* (SD)

Dark Cove is aptly named because afternoon sun is obscured here by 2,000-foot Mt. Foley on its western side. Wolferstan recommends a reasonably well-protected anchor site at the head of the cove north of Sydney Island, behind a tiny islet, avoiding a shallow patch just north of this islet.

Because nearby Goliath Bay is the site for a major log chipping operation, we prefer not to anchor here.

Goliath Bay (Prince of Wales Reach)

Charts 3312, 3514; 1.7 mi NE of Foley Head
Entrance: 49°49.47′N, 123°56.40′W

> *Goliath Bay, entered west of Dacres Point... is deep and offers no anchorage. Several large privately owned mooring buoys are in the bay.* (SD)

Vancouver Bay (Prince of Wales Reach)

Charts 3312, 3514; on the E shore of Prince of Wales Reach; 9 mi N of Egmont Pt
Entrance: 49° 54.68′N, 123°53.49′W

> *Vancouver Bay ... is too deep for anchorage. The sides of the bay are precipitous but the head is low with steep-to drying flats formed by sediments from Vancouver River and High Creek. Marine farm facilities are on the north and south shores and a house is on the south side of the Vancouver River entrance.* (SD)

Vancouver Bay lies at the base of a pleasant U-shaped valley. Unfortunately, the drying flat drops off at a 45-degree angle and this is not a good place to anchor, other than for a short stop in calm weather. The large mud flats at the outlet of Vancouver River are a good place to watch for bears.

McMurray Bay (Prince of Wales Reach)

Charts 3312, 3514; 5.7 mi NW of Vancouver Bay
Position: 49°58.18′N, 124°00.50′W

> *McMurray Bay is a small bay on the west side of the channel opposite Moorsam Bluff.* (SD)

McMurray Bay is reported to offer fair temporary shelter from downslope winds. Head for the low saddle and anchor close to the small beach. The bay is exposed to up-inlet winds.

Wolferstan recommends the small second nook north of McMurray Bay as having more shelter.

Princess Royal Reach (Jervis Inlet)

Charts 3312, 3514; connects Prince of Wales Reach to Queens Reach
Entrance (S, 0.68 mi E of McMurray Bay): 49°58.07′N, 123°59.45′W
Entrance (N, 0.7 mi E of Patrick Pt): 50°05.56′N, 123°47.05′W

> *Princess Royal Reach extends 10 miles NE from Britain River to Patrick Point.* (SD)

Soda Waterfalls (Princess Royal Reach)

Charts 3312, 3514; on the S shore of Princess Royal Reach; 3.0 mi NE of McMurray Bay
Position: 49°59.95′N, 123°56.66′W

Soda Waterfalls, around the corner from Moorsam Bluff at the beginning of Princess Royal Reach, is a remarkable cascade that drops 50 feet directly into the water. Since the shore is so steep-to, you can head in close to the plunging stream and the current will hold you off the overhanging rock. The surrounding saltwater is covered with white foam, perhaps the origin of the falls' name.

Deserted Bay (Princess Royal Reach)

Charts 3312, 3514; 1.8 mi E of Patrick Pt
Entrance: 50°05.54′N, 123°45.30′W

> *Deserted Bay, at the NE end of Princess Royal Reach, affords indifferent anchorage in its SE part in a depth of about 30 m (98 ft); it is only suitable for small vessels.* (SD)

Deserted Bay is too deep for convenient anchorage; however, it can be used as a temporary stop close to shore off the ruins in the southeast corner. Wildlife can sometimes be sighted near the creek on the Indian Reserve.

A scar high on the mountainside, 1.5 miles north of the Deserted River outlet, comes from clearcutting done in 1990. Another 1.5 miles north, on the west side of Mt. Pearkes, you can see a small glacial remnant of the last ice age, complete with crevasses.

Queens Reach (Jervis Inlet)

Charts 3312, 3514; last arm of Jervis Inlet
Entrance (S, 0.7 mi E of Patrick Pt): 50°05.56'N, 123°47.05'W

Queens Reach extends 10 miles NW from Patrick Pt to the head of Jervis Inlet. (SD)

Queens Reach proved quite a disappointment to George Vancouver who hoped it might be the answer to his search for a northwest passage.

There are a number of interesting waterfalls on both shores of the reach—some of which make a pleasant freshwater shower. There is a big logging camp at Smanit Creek and an abandoned house on the grassy point at the outlet of Lausmann Creek. Except at creek outlets, the shore along this region is steep-to and there are no protected anchorages.

Princess Louisa Inlet, the principal reason for your 30-mile journey up Jervis Inlet from Malaspina Strait, lies just beyond Malibu Rapids on the northeast shore of Queens Reach.

Princess Louisa Inlet (Queens Reach)

Charts 3312, 3514; on the NE side of Queens Reach
Entrance: 50°09.70'N, 123°51.17'W

Princess Louisa Inlet ... is entered through Malibu Rapids. The inlet extends 4 miles NE and is hemmed in by high mountains. Depths within the inlet are great. (SD)

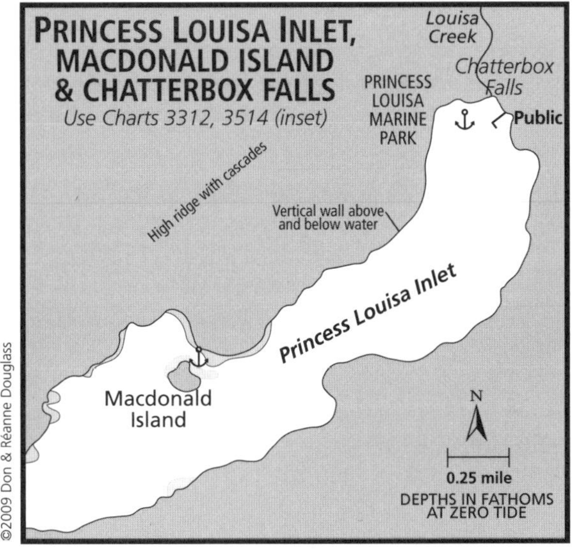

Princess Louisa Inlet, reachable only by boat or float plane, is as undeveloped and pristine a national park as any you will find.

The inlet is a magnificent granite-walled gorge cut sharply by an ancient glacier into mountains which rise 5,000 to 8,000 feet from the water's edge. It is an azure-blue jewel set in granite walls and fragrant green forests of cedars, pines and firs. The rock faces are variegated in color, and gold and copper mosses carpet the steep shores. Combined with the brilliant blue sky, white clouds and snow-capped peaks, the rocks form a masterpiece of nature.

Almost completely landlocked, the inlet is 5 miles in length and never more than three-quarters of a mile in width. The water reaches a depth of 1,000 feet and, except for Malibu Rapids at its entrance, is calm. At the head of the fjord is the awe-inspiring sight of Chatterbox Falls. In addition, until mid-June, melting snows create more than 60 waterfalls that cascade and plunge down the sheer walls.

Earle Stanley Gardiner wrote in his Log of a Landlubber: "There is a calm tranquility which stretches from the smooth surface of the reflecting waters straight up into infinity. The deep calm of eternal silence is only disturbed by the muffled roar of throbbing waterfalls as they plunge down from sheer cliffs.

There is no scenery in the world that can beat it. Not that I've seen the rest of the world, I don't need to. I've seen Princess Louisa Inlet."

Princess Louisa Inlet has been preserved so that we, our children, and our children's children, may enjoy its wonders. Please do your part by observing common courtesy and park regulations, so that the Inlet will remain a place of unparalleled beauty forever.

Basking in the sun, Princess Louisa Inlet

Malibu Rapids (Princess Louisa Inlet)

Charts 3312, 3514 inset; at the entrance to Prince Louisa Inlet
Entrance (S): 50°09.70'N, 123°51.17'W
Entrance (N): 50°09.94'N, 123°50.92'W

> *Malibu Rapids flows through a narrow gorge. It is suitable for small vessels and should be negotiated at or near slack water. Malibu Islet and several small islets lie in the south entrance. Keep in mid-channel between the light and Malibu Islet. The channel east of Malibu Islet is not recommended.*
>
> *Tidal streams in Malibu Rapids attain 9 kn on the flood and ebb on large tides.* (SD)

Malibu Rapids channel is narrow and winding. A radio check for opposing traffic on Channel 16 and an alert bow lookout are advised.

An S-shaped turn is required to stay mid-channel. Refer to the inset Chart 3312, page 7, or Chart 3514 inset, for the route, and the corrected tide tables for predicted times of slack water.

The buildings of a Christian youth camp are located on the north shore of the entrance to Princess Louisa Inlet. Visitors are allowed to tie up at their float for a short tour of the facilities. (No overnight mooring is permitted.)

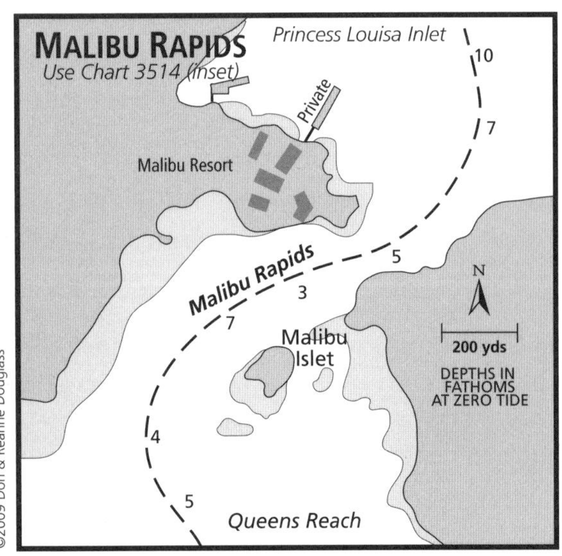

Macdonald Island (Princess Louisa Inlet)

Charts 3312, 3514 inset; 2.3 mi NE of Malibu Rapids
Position: 50°11.17'N, 123°48.24'W

> *Macdonald Island, 2 miles NE of Malibu Rapids, has a drying rock off its east end. If passage is made through the channel between Macdonald Island and the mainland care must be taken to avoid the drying ledge extending from the north shore. Anchorage, with good shelter, can be obtained by small craft inside Macdonald Island. It is reported that six mooring buoys have been installed between Macdonald Island and the mainland.* (SD)

The shoal inside Macdonald Island affords a quiet and sometimes secluded anchorage compared to the comings and goings at Chatterbox Falls. You can utilize the mooring buoys or

---

The Gift of James F. Macdonald

It is thanks to the generosity and foresight of James F. "Mac" Macdonald, a native of California, that Princess Louisa Inlet retains its pristine beauty. Eight years after his first visit to the inlet, Mac obtained the land surrounding Chatterbox Falls, and there he lived and played host to visitors from all over the globe.

In 1953, Mac gave his land in trust to the non-profit Princess Louisa International Society so that ". . . all may enjoy its peace and beauty as God created it, unspoiled by the hand of man." In 1963, with Macdonald's blessing, the Society turned over administration of the area to the Government of the Province of British Columbia and it became the Princess Louisa Marine Park.

---

anchor in desirable depths over the 300-yard-long shoal.

About 1 mile east of Macdonald Island, the rock face overhangs and you can approach by boat to study the glacier-cut granite.

Chatterbox Falls (Princess Louisa Inlet)

Charts 3312, 3514; 3.9 mi NE of Malibu Rapids
Public float: 50°12.28'N, 123°46.16'W
Anchor (off Chatterbox Falls): 50°12.33'N, 123°46.29'W

> *Chatterbox Falls, at the head of the inlet, when running strongly are spectacular and can be heard throughout the inlet.*
>
> *In settled weather small vessels can find anchorage in the narrow belt of depths under 20 m (66 ft) off the falls, being held offshore by the current, or on the west side of the head of the inlet. Mariners should be prepared to move, or have an anchor set securely to hold them offshore, in the event of a significant up-inlet wind.* (SD)

Chatterbox Falls drop 120 feet down the mountainside in a series of dizzying cascades, plunging with a roar into the calm waters beneath. You haven't begun to explore the British Columbia coast or the northwest corner of the North American continent until you ride out a storm anchored directly in front of Chatterbox Falls. From the vertical granite cliffs above, hundreds of waterfalls burst forth, swollen by the rains, tumbling 7,000 feet with a thundering crescendo.

Photo courtesy CHS, Pacific Region

Malibu Rapids

Authors at Chatterbox Falls

The public float on the east side of the inlet offers convenient access to picnic and camping facilities and two steep trails. One of the trails takes you to the base of the falls, a muddy, slippery route. The trail continues to the top of the falls, but has poorly stabilized mossy patches due to constant mist from the falls. To avoid slipping when hiking, we recommend that you wear hiking boots and walk with care. The second trail takes you to the Trapper's Cabin, about a two-hour hike. This trail is poorly maintained and makes for difficult walking.

Numerous mooring rings along the east shore facilitate using a stern tie. Intrepid boaters can try anchoring just off the creek, or slightly to the west, for a more intimate and personal experience.

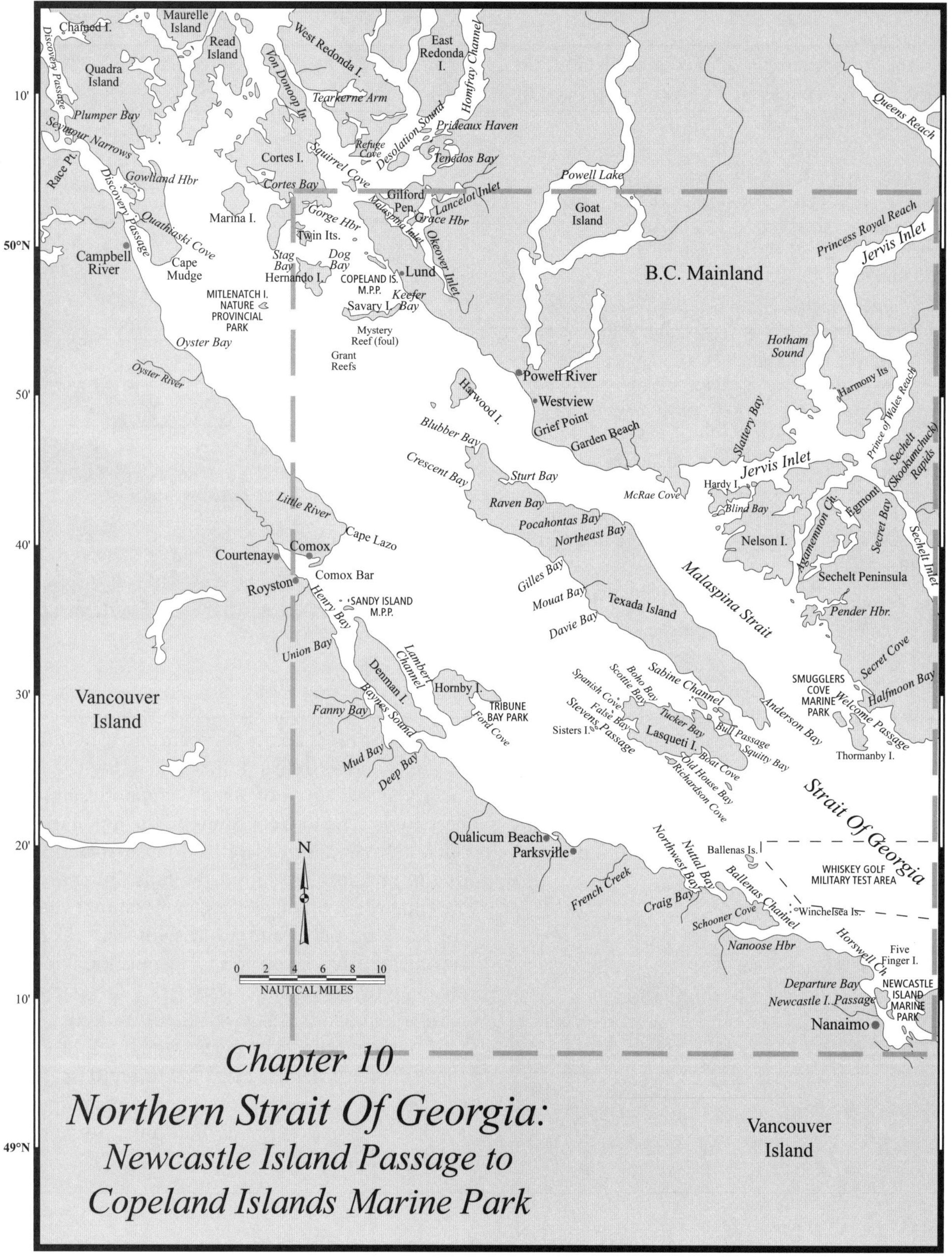

Chapter 10

Northern Strait Of Georgia:

Newcastle Island Passage to Copeland Islands Marine Park

10

NORTHERN STRAIT OF GEORGIA: Newcastle Island Passage to Copelands Islands Provincial Marine Park

The northern end of the Strait of Georgia is a complex geographical area lying between northern Vancouver Island on the west and the mainland on the east. It was explored by Captain Vancouver in the late 18th century, who named many of the places here.

When you leave Nanaimo, once you're clear of the Whiskey Golf military test area, you can head north in the Strait of Georgia, the direct route to Discovery Passage on the west side of the Strait. Routes to Desolation Sound follow either the Strait of Georgia or Malaspina Strait. The Strait of Georgia contains a number of large islands—Texada, Lasqueti, Denman, and Hornby. Malaspina Strait lies between the east side of Texada Island and the mainland

You can choose to stay close to Vancouver Island, exploring coastline coves, Denman and Hornby Islands, wandering in and out of Nanoose Bay, Tribune Bay, and Baynes Sound toward Comox Harbour, then head north to Campbell River. Although there is much to see along this route, there are relatively few anchorages.

Newcastle Island Park floats

If you wish to cross the Strait of Georgia, you can visit Lasqueti and Texada islands, enjoying many small coves, or you can head up Malaspina Strait, exploring east Texada and the mainland coast.

Malaspina Strait is also the route to take if you're heading to Jervis Inlet and Princess Louisa Inlet to the northeast. From Malaspina Strait, it's just a short hop along the mainland coast to Lund and the Copeland Islands.

The winds in the Strait of Georgia can be strong, especially afternoon northwesterlies. The area west of Cape Mudge can be quite hazardous in southeast winds on a south-flowing flood tide.

Note: Charts 3312 and 3313 are chart books in atlas format. They are designed for use by small craft, and include additional information and aerial photographs. However, these charts are not available as NDI digital charts, nor do they lend themselves easily to measurement of latitude and longitude.

Making time on a cloudy day

Newcastle Island Passage

Charts 3457, 3313, 3458; W of Newcastle Island, connects Nanaimo Hbr to Departure Bay
Entrance (S, mid-ch btwn buoys "P11" & "P12"): 49°10.54'N, 123°56.18'W
Entrance (N, mid-ch btwn Pimbury & Shaft Pts): 49°11.64'N, 123°56.89'W

> *Newcastle Island Passage, between Vancouver and Newcastle islands, leads north from the inner portion of Nanaimo Harbour to Departure Bay; it is used mainly by small vessels and recreational craft. The west shore of the passage has numerous wharves, marinas and fuel jetties.*
>
> *A ferry provides transportation for foot passengers between Nanaimo and Newcastle Island during summer months. Small craft navigators are advised to keep clear of the ferry.*
>
> *No vessel shall proceed at a speed greater than 5 kn in Newcastle Island Passage between Bate Point and Pimbury Point.*
>
> *An orange buoy, 0.1 mile southeast of Bate Point, has a speed caution sign on it.*
>
> *Oregon Rock ... lies on the west side of the fairway, 0.2 mile northwest of Bate Point.*
>
> *Passage Rock, with a 1 foot (0.2 m) over it, lies about 300 feet (91 m) north of Oregon Rock.*
>
> *A port hand buoy, identified "P13", marks Oregon Rock.*
>
> *Passage Rock daybeacon, consisting of a 5-pile dolphin displaying a port hand daymark, marks Passage Rock.*
>
> *Vessels should not pass between these markers as the channel lies on the east side, off the Newcastle Island shore.* (SD)

Newcastle Island Passage is narrow, shallow, and heavily used by local traffic and northbound pleasure craft. The channel skirts the city of Nanaimo and the many yacht facilities along its shore. A convenient fuel dock is located at the north entrance, but be careful to avoid the shoal close to the north end of the dock. A strict no-wake 5 knot speed limit is enforced in Newcastle Island to protect the numerous marinas and boat docks along the Vancouver Island shore. Avoid the shoal and rock pile north of Shaft Point marked with a yellow buoy.

Departure Bay (Vancouver Island)

Charts 3457, 3313, 3458; NW of Newcastle I
Entrance (E, 0.3 mi S of Horswell Rock light buoy "PL"): 49°12.42'N, 12355.96'W
Anchor: 49°12.33'N, 123°57.89'W

> [Departure Bay] *is well sheltered, however, few vessels anchor here due to a constant passage of ferries to and from the mainland causing large swells, which can be a problem to small craft.*
>
> *Anchorage is prohibited in the area north of Brandon Islands*
>
> *During summer months diving rafts, a water-ski raft and swimming area marker floats are moored off the west shore of Departure Bay.* (SD)

Although Departure Bay is well sheltered, no anchoring is permitted due to heavy ferry traffic and the public bathing beach. The large ferry terminal is located 0.25 mile west of Pimbury Point; small craft should avoid this busy area. The Pacific Biological Station, which monitors fish and shellfish, is located on the north shore. The east entrance to Departure Bay leads to Horswell, Rainbow and Fairway channels. Boats headed to the north coast usually exit through Horswell; those heading to the Sunshine Coast use Rainbow Channel; those heading to Vancouver use Fairway Channel.

Caution: Avoid leaving Departure Bay when gales are forecast for north of Nanaimo; the Strait of Georgia can be rough.

Anchor in 6 fathoms over mud with good holding.

Anne Vipond

Weather-worn rocks along the Vancouver Island shore

Horswell Channel

Charts 3457, 3313, 3458; 1.1 mi NE of Newcastle Island
Entrance (S, 0.25 mi W of Horswell Rock light buoy "PL"): 49°12.72'N, 123°55.57'W
Entrance (N, 0.35 mi E of Lagoon Head): 49°13.71'N, 123°56.35'W

> *Horswell Channel lies between Hudson Rocks and the coast of Vancouver Island.* (SD)

Hammond Bay (Pipers Lagoon) (Vancouver Island)

Charts 3458, 3313; 1.5 mi N of Horswell Rock; W side of Horswell Channel
Entrance: 49°13.99'N, 123°57.39'W
Anchor: 49°13.68'N, 123°57.42'W

> *Hammond Bay, entered between Lagoon Head and Neck Point, is exposed to NE weather. A launching ramp is in the south part of the bay.* (SD)

Hammond Bay has a number of private buoys used by local residents during the summer. Good anchorage can be found in the south end of the bay, avoiding the private mooring buoys. This area is well protected from southeast and westerly winds, although seas from the northwest tend to curve around Neck Point and enter the bay. Hammond Bay is a good place to anchor overnight when you want to enter Nanaimo in the daylight hours.

Page Lagoon, on the southeast side of Hammond Bay, is a regional park.

Anchor (south end of bay) in 4 fathoms over sand and mud with good holding.

Winchelsea Islands

Charts 3459, 3512; 2 mi NE of Nanoose Hbr entr
Position (radio towers): 49°17.67'N, 124°05.15'W

> *Winchelsea Islands are covered with grass and have a few stunted trees on them. The islands are a Canadian Armed Forces base; trespassing is prohibited.* (SD)

Whiskey Golf Military Test Area (Strait of Georgia)

Charts 3459, 3512; extends 14 mi E from Ballenas Islands
Position: See sidebar on next page.

When you head across the Strait of Georgia, avoid the military exercise area Whiskey Golf (WG), clearly marked on the charts listed above. This is a torpedo test area and private boats are not allowed while operations are being carried out. During these tests, the area is aggressively patrolled. To determine hours of active operation for Whiskey Golf, call the operations center, Winchelsea Control, on VHF Channels 10 or 16, or check with Comox Coast Guard Radio.

If exercises are taking place at the time you want to cross the Strait of Georgia, Winchelsea Control will direct you to pass through a narrow transit area that extends 1000 yards north of Winchelsea Island and 1,000 yards east of South Ballenas Island, before you turn northeast for Lasqueti and Texada islands.

If you want a scenic route that doesn't require checking in with Winchelsea Operations, stay close to the Vancouver Island shore, passing carefully inside Ada and Yeo islands. This route gives you maximum protection from chop, and you can duck into Nanoose Bay or the marina at Schooner Cove if a blow develops. While this route doesn't require contacting Winchelsea, it does demand careful piloting among the islets and rocks, many of which are marked only by kelp or breaking waves.

"WHISKEY GOLF"
CANADIAN FORCES MARITIME EXPERIMENTAL AND TEST RANGES

The Canadian Forces Maritime Experimental and Test Ranges tests ship and aircraft systems and torpedoes. Torpedoes may be launched by a surface vessel, submarine, or aircraft. No explosives are used; however, a hazard exists due to the possibility of the torpedo homing on vessels and then the vessel being struck by the torpedo on its way to the surface.

Testing is usually carried out from 0800 to 1730, Tuesday to Friday, and occasionally on Monday or Saturday.

During testing, Area "WG" is "Active." Any vessel within the area bounded by the following coordinates:

A. 49°21'35"N 123°07'70" W;
B. 49°21'00"N 123°48'40" W;
C. 49°14'83"N 123°48'40" W;
D. 49°16'75"N 124°00'90" W; and
E. 49°19'35"N 124°07'70" W;

will be required to clear or stop on demand from the Canadian Range Officer at "Winchelsea Island Control" or any of the range vessels or range helicopters. The positions of these coordinates are clearly marked on the diagram.

A transit area 1,000 yards north of Winchelsea Island and 1,000 yards east of South Ballenas Island has been established to enable mariners to transit safely around the active area. It also facilitates unimpeded access to marina facilities in Schooner Cove and Nanoose Bay. This area is clearly depicted on charts 3512 and 3459 by means of pecked lines.

Additional information on active hours or for safe transit through the area may be obtained from:

a. Winchelsea Island Control, 250.756.5080 or 250.468.5080 (next day's activity only);
b. CFMETR Range Officer, 250.756.5002 or 250.468.5002 (long range planning);
c. Winchelsea Island Control VHF CH 10 or 16 (for safe transit area information when approaching Area "WG");
d. VHF 21B or Weather 3 (listen only, for active times), or
e. CB Channel 9.

Area "WG" constitutes a "Defence Establishment" as defined in the National Defence Act to which the Defence Controlled Access Area Regulations apply. Vessels which do not comply with direction from either Winchelsea Control or Range Patrol Vessels may be charged for trespassing.

Range vessels exhibit a flashing red light in addition to the prescribed lights and shapes. These vessels may operate outside of scheduled hours and should not be approached within 3,000 yards because they may be in a three-point moor with mooring lines extending to buoys 1,500 yards away. Additionally, lit as well as unlit mooring buoys are randomly located within the area and mariners are advised to use caution when transitting this area.

Once you've passed Mistaken Island, you can set a direct course for Hornby Island and Lambert Channel. Mt. Geoffrey, the 1,090-foot peak on Hornby Island, is the first landmark you see directly ahead. If northwesterlies kick up, Tribune Bay makes a good stop.

Nanoose Harbour (Vancouver Island)

Charts 3459, 3512; 1.8 mi SE of Schooner Cove; 10 mi NW of Nanaimo
Entrance (0.4 mi S of Wallis Pt): 49°15.85'N, 124°06.30'W
Anchor (200 yards of Fleet Pt): 49°15.28'N, 124°07.91'W

Nanoose Harbour is entered between Blunden Point and Wallis Point, 1.2 miles NW. Wallis Point, the east extremity of a low island, has a number of stunted trees on it. Nanoose Hill, on the north side of the harbour, has two summits, which from the south appear as a notched peak.

The head of Nanoose Harbour is low and swampy; its south shore is low with no natural distinguishing features.

Arbutus Grove Provincial Park is on the south shore of Nanoose Harbour.

Caution.—Nanoose Harbour is used by Naval vessels for exercises and mooring; due caution should be exercised in their vicinity. Shore areas on the north shore, west of Ranch Point, are restricted by the Department of National Defense; camping or picnicking is prohibited.

Good anchorage can be obtained close to the drying bank behind the shelter of the breakwater at Fleet Point. The NW corner of the harbour offers a good anchorage but landing is restricted; this area is also used for marine farming. (SD)

Protection from easterlies and southeasterlies can be found behind the sandspit that extends north from Fleet Point. Logbooms sometime use this part of the bay for shelter, too, and you may have to tie to them or anchor close to shore about 200 yards west of Fleet Point.

Arbutus Grove Provincial Park—a 55-acre park reputed to have the best stand of arbutus trees on Vancouver Island—lies along the south shore of Nanoose Harbour.

Anchor in 4 fathoms off the drying mud flat over sand and gravel with fair-to-good holding.

Maude Island

Charts 3459, 3512; in the Strait of Georgia; 1.0 mi E of Wallace Pt
Position: 49°16.16'N, 124°04.71'W

Maude Island lies 0.75 mile north of Blunden Point off the entrance to Nanoose Harbour. Foul ground fringes the island to a distance of about 91 m (300 ft) offshore. (SD)

Maude Island, off the entrance to Nanoose Harbour, has a drying cove in its southeast corner. While this cove is not useful for anchoring, it does make a good kayak haul-out and camping beach.

Schooner Cove Smooth-Water Route

Charts 3459, 3512; extends 6.5 mi from Maude Island to Dorcas Pt
Waypoint #1 (1.03 mi SE of Maude I Light): 49°15.99'N, 124°03.14'W
Waypoint #2 (0.12 mi SW of Ada Is): 49°17.03'N, 124°06.07'W
Waypoint #3 (0.15 mi N of Schooner Reef Light): 49°17.77'N, 124°07.79'W
Waypoint #4 (0.10 mi SW of Amelia I): 49°18.09'N, 124°09.31'W
Waypoint #5 (0.16 mi N of Dorcas Rock light buoy "P27"): 49°19.33'N, 124°11.53'W

Schooner Cove Smooth-Water Route, a shortcut for vessels headed towards Baynes Sound, is the route we have used many times heading northbound from Nanaimo. The route avoids the Whiskey Golf military area by hugging the Vancouver Island shore about 1.4 miles west of the Whiskey Golf area. The first waypoint is just south of Edgell Banks; the route then continues past the east side of Maude Island, the west side of Ada Islands, the north side of Schooner Reef, and the west side of Amelia Island, passing 200 yards east of Cottam Reef, and ending north of Dorcas Rock. Since this route is narrow and passes within 200 yards of islands and reefs, it requires careful pilot-

Sunny B.C. afternoon

ing and is not recommended in poor visibility. When following this route, you frequently encounter less chop than the longer route through Ballenas Channel.

Schooner Cove (Vancouver Island)

Charts 3459, 3512; 1.8 mi NW of Nanoose Hbr; 3.0 mi SE of Nuttil Bay
Entrance (0.04 mi NE of breakwater light): 49°17.29'N, 124°07.94'W
Marina visitors dock: 49°17.21'N, 124°08.11'W

Schooner Cove has a rock breakwater across its entrance and a floating log breakwater lies close west of its seaward end. The cove affords good anchorage to small craft in 5.5 to 7.3 m (18 to 24 ft). A restaurant, hotel, grocery store and marine hardware are available in Schooner Cove. (SD)

Schooner Cove is a small, fairly well protected harbor with a narrow entrance. The cove holds Fairwinds Schooner Cove and Resort which has guest moorage with first-class facilities that include power (to 50 amp), showers, laundry, wireless internet connection, pumpout, fuel, and use of the resort's pool and its other amenities. A restaurant, pub and wine store are also on the premises. Reservations are advised.

Note that during periods of strong northeasterlies, we have had difficulty docking on the outer fingers, and there is very little turning room if we have to make another pass. Also, during such weather, chop enters the cove and creates a bouncy effect on the outer fingers. However, a waterside visit at the marina is worth every bit of possible discomfort!

⚓ **Fairwinds Schooner Cove Marina**
tel: 250.468.7691 or 800.663.7060; monitors VHF 66A; website: www.fairwinds.ca; email: marina@fairwinds.ca; fuel; power; restrooms; laundry; pumpout

Gerald Island Cove (Gerald Island)

Charts 3459, 3512; 2.0 mi NW of Schooner Cove
Entrance: 49°18.83'N, 124°09.92'W
Anchor: 49°18.78'N, 124°09.88'W

Several reefs and shoals lie in the vicinity of these islands; knowledge of local conditions is required to safely navigate this area. (SD)

Gerald Island, 0.8 mile east of Dorcas Point on the south side of Ballenas Channel, has several fine sandy beaches. The cove on the north side is a temporary fair weather anchorage only, with limited swinging room. However, some shelter from southeast winds and chop has been reported. The southeast beach is a good kayak haul-out spot.

Anchor in 2 fathoms. Bottom unknown.

Ballenas Islands

Chart 3512; 3.5 mi N of Schooner Cove
North island Light: 49°21.03'N, 124°09.63'W

Ballenas Islands are two in number. The north island is sparsely wooded. The south island is for the most part bare, but its north end is heavily wooded. A white radar dome on the south island is conspicuous from eastward.

Separated by a very narrow passage the islands appear from all directions as one. This passage, almost closed at its west end, is only navigable by small craft at or near HW; local knowledge is required. In the middle the channel opens out forming a sheltered cove on the north side of the south island; a sandy beach forms its south side. A large sign at the head of this cove reads "Do Not anchor in this cove—submerged cables." (SD)

Ballenas Island lighthouse, on the tip of the north island, has a buoy lying off its west side that can be used by visiting boats in fair weather. Since there is no large-scale chart of Ballenas Islands, you must use caution and maintain alert lookouts.

The protected cove on the south island has some protection from southerly winds; however, it should be used only as an emergency anchorage, avoiding the submarine cable which crosses the bay.

Nuttal Bay (Vancouver Island)

Charts 3459, 3512; 2.5 mi NW of Schooner Cove; 0.3 mi SW of Dorcas Pt
Entrance: 49°18.83'N, 124°11.91'W
Anchor: 49°18.49'N, 124°11.26'W

Nuttal Bay lies between Dorcas and Cottam Points. Several privately owned mooring buoys are in the bay. (SD)

Nuttal Bay offers good protection from southeast winds deep in the bay. When entering from the east, avoid Cottam Reef with its various shoals and rocks.

Chart 3459 is the best guide. If you're in doubt, stay north of Dorcas Rock, buoy "P27." The bay is open to prevailing northwest winds.

Anchorage can be taken in the easternmost nook. Those desiring more swinging room can anchor in the southwest side of the bay.

Anchor (easternmost nook) in 2 to 5 fathoms over sand and mud with very good holding.

Anchor (southwest corner) in 4-5 fathoms.

Northwest Bay (Vancouver Island)

Charts 3459, 3512; .6 mi SW of Nuttal Bay
Entrance (0.38 mi W of Cottam Pt): 49°18.90'N, 124°13.42'W
Entrance (marina): 49°18.05'N, 124°12.11'W
Anchor: 49°17.77'N, 124°12.15'W

Northwest Bay ... is exposed to NW winds; depths are considerable but anchorage can be obtained close to shore near the head of the bay. (SD)

Northwest Bay is completely open to prevailing northwest winds, as its name indicates. However, protection from southerlies can be found at the head of the bay southwest of the marina on its eastern shore. To avoid a reef off the breakwater and a submerged rock to the south, the marina is entered between red buoy "P30" and green buoy "P29."

Avoid the submerged rocks along the eastern shore of the bay.

Anchor in 5 fathoms 0.3 mile south of the marina entrance.

Craig Bay (Vancouver Island)

Charts 3459, 3512; 1.15 mi SW of Mistaken Island; 5 mi SE of French Creek
Entrance (0.11 mi NW of Madrona Pt): 49°18.88'N, 124°14.61'W
Anchor: 49°18.73'N, 124°14.61'W

Craig Bay, between Madrona Point and Brant Point, is filled with drying flats. Small craft are cautioned against anchoring in Craig Bay except under ideal conditions of a calm sea and rising tide. A private float, private mooring buoys and launching ramps are on the south side of the bay.

Rathtrevor Beach, on the west side of Craig Bay, has a large drying flat extending 0.6 mile offshore. Rathtrevor Beach Provincial Park has camping and picnic facilities. (SD)

The sand flats of Craig Bay, which extend a half-mile from shore, are home to large concentrations of land and seabirds. To the west is Rathtrevor Beach Park where nearly 200 species of birds have been recorded. Because of its undulating bottom, this sand flat can be treacherous to pleasure craft on ebbing tides.

Temporary protection can be found in the lee of Madrona Point with temporary anchorage 0.12 mile southwest of Madrona Point.

Anchor in about 3 fathoms over sand with fair holding.

Parksville Bay (Vancouver Island)

Chart 3512; 2.0 mi SE of French Creek
Anchor: 49°19.99'N, 124°19.10'W

Parksville Bay is almost entirely filled with a sand beach extending 0.4 mile offshore. Small craft can find anchorage in 15 to 18 m (48 to 60 ft) under ideal conditions but allowance must be made for the afternoon onshore wind.

The town of Parksville, at the head of the bay, is a summer resort. (SD)

Parksville Bay is a shallow bight useful only as a temporary stop in fair weather.

Anchor in 4 to 5 fathoms off the drying mud flat over sand with fair holding.

Haul up the dinghy—time to leave!

French Creek (Vancouver Island)

Charts 3512, 3513; 10 mi NW of Schooner Cove; 17 mi SE of Deep Bay
Entrance: 49°21.07'N, 124°21.25'W

A shallow channel, 49 m (160 ft) wide, leads into a boat basin, about 183 by 91 m (600 by 300 ft) in extent, at the mouth of French Creek. The basin and the channel leading into it are dredged to a depth of 3 m (10 ft).

Within the basin there are six public floats, with two connections to shore, which provide a total of 550 m (1,800 ft) of berthing space. Power and fresh water are available on the floats. (SD)

French Creek has a small-boat harbor sheltered by a large breakwater, the only secure small-boat shelter between Schooner Cove, 10 miles to the south, and Deep Bay, 17 miles to the northwest. The long, wide beaches on either side of French Creek are destination resorts, and small dinghies or trailer boats find these shores attractive. The harbor has full facilities that include showers and washrooms, fuel, garbage, used-oil disposal, and launch ramp. In summer, the harbor is lively with tourists who come to watch fish being offloaded and locals who come to buy fresh fish.

Although the harbor is primarily has been used primarily for fishing vessels, with the decrease in commercial activity, cruising vessels are being welcomed. The harbormaster reserves floats 2, 3, and 4 for transients; floats E and D are reserved for large vessels. Because these regulations may continue to change as the fishing industry does, check with the harbormaster before visiting the harbor.

⚓ **French Creek Boat Harbour**
tel: 250.248.5051; fax: 250.248.5123; monitors VHF Ch 66A; website: www.frenchcreekharbour.com; email: hafc@frenchcreekharbour.com; fuel; power; restrooms

Qualicum Bay, Qualicum Beach (Vancouver Island)

Charts 3527, 3513; 24.5 mi NE of Nanaimo
Entrance (Qualicum Bay): 49°24.87'N, 124°37.03'W
Position (Qualicum Beach): 49°21.49'N, 124°27.43'W

Qualicum Bay, 1 mile NW of Dunsmuir, is a slight indentation between the entrances of Qualicum River and Nile Creek. A boat launching ramp is at the Indian Reserve, SE of the bay, and a marine service station is in the bay.

Qualicum beach ... is a summer resort area. There are stores, including a liquor store, a post office, hotels, motels, campgrounds and a launching ramp. (SD)

Photo courtesy CHS, Pacific Region

Tiny Squitty Bay, Lasqueti Island

The long stretch of sandy beach in Qualicum Bay draws beachcombers, sand-castle "artists," children and sun worshipers, and kayakers. The bay, which is an open roadstead is too shallow and subject to strong winds and chop to afford anchorage for cruising boats. Qualicum Beach has become an upscale residential area and tourist destination.

Anchor (Qualicum Bay) in about 2 to 3 fathoms over a large flat bottom with fair holding.

Squitty Bay (Lasqueti Island)

Charts 3312, 3512; 6.3 mi N of Ballenas Islands; 1.3 mi S of Bull Passage
Entrance: 49°27.16'N, 124°09.72'W

Squitty Bay Marine Park encompasses the area around Squitty Bay, a small indentation on the east end of Lasqueti Island. The bay has been dredged to a depth of 2.4 m (8 ft) beyond the public float but several rocks lie in the entrance. The public float is 30 m (100 ft) long and a road leads from the bay to other settlements on the island. No garbage disposal or any other facilities are available.

The entrance to Squitty Bay is very deceptive. From east it looks much like any of the other small inlets indenting the east end of Lasqueti Island; from north it is sometimes only identifiable by sight of the masts of vessels tied alongside the public float. The peninsula which protects Squitty Bay from the north is low, grassy knolls rising 3 to 6 m (10 to 20 ft) above sea level. Several drying rocks lie just inside the entrance. The safest entrance channel is along the south shore. Although the bay appears to be open to the SE, it is in fact completely protected from all seas. Even in winter with a SE gale sending spray and small bits of driftwood over the outer rocks and above the masts of vessels tied to the public float the bay is reported to be subject only to a slight swell. (SD)

Squitty Bay, with its tiny entrance lies on the rocky south shore of Lasqueti Island, is badly exposed to southeast gales and its entrance can be intimidating. Small boats only (32 feet & under) can find moorage at the public dock and float, but it is often crowded in season, so rafting is encouraged. If you go ashore, check out the great view to the south and east from the highest rock inside the small fenced area to the left of the head of the gangway.

The entrance fairway strongly favors the southwest side. Stay very close to the large isolated granite rock to port, passing about 20 feet off. The rock to starboard has an underwater ridge that extends out to about midchannel and is awash on low tides. We call this ridge "Bottom Paint Rock" because of the interesting colors on its surface. There is no anchorage in Squitty Bay. If you want to anchor, we recommend the anchorages between Bull Passage and Scottie Bay.

Bull Passage

Charts 3312, 3512; along the NE shore of Lasqueti Island
Entrance (SE): 49°28.42'N, 124°10.16'W
Entrance (NW, 0.66 mi W of Jervis Island): 49°30.68'N, 124°15.87'W

Bull Passage ... is separated from Sabine Channel by the offshore islands. It offers good shelter in all weather and is used by tugs towing logbooms. In summer NW winds blow through the passage, but because of the islands there is seldom a rough sea or a heavy swell.

Bull Passage daybeacon, on a drying rock on the south side of the east entrance to the passage, has a port hand daymark. (SD)

Bull Passage, a pleasant and scenic route along the east coast of Lasqueti Island, has several good anchor sites. The easternmost is Rouse Bay.

Rouse Bay (Lasqueti Island)

Charts 3312, 3512; 0.6 mi W of E enrance to Bull Passage
Entrance: 49°28.51'N, 124°11.13'W
Anchor: 49°28.35'N, 124°11.13'W

Rouse Bay, SW of Bull Passage daybeacon, has a small islet close off the north shore. Anchorage can be obtained at the head of the bay, behind the islet. A submarine cable crosses the entrance to Rouse Bay. (SD)

Rouse Bay is a small, quiet cove where about three small boats can anchor southeast of the islet. The bay offers adequate protection in fair weather, but room is limited. The high, rocky south shore is covered with a lovely stand of arbutus trees. Avoid the dangerous rock awash off the entrance.

Anchor in 2 fathoms over mud with good holding.

Bull Passage Bight (Lasqueti Island)

Charts 3312, 3512; 1.1 mi NW of Rouse Bay
Entrance: 49°28.92'N, 124°12.65'W
Anchor: 49°28.77'N, 124°12.64'W

Bull Passage Bight is our name for the small bight in the Lasqueti Island shore southwest of Bull Island. Reasonable shelter from southeast weather can be found deep in the bight close to shore, or tucked in behind the east side of the small islet. The bay, which is fairly deep, shoals rapidly toward shore. A house on pilings lies at the head of the bight.

Anchor in about 12 fathoms over sand and rock; fair holding.

Little Bull Passage

Charts 3312, 3512; btwn Bull & Jedediah Islands
Entrance (E, mid-ch btwn Sheer & Rabbit Is): 49°29.10'N, 124°10.14'W
Entrance (W): 49°29.44'N, 124°12.48'W

Little Bull Passage separates the steep cliffs on the SW side of Jedediah Island from Bull Island; it is deep enough for small craft to navigate safely. A drying rock lies at the west end of the passage, close to Jedediah Island. Dangerous pinnacle rocks, resulting from a rockslide on the Bull Island shore, lie about half-way through the passage. (SD)

Bull Passage is the preferred passage close along the eastern shore of Lasqueti. Both Bull Passage and Little Bull Passage receive confused seas at the east entrance during strong southeast winds. Little Bull Passage, the small-boat route between Jedediah and Bull islands, is clear if you stay mid-channel with about 1 fathom minimum depth. Avoid the rocks off the east entrance of the north side and midway through on the south side. The high bluffs of each island are picturesque. Some skippers report finding suitable anchorage in the nooks on the east end of Little Bull Passage. Our only experience has been anchoring on a shelf at the west end, favoring the Jedediah Island shore.

Long Bay (Jedediah Island)

Charts 3312, 3512; 0.5 mi E of Boho Island
Position: 49°29.97'N, 124°12.78'W

Long Bay offers good shelter from the southeast. At high water, Long Bay is an attractive inlet but, alas, most of it dries almost to the entrance. You may frequently see one or two small boats anchored temporarily off the drying flat using shore ties.

Log Boom Cove (Jedediah Island)

Charts 3312, 3512; immediately N of Long Bay
Position: 49°30.02'N, 124°12.74'N

Log Boom Cove is the local name for the next cove north of Long Bay. It, too, largely dries at low water; however, some boats find good anchorage on the south shore by using a stern tie to shore at the entrance. Avoid the reef off the north entrance point.

Jedediah Bay (Jedediah Island)

Charts 3312, 3512; 0.15 mi SE of Paul Island
Anchor (immediately N of Log Boom Cove): 49°30.19'N, 124°12.87'W

> *Jedediah Bay is on the west side of Jedediah Island, east of Boho Island. Long Bay and Log Boom Cove are the south and north arms, respectively ... both are filled with drying sand flats. Good anchorage can be obtained in Jedediah Bay.* (SD)

Although Jedediah Bay is somewhat open, in fair weather it provides good shelter. The west side of Jedediah is relatively steep-to; some boats use a stern tie to shore to minimize swinging room.

Anchor in about 5 fathoms over sand and gravel with fair holding.

Deep Bay (Jedediah Island)

Charts 3312, 3512; immediately E of Paul Island
Anchor: 49 30.33'N, 124 12.96'W

> *Deep Bay, north of Jedediah Bay, is one of the safest anchorages on this side of Sabine Channel because of the protection from NW winds afforded by Paul Island.* (SD)

Deep Bay is the local name for the tiny bay north of Jedediah Bay and due east of Paul Island. Paul Island provides shelter from prevailing northwest winds, making this one of the most sheltered anchorages in the area; however, since swinging room is limited, this is a good place to use a stern tie to shore.

Anchor in 5 to 8 fathoms over an unrecorded bottom.

Boho Bay (Boho Island)

Charts 3312, 3512; 0.6 mi W of Long Bay
Entrance: 49°29.63'N, 124°13.30'W
Anchor: 49°29.85'N, 124°13.70'W

> *Boho Island, 0.9 mile NW of Bull Island, lies on the west side of Bull Passage. Boho Bay on the south side of Boho Island, offers good anchorage.* (SD)

Boho Bay is a favorite of large sailboats and, in the summer, you may find a number of them here. Small boats can tuck in close to shore near the eastern islets. Skerry Bay, on the west side of Boho Island, is more intimate and affords shelter from east winds.

Anchor (center of bay) in 12 fathoms over sand with fair-to-good holding.

Skerry Bay (Boho Island)

Charts 3312, 3512; W end of Boho Bay
Anchor 49°29.95'N, 124°14.04'W

> *Skerry Bay lies west of Boho Island. The bay derives its name from the Gaelic, referring to the large number of rocks in it. A drying rock lies in the middle of the north entrance to the bay. Marine farm facilities are in the northern portion of Skerry Bay and along the NW shore of the north entrance to the bay.*
>
> [It] *offers very good protection from most winds but a strong NW wind often sends gusts over the gap at the head of the bay or through*

Photo courtesy CHS, Pacific Region

Boho Bay

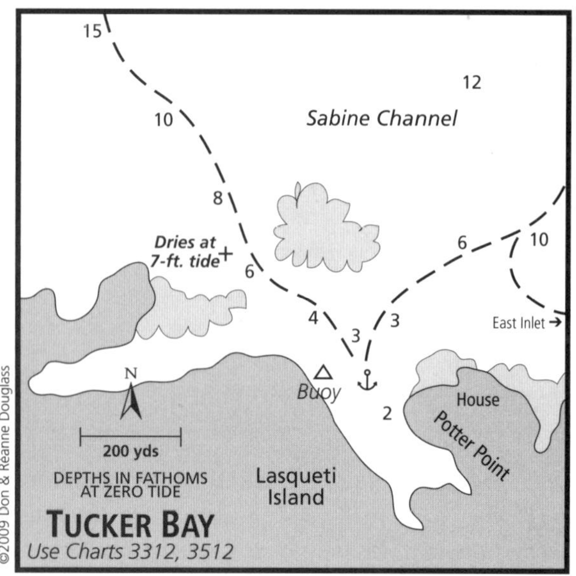

the north entrance causing anchored vessels to swing through a fairly wide arc. (SD)

Skerry Bay offers very good protection from all weather. Entering from the north, avoid the midchannel rock which dries at about 5 feet. Favor the Boho Island shore and anchor mid-bay.

Anchor in about 5 fathoms over an unrecorded bottom.

Tucker Bay (Lasqueti Island)

Charts 3312, 3512; 5 mi NW of Squitty Bay; 4 mi E of Scottie Bay
Entrance: 49°30.61′N, 124°16.40′W
Anchor (W of Potter Pt): 49°30.13′N, 124°16.33′W
Anchor (E inlet): 49°30.11′N, 124°15.67′W

Anchorage in Tucker Bay is fair in a depth of about 30 m ... Small craft can anchor south of Larson Islet in 9 to 11 m (30 to 36 ft) where they will be almost completely sheltered. When approaching this small craft anchorage pass within 90 m (300 ft) of the west end of Larson Islet. (SD)

Tucker Bay offers sheltered anchorage in several places. Some vessels prefer to anchor in the drying inlet on the east side, while others like the small nook west of Potter Point; both are quite good in settled weather. Avoid the rocks and drying flats.

A cove west of West Point, southwest of Jelina Island, can be used for protection against southeast gales. There is good swinging room. Anchor in the cove in 3 to 5 fathoms over a sandy bottom with fair holding.

Anchor (W of Potter Pt) in 3 fathoms over mud with good holding.

Anchor (E inlet) in about 5 fathoms over sand and gravel with fair holding.

Cove WSW of Jelina Island

The unnamed cove SW of Jelina Island can be used for protection against southeast gales. There is good swinging room here.

Anchor in 3 to 5 fathoms over sand with fair holding; good swinging room.

Scottie Bay (Lasqueti Island)

Charts 3312, 3512; 1.4 mi NE of False Bay; 4.1 mi NE of Sisters Islets
Entrance: 49°30.96′N, 124°20.34′W
Anchor: 49°30.80′N, 124°20.68′W

Scottie Bay, south of Lindbergh Island, is protected from virtually all winds and sea. Enter close to the Lasqueti Island shore to avoid the shoal extending south from Lindbergh Island. The wharf and slipway are privately owned. (SD)

Scottie Bay, a small landlocked bay at the northeast end of Lasqueti Island, offers nearly

Tucker Bay

Well-protected Scottie Bay

bombproof protection in most weather. A large wooden barge occupies the west center side of the bay and several local boats are usually permanently moored south and north of the barge. A few small boats (40 ft or less) can find anchorage between the barge and the entrance. Boats over 40 feet are not recommended inside the bay due to both the narrow entrance channel and the restricted swinging room.

On entering Scottie Bay, favor the south shore within 30 feet and station a lookout on your bow; rooks extend two-thirds of the way across the entrance from the north shore. A jury-rigged vertical stick, 7 feet high, marks the southern extremity of this reef. On a 3.9-foot tide, our depth sounder read a minimum of 1.2 fathoms across the entrance. During strong southeast winds, larger boats may yaw sideways when proceeding through the entrance due to lack of steerage.

In southeast gales some swells are felt inside of Scottie Bay at high water when the reef covers.

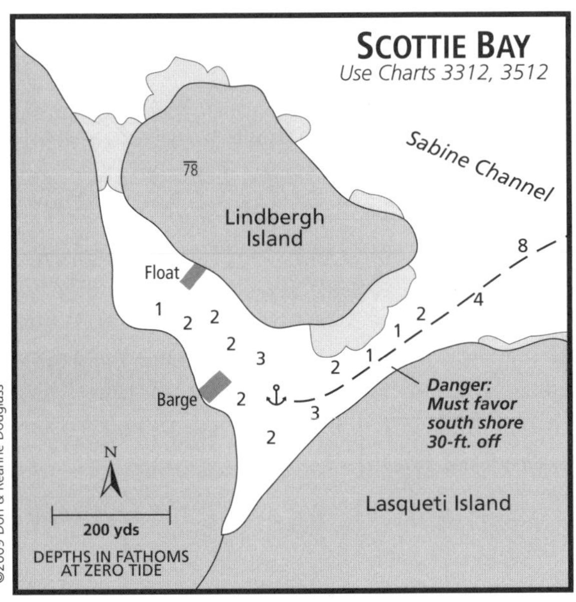

The late Allen Farrell's China Cloud *in Scottie Bay*

Lagoon, south side of False Bay

Anchor in 2-3 fathoms over sticky, brown mud with thick clam shells; very good holding.

Spring Bay, Spanish Cave (Lasqueti I)

Charts 3512, 3513; 1.0 mi NW of Scottie Bay; 3.5 mi NE of Sisters Islets
Entrance (N): 49°31.72'N, 124°22.32'W
Entrance (S): 49°30.89'N, 124°22.99'W
Anchor: 49°31.34'N, 124°21.85'W

> *Spring Bay, east of Fegan Islets, offers good anchorage in SE winds but Fegan Islets give only minimal protection from NW winds and sea. Spanish Cave is a small development at the head of the bay.* (SD)

Spring Bay, a fair weather anchorage for those fishing the Fegan Islets, is somewhat open to the prevailing northwest winds. It can be useful in a southeast storm.

Anchor is 4 fathoms. The bottom is unrecorded.

False Bay, Orchard Bay (Lasqueti Island)

Charts 3312, 3536 inset; 3512, 3513; 8.6 mi N of French Creek; 18 mi SE of Blubber Bay, Texada Island
Entrance: 49°29.00'N, 124°22.60'W
Mud Bay (public float): 49°29.51'N, 124°21.17'W
Anchor (Orchard Bay): 49°29.89'N, 124°21.46'W

> *False Bay, entered between Olsen Island and Heath Islet, is open to the Qualicum, a strong west wind which blows in from the Pacific Ocean and funnels through the Qualicum Beach area. Jeffrey Rock, 0.2 mile south of Olsen Island, has less than 2 m (6 ft) over it. A rock, with less than 2 m (6 ft) over it, lies midway between Olsen Island and Higgins Island.*
>
> *Anchorage, sheltered from most winds, can be obtained in the north part of False Bay east of Higgins Island in a depth of 13 m (42 ft). Small craft can find anchorage, with good holding ground, in shallower water closer to shore.* (SD)

The eastern end of False Bay is the site of Lasqueti village. There is a public wharf and float, and a fuel float. Water is available at the float but there is no garbage disposal. During a west wind the chop can be uncomfortable at the float.

Small craft can find very good shelter tucked into several nooks in the west and north ends of the bay. The northern nook, known as Orchard Bay, can accommodate a number of boats.

Anchor (Orchard Bay) in 3 fathoms over sand and mud with good holding.

False Lagoon (Johnson Lagoon) (Lasqueti Island)

Charts 3312, 3536 inset, 3512, 3513; 0.5 mi S of Mud Bay
Entrance: 49°29.37'N, 124°21.67'W
Anchor: 49°28.94'N, 124°21.21'W

> *The lagoon, entered east of Prowse Point, is completely protected and often used by wintering fish boats. A drying reef lies in the middle of the entrance and the entrance channel dries at about half tide. It is best to use this channel only at HW as there is a 3 to 4 kn current when the tide is running. The deepest part of the channel is on its north side but care must be taken to avoid the rock ledges projecting from shore. A rock, which dries 3.6 m (12 ft), lies about midway through the channel.* (SD)

False Lagoon, also called Johnson Lagoon, is a half-mile south of Lasqueti village. It is a totally landlocked body of water used by wintering boats and those seeking solitude and scenic surroundings. False Lagoon can be entered only at or near high water. The entrance to the lagoon dries on half-tide, so if you wish to enter its warm waters, we recommend that you consult the Tide Tables and reconnoiter by dinghy before entering on rising high water. An excellent photograph of the lagoon's entrance is on page 181 of Wolferstan's Gulf Islands.

Anchor in 3 fathoms over sand with good holding.

Jenkins Cove (Lasqueti Island)

Charts 3312, 3512; 0.25 mi NW of Jenkins Island
Entrance: 49°27.53'N, 124°18.30'W

> *Jenkins Island is separated from Lasqueti Island by a narrow, deep passage. Sea Egg Rocks lie 0.3 mile west of Jenkins Island …* (SD)

Temporary shelter can be found in Jenkins Cove or in the passage on the north side of Jenkins Island.

Richardson Cove (Lasqueti Island)

Charts 3312, 3512; 0.6 mi NE of Jenkins Island
Entrance: 49°27.45'N, 124°16.47'W
Anchor: 49°27.59'N, 124°16.53'W

> *Richardson Cove lies 0.7 mile west of Old House Bay.* (SD)

Good shelter from westerlies, but poor shelter from southerlies, can be found in Richardson Cove near the head of the bay.

Anchor in 5 to 7 fathoms.

Old House Bay, Graveyard Bay (Lasqueti Island)

Charts 3312, 3512; 3.6 mi W of Squitty Bay; 4.1 mi SE of Mud Bay
Entrance: 49°27.40'N, 124°15.24'W
Anchor (Old House Bay): 49°27.54'N, 124°15.57'W

> *Old House Bay, with Graveyard Bay indenting its SW side, lies 0.7 mile west of Boat Cove. … Anchorage, protected from NW winds, can be obtained at the head of Old House Bay and in Richardson Cove.* (SD)

Photo courtesy CHS, Pacific Region

Old House Bay

Old House Bay and adjacent Graveyard Bay offer good protection from prevailing northwest winds. Avoid the reefs and islets in the center of Old House Bay.

Anchor (Old House Bay) in 5 to 6 fathoms over a hard bottom with fair-to-good holding.

Boat Cove (Lasqueti Island)

Charts 3312, 3512; 0.7 mi NE of Old House Bay; 3.1 mi W of Squitty Bay
Entrance: 49°27.56'N, 124°14.48'W
Anchor: 49°27.90'N, 124°14.56'W

> *Boat Cove, 1.25 miles north of Seal Reef, has drying and sunken rocks in its SE approach and is exposed to the south and SE; it offers good protection from west winds.* (SD)

Boat Cove is well sheltered from westerlies. While it is a little deep, it offers good swinging room deep in the cove. Avoid the reefs at the eastern side of the entrance.

Anchor in 12 fathoms over an unrecorded bottom.

Sabine Channel

Charts 3512, 3513; lies btwn NE side of Lasqueti Island; SW side of Texada Island
Entrance (S, mid-ch btwn Rabbit I & Upwood Pt Light): 49°29.10'N, 124°09.50'W
Entrance (N, mid-ch btwn Davie Bay & Fegan Islets Light): 49°33.97'N, 124°22.95'W

> *Sabine Channel separates Lasqueti Island and the islands off its NE side from Texada Island. The main channel is deep with few off-lying dangers.*
>
> *Military exercise area.—An area, about 20 miles long and 4 miles wide, which parallels the west side of Texada Island at a distance of 1 mile, is used by low flying military aircraft during bombing exercises. Mariners should be prepared to avoid this area when warned to do so …* (SD)

Sabine Channel is a good alternative to the Strait of Georgia and is frequently smooth when the strait is kicking up. The west coast of Texada Island is seldom visited by cruising boats, most of which pass on their way to Desolation Sound. There are two or three bays that make good temporary lunch stops, particularly Davie and Mouat bays.

Home Bay (Jedediah Island)

Charts 3312, 3512; 2.4 mi NW of Upwood Pt
Entrance: 49°29.79′N, 124°11.41′W

Home Bay, on the east shore of Jedediah Island, has an island in its centre part and dries completely. (SD)

Home Bay is a good place to stop when passing through Sabine Channel because of its generally protected waters. Temporary anchorage can be found off the drying mud flat.

Cook Bay (Texada Island)

Chart 3512; 4.2 mi E of the N tip of Lasqueti I
Entrance: 49°32.60′N, 124°15′61′W

Cook Bay, 1.6 miles NW of Partington Point, is exposed to the south and too deep for anchorage. Two islets lie off the west entrance and a rock, which dries 0.2 m (1 ft), lies off the head of the bay. (SD)

Some temporary shelter from prevailing northwest winds and chop can be found at the head of Cook Bay off the steep-to shore, but the bay is exposed to southerly weather.

Davie Bay (Texada Island)

Chart 3513; 4.8 mi NW of Lasqueti Island
Entrance: 49°35.93′N, 124°23.57′W
Anchor: 49°36.14′N, 124°23.73′W

Davie Bay is exposed and only suitable for small craft. Two islets lie off the entrance and a rock awash lies NW of the east islet. Another islet, 0.7 mile SE, has a reef of drying rocks extending west from it. (SD)

Davie Bay affords moderate protection in fair weather. Temporary anchorage can be taken close to the north shore.

Anchor in about 5 fathoms, unrecorded bottom.

Mouat Bay (Texada Island)

Chart 3513; 4.0 mi NW of Davie Bay
Entrance (W, 0.35 mi S of Dick I): 49°38.61′N, 124°28.28′W
Entrance (S, 0.6 mi SE of Mouat Is): 49°37.62′N, 124°26.93′W

Mouat Bay...has Mouat Islands lying in its entrance and is fronted by a boulder foreshore.

Harwood Point, known locally as Shelter Point, is the north point of Davie Bay. Dick Island is connected to Harwood Point by a drying boulder bar.

Harwood Point Park has launching ramps, camping and picnic facilities, fresh water is obtainable. (SD)

Mouat Bay, a temporary fair weather anchorage, lies close south of Harwood Point, east of Dick Island. The area inside Mouat Islands and the above-water bare rocks offers some protection from southwest and west chop. Depths are great except near shore where temporary anchorage can be found in 10 fathoms.

There is a launching ramp in the northeast corner of the bay and a small breakwater at its southeast corner. Avoid the reef that extends 200 yards south of Dick Island.

On shore, Harwood Regional Park has picnic tables, campsites and pit toilets. Anchor and take your tender in if you wish to go ashore. Mouat Bay is exposed to southerly weather, so we advise running for Blubber Bay in a heavy southeasterly.

Anchor in 10 fathoms over sand and gravel with rocks; fair holding.

Gillies Bay (Texada Island)

Chart 3513; immediately N of Mouat Bay
Entrance (Gillies Bay): 49°39.80′N, 124°29.10′W

Gillies Bay, north of Harwood Point, is easily identified when approaching from the south by the houses around its shores. The community, on the west side of the bay, has a post office, grocery and liquor store, RCMP office, medical clinic and resident doctor. Gasoline and minor repairs are obtainable. There is no wharf or jetty in the bay. (SD)

Gillies Bay may offer temporary shelter in fair weather. A large, conspicuous cement plant, due west of Cranby Lake air strip, lies three miles north of the bay. Loading docks, with conveyor belts and tugs can be seen in the vicinity. Harwood Point Regional Park, north of Gillies Bay, is a picnic area used by local residents. The park has campsites and pit toilets; dinghy in, if you want to use the facilities.

All ashore for some exploring!

Welcome Bay, Davis Bay

(Texada Island)
Position (Welcome Bay): 49°42.56′N, 124°34.83′W
Position (Davis Bay): 49°43.15′N, 124°36.52′W

Surprise Mountain rises steeply from shore between Welcome Bay and Davis Bay, 1.3 miles NW. (SD)

Welcome Bay and Davis Bay, respectively 4.3 and 5.6 miles northwest of Gillies Bay, are shallow bights offering little or no shelter.

Favada Point (Texada Island)

Chart 3515; N of Davis Bay
Entrance: 49°44.44′N, 124°38.39′W

The land north of Favada Point trends northeast. Chop from southeast weather diminishes in tiny Maple Bay. The cove north of Favada Point is surprisingly calm during moderate southerly weather. The rocks off its entrance point are a favorite haul out spot for seals. There is room for one boat for a temporary stop.

Crescent Bay, Limekiln Bay (Texada I)

Chart 3513; Crescent Bay is 0.7 mi SW of Blubber Bay; Limekiln Bay is 1.7 mi SW of Blubber Bay
Position (Crescent Bay): 49°46′11′N, 124°37.78′W
Position (Limekiln Bay): 49°47′50′N, 124°38.02′W

Crescent Bay and Limekiln Bay, north of Favada Point, are separated by Marshall Point and have extensive shallow beaches. (SD)

Crescent and Limekiln bays are large bights with sandy, gravel beaches. They are exposed to northwest winds and swells, but have little chop from the south. They are useful as temporary stops in calm weather, in easterly winds and light southerlies. Blubber Bay, to the west of Kiddie Point, offers the only protection in the area from southeast gales.

Malaspina Strait

Charts 3312, 3512, 3513; btwn Texada Island & the mainland
Entrance (S, mid-ch btwn Epsom & Upwood Pts): 49°29.87′N, 124°04.47′W
Entrance (N, mid-ch btwn Grief & Grilse Pts): 49°48.22′N, 124°33.87′W

Malaspina Strait, 27 miles long with a least width of 2.5 miles, separates the NE side of Texada Island from the British Columbia mainland. It is entered from the south between Epsom Point and Upwood Point, or by way of Welcome Passage. (SD)

Malaspina Strait affords some protection from northwest chop, but it can get messy in a major southeast blow. We once took a near knockdown here in July while we were running for Blubber Bay from the mainland coast in a southeast gale. (We were carrying too much sail in a chartered fin keel boat we weren't accustomed to, and a weather helm got the better of us.)

Anderson Bay (Texada Island)

Charts 3312, 3512; on the SE corner of Texada Island; 1.6 mi N of Upwood Pt
Entrance (S): 49°30.62'N, 124°07.80'W
Anchor: 49°31.07'N, 124°08.24'W

> *Anderson Bay ... offers very good protection from all except SE winds. An island lies across the entrance to the bay, the passage north of this island has a drying rock lying close off the north entrance point; pass south of this rock. A log dump and booming ground are in the bay.* (SD)

Anderson Bay, which is small and deep, offers good protection inside the wooded peninsula from all but southeast gales. The anchorage tends to be rolly from passing traffic. It's a good idea to use a shore tie if you wish to remain overnight here. Enter with a bow watch to avoid rocks and keep an eye on your depth sounder – the bottom has shelves that extend from the island.

Anchor in 8 fathoms near the head of the bay using a shore tie.

Northeast Bay (Texada Island)

Charts 3312, 3512; 15.0 mi NW of Anderson Bay
Entrance: 49°42.96'N, 124°22.58'W
Anchor: 49°42.85'N, 124°22.63'W

> *Northeast Bay, 1 mile NW of Northeast Point, has McQuarry Island (a local name) near its centre and affords some shelter from west and SE winds.* (SD)

Some shelter from northwest winds is possible behind McQuarry Island, in the center of the bay. There may be emergency protection from southeasterlies on McQuarry's west side.

Pocahontas Bay (Texada Island)

Charts 3312, 3512, 3513; 2.2 mi NW of Northeast Bay
Entrance: 49°43.74'N, 124°25.84'W
Anchor: 49°43.55'N, 124°25.82'W

> *Pocahontas Bay ... is small but affords emergency shelter for small craft during SE weather. Some buildings and dolphins are at the head of the bay.* (SD)

Pocahontas Bay is too deep for convenient anchorage except at the head of the bay with limited swinging room.

Anchor temporarily at the head of the bay off the steep-to mud flat.

McRae Cove, Frolander Bay (Malaspina Strait)

Charts 3312, 3512; at the head of Jervis Inlet; 1.2 mi S of Thunder Bay
Entrance (McRae Cove): 49°44.37'N, 124°16.79'W
Anchor (McRae Cove): 49°44.87'N, 124°16.69'W
Position (Frolander Bay): 49°45.28'N, 124°17.80'W

> *McRae Cove ... offer[s] some shelter for small craft. Local knowledge is required to approach McRae Cove because of several islets and drying rocks in its entrance.* (SD)

McRae Cove, on the east side of Malaspina Strait across from Northeast Bay, lies a half-mile northwest of Scotch Fir Point (the western entrance to Jervis Inlet). Upon entering the cove, avoid the rocks on the starboard side of the fairway, awash at low tide. Although McRae Cove is well sheltered from northwest winds, but it is open to any wind and seas that blow up Malaspina Strait; however, unless it is a fresh breeze, the chop dies down before reaching the head of the cove.

Frolander Bay is immediately northwest of McRae Cove.

Anchor (McRae Cove) northeast of the 36-meter island in about 2 fathoms.

Stillwater Bay, Lang Bay, Brew Bay (Malaspina Strait)

Charts 3311, 3512, 3513; 2 mi NW of McRae Cove
Entrance (Stillwater Bay): 49°25.92'N, 124°19.16'W
Entrance (Lang Bay): 49°46.22'W, 124°21.11'W
Position (Brew Bay): 49°46.19'W, 124°22.70'W

> *Stillwater Bay, 2.5 miles NW of Scotch Fir Point, is almost filled with booming grounds.*

Stillwater settlement, at the head of the bay, is connected by road to the main highway.

Small craft can obtain temporary anchorage in a depth of about 30 m (98 ft), with the west end of the power plant bearing about 037°, distant 0.35 mile.

A large drying sand spit, west of Stillwater Bay, extends 0.3 mile offshore from the mouth of Lois River.

Lang Bay ... has a rock, with 4 m (13 ft) over it, in its entrance. The public wharf, with a depth of 3.4 m (11 ft) alongside, and a store are available.

Brew Bay, west of Kelly Point, is fronted by a sandy beach. (SD)

Some shelter from winds from the easterly quadrant can be found in the east end of Stillwater Bay. Lang Bay is 1.4 miles west of Stillwater Bay; Brew Bay is 2.5 miles west.

Beach Gardens Resort & Marina (Malaspina Strait)

Chart 3311; 0.4 mi SE of Grief Pt; 2 mi S of Westview
Entrance: 49°47.99'N, 124°31.19'W

Beach Gardens Resort & Marina, 0.4 mi southeast of Grief Point, lies in a small man-made harbor protected by two rock breakwaters. The marina has been undergoing renovation and has fuel, water, power (15 & 30 amp), showers and laundry as well as cottages and rooms. Beer and wine are available. The marina has transient moorage for cruising vessels.

⚓ **Beach Gardens Resort & Marina** tel: 604.485.6267 or 800.663.7070; monitors VHF Ch 66A; website: www.beachgardens.com; email: beachgardens@shaw.ca; fuel; power; restrooms; showers; laundry

Vananda Cove, Spratt Bay, Raven Bay (Texada Island)

Charts 3311, 3536, 3513; Spratt Bay is 1.9 mi SE of Vananda Cove; Raven Bay is 2.6 mi SE of Vananda Cove
Entrance (Vananda Cove): 49°45.64'N, 124°33.27'W
Position (Spratt Bay): 49°44.69'N, 124°30.54'W
Position (Raven Bay): 49°44.25'N, 124°29.72'W

Vananda Cove, between Marble Bluff and Vananda Point, offers no protection from the north. A drying spit and shoal water extend NW from the east entrance point.

The community of Vananda has a post office, store, liquor store, hotel and restaurant.

The public wharf, on the SE side of Vananda Cove, has depths of 3.4 to 6.4 m (11 to 21 ft) alongside the NE side of the wharfhead.

Diesel fuel, stove oil, propane, fresh and frozen provisions and fresh water are obtainable.

Raven Bay, 2.5 miles WNW of Pocahontas Bay, has a limestone quarry with loading facilities. Spratt Bay, 0.6 mile WNW of Raven Bay and close south of Butterfly Point, has a limestone quarry and a wharf for loading limestone. (SD)

Vananda Cove is open to Malaspina Strait; the government wharf is exposed and not recommended for small craft. Sprat and Raven bays are small bights offering little or no protection for small boats.

Sturt Bay (Marble Bay), Caesar Cove (Texada Island)

Charts 3311, 3536, 3513; 2.9 mi SE of Blubber Bay
Entrance (Sturt Bay, 0.08 mi E of Scott Rock): 49°45.77'N, 124°33.54'W
Entrance (Caesar Cove): 49°45.60'N, 124°33.89'W
Position (Texada Boat Club): 49°45.62'N, 124°33.81'W
Anchor (Sturt Bay, 0.07 mi NE of Ursula Rock): 49°45.67'N, 124°33.69'W

Sturt Bay, known locally as Marble Bay ... is entered between Marble Bluff and Hodgson Point. Scott Rock, 0.1 mile east of Hodgson Point, has 2.1 m (7 ft) over it. Ursula Rock, on the south side of the bay, is 1 m (3 ft) high and has a drying ledge extending north from it.

A rockfill breakwater, extending NW from the shore to Ursula Rock, protects a small boat basin with a 90 m (295 ft) float belonging to the Texada Boat Club.

Caesar Cove, entered east of Grant Bluff, is the south arm of Sturt Bay.

Anchorage can be obtained by small vessels in 25 m (82 ft) in the middle of Sturt Bay, west of Ursula Rock. Small craft can find shelter in Caesar Cove. (SD)

Sturt Bay, close west of Vananda, has good anchorage in fair weather. The small-boat basin and Caesar Cove to the southeast offer very good protection in southeast weather. The Texada Boat Club has transient moorage with water and some power. A restaurant in the Texada Island Inn, is a short walk from the dock.

Anchor (Sturt Bay) in 6 fathoms over sand and gravel with fair holding.

Blubber Bay (Texada Island)

Charts 3511, 3513; 4.0 mi SE of Westview; 14.5 mi NE of Comox
Entrance: 49°48.07'N, 124°37.05'W
Anchor (SE corner): 49°47.63'N, 124°36.87'W
Anchor (ferry dock): 49°47.63'N, 124°37.12'W

Blubber Bay is entered between Blubber Point and Treat Point; both points should be given a berth of at least 0.1 mile. Blubber Bay has a post office (V0N 1E0) and is connected by road to Vananda and Gillies Bay.

A ferry maintains a regular schedule between Blubber Bay and Westview.

Anchorage, sheltered from all but NW winds, can be obtained by large vessels off the entrance to Blubber Bay. Smaller vessels can anchor in the middle of the bay, sand and mud bottom; space is restricted and frequently used by the ferry. Do not anchor in the route of the ferry.

The public wharf, on the west side of Blubber Bay, has a float, 13 m (43 ft) long with a depth of 2.7 m (9 ft) alongside, attached to its south end.

The ferry landing is close south of the public wharf. (SD)

Despite its lack of beauty, Blubber Bay is an excellent place to find refuge in southeasterly weather. Chop from the southeast diminishes once you're northwest of Favada Point—welcome relief in a gale.

Rounding the north tip of Texada from the west, avoid the shoal with a number of submerged rocks off Kiddie Point, as well as dangerous Rebecca Rock identified with a white marker (1.2 miles northwest of Kiddie Point).

Approaching Blubber Bay from the east, avoid Cyril Rock (0.25 mile northwest of Grisle Point), marked by a white light.
Very good protection can be found in the southeast corner of the bay, off the beach, near a small creek outlet. Anchor as close to shore as depths allow.

A dock, south of the ferry landing and west of the gravel company wharf has 12-foot floats marked with yellow rails. This is a private wharf for the employees of the limestone plant operation. In strong northwest winds, you can anchor south and east of the ferry docks and the private floats, being careful not to obstruct any traffic. Swinging room at this site is limited.

From the outer entrance to Blubber Bay, Powell River is clearly visible on the mainland shore. Smoke from the pulp mill gives a good indication of wind direction.

Anchor (NW weather) in the SW corner of the bay in about 4 fathoms over mud and sand; good holding with limited swinging room.

Anchor (SE weather) in the southeast corner of the bay in about 3 fathoms over sand; very good holding.

Lambert Channel

Charts 3527, 3513; separates Hornby Island from SE side of Denman Island
Entrance (S, in the fairway btwn Chrome I & Norman Pt): 49°29.06'N, 124°40.38'W
Entrance (N, mid-fairway btwn Fillongley Park & Collishaw Pt): 49°32.83'N, 124°44.20'W

[Lambert Channel] is entered from south between Boyle Point and Norman Point, 1.25 miles NE. The Denman Island shore is free of dangers beyond 0.15 mile, except near the north end and in the vicinity of Fillongley Park. The Hornby Island shore has reefs and shoal spits close offshore. (SD)

The shortest route north to Cape Mudge from Hornby Island leads through Lambert Channel. But if you want to find protection from the northwesterlies, cross over inside Denman Island and head for Deep Harbour or Comox.

Tribune Bay Park (Hornby Island)

Charts 3527, 3513; 3.7 mi NE of Chrome I Light
Entrance: 49°30.60'N, 124°35.84'W
Anchor (0.25 mi NE of Spray Pt): 49°31.43'N 124°37.91'W

> *Tribune Bay is entered between Flora Islet and Nash Bank, 1.6 miles WSW. The NE shore of the bay is bold and cliffy; the west shore is low and shelving with drying ledges extending 0.15 mile offshore. Spray Point is a small peninsula at the head of the bay. Tribune Bay Provincial Park is undeveloped.*
>
> *Anchorage can be obtained in Tribune Bay, in 15 m (48 ft), sand bottom. The anchorage is exposed to ESE and SE winds but sheltered from other winds.*
>
> *Hornby Island is thickly wooded; on its west side it rises precipitously in terraces to the summit of Mount Geoffrey, from which it slopes more gently east. The island is easily identified from all approaches. Hornby Island has resorts and lodges.*
>
> *Hornby Island settlement and ferry landing, near Shingle Spit, has stores, campsite, launching ramp and a motel with a float.*
>
> *Because of the spit, there is usually a leeward side offering some protection from the sea. However, for small craft the most frequently used anchorage is just south of the spit, taking care to anchor well clear of the submarine cables. The predominating winds during summer months are from NW, which blow strongly at times through Lambert Channel.* (SD)

From the south, 900-foot-high Mt. Geoffrey, on the western edge of Hornby Island, looks like a small peak rising out of the water and sloping gently to the east. As you approach and the mountain grows in height, the wide expanse of the eastern part of the island and Tribune Bay come into view.

From the south, head straight into Tribune Bay and go deep until you approach the north shore, avoiding Nash Bank on the southwest side of the bay, and staying east of rocky Spray Point at the head of the bay. Although there's good protection from prevailing northwesterlies here, you're completely open to any southerly weather, as the driftlogs along the beach indicate. The Park boasts more than 1,000 meters of sandy beach and some of the warmest swimming in lower B.C. You can enjoy picnicking on shore in a covered picnic area at the east side of the bay.

When you leave Tribune Bay, clear buoy "P35" (Nash Bank) 1 mile southeast of Dunlop Point before turning west. If you are eastbound, clear the long reef extending from Flora Islet before you make your turn.

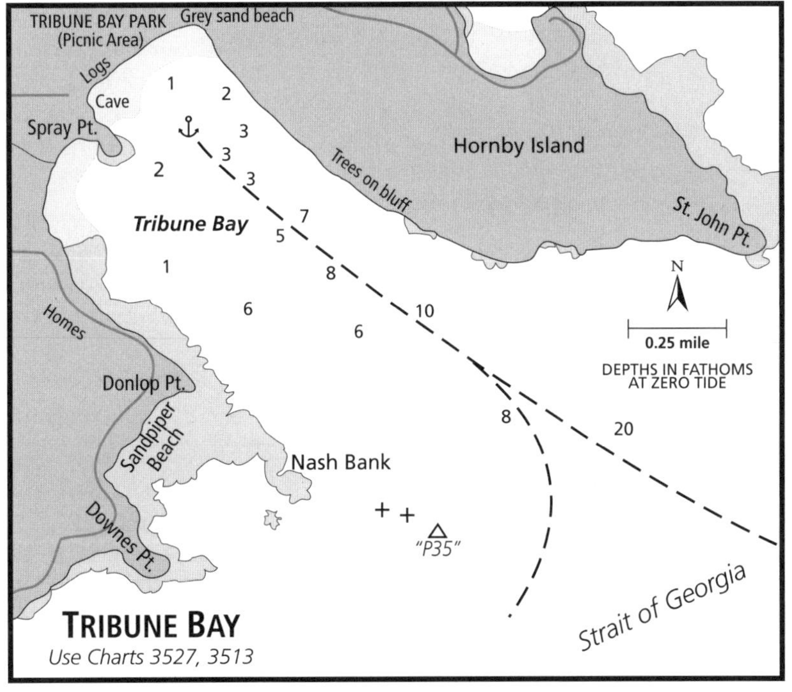

TRIBUNE BAY
Use Charts 3527, 3513

Anchor in 2 to 3 fathoms over a sandy bottom with good holding.

Ford's Cove (Hornby Island)

Charts 3527, 3513; 1.6 mi NE of Chrome I Light
Entrance (S): 49°29.79'N, 124°40.75'W
Entrance (N): 49°30.10'N, 124°41.21'W
Public float: 49°29.82'N, 124°40.53'W
Anchor: 49°29.85'N, 124°40.61'W

> *Ford('s) Cove, 0.6 mile NW of Norman Point, can be entered north or south of Maude Reef, which dries 4.6 m (15 ft).*
>
> *At the SE corner of Ford's Cove there are three public floats with a common connection to shore. The floats and pier are protected by a rock breakwater on their SW side and by a floating breakwater on the NW side; the basin within has been dredged to 2.4 m (8 ft). The SW float is a fuel dock and a 5 ton crane is on the wharfhead. Power is available on the floats.* (SD)

Small Ford's Cove, protected by a breakwater, is the only all-weather shelter in Lambert Channel. The cove has a government wharf. Ford's Cove Marina offers services to small boats. Ashore there are nice walking trails and a general store.

Anchorage may be found in about 3 fathoms over rock, sand and gravel.

⚓ **Ford's Cove Marina & Store**
tel: 250.335.2169; fax: 250.335.2312; website: www.fordscove.com; email: info@fordscove.com

⚓ **Ford Cove Harbour Authority**
power; restrooms

Gravelly Bay (Denman Island)

Charts 3527, 3513; 1.6 mi NW of Chrome I Light
Position: 49°29.68'N, 124°42.52'W

> *Gravelly Bay, 1.5 miles NW of Boyle Point, is the site of Denman East Ferry Landing. Regular ferry service for passengers and automobiles operate to and from Hornby Island.* (SD)

Shingle Spit (Hornby Island)

Charts 3527, 3513; 1.5 mi NW of Ford Cove
Anchor (S side): 49°30.70'N, 124°42.45'W

> *Shingle Spit, 0.5 mile NW of Savoie Rocks, has a clump of trees near its extremity then projects as a drying spit into the channel.* (SD)

Shingle Spit, a remarkable feature extending from Hornby Island into Lambert Channel, makes an excellent rest stop on a north- or southbound trip, with fair protection from prevailing northwest winds. Anchorage can be taken between the ferry dock and the end of the spit as desired.

Anchor (south side) in 1 fathom over sand and gravel with fair holding.

Baynes Sound

Charts 3527, 3513; separates Denman Island from Vancouver Island
Entrance (S, 0.52 mi SW of Chrome I Light): 49°28.23'N, 124°41.89'W
Waypoint (mid-fairway btwn buoys "P40" & "P39"): 49°29.22'N, 124°43.67'W
Entrance (N, via Comox Bar):

> [Baynes Sound] *is entered from the south between Chrome Island and Mapleguard Point; from the north it is entered by way of Comox Bar.*
>
> *Baynes Sound is one of the largest oyster producing regions on the British Columbia coast.*
>
> *Tidal streams in Baynes Sound attain 2 or 3 kn in the south entrance, but within the sound the rate is considerably less, decreasing as the channel widens. When flowing against an opposing wind a nasty chop can be raised which can be uncomfortable for small craft.*
>
> *A regular ferry services crosses Baynes Sound, connecting Denman Island to Buckley Bay on Vancouver Island ... Small craft navigators should, at all times, keep clear of the ferry and the ferry landings.* (SD)

Deep Bay (Vancouver Island)

Charts 3527, 3513; 2.0 mi W of Chrome I Light; 14.3 mi SE of Comox Hbr
Entrance (0.3 mi W of Mapleguard Pt): 49°27.96'N, 124°44.62'W
Anchor: 49°27.86'N, 124°43.94'W

Deep Bay has a marina and public floats near its SE end. Public floats, 18 to 146 m long, have a common connection to a pier and are protected by a floating breakwater. A 3 tonne crane, public telephone, garbage and used oil disposal facilities are on the pier. A sewage pumpout facility is located on the main off-loading float. Washroom and shower facilities are located near the office at the pier entrance and near the parking lot. Tidal grids lie on both sides of the pier. Power and fresh water are available on the floats, groceries are obtainable nearby. Several private floats and mooring buoys are in the bay. The wreck of a 14 m fishing vessel, sunk on 2003, is 0.1 mile WNW of the public floats. It is reported to lie in 18 m of water.

Marine farm facilities, in Deep and Mud Bays, consist of longline oyster culture rafts and buoys.

Anchorage can be obtained in Deep Bay in a depth of about 30 m, mud bottom. (SD)

Deep Bay offers the best-sheltered anchorage between Nanaimo and Comox. The current at the south entrance to Baynes Sound can run as high as 3 knots at spring tides, and a nasty chop can develop if the wind opposes the current. Pass midchannel between green buoy "P39" and red buoy "P40" to avoid the large sandbars and drying reefs off Mapleguard and Repulse points. Avoid the aquaculture in the southwest corner of the bay, as well as the numerous private buoys and floats. Anchorage can be taken north of the breakwater.

Anchor approximately 300 yards southeast of Mapleguard Point in about 7 fathoms over mud with good holding.

⚓ **Deep Bay Harbour Authority**
tel: 250.757.9331; monitors VHF Ch 66A; power; restrooms; showers; pumpout

Mud Bay (Vancouver Island)

Charts 3527, 3513; 2 mi NW of Deep Bay
Entrance: 49°28.99'N, 124°46.78'W

Mud Bay is encumbered with mud flats with numerous boulders, and fronted by steep-to drying reefs. A rock awash is in the centre of the south entrance. The bay has a booming ground and a marina, which is protected by a breakwater. The channel leading to the marina dries. (SD)

Mud Bay is a large, shallow bight which mostly dries at low water. Temporary anchorage can be found in a 2- to 3-fathom hole which extends from northwest to southwest of the drying sandbar in the middle of the bay. Avoid the boulders as mentioned in Small Craft Guide. The bottom is mud, gravel and shells.

Fanny Bay (Vancouver Island)

Charts 3527, 3513; 4.0 mi NW of Deep Bay
Entrance: 49°30.78'N, 124°48.88'W
Anchor: 49°30.47'N, 124°49.27'W
Public float: 49°30.46'N, 124°49.62'W

Fanny Bay is bounded on its south side by a drying mud flat and on its NW side by the drying flat off Base Flat. When entering from the south, give Ship Point a berth of not less than 0.3 mile. Maine farm facilities and a booming ground are in the bay.

The settlement of Fanny Bay has a store, hotel and restaurant, the post office is 1.6 km north.

A conspicuous white tower, close SW of the public wharf, is 39 m high.

The public wharf in Fanny Bay has a depth of 4.6 m at its head. A float is attached to the NW end of the public wharf.

Anchorage in Fanny Bay can be obtained in 13 to 15 m mud bottom, with the extremity of Ship Point in line with the SW extremity of Denman Island bearing 117° and Denman Island light structure bearing 345° (SD)

Denman Island Public Floats (Denman Island)

Charts 3527, 3513; public floats 5.1 mi NW of Deep Bay
Public floats: 49°32.05'N, 124°49.33'W

Denman Island village, on the east side of Baynes Sound opposite Buckley Bay, is the site of a ferry landing that provides regular service to Buckley Bay. A post office and store are within walking distance of the public wharf.

There is road connection to the ferry landing at Gravelly Bay, then by ferry to Hornby Island. ...

The public wharf, close south of the ferry landing, has a berthing length of 34 m with a depth of 5.5 m alongside. A float, attached to the inner side of the wharfhead, is 24 m long. (SD)

Buckley Bay (Vancouver Island)

Charts 3527, 3513; 1.4 mi NW of Fanny Bay
Position: 49°31.58'N, 124°50.82'W

Buckley Bay, close north of Base Flat, is the site of the ferry landing from which regular service operates to Denman Island. The south part of the bay is a booming ground with a barge loading berth. (SD)

Union Bay (Vancouver Island)

Charts 3527, 3513; 0.5 mi SW of Union Pt
Entrance: 49°35.07'N, 124°52.86'W
Anchor: 49°35.06'N, 124°52.97'W

Unions Bay ... was a bunkering and shipping port for coal, facilities and mines closed in 1959. The settlement of Union Bay is connected to the Island Highway and the E&N railway, it has a hotel, post office and a store. A log dump and booming ground are in the bay. A rockfill breakwater protects a launching ramp. (SD)

Union Bay is a small bight offering temporary anchorage in the lee of Union Point.

Anchor in 2 to 3 fathoms over mud and gravel with fair holding.

Henry Bay (Denman I)

Charts 3527, 3513; 1 mi SE of Sandy Island, 5.0 mi SE of Comox Hbr
Entrance: 49°36.08'N, 124°50.62'W
Anchor: 49°36.13'N, 124°50.08'W

Henry Bay ... is the site of commercial oyster beds. A sand and mud drying spit extends 2.5 miles NNW from Longbeak Point, the north extremity of Denman Island, and terminates at White Spit (SD)

Although Henry Bay is a nice anchorage with some protection from east to southeast winds, our choice in stable weather is nearby Sandy Island—or Comox in a real blow.

It is easier, however, to anchor in Henry Bay than at Sandy Island; the bottom here is flatter and shallower over a larger area, allowing more swinging room. We frequently see flocks of mergansers, Bonaparte gulls and other species of birds along the spit to Longbeak Point.

Anchor in 3 to 4 fathoms over sand, gravel, and shells with fair-to-good holding.

Sandy Island Marine Provincial Park (Sandy Island)

Charts 3527, 3513; 4.2 mi SE of Comox Hbr
Entrance: 49°36.78'N, 124°51.17'W
Anchor: 49°36.97'N, 124°50.99'W

Sandy Island Marine Park is undeveloped; good temporary anchorage can be obtained to the west of Sandy Island where the sand bank drops off sharply, or south of the island with

Sailboat at Sandy Island

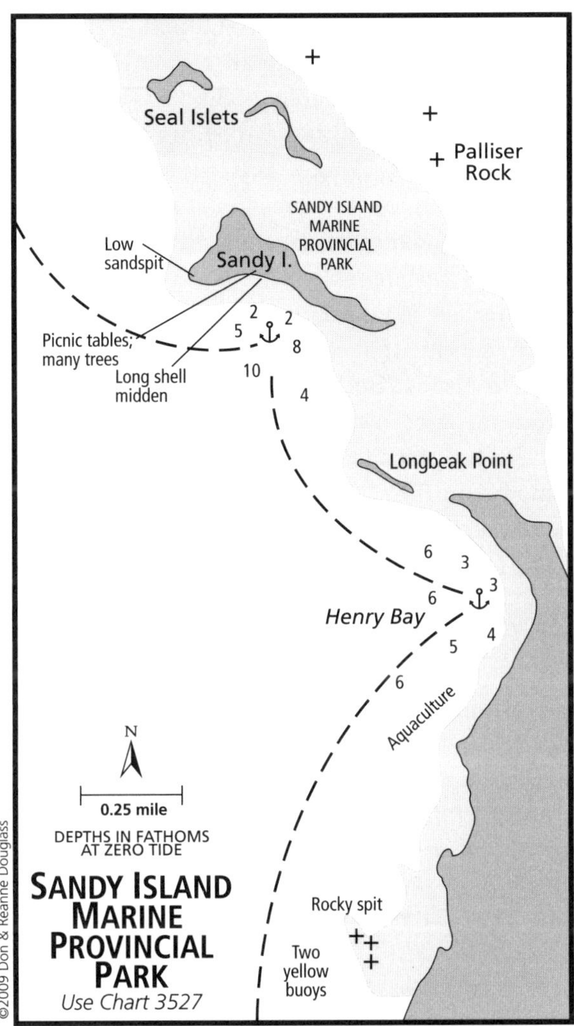

good protection from the NW. The sand bank between Sandy Island and Longbeak Point protects the anchorage from SE seas but not from SE winds. (SD)

Sandy Island Marine Provincial Park is a small undeveloped park with its own charm. This low-lying island has trees that give it the local name "Tree Island". The beautiful white sand spits projecting west and east make for pleasant beachcombing and bird watching. Shell middens attest to the island's popularity with early native peoples, and modern-day kayakers find it to their tastes as well. Primitive camping is allowed ashore but there are no facilities.

The cove is steep-to, but since surf is usually minimal, you shouldn't have trouble getting ashore to stretch your legs and look for wild asparagus or dig for clams.

Although Sandy Island does offer some protection from northerly and easterly chop it's good only for overnight anchoring during calm and stable weather. It is not the place to be caught in a blow. If southerly weather is expected, head inside Comox Harbour.

Anchoring off the beach is a little tricky because the bottom shoals rapidly from about 15 fathoms. If you wish to anchor close to shore, you may need to use two anchors.

Anchor in 2 to 8 fathoms over a steep-to bottom of sand, shells, and grass with fair-to-good holding.

Comox Harbour (Vancouver Island)

Charts 3527 inset, 3513; 3.5 mi SW of Cape Lazo Light; 18.7 mi SW of Powell River
Entrance (0.28 mi S of Goose Spit Light): 49°39.34'N, 124°55.51'W

Marina entrance (0.15 mile W of public wharf and 40 yards W of the W breakwater light): 49°40.16'N, 124°55.87'W

East public floats entrance (40 yards southeast of east breakwater light): 49°40.06'N, 124°55.47'W

Comox Harbour, entered between Gartley Point and Goose Spit, is a well protected anchorage available to all classes of vessels. Drying mud flats extend a considerable distance from its shores.

The harbour affords anchorage almost anywhere, in 20 to 26 m (66 to 84 ft), as convenient. Small craft can obtain anchorage off Royston; it is partially protected from southeasterlies by the mud flats of the Trent River off Gartley Point.

Comox, a town on the north shore of the harbour, is the centre of an agricultural district and the site of a Canadian Armed Forces Base. It has a population of 6,607 (1981) and the local facilities include numerous retail stores, including a liquor store, a post office (V9N 3Z0), banks and laundromat.

Customs clearance can be made at Courte-

nay. The public wharf and extensive floats are west of the last-mentioned DND wharf [on the north shore of the harbour]. Public telephones, garbage and used oil disposal facilities are available at the wharfhead; power and water are available on the floats. A tidal grid is on the north side of the wharfhead. A float reserved for seaplanes is attached to the end of the south public float. (SD)

Although entering Comox over the bar can be a challenge, once you're safely inside the breakwater, it's worth it. Comox is a delightful town that has done a magnifent job of improving its waterfront—green spaces, upgraded harbor facilities and a lovely walkway. Comox Valley Harbour Authority's Fisherman's Wharf now has excellent facilities for cruising vessels. Their attractive office building, on-site showers, laundry facilities, pump-out and oil disposal are the latest improvements to the public marina, and their personnel are friendly and accommodating; power (to 20 amp) and water.

Comox Municipal Marina, to the immediate west of Fisherman's Wharf does not accept transients. Comox Bay Marina, west of Municipal Marina, has permanent moorage only, although from time to time they may have a few slips available. Black Fin fuel dock (gasoline and diesel) has very limited space.

The town of Comox has a supermarket, liquor store, bookstore, restraurants and pubs and boutiques, within short a short walk above the harbor.

Comox is also home to the Coast Guard radio station that covers the coast northward to almost Bella Bella, as well as to the Canadian Air Force. The Comox airport is a convenient place to arrange for crew or guests to meet you. The B.C. ferry at the north end of town runs between Comox and Powell River.

For family and adult fun, the entire Comox Valley offers a wide choice of outdoor activities several museums (Courtney Museum and the Air Force Museum), a live theater and numerous restaurants and bistros. The Old House Restaurant on the west side of the slough is our favorite (reservations a must tel: 250.338.5406). For the myriad possibilities check out the Comox Valley Chamber of Commerce website www.comox-valley-tourism.ca. From Comox harbor, you can take a tender north to Courtenay through the slough and dock at the city float. (Ask for information at Fisherman's Harbour before you head up Courtenay Slough.)

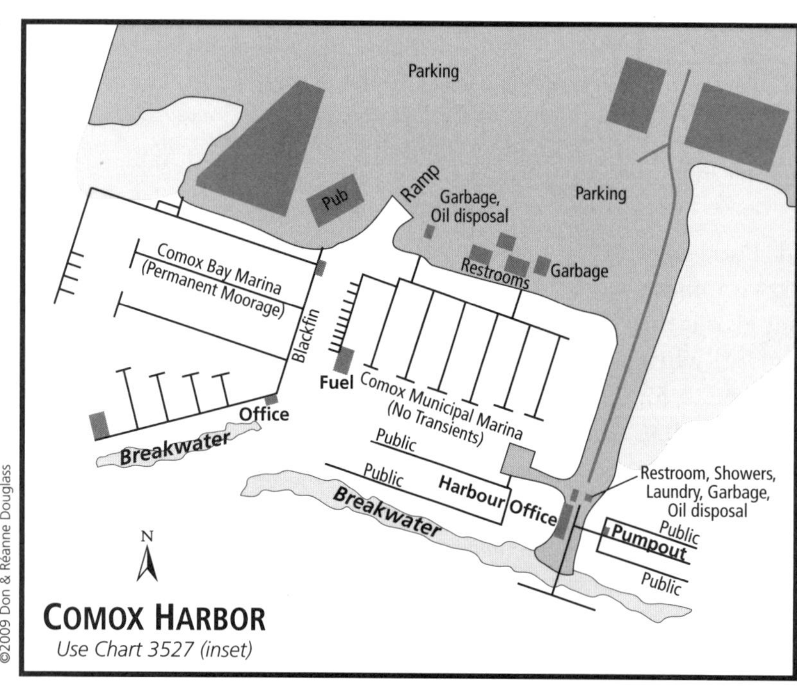

If you want to anchor, instead of mooring, tuck inside the harbor, behind Goose Spit. Be aware, though, that this site may be crowded in summer.

The town itself has a supermarket, bookstore, liquor store, and restaurants within walking distance of the harbor. If you need to do heavy provisioning, Courtenay is just a short taxi ride to the

Fun on Comox Nautical Days

west and has a greater choice of stores.

Small vessels can tuck inside the harbor behind Goose Spit; although the area is small and sometimes crowded, it offers good protection in all weather.

⚓ **Comox Valley Harbour Authority** tel: 250.339.6041; fax: 250.339.6057; monitors VHF Ch 66A; website: www.comoxfishermanswharf.com; email: info@comoxfishermanswharf.com; power; wireless internet access; garbage disposal; best to call ahead during high season

⚓ **Comox Bay Marina** tel: 250.339.2930; monitors VHF Ch 66A; mostly permanent moorage; call ahead for possible moorage

⚓ **Gas N Go Marina** tel: 250.339.4664; monitors VHF Ch 66A; fuel; power

⚓ **Chamber of Commerce** tel: 250.334.3234; toll free US & Canada: 888.357.4471; website: www.comox-valley-tourism.ca

Courtenay River and Slough

(Vancouver Island)
Charts 3527 inset, 3513; 2 mi W of Comox marinas
Entrance (0.52 mi W of Goose Spit Light): 49°39.64'N, 124°56.29'W

Courtenay River has an estuary filled with drying mud flats. The channel across these drying flats is marked by daybeacons and ranges and was dredged in 1982 to a width of 35 m [115 ft] and a depth that dries 1 m [3 ft]. The river is fed, partly by tributaries leading from by glaciers and snowfields on Forbidden Plateau. Even in late summer, when most other island rivers are almost dry, there is usually 1.8 m (6 ft) of water up to the Courtenay Bridge south of Lewis Park.

Water levels in the estuary are affected by tidal and weather conditions along with fresh water runoff that is controlled by a B.C. Hydro dam upstream. It is essential that mariners check local water level conditions before attempting to navigate the river.

The mouth of the Courtenay River is a water aerodrome.

...Local knowledge and familiarity with local conditions are advised before attempting to navigate the river. Numberous deadheads can be encountered in the channel. (SD)

The largest navigable river on Vancouver Island is the Courtenay River. Entrance is made just west of Comox Harbour across the drying mud flats. Small boats (less than 6 feet draft) can trace the saltwater bay across the mud flats into the river and find fresh water moorage at the public floats in Courtenay Slough; the scenery is reminiscent of the French canals. Because the outer route across the bar changes over time, you should make local inquiries before attempting this interesting side trip. The perfect way to visit Courtney Slough is via a dinghy or kayak that won't require the drawbridge to be opened for you.

Comox Bar

Charts 3527, 3513; 3.3 mi S of Cape Lazo; extends from Goose Spit to White Spit at Sandy Island
Entrance (SW, 0.2 mi SW of buoy "P50"): 49°38.77'N, 124°52.61'W
Entrance (NE, 0.2 mi NE of buoy "P54"): 49°39.61'N, 124°51.43'W

Comox Bay extends NNW from White spit to the beach fronting Willemar Bluff... . The passage across the bar is marked by range lights and the least depth on this range, cleared by a wire drag, was 2.4 m in 1969. Several vessels have reported grounding while crossing the shallowest part of the bar. Tide sea state, and vessel draught must be carefully considered before a decision is made to cross the bar.

To assure clearing the shallow spit extending SE from Cape Lazo, when approaching Comox Bar from the north, do not haul in for the leading line until Willemar Bluff bears more than 250. When departing Comox note the range is obscured by houses and trees until about 0l1 mile from the leading line.

Comox Bar range lights (501, 502), on the west shore of Baynes Sound about 2 miles west of Sandy Island, when in line bearing 222° indicate the track across Comox Bar.

Comox Bar light and bell buoy "P54" (500), at the east edge of Comox Bar and close north of the leading line, is a starboard hand buoy.

Starboard hand buoys "P50" and "P52" are on Comox Bay SW of the light buoy; buoy "P50" has a radar reflector. (SD)

The route across Comox Bar is marked with three buoys and a set of lighted range markers on the Vancouver Island shore to the southwest. Depth in the water across the bar is only 1 to 2 fathoms for a distance of one mile.

When crossing the bar as you leave Comox, be sure to line up the range lights on shore behind you and keep them in line, using the three buoys as references. A course made good of about 020° magnetic will carry you across the bar. However, at times, there is significant current. As you crab against the current, your actual heading can differ considerably as you attempt to keep the range markers in line behind you.

Avoid cutting the corner of Cape Lazo before you round to the northwest. Foul ground extends off the cape for over a half-mile. It's best to remain outside the two buoys one mile off Cape Lazo.

Boats continuing to Campbell River after crossing Comox Bar will find no harbors along the stretch between Comox and Campbell River, although some bights along shore can be used as temporary, fair-weather anchor sites. Our preference, however, is to head to the tiny cove at Mitlenatch Island Nature Park, strategically located at the north end of the Strait of Georgia, and spend a night there.

Wind- and human-powered vessels meet

Cape Lazo (Vancouver Island)

Charts 3527, 3513; 25 mi SE of Campbell River; 32 mi NW of Ballenas Islands
Buoy "PK" (0.8 mi NE of Cape Lazo): 49°42.73'N, 124°50.95'W
Buoy "PJ" (1.33 mi SE of Cape Lazo): 49°41.51'N, 124°49.71'W

Cape Lazo ... known locally as Point Homes, is a prominent headland with a flat summit, its seaward sides are faced with yellow clay. From the SE, this headland appears to be an island and it is not until north of Hornby Island that it can be seen to be part of Vancouver Island. Drying rock ledges surround the cape and Kye Bay, on its north side, dries completely.

Comox Aeronautical Beacon light (508) is 1.25 miels NW of Cape Lazo.

East cardinal buoy "PJ" and Cape Lazo east cardinal light buoy "PB" (507.5) mark the outer edge of the shoal area east of Cape Lazo.

A large white radar dome, 1.1 miles NW of Cape Lazo at Comox Airport, has fixed red lights and is the first identifiable feature when approaching Cape Lazo from north. A microwave tower, 42 m high, and a radio tower are at the north end of Cape Lazo. (SD)

As you approach Cape Lazo from the south, from a distance the bluffs of the cape look like an island on the horizon. Much of the steep yellow clay of the bluffs has worn away over the eons and been deposited as much as a mile off shore. It is easy to think you can take a short cut across the shoals of the cape whether you are heading to or from Comox Harbor. Lazo means "snare," and we have seen commercial fishing boats caught and grounded by this snare while trying the short cut. To avoid high anxiety, be sure to follow the navigation aids; buoys "PK" or "PJ" mark the safe turning points.

Little River (Vancouver Island)

Charts 3527, 3513; 3.2 mi NW of Cape Lazo
Position: 49°44.43'N, 124°55.27'W

Ferry Landing. Close east of the mouth of Little River, 3 miles NW of Cape Lazo... Small craft navigators are advised to keep clear of the ferry and the ferry landing. (SD)

Little River is the terminal for the ferry that runs back and forth between Comox and Powell River. Al thought locals have told us that the bight on the south side of the ferry landing is protected by the Little River Spit and that boats do anchor there at times, we have never tried it; it appears too open to northwest winds and chop.

Elma River (Vancouver Island)

Chart 3513; 12.7 mi NW of Cape Lazo
Position: 49°51.31'N, 125°05.38'W

Elma Bay ... at the entrance to Black Creek, has a resort with boat launching ramp. (SD)

Elma Bay is an open roadstead. Camping, picnic facilities, and fresh water are available at Miracle Beach Provincial Park.

Oyster River (Vancouver Island)

Chart 3513; 14.1 mi NW of Cape Lazo
Entrance: 49°52.30'N, 125°06.45'W

Oyster River, 1.5 miles NW of Elma Bay, is a stream of considerable size, with a drying bank of shingle extending 0.3 mile from its mouth. A dredged channel, leading to a marina and boat basin in the mouth of Oyster River, is marked by a series of piles. Due to storms and an unstable shoreline the channel and boat basin require dredging annually. Local knowledge should be acquired before entering the channel.

Anchorage, open to most winds, can be obtained about 0.5 mile from shore midway between Elma Bay and Oyster River, in 18 to 30 m (SD)

The dredged channel mentioned in SD leads to Pacific Playgrounds Resort on the south side of Oyster River outlet. The channel does not necessarily follow a straight line from the two poles marking the outer entrance. A transit of the several hundred-yard channel is best done when the channel banks can been seen for reference. The resort is open year round, with fuel, power, laundry and showers. Telephone 250.337.5600 for the latest information on depths in the channel and moorage availability.

⚓ **Pacific Playgrounds International**
tel: 250.337.5600; fax: 250.337.5979;
website: www.pacificplaygrounds.com;
power; restrooms; showers; laundry

Fresh halibut

Kuhushan Point (Salmon Point Marina) (Vancouver Island)

Chart 3513; 0.6 mi N of Oyster River
Entrance: 49°53.50'N, 125°07.45'W

> *Kuhushan Point ... is a low, sandy projection. Trees, which in thick weather can be mistaken for the extremity of the point, are about 0.15 mile inlalnd. Several houses are near the point and close north of the light structure there is a large low building with a conspicuous pyramidal roof marked "Pub", which in daytime, can be seen long before the light sructure can be identified. A dredged channel close north of Oyster Pond leads to a boat basin and resort. It requires annual dredging therefore local knowledge is advised.* (SD)

On the north side of Oyster River and just behind the beach is Oyster Pond. At the north end of Oyster Pond, a small rectangle has been dredged to form a private marina. The channel to the entrance is shorter than that of Oyster River and easier to negotiate. The Kuhushan Point Light is actually a half-mile north of Kuhushan Point as marked on the chart and is recognizable as a white square, skeleton tower.

Oyster Bay (Vancouver Island)

Charts 3538, 3513; 0.5 mi SE of Shelter Pt
Entrance: 49°56.05'N, 125°10.02'W
Anchor: 49°56.10'N, 125°10.70'W

> *Anchorage, with fair protection from SE winds, can be obtained in Oyster Bay in 10 to 20 m (33 to 66 ft), about 1 mile offshore.* (SD)

Oyster Bay is a large bight on the Vancouver Island shore between Kuhushan Point to the south and Shelter Point to the north. The latter, the southern entrance to Discovery Passage, is 3 miles due south of Cape Mudge. Shelter Point has drying reefs with boulders extending 0.4 mile offshore.

Temporary anchorage, with fair protection from prevailing northwest winds, can be found in the lee of Shelter Point, as well as at Mitlenatch Island, 7 miles east. Both are good places to await proper tide conditions in Discovery Passage.

Anchor in 2 to 4 fathoms over a mixed bottom with fair holding.

Powell River, Westview

Charts 3311, 3536 inset, 3513; on the mainland coast; 29 mi ESE of Campbell River; 49 mi NW of Nanaimo
Westview S basin breakwater light: 49°50.03'N, 124°31.79'W

> *Westview is a suburb of Powell River. Numerous stores, including a liquor store, restaurants, a laundromat and post office (V8A 4Z4) are available. A RCMP vessel and a Canadian Coast Guard search and rescue vessel operate year round from Westview.*
>
> *The ferry landing is attached to the south side of the public wharf; regular passenger and automobile services are maintained between Westview and Little River, near Comox on*

Vancouver Island, and Blubber Bay, on Texada Island.

The public wharf, between the north and south basins, is used mainly for handling petroleum ...

The ferry landing is attached to the south side of the public wharf.

A public fishing harbour, on the south side of the public wharf, is protected by breakwaters to the west and south and was dredged to 2.4 m (8 ft) (1975). A long float extends south with a series of finger floats extending SW from it. Water and power are laid on the floats; garbage and used oil disposal facilities are available.

A marina, on the north side of the public wharf, is operated by the municipality of Powell River; there are no transient facilities.

Diesel fuel, gasoline, lubricants, fresh water, marine hardware and provisions are obtainable.

Repairs for small craft, including a marine railway, hoist and boat grid are available. (SD)

Powell River, the site of the large pulp and paper mill, is largely an industrial town. Westview, 2.5 miles south and a suburb of Powell River, has the only harbor for pleasure craft. The breakwater near the mill, formed by the hulls of two Liberty ships, is a tourist curiosity.

At Westview, there are two basins protected by stone breakwaters. The north basin is used for permanent moorage. The south basin, located immediately southeast of the ferry landing, is open to transient vessels and has been upgraded since our last edition. Power, water, showers, laundry, garbage disposal and fuel dock are inside the basin. Marine Traders is above the dock. There are several sizeable malls within taxi distance of the harbor.

For boaters that have kayaks and want to get in some fresh-water "cruising", the Powell Forest Canoe Route has a lot of quiet areas. One year we spent two days kayaking Powell Lake for a respite from saltwater.

Fuel and water can be obtained in the boat basin. All other supplies and services (including propane) are within walking distance of the harbor. There are several sizable malls within taxi distance of the harbor.

⚓ **Westview Harbour** tel: 604.485.5244; fax: 604.485.5286; monitors VHF Ch 66A; website: www.discoverpowellriver.com; open year-round; power; restrooms; shower; laundry

⚓ **Westview Fuels Fuel Dock** tel: 604.485.2867; monitors VHF Ch 66A; fuel; restrooms; supplies

Shearwater Passage (Mystery Reef)

Charts 3311, 3513; btwn Harwood Island & Mystery Reef
Entrance (SW, mid-ch btwn Grant Reefs & Harwood I, 2.7 mi S of Mystery Reef): 49°51.65'N, 124°43.11'W
Grant Reef light buoy "QM" (S extremity of reef): 49°52.07'N, 124°46.08'W
Mystery Reef buoy "Q25" (close NE of reef): 49°54.76'N, 124°42.83'W

Shearwater Passage is bounded on its SE side by Harwood Island and on its NW side by Grant Reefs, Savary Island and Mystery Reef. The fairway is about 2.5 miles wide.

Caution. The shallow waters over Grant Reefs and between Mystery Reef and Savary Island can become very rough when a strong wind opposes the tide; under these conditions it would be wise to give the reefs a wide berth.

Grant Reefs, 3 miles NW of Vivian Island, have drying rocks and a rock awash near their east end.

Mystery Reef, 3 miles SE of Savary Island, is a group of drying boulders connected to Savary Island by a shoal spit. It is steep-to on its SW, south and SE sides. Do not pass between Mystery Reef and Savary Island. (SD)

When using Shearwater Passage, avoid Grant Reefs and Mystery Reef, as well as the entire shoal area between Mystery Reef and Savary Island. Over the entire area, kelp-infested waters and isolated rocks (unmarked) pose a danger to all craft.

Harwood Island

Charts 3311, 3513; 4 mi W of Powell River
Harwood Island S Pt: 49°50.23'N, 124°40.12'W

> *Harwood Island is flat topped and wooded. Its south extremity is steep-to, its east side is fringed with boulders and drying reefs extending up to 0.5 mile offshore and its west side is fringed with steep-to banks of stones and boulders. Harwood Island is an Indian Reserve.* (SD)

Avoid the steep-to mud flats on all sides of the shore and the numerous sportfishing boats in the vicinity.

Keefer Bay (Savary Island)

Charts 3538, 3311; 10 mi NW of Powell River
Keefer Public Wharf: 49°56.76'N, 124°46.78'W

> *Savary Island is thickly wooded and surrounded by sandy beaches, strewn with boulders. The island is a summer resort.*
>
> *It is reported that the soft sand bottom off Savary Island affords poor holding ground.* (SD)

Low and flat, Savary Island extends 4 miles from east to west. Tidal flats around the island are steep-to and require care in approaching. The island is well known for its uncrowded, long sandy beaches. There are some lovely homes, and roads and trails allow visitors to admire the beautiful woods and meadows filled with wildflowers.

There's a small public wharf in Keefer Bay on the northeast corner of Savary Island. Anchorage can be taken on either side of the wharf in stable weather, offering good protection from southeasterlies but somewhat open to northwesterlies. The small wharf is used principally as a loading zone for the Lund water taxi. Boats mooring here should not be left unattended.

There are dozens of private mooring buoys east and west of the public dock.

Anchor in 5 fathoms over sand and gravel with poor-to-fair holding.

Hernando Island

Charts 3538, 3513, 3311; 5.5 mi NW of Keefer Bay

> *Hernando Island is thickly wooded with some cleared areas on its north side. The island is fringed with extensive beaches, studded with large boulders, and shoal water; it should be given a good clearance.* (SD)

Since Hernando Island, like Savary Island, is a remnant of a glacial terminal moraine, its drying flats of sand and gravel with isolated boulders extend some distance from shore. While it is not generally visited by cruising boats, temporary anchorage can be found along its eastern shore. Summer afternoons here can be quite balmy even when Desolation Sound itself is covered by low clouds.

Dog Bay (Hernando Island)

Charts 3538, 3513, 3311; immediately SE of Hidalgo Pt
Entrance: 49°59.69'N, 124°53.88'W
Anchor: 49°59.66'N, 124°54.10'W

> *Dog Bay ... has a rock, with less than 2 m (6 ft) over it, in its north part. Dog Rock, in the centre of Dog Bay, is 2 m (7 ft) high.* (SD)

Both Dog Bay, and the area off the easternmost tip of Hernando Island, are the preferred anchorages; avoid numerous rocks.

Anchor in about 2 fathoms over sand and gravel with fair-to-good holding.

Stag Bay (Hernando Island)

Charts 3538, 3513, 3311; btwn Spilsbury & Hidalgo Pts
Entrance (0.4 mi NW of Hidalgo Pt): 49°59.95'N, 124°54.73'W
Anchor: 49°59.82'N, 124°54.63'W

> *Stag Bay ... has a conspicuous white boulder on its shore about 0.7 mile west of Hidalgo Point.* (SD)

Stag Bay is open to the northwest but offers fair protection during southeast blows. The float at the east end of Stag Bay is private.

Anchor in 6 fathoms over sand and gravel with fair holding.

A water taxi at Keefer Bay's public float, Savary Island

Lund (Malaspina Peninsula)

Charts 3538, 3311; 10.5 mi NW of Powell River; 2.1 mi NE of Keefer Bay on Savary Island
Entrance: 49°58.84'N, 124°46.09'W
N breakwater light: 49°58.84'N, 124°45.79'W

> *Lund ... is a small settlement at the northern terminus of the main highway from Vancouver. A post office, store, hotel and marinas are in the settlement. ...*
>
> *Public floats, south of the public sharf, are 75 m long and have a common connection to an approach structure. Water and power are available on the floats and washrooms and showers on shore. A water taxi float is in the harbour between the public floats and the wharf head. A rockfill breakwater is south and a floating three section concrete breakwater is west of the floats and also used for mooring.*
>
> *Close north of the public floats are floats belonging to the hotel, the south float is a fuel dock.* (SD)

Lund has made the tourist circuit. You may now hear French, German or Japanese spoken as summer visitors arrive in their rental cars, motorcycles or motor coach to check out the most northerly settlement on Highway 101. The recently restored Lund Hotel includes a restaurant, general store, liquor store, a gift shop and art gallery (Tug Ghum Gallery). The area outside the hotel has an ice cream shop and deli. The harbor, too, has upgraded its facilities to include a new office complex with showers. Nancy's Bakery, also in a new building above the docks is a must for tourists and locals, alike.

Unfortunately, dock space at Lund is limited. The southern float is reserved for commercial craft (although you can moor temporarily when space is available); the north float accommodates transient vessels, but arrive early to get a space; otherwise you'll have to raft or moor on the floating breakwater and take your dinghy to shore.

Boat charter tours of Desolation Sound and surrounding waters can be arranged at the hotel or you can rent a kayak; a small water taxi runs back and forth from Lund to Savary Island.

⚓ **Lund Harbour Authority Wharf** tel: 604.483.4612; monitors VHF Ch 66A (we had better luck on 68, but this may change); power; restrooms; showers

⚓ **Lund Hotel** tel: 604.414.0474; website: www.lundhotel.com; fuel

Finn Cove (Malaspina Peninsula)

Charts 3538, 3311; 0.4 mi N of Lund
Entrance: 49°58.98'N, 124°46.04'W

> *Finn Cove ... offers protection from west winds.* (SD)

Finn Cove is home to a small fishing community; fresh fish or ice may sometimes be procured at the fish freezing plant at the head of the bay. Swinging room is limited and anchorage is recommended only in an emergency.

Thulin Passage

Charts 3538, 3311; btwn Copeland Islands & Malaspina Peninsula
Entrance (S): 49°59.67′N, 124°47.43′W
Entrance (N): 50°01.98′N, 124°49.56′W

Copeland Islands Marine Provincial Park (Ragged Islands)

Charts 3538, 3311; 2.5 mi NW of Lund
Anchor: (See diagram)

"A"	50°00.04′N,	124°48.23′W
"B"	50.00.46′N,	124°48.60′W
"C"	50°00.72′N,	124°48.70′W
"D"	50°00.62′N,	124°48.88′W
"E"	50°00.58′N,	124°49.12′W

Copeland Islands, NE of Major Islet, are known locally as the Ragged Islands. This long chain of four large islands and numerous islets and rocks lie parallel to the west shore of Malaspina Peninsula.

Copeland Islands Marine Park encompasses the Copeland Islands group; it is undeveloped. Temporary anchorage is available in several nooks throughout the islands.

Thulin Passage separates the Copeland Islands from the mainland and is not less than 137 m (450 ft) wide. The passage is used by tugs with logbooms or scows and other small craft. Logbooms are often secured to the east shore, for which purpose a number of concrete abutments have been constructed.

Tidal streams within Thulin Passage are weak. (SD)

Copeland Islands Marine Provincial Park consists of 1,080 acres, 635 of which are water! There is no development here. Formerly called the Ragged Islands, there are four major islands and numerous islets, nooks and channels. This small, intimate area, protected from prevailing weather patterns, is an excellent place to explore by canoe, kayak or dinghy.

Rocky ledges onto which you can step directly from your dinghy make wonderful swimming platforms. There is good fishing and scuba diving in the Islands. Inter-tidal shelves are laden with oysters, and the tide pools invite exploration. The steep-sided islands are covered with arbutus and wildflowers, but there are no real trails. Most wildlife and plant life can be seen from the shore or a small craft. It has been reported that pictographs can be seen on rocky surfaces in Thulin Passage.

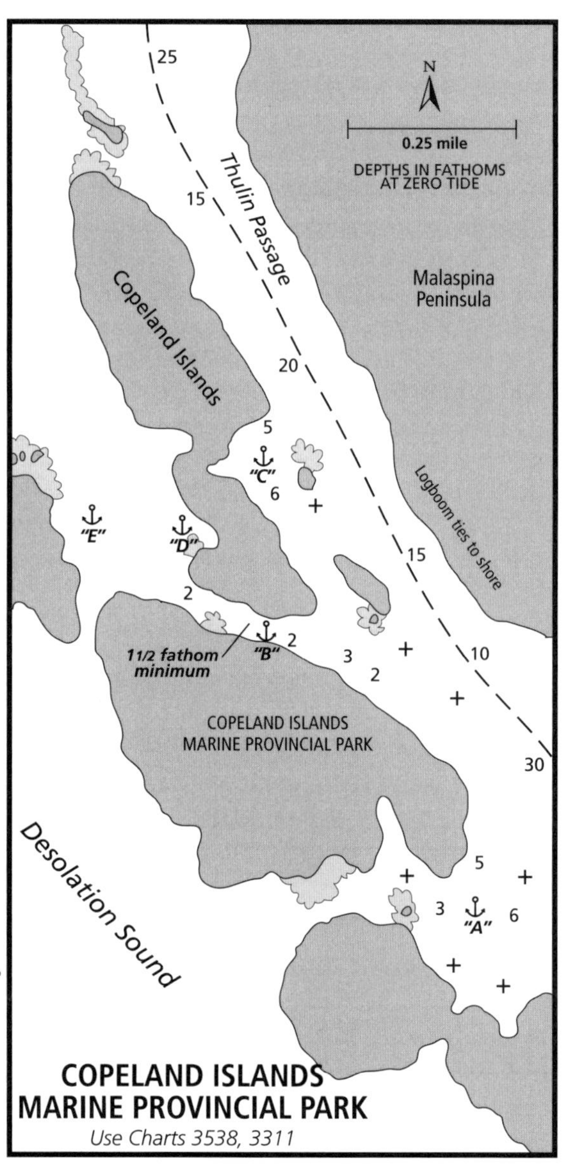

COPELAND ISLANDS MARINE PROVINCIAL PARK
Use Charts 3538, 3311

There are a number of places where you can find temporary fair-weather anchorage in the Copelands. The diagram shows five sites listed as "A" through "E"; other anchorages are used also, such as the west side of the long island. Anchor site "C" offers the best kayak haul-out and campsites, as well as an evening view. Anchor site "D" is a sand and gravel hole with a shore tie to an arbutus tree. A shore tie to an old chain is recommended at anchor site "E."

Floats at the Lund resort

The best anchorages in a southerly are reported to be the two spots on the west shore of island "87" using a shore tie; and in a northerly sites "C" and "B".

The bottom within these islands is irregular, indicating the presence of rocks. The depths are generally deeper than those shown on the diagram. Swinging room is limited and a shore tie is a good idea.

You can pass between the major islands, as noted, but watch out for submerged isolated rocks here and there. Except for the wake from passing vessels, it is quite calm here. Be sure to test the set of your anchor.

Entrance to Mitlenatch Cove

Anchor, depending on the site, in 2 to 5 fathoms over a sand, gravel and rocky bottom with poor-to-good holding.

Turner Bay, Bliss Landing

Charts 3538, 3311; 4.0 mi NW of Lund
Entrance: 50°02.13'N, 124°49.32'W

> *Bliss Landing is at the head of Turner Bay. Private homes and floats line the shores of the bay.* (SD)

Private mooring is available with shore power.

Mitlenatch Island Nature Provincial Park

Chart 3538; 9.3 mi W of Lund; 10.2 mi SE of Campbell River
Entrance: 49°56.98'N, 124°59.57'W
Anchor: 49°57.06'N, 124°59.91'W

> *Mitlenatch Island ... is rocky with two bare peaks separated by a grassy valley, A shoal spit extends 0.5 mile north from its north extrem-*

Pinniped families, Mitlenatch Island

ity, otherwise, the island is steep-to. The best landing is in semi-protected cove at the SE corner of the island, a small cabin is on the shore of this cove. The island and adjacent waters to 305 m comprise Mitlenatch Island Nature Park. (SD)

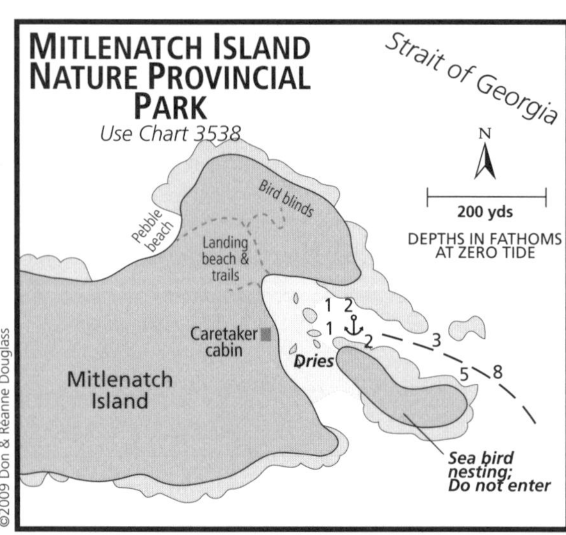

Tiny Mitlenatch Island has a cove on its southeast side that can give protection to a few small vessels in prevailing northwesterlies during stable weather. In southeast gales, temporary shelter can be found on the northwest side off a pebble beach, avoiding a rock 0.17 mile north, awash at a 1-foot tide. The attraction of Mitlenatch is the abundance of birds protected by the island's status as a nature preserve (and by the kindness of voluntary watchmen who live in a cabin ashore during summer). The island hosts harlequin ducks, oyster catchers, guillemots, gulls, and other beautiful birds, as well as a large colony of seals and, occasionally, Steller sea lions. The small islet to the south, and parts of the main island, are off-limits during nesting season, so please observe all signs and check with the caretaker to learn where you may go. A short trail leads across the island to a pebble beach on the northwest shore where you can watch magnificent summer sunsets. Another trail leads east and uphill where, from bird blinds overlooking the Strait, you can watch the bird life.

Peter Fromm

Beach rocks

Anchoring at Mitlenatch is marginal at best, due both to the lack of swinging room and the shallow drying area at the head of the cove. Although it's possible for boats over 36 feet in length to enter the cove, we don't recommend anchoring unless you have an all-chain anchor rode and/or you can use a shore tie. We've anchored overnight here in calm weather, tucked well into the cove, but only when tides are not expected to be low (a number of isolated flat rocks dry at low tides). Because this is such a fragile natural environment, cruising boats should be careful to observe the regulations and to follow common sense so that all boaters will continue to be welcomed.

Anchor in 1 to 2 fathoms east of the north end of the south islet, over a mixed bottom of mud, sand, shells, and grass with fair holding.

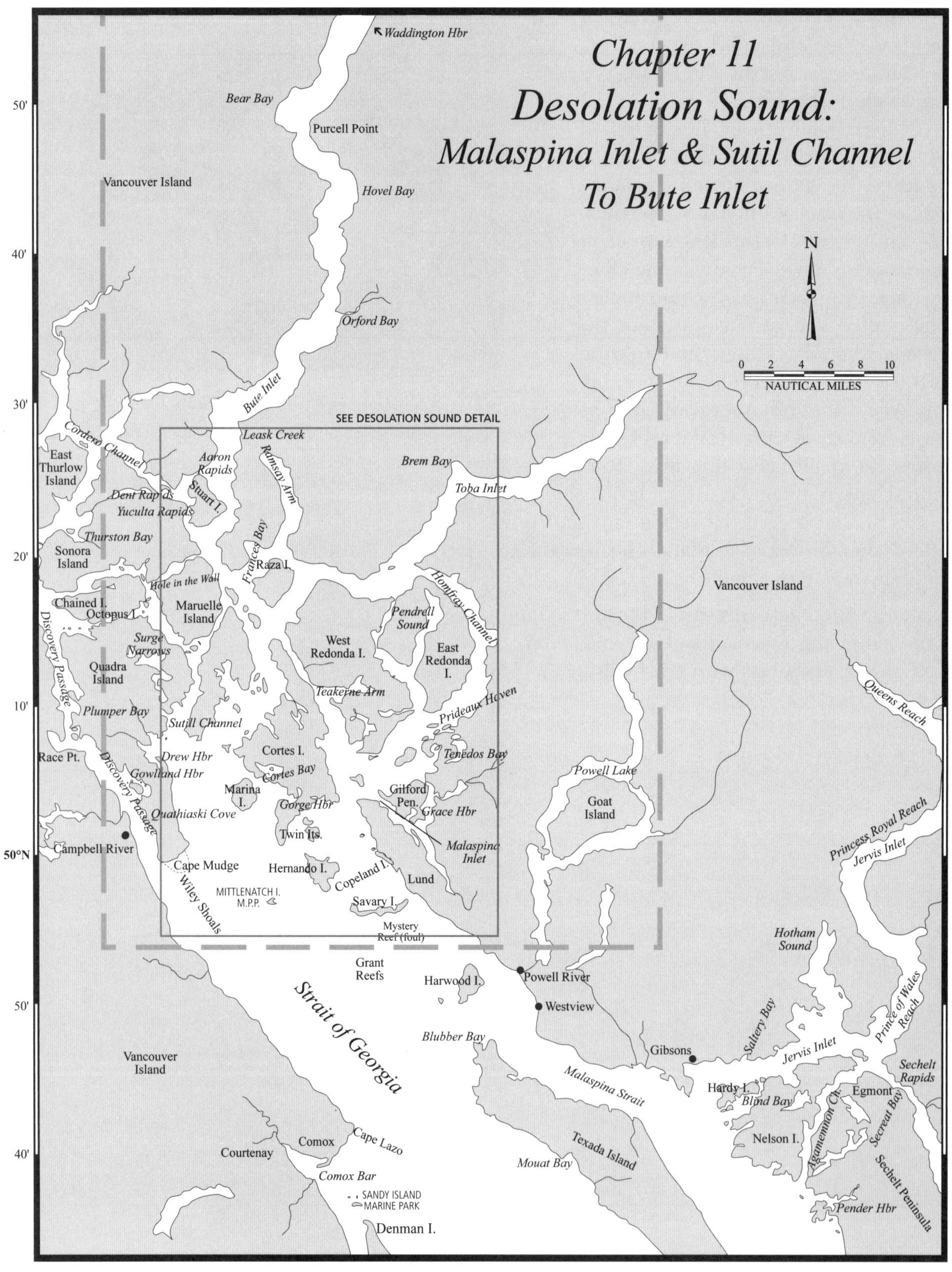
Chapter 11
Desolation Sound:
Malaspina Inlet & Sutil Channel
To Bute Inlet
N
0 2 4 6 8 10
NAUTICAL MILES
SEE DESOLATION SOUND DETAIL
50'
40'
30'
20'
10'
50°N
50'
40'
Waddington Hbr
Bear Bay
Purcell Point
Vancouver Island
Hovel Bay
Orford Bay
Bute Inlet
Leask Creek
Cordero Channel
East Thurlow Island
Aaron Rapids
Ramsay Arm
Brem Bay
Toba Inlet
Dent Rapids
Yuculta Rapids
Stuart I.
Frances Bay
Thurston Bay
Sonora Island
Raza I.
Hole in the Wall
Homfray Channel
Vancouver Island
Chained I.
Octopus I.
Maruelle Island
Pendrell Sound
Discovery Passage
Surge Narrows
West Redonda I.
East Redonda I.
Quadra Island
Teakerne Arm
Queens Reach
Plumper Bay
Sutil Channel
Prideaux Haven
Race Pt.
Drew Hbr
Cortes I.
Tenedos Bay
Gowlland Hbr
Cortes Bay
Powell Lake
Marina I.
Gilford Pen.
Goat Island
Discovery Passage
Quathiaski Cove
Gorge Hbr
Grace Hbr
Twin Its.
Malaspina Inlet
Princess Royal Reach
Campbell River
Jervis Inlet
Cape Mudge
Hernando I.
Copeland I.
Lund
Wiley Shoals
MITTLENATCH I. M.P.P.
Savary I.
Mystery Reef (foul)
Hotham Sound
Grant Reefs
Harwood I.
Powell River
Strait of Georgia
Westview
Saltery Bay
Prince of Wales Reach
Blubber Bay
Vancouver Island
Gibsons
Jervis Inlet
Sechelt Rapids
Malaspina Strait
Hardy I.
Egmont
Blind Bay
Agamemnon Ch.
Secreat Bay
Nelson I.
Cape Lazo
Comox
Texada Island
Courtenay
Mouat Bay
Sechelt Peninsula
Comox Bar
SANDY ISLAND MARINE PARK
Pender Hbr
Denman I.

11

DESOLATION SOUND: Malaspina Inlet and Sutil Channel to Bute Inlet

Desolation Sound, the beautiful and popular cruising ground north and east of Malaspina Peninsula, was set aside in 1973 as the largest marine park in southern British Columbia. The sound was named by Captain Vancouver in 1792, who wrote: "Our residence here was truly forlorn; an awful silence pervaded the gloomy forests ..." In the eyes of today's visitors, Desolation Sound is a place of calm, clear water, lush scenery, and abundant wildlife such as beaver and bald eagles. It contains some of the warmest coastal waters, ideal for swimming, snorkeling and diving, canoeing and kayaking. Oysters and clams can be found in some sheltered bays and lagoons, and sportfishing is good here. On the eastern horizon, the snowcapped peaks of the Coast Mountains provide a beautiful and fascinating backdrop.

Desolation Sound: a great place for kayaks, power boats, and sailboats

There are several off-shore islands, and the gradually rising upland coast contains a number of lakes, waterways, and waterfalls. Whether you're travelling by motor vessel, sailboat or kayak, this area is a marvelous place for exploring. You will see the remains of many old settlements—Indian, loggers, and farmers—with some fascinating ruins.

Note: Many of Desolation Sound bays and harbors are designated 'No discharge zones."

Desolation Sound

Charts 3312, 3538; E of Cortes Island; S of West Redonda & E Redonda Islands; NW of mainland Entrance (mid-ch btwn Mary & Sarah Pts): 50°03.59'N, 124°51.81'W

> *Desolation Sound is entered from the south between Mary and Sarah Points.*
>
> *Tidal streams. Because this is a region where the flood stream from Queen Charlotte Sound via Johnstone Strait meets that from Juan de Fuca Strait via the Strait of Georgia, the tidal streams are inconsistent and weak, seldom exceeding 2 kn, and are strongly affected by*

Note: Charts 3312 and 3313 are chart books in atlas format. They are designed for use by small craft, and include additional information and aerial photographs. However, these charts are not available as NDI digital charts, nor do they lend themselves easily to measurement of latitude and longitude.

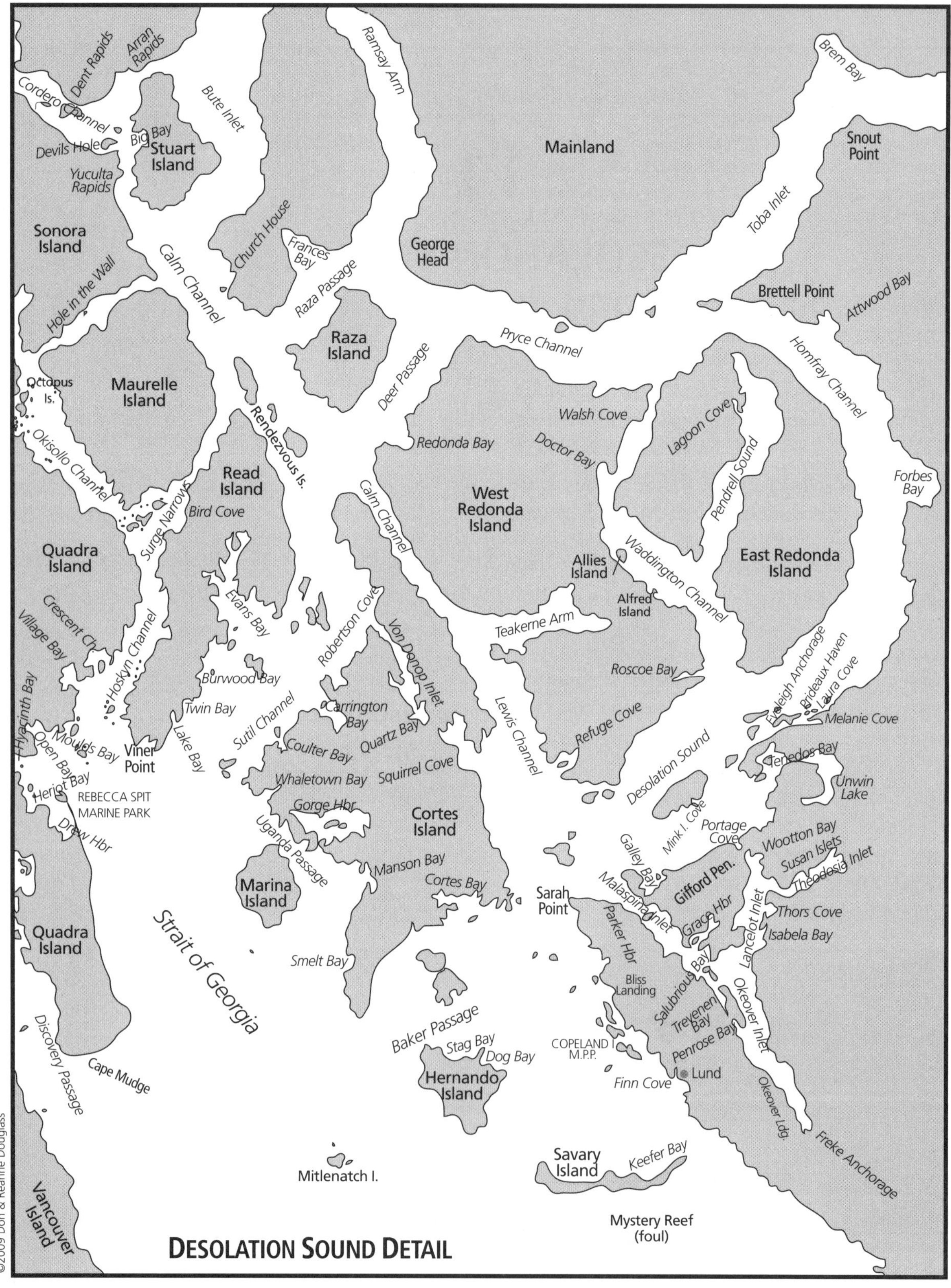
Dent Rapids
Arran Rapids
Cordero Channel
Devils Hole
Big Bay
Stuart Island
Yuculta Rapids
Bute Inlet
Ramsay Arm
Mainland
Brem Bay
Snout Point
Sonora Island
Church House
Frances Bay
George Head
Toba Inlet
Hole in the Wall
Calm Channel
Raza Passage
Brettell Point
Atwood Bay
Raza Island
Pryce Channel
Octopus Is.
Maurelle Island
Deer Passage
Homfray Channel
Rendezvous Is.
Walsh Cove
Redonda Bay
Doctor Bay
Lagoon Cove
Okisollo Channel
Read Island
Pendrell Sound
Forbes Bay
West Redonda Island
Bird Cove
Surge Narrows
Calm Channel
Quadra Island
Allies Island
Waddington Channel
East Redonda Island
Crescent Ch.
Evans Bay
Alfred Island
Village Bay
Robertson Cove
Von Donop Inlet
Teakerne Arm
Hoskyn Channel
Burwood Bay
Roscoe Bay
Hyacinth Bay
Twin Bay
Carrington Bay
Lewis Channel
Refuge Cove
Eveleigh Anchorage
Prideaux Haven
Laura Cove
Melanie Cove
Moulds Bay
Viner Point
Lake Bay
Sutil Channel
Quartz Bay
Coulter Bay
Open Bay
Heriot Bay
Whaletown Bay
Squirrel Cove
Desolation Sound
Tenedos Bay
Unwin Lake
REBECCA SPIT
MARINE PARK
Gorge Hbr
Cortes Island
Mink I. Cove
Portage Cove
Drew Hbr
Uganda Passage
Galley Bay
Wootton Bay
Susan Islets
Theodosia Inlet
Manson Bay
Gifford Pen.
Marina Island
Cortes Bay
Sarah Point
Malaspina Inlet
Quadra Island
Strait of Georgia
Parker Hbr
Grace Hbr
Lancelot Inlet
Thors Cove
Isabela Bay
Smelt Bay
Bliss Landing
Salubrious Bay
Okeover Inlet
Discovery Passage
Baker Passage
Trevenen Bay
Stag Bay
Dog Bay
COPELAND I M.P.P.
Penrose Bay
Cape Mudge
Hernando Island
Lund
Finn Cove
Okeover Ldg.
Freke Anchorage
Savary Island
Keefer Bay
Mitlenatch I.
Vancouver Island
Mystery Reef (foul)
DESOLATION SOUND DETAIL
©2009 Don & Réanne Douglass

winds. The flood stream flows north up the west side of Kinghorn Island, SE down the east side of the island then NE through Desolation Sound. The boundary between the flood streams from north and south can be abreast Squirrel Cove in settled weather or as far north a the north entrance of Lewis Channel in sustained SE winds.

Desolation Sound Marine Park, on Gifford Peninsula, includes Prideaux Haven, Tenedos Bay and Grace Harbour. (SD)

Aquaculture in Malaspina Inlet

Malaspina Inlet

Charts 3559, 3312, 3538; 4 mi SE of Refuge Cove
Entrance (0.48 mi SW of Zephine Head): 49°04.28′N, 124°48.86′W

Malaspina Inlet, a popular small craft cruising area, extends 4 miles south and leads to Okeover and Lancelot Inlets. The first 2 miles of Malaspina Inlet has numerous islands, drying rocks and shoals. Limited supplies are obtainable in Malaspina Inlet. Numerous logging camps are scattered throughout the area.

Tidal streams in the entrance to Malaspina Inlet attain 2 to 4 kn, but within the inlet they are weak. (SD)

Malaspina Inlet has a number of small islands, islets and rocks in its entrance that require alert navigation to avoid, but which also create some isolated small coves. Some of these coves are out of the current and offer good exploring and solitary anchor sites. There are aquacultures in some of the more protected spots, but you can find your own spot by carefully poking around. For instance, the shore south of Cochrane Islands is part of Desolation Sound Marine Park, along with Gifford Peninsula, and is worth visiting. Parker Harbour is a comfortable fair-weather anchorage.

Limited flushing of the entire waterway south and east of Malaspina Inlet causes the water to warm up to surprisingly pleasant temperatures. Unfortunately, large jellyfish find such warm, calm water to their immense satisfaction and sometimes procreate to fill every cubic meter.

The most protected and popular anchorage in Malaspina Inlet is the basin at the head of Grace Harbour.

Parker Harbour (Malaspina Inlet)

Charts 3559, 3312, 3538; 1.3 mi inside entrance to Malaspina Inlet
Anchor (N bay): 50°03.44′N, 124°47.76′W
Anchor (S bay): 50°03.18′N, 124°47.52′W

Beulah Island and the large island close SE are joined together and to the mainland by drying ridges. The coves north and south of these drying ridges are known locally as Parker Harbour; temporary anchorage can be obtained in the north part of the harbour. The float on the mainland shore is private. It is reported that more protected anchorage can be found in the south part of Parker Harbour which is entered north of the drying reefs lying north of Thorp Island. (SD)

Parker Harbour is the well-protected area northwest of Thorp Island along the Malaspina Peninsula. There are good anchor sites in both north and south bays out of the current of the narrows. Give Thorp Island a wide berth when entering Parker Harbour since there are rocks and two shoals on its north side.

The breeze freshens, but Coast Eagle *is safely anchored at Cochrane Island*

Anchor mid-bay or as desired, avoiding kelp and reefs near the islets. Check your anchor set since the bottom is quite rocky.

Anchor (N bay) in 3 fathoms over sand and gravel with fair-to-good holding.

Anchor (S bay) in 4 fathoms over a rocky mixed bottom with poor-to-fair holding.

Entrance to Grace Harbour

Cochrane Islands (Malaspina Inlet)

Charts 3559, 3312, 3538; 0.7 mi SE of Josephine Is
Entrance: 50°02.49'N, 124°46.36'W
Anchor: 50°02.59'N, 124°46.72'W

> *Cochrane Islands ...consist of two large islands joined by a drying ledge with several rocks and islets on it. Several detached drying rocks lie north and west of Cochrane Islands. Marine farm facilities lie along the shore behind Cochrane Islands. Good anchorage can be found behind the islands.* (SD)

Grace Harbour (Malaspina Inlet)

Charts 3559, 3312, 3538; 2.9 mi SE of entrance to Malaspina Inlet
Entrance (mid-ch btwn Scott & Moss Pts): 50°02.49'N, 124°45.40'W
Anchor: 50°03.22'N, 124°44.72'W

> *Grace Harbour ...extends 1 mile NE.*
>
> *Grace Harbour ... affords anchorage for small vessels in about 25 m. The inner par tof the harbour provides completely sheltered anchorage for small craft.*
>
> *Anchorage for small vessels can be obtained about 0.1 mile NE of Jean Island in about 25 m (82 ft). The inner part of the harbour provides completely sheltered anchorage for small craft.* (SD)

Grace Harbour is a well-protected anchorage with shallow water and plenty of swinging room. The water temperature is quite warm due to its remoteness and, because of this, it's frequently full of medium-sized jellyfish during the mid- to late-summer months. The small creek at the head of the bay has some

Photo courtesy CHS, Pacific Region

Grace Harbour

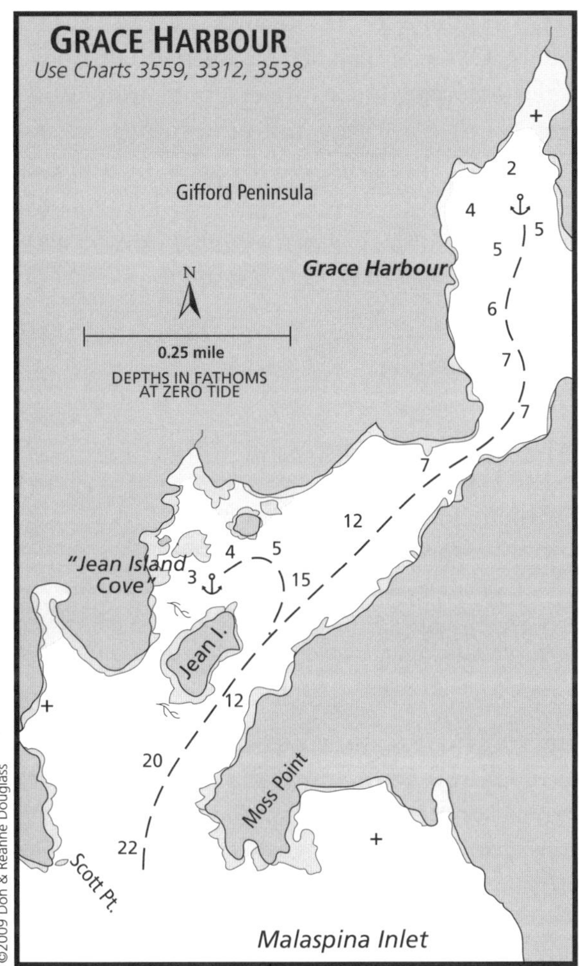

lovely small pools for freshwater bathing, and you can enjoy the rain forest as you splash.

Anchor in 3 to 5 fathoms deep into the harbor, over sticky mud with very good holding.

Rafting is often necessary in Grace Harbour

Jean Island Cove (Grace Harbour)

Charts 3559, 3312, 3538; mid-ch 0.2 mi within harbor entrance
Entrance: 50°02.82'N, 124°45.21'W
Anchor: 50°02.80'N, 124°45.29'W

> *The passage west of Jean Island has several drying rocks and ledges in it.* (SD)

There is room for one or two boats in Jean Island Cove; it is much quieter than Grace Harbour.

Anchor in 1 to 3 fathoms over sand with good holding. Swinging room is limited. Avoid the reefs in the center of the bay and along the shoreline.

Trevenen Bay (Malaspina Inlet)

Charts 3559 inset, 3312, 3538; 4 mi from entrance to Malaspina Inlet
Entrance: 50°02.00'N, 124°45.27'W
Anchor: 50°01.00'N, 124°44.16'W

> *Anchorage, sheltered from SE winds, can be obtained in Trevenen Bay.* (SD)

Trevenen Bay is the long bay to the west of Coode Island and Coode Peninsula. While some southeast wind will gust through the low wooded isthmus at its head, the bay is quite protected from southerly storms. The road connecting to Lund terminates in the isthmus. Avoid the wall-to-wall aquaculture sites which fill Trevenen Bay.

Anchor in 2 fathoms over gravel, sand and shells with fair holding.

Okeover Inlet (Malaspina Inlet)

Charts 3559, 3312, 3538; 4 mi from entrance to Malaspina Inlet
Entrance: 50°01.78'N, 124°43.97'W

> *Okeover Inlet is entered between Hillingdon Point and the NW end of Coode Peninsula 1 mile west.* (SD)

Okeover Inlet, the continuation of Malaspina Inlet to the south, terminates in Freke Anchorage off its drying mud flats. A number of aquacultures are found along both shores.

Penrose Bay (Okeover Inlet)

Charts 3559, 3312, 3538; S end of Coode Peninsula; 2.75 mi SE of Grace Hbr
Entrance (0.17 mi S of Boundary Rock): 50°00.24′N, 124°43.09′W
Public float: 49°59.49′N, 124°42.67′W
Anchor: 50°00.52′N, 124°43.68′W

> *Penrose Bay ...has a shoal spit extending north from its south entrance point. A marina is on the west side of the bay. Anchorage can be obtained in a depth of 7.4 m (24 ft) at the head of Penrose Bay. Marine farm facilities line the east shore of Okeover Inlet.* (SD)

Penrose Bay is the south bay formed by the mushroom-shaped Coode Peninsula. Shelter from northwest winds is very good, but the bay is open to strong southerlies. When entering the bay, avoid Boundary Rock 200 yards off Coode Peninsula.

Penrose Bay offers good protection from prevailing northwest winds. The landing is at the end of the road from Lund and is used by kayakers and other small craft.

Anchor in 2 fathoms over sand with fair holding.

Okeover Landing (Okeover Inlet)

Charts 3559, 3312, 3538; 1.2 mi SE of Penrose Bay
Public float: 49°59.49′N, 124°42.67′W

> *Okeover Arm Provincial Park ...has camping and picnic facilities and a launching ramp.* (SD)

Okeover Landing has a convenient public float with a nearby launching ramp which serves as a base for trailerable boats, canoes and kayaks. An unusual First Nation's pictograph of a human form lies across the inlet on the east shore.

Freke Anchorage (Okeover Inlet)

Charts 3559 inset, 3312, 3538; 1.7 mi SE of Okeover Landing
Anchor: 49°58.18′N, 124°40.98′W

> *Marine farm facilities are off the west shore of Freke Anchorage.* (SD)

Freke Anchorage is located at the bitter end of Okeover Inlet. The head of the bay is rather open, but it offers good protection from southeast storms for large vessels wanting lots of swinging room and a minimum of fetch. Avoid the submerged waterline that crosses the inlet to the seafood plant. Freke Anchorage ices over in the winter.

Anchor in 6 fathoms over sand and gravel with fair holding.

Lancelot Inlet (Malaspina Inlet)

Charts 3559, 3312, 3538; 4 mi inside entrance to Malaspina Inlet
Entrance: 50°02.15′N, 124°43.60′W

> *Lancelot Inlet, the north branch of Malaspina Inlet, is entered between Edith Island and Hillingdon Point, a bold, steep-to projection 0.6 mile east.* (SD)

Lancelot Inlet turns north from the southern tip of Gifford Peninsula. This protected water is deep and clear. Isabel Bay, on the west shore, provides some very calm anchorages with favorable holding ground.

Isabel Bay (Lancelot Inlet)

Charts 3559, 3312, 3538; 0.6 mi E of Grace Hbr
Entrance: 50°03.32′N, 124°43.49′W
Anchor (N): 50°03.29′N, 124°43.81′W
Anchor (S): 50°03.03′N, 124°43.79′W

> *Isabel Bay ... is entered between Polly Island and Madge Island. A rock, which dries 0.4 m, lies 90 m NE of Polly Island and drying ledges extend north and NE from Madge Island. Isabel Bay is a popular anchorage for small craft ...* (SD)

Isabel Bay is an indentation on the east side of Gifford Peninsula with a quiet, calm aspect. Madge and Polly islands are tree-covered and fun to explore by dinghy or kayak. The entrance bar is deeper than Grace Harbour, and a shore tie can be used to advantage since much of the bay is steep-to.

Our favorite spot is in the narrow finger

west of Madge Island. Swinging room is limited.

Anchor (N) in 3 fathoms over a sandy bottom with fair holding.

Anchor (S) in 4 to 8 fathoms over mud with fair-to-good holding.

Thors Cove (Lancelot Inlet)

Charts 3559, 3312, 3538; 0.9 mi NE of Isabel Cove
Entrance: 50°03.58′N, 124°42.58′W
Anchor: 50°03.47′N, 124°42.30′W

> *Thors Cove, entered north of Bunster Point, offers good anchorage behind the island close off the south shore. Marine farm facilities line the south shore of the cove.* (SD)

Thors Cove can provide very good shelter for two boats behind the unnamed islet off the south shore. Swinging room is limited. It is better to enter on the north side of the islet to avoid the shoal and aquaculture to the south.

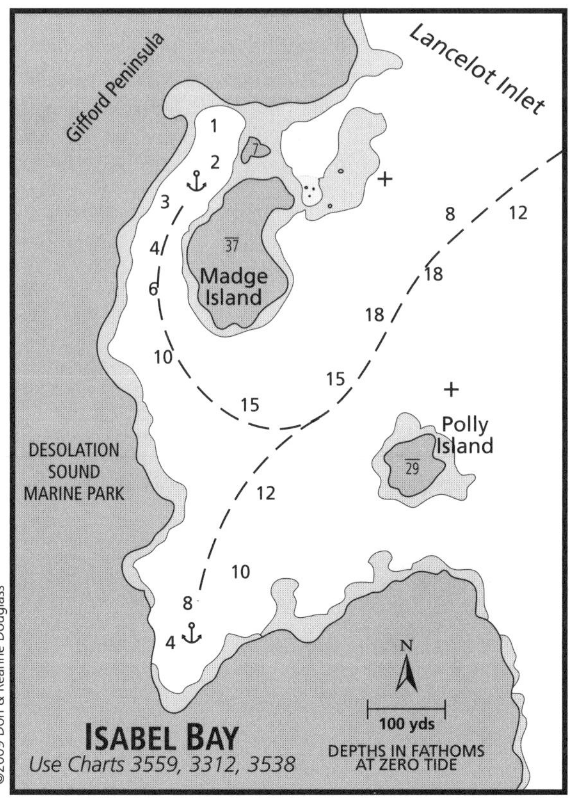

Anchor in 3 fathoms over sand and shells with fair-to-good holding.

Wootton Bay (Lancelot Inlet)

Charts 3559, 3312, 3538; extreme N end of Lancelot Inlet; 1.9 mi N of Isabel Bay
Entrance: 50°04.64′N, 124°42.85′W
Anchor: 50°05.00′N, 124°43.14′W

> *Wootton Bay, at the head of Lancelot Inlet, affords anchorage in about 20 m (66 ft.).* (SD)

Wootton Bay is barely 200 yards from Portage Cove in Desolation Sound. This isthmus was an excellent portage for canoers and kayakers before the No Trespassing signs went up from the in-holding. This can be a very quiet, calm anchorage, but it is partially exposed to southerlies.

Anchor in 6 fathoms over mud, shells and some rocks with fair-to-good holding.

Theodosia Inlet (Lancelot Inlet)

Charts 3559, 3312, 3538; 2.2 mi NE of Isabel Bay
Entrance: 50°04.11′N, 124°41.98′W
Entrance (narrows): 50°03.96′N, 124°41.72′W
Anchor: 50°04.39′N, 124°40.60′W

> *Theodosia Inlet, the head of which dries, is entered SE of Galahad Point through a narrow passage with a least depth of 2.4 m (8 ft) in the fairway. A rock awash lies off the north side of the channel. The inner basin, used extensively as a booming ground, provides good anchorage for small craft.* (SD)

Theodosia Inlet cuts into the mainland at the upper end of Lancelot Inlet and offers very good shelter from all weather. The entrance has a narrow fairway with a shallow bottom of sand and gravel. The upper basin opens up to a very large drying mud flat and is largely filled with clear-cut forests and numerous logbooms offering little interest for cruising boats. This may become a major habitat for birds and other creatures when it returns to its natural state.

Anchor in 5 fathoms over sand and gravel with good holding and swinging room

Susan Islets Cove (Theodosia Inlet)

Charts 3559, 3312, 3538; N side of entrance to Theodosia Inlet
Entrance (mid-ch btwn Susan Islets & Galahad Pt): 50°04.16'N, 124°42.11'W
Anchor: 50°04.24'N, 124°42.22'W

> *Susan Islets, 0.2 mile SE of Grail Point, lie nearly in the middle of the entrance to Theodosia Inlet. The NW and smaller islet has a prominent pointed rock on its summit and between it and Grail Point there is a large drying rock.*
>
> *Anchorage can be obtained by small craft behind Susan Islets, mud bottom.* (SD)

Susan Islets Cove is formed by Grail Point on the west and Susan Islets on the south. Entrance is best made east of wooded Susan Islets. Once private property, the cleared foreshore is reverting to a more natural condition.

Look for the 4-fathom hole just east of a large drying reef. Avoid the 1-fathom shoal north of Susan Islets. We find this small anchorage quite secure and one of the quietest in the area.

Anchor in 4 fathoms over a mixed bottom of mud, rock and shells.

Galley Bay (Gifford Peninsula)

Charts 3559, 3312, 3538; N side of Gifford Peninsula
Entrance: 50°04.53'N, 124°47.37'W
Anchor (W nook): 50°04.20'N, 124°47.59'W
Anchor (E island): 50°04.32'N, 124°46.77'W

> *Drying reefs lie in the central portion of the bay and a rock with 1.3 m over it lies south of the island in its east part.* (SD)

Galley Bay is a popular small-craft anchorage. The best anchorages are found in the westernmost cove and behind the island in the eastern part of the bay. Both offer good protection in almost all weather. The western

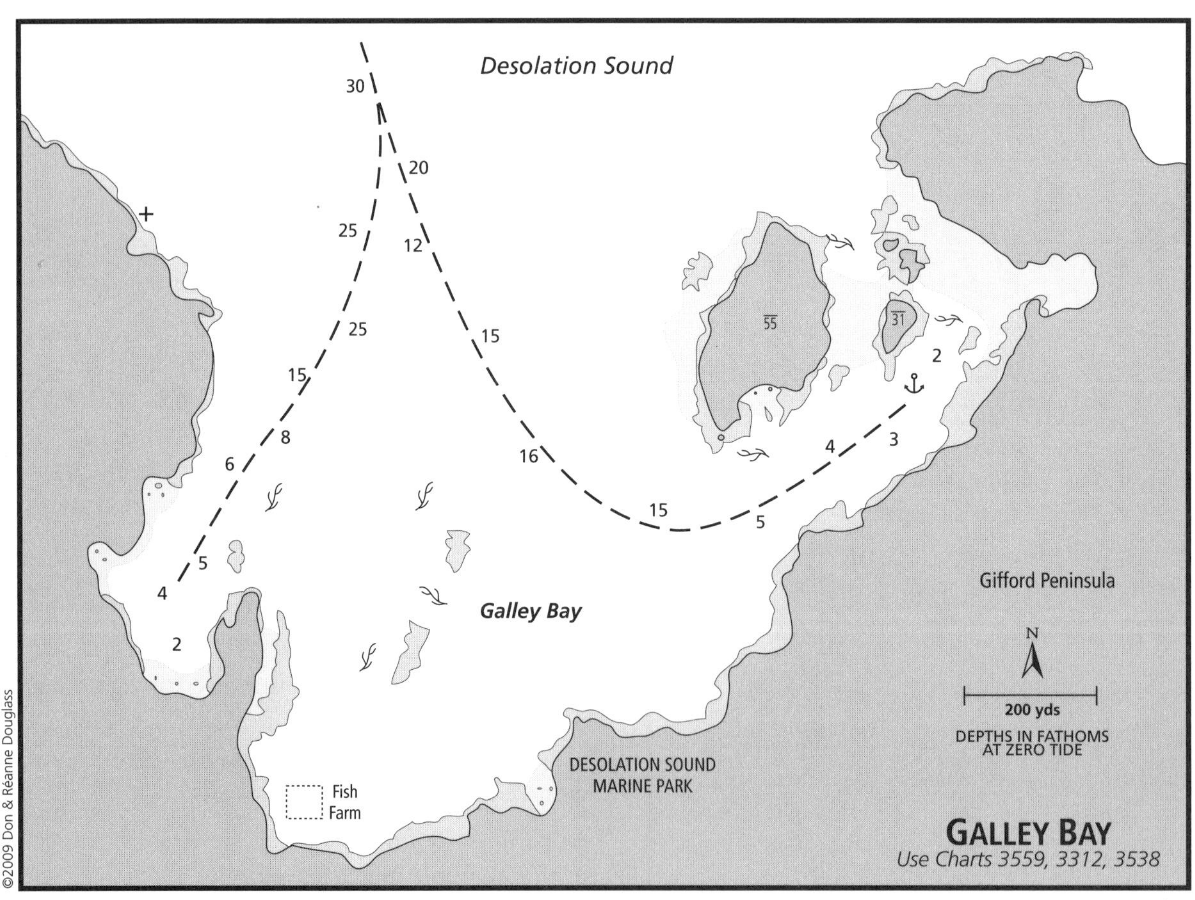

This snug anchorage is in Galley Bay

nook is partially exposed to down-inlet winds and chop. Shore ties are useful along the edge of the west bay.

Galley Bay is part of Desolation Sound Marine Park, but evidence of private inholdings can still be seen; there are cabins along the northwest shore and a few homes along the southeast shore with private floats. This was once a large commune supporting 100 people, and the clearing can still be found on the western shore. A small lake is 0.25 mile east of the island anchor site.

Anchor (W nook) in 4 fathoms over a mixed bottom with fair holding.

Anchor (E island) in 2 fathoms with limited swinging room over sand and gravel with fair-to-good holding.

Portage Cove (Gifford Peninsula)

Charts 3312, 3538; 1.8 mi SW of Tenedos Bay
Entrance: 50°05.33′N, 124°43.71′W
Anchor: 50°05.18′N, 124° 43.63′W

Portage Cove, on the mainland SE of Mink Island, has drying rocks on its east side. (SD)

Portage Cove is the small indentation in Gifford Peninsula which almost connects to Wootton Bay, nearly making the peninsula an island. It is well sheltered except for rare gusts across the isthmus which is still a private inholding. The cove is best entered near high water because of the entrance reef. Swinging room is limited.

Anchor in 2 fathoms over mud, sand and gravel.

Mink Island Cove

Charts 3538, 3312; 2.6 mi SW of Tenedos Bay; 3.0 mi NE of entrance to Malaspina Inlet
Entrance: 50°06.30′N, 124°45.06′W
Anchor: 50°06.28′N, 124°45.45′W

Anchorage can be obtained in the bay on the SE side of Mink Island. (SD)

Mink Island Cove has long been a favorite hideaway of cruising boats. The deeper outer anchorage is exposed to down-inlet winds from the east — particularly early and late in the season. Although the head of the cove behind the wooded islet is very well protected, it is filled with many private floats and mooring buoys, so you may have to anchor in deeper water. Larger boats anchor outside in deeper water.

The shoreline is rocky and a shore tie is now required in all but the winter season because of the cove's increased popularity and limited swinging room. The small shallow lagoon at the north side of the islet is

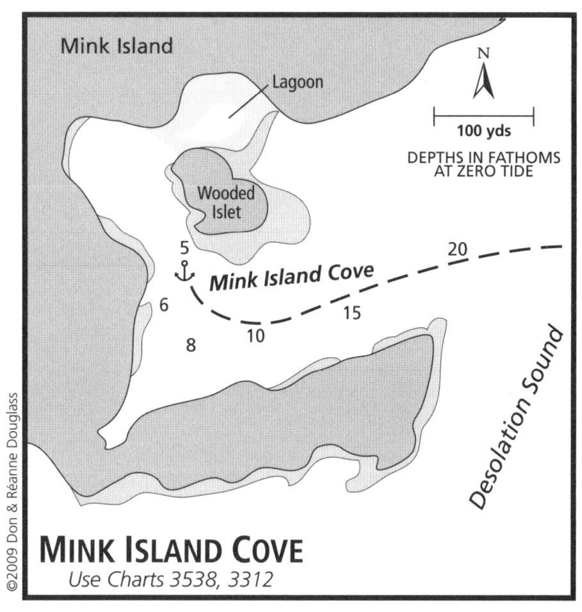

Storm Haven at anchor at Mink Island

like a big outdoor hot tub and is interesting to explore.

Mink Island is outside the Desolation Sound Marine Park. Please respect private property. Anchor in 5 to 6 fathoms over sand, gravel and rock; fair holding.

Tenedos Bay

Charts 3312, 3538; enter E of Bold Head; 5.6 mi NE of entrance to Malaspina Inlet; 1.2 mi S of Prideaux Haven
Entrance (0.43 mi SE of Ray Rock): 50°06.41′N, 124°42.86′W
Anchor (NE corner): 50°07.37′N, 124°41.55′W
Anchor (NW Unnamed Island): 50°07.57′N, 124°42.47′W
Anchor (3-fathom hole): 50°07.40′N, 124°42.71′W
Anchor (Bare Islets): 50°07.08′N, 124°42.65′W

> *Tenedos Bay ... affords good anchorage for small vessels in its north extremity in 12 m (39 ft). Small craft can find good anchorage in several coves in the bay.* (SD)

Tenedos Bay, on the mainland shore, is deep and steep-to, but it has been one of the more popular cruising areas for years. The bay is well sheltered, and anchorage can be found

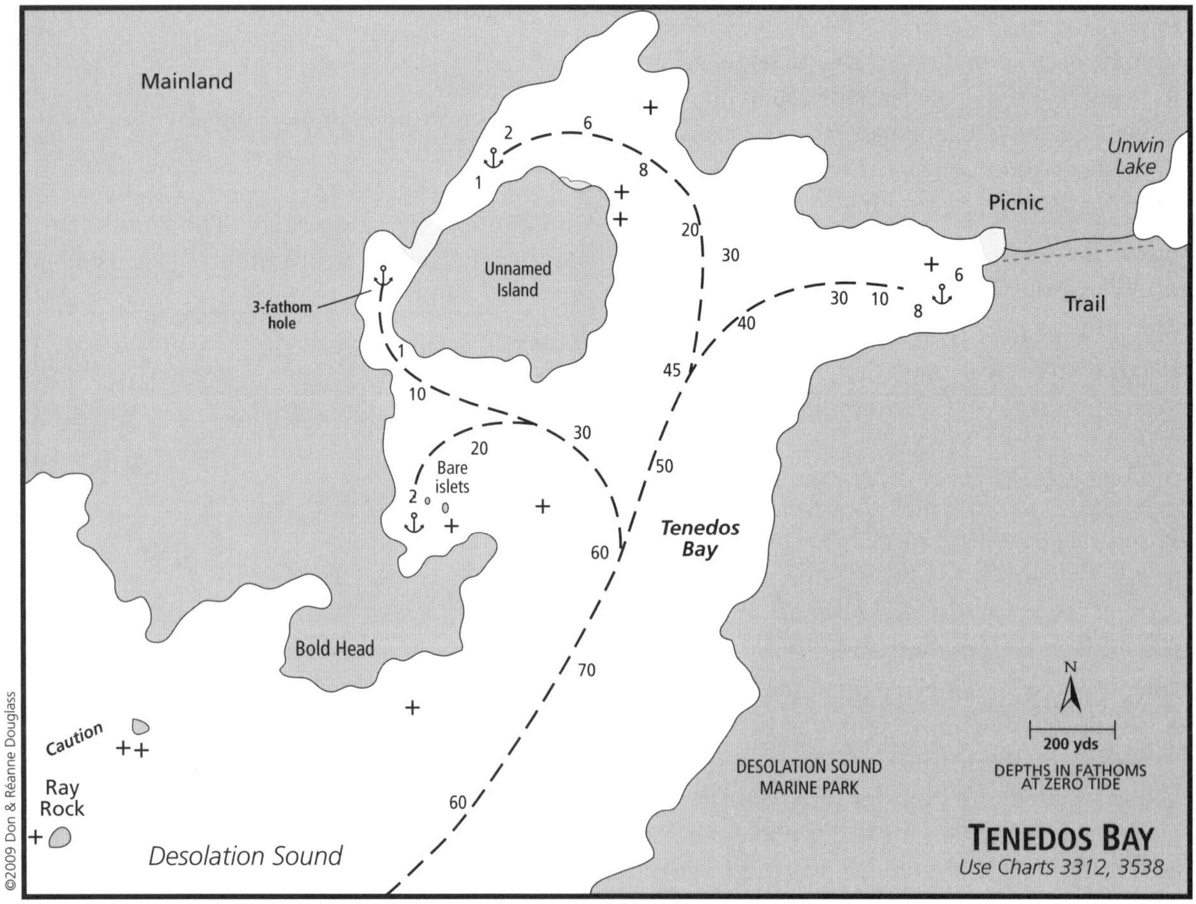

Mainland
Unnamed Island
3-fathom hole
Bare islets
Bold Head
Unwin Lake
Picnic
Trail
Tenedos Bay
Caution
Ray Rock
Desolation Sound
DESOLATION SOUND MARINE PARK
N
200 yds
DEPTHS IN FATHOMS AT ZERO TIDE
TENEDOS BAY
Use Charts 3312, 3538

Anchored in Tenedos Bay

Anchor (NE corner) in 8 fathoms over a mixed bottom of sand, gravel and small rocks with good holding.

Otter Island

Charts 3538, 3312; 0.25 mi S of Sky Pilot Rock; 0.8 mi NE of Mink Island
Entrance (S): 50°07.38'N, 124°43.76'W
Entrance (N): 50°07.69'N, 124°43.56'W
Anchor: 50°07.51'N, 124°43.59'W

Otter Island ... approaching this anchorage from the north take care to avoid Sky Pilot Rock, which dries 2.1 m. (SD)

The passage on the east side of Otter Island has long been a favorite hideout for two or

almost anywhere along the shore. When swinging room is limited, a stern tie is useful and almost mandatory in summer season.

Boats tend to crowd into the northeast corner to be close to the Unwin Lake trail and the primitive camping, picnicking, and outhouse along the creek. They anchor southeast of the submerged rock west of Unwin Creek outlet. Unwin Lake offers a refreshing freshwater swim; however, there are no convenient beaches and the lake outlet is clogged with slippery, rolly logs. Use caution!

Small boats wanting more solitude anchor in the shallow water on the north side of the unnamed island or in the 3-fathom hole on the west side, entering by way of the shallow rocky south entrance at mid-tide or higher. Swinging room is limited, so a shore tie is a good idea. You can circumnavigate the unnamed island in a dinghy or kayak near high water. Another attractive hole is at the very southwest corner of Tenedos Bay behind the bare islets. The passage east of Otter Island makes a scenic transit when tide levels permit.

The entrance to Tenedos Bay

three small vessels nestled together on the east side of the passage north of the narrows. Be aware that small runabouts may often race through this passage at full speed.

Homfray Channel

Charts 3538, 3541, 3312; separates East Redonda Island from the mainland
Entrance (S, 0.66 mi S of Horace Head): 50°09.22'N, 124°43.53'W
Entrance (N, mid-ch btwn Brettell & Hepburn Pts): 50°18.88'N, 124°44.01'W

> *Homfray Channel, entered south of Horace Head on East Redonda Island, leads 13 miles north to join Pryce Channel at Hepburn Point. The channel is very deep with no off-lying dangers. The east half of East Redonda Island is a Provincial Ecological Reserve; camping, fires, or disturbance of animals or vegetation are prohibited.* (SD)

Eveleigh Anchorage (Homfray Channel)

Charts 3555, 3312; on the S side of Eveleigh I
Entrance: 50°08.31'N, 124°42.17'W
Anchor: 50°08.41'N, 124°41.74'W

> *Eveleigh Anchorage ...offers anchorage in a depth of about 70 feet (21 m). The south extremity of Eveleigh Island is connected to the mainland shore by a drying gravel bank, which restricts passage east into Prideaux Haven.* (SD)

Eveleigh Anchorage, although considered part of Prideaux Haven, gets less usage; however, in July and August it may be "claimed" by larger yachts. It is well protected and has easy access. The flat bottom is composed of sand and mud. A sand and rock spit attaching Eveleigh Island to Gifford Peninsula is dry except at spring tides.

Anchor in 10 fathoms over sand and mud with good holding.

Prideaux Haven (Homfray Channel)

Charts 3555, 3538, 3312; 6.4 mi E of Refuge Cove; 3.3 mi SE of Roscoe Bay
Entrance (0.05 mi SW of Scobell I): 50°08.79'N, 124°41.12'W
Anchor: 50°08.65'N, 124°40.81'W

> *Prideaux Haven, with Melanie and Laura Coves to the east and Eveleigh Anchorage to the west are popular small craft anchorages and shelter areas.*
>
> *Tidal streams in the north approach to these anchorages are weak, influenced by winds, and seldom exceed 1.5 kn.*
>
> *Prideaux Haven, south of Scobell Island, is entered between Lucy Point on the west and William Islands and Oriel Rocks on the east. A rock, which dries 3 feet (0.9), lies close off Lucy Point and drying ledges extend from Oriel Rocks and Eveleigh Island which narrow the passage to about 100 feet (30 m); the least depth in the fairway is 8 feet (2.4 m).*
>
> *Anchorage can be obtained in a depth of about 40 feet (12 m) south of Eveleigh Island.* (SD)

Prideaux Haven, with its spectacular views of the snow-covered peaks to the north, is perhaps the quintessential anchorage in all of greater Desolation Sound. There are several attractive coves to choose from and, through "windows" in each, you can enjoy these views while appreciating the meaning of haven. In addition, it's relatively shallow in these areas and the mud bottom provides very good holding, so you can get a good scope/rode ratio with a small amount of line out; a shore tie can also be useful. This area offers such excellent exploring by dinghy or kayak that you'll lose track of time.

The entrance to Prideaux Haven on the east side of Eveleigh Island is narrow, with as little as 7 feet of water at zero tide. Stay midchannel

Photo courtesy CHS, Pacific Region

Prideaux Haven entrance

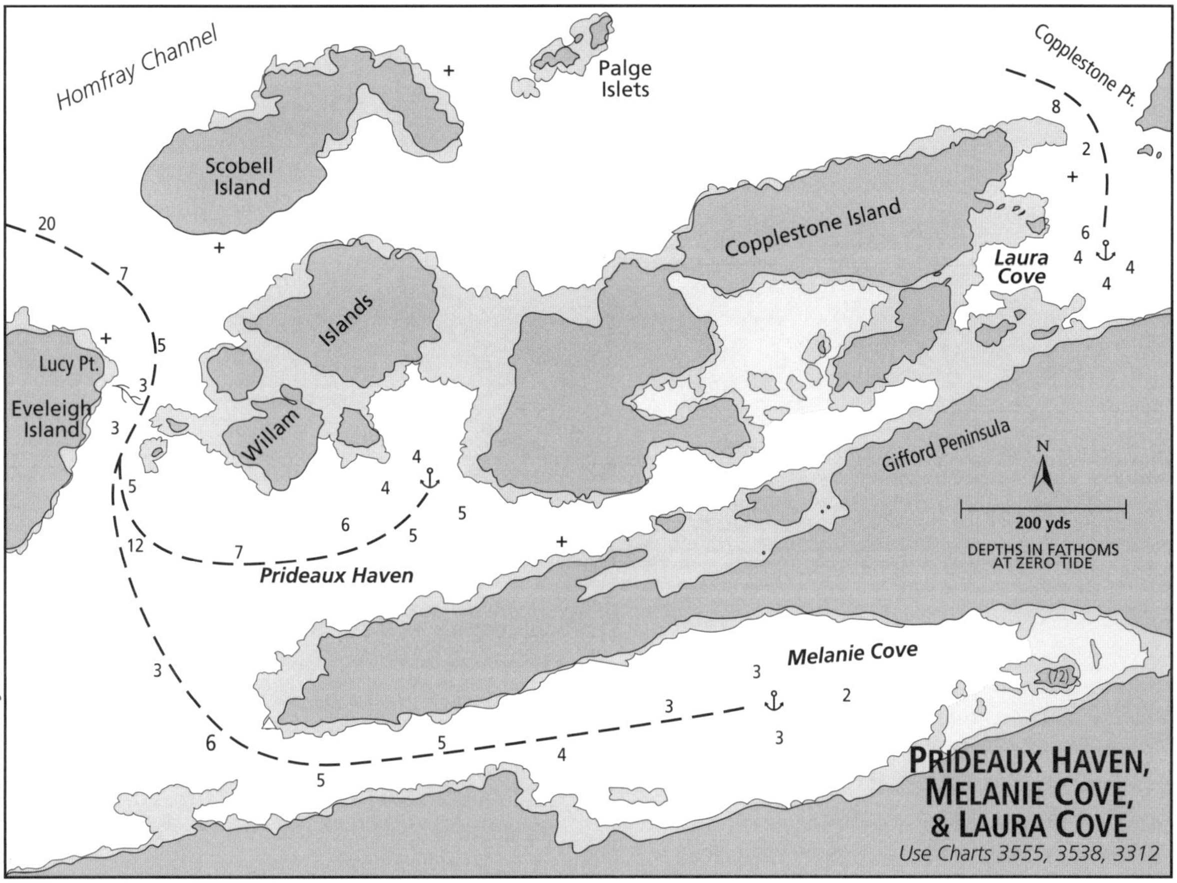

PRIDEAUX HAVEN, MELANIE COVE, & LAURA COVE
Use Charts 3555, 3538, 3312

with alert lookouts, and avoid the rock and rocky shelves south of Lucy Point.

For great views on a clear day, anchor just south of the drying bar between the William Islands and Copplestone Island in as shallow water as your draft or tide levels permit.

Caution: The tidal range in Prideaux Haven is over 18 feet during spring tides.

Anchor in 4 to 5 fathoms over mud with very good holding.

Melanie Cove (Homfray Channel)

Charts 3555, 3538, 3312; 0.4 mi SE of Prideaux Haven
Entrance: 50°08.49'N, 124°40.97'W
Anchor: 50°08.53'N, 124°40.46'W

Float plane taxi delivers crew to Prideaux Haven

Looking north from Prideaux Haven

Rafting in Prideaux Haven

near islet (72). Boats wanting to be in close proximity to one another, or those wishing to conserve open spaces, can anchor with a stern tie to the north shore, since the bottom there is steep-to.

Anchor in 3 fathoms over a sticky mud with very good holding.

> *Melanie Point, 0.15 mile SSE of Oriel Rocks, is the north entrance to Melanie Cove, the east arm of Prideaux Haven. The entrance to Melanie cove is narrowed to about 200 feet (61 m) by a drying ledge projecting from the south shore. A garbage scow is moored just outside the entrance to the cove.*
>
> *Anchorage can be obtained in depths of 13 to 35 feet (4 to 11 m) in Melanie Cove.* (SD)

Melanie Cove, the southern corner of Prideaux Haven, has even more shelter than Prideaux Haven, although it has a less picturesque view. There is very good anchorage anywhere in the long cove, except in the drying flat

Beyond Prideaux Haven

Laura Cove (Homfray Channel)

Charts 3555, 3538, 3312; 0.7 mi NE of Prideaux Haven
Entrance (0.04 mi NW of Copplestone Pt): 50°08.88'N, 124°40.17'W
Anchor: 50°08.79'N, 124°40.00'W

> *Laura Cove, 0.2 mile SW of Roffey Island, is entered between Copplestone Point and the NE extremity of Copplestone Island. The entrance channel, which leads east of a rock drying 1 foot (0.3 m), has a least depth of 11 feet (3.4 m) in the fairway and a width of about 135 feet (41 m).*
>
> *Anchorage can be obtained in Laura Cove in a depth of about 30 feet (9 m).*
>
> *The land area at the head of Laura Cove has been deeded to the University of British Columbia as an ecological reserve.* (SD)

Laura Cove, located to the east of Copplestone Island, is a favorite of boats wanting a little more solitude, if that's possible during summer months in Prideaux Haven! Shelter is excellent in all weather and this tidal wonderland is a great base from which to explore. (Don't miss Roffey Island.)

The entrance is from the north (Copplestone Point); the fairway is very narrow and S-shaped. Avoid the submerged reef on the port hand and the rock awash at low water to starboard.

Anchor in 5 fathoms over mud with good holding.

Roffey Island (Homfray Channel)

Charts 3555, 3312; 0.3 mi NE of Laura Cove
Position: 50°09.00'N, 124°39.84'W

> *Roffey Island at the NE extremity of the approach to Prideaux Haven, is surrounded by drying ledges. The passage between the island and the mainland to the east is encumbered by numerous drying rocks and ledges.* (SD)

Temporary anchorage can be found in about 9 fathoms over sand and rocks with fair holding.

Forbes Bay (Homfray Channel)

Charts 3541, 3312; E side of the channel; 5.7 mi NE of Prideaux Haven
Entrance: 50°14.70'N, 124°36.77'W
Anchor (S nook): 50°14.08'N, 124°36.04'W

> *Forbes Bay ... is too deep for anchorage except for smaller vessels near shore, and offers little shelter. Attwood Bay affords anchorage with good shelter for small vessels.* (SD)

Temporary anchorage is reported in the small delta off the outlet to the creek in the south side of Forbes Bay.

Anchor (S nook) in 2 fathoms over a sand and gravel bottom with fair holding.

Attwood Bay (Homfray Channel)

Charts 3541, 3312; near N end of Homfray Channel; 4.8 mi NW of Forbes Bay
Entrance: 50°18.54'N, 124°40.25'W
Position (N cove): 50°18.97'N, 124°40.02'W

> *Attwood Bay affords anchorage with good shelter for small vessels. Marine farm facilities are on the east side of the bay.* (SD)

Attwood Bay provides good anchoring opportunities close to shore if you're not inhibited by the aquacultures and logging operations. The entire bay is steep-to and a shore tie is recommended.

Waddington Channel

Charts 3538, 3541, 3312; separates W & E Redonda I; direct route to Toba Inlet & Pryce Ch
Entrance (S, 4.7 mi NE of Refuge Cove): 50°09.77'N, 124°44.27'W
Entrance (N): 50°17.21'N, 124°47.11'W

Bow Watch—An Extra Pair of Eyes

Going through rapids, traversing rocky, narrow, twisting passages, crossing rough sounds or rounding difficult capes—these are the things that excite some people.

As for me, I'm just glad when that part of a cruise is over. After a day's run, I look forward to the adventure of finding the right cove for our night's anchorage. I *like* the job of being the bow watch. And even though it may be freezing outside, for me this is one of the most thrilling adventures.

Of course I'm on the bow as an extra pair of eyes, and my job is to inform the captain of any obstacles that might impede the boat's smooth progress. All of my senses are bombarded with stimuli that only the sea meeting the land can impart. I might see a pair of loons off to one side, a sea lion peering up at me with half-submerged face, large orange masses of undulating jellyfish, walls of ferns and lichens; a stream, a bear, eagles, wildflowers, and the forest walls hugging the cove.

Sometimes I feel a change of temperature or a drop in the force of the wind. I love the shrill sounds of a thousand small birds emanating from all directions, echoing through the branches of cedar and spruce.

Bow watches looking for Prideaux Haven

Wet earth and sea life have their own fragrance which means land and a quiet cove. A haven for the night!

—Gloria Burke, First Mate, M / V *Carousel*

Heading toward another beautiful marine park

Waddington Channel, entered from south between Marylebone Point ... and Horace Head, separates East and West Redonda Islands and connects Desolation Sound to Pryce Channel.

Marine farm facilities are west of the unnamed island 1 mile NW of Church Point, west of Allies Island, in Doctor Bay and 0.4 mile SE of Butler point.

Tidal streams in Waddington Channel flood north and seldom exceed 1 kn.

Anchorage for small vessels is available in Walsh Cove. Small craft can find anchorage in Roscoe Bay, but note the drying bar 0.3 mile inside the entrance. Anchorage can also be obtained behind the unnamed island 1 mile NW of Church Point, clear of the marine farm facilities.

False Passage (50°16'N, 124°48'W.) leads north of Gorges Islands. The recommended approach to Walsh Cove is from the south. (SD)

Roscoe Bay Marine Park

(West Redonda Island)

Charts 3538, 3312 inset; 4 mi NE of Refuge Cove; 3.3 mi NW of Prideaux Haven
Entrance: 50°09.75'N, 124°45.11'W
Anchor: 50°09.59'N, 124°46.21'W

Small craft can find anchorage in Roscoe Bay, but note the drying bar 0.3 mile inside the entrance. Anchorage can also be obtained behind the unnamed island 1 mile NW of Church Point, clear of the marine farm facilities. (SD)

Roscoe Bay Marine Park, protected from all weather, is a cruising delight, landlocked and close to Black Lake where you can enjoy a dip in relatively warm water. There are picnic tables along the north shore of the bay.

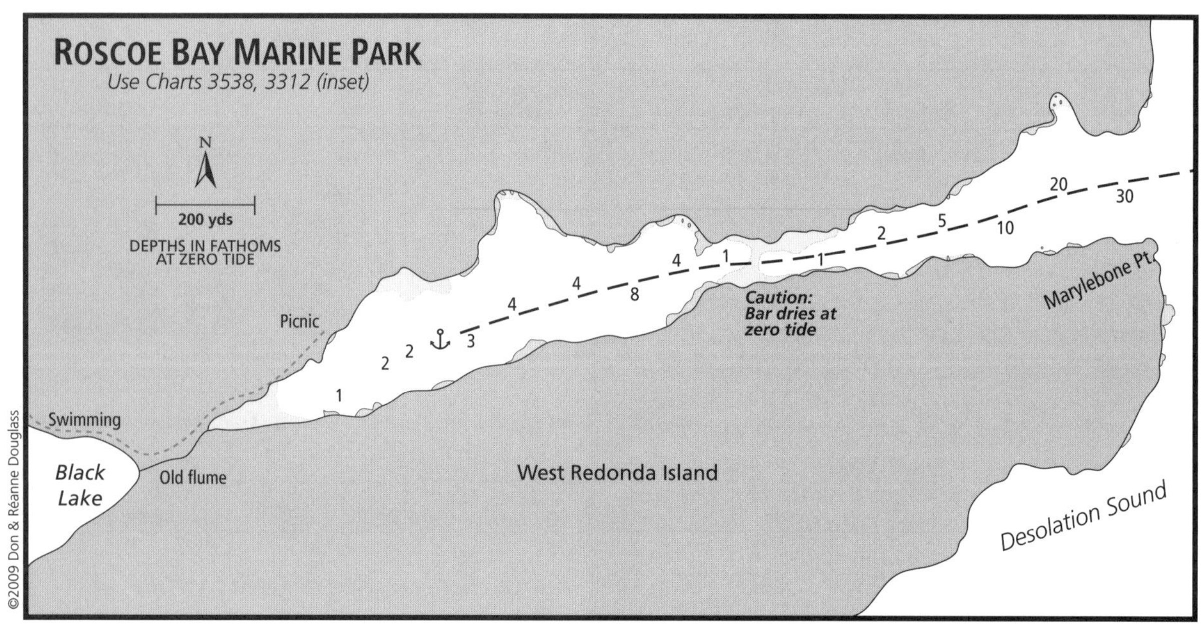

Roscoe Bay

Black Lake is only 10 feet above high water. The 100-yard trail that takes off from the head of the cove follows the north side of a flume once used for moving logs from the lake into the bay. Clean, flat rocks extending into Black Lake from the north shore make excellent "diving" platforms from which to launch your swim. But beware—the water is considerably colder below the surface; proceed inch by inch if you don't like surprises! (An added caveat: Rubber boots are the best footwear, unless it's a dry season!)

Caution: Every summer, several boats entering Roscoe Bay end up grounded on the drying bar, much to their chagrin and the smug amusement of boaters anchored safely inside. (See Chart 3312 inset.) Enter at an appropriate tide level for the draft of your boat and keep an alert bow watch for an otherwise easy entry—the minimum depth across the bar is close to the chart's zero datum. You may be surprised to find some fairly large cruising boats anchored inside.

A number of boats can anchor in Roscoe Bay in depths of one to 8 fathoms.

Anchor in 3 fathoms over mud with good holding.

Alfred Island (Waddington Channel)

Charts 3538, 3312; 1.1 mi NW of Church Pt; across the channel from Pendrell Sound
Entrance: 50°12.03'N, 124°47.25'W
Position: 50°11.87'N, 124°47.42'W

Alfred Island, also known as Elworthy Island, is reported to offer temporary anchorage with fair shelter. Avoid the rocks off the north end of the island and find suitable depths between the island and West Redonda Island.

Allies Island (Waddington Channel)

Charts 3541, 3312; 2.4 mi NW of Church Pt
Entrance: 50°13.14'N, 124°48.64'W
Anchor: 50°12.84'N, 124°48.94'W

Allies Island, formerly Prussian Island, on the west side of Waddington Channel, is reported to provide good shelter northwest of the small islet. At one time there was an aquaculture in the cove. The passage along West Redonda Island that dries at 10 feet has been under an oyster lease.

Anchor in about 4 fathoms over a sand and gravel bottom with fair holding.

Doctor Bay (Waddington Channel)

Charts 3541, 3312; 0.3 mi NW of Bishop Pt
Entrance: 50°14.73'N, 124°49.14'W
Anchor: 50°15.12'N, 124°49.18'W

Marine farm facilities are west of the unnamed island 1 mile NW of Church Point, west of Allies Island, in Doctor Bay and 0.4 mile SE of Butler Point. (SD)

Doctor Bay offers good protection in the head of the bay. A reef protrudes east of the small islet about 100 yards. The bay is open to the south, but there is little sign on shore of drift or heavy chop. Friends report that this is also good oyster country.

Anchor in 5 fathoms over an unrecorded bottom.

Walsh Cove Marine Park (Waddington Channel)

Charts 3541, 3312; near the N end of Waddington Channel; 4.6 mi NE of Roscoe Bay
Entrance (0.14 mi SW of Gorges Islands): 50°15.93'N, 124°48.13'W
Anchor: 50°16.12'N, 124°48.10'W

Anchorage for small vessels is available in Walsh Cove.

False Passage leads north of Gorges Islands. The recommended approach to Walsh Cove is from the south. (SD)

Walsh Cove has differing reputations depending upon whom you ask. North winds are said to howl here occasionally! The Gorges Islets shield the cove from passing wake, but the bottom is mixed, and what presents anchoring problems for one boat may offer great possibilities for another. This is a good base from which to explore Toba Inlet. The Marine Park is undeveloped.

Anchor in about 6 fathoms over a mixed bottom with fair holding.

Toba Inlet

Charts 3541, 3312; on the N side of East Redonda Island
Entrance (mid-ch btwn Double & Channel Is): 50°19.10'N, 124°46.37'W

Toba Inlet, entered west of Brettel Point, between Channel Island and Double Island, leads 20 miles NE to the sand and mud flat estuary of the Toba River at its head.

Anchorage can be obtained at the head of the inlet in 35 m (115 ft). Caution is advised because depths shoal rapidly and the bottom is not visible through the milky white water. (SD)

Toba Inlet is a classic glacier-carved fjord surrounded by beautiful high peaks. The inlet is quite deep with vertical sides that plunge straight into the sea. Anchoring is marginal along shore. For more information, refer to Wolferstan, Desolation Sound, Vol. 2, page 110.

Brem Bay (Toba Inlet)

Charts 3541, 3312; 7.8 mi inside entrance to Toba Inlet
Entrance: 50°25.61'N, 124°39.66'W
Anchor (W shore): 50°25.92'N, 124°40.37'W

Brem Bay is the site of a large abandoned logging camp. An old stone breakwater is reported to provide indifferent shelter for small craft. (SD)

Temporary anchorage may be possible on the west shore off the drying flat.

Stapleton's Bay (Toba Inlet)

Chart 3541 inset; small cove due N of the only islet in Toba Inlet
Position: 50°25.93'N, 124°32.08'W

According to Wolferstan (Vol. 2, p. 110), Stapleton's Bay may provide safe temporary anchorage.

Friends verify that Stapleton's Bay is a good little anchorage.

Roscoe Bay Stranding

The entrance to Roscoe Bay on the east side of West Redonda Island is a pass of sorts. It has the added feature of drying at low tide. We wanted to go in for a quick tour even though we were well into an ebb. We made it in, did our tour and headed out again 10 minutes later. But with three distinct bumps, we stopped and immediately started to list to starboard.

Dave Young

Stranded on Roscoe Bay Bar

The slapping of the wire halyards on the aluminum mast got the attention of everyone anchored in the bay. Soon there were skiffs all around. One man helped us find some wood to put under the bilge for the boat to lie on, while the rest took the mandatory photographs. Later, we set an anchor out ahead to keep the boat in mid-stream as it rose on the flood tide. The only damage was to our egos and to the contents of a locker which was filled by the galley pump as it siphoned out the fresh-water tank. **—Dave Young**

Pendrell Sound

Charts 3541, 3312; enter from Waddington Channel; nearly bisects East Redonda Island
Entrance (mid-ch btwn Durham & Walter Pts): 50°12.37'N, 124°45.17'W

> *Pendrell Sound is entered between Durham Point ... and Walter Point. Small craft can find anchorage off the mouth of a drying lagoon on the west side, 2 miles from the head, but there is no good anchorage for larger craft.*
>
> *The waters of Pendrell Sound, being warmer than most in this region, allow the production and collection of oyster spat, usually in July. To avoid damage to the spat collection gear, speed in the north half of the sound should not exceed 4 kn.* (SD)

Pendrell Sound, known for the warmest waters along the B.C. coast, has had recorded surface temperatures as high as 78° F (25.5°C). This is apparently due to its great depths; there is very little freshwater inflow and not much horizontal water movement, and the wind seldom reaches the surface because of the surrounding peaks.

In July when water temperatures peak, oysters breed and reproduce by the millions. This spat is fragile and can be damaged by wake from boats. Please respect the no-wake speed limit in force in these areas.

Lagoon Cove (Pendrell Sound)

Chart 3541, 3312; 6.65 mi N of Roscoe Bay
Anchor: 50°16.32'N, 124°43.69'W

> *Small craft can find anchorage off the mouth of a drying lagoon on the west side, 2 miles from the head, but there is no good anchorage for larger craft.* (SD)

Lagoon Cove is the most protected anchorage in this region of oyster culture, and the view across the sound to Mt. Addenbroke is impressive.

Anchorage can be taken in from 3 to 8 fathoms, west of the islet, south of the entrance to the lagoon, or on the north side of the islet. Shore ties are useful.

Anchor west of the islet in 8 fathoms over mixed bottom; fair holding.

Lewis Channel

Charts 3538, 3312, 3541; btwn W Redonda Island & NE side of Cortes Island
Entrance (S, 0.86 mi SE of Junction Pt): 50°07,76'N, 124°52.77'W
Entrance (N, 0.66 mi NE of Bullock Bluff): 50°14.60'N, 124°59.31'W

> *Lewis Channel leads about 7 miles NNW from Junction Point, joining Sutil Channel abreast Bullock Bluff.* (SD)

Lewis Channel is the main route from

Oysters

Oysters are grown commercially all over the British Columbia coast. Pendrell Sound, in the Desolation Sound area, is the main producer of seed oysters for commercial growers. It is an ideal area because the temperature of the summer waters usually exceeds 68° F. Pendrell Sound, it has been said, has the "warmest saltwater north of Mexico."

An oyster can spawn as a male one year and a female the next. Each produces millions of eggs, only a tiny fraction of which are fertilized; still fewer survive floating free. The survivors eventually wash to shore and fasten to a smooth surface, where they begin to grow.

In seed oyster culture, strings of cultch material, often empty oyster shells, are suspended from floats until the oyster spat adheres. They are then harvested and shipped to oyster farms. ***Please note:*** Seed oyster growers ask that you observe a 4-knot speed limit in their area.

Free-growing oysters can be found in many of the bays and lagoons of Desolation Sound. They are intertidal creatures, covered with water at high tide and exposed at low tide. Oysters can be eaten at any time of year, although in summer, plankton gives them a greenish tinge and slight iodine taste.

You will most often find the larger, Japanese variety of oyster. Imported into the area for oyster culture, it is now rapidly driving out the native Olympic oyster, which is smaller, slower-growing, rounded, and about the size of a silver dollar. Because these Olympic oysters are threatened, please do not harvest them.

Desolation Sound for boats heading north to Cordero Channel and Johnstone Strait.

Refuge Cove (West Redonda Island)

Charts 3555, 3538, 3312; 3.0 mi E of Squirrel Cove; 3.7 mi N of Sarah Pt; 5 mi NE of Cortes Bay
Entrance (0.15 mi NW of light): 50°07.11 N, 124°51.06'W
Public float: 50°07.41'N, 124°50.41'W
Anchor (N cove): 50°07.58'N, 124°50.48'W
Anchor (larger boats): 50°07.54'N, 124°50.78'W

Public floats with 850 feet (259 m) of berthing space and private floats with about 150 feet (46 m) are on the east side of Refuge Cove. Depths of 8 to 16 feet (2.4 to 4.9 m) exist alongside. (SD)

Refuge Cove—a central meeting place

Refuge Cove is a central meeting place for Desolation Sound where summer boaters stop to provision, buy fuel, take showers, and do their laundry. This is such a popular place that the Refuge Cove Store owners suggest avoiding the mid-day rush, particularly if you want to moor for the night. Standing off and taking a dinghy to the dock is common during busy hours. (We advise arriving before 10:00.)

The store, which is open June through September, has an excellent choice of groceries, deli items, wines, gifts and books and magazines; the Refuge Cove post office is located inside the store. In summer it is difficult to find dock space at this busy place; standing off or anchoring and taking a dinghy ashore is becoming more common. The store and gift shop in the cove have a good selection of provisions, wine and gifts. Telephones and showers are available, but you may have to stand in line a while for both. Protected anchor sites may be found along the north and northeast shore. Take care to anchor outside the main passage! In high season, it may be difficult to find a spot with convenient depths.

In summer, Dave's Garbage Barge is moored off the north side of Centre Island; fee for drop-off. A sign at the dock

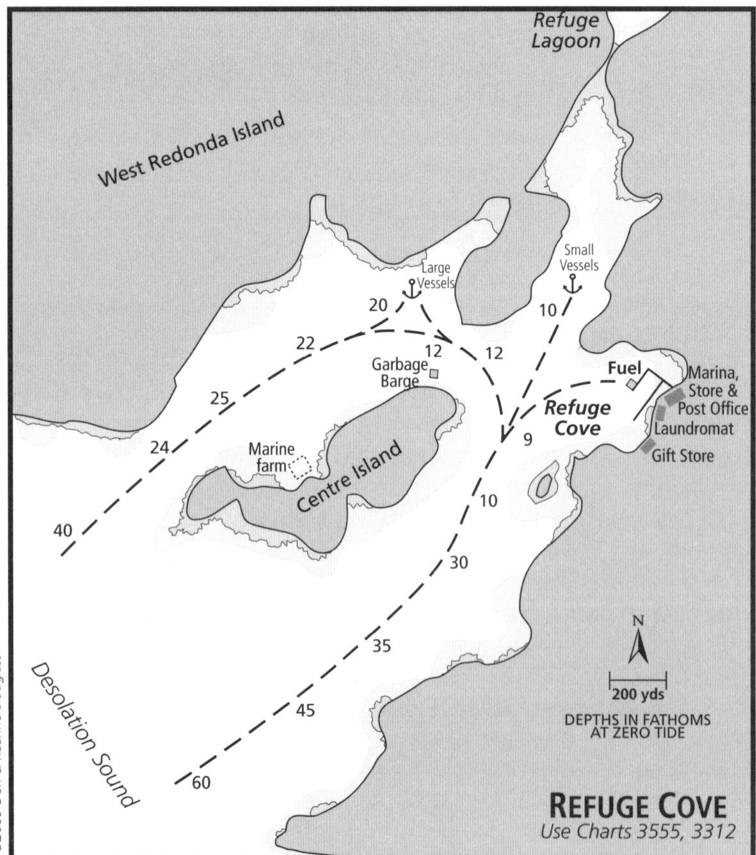

stipulates that water from natural sources should be boiled. Although we have never had a problem with an anchor site be aware that, since Refuge Cove was once a thriving logging settlement, there could be slash or logs on the bottom.

Anchor (north) in about 8 fathoms, outside the main passage over soft mud with fair-to-good holding.

⚓ **Refuge Cove Genreal Store** (seasonal) tel: 250.935.6659; website: www.refugecove.com/ email: refcov@twincomm.ca; gas, diesel, propane; showers; laundry; post office; no reservations for moorage

Teakerne Arm (West Redonda Island)

Charts 3538, 3312; enter from Lewis Channel, 4.2 mi NW of Refuge Cove
Entrance: 50°10.78′N, 124°54.33′W
Anchor: 50°11.94′N, 124°50.93′W

> *Teakerne Arm, entered north of Joyce Point, is not recommended for anchorage because it is exposed to the NW. ... A waterfall cascades down the north shore at the outlet of Cassel Lake.* (SD)

Teakerne Arm is a popular stop along the Desolation Sound route for its waterfall and for Cassel Lake just a short hike above the cascade. Teakerne Arm Provincial Park encompasses the head of the inlet, along with a portion of Cassel Lake.

Although the entire arm is too deep for small craft anchoring, vessels can drop crew at the park float and drift or tie up at a log boom and dinghy to the float. During off-season, you may be able to moor temporarily at the float.

Cassel Lake offers warm, fresh water for swimming—a secret George Vancouver may have discovered over 200 years ago.

A trail from shore to the swimming area leads up the west side of the creek above the falls. To go ashore, you can make a temporary stop in the small bight just west of the falls. Although the water is too deep for convenient anchoring, and holding is marginal, it's possible to get an adequate set for a shore party to enjoy the walk to the lake and a swim. However, an attendant should remain on board.

Anchor in about 12 fathoms using a shore tie.

Talbot Cove (West Redonda Island)

Charts 3538, 3312; 3.3 mi NW of Refuge Cove
Entrance: 50°10.53′N, 124°53.20′W
Anchor: 50°10.41′N, 124°53.65′W

> *Talbot Cove is not recommended for anchorage because the holding is reported to be poor.* (SD)

Good protection from southeast gales may be found in this tiny cove west of Talbot Islet.

Squirrel Cove (Cortes Island)

Charts 3555, 3538, 3312; 3 mi W of Refuge Cove
Entrance: 50°07.33′N, 124°54.32′W
Anchor: 50°08.50′N, 124°55.16′W

> *Squirrel Cove is a popular small craft anchorage. Boulder Point, on the north side of the entrance, is low with a drying reef projecting south from it and a conspicuous above-water boulder lying on its south shore. Squirrel Cove settlement has a population of 45 (1986), a general store and liquor store.*
>
> *Wharf. The public wharf on the south shore of Squirrel Cove just within the entrance has a depth of 16 feet (4.9 m) at its outer end. A 3 tonne crane and garbage disposal facilities are on the wharf. Floats attached to the wharf provide about 400 feet (122 m) of berthing space.*

Photo courtesy CHS, Pacific Region

Squirrel Cove, Cortes Island

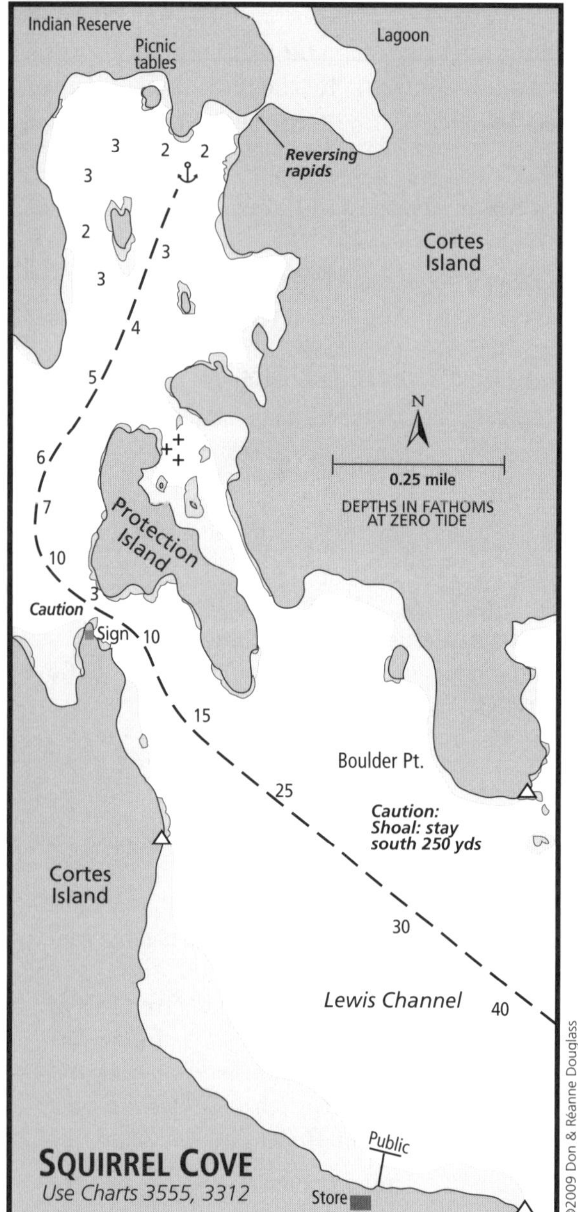

Anchorage for small vessels is available off the wharf or in the inner part of the cove, entered SW of Protection Island through a channel with a least depth in the fairway of 15 feet (4.6 m). A wreck (position approximate) is close north of Protection Island and a drying rock is close offshore in the NW part of the cove. There is a risk of anchors being fouled by numerous sunken logs and logging cables on the bottom of the inner cove. Holding is good in mud. (SD)

A good day for exploring

Squirrel Cove is one of the most popular stops in Desolation Sound. Its landlocked inner basin provides excellent all-weather protection, and its fairly flat bottom overall offers anchorage for many boats. (However, space during high-season is sometimes at a premium.) The Squirrel Cove General Store is located at the head of the public wharf in the outer basin. The store has a good supply of groceries and liquor, hardware, and books and magazines. Showers and laundry are available through the store. A public telephone is at the head of the dock; garbage may be dropped for a fee.

Entering Squirrel Cove's outer basin from the north, be sure to give Boulder Point plenty of clearance to avoid the rocks in its shoal area. Every year, some boat leaves bottom paint here or, worse yet, takes a chunk out of its keel.

Entrance to the inner cove is made through the passage to the west of Protection Island, remaining in the center of the fairway. Entering through the east side of Protection Island is not advised for other than kayaks or dinghies, due to rocks and reefs. Study the chart carefully before choosing your anchor site. Excellent anchorage can be found almost anywhere north of Protection Island. Be aware, however, that although we have never had a problem snagging a log or cable, we have heard reports of boaters who have.

Photo courtesy CHS, Pacific Region

Cortes Bay

The lagoon to the northeast is fun to explore by dinghy, but beware of the reversing rapids—we've been caught inside more than once.

Anchor in 2 to 3 fathoms over sticky mud; very good holding.

⚓ **Squirrel Cove Public Wharf** power; garbage

⚓ **Squirrel Cove Trading Co. Ltd.** tel: 250.935.6327; website: www.cortesisland.com/squirrelcove; restrooms; showers; laundry

Tiber Bay (Cortes Island)

Chart 3538; 0.7 mi N of Mary Pt; 3.2 mi SE of Squirrel Cove
Entrance: 50.04.26'N, 124°52.85'W

> *Tiber Bay ... has a submarine cable laid across it.* (SD)

Temporary anchorage may be found in the south finger of Tiber Bay, avoiding the submarine cable and the rock awash in the center of the bay.

Cortes Bay (Cortes Island)

Charts 3538, 3312, 3513; 2.9 mi W of Sarah Pt; 3.8 mi SW of Gorge Hbr
Entrance: 50°03.48'N, 124°55.12'W
Public float: 50°03.78'N, 124°55.95'W
Anchor: 50°03.85'N, 124°56.06'W

> *Cortes Bay ... has a narrow entrance encumbered with a drying rock with a light on it. When entering Cortes Bay pass to the south of* [Cortes Bay] *light. A rock, with 2.7 m over it, lies in the centre of the bay.*
>
> *Anchorage can be obtained in Cortes Bay in depths of 9 to 15 m, soft mud bottom, holding ground is poor. NW winds funnel in from the head of the bay and with strong SE winds a confused sea can be encountered.* (SD)

Cortes Bay offers good protection in all weather and, in our opinion, is not as difficult or as exposed as Sailing Directions indicates. The entrance to the bay is narrow and shallow which may cause confused seas on an ebb tide with a strong southeasterly; under these conditions, as swell can enter the bay. However, it's rare in summer.

The entrance fairway, to the south of the rock with light on it, has a minimum depth of about 3 fathoms. The mud bottom inside the bay is soft, requiring that you check the set of your anchor carefully.

Out for a row in Cortes Bay

Anchorage can be taken in the west end of the bay during northerly winds and in the south end during southerlies. The Seattle Yacht Club owns the facility on the south side of the bay; the Royal Vancouver Yacht Club owns the one on the north side of the bay. You must be a member of either yacht club to moor at their float. (No reciprocals.)

Anchor, as desired, in 4 to 7 fathoms over mud and some rock; generally fair holding.

Sutil Channel

Charts 3538, 3312; btwn W shore of Cortes I; SE shore of Quadra I; E shore of Read I
Entrance (S, 2.0 mi E of Francisco Pt): 50.00.69'N, 125°05.68'W
Entrance (N, 0.675 mi W of Bullock Bluff): 50°14.29'N, 125°01.31'W

> *Sutil Channel ... leads 17 miles north and NNE along the west side of Cortes Island and connects the Strait of Georgia to the junction of Calm Channel, Lewis Channel and Deer Passage.*
>
> *Tidal streams in Sutil Channel are weak, rarely exceeding 2 kn. The flood stream flows north in the south portion, south in the north portion, meeting about Penn Islands.* (SD)

Sutil Point marks the southern boundary of Sutil Channel. When going to or coming from Desolation Sound, beware of the shoals which extend nearly 1 mile southwest of Sutil Point. Strong flood currents of 3 knots set north on spring tides. From a distance, during mid-tide, the rocks looks like a South Pacific atoll. Give this area a wide berth, staying outside bell buoy "Q20."

Smelt Bay (Cortes Island)

Charts 3538, 3312; 1.5 mi N of Sutil Pt
Entrance: 50°02.16'N, 125°00.00'W
Anchor: 50°02.12'N, 124°59.75'W

> *Smelt Bay ... is the site of Smelt Bay Provincial Park; fresh water, camping and picnic facilities are available. A sand bottom provides good holding for anchorage in fair weather. The shores of Smelt Bay are lined with houses.* (SD)

Smelt Bay is a shallow bight along the southwest corner of Cortes Island with Smelt Bay Provincial Park on its south end. It has a beautiful sand and gravel beach and is a good place to go ashore to picnic.

The bay itself is really an open roadstead off a wide sand flat that dries and has submerged rocks or boulders both to the north and south. In fair weather, small boats find temporary anchorage along the shore for swimming and beachcombing. At low water, cars can be seen driving on the hard sand.

Anchor in 4 fathoms over hard sand with fair holding if well set.

Manson Bay, Manson's Landing Marine Park (Cortes Island)

Charts 3538, 3312; 1.4 mi SE of entrance to Gorge Hbr; 3.5 mi N of Sutil Pt
Entrance: 50°04.21'N, 124°59.39'W
Public float: 50°04.31'N, 124°59.00'W

> *Manson Bay ... is exposed to SW winds but affords temporary anchorage for small craft, some shelter is available behind the islets off its west entrance point. A private float and piles are at the head of the bay.*
>
> *Mansons Landing Provincial Park, with beaches fronting on Sutil Channel and Hauge Lake, has picnic and sanitary facilities.*

Sewage disposal in the waters of Mansons Bay and Mansons Landing Provincial Park is prohibited under the "Pleasure/Non-Pleasure Craft Sewage Pollution Prevention Regulations."

Mansons Landing is on a spit fronting a drying lagoon along the east side of Manson Bay.

The public wharf at Mansons Landing has a berthing length along its T-shaped head of 22 m and a least depth of 5.2 m alongside. Floats with a berthing length of 110 m are attached to the north side of the wharf. The end float is reserved for seaplanes. A telephone is near the wharf. (SD)

Manson's Landing beach and float

Manson Bay offers sheltered water from all but southwest wind and swells.

Manson's Landing Marine Park encompasses a lovely sandspit and lagoon at the east side of Manson Bay. A public float on the east shore provides easy access to the beautiful sandy beaches from here south. A short trail to the east of the public float leads to the lagoon, a great swimming hole for kids. The lagoon can be entered by small boats on a spring tide only. The mooring buoys at the north end of the park are private.

June Cameron and Réanne Douglass talk about old times at Manson's Landing

If you want more protection than found here, anchor northeast of Sheep and Cat islands near the head of the bay. In a southerly blow, you might want to head to Gorge Harbour.

The Gorge (Cortes Island)

Charts 3538, 3312; 1.5 mi NW of Manson Bay
Entrance (S): 50°04.99'N, 125°00.95'W
Entrance (N): 50°05.47'N, 125°00.88'W

The Gorge, north of Guide Islets, is the narrow entrance to Gorge Harbour. It is about 0.5 mile long and less than 61 m wide in places. Least depth in the fairway is 11 m (36 ft). On the west side of The Gorge there are Indian rock paintings on flat patches of rock, and on the east side there are huge boulders which formed burial caverns.

Tidal streams attain 4 kn at the entrance to The Gorge. (SD)

The Gorge is the spectacular opening into Gorge Harbour. The fairway is narrow but fair; while the current runs fast (up to 4 knots), it is a laminar flow over a minimum depth of about 6 fathoms.

The nearly vertical, high west wall of The Gorge contains the remnants of the rock paintings mentioned in Sailing Directions. These earlier paintings were thought to have been done by natives lowered from the cliff above by cedar bark rope. They must have been an impressive sight for tribes paddling in through The Gorge for the first time!

As you enter through the north, avoid Tide Islet by favoring the west shore.

Gorge Harbour (Cortes Island)

Charts 3538, 3312; enter through The Gorge (see above)
Entrance (N, The Gorge): 50°05.47′N, 125°00.88′W
Public float: 50°05.97′N, 125°01.20′W
Anchor (far W end): 50°06.00′N, 125°01.73′W

Gorge Harbour affords good anchorage for vessels of moderate size and is a popular small craft anchorage although squalls sweep down the surrounding hills.

The public wharf and float, with depths of 2.4 to 3 m (8 to 10 ft) alongside and 32 m (106 ft) of berthing space, is on the north shore near the west end of the harbour.

The best anchorage is in the area south of the public wharf in 18 to 22 m (60 to 72 ft). In strong westerly winds the preferred anchorage is along the north shore or at the west end of the harbour. (SD)

Gorge Harbour is a natural, landlocked harbor affording very good shelter in all weather. In strong prevailing northwest weather, the best shelter is found in the upper west end of the harbor. In southeast weather, the best shelter is in the south end, the east end, or on the north side of Tan Island.

Gorge Harbour Marina Resort—one of the nicest along the South Coast—has 7.5 acres of waterfront land, 1,800 feet of moorage for cruising boats, a guest lodge and camping sites. The resort offers full amenities, including fuel, a well-stocked store and the Old Floathouse Restaurant which has excellent meals. Reservations are recommended for both the marina and the restaurant.

The public float on the north side of Gorge Harbour has little space available. Many boats are found anchored here or moored to private buoys.

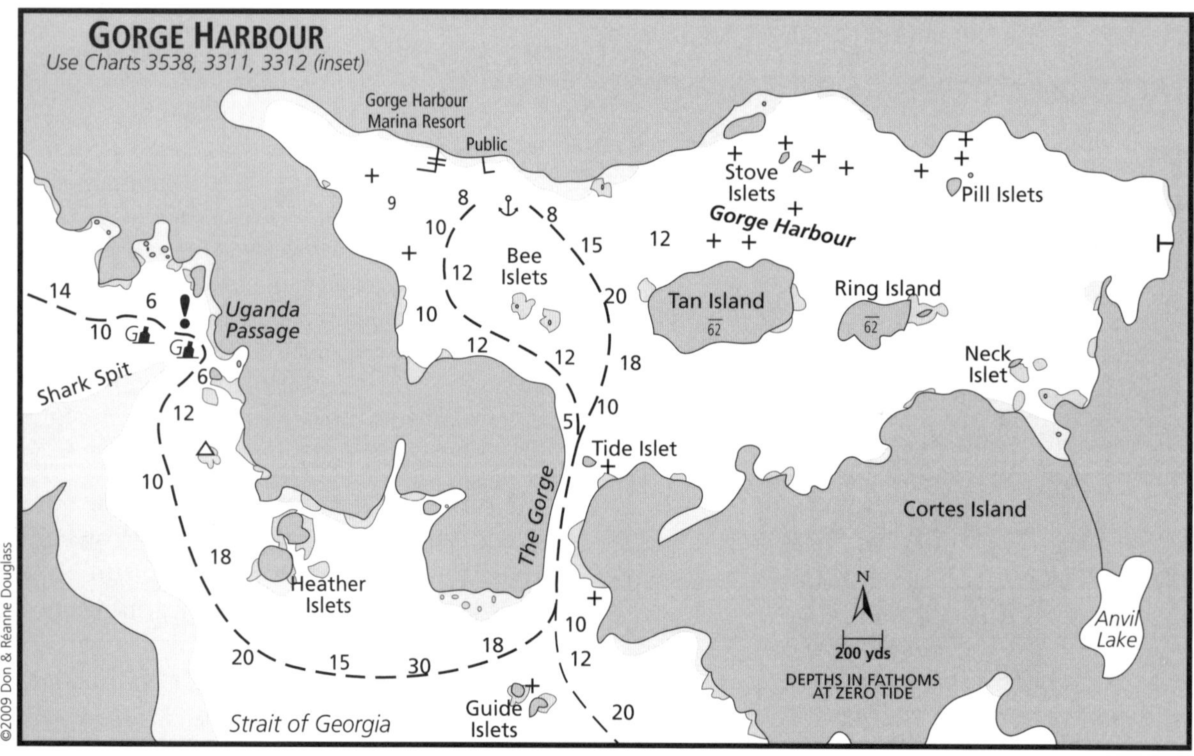

Photo courtesy CHS, Pacific Region

Gorge Harbour

Anchor in 5 fathoms over mud with fair holding.

⚓ **Gorge Harbour Marina** tel: 250.935.6433; fax: 250.935.6402; website: www.gorgeharbour.com; email: info@gorgeharbour.com; monitors VHF Ch 66A; fuel; power; restrooms; showers; laundry

The entrance to Gorge Harbour

Uganda Passage

Charts 3312 inset, 3311, 3538; btwn Marina & Cortes Islands, 1 mi NW of The Gorge
Entrance (S, 100 yards S of buoy "Q13"): 50°05.52'N, 125°02.23'W
Entrance (N, 100 yards N of buoy "Q11"): 50°05.65'N, 125°02.38'W

> *Uganda Passage which leads around the end of Shark Spit, at the north end of Marina Island, turns through more than 90°. It is encumbered with rocks and shoals. The least depth is 11 m.*
>
> *Tidal streams in Uganda Passage are reported to be 2 to 3 kn.* (SD)

Uganda Passage is used extensively by small-boat traffic during the summer, but requires careful piloting.

Shark Spit Anchorage (Uganda Passage)

Charts 3312 inset, 3311, 3538; 1 mi W of The Gorge
Anchor: 50°05.25'N, 125°02.46'W

Temporary anchorage can be found inside Shark Spit in what we call Shark Spit Anchorage. It can be useful in calm weather or prevailing westerlies. During low tide, the spit is a good place to dig for clams.

Anchor in 8 fathoms. *Caution:* Shark Spit shoals rapidly.

Whaletown Bay (Cortes Island)

Charts 3312, 3538; 1 mi NW of Uganda Passage; 5.5 mi E of Rebecca Spit Marine Park
Entrance (W, 0.13 mi NW of buoy "Q10"): 50°06.33'N, 125°03.74'W

Photo courtesy CHS, Pacific Region

Shark Spit (east from Marina Island), Uganda Passage

Whaletown general store

The public wharf is 15 m long, along its north face, with a least depth of 3.4 m alongside. Floats, with 96 m of berthing space, extend NE from the SE corner of the wharf, the outer float is reserved for seaplanes. A 3 tonne crane and garbage disposal facilities are on the wharf. (SD)

When entering Whaletown Bay, identify red spar buoy "Q10" that marks a rock in the center of the entrance. You can enter the bay by passing on either side of "Q10," but do not pass north of the flashing green buoy off the point that shoals rapidly.

Whaletown Bay has a public float behind the peninsula on its east shore which affords fair-to-good protection in all weather. Whaletown General Store, located at the head of the small wharf, has groceries, a small post office and pay telephone. Southwest swells can enter the bay on occasion. The B.C. ferry landing, with connections to Heriot Bay, is located on the north side of the bay. Upon entering the bay, avoid the mid-bay rock marked with a daymark.

Temporary anchorage can be found east of the ferry dock avoiding the shoal between the ferry dock and the public float. There is limited swinging room.

Anchor in 2 fathoms over mud with good holding.

⚓ **Whaletown General Store**
tel: 250.935.6562

Entrance (W, 0.17 mi SE of buoy "Q10"): 50°06.18'N, 125°03.35'W
Public float: 50°06.49'N, 125°03.06'W
Anchor: 50°06.56'N, 125°03.13'W

Whaletown Bay ... has a drying rock marked by starboard hand buoy "Q10" in the middle of its approach. A drying rock in the bay is marked by a daybeacon with a port hand daymark. The ferry landing, with service to Quadra Island, is on the north shore of the bay. Whaletown, on the south shore, has a post office and store.

Whaletown Bay Entrance light (483.3) is on a drying rock off the west entrance point.

A private light is shown from the ferry landing.

This Chinese junk rig is at the Whaletown float

Drew Harbour (Quadra Island)

Chart 3538; immediately SE of Heriot Bay
Rebecca Spit Light: 50°06.47'N, 125°11.74'W
Entrance (0.19 mi W of flashing green light): 50°06.47'N, 125°12.03'W
Anchor (head of harbour): 50°05.58'N, 125°11.52'W

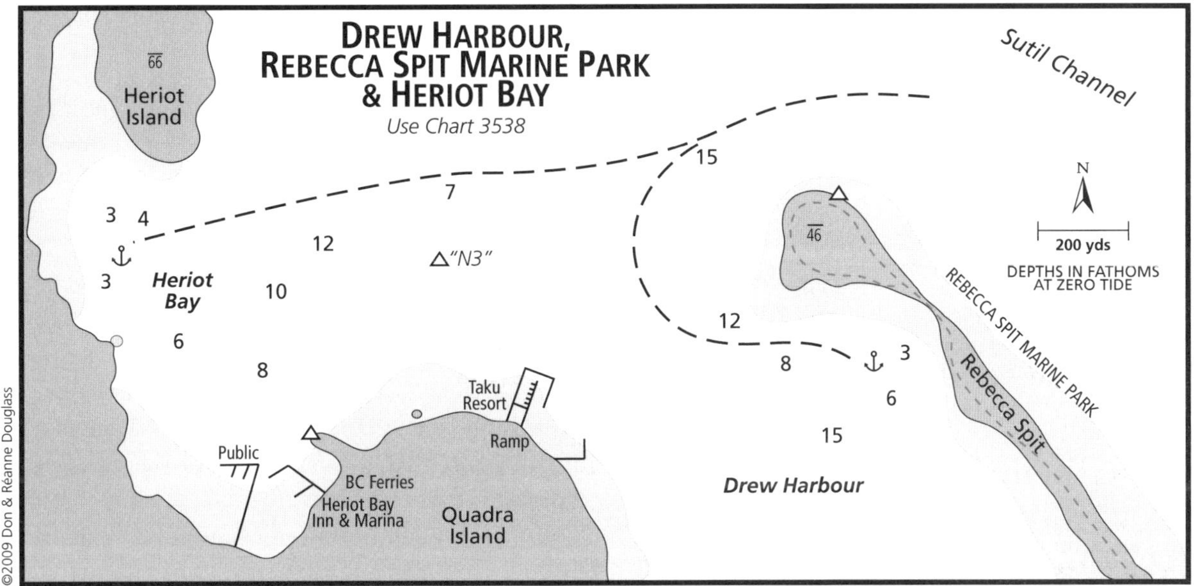

Drew Harbour, sheltered by Rebecca Spit, affords good anchorage but the bottom is hard, small craft may have difficulty in getting an anchor to hold. The harbour is subject to strong squalls during south or SE gales. The best shelter for small craft is close south of the north tip of Rebecca Spit. (SD)

Drew Harbour is a large, flat-bottomed bay surrounded on three sides by Quadra Island. It is fully protected from most weather and there is unlimited swinging room for a number of boats.

There are a few private mooring buoys off the southern and western sides in front of some lovely homes which indicates that these areas are well sheltered. Rebecca Spit Marine Park, like the entire east side of Drew Harbour, is a popular cruising anchorage.

Rebecca Spit

Rebecca Spit Marine Provincial Park

(Quadra Island)

Chart 3538, 3539; at NE corner of Drew Hbr; 0.7 mi E of Heriot Bay

Anchor: 50°06.29′N, 125°11.65′W

The harbour is surrounded by a white sandy beach and Rebecca Spit, the site of a marine park, has picnic and sanitary facilities, a launching ramp and fresh water. A resort with marine facilities is in the harbour. (SD)

Rebecca Spit offers well-sheltered anchorage off the west side of the mile-long sandy spit. The north end, where the spit is low and treeless, offers the easiest access to the beach on the east side. The exposed outer beach often collects enough driftwood to keep adults and kids occupied for hours. Hiking trails lead along both sides of the sandy spit to the grassy picnic area. The park has drinking water, picnic area, and pit toilets. Camping is available only at the private We Wai Kai Campsites. Rebecca Spit MP is an extremely popular cruising destination, so be forewarned that anchoring sites may be difficult to find in high season. Taku Resort and Heriot Bay Inn

Kayak instruction, Rebecca Spit Marine Park

and Marina have moorage for transient vessels, but reservations are a must in summer.

Although the sand along the bottom of Drew Harbour and the Park is well packed, if you set your anchor slowly and carefully, it should dig in well.

Anchor in 6 to 8 fathoms over a hard, sandy bottom with fair-to-good holding if well set.

Heriot Bay (Quadra Island)

Chart 3538, 3539; 6 mi W of Whaletown; 5 mi NE of Campbell River
Entrance: 50°06.52'N, 125°12.58'W
Public floats: 50°06.18'N, 125°12.81'W
Anchor: 50°06.42'N, 125°12.94'W

Heriot Bay ... is entered between a rock with 1.8 m over it close SE of Heriot Island and a shoal spit marked by port hand buoy "N3" projecting from the east entrance point. The bay affords fair anchorage in its west part, away from the ferry route.

A private light is shown from the ferry landing.

The public wharf, at the head of Heriot Bay, has a berthing length of 12 m with floats at the outer end providing 397 m of berthing. A 3 tonne crane is on the wharf. Power, water, garbage disposal facilities, and a launching ramp are available. (SD)

Anchored at Rebecca Spit Marine Park

Heriot Bay, the hub of the eastern side of Quadra Island has public floats close west of the ferry landing and two marinas where cruising vessels can moor. The only facilities at Heriot Bay Public Wharf are water, garbage disposal, power and launch ramp; space is limited and, in high season, rafting is the norm.

Both Heriot Bay Inn and Marina (southwest side of the Ferry Dock) and Taku Resort (to the northwest) have moorage for transient vessel with excellent facilities. Tru Value Foods has a complete selection of groceries as well as hardware and liquor. They offer free dock delivery service. The town has a post office; the ferry runs between Heriot Bay and Whaletown on Cortes Island.

Anchor sites within the bay may be crowded in the summer. If you choose to anchor, avoid all private mooring buoys. Our suggested site lies in the northwestern section of the bay in the lee of Heriot Island.

Anchor in 4 fathoms over sand and mud with fair holding.

Ferry boat and dock at Heriot Bay

Hyacinthe Bay (Quadra Island)

Charts 3539, 3312; 1 mi NW of Heriot Bay
Entrance: 50°07.15′N, 125°13.08′W

Hyacinthe Bay and Open Bay, separated by Hyacinthe Point, are open with scattered rocks and shoals and not suitable as anchorages. (SD)

Hyacinthe Bay is well sheltered from prevailing northwest winds but is exposed to the southeast. Avoid the charted rocks in the entrance. Temporary anchorage can be found along the south shore.

⚓ **Heriot Bay Inn and Marina** tel: 250.285.3322 or 888.605.4545; fax: 250.285.2708; monitors VHF 66A; website: www.heriotbayinn.com; fuel; power; propane; showers; laundry; restaurant & pub; internet

⚓ **Heriot Bay Public Wharf**

⚓ **Taku Resort** tel: 250.285.3031; fax: 250.285.3712; monitors VHF Ch 66A; website: www.takuresort.com; email: info@takuresort.com; power; showers; laundry; internet; open March to October

Open Bay (Quadra Island)

Charts 3538, 3539, 3312; 1.2 mi N of Heriot Bay
Entrance (0.24 mi NE of Hyacinthe Pt): 50°07.67′N, 125°12.39′W
Anchor: 50°08.24′N, 125°12.62′W

Open Bay offers protection from northwest winds but is open to southeast weather. Sheltered anchorage can be found on the northwest side of the bay.

Anchor in 5 fathoms over sand and mud with good holding.

(For Hoskyn Channel, see next chapter.)

Lake Bay (Read Island)

Charts 3539, 3538; 4.0 mi NE of Heriot Bay
Entrance: 50°08.30′N, 125°07.00′W

Lake Bay is too deep for convenient anchoring and is exposed to the south.

Backpacker *and friend in Heriot Bay*

Twin Bay (Read Island)

Charts 3539, 3538; 0.5 mi NE of Lake Bay
Entrance: 50°08.80′N, 125°06.50′W

Although Twin Bay is sheltered from westerlies, it is too deep for convenient anchoring and is exposed to the south.

Water fun in Desolation Sound

Anchor in 2 to 3 fathoms over sand and gravel with fair holding.

Read Island Settlement

Charts 3539, 3312; 1.3 mi NE of Burdwood Bay
Public float: 50.11.08'N, 125°05.28'W

Read Island settlement has public floats providing about 30 m (98 ft) of berthing. The floats are reported to be well protected from all winds although strong SE winds sometimes raise an uncomfortable sea.

The east coast of Read Island north of Penn Islands is rocky and steep-to but fringed in places by shoals and rocks. (SD)

Burdwood Bay (Read Island)

Charts 3538, 3312; 1.6 mi SW of Evans Bay; 5.5 mi NE of Heriot Bay
Entrance (0.1 mi NE of S islet): 50°09.57'N, 125°05.52'W
Anchor: 50°09.84'N, 125°05.77'W

Burdwood Bay has several islets and rocks in it. An islet in the south part of the bay has a drying rock close north of it marked by a daybeacon with a port hand daymark.

Marine farm facilities are on the NW side of the island with the daybeacon and north and west of the islets known locally as Wild Flower Islands.

Anchorage for small vessels is available west of the Wild Flower Islands but is exposed to southerly winds and seas. Unsheltered anchorage can be obtained in the north part of Burdwood Bay. (SD)

Burdwood Bay, surrounded by islets, offers a remarkably calm and scenic temporary anchorage. Since the bay is somewhat open to southerlies, swell or chop can be uncomfortable.

Avoid the aquaculture to the south and north, as well as the submerged rock 150 yards north of the daymark. This can be a good base for exploring the many indentations of Read Island.

Evans Bay/Bird Cove (Read Island)

Charts 3312, 3539, 3538, 3541; E side of Sutil Channel; 4 mi NW of Carrington Bay
Entrance (Evans Bay, 0.66 mi SW of Frederic Pt): 50°10.84'N, 125°04.00'W
Entrance (Bird Cove): 50°11.82'N, 125°05.14'W
Anchor (Bird Cove): 50°12.14'N, 125°05.47'W
Entrance (E arm): 50°12.80'N, 125°04.45'W
Anchor (E arm): 50°13.19'N, 125°04.23'W

Evans Bay ... entered SW of Frederic Point, which is bold, does not afford suitable anchorage for large vessels but small craft can find anchorage, open to southerly winds, in Bird Cove and in the NE arm of the bay which has booming grounds and a log dump at its head (1984). It is reported that the last-mentioned arm, which can be recognized by its logged off hillside, affords the best all weather shelter in Evans Bay. (SD)

Read Island, as well as Evans Bay, offers a chance to get away from the Desolation Sound crowd in a number of small anchorages along the edges of the island.

Evans Bay is open to the south, but unless a front is moving through, the bay provides calm anchorage during the summer.

Anchor (head of Bird Cove) in 3 to 5 fathoms over sand and gravel with fair holding.

Anchor (E arm) in 5 fathoms over sand with fair holding.

Subtle Islands (Plunger Passage)

Charts 3538, 3312; E side of Plunger Passage; 1.2 mi NW of Whaletown Bay
Position (E side of sand spit): 50°07.13'N, 125°04.66'W

> *Subtle Islands ... connected by a causeway, are separated from the west extremity of Cortes Island by Plunger Passage. The passage between Subtle Islands and Centre Islet, which is treeless, is restricted by a drying spit projecting from Subtle Islands. Both passages are suitable for small craft.* (SD)

Temporary anchorage in settled weather can be found in the shallow water off the spit joining the two islands, or at the head of the small cove on the north island.

Coulter Bay (Cortes Island)

Charts 3538, 3312; 1.4 mi N of Whaletown Bay
Entrance: 50°08.32'N, 125°02.43'W
Anchor: 50°07.90'N, 125°02.74'W

> *Coulter Bay is reported to afford good anchorage for small craft, with fair protection from westerly winds being found close to Coulter Island.* (SD)

Coulter Bay is a small, scenic and well-sheltered bay. We prefer to anchor between Coulter Island and the islet to the south close to the drying spit between them. There is a private water line between the southeast corner of Coulter Island and Cortes Island marked with a sign reading Water line, do not anchor. (Avoid the private dock on the south tip of Coulter Island.) There is limited swinging room here.

Anchor in 3 to 5 fathoms over a hard mixed bottom of poor-to-fair holding.

Carrington Bay (Cortes Island)

Charts 3538, 3312; btwn Coulter & Quartz Bays
Entrance: 50°08.98'N, 125°01.21'W
Anchor (0.2 mi N of lagoon bar): 50°08.33'N, 125°00.12'W

> *Carrington Bay has Jane Islet near its centre and Carrington Lagoon at its head. It is reported that the bottom is rocky and holding ground poor.* (SD)

Temporary anchorage is available behind the two islets on the east side of Carrington Bay, or near the outlet of Carrington Lagoon. The bay is open to the northwest, and driftwood along the shore is evidence that winds can blow hard into the bay.

Carrington Lagoon is separated from the bay by a narrow bar; small dinghies and kayaks can easily be portaged across the bar.

Anchor in 10 fathoms over sand and gravel with fair holding.

Quartz Bay (Cortes Island)

Charts 3538, 3312; 0.8 mi N of Carrington Bay; 1.6 mi SW of Von Donop Inlet
Entrance: 50°09.68'N, 125°00.29'W
Anchor: 50°09.37'N, 125°00.26'W

> *Quartz Bay is reported to provide limited anchorage for small craft. Marine farm facilities are located throughout Quartz Bay.* (SD)

The south arm of Quartz Bay affords good temporary shelter from all wind directions over a large, flat area. Avoid the oyster farm, the private floats and dock, and the two mooring buoys.

The east arm is full of private floats, and since it dries almost completely, little swinging room remains.

Anchor in the south arm in 7 fathoms over a hard bottom with some rocks; fair holding.

Ha'thayim Provincial Marine Park (Von Donop Inlet)

Charts 3538, 3312; at NW tip of Cortes Island; 6.5 mi NW of Refuge Cove
Entrance: 50°11.06'N, 124°58.90'W
Anchor: 50°08.56'N, 124°56.72'W

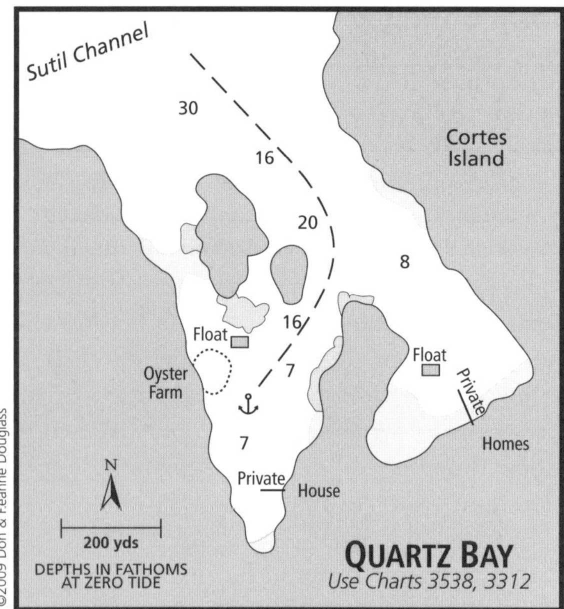

Von Donop Inlet is a good anchorage for small craft, the most popular berths being at the head, with good holding reported. In the narrowest part of the inlet, about 50 m wide, a rock with less than 2 m over it lies in mid-channel. It is usually marked by kelp and only visible at LW. The preferred route leads west of this rock. A rock that dries 2.8 m is at the head of the inlet. (SD)

Three-mile-long Von Donop Inlet, encompassed within Ha'thayim Provincial Marine Park which was established in 1993, is entirely landlocked and fully protected from all weather. Upon entering, winds quickly die out and the waters are calm. Overhanging cedars line the shores, and there is an overpowering silence as you glide in.

Use caution at the narrows (as noted in *Sailing Directions*). Local knowledge is to hug the south shore—"with the branches brushing the sides of the boat." The lagoon at the northeast corner of the inlet can be entered by dinghies and kayaks at high-water slack. Note: The outlet to the lagoon becomes a raging waterfall at low water. The dinghy route into the lagoon initially follows the south shore until you reach the rapids where you favor the north shore.

You can anchor along either shore with a stern tie recommended. To picnic ashore, note the location of picnic tables on the diagram. For more swinging room, continue to the head of the inlet where there's plenty of space to anchor on a single hook.

If you want to stretch your legs, there's a nice trail to Squirrel Cove from Von Donop. It's a bit of a problem locating the trailhead at first, because the small sign on the beach is somewhat misleading. To avoid taking a long, long walk that ends at Squirrel Cove store, take the trail to the left of the outhouse (i.e., keep the outhouse to starboard!). This trail climbs a small hill and heads southeast, dropping down to Squirrel Cove mud flats within about a half-mile.

If you do want to go to the store, the trails are unmarked and confusing. You take the right-hand trail that meanders interminably along overgrown logging roads, eventually connecting to the Cross Island road that goes from Whaletown Bay to the Squirrel Cove wharf. The far left trail heads north along the inlet.

Anchor at the south end of the inlet in 3 fathoms over sticky mud with very good holding.

Rafted in Von Donop Inlet

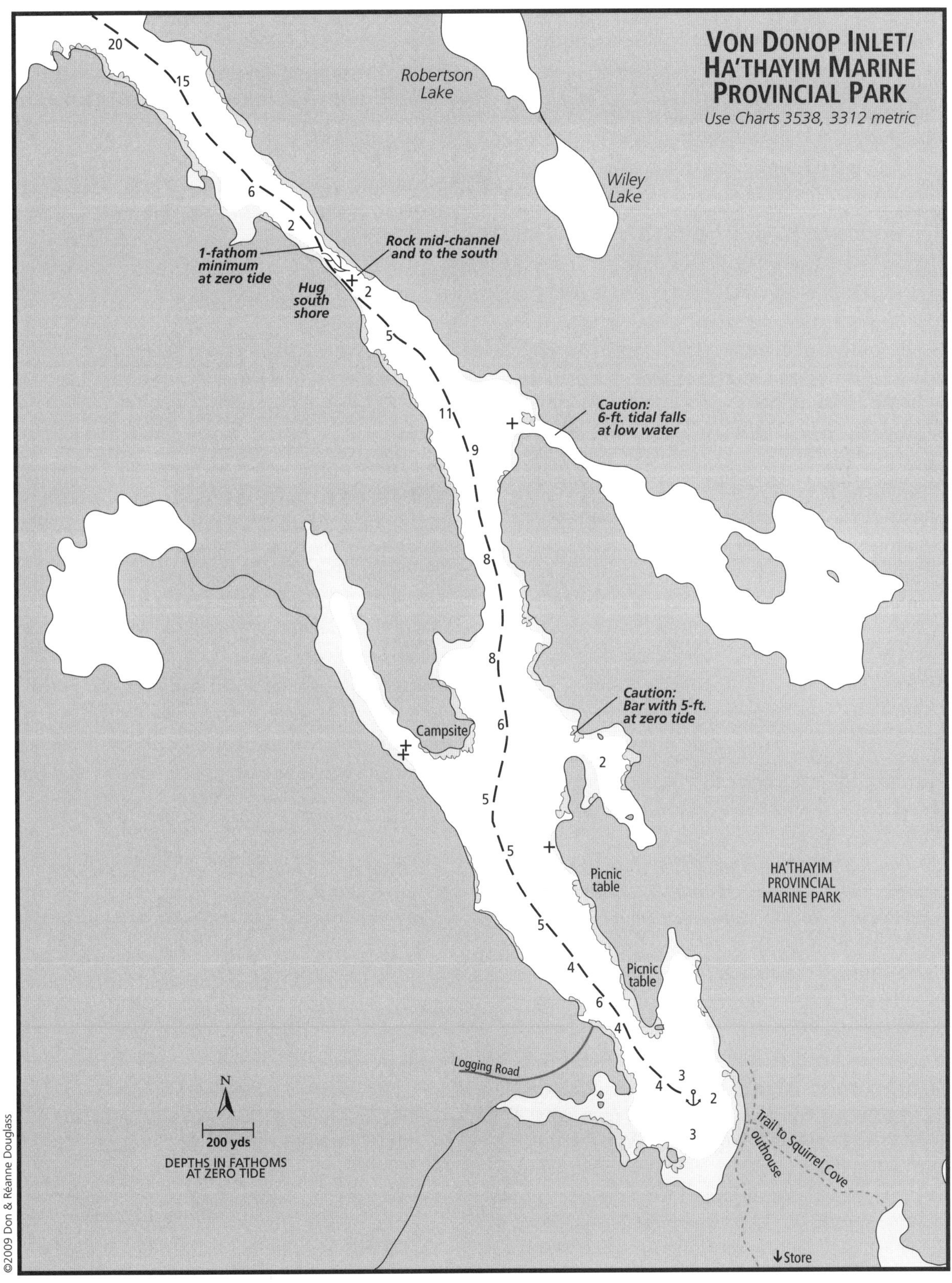
VON DONOP INLET/
HA'THAYIM MARINE
PROVINCIAL PARK
Use Charts 3538, 3312 metric
Robertson Lake
Wiley Lake
1-fathom minimum at zero tide
Rock mid-channel and to the south
Hug south shore
Caution: 6-ft. tidal falls at low water
Caution: Bar with 5-ft. at zero tide
Campsite
Picnic table
Picnic table
HA'THAYIM PROVINCIAL MARINE PARK
Logging Road
Trail to Squirrel Cove
outhouse
Store
N
200 yds
DEPTHS IN FATHOMS AT ZERO TIDE
20
15
6
2
2
5
11
9
8
8
6
5
5
5
4
6
4
4
3
2
3
2

Robertson Cove (Cortes Island)

Charts 3538, 3312; at outlet to Robertson Lake; 0.77 mi N of Von Donop Inlet entrance
Entrance: 50°11.79'N, 124°58.77'W

The bottom of the cove is reported to be undependable for holding.

Marine farm facilities are in the cove north of Robertson Cove. (SD)

Robertson and Wiley lakes to the north of Von Donop Inlet are within the park boundaries and accessible by trail. It's reported that you can anchor temporarily in Robertson Cove at the outlet of the lakes. The trail from the beach follows the south shore of Robertson Lake as far as Wiley Lake where you can find good swimming and fishing.

Redonda Bay (West Redonda Island)

Charts 3555, 3541; 3.3 mi E of Rendezvous I; 5.6 mi NW of Teakerne Arm
Entrance: 50°15.87'N, 124°58.07'W

It is too exposed for comfortable anchorage as seas form with almost any wind. (SD)

Calm Channel

Chart 3541; runs from N end of Cortes Island to S end of Stuart Island
Entrance (S, mid-ch btwn Rendezvous Islands & Raza Island): 50°15.90'N, 125°00.75'W
Entrance (N, 0.4 mi SW of Harbott Pt): 50°21.37'N, 125°08.52'W

Calm Channel, entered SW of Raza Island, leads about 8 miles NW from Sutil and Lewis Channels, joining Bute Inlet and Cordero Channel at Stuart Island. (SD)

Calm Channel leads northwest to the Yuculta Rapids and, true to its name, usually has calm seas and little wind.

Rendezvous Island Cove (Drew Passage)

Charts 3541, 3312; 1.25 mi E of N entrance to Whiterock Passage; 5.9 mi NW of Von Donop Inlet entrance
Anchor: 50°16.38'N, 125°03.08'W

Drew Passage, which leads west of Rendezvous Islands, is clear of dangers. The passage between the middle and south Rendezvous Islands is foul but small craft can carry 8 m (26 ft) through it; local knowledge is required. (SD)

Of the three Rendezvous Islands, the northernmost where a lodge is located, and the middle are private, with homes, some of which have floats. The southernmost island is entirely Rendezvous Island South Provincial Park, part of the B.C. Marine Trail network.

Raza Passage

Chart 3541; joins Calm Channel to Ramsay Arm & Pryce Channel
Entrance (W): 50°18.59'N, 125°02.69'W
Entrance (E): 50°20.21'N, 124°59.62'W

Raza Passage [is] entered north of Raza Point. (SD)

Frances Bay (Raza Passage)

Charts 3541, 3312; on NW side of Raza Passage
Entrance: 50°20.11'N, 125°01.18'W
Anchor: 50°20.97'N, 125°02.50'W

Frances Bay affords anchorage for small craft at its head with protection from all but SE winds. (SD)

Frances Bay can be used when a temporary anchorage is needed in stable weather. There is good northwest protection and shelter from up- or downslope winds. It is somewhat exposed to southeast chop blowing across Pryce Channel. However, the water is deep and you must anchor close to shore; swinging room is limited.

We have used Frances Bay as a staging area for Bute Inlet and Yuculta Rapids.

Anchor in 7 to 9 fathoms over a unrecorded bottom.

Ramsay Arm

Chart 3541; enter W of George Head
Entrance: 50°20.73'N, 124°58.75'W
Position (Quatam River): 50°22.65'N, 124°56.53'W

Ramsay Arm ... is deep with no good anchorages. Quatam Bay is the site of a logging camp with a private sand and gravel airstrip 640 m (2,100 ft) long, on the north side of Quatam

River. Marine farm facilities are off the east side of the arm, 1 mile north of George Head. (SD)

Church House (Calm Ch)

Chart 3541; 1.9 mi E of Hole in the Wall's E entrance
Public float: 50°20.13'N, 125°04.66'W

Church House is a First Nations settlement with a conspicuous church and a public wharf with floats. (SD)

Temporary anchorage can be found in calm weather in the passage west of Bartlett Islet.

Logboom waiting to be hauled to market

Bute Inlet

Charts 3542, 3541, 3312; N of Calm Channel; E of Stuart Island
Entrance: 50°21.10'N, 125°06.50'W

Bute Inlet, entered WNW of Johnstone Bluff, has mountains on both sides rising abruptly to high peaks. Several large rivers empty into the inlet and the water is often milky.

Henrietta Point, the east extremity of Stuart Island, lies on the west side of Bute Inlet 2 miles within the entrance. A log dump and booming ground are SW of the point.

Due to land drainage, a definite overlay of fresh water flows almost constantly out of the inlet at 1 to 2 kn, being strongest during spring runoff and weakest during a dry summer. This overlay, augmented by runoff along the way, increases in volume and rate as it flows from the head toward the foot of the inlet.

...Lawrence Point, Amor Point, Alpha Bluff, Boyd Point, Mellersh Point, Bear Bay and Littleton Point are on the west side of Bute Inlet. On the east side are Fawn Bluff, Clipper Point, Orford Bay, Hovel Bay, Purcell Point and Ward Point. (SD)

Bute Inlet, one of the most striking fjords on the British Columbia coast, has the highest mountains towering above its entire length, and is one of the deepest and widest.

Note: Chart 3542 was reissued in 1994 with new horizontal datum. The scale is twice the size of the previous one, which can be quite useful. However, the underlying surveys are still 50 years old and there may have been a number of changes in the topography since then. For example, our notes on Waddington Harbour, first taken in 1987, indicate that the mud flat extending from the south shore is about twice the size of that indicated on Chart 3542. Use this chart with care when you approach the head of a major river.

Leask Creek (Bute Inlet)

Charts 3542, 3312; 0.64 mi S of Fawn Bluff
Position: 50°28.11'N, 125°02.80'W

Temporary anchorage with some shelter from down-inlet winds can be found off the outlet of Leask Creek 0.64 miles south of Fawn Bluff. Because swinging room is limited, a shore tie may be required. We have seen a boat anchored there, but have no further information. There are buildings at the outlet to Moh Creek on the west shore with lights showing. This is just below a large clear-cut patch (1987).

Estero Basin Cove (Bute Inlet)

Charts 3542, 3312; 5 mi N of Arran Rapids
Entrance: 50°30.03'N, 125°06.30'W

A trail is said to lead 1.5 miles over a shallow pass to Estero Basin which empties into Frederick Arm.

Orford Bay (Bute Inlet)

Charts 3542, 3312; 14 mi NE of Arran Rapids
Entrance: 50°35.68'N, 124°52.18'W

Booming grounds and logging camps are ...in Orford Bay. (SD)

Orford Bay has had a logboom storage area in its southeast corner. There may be adequate shallow water off the large drying flat of the Orford River for emergency or temporary anchorage. This area is open to southeast gales and williwas.

We've seen grizzlies walking the drying mud flat along here.

Hovel Bay (Bute Inlet)

Charts 3542, 3312; 5 mi N or Orford Bay
Position: 50°39.94'N, 124°51.31'W

Hovel Bay is a bight on the east shore of Bute Inlet. This bay is named after a pioneer whose dinghy accidentally blew away while he was on an excursion. He died while attempting to hike back along the rugged shoreline.

There is no local knowledge available on Hovel Bay.

Waddington Harbour (Bute Inlet)

Charts 3542, 3312; at head of Bute Inlet; 32 mi NE of Arran Rapids
Breakwater (Southgate River): 50°53.68'N, 124°47.57'W
Logbooms (Homathko River): 50°55.06'N, 124°51.06'W

Waddington Harbour has Southgate River flowing into its SE part through Pigeon Valley, and Homathko River flowing into its NW Corner.

Getting Hooked Deep

In the glacier-cut waterways of the southern British Columbia coast, anchoring can sometimes be a challenge. The classic U-shaped valleys are steep-to for miles. It is often possible to cruise within a few yards of shore and still find readings of over 100 feet on the echo sounder. I have often nosed *Forevergreen* up to a waterfall and grabbed a few buckets of sweet drinking water without the slightest concern for underwater obstacles. But what about spending a peaceful night?

There are several solutions. At the head of almost every inlet, streams or rivers have deposited extensive mud flats. They afford good holding, but be careful. Frequently, the water under your keel changes from 50 feet to shoal depths of six feet or less in just a few yards. The trick is to survey the location first using an echo sounder, drop the bow anchor on the down-sloping flat, then back off (or use the dinghy) and set a stern anchor on the flat in the shallow water. This holds the bow rode in a position roughly parallel to the upslope with the anchor well dug in. If a falling tide cuts the depth under your keel to a level you're not comfortable with, just slack off the stern rode and take in the bow. Of course, if a strong katabatic (downslope) wind kicks up during the night, you'll be hanging on the aft hook, but the fetch will be short and the waves inconsequential.

The other alternative is to try to make those steep-to places work. Use the same basic concept: drop the bow anchor in deep water; then with the dinghy take the stern line (but not the anchor) to shore, double it around a tree and lead it back to a cleat. Try to choose a place that won't jam the line, and you can simply pull it through the next morning without getting your feet wet! Creativity helps. Once in Talbot Cove off Teakerne Arm, my friend Ronn Hayes found a huge log embedded in the sand. No way to get a line around the monster. But further inspection revealed a perfect one-inch hole drilled through the log. Apparently it had once served as a boom to contain other logs. We jumped on the opportunity, making sure to put in protection against chafing. A short section of ordinary garden hose works well for this purpose. Run your line through it and duct tape it in the right place.

Happy British Columbia anchoring!

—Roderick Frazier Nash

Roderick Frazier Nash is Professor Emeritus of History and Environmental Studies, University of California, Santa Barbara

Hamilton Point and Potato Point are on the west side of the harbour.

Booming grounds are north of Hamilton Point. Water is pale green due to the mineral content of runoff from Homathko Icefield, 5 miles NE. A float with 4.3 m (14 ft) alongside and protected by a breakwater lies abreast a logging camp on the north side of Southgate River.

Indifferent anchorage, unsafe in strong SW winds, can be obtained close to the edge of the drying flats. As the bottom shoals rapidly and the flats are subject to change, pay close attention to depths. (SD)

Low bridge, Gilford Island

Southgate River flows into Waddington Harbour through Pigeon Valley from the east. There are many large glaciers up the valley and their runoff greatly affects the color and visibility of the water in Waddington Harbour. Homathko River, flowing in from the north, generally contains less glacial flour. When you approach Waddington Harbour, passing Boyd Point, you will observe that the water becomes light turquoise. North of Purcell Point, it becomes a vanilla-pudding color with heavy flotsam of logs and limbs. At Ward Point, the color of the water turns to butterscotch-pudding, and directly off Southgate River, it's chocolate pudding. You may find green water off of Hamilton Point due to the dominance of the Homathko River on that side.

We have found that the drying flat on the south side of Southgate River extends farther than shown on Charts 3312 and 3542—about 0.6 mile from shore. The bottom north of this shoal is highly irregular and, since most echo sounders do not work well in heavily-silted water with visibility no more than half an inch, skippers will find this high-anxiety cruising.

Waddington Harbour is a wild and exposed place. Chart 3542 gives skippers more confidence for visiting this beautiful area, but until there is more documented exploration, this is a place for a short day visit in fair weather only.

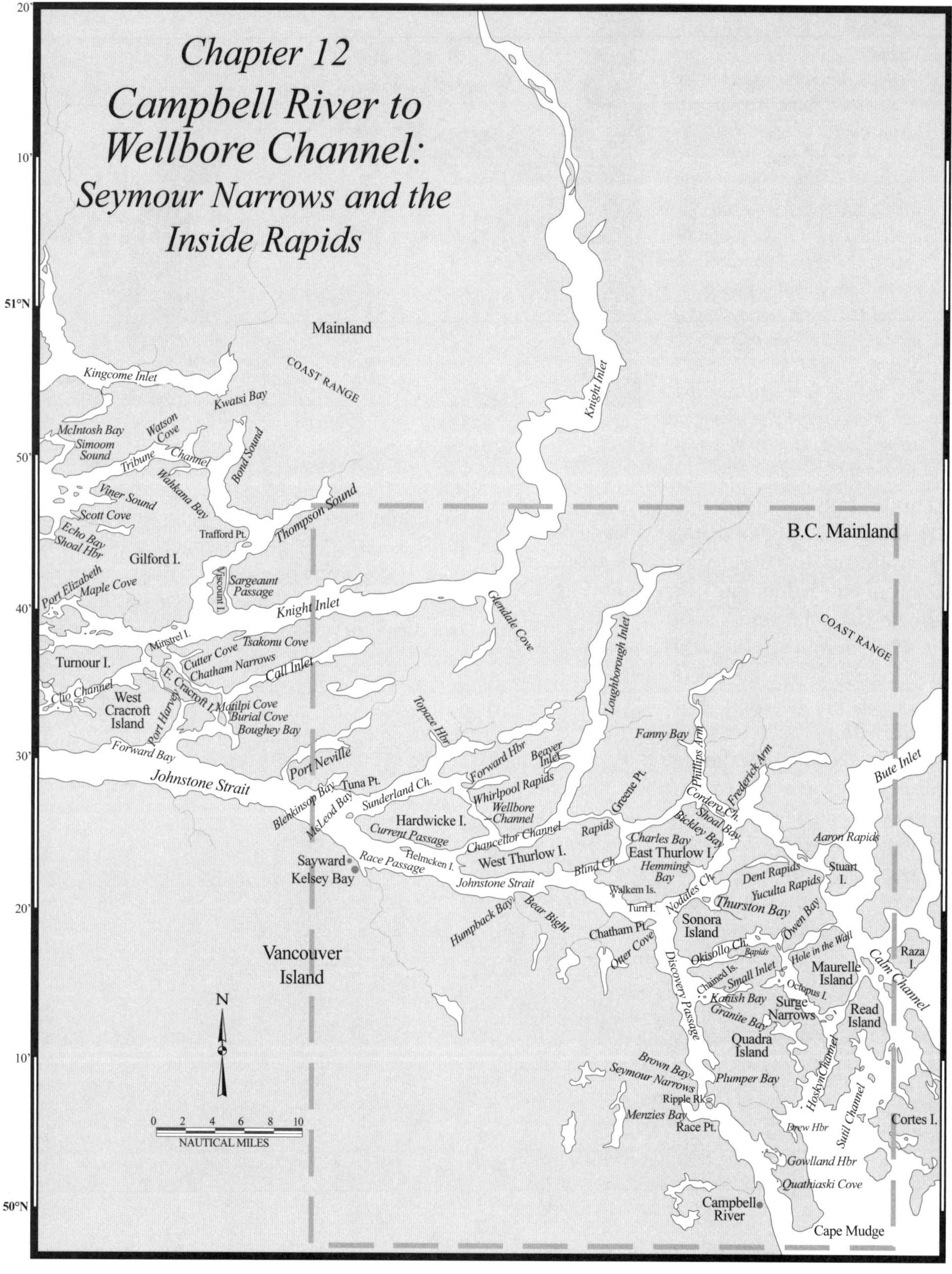

Chapter 12
Campbell River to Wellbore Channel:
Seymour Narrows and the Inside Rapids
20'
10'
51°N
50'
40'
30'
20'
10'
50°N
Mainland
COAST RANGE
Kingcome Inlet
Kwatsi Bay
McIntosh Bay
Simoom Sound
Watson Cove
Tribune Channel
Bond Sound
Wahkana Bay
Viner Sound
Scott Cove
Echo Bay
Shoal Hbr
Trafford Pt.
Thompson Sound
Gilford I.
Port Elizabeth
Maple Cove
Viscount I.
Sargeaunt Passage
Knight Inlet
Glendale Cove
Loughborough Inlet
B.C. Mainland
COAST RANGE
Minstrel I.
Tsakonu Cove
Cutter Cove
Chatham Narrows
Call Inlet
Turnour I.
E. Cracroft I.
Clio Channel
West Cracroft Island
Port Harvey
Matilpi Cove
Burial Cove
Boughey Bay
Topaze Hbr
Fanny Bay
Phillips Arm
Frederick Arm
Forward Bay
Johnstone Strait
Port Neville
Tuna Pt.
Blenkinsop Bay
McLeod Bay
Sunderland Ch.
Forward Hbr
Beaver Inlet
Whirlpool Rapids
Wellbore Channel
Greene Pt.
Cordero Ch.
Shoal Bay
Bickley Bay
Bute Inlet
Hardwicke I.
Current Passage
Chancellor Channel
Rapids
Charles Bay
East Thurlow I.
Aaron Rapids
Sayward
Kelsey Bay
Race Passage
Helmcken I.
West Thurlow I.
Blind Ch.
Hemming Bay
Dent Rapids
Stuart I.
Johnstone Strait
Walkem Is.
Nodales Ch.
Yuculta Rapids
Thurston Bay
Humpback Bay
Bear Bight
Turn I.
Sonora Island
Owen Bay
Chatham Pt.
Otter Cove
Okisollo Ch.
Rapids
Hole in the Wall
Maurelle Island
Raza I.
Calm Channel
Vancouver Island
Discovery Passage
Chained Is.
Small Inlet
Octopus I.
Kanish Bay
Granite Bay
Surge Narrows
Read Island
N
Quadra Island
Brown Bay
Seymour Narrows
Plumper Bay
Hoskyn Channel
Sutil Channel
Ripple Rk
Menzies Bay
Race Pt.
Drew Hbr
Cortes I.
0 2 4 6 8 10
NAUTICAL MILES
Gowlland Hbr
Quathiaski Cove
Campbell River
Cape Mudge

12

CAMPBELL RIVER TO WELLBORE CHANNEL: Seymour Narrows and the Inside Rapids

Discovery Passage is the long, narrow stretch of water lying between Vancouver Island to the west and what are sometimes called the Discovery Islands—Quadra, Sonora, East Thurlow—to the east. It is the main waterway that links the Strait of Georgia with Johnstone Strait. All commercial traffic funnels through Discovery Passage, and the area is a big draw for sport-fishermen and recreational boaters.

Discovery Passage and the channels above Desolation Sound, known for their rapids, mark the beginning of a wilder and less-traveled wilderness. South of Seymour Narrows, the shorelines are less steep, the land is thickly covered with cedars and fir, and there are many delightful coves and bays, sandy cliffs and beaches. You will find old settler ruins and active Indian settlements. Farther north, the shorelines become rugged, and Mount Menzies can be seen on the western skyline.

Approximately one-third of the tidal waters of the Strait of Georgia attempt to squeeze through narrow Discovery Passage. The resulting activity requires heads-up navigating. Since the removal of Ripple Rock in Seymour Narrows (1958)—previously a major obstacle to navigation—Discovery Passage is both more convenient and a faster route for reaching the north coast.

Here, the colder currents flowing south from Queen Charlotte Sound through Johnstone Strait meet warmer ones, and the protected waters have a chance to heat up. In summer, water temperatures often reach the mid-to-high sixties (F)—warmer than those of southern California.

Cat boat enjoys fall weather

Complex flow patterns along the northern channels require study and decision-making. Until you've tested your skills in these rapids and become accustomed to navigating them, they can be a concern. Adequate planning and careful timing are your key to a safe, enjoyable (yes, and even fun!) passage through these rap-

---

Note: Charts 3312 and 3313 are chart books in atlas format. They are designed for use by small craft, and include additional information and aerial photographs. However, these charts are not available as NDI digital charts, nor do they lend themselves easily to measurement of latitude and longitude.

ids. Several routes through this maze are possible. You can take either the west side (direct route) or one of the routes along the mainland coast.

To compare slack waters and maximum currents for the various rapids of this region, refer to Canadian Tide and Current Tables to eliminate guesswork.

Discovery Passage

Chart 3539; separates Quadra & Sonora Islands from Vancouver Island
Entrance (S, 0.9 mi S of Cape Mudge Light): 49°59.00′N, 125°11.50′W
Entrance (N, 0.6 mi N of Chatham Pt Light): 50°20.00′N, 125°25.54′W

> *Discovery Passage ... is the main shipping channel leading NW from the north end of the Strait of Georgia. It is entered from the south between Cape Mudge and Willow Point. The north limit of Discovery Passage is Chatham Point. South of Seymour Narrows shores are relatively low lying. North of the narrows they become steep and mountainous, especially on the west side. Mount Menzies, NW of Menzies Bay, attains an elevation of 1,239 m and snow often remains on its summit until late June.*
>
> *Between Cape Mudge and dWillow Point there is a heavy race on south-going streams. When opposed by strong SE winds short steep swells and a rough sea form that can be very dangerous. Under such conditions small vessels are advised to pass through the area at or after HW slack.* (SD)

Discovery Passage is the shortest and quickest route for boats bound for Johnstone Strait and points north. It is a fast moving "river," and the strength of its currents at flood tides will amaze you. Except in areas of rocks or points, the flow tends to be laminar and is not dangerous, especially if your vessel has sufficient speed to overcome the current.

Counter-flood currents along both shores can be used to advantage against the strong midchannel flood. Since fishing is excellent around this tidal face, you'll encounter many small sportfishing boats in season. Chinook salmon run early, starting in June; Coho run through the middle of October.

To plan your transit of Discovery Passage, study Canadian Tide and Current Tables, paying particular attention to the tidal calendar for Campbell River. This graph, for each day of the year, can help you choose a time when adjacent tidal differences are minimal. If you want the strongest favorable current, pick a time of high difference. A near-horizontal line on the graph means little current; a steep vertical line means maximal currents.

If you want to remain overnight in Discovery Passage, you can usually find moorage in Campbell River or you can cross Discovery Passage and stay in Quathiaski Cove, "April Point Cove," or Gowlland Harbour.

Cape Mudge (Quadra Island)

Charts 3539, 3540; at S end of Quadra Island; marks southern limits of Discovery Passage
Light: 49°59.91′N, 125°11.75′W

> *Cape Mudge is flat, wooded, and ends in a conspicuous whitish yellow earth cliff covered with scattered vegetation; the cliff faces SE. During summer months numerous small pleasure craft will be encountered here. There are several resorts located at Cape Mudge.*
>
> *Tidal streams in the vicinity of Cape Mudge attain 7 to 9 kn; the flood flowing south and the ebb north. On a strong flood there is a strong counter current along the edge of Wilby Shoals as far as the lighthouse, small craft can take full advantage when proceeding north. On the ebb, a similar backeddy is evident along the shore between Cape Mudge lighthouse and Yaculta village.*
>
> *Caution. Between Cape Mudge and Willow Point there is a heavy race on south-going streams. When opposed by strong SE winds ~~sets up~~ short steep swells and a rough sea form that can be very dangerous. Under such conditions small vessels are advised to pass through the area at or after HW slack.* (SD)

Cape Mudge is the exit for much of the flood tide flowing south from Johnstone Straits. In

Heading past Cape Mudge

addition to the TV tower mentioned above in *Sailing Directions*, the traditional white lighthouse buildings with their red roofs are leading landmarks. If you're heading north from Mitlenatch Island, avoid Wilby Shoals by clearing the spar buoy.

During southeast winds, flood tides create a nasty and dangerous chop off Cape Mudge, and small vessels should avoid this area at such times.

Yaculta (Quadra Island)

Chart 3540; 1.5 mi E of Campbell River public floats
Public float: 50°01.39'N, 125°11.87'W

> *The village of Yaculta, on Quadra Island opposite Yaculta Bank, has a public wharf, with a berthing length of 86 m (282 ft), protected on its south side by a pile and timber breakwater.* (SD)

The public float here is used primarily for sportfishing craft.

Campbell River (Vancouver Island)

Chart 3540; 24.5 mi NW of Comox; 8.5 mi SE of Seymour Narrows
Entrance (Discovery Hbr Marina): 50°02.19'N, 125°14.50'W
Campbell River breakwater light: 50°01.48'N, 125°14.26'W
Public floats entrance (100 ft N of bkw light): 50°01.50'N, 125°14.26'W

> *Campbell River municipality ... is a logging and commercial fishing centre and a resort area*

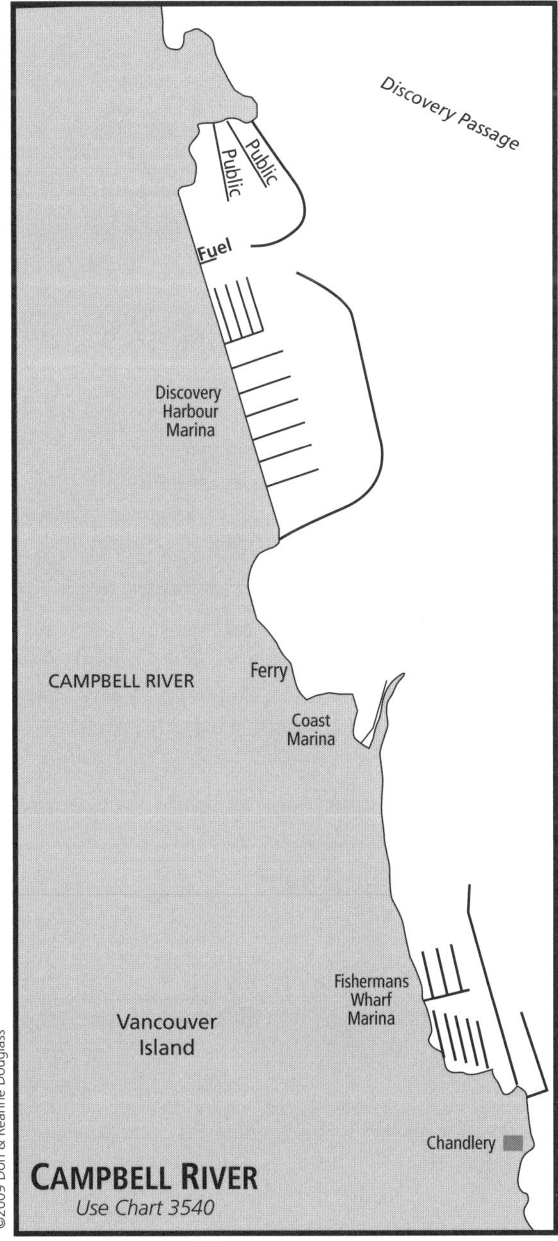

noted for its sport fishing; the population is 16,986 (1986).

Hotels, motels, banks, restaurants, numerous stores (including a liquor store) and complete postal (V9W 4Z8) service are available. Several marinas and launching ramps are available for boaters.

A public fishing and recreation pier extends east the north from the south end of the south breakwater at the boat basin. It is lighted at night and not designed for berthing.

As the tidal streams are strong and the holding ground poor, only temporary anchorage during calm weather should be considered in the vicinity of Campbell River. During rough weather, Duncan Bay provides the only safe anchorage for large vessels. Small craft can obtain shelter within the boat harbours, or in Quathiaski Cove or Gowlland Harbour.

The maximum tidal range for Campbell River is 4.6 m. (SD)

Campbell River, the supply center for north central Vancouver Island and the islands north and east, has become one of the most popular areas for tourism on the island. The town has renovated its waterfront and The list of resorts, guide services and charter operations is lengthy, covering everything from fishing , kayaking, diving, mountain biking and whale watching.

The town is home to the lovely Campbell River Museum where you can view First Nations' artifacts, as well as a film that gives insight into their heritage. Also available at the museum is a fascinating documentary film that recounts the explosion of Ripple Rock in Seymour Narrow (reported to have been the large non-nuclear, man-made explosion).

There are three possible transient moorage basins in Campbell River. From south to north, Campbell River Harbour Authority's Fisherman's Wharf at the south end of town; Coast Marina north of Fisherman's; Discovery Harbour Marina at the north end.

Fisherman's Wharf, while primarily commercial, welcomes pleasure craft when there is room (best to call ahead); their facilities include power and water, pumpout, and showers, and they are the closest to marine supply stores. The upscale Coast Marina has power (30 to 100 amp), pumpout, showers, laundry; wirelss internet and access to its hotel.

Discovery Harbour Marina, owned and run by the Campbell River Band and the northernmost marina, has a large pleasure-craft basin with power (20-100 amp) and water, showers, laundry. It is located to the south of the Esso Fuel Dock. Although the basin to the north of the fuel dock is primarily home to local fishing boats, transients may be able to find moorage here.

Discovery Harbour Marina is close to the Discovery Harbour Centre where the choice at the supermarket could supply several cruise ships. You'll also find restaurants, boutiques, a marine store, clothing and gift shops and a Postal Centre in the shopping center.

⚓ **Campbell River Harbour Authority** (Fisherman's Wharf)
tel: 250.287.7931; monitors VHF Ch 66A; open year-round

⚓ **Coast Marina** tel: 250.287.7455; monitors VHF Ch 66A; website: www.coasthotels.com; (reservations advised)

⚓ **Discovery Harbour Marina**
tel: 250.287.2614; monitors VHF Ch 66A; website: www.ciscoveryharbourmarina.com; office is closed at night

Quathiaski Cove (Quadra Island)

Chart 3540; 1.4 mi NE of Campbell River public floats
Entrance (S): 50°02.60′N, 125°13.38′W
Entrance (N): 50°02.99′N, 125°13.76′W
Public float: 50°02.58′N, 125°13.02′W
Anchor: 50°03.10′N, 125°13.46′W

Quathiaski Cove affords shelter for small vessels. Much of the bottom is rocky and, at times, a strong current sets through the cove. It can be entered north or south of Grouse Island, but the south entrance is generally used. Two rocks with 0.2 m (1 ft) over them lie close west and north of the fish processing plant in the SE corner of the cove.

Quathiaski Cove light (512.5) is on the drying reef extending SE from Grouse Island.

A ferry landing, in the south part of the cove, provides regular service to Campbell River. Give the ferry a wide berth. (SD)

Quathiaski Cove, directly northeast across Discovery Passage on Quadra Island, is well sheltered. At the south end of the cove is the Campbell River ferry landing with a public wharf close north. The shore along the north end of Quathiaski Cove has a number of private docks and attractive homes.

Anchorage can be taken in the center and north end of Quathiaski Cove in 5 to 10 fathoms. To avoid the occasional currents, anchor near the outlet of the drying Unkak Cove. In the center of the north entrance, there is a rock with one fathom of water over it and you can easily pass on either side.

Anchor in 5 fathoms over a mixed bottom with fair holding.

April Point Cove (Quadra Island)

Charts 3540, 3539; 1.2 mi N of Quathiaski Cove
Entrance (0.18 mi NE of April Pt): 50°04.04'N, 125°14.14'W
Anchor: 50°03.72'N, 125°13.52'W

A boat passage between the SW extremity of Gowlland Island and April Point is encumbered with drying and below-water rocks but gives access to the south part of Gowlland Harbour. (SD)

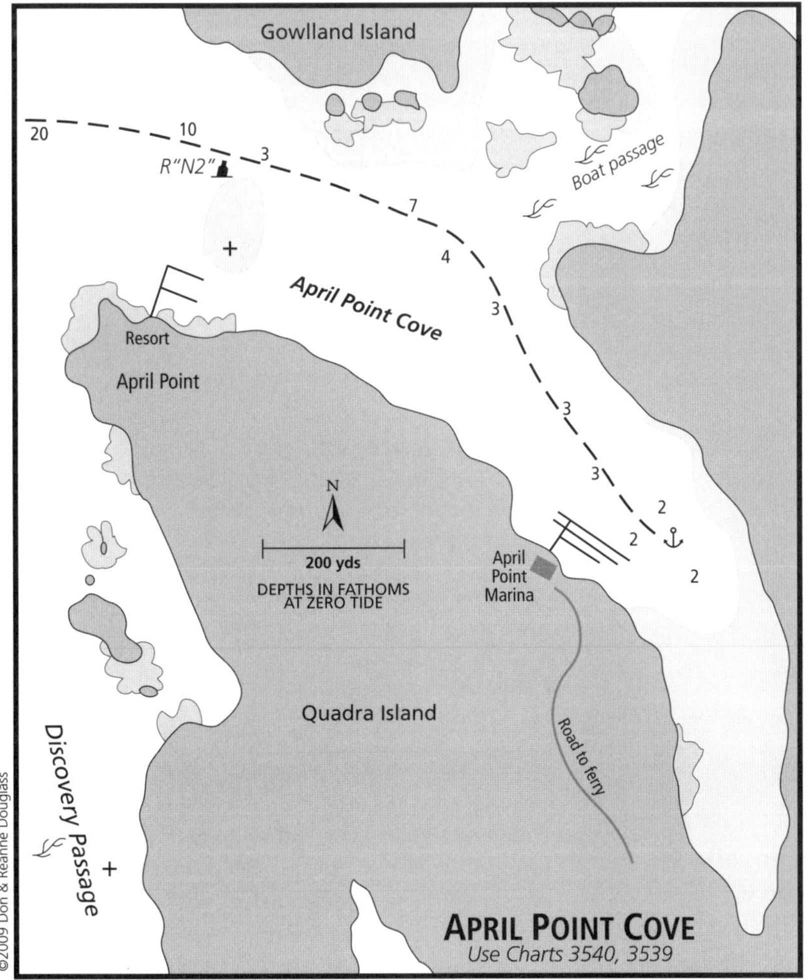

April Point Cove is the well-sheltered area east of April Point, a mile north of Quathiaski Cove. Except for April Point Lodge and April Point Marina the cove has little noise. However, room to anchor is restricted due to docks and shoal area. Where you can find room clear of any floats, you'll spend a quiet night since there is no current here. The cove has a flat mud bottom.

A narrow, dinghy passage in the northeast corner of the harbor of April Point Cove connects to Gowlland Harbour. The least depth throughout this passage is about half a fathom, is use caution as currents can be strong here. Avoid the shoals and rocks on either side of the curving route.

Anchor (north end) in 2 fathoms, mud with good holding.

⚓ **April Point Resort & Marina**
tel: 250.285.2222; fax: 250.285.2016; monitors VHF 66A; power; laundry

Gowlland Harbour (Quadra Island)

Chart 3540; 3 mi due N of Campbell River
Entrance (0.12 mi NW of Vigilant Islets): 50°05.10′N, 125°14.86′W
Anchor (Vigilant Islets): 50°04.96′N, 125°14.63′W
Anchor (NW of Fawn Islet): 50°04.81′N, 125°13.47′W
Anchor (S of Stag I): 50°04.33′N, 125°12.93′W

Gowlland Harbour, entered between Vigilant Islets off the north end of Gowlland Island and Entrance Rock, is encumbered by several islets and rocks. Its south end is a fine land-locked anchorage. Spoil Rock, 0.1 mile east of Vigilant Islets, has 6.4 m over it and like Entrance Rock is marked by kelp. Entrance Bank between Entrance Rock and May Island, has 0.2 m over it, sand bottom. Wren Islet, Crow Islet, Mouse Islets, Fawn Islet, Stag Island and Doe Islet are on the north and east sides of the harbour and are Provincial Park Reserves.

Anchorage can be obtained in Gowlland Harbour as convenient, south of Doe Islet, in 15 m (49 ft), mud. (SD)

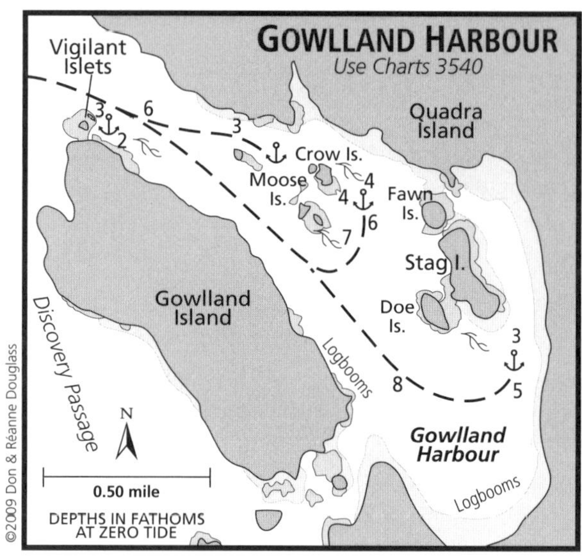

Gowlland Harbour provides good shelter close to the action at Seymour Narrows. From this point, you can gauge conditions easily without venturing into the channel.

To enter Gowlland Harbour, study Chart 3940 carefully ahead of time and follow the directions given in *Sailing Directions*.

We like to tuck in behind the rocky spit at the north tip of Gowlland Island, to the east of Vigilant Islets. At high tide, most of the spit is at or under water, so you must pass well east to avoid its off-lying rocks; there is no current at this site.

We have also anchored south of Stag Island, near the booms in the south part of the harbor where depths are a little greater. Friends, who have a smaller boat than ours, prefer anchor southeast of Stag Island in 3 to 5 fathoms.

Avoid the logboom areas around the harbor which can change from season to season and create challenges for anchoring, if you're not careful. However, all-in-all, Gowlland is a good place to monitor conditions in Discovery Passage.

Anchor (Vigilant Islets) in 2 to 3 fathoms over hard mud and gravel with fair-to-good holding.

Anchor (NW of Fawn Islet) in 6 fathoms over mud with good holding.

Anchor (S of Stag Island) in 5 to 8 fathoms over mud; fair-to-good holding

Seymour Narrows

Charts 3539 inset, 3540; btwn Quadra & Vancouver Islands; the narrowest part of Discovery Passage
Entrance (S, 0.38 mi N of Race Rock Light): 50°07.18′N, 125°19.50′W
Ripple Rock: 50°07.91′N, 125°21.25′W
Entrance (N, 0.3 mi W of Plumper Pt): 50°09.50′N, 125°21.40′W

Seymour Narrows ... commences about 1 mile NW of Race Point; it is nearly 2 miles long and not less than 0.4 mile wide. The shores on either side are high, rugged and steep-to. Ripple Rock, almost in the middle of the channel, causes considerable turbulence when tidal streams are running at strength.

Mariners are advised to navigate Seymour

Narrows only at or near slack water if their vessel is of low power, towing other vessels, or is a small vessel, under about 20 m (66 ft) long. Fatal accidents have occurred to small vessels when attempting to navigate this narrows when the tidal stream is running at full strength.

Small vessels have been capsized with loss of life while navigating Seymour Narrows even near slack water and in reasonable weather conditions; they were in light condition with considerable top weight. Precautions should be taken to maintain adequate stability and trim even when planning to transit at slack water. All crew members should be alert and ready to cope with any emergency.

If one must go through on the flood stream the west side of the narrows should be avoided.

Tidal streams in Seymour Narrows attain 16 kn; the flood sets south and the ebb north. When either stream is running at strength, the eddies and swirls are extremely heavy, and when these are opposed by a strong wind, the races become very dangerous to small vessels. In the vicinity of Ripple Rock, near the shallowest parts, there are up-wellings which vary in strength with the velocity of the stream; these up-wellings occur about every 5 seconds, increase in size and are swept away in the current causing eddies and whirlpools.

Daily predictions of the times of slack water, and of the times and rates of maximum flood and ebb streams, are given in the Tide Tables, Volume 6. The duration of slack water can be as much as 12 or 15 minutes, but when there is a large range of tide, the interval of change can be considerably less. Local weather conditions, particularly when these are severe, can affect the duration of slack water very considerably. (SD)

Waterfront real estate

To proceed against the tidal stream during the period of spring tides, and to ensure maximum control, a speed of 13 kn is necessary during the first and last hours of the tidal stream, 15 to 16 kn during the second and fourth hours, and 17 kn to drive through at the full strength of the tide. The vessel should be quick and handy to answer the helm to achieve full control.

Despite *Sailing Directions*' frightening details regarding the transit of Seymour Narrows, Baidarka's first mate prefers the short turbulence of Ripple Rock in Seymour Narrows to the more protracted whirlpools of the narrows further east.

To learn more about this passage, be sure to watch the documentary about the explosion of Ripple Rock at the Campbell River Museum.

Race Point (Vancouver Island)

Chart 3539 inset; 6.2 mi NW of Campbell River public floats; 1.0 mi SE of Maud Island
Light: 50°06.80'N, 125°19.50'W

Race Point ... is a bold, rocky bluff which is steep-to.

When the flood, or south-going, tidal stream is running at strength through Seymour Narrows, it strikes the shore about midway between Race and Huntingford Points. Part flows east past Race Point, and the other turns west to Huntingford Point, where it is deflected NW and lost in the middle of Menzies Bay.

The flood stream attains 11 kn off Race Point causing overfalls and eddies extending some distance east. With fresh east or SE winds, this race becomes very dangerous to small craft. Between Middle and Race Points, there is a strong counter current along the shore when the south-going stream is strong. (SD)

The sight of spring tides off Race Point, where much of the flood current hits, can make the hair on the back of your neck bristle. On one of the highest spring tides of the year, in order to watch this incredible sight, we worked our way north along the shore of Vancouver Island, using the well-developed back eddies along shore from Duncan Bay and Orange Point. Once we were close abeam Race Point light, we turned the engine off and, for two hours, we drifted in clockwise circles, listening to the rush of the water and watching eruptions that occurred just 50 to 100 yards to the northeast. (Better than fireworks! We recommend this experience as a demonstration of the tremendous power of water.) When the current diminished enough, we dashed into Menzies Bay and used a back eddy to carry us to Nymphe Cove.

On the other hand, on neap tides near slack water, Race Point can be calm enough to pass by in a dinghy.

Menzies Bay (Vancouver Island)

Chart 3539 inset; on the W side of the S entrance to Seymour Narrows
Entrance (center of bay): 50°07.34'N, 125°22.00'W
Position (logbooms, N side): 50°07.96'N, 125°22.45'W

> *Menzies Bay, on the west side of the approach to Seymour Narrows, has a ruined pier on Josephine Flat near the entrance to Mohun Creek. Booming grounds with numerous dolphins, a mooring buoy and barge loading ramp are close-off Huntingford Point. Bloedel, on the south side of Menzies Bay, is fronted by booming grounds and has a log dump and conveyor for loading barges.* (SD)

The west end of Menzies Bay dries and there is a large shoal area along the edge of the flood back eddy. However, behind Defender Shoal, and along the northeast shore where logs are tied, you can find excellent protection.

We've found that the area southwest and west of Defender Shoal carries less water than that indicated on the chart, so be cautious. Also, this area is subject to extensive log operations and storage which make the south shore congested.

Tying to Logbooms

If you are a visitor to these waters, it may surprise you to hear that many northwest cruising boats tie up to parked logbooms and that guidebooks may even suggest doing so. A logboom is a large bundle of logs rafted together, tied to shore, and stored until taken to market.

Sometimes an anchorage is completely filled with logbooms and your anchor choices are severely limited. If you tie to a logboom, which is unlikely to move at night, you are doing so at your own risk. Trying to anchor where log booming operations have been located can be futile. Extensive amounts of bark, slash and, occasionally, old cables litter the bottom which prevents setting your anchor well.

Nymphe Cove (Vancouver Island)

Chart 3539 inset; NE of Menzies Bay, close E of Stephenson Pt
Entrance: 50°07.66'N, 125°21.79'W
Anchor (Nymphe Cove): 50°07.75'N, 125°21.88'W

> *Nymphe Cove ... does not offer good anchorage as it is exposed to the SE and has poor holding ground. The bottom, south of the drying mud flats at its head, is bare rock. An overhead cable, with a vertical clearance of 21 m (69 ft), crosses the mud flats at the head of the cove.* (SD)

Although Nymphe Cove is a good place to observe Seymour Narrows and Ripple Shoal, the cove is steep-to and offers only marginal protection from weather; it is close to the eddy currents which sometimes swirl through. However, it's an excellent place from which to watch large ships and barges passing through the narrows on the last of the flood. Their response to the turbulence as they start their turn to avoid Race Point is interesting.

The water in Nymphe Cove is so clear, you can see crabs walking along the bottom.

Anchor directly below the overhead power lines and check your anchor set because of the eel grass and the steepness of the bottom. Swinging room is limited.

Anchor (Nymphe Cove) in 2 to 4 fathoms over sand with eel grass; fair holding.

Maud Island Cove (Maud Island)

Chart 3539 inset; lies on the E side at the S end of Seymour Narrows; on the N side of the I
Entrance: 50°07.71'N, 125°20.00'W
Anchor: 50°08.14'N, 125°20.63'W

Temporary anchorage can be found in Maud Island Cove out of the outside current and chaos. This is a fair weather anchorage only as it is exposed to the southeast. Anchor at the head of the bay, close to the causeway that connects Maud Island to Quadra Island. (This causeway provided access for the miners who drilled the tunnels from Maud Island to Ripple Rock under Seymour Narrows.) In this area, you can see the concrete bunkers and remains of the test core samples taken by the miners.

The cove has become a popular scuba diving area since the sinking of the vessel Columbia.

Saltwater Lagoon can be explored by dinghy.

Anchor in 2 to 4 fathoms over sand, gravel and some rocks with fair holding.

Ripple Rock (Seymour Narrows)

Charts 3539, 3540; mid-ch btwn Maud Island & Wilfred Pt; 7.8 mi NW of Campbell River ppubic floats
Position: 50°07.91'N, 125°21.25'W

> *Ripple Rock, which has two heads with 13.7 and 15.2 m (45 and 50 ft) over them, is about 0.2 mile in extent and slightly to the west of midchannel, with the south and shallowest head about 0.25 mile west of Maud Island light. The channels on either side of the rock have depths in excess of 50 m (164 ft).* (SD)

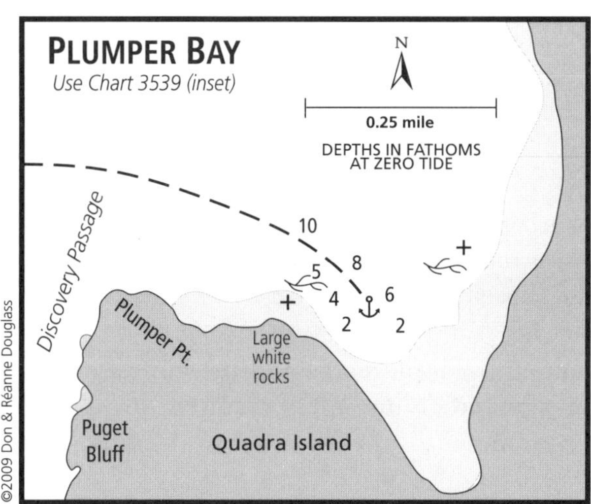

In 1958, the horns of the infamous Ripple Rock were blown to smithereens in the biggest non-atomic explosion up to that time. In 1951, Don remembers seeing a stream of ships and barges waiting in a line for slack water at the south end of Seymour Narrows. He experienced the thrill of being at the helm of the U.S. Coast Guard ice breaker, *Storis*, as she passed directly over Ripple Rock on the last of a strong flood tide with only a few feet of water below the keel. In those days, Don didn't have a lot of helm experience on power vessels and was a little slow to turn it hard-over. *Storis* hit the whirlpools on the lee side and was turned end-for-end. The skipper had to grab the helm and yell for flank speed ahead in an effort to regain control. In a chastising response to this maneuver, the Alaska steamship and Canadian Pacific Railway (CPR) boats waiting to head north sounded their whistles as *Storis* passed them going south.

Plumper Bay (Quadra Island)

Chart 3539 inset; 1.2 mi E of Brown Bay, 3.0 mi NW of Race Pt
Entrance: 50°09.80'N, 125°20.65'W
Anchor: 50°09.48'N, 125°20.36'W

> *Plumper Bay is a convenient stopping place for vessels awaiting the turn of the tidal stream in Seymour Narrows ... Good anchorage, well sheltered and out of the tidal stream, can be obtained in Plumper Bay, in 15 to 18 m (48 to 60 ft), mud and sand, about 0.5 mile ENE of Plumper Point.* (SD)

Plumper Bay was a major waiting place for southbound steamships when Ripple Rock was only 9 feet below zero tide. Although it offers good protection from southerlies, it is wide open to the northwest. The head of the bay shoals rapidly to a sand and grass bottom.

Anchor in 6 to 8 fathoms over hard mud with fair-to-good holding.

Brown Bay (Vancouver Island)

Chart 3539 inset; 1.9 mi NW of Ripple Rock; 10.4 mi S of Chatham Pt
Entrance: 50°09.80'N, 125°22.22'W

> *Brown Bay...is the site of a marina, but too deep for anchorage.* (SD)

In gale force winds or strong northwesterly winds, emergency moorage for small craft is safer behind the breakwater in Brown Bay than in Plumper Bay across the channel. Brown's Bay Marina and RV Park is particularly popular amongst North Central Islanders. The small marina, that caters mostly to vessels under 30 feet, has gas and diesel, 15 to 30 amp power, showers and laundry.

⚓ **Brown's Bay Marina & RV Park**
tel: 250.286.3135; fax: 250.286.0951; monitors VHF 66A; website: www.brownsbayresort.com; email: marina@brownsbayresort.com; fuel; restrooms; showers; laundry

Deepwater Bay (Quadra Island)

Chart 3539; 1.8 mi NE of Brown Bay
Entrance: 50°11.12'N, 125°20.67'W
Anchor: 50°10.37'N, 125°20.15'W

> *Deepwater Bay, NE of Separation Head, has depths in excess of 40 m (131 ft) with sand and mud bottom. A small vessel can anchor in 20 m (66 ft) close inshore in the south corner of the bay.* (SD)

Deepwater Bay provides good protection from any southerly weather.

Anchor in 6 to 10 fathoms over sand and mud with good holding.

Kanish Bay (Quadra Island)

Chart 3539; 5.1 mi SE of Chatham Pt; 7.6 mi N of Ripple Rock
Entrance (0.27 mi SW of Nixon Rock): 50°15.58'N, 125°22.19'W

> *Kanish Bay, entered between Bodega Point and Granite Point, has the Chained Islands along its south shore.* (SD)

Kanish Bay has several well-sheltered anchor sites—Granite Bay, "Kanish Bay Cove," Small Inlet—all close to the Chained Islands and to Discovery Passage.

Granite Bay (Quadra Island)

Chart 3539; in the SE corner of Kanish Bay
Entrance: 50°14.64'N, 125°19.24'W
Anchor: 50°14.36'N, 125°18.45'W

> *Granite Bay ... has a rock with less than 2 m (6 ft) over it in its approach and its entrance fairway is less than 90 m (295 ft) wide.* (SD)

Granite Bay, an almost landlocked bay, offers excellent protection in all weather. It is a good cruising stop because of its excellent shelter, shallow water, and ample swinging room.

Enter through the narrow channel in the southeast corner of Kanish Bay; avoid the charted rock north of the narrows, staying midchannel through the narrows which has a minimum depth of 3 to 4 fathoms. There are old pilings, logboom floats, and drying flats at the head of the bay. Many of the cabins along the shore are being renovated to serve as year-round homes.

We like to anchor off the tiny bight on the east side of the bay.

Anchor in 3 fathoms over sticky mud with very good holding.

Kanish Bay Cove (Quadra Island)

Chart 3539; E of island (102); 0.6 mi N of Granite Bay
Entrance: 50°14.81'N, 125°19.09'W
Anchor: 50°14.93'N, 125°18.68'W

Kanish Bay Cove is easy to enter and sheltered from most weather, but it may receive some southwest chop at times.

There are two storage floats at its north entrance. An old barge and the hull of a boat lie aground on the spit at the north side of the cove; the head of the cove has a drying mud flat.

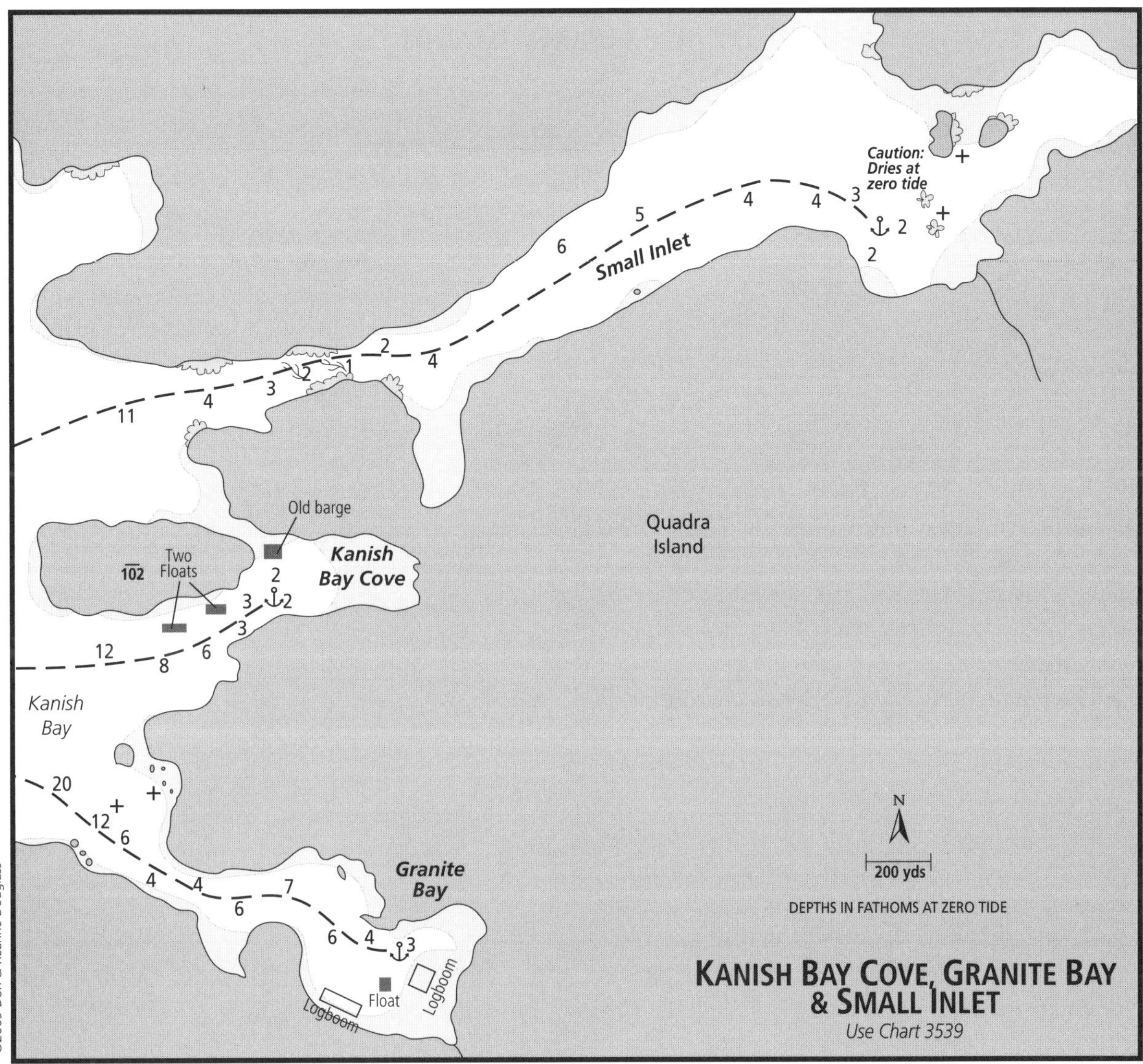

In late summer, as water temperatures rise to about 64°F, red tide and thousands of jellyfish are found in the entrance. The shores are surrounded by second-growth, and sometimes you can spy osprey perched in the branches of the alders.

Anchor in 2 fathoms over sticky grey mud and shells with very good holding.

Small Inlet (Quadra Island)

Chart 3539; at the NE end of Kanish Bay;
1.8 mi E of Bodega Pt
Entrance: 50°15.21'N, 125°19.02'W
Anchor: 50°15.48'N, 125°17.13'W

Small Inlet ... has a narrow entrance with depths of 2.4 m (8 ft). (SD)

Small Inlet is a special place with no development of any kind. Although it can present a foreboding aspect on dark, drizzly days, on sunny summer days it has the feel of an isolated Alpine lake with water that warms to the mid-sixties (F). During these times, red tide may appear in the western half of the inlet, limiting visibility through the water to a few inches.

The inlet is fully protected from all weather; there is no driftwood along shore, and the

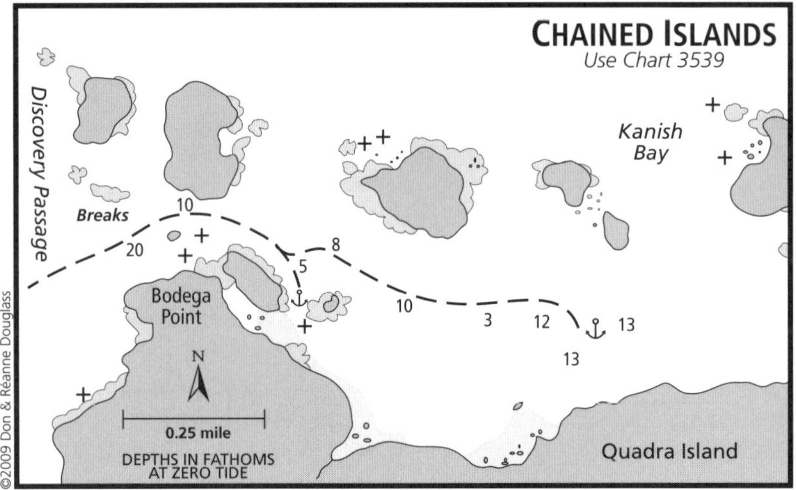

margins are grassy, indicating that chop never enters here. Wind gusts may possibly blow across the 0.5 mile isthmus to Waiatt Bay in Okisollo Channel, but we haven't experienced such gusts.

The entrance to Small Inlet is narrow with a kelp-filled bar just inside its narrows. Favor the south shore to avoid the kelp; the fairway carries about 6 feet at zero tide.

Fishing boats occasionally anchor off the west side of the islets. We prefer the bight deep in the inlet to the south off a gravel and cobblestone beach. The bitter end of the inlet may also offer good anchorage, but the charts may not show all the rocks.

Anchor in 2 fathoms over a mixed bottom of sand and gravel with fair holding.

Chained Islands (Kanish Bay)

Chart 3539; along the S shore of Kanish Bay; immediately E of Bodega Pt
Entrance (0.1 mi NW of Bodega Pt): 50°14.93'N, 125°22.16'W
Anchor (W): 50°14.87'N, 125°21.60'W
Anchor (E): 50°14.81'N, 125°20.71'W

> *Anchorage for small craft can be obtained 0.7 mile east of Bodega Point, south of Chained Islands, in 26 m (85 ft), mud. Good sheltered anchorage can also be obtained in Granite Bay in 7 to 13 m (23 to 43 ft), mud bottom, or in Small Inlet.* (SD)

In the Chained Islands, there are two places where small craft can find protection from southerly winds and chop. The first site is just east of the small island inside Bodega Point (see anchor west above). Avoid the detached rocks awash in the entrance and a somewhat shoaling and rocky south shore. In the cove, most rocks lurk below the surface! There is little swinging room here.

The east anchorage is in the middle of the bay formed by the Chained Islands and the Quadra Island shore. Although depths are fairly substantial, there is a lot of swinging room.

Do not attempt to enter the Chained Islands at night or with restricted visibility—it's too difficult to see the entrance reefs and rocks. If serious southerly weather is expected, we recommend heading to Granite Bay or Small Inlet.

Anchor (west) in 4 fathoms over a hard, rocky bottom with poor holding.

Anchor (east) in 13 fathoms over a rocky bottom with poor-to-fair holding.

Elk Bay (Vancouver Island)

Chart 3539; 4 mi NW of Kanish Bay; 3 mi S of Chatham Pt
Entrance: 50°16.89'N, 125°25.69'W
Anchor: 50°17.00'N, 125°26.15'W

> *Fair anchorage, open to north and east but out of the strength of tidal streams, can be obtained in Elk Bay in a depth of about 26 m (85 ft), mud and sand. The anchorage is often used when awaiting slack water at Seymour Narrows.* (SD)

Elk Bay is a wide bight on the coast of Vancouver Island. It is open and rather deep for cruising boats. For better protection from winds, chop and current, try Otter Bay, 2.5 miles north, or Kanish Bay.

Otter Cove (Vancouver Island)

Chart 3539; immediately S of Chatham Pt
Entrance (mid-ch btwn Snag Rock & Rocky Islets): 50°19.54′N, 125°26.37′W
Anchor: 50°19.47′N, 125°27.10′W

> *Otter Cove … offers sheltered anchorage to small craft.*
> [It] *affords sheltered anchorage to small craft near its head. The approach should be made between Rocky Islets and Limestone island; the passage south of Limestone Island is encumbered by foul ground.* (SD)

Otter Cove is a haven for vessels needing to time their entry northbound into Johnstone Strait or southbound into Discovery Passage.

Otter Cove is a welcome anchorage if Johnstone Strait turns nasty or darkness sets in. You can carefully enter using radar if necessary—the north rock wall makes a very good target—and if you go deep into the apex of the cove, you find protection from most seas. Use the north entrance; there is a large patch of foul ground on the south side. The water is clear, however, and in good visibility you can find a 4-fathom fairway south of Limestone Island if you want a short cut.

Use caution upon anchoring since there are a number of saturated logs lying along the bottom of the cove; in addition, there are rocks and deadheads on the southwest shore. It is a good idea to tie a line to the head of your anchor in case it snags a log. *Caution:* The bottom here is steep-to, rising from 4 fathoms to just one fathom within 30 feet! The anchorage behind Turn Island, 2 miles northwest, is a good alternative and doesn't have this problem.

Anchor in 6 fathoms over mud, sand and shells (and some logs, too!) with good holding.

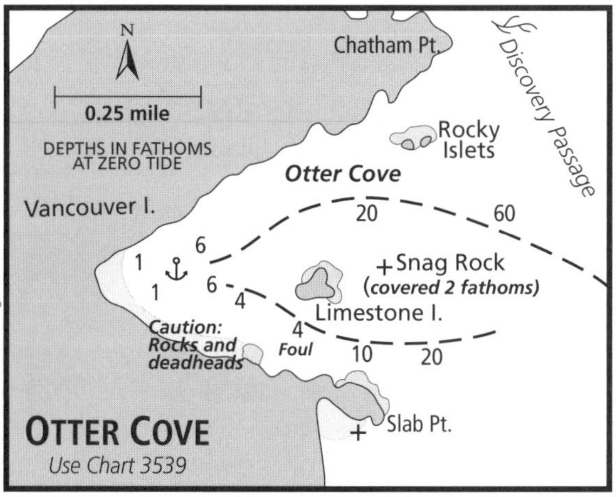

Hoskyn Channel to Surge Narrows

Chart 3539; leads N btwn Quadra Island & Read Island to Surge Narrows
Entrance (S): 50°07.58′N, 125°09.54′W
Entrance (N) (S end of White Rock Passage): 50°14.58′N, 125°06.09′W

Hoskyn Channel and Okisollo Channel are on the east and north shores of Quadra Island. These well-sheltered waters generally receive light traffic and offer nice cruising grounds. Hoskyn Channel meets Okisollo Channel at Surge Narrows. Surge Narrows, Hole in the Wall (which separates Maurelle Island and Sonora Island) and Upper Rapids, north of Hole in the Wall, all have extremely hazardous turbulence and eddies that require careful navigation.

Moulds Bay (Quadra Island)

Charts 3539, 3538, 3312; at the S end of Hoskyn Channel; 0.5 mi NW of Breton Islands
Entrance (S): 50°07.90′N, 125°11.50′W
Entrance (E): 50°08.40′N, 125°10.95′W
Anchor: 50°08.35′N, 125°11.52′W

> *Moulds Bay … is reported to offer good anchorage to small craft in 7 to 10 m (23 to 33 ft). Marine farm facilities are on its east side.* (SD)

Moulds Bay, a small cove on the eastern shore of Quadra Island, affords temporary shelter from west, north and east winds. It is exposed to south and southwest chop. Breton Islands provide some protection from southeasterlies.

As a temporary anchorage there is a small, steep-to site near the west shore of Moulds Bay, in front of a cabin and north of the rock that dries at 10 feet.

The tiny passageway to the northeast of Moulds Bay carries a minimum of 3 to 4 fathoms through the midchannel fairway and is a scenic transit.

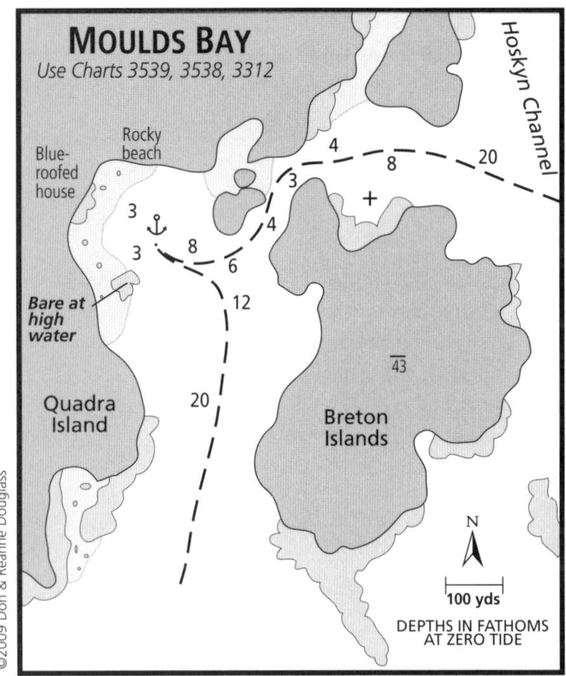

The waters surrounding Moulds Bay contain a variety of sea creatures, including the huge sun star.

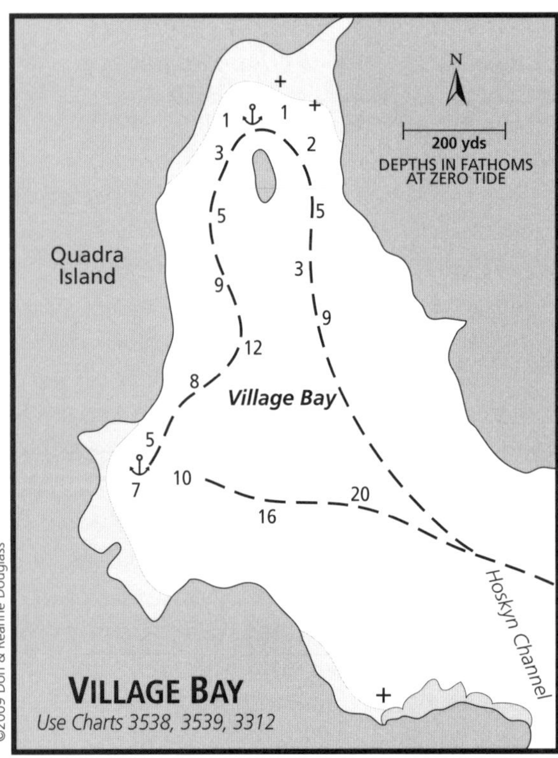

Anchor in 6 to 8 fathoms over a mixed bottom with fair holding.

Village Bay (Quadra Island)

Charts 3538, 3539, 3312; E facing cove at S entrance of Hoskyn Channel
Entrance: 50°09.33'N, 125°10.79'W
Anchor (N nook): 50°09.82'N, 125°11.45'W
Anchor (S): 50°09.43'N, 125°11.65'W

> *Village Bay, in the SE part of Quadra Island, is open to SE but affords temporary anchorage for small vessels in its centre part and for small craft in the SW corner near the head ... A marine farm is in the south part of the bay.* (SD)

Village Bay was formerly the site of a nudist colony visited by early cruising skippers. Only a fish farm and an old cabin on the northern islet remain. The cove offers good shelter from northwest winds, but some driftwood and rocky bluffs indicate that east winds or chop enter Village Bay on occasion.

You can find anchorage north of the fish farm offshore from a cabin and a small rocky beach or in the more protected and secluded north nook. In late summer, jellyfish take over.

The creek delta on the north side of the islet can provide good anchorage. Shelter is very good but swinging room is limited.

Anchor (N nook) in 1 fathom over brown mud and shells with good holding.

Anchor (S) in 4 to 6 fathoms over a hard, rocky bottom with poor-to-fair holding.

Crescent Channel and Bold Point

Chart 3539; 0.6 mi NW of Village Bay; 3.9 mi SW of Surge Narrows
Entrance (W): 50°09.59'N, 125°10.21'W
Entrance (E): 50°09.79'N, 125°09.76'W
Anchor (W): 50°10.01'N, 125°10.54'W
Anchor (N tip Bold Island): 50°10.26'N, 125°10.04'W

> *Crescent Channel ... is entered west of Bold Point, a prominent point at the south end of Bold Island. Marine farm facilities are in Crescent*

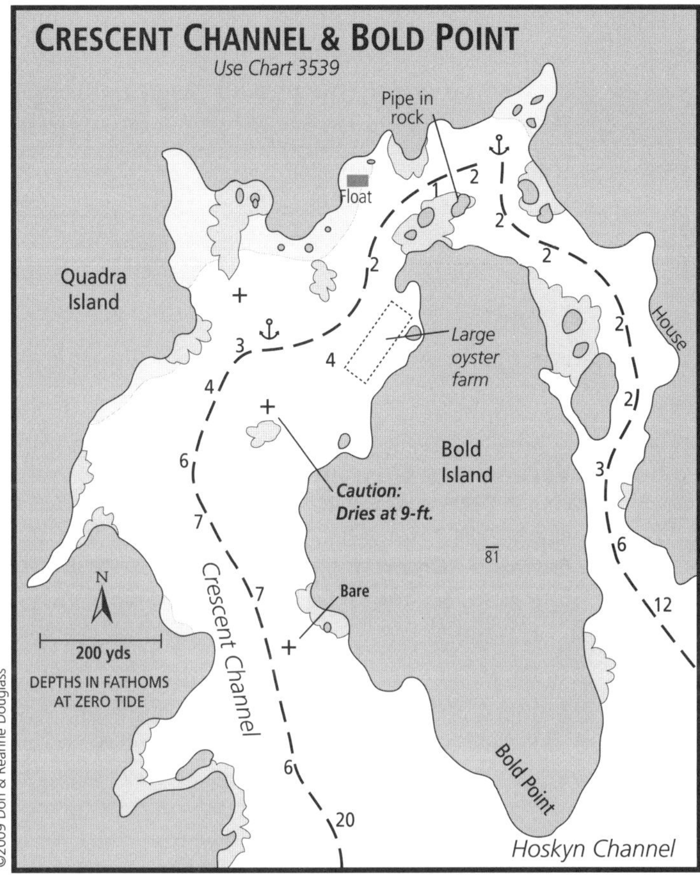

Channel. Well protected anchorage for small craft is available in the channel. Take care to avoid drying rocks and rocks with less than 2 m over them.

Marine farm facilities front Bold Point settlement. (SD)

Crescent Channel oyster culture

Crescent Channel is a unique, tiny channel (almost a canal) surrounding Bold Island. It has the feel and appearance of a turn-of-the-century hideout for smugglers and fish pirates. Small boats can navigate the entire Crescent Channel (slowly) and find good shelter and anchorage with limited swinging room. Today the large oyster farm is the latest in technology, and the home on the north channel is 21st century outback.

When entering the south entrance, avoid the bare rock and the rock to starboard which dries at 9 feet. Once abeam the oyster farm, avoid the tiny bare rock to port awash at high water. A near dead-slow speed and alert lookouts are prudent north of the oyster farm.

The northern tip of Bold Island has a hooked reef extending northeast with a steel pipe that marks rocks near the outer end. Between these rocks and the wooded islets are one or two private mooring buoys, and a small boat can find very sheltered anchorage with limited swinging room. The upper reaches of the channel carry about 1 fathom of water.

Anchorage for larger boats can be found west of the oyster farm; small boats can anchor at the end of the channel.

Anchor (W) in 3 fathoms over a hard, rocky bottom with poor holding.

Anchor (N tip) in 1 fathom, sand and cobblestone bottom with poor-to-fair holding.

Conville Bay (Quadra Island)

Chart 3539; on the W side of Hoskyn Channel; 1 mi NE of Bold Island
Entrance: 50°10.76'N, 125°08.95'W

An isolated 5.8 m shoal lies 0.3 mile south of Conville Point. Marine farm facilities in Conville Bay... (SD)

Conville Bay is an open bight affording shelter from westerlies but is exposed to the south.

Hjorth Bay (Read Island)

Chart 3539; 1.8 mi NE of Bold Island; 2.9 mi SE of Surge Narrows
Entrance: 50°10.77'N, 125°07.69'W
Anchor: 50°10.62'N, 125°07.33'W

> *Anchorage for small craft can be obtained on the east side of Hoskyn Channel in Hjorth Bay* ... (SD)

Hjorth Bay provides good protection from southerly weather deep in the cove. The islets and the shallow drying flat on the east shore provide excellent kayak haul-outs and campsites and are interesting to explore.

The south beach of Hjorth Bay is steep-to, but anchorage can be found close offshore.

Anchor in 6 to 8 fathoms over a mixed bottom of unrecorded holding.

Boulton Bay ("Melibe Anchorage"), Sheer Point (Read Island)

Chart 3539; 1.2 mi N of Hjorth Bay; 1.7 mi SE of Surge Narrows
Entrance: 50°11.81'N, 125°07.62'W
Anchor: 50°12.01'N, 125°07.53'W

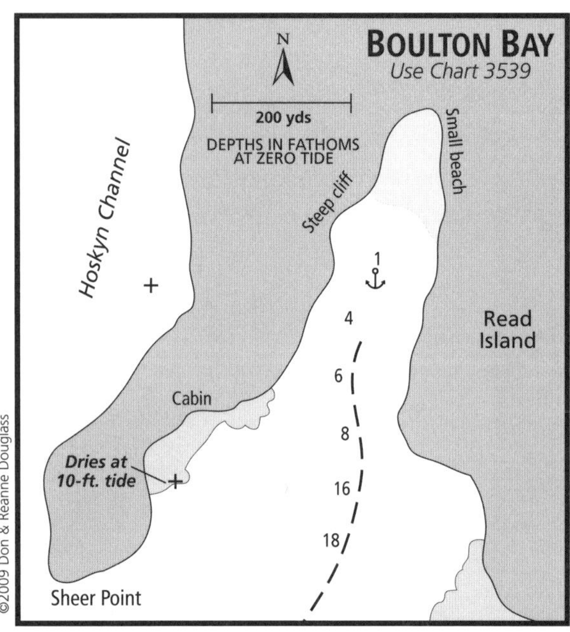

Boulton Bay, also known as Melibe Anchorage, offers very good shelter from prevailing northwest winds by virtue of bold Sheer Point, but is exposed to southerlies. There is a cabin on the west shore just north of the off-lying rock which dries at 10 feet. This is a quiet and picturesque place.

Anchorage can be taken off the small sand and gravel beach at the head of the bay.

Anchor in 4 fathoms over a mixed bottom of unrecorded holding.

Whiterock Passage

Chart 3537 inset, 3539, 3312; btwn Read & Maurelle Is; connects Hoskyn Ch to Calm Ch
Entrance (S range): 50°14.58'N, 125°06.87'W
Entrance (N range): 50°15.07'N, 125°06.09'W

> *Whiterock Passage ... [provides] a route to avoid the strong currents in Surge Narrows and Hole in the Wall. The passage has drying banks on both sides and is obstructed at the south end by an islet and several drying rocks. A channel with a least depth of 1.5 m (5 ft) has been dredged through the bank. Several cabins lie along the shores of the passage,*
>
> *Tidal streams in Whiterock Passage are weak, usually less than 2 kn. The flood stream sets north.*
>
> *Whiterock Passage range 1 lights ... bearing 065 1/2° lead through the south part of the dredged channel.*
>
> *Whiterock Passage range 2 lights ... bearing 211 1/2° lead through the north part of the dredged channel.* (SD)

Whiterock Passage is a good small-boat route but it requires careful navigation. The dredged channel cuts across a rock and a boulder shoal between Read and Maurelle islands. Two sets of range marks (yellow flashing lights) define the proper route. Current seldom exceeds 2 knots, but sailboats or other deep-draft boats need to make sure they are not set sideways by the current. Follow Chart 3537 inset. Note: The bearings noted in the *Sailing Directions* are true bearings and refer to entering from the south and north ends respectively. (Subtract 22° from true bearings to give magnetic bearings.)

Surge Narrows Settlement

Charts 3537 inset, 3539; on the E side of Hoskyn Ch; 1.1 mi E of Beazley Passage; 0.9 mi S of Whiterock Passage
Entrance: 50°13.64'N, 125°06.84'W
Public float: 50°13.62'N, 125°06.71'W

> *Surge Narrows settlement, ... NE of Surge Point, has a post office (V0P 1W0) on the public wharf.* (SD)

The public float at Surge Narrows Settlement, with its characteristic red painted gangway, serves the residents of this part of Read Island. Surge Narrows General Store now has its own float, so you don't have to rely on the public float if you need to pick up a few provisions. This area is a good place to wait for slack water at Beazley Passage or Whiterock Passage. Be careful to avoid the rock marked with buoy Q1 west of the public float.

Approaching Surge Narrows

Surge Narrows (Beazley Passage)

Charts 3537 inset, 3539; 7.5 mi NE of Heriot Bay; 4.2 mi SE of Octopus Islands Marine Park
Entrance (E): 50°13.47'N, 125°08.33'W
Entrance (W, Beazley Passage): 50°13.65'N, 125°09.01'W

> *Surge Narrows ... joins Hoskyn Channel to Okisollo Channel leading SW of Antonio Point. It is obstructed at its SE end by the Welsford Islands and the Settlers Group. The name Surge Narrows is applied locally to the entire route, from Hoskyn Channel through Beasley Passage, described below, to Okisollo Channel. This route should be navigated only at or near slack water.*
>
> *Beasley Passage, between Sturt Island and Peck Island, is the only navigable passage through or around Settlers Group into Okisollo Chanel. It has a minimum width of 60 m. Tusko Rock, which dries 1.6 m, lies at the west end of the passage.*
>
> *Anchorage in the vicinity of Settlers Group is not recommended because of strong tidal streams and poor holding.*
>
> *Tidal differences for Surge Narrows (Index No. 8045), referenced on Point Atkinson, are in "Tide Tables, Volume 5."*
>
> *The strongest tidal streams in the Surge Narows area occur in Beasley Passage, where at large tides they reack 11½ kn on the flood and 9½ kn on the ebb. Duration of slack water throughout Surge Narrows varies from 5 to 11 minutes. Daily predictions for times of slack water, and times and rates of maximum flood and ebb streams, are tabulated for current station Beasley Passage (Index No. 5200) in "Tide Tables, Volume 6."* (SD)

Surge Narrows (Beazley Passage) is much smaller than the other rapids, but it can pack a similar punch over its short distance. Beazley Passage is the recommended route through the Settlers Group Islands. It is recommended that transit of Surge Narrows be made at slack water. Check Tide Tables, Volume 6, for the predicted time and arrive early. If your boat has the power, it is not difficult to push through on moderate floods by using back eddies on the north shore to approach the narrowest point and then powering through. *Caution:* Tusko Rock is marked with a large kelp patch. On an ebb current, reduced steering may be a problem. If the ebb is strong enough, it may drag the kelp under, making identification of Tusko Rock difficult. Tusko Rock is located on the northeast side of Beazley Passage west of Sturt Island.

Okisollo Channel

Chart 3537, 3539; separates Quadra Island from Mauralle & Sonora Islands
Entrance (S): 50°14.19'N, 125°09.97'W
Entrance (W): 50°17.18'N, 125°23.20'W

> *Okisollo Channel leads from Surge Narrows to Discovery Passage ... Because of the currents and shoal rocks in Surge Narrows, Upper and Lower Rapids and Hole in the Wall, the route through Okisollo Channel is suitable only for small vessels and small craft.* (SD)

Okisollo Channel has little, if any, through-traffic and the winds are calm most of the time, making this a quiet and secluded cruising ground. Old clearcuts are visible along the north shore.

Spacious and lovely Okisollo Channel

Yeatman Bay (Quadra Island)

Chart 3537; 1.5 mi NW of Beazley Passage
Entrance: 50°14.12'N, 125°10.90'W
Anchor: 50°14.01'N, 125°10.86'W

> *Anchorage for vessels awaiting slack water in Surge Narrows can be obtained in Yeatman Bay. Bottom near shore is rock and the holding ground indifferent.* (SD)

Yeatman Bay is somewhat open to occasional northwest winds. Several nooks on Maurelle Island offer shelter from northwest winds for small boats, and can be used to wait for slack water at Surge Narrows. Temporary anchorage can be found in the head of the bay off the drying flat that is steep-to.

Anchor in about 6 fathoms over sand and gravel with fair holding.

Waiatt Bay (Quadra Island)

Chart 3537, 3539; immediately S of Octopus Is Marine Park; 4.0 mi NW of Surge Narrows
Entrance: 50°16.13'N, 125°12.90'W
Central narrows (mid-ch): 50°16.18'N, 125°13.55'W
Anchor (head of bay): 50°15.82'N, 125°15.31'W

> *Waiatt Bay affords well protected anchorage for small vessels in its centre and for small craft near its head or in small bays in the marine park. The bottom is mud with some sand and shale near shore.* (SD)

Waiatt Bay, two miles south of Hole in the Wall, is a large, landlocked bay with room for a number of boats; unlimited swinging room is available over a flat, shallow bottom. The bay can be entered by three main routes; each is narrow with submerged rocks difficult to position correctly. *Caution:* Alert bow lookouts and slow speed are required. The northern route, perhaps the safest, passes just west of islands (50) and (71) along the eastern border of Octopus

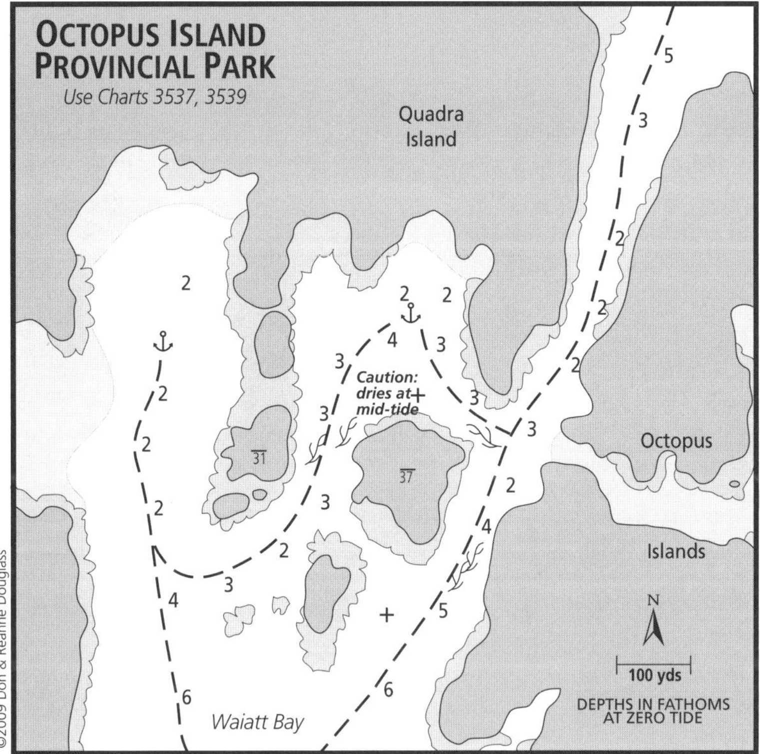

Islands Marine Park. The central approach passes north of island (55) and south of island (71), avoiding the islets and reef as well as the rock which dries at 4 feet on the starboard side. In summer, kelp usually marks the route, but don't count on it. The third route, to the south, passes south of island (55) and follows the south shore west. The large-scale Chart 3537 is very useful.

Anchorage is frequently taken along the south shore or deep near its head where a primitive trail connects with Small Inlet 0.5 mile west.

Anchor in 3 fathoms over mud and shells with very good holding.

Puffin *at Octopus Islands Marine Park*

Octopus Islands Provincial Park

Charts 3537, 3539; on N side of Waiatt Bay;
1.4 mi SW of Hole in the Wall
Entrance (NE): 50°16.99'N, 125°13.32'W
Entrance (S, Waiatt Bay): 50°16.39'N, 125°13.82'W
Anchor (W): 50°16.74'N, 125°13.96'W
Anchor (E): 50°16.76'N, 125°13.68'W

> *Octopus Islands Marine Park ... is undeveloped.* (SD)

Octopus Islands Provincial Park, on the east side of Quadra Island, is a landlocked area offering seclusion. It is a great place for exploring the shoreline and islets by dinghy or kayak. Large vessels do not enter Okisollo Channel and, except for a few small commercial fishing boats working the area, there is no through-traffic; the area is undeveloped and pristine. Kayakers can haul out and camp ashore at the creek outlet on the western shore.

Entrance can be made by the north entrance shown on the diagram or by the central entrance to Waiatt Bay described above.

Anchorage can be taken in either of the north areas with good shelter. The area is open to the south and, in heavy weather, the east arm would be more protected, but swinging room is limited. Stern ties are useful in Octopus Island Marine Park since fir and cedar grow right to the water's edge.

Anchor in either arm in 2 fathoms over mud with good holding.

Bodega Anchorage (Quadra Island)

Chart 3537; N of Octopus Islands; 1.2 mi SE of Upper Rapids
Entrance (0.18 mi W of Chasina Island): 50°17.16′N, 125°13.28′W
Anchor: 50°17.16′N, 125°13.49′W

> *Bodega Anchorage … is useful for craft awaiting slack water for passage through Hole in the Wall or Upper Rapids. Holding is reported to be good. Booming grounds line the south shore.* (SD)

Bodega Anchorage is an open bight on Quadra Island's east shore, 0.7 mile southwest of Hole in the Wall. It is used principally to store logbooms or as a temporary anchorage with a good view of conditions at the entrance to the rapids.

Anchor in 5 fathoms over a mixed bottom of unrecorded holding.

Hole in the Wall

Chart 3537, 3539; 0.7 nile NE of Bodega Anchorage; leads from Okisollo to Calm Chs
Entrance (W): 50°17.85′N, 125°12.82′W
Entrance (E): 50°19.80′N, 125°07.60′W

> *Hole in the Wall [is] entered between Springer Point and Etta Point … Hole in the Wall is normally used by commercial traffic in preference to Surge Narrows, as the channel in the former is wider. Hole in the Wall should only be navigated at or near slack water.*
>
> *Two shoals lie in the middle of the west entrance to Hole in the Wall. In the narrows a drying rock lies close off the north shore and another lies close off the south shore.*
>
> *Tidal streams in Hole in the Wall reach 12 kn on the flood and 10 kn on the ebb in the narrows at the west entrance of the channel. The flood sets NE and the duration of slack, on the average, is 4 minutes. The stream in the east entrance, between Bernard Point and Bassett Point, is about 2 kn. Secondary current station Hole in the Wall, referenced on Seymour Narrows, is given in the Tide Tables, Volume 6.* (SD)

Calm cruising in the wind shadow, Octopus Islands

Hole in the Wall can have strong turbulence and eddies along the north side of the west entrance on flood tides, and west and south of the west entrance on ebb tides. Once clear of the west narrows, the current quickly dies down to about 2 knots through the rest of the eastern end of the passage.

When approaching Hole in the Wall from the southwest side, stay north and avoid the two 3- to 4-fathom rocks off the west entrance which cause a good part of the turbulence and eddies.

Florence Cove (Hole in the Wall)

Charts 3537, 3539; indents the S shore of Hole in the Wall
Entrance: 50°18.78′N, 125°10.09′W
Anchor: 50°18.62′N, 125°10.09′W

> *Florence Cove indents the south shore of Hole in the Wall. Well positioned as an anchorage for small vessels, reports of its suitability are mixed. It has been reported that log hauling cables were dumped in the sound end of the cove and weed has fouled anchors. Other reports indicate that it offers good, quiet anchorage.* (SD)

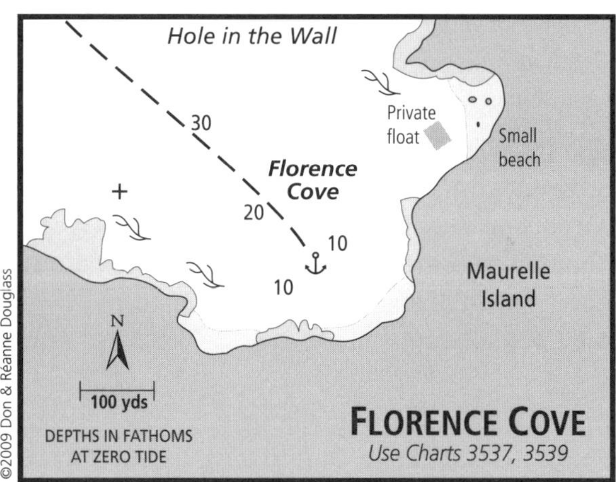

Florence Cove provides temporary anchorage close to the southern steep-to shore and out of the tidal stream. It is a good place to wait for slack water when you are westbound. Avoid the rock off the western islet and the logbooms and private float on the east shore. Bodega Anchorage is the preferred place to wait and watch on the west side of the narrows.

Anchor in about 10 fathoms over gravel with poor-to fair-holding.

Diamond Bay (Sonora Island)

Chart 3537; halfway btwn Hole in the Wall & Upper Rapids
Entrance: 50°18.05'N, 125°13.40'W
Anchor: 50°18.12'N, 125°13.38'W

Diamond Bay and the bay close north have private floats in them (1984). (SD)

Diamond Bay is out of the main tidal stream and can provide temporary or emergency anchorage or a place to await calmer water during spring tides.

Anchor in 2 to 3 fathoms near the head of the bay.

Upper Rapids

Chart 3537, 3539; btwn Cooper Pt on Quadra Island & islands off E shore of Sonora Island
Entrance (NW): 50°18.47'N, 125°14.23'W
Entrance (SE): 50°17.81'N, 125°13.40'W

Upper Rapids ... has a maximum rate of 9 kn; overfalls and eddies are extremely dangerous. Secondary current station Okisollo Channel (Upper Rapids), referenced on Seymour Narrows, is given in the Tide Tables, Volume 6. Upper Rapids should be navigated only at or near slack water.

Dangers.—Bentley Rock, which dries 0.1 m (awash), and a reef with 3.4 m (11 ft) over it close SE, lie near mid-steam at the SE end of Upper Rapids. A rock, which dries 0.1 m (awash) lies close offshore SE of Cooper Point. (SD)

While the currents on spring tides (9 knots) are not as great as the other major rapids in this part of the British Columbia coast, Upper and Lower Rapids need to be treated with respect. They have an added obstacle—shallow rocks in the fairway causing overfalls, especially on large ebbs—as well as turbulence and eddies. The upper overfalls are not difficult for most boats on neap tides and when the current is 3 knots or less.

Owen Bay (Sonora Island)

Chart 3537, 3539; immediately NE of Upper Rapids; 1.1 mi E of Lower Rapids
Entrance (0.17 mi SE of Walters Pt): 50°18.79'N, 125°14.10'W
Public float: 50°18.63'N, 125°13.41'W
Anchor (head of bay): 50°19.41'N, 125°13.40'W

Owen Bay settlement, on the SE shore, has no fuel, supplies or other services. The public wharf has floats providing 17 m of berthing.

Good anchorage is available in Owen Bay over mud bottom. It is reported that the islands SW of the wharf should be avoided as the tidal currents rush between them with remarkable force. (SD)

Owen Bay is well sheltered from all the wind, chop and chaos of the saltwater "rivers" to the west and south. The recommended entrance is on the north side of Grant Island; the south side is foul. The south side can be used as a dinghy passage near high water slack. The public float serves the local houses and allows you to use the trail that leads to Hole in the Wall. The trail becomes overgrown near its end.

Underpowered boats, transiting Okisollo

Channel from the north, should time their arrival at Owen Bay at slack. Be aware that the entrance to Owen Bay can have whirlpools and rip tides that carry you towards the reefs.

Good protection is available in all weather. You can anchor off the public float or almost anywhere in the big bay with plenty of swinging room, avoiding the logbooms and the narrow fast-flowing channels between the islands immediately west.

Anchor (head of bay) in 4 fathoms over mud with very good holding.

Lower Rapids

Chart 3537, 3539; S of Okis Islands
Position: 50°18.60'N, 125°15.80'W

> *Lower Rapids ... are obstructed by Gypsy Shoal, which has two heads; the SW rock dries 0.4 m (1 ft) and the NE rock has 0.2 m (1 ft) over it. The fairway passes south of Gypsy Shoal; it should be navigated only at or near slack water. Lower Rapids can be avoided by passing north of Okis Islands where the channel is free of dangers although the currents are still strong.* (SD)

The fairway south of Gypsy Shoal is about 15 fathoms and not difficult when the current is 3 knots or less. The overfalls created by Gypsy Shoal can be avoided by taking a short detour north into Barnes Bay, staying north of all of the Okis Islands.

Owen Bay

A government dock in Owen Bay provides access to a nearly uninhabited part of Sonora Island. From the dock you can take a 30-minute hike, ending just east of Springer Point for a view of Okisollo Channel and Hole in the Wall as well as the Octopus Islands.

The placid waters of the bay reflect tree-covered knolls. In contrast to the turbulent channels boaters must pass through on the way, the calm of Owen Bay is remarkable—even downright eerie, some say.

Author Liv Kennedy lived here as a child and has visited several times since. In her book *Coastal Villages* (Harbour Publishing, 1991), she recounts her own and others' tales of creepy happenings. Boaters have reported unexplained noises, giant footprints on shore and eccentric inhabitants. Kennedy also tells about meteorites, drownings and lodges constructed and then abandoned. Her friends Alex and Margaret Cameron disappeared from their boat one day after writing in their logbook, leaving behind a pet cat; a search turned up no bodies. Over the years Owens Bay has had its share of sinister events.

Ghost stories have a way of perpetuating themselves. The only way to combat them is to visit Owen Bay yourself—if you dare.

Barnes Bay (Sonora Island)

Chart 3537, 3539; on Okis Islands; 0.7 mi N of Lower Rapids
Entrance: 50°19.38'N, 125°15.90'W
Anchor: 50°19.43'N, 125°15.37'W

> *Barnes Bay affords anchorage for vessels in its east part and is reported to afford safe anchorage for small craft behind the islet in its east extremity. The bottom is reported to be rock. Booming grounds line its shores.* (SD)

Barnes Bay and the cove to its west are active logboom areas. While safe anchorages can be found there, the bay tends to be noisy and the bottom foul. During recent trips, we have found good secure anchorage deep in the bay on the southwest side of the islet.

Anchor in 4 fathoms over sand and mud with good holding.

Pulton Bay (Quadra Island)

Chart 3537; 0.5 mi SW of Lower Rapids
Entrance: 50°18.36'N, 125°16.35'W

> *Pulton Bay has a drying reef close off its SE shore and a house with a boathouse and private floats on its SW shore.*
>
> *Booming grounds line the south shore 0.5 mile west of Pulton Point.* (SD)

Pulton Bay offers easy access to protection from southerly winds if needed.

Chonat Bay (Quadra Island)

Chart 3537; 2.2 mi SW of Lower Rapids
Entrance: 50°17.53'N, 125°19.13'W

> *Chonat Bay ... is used for storing logbooms.*
>
> *Anchorage is available in the middle of the*

bay, but note the shoal 0.1 mile SW of Chonat Point. (SD)

The logbooms mentioned in *Sailing Directions* are no longer in Chonat Bay. Anchorage can be found off the drying mud flat, avoiding the rocks marked by kelp.

Metcalf Islands Bight (Quadra Island)

Chart 3537; 1.8 mi SW of Chonat Bay; 1.5 mi SE of the Cinque Islands
Entrance: 50°17.07′N, 125°21.94′W

Metcalf Islands lie close to the south shore near the west entrance of Okisollo Channel.

Fresh water is reported to be obtainable from a waterfall on the Sonora Island shore, north of Metcalf Islands. (SD)

Metcalf Islands Bight can be a noisy log dump on occasion; however, commercial fishing boats use this as a convenient anchorage away from Discovery Passage traffic.

The tiny unnamed cove on the north side of the Okisollo Channel and 0.35 mile north of Metcalf Islands Bight is a good kayak haul-out site. The small cove 0.53 mile west of the kayak haul-out provides good anchorage in fair weather.

Cordero Channel from Yuculta Rapids to Chancellor Channel

Chart 3543; extends from Yuculta & Arran rapids on the E to 3.5 mi W of Green Pt Rapids
Entrance (E, 0.4 mi SW of Harbott Pt): 50°21.37′N, 125°08.52′W
Bute Inlet entrance (0.17 mi NE of Turnback Pt): 50°25.42′N, 125°07.73′W
Entrance (W, 0.27 mi SW of Lyall Island): 50°26.46′N, 125°35.86′W

Cordero Channel, whose east end is entered either SW or north of Stuart Island, leads about 20 miles NW and west to join Chancellor Channel north of West Thurlow Island. The route between the Strait of Georgia and Johnstone Strait leading through Calm and Cordero Channels is more protected and has less traffic than that through Discovery Passage. (SD)

Cordero Channel is a saltwater, two-way reversible "river;" the strong currents favor skippers who are alert and study the tide and current tables and punish those who do not.

Yuculta Rapids

Chart 3543 inset; 22 mi N of Campbell River; 27.5 mi NW of Lund; 37.5 mi E of Port Neville
Entrance (S, 0.4 mi SW of Harbott Pt): 50°21.37′N, 125°08.52′W
Entrance (N, mid-ch btwn Whirlpool Pt & Sea Lion Rock): 50°23.11′N, 125°08.94′W

The Yucultas is a local name used to cover the Yuculta Rapids proper, Gillard and Barber Passages and Dent Rapids.

Strong tidal streams with overfalls and, at times, violent eddies and whirlpools exist in parts of Cordero Channel. These streams reach maximum velocities during large tides of 7 kn in Yuculta Rapids, 13 kn in Barber and Gillard Passages, 9 kn in Arran and Dent Rapids and 7 kn in Greene Point Rapids.

Predictions for the times of turn to flood and ebb and maximum rates in Gillard Passage, and time differences and maximum rates for secondary current stations Yuculta Rapids and Dent Island, referenced on Gillard Passage, and for Greene Point Rapids, referenced on Seymour Narrows, are given in the Tide Tables, Volume 6. The times of turn to flood and ebb at Arran Rapids are the same as at Dent Rapids.

Due to the strength of the tidal streams and the turbulence that develops in various areas, navigation of Yuculta, Arran, Dent and Greene Point Rapids, and Gillard and Barber Passages, should not be attempted other than at or near slack water, at which time they can be taken without difficulty.

Small craft with low power bound westward are advised to approach Yuculta Rapids about 1 hour before turn to ebb, taking advantage of a backeddy along the Stuart Island shore until off Kellsey Point, then to cross to the Sonora Island shore where there is a prevailing northerly current. This should allow time to transit Gillard and Dent Rapids before the ebb current reaches full force. If late for slack water and unsure of Dent Rapids, small craft are advised to wait in Big Bay for the next slack water. (SD)

The Yucultas can be vicious and are worth taking seriously! (See sidebar.) We once followed an overloaded fishing boat through the rapids well after the flood had begun and watched it take some alarming deep rolls in Devils Hole 0.2 mile south of Little Dent Island. (See photos.) We also heard the story from residents of Big Bay about a drum seiner that went through the rapids on a huge flood in the 1990s against the advice of the locals and flipped with four people aboard; all were lost. If you follow *Sailing Directions*, you should have no trouble.

After traversing Dent Rapids, you can enter Johnstone Strait at Turn Island by heading southeast on the east side of East Thurlow Island, with a possible stop at Thurston Bay. Or you can pass between the two Thurlow Islands and stop by the resort at Blind Channel.

If you want maximum protection from the current, wind, and chop of Johnstone Strait, continue west through Green Point Rapids, joining Johnstone Strait in Current Passage. Or you can hug the mainland coast, passing through Whirlpool Rapids and entering Johnstone Strait near Blenkinsop Bay, just east of Port Neville.

We have tried all the various combinations; under strong westerlies or in unsettled weather, we recommend hugging the mainland coast. This slower route is also the more scenic route.

Big Bay (Stuart Island)

Chart 3543 inset; on W shore of Stuart Island; midway btwn Yuculta & Dent Rapids
Entrance: 50°23.51'N, 125°08.63'W
Public float: 50°23.51'N, 125°08.20'W

Big Bay, formerly the home of Big Bay Resort, has been closed and returned to its natural state. The Stuart Island Community Association Dock re-decked and re-floated the public docks in 2005, and additional floats are planned for the future. Also in process are other facilities for pleasure craft, including a store with a large deck that overlooks the bay.

Least depth at the inner float is about 1 fathom at zero tide. Boats of deep draft should moor at the outer float. Be aware that even at the float, strong current can be felt at times.

Yuculta Rapids

At Yuculta Rapids, don't be surprised to find Boston Whalers with 50-hp outboards and 10-hp kickers darting in all directions and on all stages of the tide. They are in search of the famous salmon found in these fast, turbulent waters. These boats are skippered by professional guides who do this every day in the summer and they know the rapids well—or they don't survive! Everyone on board wears a full survival suit, regardless of the air temperature. The boats plane across the surface, with little area below water for the eddies to act upon. Stories are heard about these agile, aggressive rigs flipping over and people being lost in whirlpools while their friends watch helplessly. So don't be intimidated by these planing boat antics or be bullied into thinking that the laws on prudence have been repealed! Boats that are slow or under-powered, have deep draft, low freeboard or are top-heavy, are at risk in traversing Yuculta Rapids. You should carefully plan and execute your strategy to transit the rapids with your own limitations in mind.

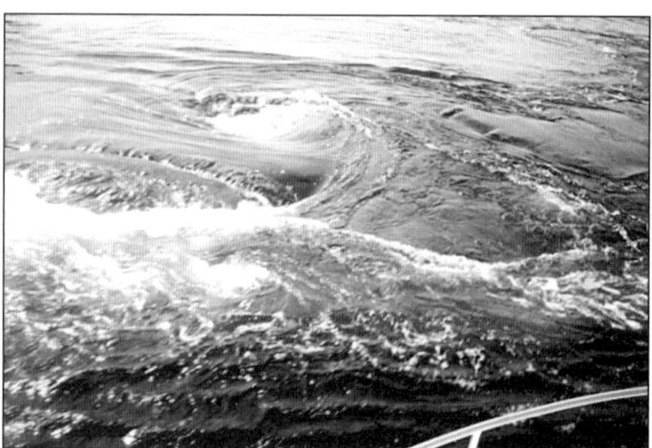

Yuculta Rapids are worth taking seriously!

From the floats you can watch the heavy tidal action churning a half mile west. Locals do not advise anchoring in the bay. The surrounding passageways and islands are swept by strong currents. Take care when traversing the waterways.

Gillard Passage

Chart 3543 inset; lies btwn Gillard & Jimmy Judd Islands
Entrance (E): 50°23.55'N, 125°09.24'W
Entrance (W): 50°23.62'W, 125°09.78'W

Stuart Island

Approaching Stuart Island from the south through the Yuculta Rapids, you might feel a little like Odysseus as he sailed between the six-headed monster Scylla and the whirlpool Charybdis. You'll go between Sea Lion Rock and Whirlpool Point before turning right into the island's docking area at Big Bay. Hopefully, unlike Odysseus, you won't lose any of your crewmembers to the perils of the journey.

In 2004 the government dock was acquired by the Stuart Island Community Association and many upgrades have taken place. Besides 1,100 feet of public moorage, there is fresh water, a store, laundromat, shower and espresso bar. Boaters can visit the refurbished Community Hall and enjoy the grassy uplands.

Stuart Island is also home to resorts owned by wealthy businessmen who fly in deep-pocketed tourists for sport fishing, golf, hot-tubbing and other recreational pursuits.

A controversy over fish farms is ongoing. An alliance of conservationists, lodge owners and the Homalco First Nations oppose fish farming on the island because they are afraid escaping fish might spread disease to wild stock.

Besides five species of salmon, the neighboring waters and lands are home to bald eagles, Dall's porpoises, otters, orcas and black bears. Grizzly bears can be seen roaming the beaches along Bute Inlet. At the Community Store you can arrange for a fishing guide or a wildlife tour.

The island's highest point is Mount Muehle at 1,634 feet, accessible by foot from Big Bay. Another popular hike goes through the forest to Eagle Lake.

Dock space can be reserved by calling 250.202. DOCK (3625).

Gillard Passage ... is used by vessels bound east or west. Shoal depths, including Jimmy Judd Reef, fringe the south shore of Jimmy Judd Island.

Dangerous whirlpools form east of Gillard Islands between 2 hours after turn to flood and 1 hour before turn to ebb. (SD)

Barber Passage

Chart 3543 inset; leads btwn Jimmy Judd & Stuart Islands
Entrance (S, 0.13 mi SW of Hesler Pt): 50°23.61'N, 125°02.00'W
Entrance (N, 0.14 mi NE of Jimmy Judd I): 50°23.88'N, 125°09.22'W

A drying rock and shoal depths fringe the east side of the passage near Hesler Point. A private float is in the cove 0.7 mile NNE of Asman Point. (SD)

Arran Rapids

Chart 3543; connects Cordero Channel to Bute Inlet
Entrance (W, 0.15 mi W of Arran Pt): 50°25.10'N, 125°08.60'W
Entrance (E): 50°25.42'N, 125°07.73'W

Arran Rapids ... have Arran Point and Turnback Point on the south side. (SD)

Arran Rapids are swift (up to 14 knots at spring tides), but the channel is deep with mostly laminar flow.

Mermaid Bay (Dent Island)

Chart 3543 inset; S side of Dent Island
Entrance: 50°24.14'N, 125°11.36'W
Anchor: 50°24.22'N, 125°11.12'W

Mermaid Bay ... is a mooring ground for tugs with logbooms awaiting slack water to navigate the rapids. (SD)

Mermaid Bay is known for the tugboat name signs tacked to trees on the north side of the bay, attesting to the fact that vessels missing slack water take refuge between the rapids.

Anchor in 5 fathoms over sand with unrecorded holding.

Air photo by permission of Ministry of Environment, Lands and Parks, Geographic Data B.C.

Yuculta and Arran Rapids on ebb

Air photo by permission of Ministry of Environment, Lands and Parks, Geographic Data B.C.

Dent Rapids on flood

Dent Rapids

Chart 3543 inset; lies btwn Little Dent & Sonora Islands
Entrance (E): 50°24.02'N, 125°11.91'W
Entrance (W): 50°24.60'N, 125°12.92'W

Dent Rapids: Devil's Hole starting to develop on flood

Dent Rapids ... are swift and turbulent with dangerous overfalls and eddies.

Caution.—A shoal, with 6.4 m (21 ft) over it, 0.5 mile NW of Dent Islands light, creates dangerous turbulence and a large overfall on ebb tides.

Dangers.—Secord Rock, a drying rock NNW of Horn Point, and Denham Rock, ESE of Denham Islet, sometimes marked by kelp, are isolated dangers. Secord Rock is marked by a private buoy (1984). A shoal with 3.7 m (12 ft) over it lies 0.1 mile offshore, 0.5 mile north of Horn Point. (SD)

Devils Hole (Dent Rapids)

Chart 3543 inset; 0.45 mi W of Dent Island; 0.15 mi SW of Little Dent Island
Position (approximate): 50°24.23'N, 125°12.37'W

Deep roll to starboard

Deep roll to port

Dent Rapids

As the *Bella Nova* steamed westward through Gillard Passage toward Dent Island, the water was like satin, and ahead, a faint line of white indicated the beginning of the flood current. Since it was just the beginning of the flood, I chose to push my 7-knot-fishboat through, definitely a mistake. By the time I realized the state of the current, I discovered just how turbulent Dent Rapids can be and also how limited my options had become. Dent Point was spitting out whirlpools thirty feet across, and between two of these whirlpools, the *Bella Nova* chugged up a three-foot overfall. I could not turn my small boat around, because to do so would have put me smack in the middle of one or another of these violent eddies. *Bella Nova,* whirlpools and all, were propelled laterally across the channel at a horrifying speed and I feared being dashed onto the shore of Sonora Island. Slowly, slowly, I could see that we were creeping ahead of the point and, after a few minutes, we were once again in smooth water, making a couple of knots or so.

It seems that I had planned on reaching Yuculta Rapids, not Dent, at the time of slack water. And upon reading the tide tables a little more closely, I discovered that I had done this on the second largest tide of the year!

After that experience, I have learned to arrive at Gillard Passage exactly at slack; when westbound, I will time my arrival for slack water at Dent Rapids.

—Kevin Monahan

In Devils Hole, violent eddies and whirlpools form between 2 hours after turn to flood and 1 hour before turn to ebb. Favour the Sonora Island shore of Dent Rapids. (SD)

Devils Hole is a major turbulent patch of water on a flood tide and can be dangerous to small or top-heavy vessels. (See photos taken by the authors less than one hour after flood began.)

Tugboat Passage

Chart 3543; btwn Dent & Little Dent Islands
Entrance (S): 50°24.30'N, 125°12.00'W
Entrance (N): 50°24.62'N, 125°12.02'W

Tugboat Passage ... is not recommended because of islets, shoals and confused currents, but is used extensively by tugs; local knowledge is necessary.

Tugs towing logbooms will frequently be found moving with the last of the ebb from Horn Point to Burnt Bluff and from there through Tugboat Passage to Mermaid Bay, or from Mermaid Bay through Gillard Passage. Tugs with booms can also be encountered at Dent Rapids on the turn of the flood. (SD)

Passing between Dent and Little Dent islands, Tugboat Passage is an alternative to Dent Rapids and Devils Hole. We have no quantitative information on their differences. The local aluminum school boat that services the students on either side of Dent Rapids uses the tiny, narrow passage on the east side of Dent Island, frequently finding a steep standing wave in the process.

Horn Bay

Chart 3543; due N of Little Dent Island
Entrance: 50°25.25'N, 125°12.52'W
Anchor: 50°25.27'N, 125°12.39'W

Anchor in 1 to 2 fathoms over sand and gravel with fair holding.

Frederick Arm

Chart 3543; enter W of Gomer Island
Entrance: 50°27.41'N, 125°17.02'W

Frederick Arm ... has no dangers beyond 0.15 mile from its shores ... Depths under 30 m (98 ft) extend 0.5 mile from the head of Frederick Arm, appearing to afford better anchorage than is found in most mainland inlets. A logging camp and booming ground are on the east side of the arm. Marine farm facilities are on the east side of the inlet, 0.5 mile north of Gomer Island (1989). (SD)

Gomer Island

Chart 3543; just off Pt at E entrance to Frederick Arm
Anchor (S of spit): 50°27.43'N, 125°16.14'W

Gomer Island offers temporary anchorage on either side of the spit which connects to the mainland. This can be used as a lunch stop or a place to wait for favorable conditions.

Anchor in 2 fathoms over sand and gravel with fair holding.

Estero Peak

Chart 3543; 3 mi N of Dent Rapids
Position: 50°27.60'N, 125°11.61'W

A remarkable image caps Estero Peak (5,420 ft.)—it looks like either a profile of George Washington or a sleeping Indian maiden, depending on the viewing angle.

Estero Basin

Chart 3543; at the head of Frederick Arm
Entrance: 50°30.08'N, 125°15.11'W

Estero Basin, about 4 miles long and unsounded, flows into the head of [Frederick Arm] over a shallow flat. (SD)

The entrance to Estero Basin, known as "The Cut," is said to be 3 to 4 feet deep at high water; otherwise it is a waterfall at low tides. The basin, about 4 miles long and uncharted, sits among magnificent high peaks like an alpine lake. The east end of Estero Basin is just 1.5 mile from what we call Estero Basin Cove in Bute Inlet. (See previous chapter.)

Exploring the B.C. coast

Nodales Channel

Chart 3543; joins Cordero Channel to Discovery Passage
Entrance (NE): 50°26.70'N, 125°18.23'W
Entrance (SW, mid-ch btwn Suffolk Pt & Howe I): 50°20.84'N, 125°25.29'W

> *Nodales Channel ... is entered between Hall Point and Johns Point, on East Thurlow Island. A log dump is south of Thurlow Point, and a booming ground is north of Sonora Point.*
>
> *Tidal streams in Nodales Channel attain 3 kn, the flood stream flowing northward, with turbulence off Johns Point where the flood streams meet.*
>
> *Marine farm facilities are off the west shore 0.8 mile SSW of Thurlow Point and 0.3 mile north of Brougham Point.* (SD)

Thurston Bay (Sonora Island)

Charts 3543, 3539; 5 mi NE of Chatham Pt
Entrance (N, mid-ch btwn Davis Pt & Block I): 50°22.39'N, 125°19.93'W
Entrance (S, mid-ch btwn Wilson Pt & Block I): 50°21.99'N, 125°19.86'W
Entrance (lagoon): 50°21.84'N, 125°19.32'W
Anchor (lagoon): 50°21.61'N, 125°19.13'W

> *Thurston Bay, entered between Davis Point and Wilson Point, has Block Island in its north part. A detached drying and above-water reef lies close off the south shore of the bay. The north part of Thurston Bay, and the north part of Cameleon Harbour, is a marine park; there are no facilities.*
>
> *Anchorage. It is reported that reasonably sheltered anchorage can be obtained behind Block Island, and by small craft, in the lagoon on the south shore of the bay. The lagoon has a depth of 0.6 m (2 ft) in its entrance channel.* (SD)

Thurston Bay Marine Park, on the west side of Sonora Island, has two parts: the northern one behind Block Island and the southern section between Wilson Point and Handfield Bay. The lagoon on the south side of Thurston Bay, outside the park boundaries and extremely well protected, is only useful as a small-boat anchorage due to its shallow entrance.

The lagoon has a fairway depth of about 2 feet at zero tide; a bow watch can easily view the bottom the entire way into the lagoon. We find the seclusion and natural setting here a pleasure. A fairly large 2-fathom shoal in the center of the lagoon makes for easy anchoring. The bottom is largely gravel with indifferent holding, but conditions in summer are so calm this shouldn't be a problem since there is almost no pull on your rode.

The southern section of Thurston Bay Marine Park, also undeveloped, has several names which can be a bit confusing. Cameleon Harbour is the name of the well-protected anchorage east of Bruce Point. Piddell Bay is a shallow bight in the eastern part of the harbor; Handfield Bay, the northern part of Cameleon Harbour, is within the Thurston Bay Marine Park boundaries and has a well-sheltered anchorage at its head. A number of reefs and islets make the bay picturesque and fun to explore. However, you need to make a cautious entry, avoiding Douglas Rock, awash at low water, southwest of Bruce Point.

Anchor (lagoon) in 2 fathoms over a sand and gravel with poor-to-fair holding.

Anchorage can also be found north of Block Island in 8 to 10 fathoms over sand and mud with good holding.

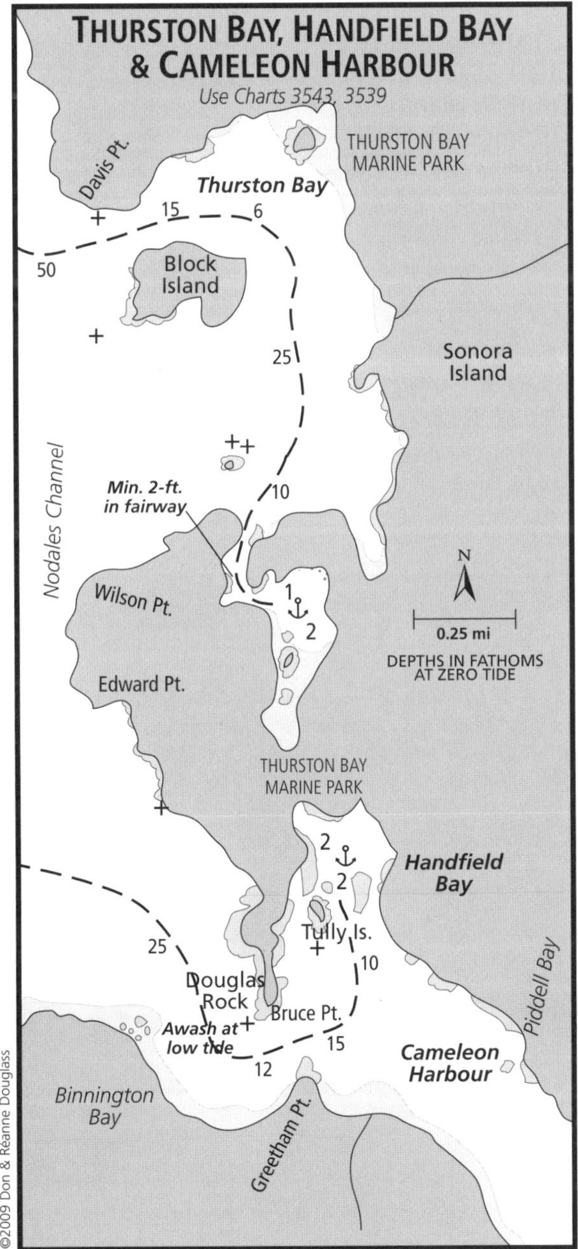

Cameleon Harbour (Burgess and Young Passages) (Sonora Island)

Chart 3543; immediately S of Thurston Bay Marine Park
Entrance (Burgess Passage): 50°21.83'N, 125°20.59'W
Entrance (Young Passage): 50°21.44'N, 125°21.98'W
Entrance (Cameleon Hbr, 0.19 mi NW of Bruce Pt): 50°20.79'N, 125°19.55'W
Anchor (Cameleon Hbr): 50°20.21'N, 125°18.18'W

Cameleon Harbour can be approached either side of Hardinge Island through Burgess Passage or Young Passage, and is entered between Bruce Point and Greetham Point.

Dangers. Maycock Rock and Entry Ledge lie on the south side of the inner approach; Douglas Rock lies close SW of Bruce Point. A drying rock lies off the south side of Young Passage.

Anchorage, sheltered from all winds, can be obtained by small vessels near the SE end of the harbour. (SD)

Cameleon Harbour to the south of Thurston Bay offers good shelter in a rather wild environment.

Commercial fishing boats prefer the ease of access and greater swinging room of Cameleon. They also like to anchor in Young Passage southwest of Hardinge Island against the south shore.

Anchor in 5 fathoms over mud with good holding.

Handfield Bay (Cameleon Harbour)

Chart 3543; N part of Camelion Hbr
Entrance (0.22 mi NE of Bruce Pt): 50°20.75'N, 125°18.95'W
Anchor: 50°21.04'N, 125°18.99'W

Small craft can find anchorage in Handfield Bay and at the head of the harbour. (SD)

We prefer Handfield Bay for its intimate, wild setting. There are a number of rocks and reefs to avoid in the bay but, in good visibility, entering presents no difficulty. Proceed slowly and maintain a lookout on the bow.

Anchor deep in Handfield Bay in 2 fathoms over mud or gravel with fair-to-good holding; limited swinging room.

Hemming Bay (East Thurlow Island)

Chart 3543; W of Lee Is; 1.5 mi NW of Block I
Entrance (0.25 mi SW of Lee Is): 50°22.96′N, 125°22.02′W
Anchor: 50°23.93′N, 125°23.02′W

> *Anchorage for small vessels can be obtained in the NE part of the head of Hemming Bay. Small craft can find anchorage close north of the islet 44 m (144 ft) high near the head, also SW of this islet in an enclosed nook.* (SD)

Hemming Bay is open to the southeast, but the islets at the head of the bay provide good shelter in prevailing summer weather. If a southeast storm is forecast, the lagoon in Thurston Island Marine Park or the bottom of Cameleon Harbour provides better protection.

Two fish farms are located in the two nooks on the north side of Hemming Bay. Boats coming from Cordero Channel can pass inside (north) of Lee Islands over a 2-fathom minimum depth, keeping the midchannel rock to port. Most of the rocks in the bay are marked by kelp.

The islet at the northwest corner of island (44) has an iron ring on its east side that can be used for a stern tie. The tiny nook in front of this islet makes a picturesque, calm anchorage.

Anchor deep in the bay in 1 fathom over sand and mud with fair-to-good holding.

Channe Passage

Chart 3543; separates Channe Island from E Thurlow Island
Entrance (E): 50°26.89′N, 125°19.41′W
Entrance (W): 50°27.27′N, 125°20.32′W

> *Channe Passage, which leads SE of Channe Island, has rocks and shoal water projecting from its SW shore to midchannel and shoal water fringing its NE shore for 90 m (295 ft) off.* (SD)

Channe Passage, south of Channe Island, can be safely transited (5 fathoms) by favoring the north shore and avoiding the rock on the south shore.

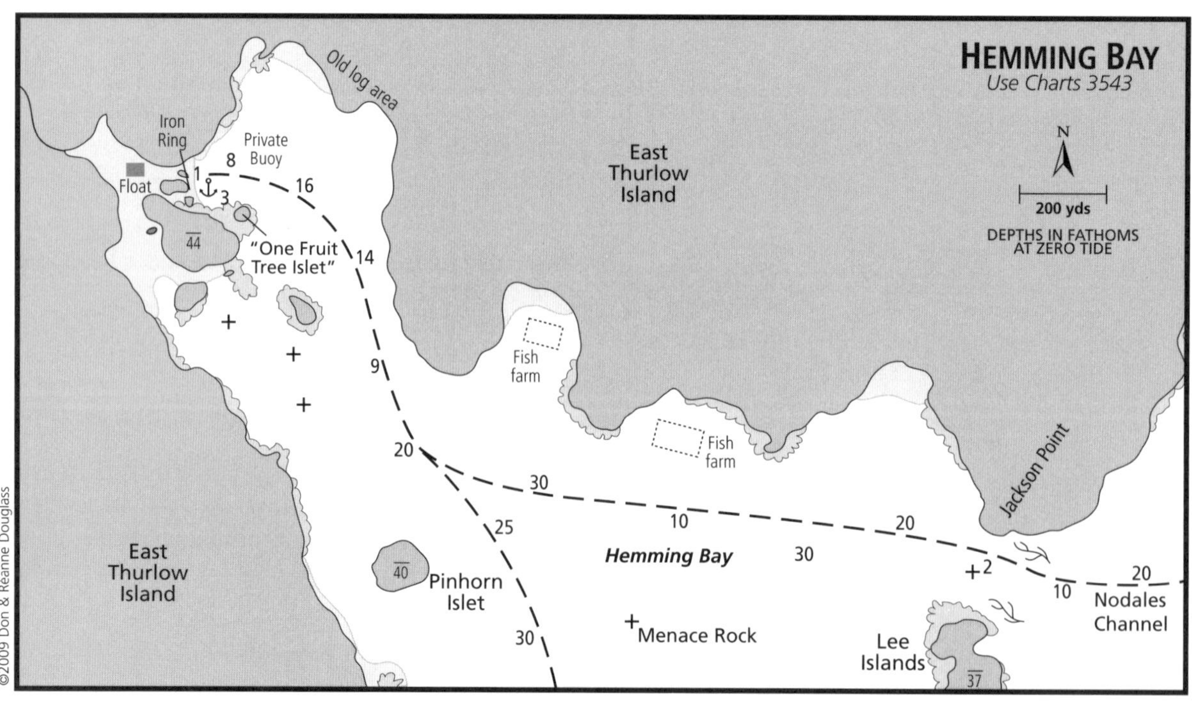

Shoal Bay (East Thurlow Island)

Chart 3543; 6.5 mi NW of Dent Rapids; 5.7 mi NE of Blind Channel
Entrance: 50°27.76'N, 125°21.87'W
Anchor: 50°27.51'N, 125°21.93'W

Shoal Bay, entered 1 mile WNW of Channe Island, has a public wharf and floats with 200 m (656 ft) of berthing space and fresh water. Gold was at one time mined in this area but the former settlement Thurlow is abandoned. (SD)

Shoal Bay features a long public float and offers a magnificent view across Cordero Channel and northward up Phillips Arm. The public float is used for access to a resort set in a grass-covered expanse. The bay is open to northerlies and the wakes of passing ships and the water shallows at the head of the bay. The Shoal Bay Lodge & Pub is planning on updating their fresh water system. The pub offers alcohol, beer and wine and limited food. Showers, laundry, and wi-fi internet access are available at Shoal Bay Lodge.

Anchor in 5 fathoms over sand and gravel with poor-to-fair holding.

⚓ **Shoal Bay Lodge** tel: 250.287.6818; website: shoalbaylodge.com

Phillips Arm

Chart 3543; 7.5 mi NW of Dent Rapids; 6.0 mi NE of Greene Pt Rapids
Entrance (0.63 mi W of Don Creek): 50°28.89'N, 125°21.78'W

Extensive logging operations are carried out at the head of the arm and in Fanny Bay. Marine farm facilities are off the east shore, 0.5 mile south of Richard Point. (SD)

Fanny Bay (Phillips Arm)

Chart 3543; 3.0 mi N of Phillips Arm entrance
Entrance: 50°31.41'N, 125°23.02'W
Anchor: 50°31.83'N, 125°23.98'W

Phillips Arm affords anchorage close to the drying flat at its head and, for small vessels, in Fanny Bay. (SD)

Anchor in about 5 fathoms over mud near the drying mud flat.

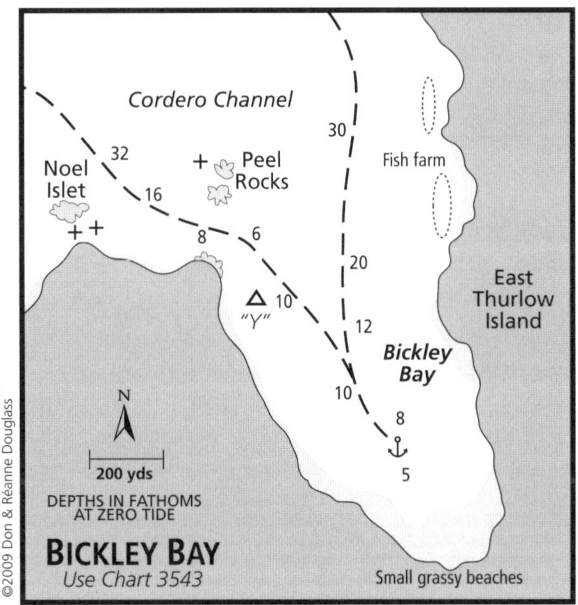

Bickley Bay (East Thurlow Island)

Chart 3543; 1.4 mi SW of Shoal Bay; 4.2 mi E of Greene Pt Rapids
Entrance (0.15 mi N of Peel Rocks): 50°27.28'N, 125°24.12'W
Anchor: 50°26.74'N, 125°23.71'W

Bickley Bay affords anchorage for vessels awaiting slack water in Green Point Rapids, 4 miles west, in its inner part and for small craft close to its head, mud bottom.

Dangers. Noel Islet, Peel Rocks, and a rock with 4.9 m (16 ft) over it, close SE of Peel Rocks, lie on the west side of Bickley Bay and its approach. (SD)

Bickley Bay, a well-sheltered anchorage in most summer weather, is a popular anchorage strategically located between Dent Rapids and Greene Point Rapids. Some people have reported experiencing a rocky bottom with poor holding. We found the sticky grey mud at the head of the bay to be the most secure we've seen in the vicinity.

Anchor in 6 to 10 fathoms over sticky grey mud with very good holding.

Cordero Lodge (Lorte Island)

Chart 3543; 2 mi E of Greene Pt Rapids
Entrance (0.11 mi NE of Lorte Island Light): 50°26.58'N, 125°27.12'W
Float: 50°26.81'N, 125°27.15'W

Lorte Island, on the Cordero Channel, provides protection for the Cordero Lodge. The lodge, an attractive log floathouse run by the Küppers family, caters to sportfishing enthusiasts who arrive by float plane or boat. Overnight moorage (without power) is available for small cruising boats. Call ahead on VHF Channel 66A for reservations or telephone 250.287.0917. Docking at the float often presents a challenge for small boats due to the strong currents. Be forewarned. The lodge restaurant features an excellent German cuisine; best to call ahead to verify that they can take you.

⚓ **Cordero Lodge** tel: 250.287.0917; monitors VHF Ch 66A; website: www.corderolodge.com; email: info@corderolodge.com

Crawford Anchorage (East Thurlow I)

Chart 3543; on S side of Erasmus Island; 1.9 mi E of Greene Pt Rapids
Anchor: 50°26.12'N, 125°27.66'W

Crawford Anchorage, sheltered by Erasmus Island and Mink Island, is suitable for small vessels but is reported to afford poor anchorage for small craft. Approach this anchorage from west. (SD)

Crawford Anchorage is the name for the moderately-protected area between Erasmus Island and East Thurlow Island. A shoal extending south from Erasmus Island is covered with kelp which acts as an effective breakwater for any easterly chop. Small cruising boats can find temporary anchorage west of the kelp patch near Erasmus Island, but we don't recommend it as an overnight anchorage. In 2005, there was a large logging operation in the bay.

Anchor in 6 fathoms over a hard and rocky bottom with poor-to-fair holding.

Tallac Bay

Chart 3543; on N side of Cordero Ch; 1.3 mi E of Greene Pt Rapids; 0.9 mi W of Cordero Lodge
Entrance: 50°26.49'N, 125°28.42'W
Anchor: 50°26.65'N, 125°28.54'W

Tallac Bay has a reef with three heads, with less than 2 m (6 ft) over them lying close SE of its entrance. (SD)

Tallac Bay is a small cove north of Erasmus Island. It is out of the 5-knot current which can run in this part of Cordero Channel on spring tides. The head of Tallac Bay dries as

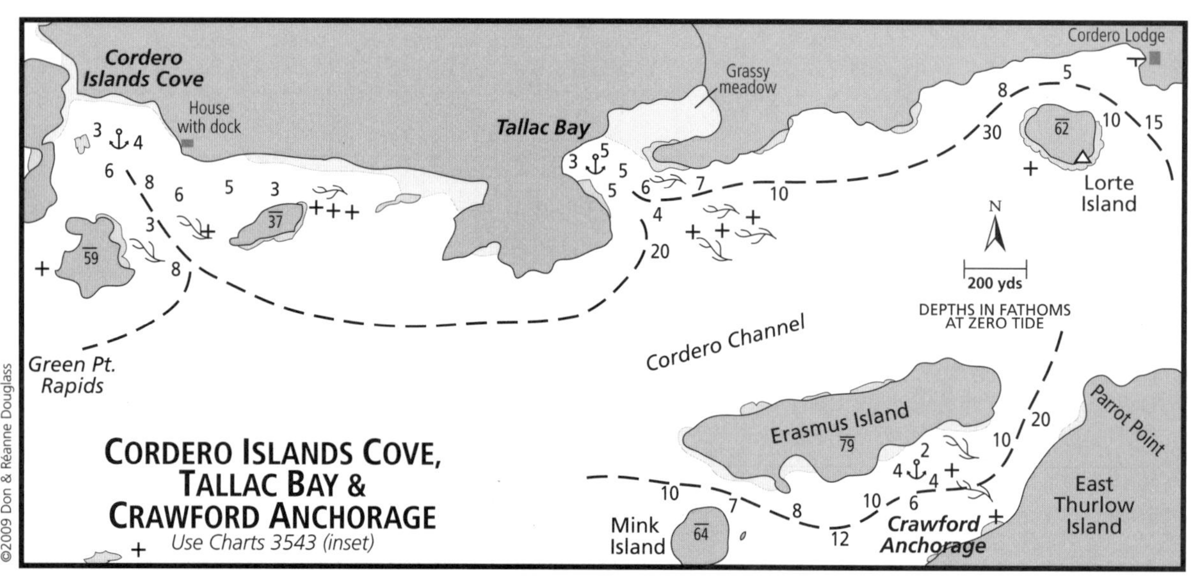

CORDERO ISLANDS COVE, TALLAC BAY & CRAWFORD ANCHORAGE
Use Charts 3543 (inset)

Cordero Lodge, Lorte Island

far out as the bay's eastern peninsula. The flat is steep-to and has a grassy meadow at its head. Temporary anchorage can be found off the steep bank on the west side of the bay. Avoid the reefs mentioned above by staying close to shore or entering west of the reef. The reef is well marked by kelp in the summer. Tallac Bay is out of the current streaming past.

Anchor in 4 to 5 fathoms over sand and gravel with fair holding and limited swinging room.

Cordero Islands Cove

Chart 3543 inset; 1.8 mi N of Blind Channel
Entrance: 50°26.47'N, 125°29.67'W
Anchor: 50°26.71'N, 125°29.86'W

> *Anchorage with fair shelter is available to small vessels between Cordero Islands and the north shore.* (SD)

Cordero Islands Cove is our name for the well-protected area immediately east of Greene Point Rapids. The Cordero Islands and strategically-placed kelp patches keep out all turbulence and eddies that are within shouting distance to the west.

Look for an entrance (minimum kelp) in the center of the south channel midway between islands (37) and (59). A house and dock are on the east side of the cove. Anchor as desired near the north end of the cove.

Anchor in 4 to 6 fathoms over soft sand and kelp with poor-to-fair holding.

Mayne Passage (Blind Channel)

Chart 3543; connects Cordero Channel to Johnstone Strait
Entrance (N): 50°25.95'N, 125°29.50'W
Entrance (S, 0.68 mi NW of Edith Pt): 50°22.90'N, 125°34.06'W

> *Mayne Passage [is] known locally as Blind Channel.* (SD)

Mayne Passage (Blind Channel) is only 4 miles north-northeast of Chatham Point and is used as part of a loop or to escape from Johnstone Strait. Boats continuing west use Johnstone Strait or go west via Greene Point Rapids. In Chancellor Channel, they can also join Johnstone Strait or delay entry again by going northwest through Wellbore Channel and Whirlpool Rapids.

Fuel and modest supplies are available at Blind Channel Resort on the east shore of West Thurlow Island, 1.5 miles south of Greene Point Rapids.

Blind Channel floats

Blind Channel (West Thurlow Island)

Chart 3543; settlement if on W side of Mayne Passage
Public float (fuel dock): 50°24.82′N, 125°30.08′W

> *Blind Channel settlement ... has a resort with a store, a liquor store, restaurant and post office (V0P 1B0). The public wharf and float provide 37 m (121 ft) of berthing. Part of the float is reserved for aircraft and a private float extends north from the public wharf. Gasoline, diesel fuel and fresh water are obtainable.*
>
> *Anchorage is available in midchannel south of Butterfly Bay.* (SD)

Blind Channel Marina and Resort is a popular cruising stop with full amenities that include an excellent restaurant, well-maintained floats, fuel dock, store (with homemade bread for sale!) and liquor. Power and water are available on the floats; laundry and showers on shore. You may stay at the public fuel dock for a short time free of charge, or overnight at the marina floats. If you're just passing by, take time to look at the interesting mosaic "tableaux" mounted along the concrete float, created by the late Annamarie Richter from shards of glass, pottery and pieces of junk she found along shore. Also, don't miss the forest trails: you can take the Viewpoint Trail (30 min.), the Big Cedar Trail (45 min.), or the Forest Management Trail (60 min. or more). The trails lead west across the creek and up its north side through a large and beautiful old-growth cedar rain forest. An 800-year-old cedar tree, 16 feet in diameter, is the pièce de résistance!

⚓ **Blind Channel Resort** tel: 250.949.1420 or 888.329.0475; monitors VHF Ch 66A; website: www.blindchannel.com; email info@blindchannel; fuel; power; restrooms; showers; laundry

Blind Channel nature trail

800-year-old "grandfather cedar," Blind Channel

Charles Bay (East Thurlow Island)

Chart 3543; on E side of Mayne Passage
Entrance: 50°25.22'N, 125°29.49'W
Anchor: 50°25.09'N, 125°29.22'W

> *Charles Bay, entered south of Shell Point, is shallow. Eclipse Islet stands on a boulder bank near the centre of the bay.* (SD)

Charles Bay, although interesting for its marine environment, does not offer easy access or convenient anchoring. There's a nice 2-fathom hole southeast of Eclipse Islets, but the approach at zero tide is shallow (2 to 3 feet on the west, 1 foot on the north) and choked with long eel grass that can foul your anchor and your engine cold-water intake filter. The bottom is black mud, however, and if you can finally penetrate the eel grass, you'll have good holding.

Anchor (reluctantly) in the 2-fathom hole over eel grass and black mud with poor holding unless your anchor is well set.

Grass and kelp foul anchor, Charles Bay

Old-growth cedar, Blind Channel

Greene Point Rapids

Chart 3543; leads btwn Cordero Islands to NE & West Thurlow Island to the SW
Entrance (E): 50°26.26'N, 125°29.95'W
Entrance (W): 50°26.83'N, 125°31.09'W

> *Tidal streams in the rapids reach 7 kn with considerable overfalls, whirlpools and eddies, particularly with large tides. Passage at slack water is recommended. Secondary current station Greene Point Rapids, referenced on Seymour Narrows, is given in the Tide Tables, Volume 6.*
>
> *Caution. Low powered vessels and vessels towing, when eastbound through the rapids with the flood current, should take care not to be set on Erasmus Island.*
>
> *Anchorage with fair shelter is available to small vessels between Cordero Islands and the north shore.* (SD)

At spring tides, a whirlpool 200 yards south of Griffiths Islet Light puts on an impressive show, dropping 3 feet for a width of 60 to 75 feet. Although the whirlpool appears to remain fairly stationary, you should stay clear of it. We've found that we can buck small flood or ebb currents successfully with adequate power. Due to the narrow width of Cordero Channel west of Greene Point Rapids, the current remains strong until you're well into Chancellor Channel.

In addition to the anchorage mentioned in *Sailing Directions*, temporary anchorage is available along the north shore opposite Greene Point.

Loughborough Inlet

Chart 3543, 3555; at junction of Cordero & Chancellor channels; 4.7 mi NE of Blind Channel
Entrance: 50°27.02'N, 125°36.42'W

> *Loughborough Inlet, entered between Grismond Point and Styles Point, lies between high wooded mountains rising abruptly from its shores. There is a considerable amount of logging in the inlet. Because of its deep water and steep-to shores, anchorages are scarce, the only good ones being in Beaver Inlet.*
>
> *Tidal streams in Loughborough Inlet seldom exceed 2 kn. Due to land drainage, an overlay of fresh water flows almost constantly out of the inlet at 1 to 2 kn, being strongest during the spring runoff and weakest during a dry summer. This overlay, augmented by runoff along the way, increases in volume and rate as it flows from the head toward the foot of the inlet.* (SD)

Loughborough Inlet is a deep fjord that extends over 18 miles into the coast range. As logging operations wind down, this area will take on additional charm for cruising boats. The high peaks with their granite slabs and snowfields on the east shore have been largely clearcut and are crisscrossed with logging roads; however, a period of healing and re-growth is now taking place. Because of its configuration, Loughborough Inlet appears to receive more moderate wind than do the channels to the south.

Beaver Inlet (Loughborough Inlet)

Chart 3555 inset; 3 mi N of entrance to Loughborough Inlet
Entrance: 50°30.60'N, 125°35.14'W
Anchor: 50°29.73'N, 125°38.02'W

> *Beaver Inlet ... is entered between William Point and Mary Point. Small vessels can find anchorage with good holding in mud near the head of the inlet.* (SD)

Beaver Inlet provides good protection at its head over a long, flat mud bottom. There is some down-channel wind from the northeast.

Anchor in 3 to 5 fathoms over mud with good holding.

Edith Cove (Beaver Inlet)

Chart 3555 inset; on S shore of Beaver Inlet; 1.0 mi W of William Pt
Anchor: 50°30.22'N, 125°36.36'W

Edith Cove provides good temporary anchorage for small boats off the drying flat south of Hales Point. The last time we checked, there was a float house in the cove, which if still there, may restrict the room for anchoring.

Anchor in 2 fathoms over an unrecorded bottom.

Sidney Bay (Loughborough Inlet)

Charts 3555 inset, 3543; 0.6 mi N of Beaver Inlet
Entrance: 50°31.07'N, 125°35.41'W

> *Sidney Bay has booming grounds, private floats and affords anchorage for small vessels near its head.* (SD)

Sidney Bay is too deep for convenient anchoring but there is a private float at the head of the bay. The float belongs to a homesteader who is well prepared for self-sufficiency with a water-powered electric generator.

Heydon Bay (Loughborough Inlet)

Chart 3543; 4.5 mi N of Beaver Inlet
Entrance: 50°34.93'N, 125°33.79'W

> *Heydon Bay is partially filled by a drying mud flat with a steep-to edge. A logging camp float is at the head of the bay and booming grounds lie off the north side.* (SD)

McBride Bay, Frazer Bay (Cooper Reach, Loughborough Inlet)

Chart 3543 inset; at head of Loughborough Inlet
Entrance (McBride Bay): 50°42.66'N, 125°26.59'W
Entrance (Frazer Bay) : 50°42.54'N, 125°27.65'W'
Anchor (0.14 mi NW of Heard Pt): 50°43.11'N, 125°25.95'W

Towry Head, at the south end of Cooper Reach, is prominent and cliffy on its south side. At Latelle Creek, 2 miles east, there is a logging camp and a float.

Frazer Bay lies west of Pan Point. McBride Bay, between Pan Point and Heard Point, has a shoal with 3.7 m (12 ft) over it in its central part and drying reefs close south of Heard Point. (SD)

McBride Bay, the eastern head of Cooper Reach, is at the outlet of beautiful Apple River Valley. McBride Bay has been a great salmon fishing area because of extensive spawning grounds in Apple River. By contrast, Frazer Bay has yielded little salmon; there is such a large waterfall on the Stafford River that salmon cannot get up the river to spawn.

Temporary anchorage is reported off the drying flat of Apple River northwest of Heard Point.

Kelp with shell bottom

Chancellor Channel

Charts 3543, 3544; joins Cordero Channel to Johnstone Strait; 2.5 mi E of Helmcken Island
Entrance (E, 0.5 mi W of Tucker Pt): 50°26.13'N, 125°37.20'W
Entrance (W, 0.48 mi NW of Eden Pt): 50°24.32'N, 125°47.71'W

Chancellor Channel leads 8 miles WSW from its junction with Loughborough Inlet and Cordero Channel, joining Johnstone Strait east of Current and Race Passages.

Tidal streams in Chancellor Channel seldom exceed 2 kn, are free of turbulence and run parallel to shore throughout its length.

It is reported that the bay east of Shorter Point affords anchorage for vessels waiting for the tide to turn. (SD)

Shorter Point Cove (West Thurlow Island)

Charts 3544, 3543; 0.6 mi E of Shorter Pt
Entrance: 50°24.70'N, 125°42.46'W
Anchor: 50°24.53'N, 125°42.79'W

Shorter Point Cove is the name we give this bight which is well protected from westerlies. A recent aquaculture fills a good part of the cove, but shelter can be found close to shore.

Anchor in 4 fathoms over sand, mud and gravel with fair holding.

Wellbore Channel

Chart 3544; separates Hardwicke Island from mainland to the E
Entrance (S, 0.19 mi SE of Bulkely Island): 50°25.57'N, 125°43.34'W
Entrance (N, mid-ch btwn Althorp & Thynne Pts): 50°28.63'N, 125°47.28'W

Wellbore Channel ... joins Chancellor and Sunderland Channels, providing a route to

Johnstone Strait which by-passes Current and Race Passages, where wind against current can cause heavy tide-rips. (SD)

Wellbore Channel allows you to delay entering Johnstone Strait until you reach its wider part where the current is less boisterous. Here in Wellbore, you often see bear combing the mainland shore at low tide.

Wellbore Cove (Hardwicke Island)

Chart 3544; immediately S of Whilrpool Rapids
Entrance: 50°27.09'N, 125°45.87'W
Anchor: 50°27.15'N, 125°46.07'W

Wellbore Cove is our name for the small bight on the Hardwicke Island shore. We have talked with owners of small boats who anchored close to shore in 5 fathoms (avoiding the rock which dries at 7 feet) and reported that this is a snug anchorage in westerlies, out of nearby current and eddies.

Whirlpool Rapids (Wellbore Channel)

Chart 3544; narrowest part of Wellbore Channel; just off Carterer Pt
Entrance (S, 0.4 mi SE of Carterer Pt Light): 50°27.19'N, 125°45.45'W
Entrance (N, 0.2 mi NW of Carterer Pt Light): 50°27.72'N, 125°45.96'W

Tidal streams in Whirlpool Rapids create strong whirlpools, upwellings and backeddies. The turbulence occurs south of Carterer Point with the flood tide and north of the point with the ebb. The flood sets SE and the ebb NW. Secondary current station Whirlpool Rapids, referenced on Seymour Narrows, is given in the Tide Tables, Volume 6. (SD)

Whirlpool Rapids has given us fewer problems over the years than other rapids; while the water can be turbulent with eddies, we have never seen whirlpools here the size of those at Yuculta and Greene Point. At 20 minutes before slack tide there are still small whirlpools in the rapids.

Althorp Point Cove (Hardwicke Island)

Chart 3544; 1.5 mi N of Whirlpool Rapids
Entrance: 50°28.35'N, 125°47.57'W
Anchor: 50°28.38'N, 125°47.72'W

Althorp Point Cove is the shallow cove on the southeast side of Althorp Point. We find the shelter more than adequate in fair weather and it saves the extra effort of using Douglas Bay in Forward Harbour.

Anchor in 2 to 3 fathoms over sand, gravel, mud and shells with fair-to-good holding.

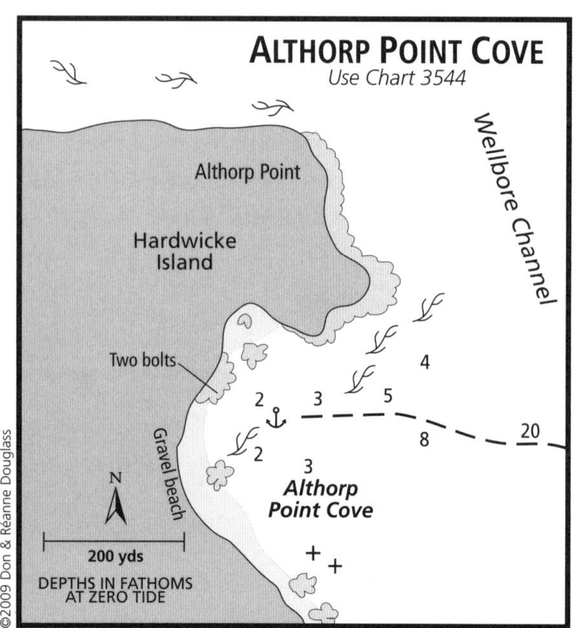

Douglas Bay (Forward Harbour)

Chart 3544; in an open bight on E side of Thynne Peninsula
Entrance (0.1 mi SE of Louisa Pt): 50°28.37'N, 125°46.08'W

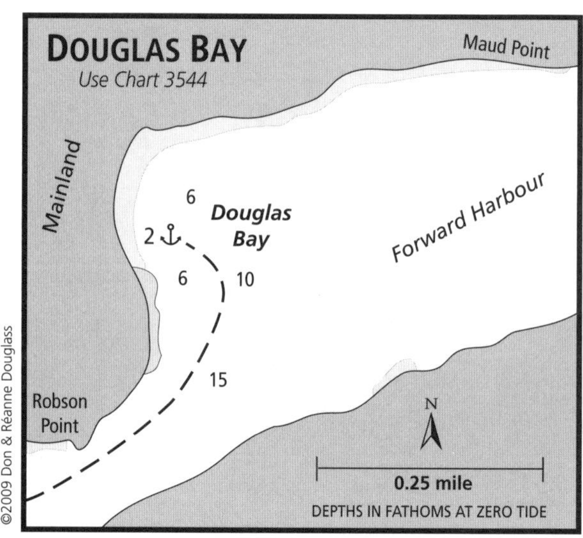

Anchor: 50°28.93'N, 125°45.29'W

Forward Harbour, entered south of Louisa Point, affords anchorage anywhere in the harbour, the best location being off Douglas Bay, where there is shelter from west winds. (SD)

Douglas Bay, at the west end of Forward Harbour, offers good protection for several boats from the westerlies that blow through Johnstone Strait so much of the time. It is open to easterlies flowing down Wortley Creek.

Anchor in 5 fathoms over mud and shells with good holding.

Sunderland Channel

Chart 3544; separates NW side of Hardwicke Island from the mainland
Entrance (E, mid-ch btwn Althorp & Thynne Pts): 50°28.63'N, 125°47.28'W
Entrance (W, 0.6 mi NW of Fanny Island Light): 50°27.76'N, 126°00.00'W

Sunderland Channel, entered from SE between Althorp Point and Thynne Point, leads 8 miles WSW to Johnstone Strait.

Tidal streams of 4 kn with heavy tide-rips sometimes occur in the west entrance of Sunderland Channel, but farther east rates seldom exceed 1.5 kn. (SD)

Bessborough Bay

Chart 3544; at the E end of Sunderland Channel
Entrance (0.37 mi N of Thynne Pt): 50°29.08'N, 125°46.91'W
Anchor: 50°28.98'N, 125°45.92'W

Bessborough ... affords anchorage for small vessels in its SE part, with no protection from west winds. (SD)

Bessborough Bay, at the apex of Wellbore Channel, Topaze Harbour, and Sunderland Channel, is an interesting anchorage. We feel its usefulness is underrated when there are light to moderate westerlies. Along the north side of Thynne Peninsula, such winds diminish to near calm when you approach the southeast head of the bay. The reason for this phenomenon may be that the turbulent water (such as tide rips) flowing up Wellbore Channel, particularly on ebb, knocks down westerly chop. The south shore of Bessborough Bay has a moderate number of drift logs, indicating that it escapes the full brunt of storms.

From here, you can see almost all the way to Johnstone Strait, so it's a good place to check for fog banks.

The mud flat at the north side dries and is steep-to. The southeast beach is sand and gravel. Two flat areas off the beach make for good anchoring. One is about $6^1/_2$ fathoms deep, the other, a little closer to the beach, is 2 to 3 fathoms. Some grass, sand and shells lie close to shore.

Anchor in 3 fathoms over mud and clay with very good holding.

Murray Island Anchorage (Topaze Harbour)

Chart 3544; at the entrance to Topaze Hbr
Entrance (S): 50°29.62'N, 125°49.26'W

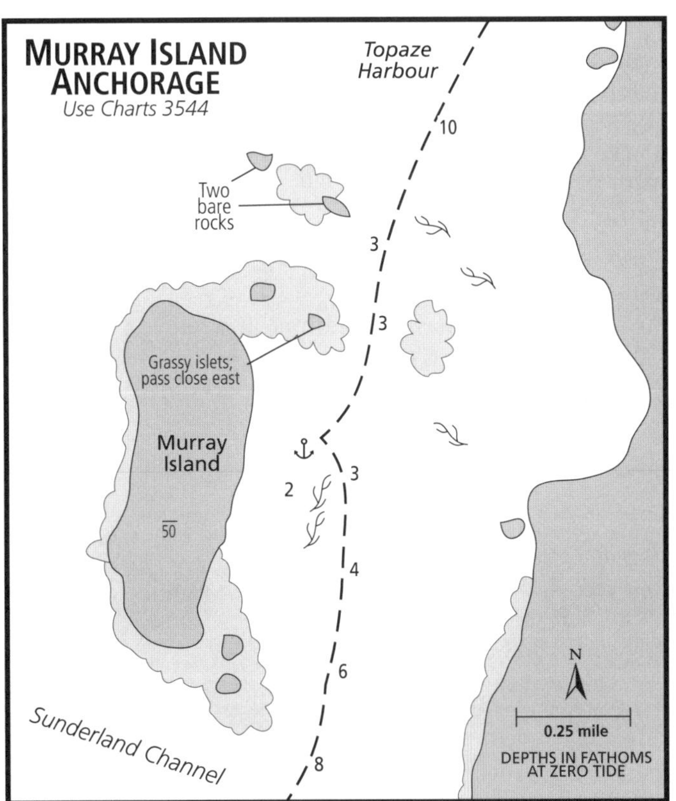

Entrance (N): 50°29.93′N, 125°49.14′W
Anchor: 50°29.77′N, 125°49.23′W

Murray Island Anchorage offers temporary, fair-weather anchorage on its east side. This small cove is formed by the lee of Murray Island and the reefs and kelp that extend east off each tip. You can enter from either end of the cove and find calm water close to the island. Approach slowly and cautiously, avoiding the charted reefs. This area makes a scenic lunch stop and is a good place to explore by dinghy or by diving.

Anchor in 2 to 3 fathoms over a sandy bottom with fair holding.

Topaze Harbour

Chart 3544; at NE end of Sunderland Channel; 3.5 mi NE of Whilrpool Rapids
Entrance: 50°29.78′N, 125°49.89′W
Buoys (Hill Pt landing): 50°31.15′N, 125°45.30′W
Entrance (Jackson Bay): 50°31.14′N, 125°49.21′W

> *Topaze Harbour is entered between Geneste Point and Murray Island.*
>
> *Good anchorage can be obtained almost anywhere in Topaze Harbour or in Jackson Bay, but there is little shelter for small craft.* (SD)

Topaze Harbour is a somewhat unique 4.5 mile inlet with an almost flat 10- to 12-fathom bottom its entire length. It doesn't appear to be glacier-cut nor does it have an outlet bar. Alas, it is being heavily logged. Very large, old and rusty mooring buoys located at Jackson Bay Landing (Hill Point) on the south shore could be used in an emergency. A very large logbooming area on the north shore of Topaze Harbour is called Jackson Bay.

Shaw Point Cove

Chart 3544; on N side of Sunderland Channel; 3.8 mi E of Blenkinsop Bay
Entrance: 50°28.63′N, 126°54.53′W

Temporary shelter from westerlies can be found tucked in behind Shaw Point. This has been used as a logboom storage area, and at last check (1995), there was still a floating log across the head of the cove. A number of cables left dangling from the shore indicate that the bottom may be fouled.

Craven Hill Bight (Hardwicke Island)

Chart 3544; 2.2 mi E of Yorke Island
Anchor: 50°27.14′N, 126°54.80′W

Commercial fishing boats frequently anchor along the south shore of Sunderland Channel north of islet (45), avoiding a charted rock which dries at 4 feet. There is fair protection from southerlies 2.5 miles east of Hardwicke Point.

McLeod Bay

Chart 3544; 0.5 mi E of Mary Island
Entrance: 50°28.18′N, 125°58.65′W
Anchor (E side): 50°28.29′N, 125°58.61′W
Anchor (W side): 50°28.22′N, 125°58.70′W

> *McLeod Bay ... has booming grounds in it.* (SD)

As you approach Tuna Point, McLeod Bay offers the first good protection from westerlies out of Sunderland Channel. Access is easy, but the bay shoals rapidly over a wide area and is largely dry on zero tides. We have tried both McLeod Bay anchor sites and we prefer the easterly one in calm conditions, the west side in blustery conditions. The logbooming grounds mentioned in *Sailing Directions* have been gone for some time, but the log loading ramp is still visible on the west side, as are several chain and cable ties along the rocky bluffs near the west point.

Anchor (E side) in 2 to 3 fathoms over sand with good holding and limited swinging room.

Anchor (W side) in 1 fathom, sand bottom with good holding; limited swinging room.

Tuna Point

Chart 3544; marks the W end of Sunderland Ch
Entrance (E): 50°28.21′N, 125°59.23′W
Entrance (W): 50°28.34′N, 125°59.84′W
Anchor: 50°28.54′N, 125°59.73′W

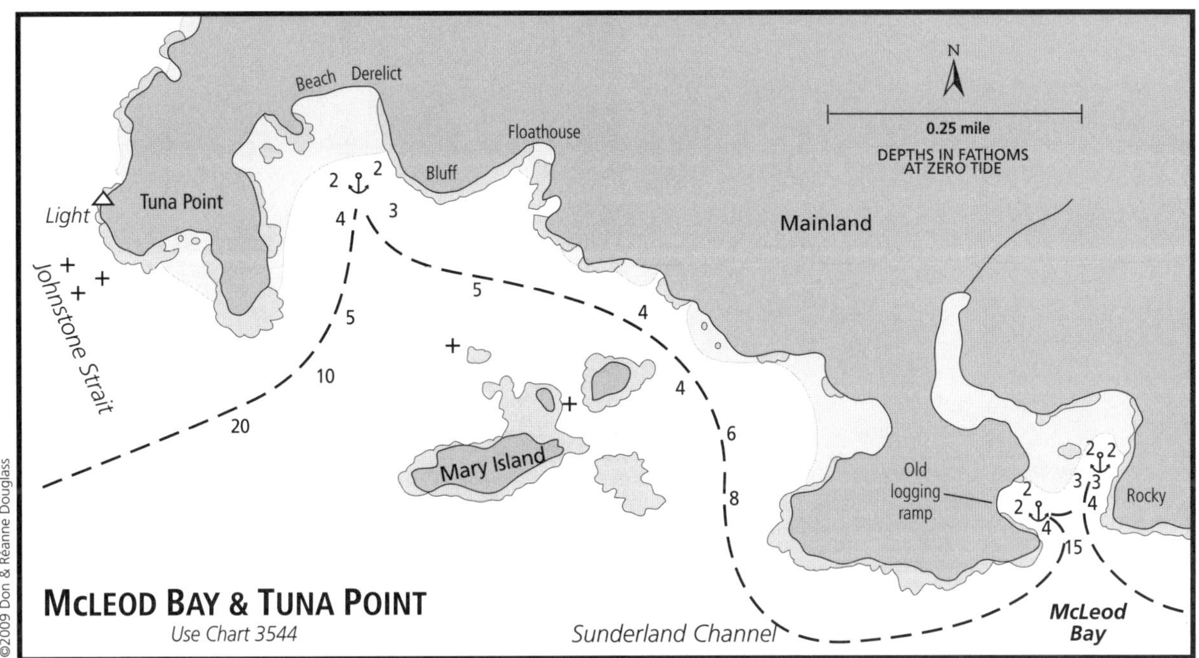

Tuna Point … has foul ground extending 0.1 mile SW from it. The bay north of Mary Island is reported to provide shelter during west winds … (SD)

Tuna Point offers good protection on the east side of the peninsula off the shoaling beach. Access can be made carefully from either side of Mary Island.

Anchor in 2 to 3 fathoms over sand with good holding.

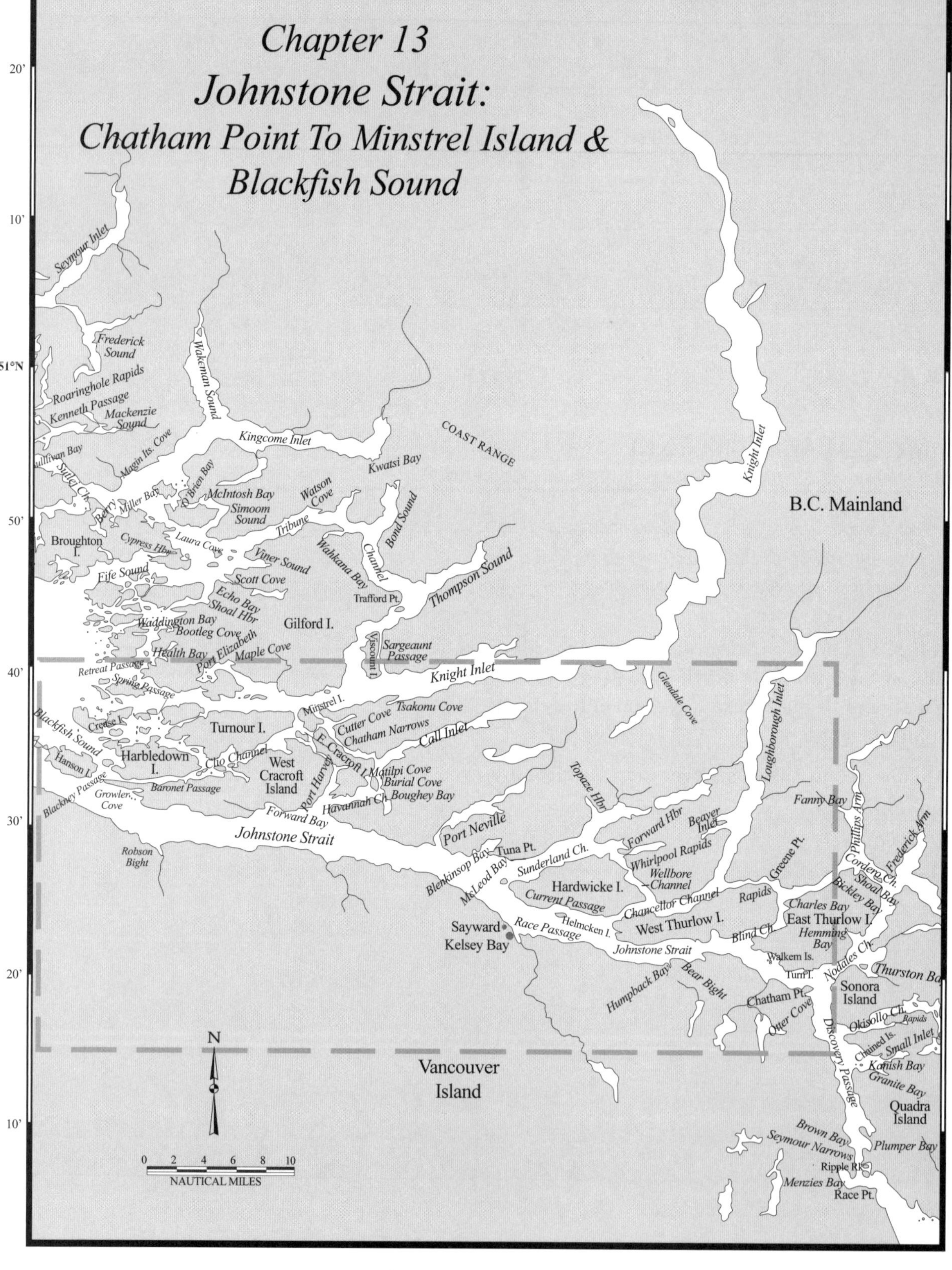
Chapter 13
Johnstone Strait:
Chatham Point To Minstrel Island &
Blackfish Sound
B.C. Mainland
Vancouver
Island
COAST RANGE
Knight Inlet
Kingcome Inlet
Wakeman Sound
Seymour Inlet
Frederick Sound
Roaringhole Rapids
Kenneth Passage
Mackenzie Sound
Sullivan Bay
Sutlej Ch.
Mogin Its. Cove
Miller Bay
O'Brien Bay
McIntosh Bay
Simoom Sound
Watson Cove
Kwatsi Bay
Bond Sound
Tribune Channel
Broughton I.
Cypress Hbr
Laura Cove
Viner Sound
Wahkana Bay
Fife Sound
Scott Cove
Echo Bay
Shoal Hbr
Trafford Pt.
Thompson Sound
Waddington Bay
Bootleg Cove
Gilford I.
Viscount I.
Sargeaunt Passage
Health Bay
Port Elizabeth
Maple Cove
Retreat Passage
Spring Passage
Minstrel I.
Tsakonu Cove
Cutter Cove
Chatham Narrows
Call Inlet
Crease I.
Turnour I.
Glendale Cove
Loughborough Inlet
Blackfish Sound
Harbledown I.
Clio Channel
West Cracroft Island
E. Cracroft I.
Port Harvey
Matilpi Cove
Burial Cove
Boughey Bay
Havannah Ch.
Hanson I.
Blackney Passage
Growler Cove
Baronet Passage
Topaze Hbr
Forward Bay
Johnstone Strait
Port Neville
Fanny Bay
Phillips Arm
Frederick Arm
Robson Bight
Forward Hbr
Beaver Inlet
Tuna Pt.
Blenkinsop Bay
McLeod Bay
Sunderland Ch.
Whirlpool Rapids
Wellbore Channel
Greene Pt.
Cordero Ch.
Shoal Bay
Bickley Bay
Hardwicke I.
Current Passage
Chancellor Channel
Rapids
Charles Bay
East Thurlow I.
Sayward
Kelsey Bay
Race Passage
Helmcken I.
West Thurlow I.
Blind Ch.
Hemming Bay
Walkem Is.
Nodales Ch.
Thurston Ba
Turn I.
Humpback Bay
Bear Bight
Chatham Pt.
Otter Cove
Sonora Island
Okisollo Ch.
Rapids
Discovery Passage
Chained Is.
Small Inlet
Kanish Bay
Granite Bay
Quadra Island
Brown Bay
Seymour Narrows
Plumper Bay
Ripple Rk.
Menzies Bay
Race Pt.
N
0 2 4 6 8 10
NAUTICAL MILES
20'
10'
51°N
50'
40'
30'
20'
10'

13

JOHNSTONE STRAIT: Chatham Point to Minstrel Island and Blackfish Sound

Johnstone Strait, flanked by Vancouver Island on the south and the dark, forested shores of upcoast British Columbia on the north, extends 54 miles from Chatham Point to the west end of Hanson Island. The strait was named for James Johnstone, master of the Chatham, cutter to Captain Vancouver's Discovery.

At Chatham Point you say good-bye to the balmy conditions of the Strait of Georgia and meet the cool, strong winds and currents and choppy seas of Johnstone Strait. There are few secure anchorages along this stretch and, in the summer months especially, a strong westerly breeze springs up at midday and roars down-strait until after dark.

In this region, you pass range after range of hills and high mountains with few buildings or settlements to be seen. This was once home to the Kwakiutl Indians, as well as settlers, entrepreneurs, loggers and fishermen. After potlatches were outlawed in the early 1880s, the indigenous population began to decline. The Kwakiutls built great lodges and erected many totem poles, some of which were used and maintained into the 1930s. Now the forest has swallowed up most signs of these native people.

Early settlements along the north side of Seymour Narrows were groups of floating homes, gardens—even a hospital—built on huge log rafts. If an area became "played out," the rafts could be towed to another location. Again, little sign of these early settlers remains.

Because of the strong winds and rough seas, many skippers report that this section of the coast is the least enjoyable part of an otherwise exciting trip. But there are frequent periods of fair weather in this region and, with adequate preparation, you can minimize the discomfort to your crew and boat; please see the sidebar below for suggestions for doing so.

Reefed down with an afternoon westerly, Johnstone Strait

Johnstone Strait

Charts 3543, 3544, 3545, 3546; extends along NE coast of Vancouver Island for 54 mi
Entrance (E, 0.4 mi N of Chatham Pt Light): 50°20.56'N, 125°26.44'W
Entrance (W, 0.6 mi N of Blinkhorn Light): 50°33.22'N, 126°46.98'W

Johnstone Strait ... extends from Chatham Point at its east end to Blinkhorn Peninsula at its west end, a distance of about 54 miles. Mountain ranges separated by valley through which flow streams of considerable size, rise abruptly from the water's edge along the southshroe. Some of the highest peaks are snow covered year round.

Tidal streams in Johnstone and Broughton Straits are predominantly semi-diurnal with the flood setting east and the ebb west. There is also a large residual westerly current at the surface where the strongest average currents are on the mainland side of the channel. This residual current results in much stronger ebbs than floods. In fact, many days can pass before there is any appreciable surface flood current in Johnstone Strait. In winter the prevailing SE winds tend to increase the ebb and reduce the duration of the flood current. In summer the prevailing NW winds have the opposite effect.

At the junction of Discovery Passage and Johnstone Strait maximum flood occurs 30 minutes later than at Johnstone Strait–Central, and maximum ebb 50 minutes later. Times of slack water are very close to those at Seymour Narrows. At Bear Point, about 9 miles west, maximum flood and ebb occur 30 and 20 minutes later respectively, than at Johnstone Strait–Central but times of slack water are quite different. Turn to flood occurs 35 minutes earlier and turn to ebb 1 h 35 later than at Johnstone Strait–Central. In this stretch of Johnstone Strait during spring tides both daily ebbs have the same velocity of 2½ kn. The current appears to level off at this speed, and to maintain it for 2½-3 hours. When the range of tide is less than 1 m there is diurnal inequality in the ebbs and the maximum speed drops to 1½ kn. The flood stream has a large diurnal inequality with a maximum just over 2 kn. When the range of tide is less than 1 m there will be no flood current for that period. (SD)

Traversing Johnstone Strait

Johnstone Strait can be one of the most uncomfortable stretches of the Inside Passage. Since heavy river runoffs in the spring add to the already strong ebb flows, it doesn't take much more than a light northwesterly to create a nasty chop. Sometimes the strong ebb currents completely overcome the surface flood current! When this happens, decrease your cruising speed—continuous spray over the bow may seem fun at first, but it can put a strain on your boat and crew.

Likewise, if a nasty chop develops on your stern, avoid surfing large following waves; a small boat could lose control, veer sideways, and broach. In such conditions, slow down, find protection from the chop, drop anchor in a cove and relax while you wait for the current to slack; there are a number of small coves and bights along Johnstone Strait that offer protection.

Plan your traverse of the strait during neap tides (first and third quarter of the moon). To minimize the velocity of the current and the presence of standing waves, avoid spring tides (full and new moon).

Consider delaying entry into Johnstone Strait by hugging the mainland coast to the west end of Hardwicke Island, 22 miles west of Chatham Point. Then, by heading north at Havannah Channel and continuing to Minstrel Island before you turn west, you can avoid the westernmost 20 miles of the strait.

Monitor COMOX weather channel as you approach Johnstone Strait and adjust your timing to take advantage of favorable currents and winds. Travel in the early morning when winds are minimal. Avoid mid-afternoon and periods when a strong wind is forecast that might oppose the current. In both Current and Race passages, currents can develop high speeds and strong turbulence. Avoid tide rips and breaking water.

While you're underway, if conditions should deteriorate, duck into any of the small coves that offer shelter and wait for a better time.

Johnstone Strait is a spectacular passage. With careful preparation and a flexible schedule, you can minimize discomfort and use the powerful natural forces to your benefit.

Chatham Point (Vancouver I)

Charts 3539, 3543; at the junction of Discovery Passage & Johnstone Strait
Chatham Pt Light: 50°20.02'N, 125°26.42'W

Chatham Point ... is low, wooded and rocky; some white buildings with red roofs on the point are prominent. Foul ground, in which there are drying and sunken rocks, extends from the shore north of the point. Beaver Rock, with less than 2 m (6 ft) over it, lies close NNE of Chatham Point light.

Chatham Point at the entrance to Johnstone Strait

Chatham Point Light (518), on a drying rock 0.2 mile north of the point, has an emergency light and a heliport. The fog signal consists of one blast on two horns every 20 seconds.

When the prevailing west wind is blowing against an ebb tide it can be very rough off Chatham Point. (SD)

At Chatham Point, northbound boats start watching for steep, choppy seas on strong ebb tides. Otter Cove or Turn Island across the channel to the northwest are good places to wait for better conditions.

Chatham Point has been a key light station for cruising boats with accurate and up-to-date weather reports, and its lightkeepers are responsive to small-boat requests for information.

Turn Bay (Turn Island)

Charts 3539, 3543; on N side of Turn Island; 1.5 mi NW of Chatham Pt
Entrance (E, 0.29 mi N of Turn Island Light): 50°20.83'N, 125°27.52'W
Entrance (W, 0.61 mi NW of Turn Island Light): 50°21.06'N, 125°28.70'W
Anchor: 50°21.12'N, 125°27.79'W

Turn Island is wooded and about 0.1 mile off the south extremity of East Thurlow Island.

Anchorage for small vessels can be obtained in 13 to 15 m (43 to 49 ft) in the middle of Turn Bay, north of Turn Island. The bay is protected from seas but exposed to winds. A considerable tidal stream sets through Turn Bay. (SD)

Turn Bay is a good vantage point from which to get an idea of the wind and sea conditions in Johnstone Strait. Protection is good here and access is easy.

Upon entering the bay, avoid the rocks off East Thurlow Island marked by ripples and kelp, and head into the calm waters off the small beach. If you stay close to shore in the northeast corner, you can avoid the current that flows through the bay. You can find a good anchor site just outside the eel grass growing near shore.

Anchor in 3 fathoms off the beach over mud, sand, shells and grass with good holding.

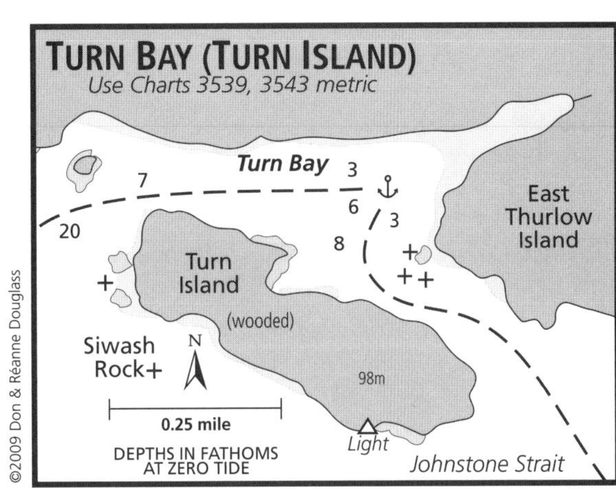

Log ship in Johnstone Strait

Rock Bay (Vancouver Island)

Chart 3543; btwn Chatham & Rock Pts
Entrance (1.7 mi W of Chatham Pt): 50°20.00'N, 125°28.70'W
Ramp: 50°19.92'N, 125°29.15'W

> *Rock Bay ... has the ruins of a pier on its west side. A road from the bay connects with the main highway system.* (SD)

A float and launching ramp are located behind the log breakwater for sportfishing boats.

Little Bear Bay (Vancouver Island)

Chart 3543; 3.1 mi W of Chatham Pt
Entrance: 50°20.52'N, 125°31.22'W

> *Little Bear Bay, west of Rock Point, is almost completely filled with a moderately steep-to drying bank. Booming grounds with dolphins are in the bay and, blue tanks of a salmon hatchery are on shore west of the drying flats. A submarine pipeline extends into the bay from the hatchery.* (SD)

RV campers along the south shore launch their runabouts and trailerable boats via a logging road.

Walkem Islands

Chart 3543; lie btwn Vancouver Island & East Thurlow Island
Entrance (E): 50°21.49'N, 125°30.55'W
Entrance (W): 50°21.86'N, 125°32.21'W
Anchor: 50°21.68'N, 125°30.96'W

> *Tidal streams are strong in the vicinity of Walkem Islands, therefore, they should not be approached within a distance of 0.2 mile. Anchorage in the channel north of the largest island is not recommended, although depths are suitable.* (SD)

Walkem Islands offer temporary protection from strong westerlies at the southeastern end of the largest island, 0.5 mile northeast of the light. Although you can't escape a heavy ebb current here, you can get out of the chop and wait for better conditions. Avoid the bare rock as you enter, and set your anchor well so it doesn't drag. Current eddies swirl throughout the bight from time to time.

Anchor in 4 fathoms over a mixed bottom; good holding if your anchor is well set.

Knox Bay (West Thurlow Island)

Chart 3543; 7.2 mi NW of Chatham Pt; 2.6 mi NE of Bear Pt
Entrance: 50°23.08'N, 125°36.63'W
Anchor: 50°23.54'N, 125°37.16'W

> *Knots Bay, an indentation in the shore of west Thurlow Island, has a log dump and booming ground on the west shore. Depths in the bay are too great for anchorage. It is reported that small craft can obtain anchorage in 15 m (49 ft) close to shore in the NW corner. Heavy tide-rips often form off Needham Point. A drying rock lies about 0.1 mile off the west entrance point of the bay.* (SD)

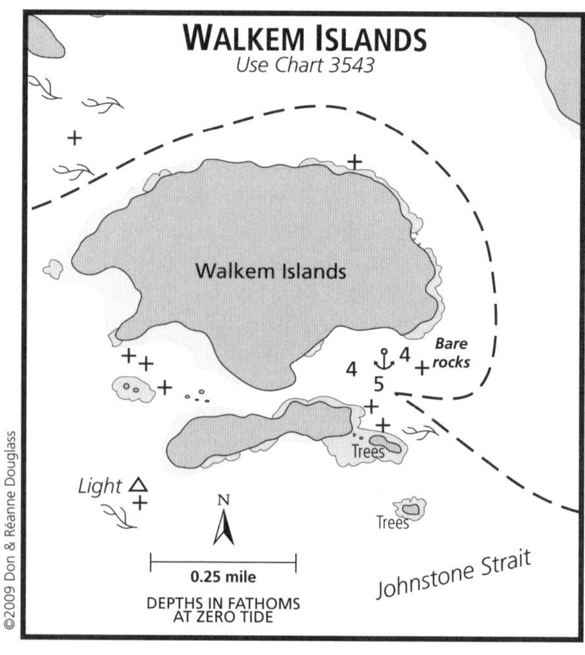

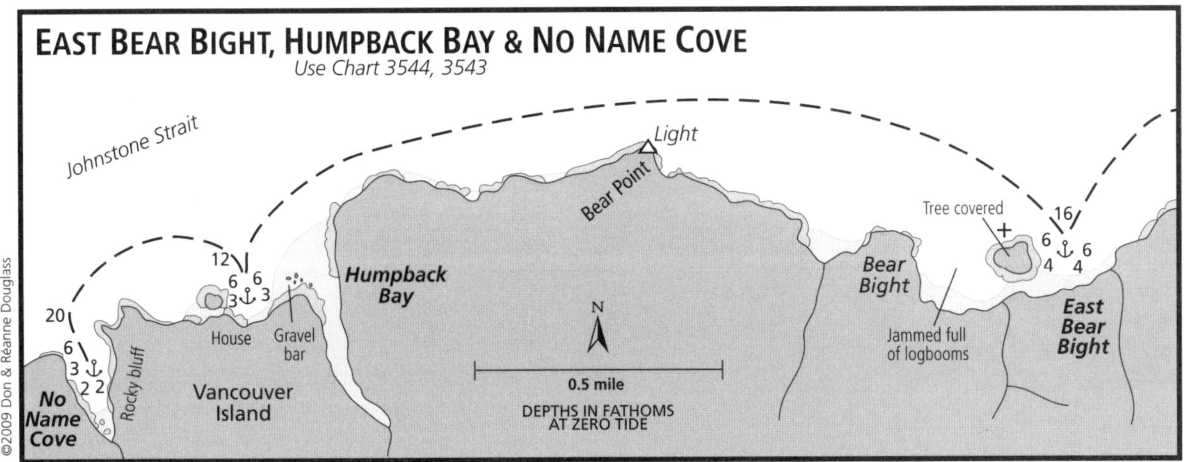

Knox Bay is a large bay that may offer temporary protection for boats over 45 feet when Johnstone Strait kicks up. Its depths are so great, except near shore, that smaller boats may not choose to anchor here. Better anchorage for smaller boats can be found along the south shore of Johnstone Strait between No Name Cove and East Bear Bight.

Anchor in 7 fathoms over an unrecorded bottom.

Bear Bight and East Bear Bight (Vancouver Island)

Chart 3543; 8.5 mi W of Chatham Pt
Entrance (Bear Bight): 50°21.76'N, 125°39.32'W
Entrance (East Bear Bight): 50°21.79'N, 125°38.95'W
Anchor (East Bear Bight): 50°21.72'N, 125°39.00'W

Bear Bight ... affords shelter to small craft east or west of the islet. (SD)

East Bear Bight is one of the small indentations offering shelter in Johnstone Strait. Behind the tree-covered islet, you can get out of the bulk of the chop by hugging the shore. The bottom is flat and offers good, if not full protection, from westerlies; the approach is easy and there is room for several boats. A road sign on West Point says: Rest Area 400 meters, next one 31 km. The bight to the west side of the island has dols, and the last time we were there it was full of logbooms.

Anchor (East Bear Bight) in 4 to 5 fathoms over hard mud with good holding if you set your anchor well.

Humpback Bay (Vancouver Island)

Charts 3544, 3543; 1.35 mi W of Bear Bight
Entrance: 50°21.81'N, 125°41.54'W
Anchor: 50°21.64'N, 125°41.55'W

Humpback Bay ... forms the mouth of Amor de Cosmos Creek ... (SD)

The small cove west of Humpback Bay offers fair protection from westerlies and marginal protection from easterlies between the islet with trees and the gavel bar at the mouth of the creek.

Anchor in 3 fathoms near the steep-to gravel beach over mud, gravel, grass and shells with good holding when your anchor is well set.

No Name Cove (Vancouver Island)

Charts 3544, 3543; just W of Humpback Bay
Entrance: 50°21.62'N, 125°42.10'W
Anchor: 50°21.46'N, 125°42.02'W

You'll find calm waters in what we call No Name Cove, a narrow indentation unaffected by current. There appear to be no rocks in the cove, and you can go deep into the head of the cove to find good shelter. It is sometimes used by large fishing boats which use shore ties to both sides of the cove. The cove is subject to strong westerlies. If you choose to anchor here, we suggest you use a shore tie, as swinging room is limited.

Anchor in 2 to 3 fathoms deep in the cove over mud and gravel with fair-to-good holding and limited swinging room.

Palmer Bay (Vancouver Island)

Chart 3544; a small bight 0.83 mi W of No Name Cove
Entrance: 50°21.49′N, 125°43.28′W

> *Palmer Bay lies 1.2 miles west of Humpback Bay.* (SD).

Palmer Bay offers no real protection; use it only in fair weather as a temporary stop.

Vere Cove (West Thurlow Island)

Chart 3544; indents the W end of West Thurlow Island
Entrance: 50°23.44′N, 125°46.88′W
Anchor: 50°23.34′N, 125°46.54′W

> *Vere Cove, entered between Tyee Point and Eden Point at the west end of West Thurlow Island, has steep wooded shores and affords anchorage to small vessels in 20 to 30 m (66 to 98 ft), well out of the tidal streams; it is exposed to the west. Dorothy Rock, off the south shore, dries 4 m (13 ft).* (SD)

Vere Cove is a good place to find temporary anchorage and observe the situation at Ripple Shoal. The cove provides good protection from southeast winds and some protection from westerly chop in the lee of Dorothy Rock. Ripple Shoal dissipates a lot of the energy that comes from the west. Dorothy Rock and its kelp bed provide some shelter for small boats able to tuck behind it. Large boats need to anchor in the center of the cove.

Anchor in 5 fathoms over mud and sand with good holding.

Current and Race Passages

Chart 3544; Current Passage lies to the N of Helmcken I; Race Passage lies to the S of the I
Entrance (Current Passage E, W-bound vessels): 50°22.59′N, 125°46.16′W
Exit (Current Passage W): 50°25.34′N, 125°58.21′W
Entrance (Race Passage W, E-bound vessels): 50°25.05′N, 125°58.45′W
Exit (Race Passage E): 50°22.28′N, 125°46.59′W

> *In Race and Current Passages, 8 miles west of Bear Point, maximum flood and ebb occur at the same time as those for Bear Point. Slack water times however are greatly affected by the difference in the residual current between the surface and the bottom in Johnstone Strait. The turn to flood in both Race and Current Passages occurs at the same time but the turn to ebb in Current Passage occurs 1 h.15 min. earlier than that in Race Passage. …*
>
> *Tide-rips, dangerous to small craft, are encountered off Ripple Point, in Race and Current Passages and between Kelsey Bay and Port Neville. …*
>
> *In some instances a large vessel or a towboat with rafts proceeding westbound on an ebb tide may have difficulty in making the turn to starboard into Current Passage and clearing Ripple Shoal. Under such circumstances the Master may decide to proceed against the traffic flow through Race Passage and should bake every effort to warn traffic in the area.*
>
> *Mariners should follow procedures set out for Vessel Traffic Services "Sector Four" of othe "Vancouver Traffic Zone" administered by "Comox Traffic." Assigned frequency is 156.575 MHz, Channel 71. Calling-in points east and west of the Traffic Separation Scheme are off Vansittart Point light and off Fanny Island light.*
>
> *Tidal differences, referenced on Alerr Bay, are given for Billygoat Bay (Index No. 8210), Kelsey Bay (Index No. 8215) and Yorke island (Index No. 8233) in "Tide Tables, Volume 6."*
>
> *Tidal streams in the vicinity of Camp Point and Riple Shoal attain 6 kn with heavy tide-rips at times. Tidal streams are alos very strong off Tyee Point, and there are often heavy tide-rips usually with the flood stream when it is opposed by a strong SE wind.*
>
> *Tidal streams run strongly through Current and Race Passages. They attain 5 kn on the ebb and flood in Current Passage and 6 kn on the ebb and flood in Race passage. Eddies and swirls in these passages are numerous and frequently*

strong. When wind opposes the tidal stream they can become dangerous to small vessels.

Over and around Earl Ledge heavy tide-rips and swirls are sometimes formed. The west approach to Race and Current Passages can be extremely dangerous to small craft when winds oppose the ebb tidal stream. (SD)

Both Current and Race passages are fast-flowing saltwater rivers. To avoid opposing traffic, follow the flow or the red arrows on Chart 3544. During neap tides, the flow is linear and you get an easy ride with a following current; on spring tides, turbulence and tide rips are significant. In any case, this is not the place to be caught if a wind opposing the current picks up. In such conditions, Billygoat Bay on Helmcken Island offers welcome relief.

Billygoat Bay (Helmcken Island)

Chart 3544; on the NW side of Helmcken Island; 3.6 mi E of Kelsey Bay
Entrance: 50°24.17'N, 125°51.88'W
Anchor: 50°23.93'N, 125°52.00'W

Anchorage for small craft, sheltered from west winds, can be found on the north side of Helmcken Island, east of the north peninsula. Billygoat Bay offers anchorage with mud bottom but the holding ground is poor; running mooring lines to shore is recommended. (SD)

Helmcken Island offers two fairly well-sheltered anchorages on its Current Passage side. Contrary to *Sailing Directions*, when we tucked up against the south shore, we found Billygoat Bay to be a satisfactory anchorage. Avoid the reefs and the rocks awash, and enter only from north of the island where the weather antenna is located. We find no current here.

Anchor close to shore in 2 fathoms, using a stern tie if warranted. The bottom is soft mud with sand and grass, good holding.

North Cove (Helmcken Island)

Chart 3544; 0.5 mi NW of Billygoat Bay
Entrance: 50°24.27'N, 125°52.25'W
Anchor: 50°24.24'N, 125°52.57'W

The north cove of Helmcken Island is easier to enter than Billygoat Bay and equally well protected from west winds. There is a good landing beach on its west side and a cabin and old log operation on the south shore. Both sides of the cove have rocky bluffs.

Anchor in 2 to 3 fathoms over soft mud and grass with fair-to-good holding.

Earl Ledge (Hardwicke Island)

Chart 3544; extends 0.25 mi S from the S shore of Hardwicke Island
Breakwater light: 50°24.66'N, 125°55.24'W

Earl Ledge ... extends 0.25 mile south from the south shore of Hardwicke Island and is steep-to on its west side with shoal ground, over which there is extensive kelp, extending 0.3 mile from its east side. The ledge is covered by the red sector of Helmcken island South Sector light. Hardwicke Island locality is close NE of Earl Ledge. A float and fishing boundary marker are west of the ledge. (SD)

For temporary protection from wind chop, try the lee side of Earl Ledge on the southwest side

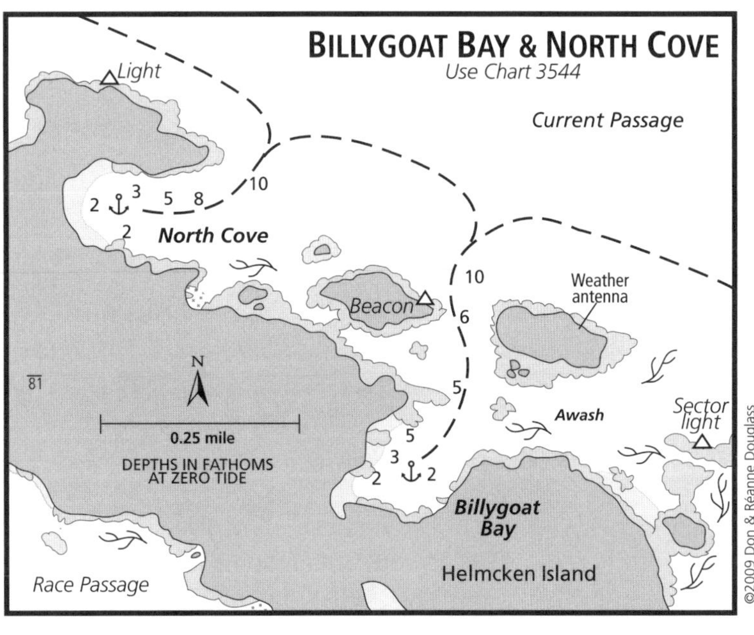

of Hardwicke Island. *Caution:* The currents are especially strong on an ebb tide and kelp patches choke the eastern approach.

Hkusam Bay (Vancouver Island)

Chart 3544; 0.5 mi W of Peterson Islet; 1.5 mi SE of Kelsey Bay
Entrance: 50°23.41′N, 125°55.34′W
Anchor: 50°23.27′N, 125°55.43′W

> *Hkusam Bay ... is suitable only for small craft. Three rocks, with less than 2 meters (6 feet) over them, lie about 0.15 mile offshore between Peterson Islet and Hkusam Bay. The remains of the Indian village Hkusam lie on the west shore of Hkusam Bay.* (SD)

Hkusam Bay is strategically located at the western junction of Race and Current passages where the turbulence can be rough for small boats. The bay's south shore may provide temporary shelter under such circumstances. The rocks and kelp patches on the shoal reduce and deflect current and chop to a large extent. Seiners also anchor on the lee side of Peterson Islet, 0.4 mile to the east.

Anchor in about 4 fathoms over sand, gravel and some rocks with fair holding.

Kelsey Bay (Vancouver Island)

Chart 3544; at the W entrance to Salmon Bay; 7.5 mi SE of Port Neville; 20.25 mi NW of Chatham Pt
Entrance: 50°23.81′N, 125°57.52′W
Public float: 50°23.78′N, 125°57.60′W

> *Kelsey Bay ... along the west side of Salmon Bay is a logging settlement with a few stores and a RCMP detachment.* (SD)
>
> *A float, attached to and parallel with the west side of the wharf, is 31 m long and suitable for small craft. It is protected by a timber breakwater built on the west side of the wharf. During strong SE winds a considerable sea sets on to the wharf. Westerly winds also cause a sea to curl around the breakwater into the wharf area.* (SD)

Kelsey Bay on Vancouver Island is a small nook that affords some relief if you're caught in a blow or unfavorable currents, but it is small

Entrance to Kelsey Bay

and crowded, and maneuvering inside can present difficulties. Watch for heavy countercurrent at the entrance on ebb tides. There are three fingers of public floats behind the old ferry landing, but there is little turning room here. Two pay telephones are located at the top of the gangway. The village of Sayward, which has provisions, is about a mile by road from Kelsey Bay

The fuel tanks previously located on the hill above the floats are no longer there, and the hillside has been logged over.

Salmon Bay (Vancouver Island)

Chart 3544; immediately E of Kelsey Bay
Logging area entrance: 50°23.75′N, 125°57.39′W

> *Salmon Bay, the estuary of Salmon River, is filled with drying mud flats that are steep-to along their outer edge. ... Small craft frequently use the estuary. The river is of considerable*

Kelsey Bay public floats

size and flows through a valley that separates Prince of Wales Range from Newcastle Ridge. (SD)

The old ship hulks in the Bloedel logging area form a breakwater

Nichols Bay (Hardwicke Island)

Chart 3544; on the W end of Hardwicke Island; 2.4 mi N of Kelsey Bay
Entrance: 50°26.11′N, 125°58.04′W
Anchor: 50°26.19′N, 125°58.06′W

The head of Nichols Bay, off the gravel beach, provides indifferent shelter. In fair weather it can be used as a base from which to visit the old fortifications on Yorke Island. However, we prefer to anchor temporarily off the south tip of Yorke Island.

Anchor in the head of the bay in 5 fathoms.

Yorke Island

Chart 3544; at the W entrance to Sunderland Channel; 0.4 mi NW of Hardwicke Pt
Anchor: 50°26.60′N, 125°58.61′W

Two buildings, halfway up the slope on the SW side of Yorke Island, are the remains of a war time military installation. (SD)

Temporary anchorage in fair weather can be found off the southwest tip of the island in the lee of the small spit and off-lying rocks.

Anchor in 3 fathoms over sand and gravel with fair holding.

Blenkinsop Bay

Charts 3564, 3544; 5.2 mi NW of Kelsey Bay
Entrance: 50°28.54′N, 126°00.57′W
Anchor: 50°29.20′N, 126°00.57′W

Anchorage in Blenkinsop Bay is well protected with good holding ground... . The small bay west of Point George also affords good anchorage with shelter from west winds. (SD)

Blenkinsop Bay, a large indentation in the mainland shore, offers moderately good shelter for small craft almost anywhere off its drying mud flat. The bay is shallow and flat over a wide area, providing unlimited swinging room. It is out of the current streams and most of the chop. Temporary anchorage can be taken just east of White Bluff with maximum protection from westerlies.

Anchor in 4 fathoms over mud, sand and eel grass with fair-to-good holding.

West Blenkinsop Cove

Charts 3564, 3544; immediately W of Pt George
Entrance: 50°28.65′N, 126°01.54′W
Anchor: 50°28.72′N, 126°01.70′W

We call the small circular cove immediately east of Blenkinsop Bay "West Blenkinsop Cove." It is deeper than the bay, but the anchorage is less exposed. Good westerly protection can be found off a small log float in the far west end, just north of the rock awash at low water.

Anchor in 4 to 5 fathoms over a mixed bottom of gravel, mud and grass with fair-to-good holding.

WW II gun emplacement, Yorke Island

Port Neville public float

Port Neville

Charts 3564, 3545; entered btwn Ransom & Neville Pts; 7.5 mi NW of Kelsey Bay
Entrance: 50°29.11'N, 126°05.30'W
Public float: 50°29.56'N, 126°05.26'W
Anchor (mid-ch of public float): 50°29.57'N, 126°05.56'W
Anchor (July Pt): 50°30.38'N, 126°04.21'W
Anchor (Baresides Bay): 50°31.60'N, 125°59.63'W

> *Port Neville … affords secure anchorage for small craft. Milly Island, close south of Neville Point, is wooded. The entrance channel, between Ransom Point and July Point, 1.4 miles north, is 0.3 mile wide and during summer months kelp grows across it. Channel Rock, 0.3 mile SW of July Point, and three other rocks with less than 2 m (6 ft) over them, lie on the sill which crosses the entrance channel.*
>
> *Tidal streams in the entrance to Port Neville attain 3 kn at times.*
>
> *A public float, attached to two dolphins, is 15 m (49 ft) long at its outer end and has a depth of about 6 m (20 ft) alongside … An extension float for small craft is attached to the north end of the main float.*
>
> *A private wharf with a float 30 m (98) ft) long lies close south of the public float.* (SD)

Port Neville store (closed)

Since the early part of the Twentieth Century, Port Neville has been a popular stop for cruising and fishing boats. An old log store run by the Hansen family operated here from 1924 to 1960, selling supplies and provisions to visiting boats. After the roads on Vancouver Island were improved and boaters could drive to Kelsey Bay, leave their car and hop into a skiff to catch the fishing openings on Johnstone Strait, the traffic at the Hansen store decreased, and it was eventually closed. The handsome log building is now used as a small gallery and potlucks are held frequently in the old kitchen during cruising season.

Ollie Hansen, the son of the original settlers, was just seven years old when his father brought the family to the area in 1916. We are sorry to report that Ollie died in 1997. Friends and visitors miss his droll sense of humor and the many stories he had to tell about his life at Port Neville. Lily, his widow, and Lorna Hansen Chesluk still live on the well-tended property. Lorna is the postmistress of the small post office located north of the gangway. Mail is picked up here by air once or twice a week, or as weather permits. Lorna will hold mail for passing boats. She asks that it be addressed with your name and your boat name in care of Postmistress, Port Neville, B.C. V0P 1M0 and marked, "Please hold for arrival."

Alders

Look across Port Neville public float to the western shores of the inlet. In 1925, when a mill caught fire, the entire forest of cedars and fir went too. Alders quickly take hold after a fire where nitrogen is plentiful. Their leaf litter adds even more nitrogen to the soil, and soon cottonwoods spring up, creating tight thickets where the sun never reaches the soil. Lack of sunshine inhibits the regrowth of firs and cedars.

Petroglyphs, Port Neville

The public float directly below the old store is usually filled in summer; during fishing openings, the center of the inlet is crammed with fishing boats anchored side by side. The float on the starboard hand as you enter Port Neville is the Hansen's private dock, please respect their property. Visitors with pets are asked to keep them on a leash and walk them on the beach, not on the Hansen property.

Artist Peggy Sowden maintains a lovely gallery on the hill across from the public dock where you can purchase arts and crafts done by coastal residents. In addition, Peggy paints watercolors of visiting boats on commission.

Vessels wishing to stay in Port Neville for a longer term can find protection by anchoring east of July Point, at the head of Baresides Bay, or in the upper basin east of Collingwood Point. *Caution:* If you continue beyond Port Neville float, use Chart 3564. Fishing boats that want to hide from easterly winds use the bight 1.7 miles northwest of Stimpson Reef.

There are petroglyphs in the vicinity of Robbers Nob and Collingwood Point. Robbers Nob is privately owned, so ask permission before you do any looking.

Anchor (midchannel) in 2 to 3 fathoms over mud and sand with good holding. Set your anchor well because of the current; keep your anchor light on in case fishing boats enter during the night.

St. Vincent Bight (Vancouver Island)

Chart 3545; 3 mi SW of the entrance to Port Neville
Entrance: 50°27.57′N, 126°09.97′W
Anchor: 50°27.47′N, 126°10.17′W

> *St. Vincent Bight, east of Windy Point, offers shelter from west winds for small craft close inshore at its west end.* (SD)

While Port Neville offers better protection, St. Vincent Bight can be used temporarily to duck out of strong westerlies. Fishing boats often use this site for short term anchoring.

Anchor in the head of the bight in about 6 fathoms.

Broken Islands

Charts 3545, 3564; 8 mi W of Port Neville
Entrance (S): 50°30.70′N, 126°17.38′W
Entrance (N): 50°31.24′N, 126°17.72′W
Broken Islands Light: 50°30.67′N, 126°17.92′W

Broken Islands—not to be confused with the Broken Group of Vancouver Island's West Coast—are a good fishing spot and fun to explore by dinghy. They also offer a tiny shortcut into Havannah Channel which is an alternate smooth-water-route to the west end of Johnstone Strait.

Havannah Channel allows you to avoid the 20-mile stretch of open water in Johnstone Strait to the west end of Hanson Island. From Minstrel Island, you can continue west in sheltered waters, or cross Knight Inlet and hug the mainland coast.

Caution: You need to station a bow lookout through the narrow passage that leads through the Broken Islands. Minimum depth of the fairway off the northern tip of the largest island is 1.5 fathoms. Proceed north, passing between two reefs awash, then into Havannah Channel.

(We will return to the Havannah Channel route after continuing west in Johnstone Strait to Blinkhorn Peninsula.)

Forward Bay (West Cracroft Island)

Chart 3545; 5 mi W of Port Harvey
Entrance (NE of Bush Islets): 50°31.12′N, 126°24.37′W
Entrance (SW of Bush Islets): 50°30.88′N, 126°24.80′W
Anchor: 50°31.10′N, 126°24.70′W

> *Forward Bay affords fair anchorage in 27 to 29 m (89 to 95 ft) near its north end. Small craft can find shelter from strong westerly winds north of Bush Islets in the west part of the bay.* (SD)

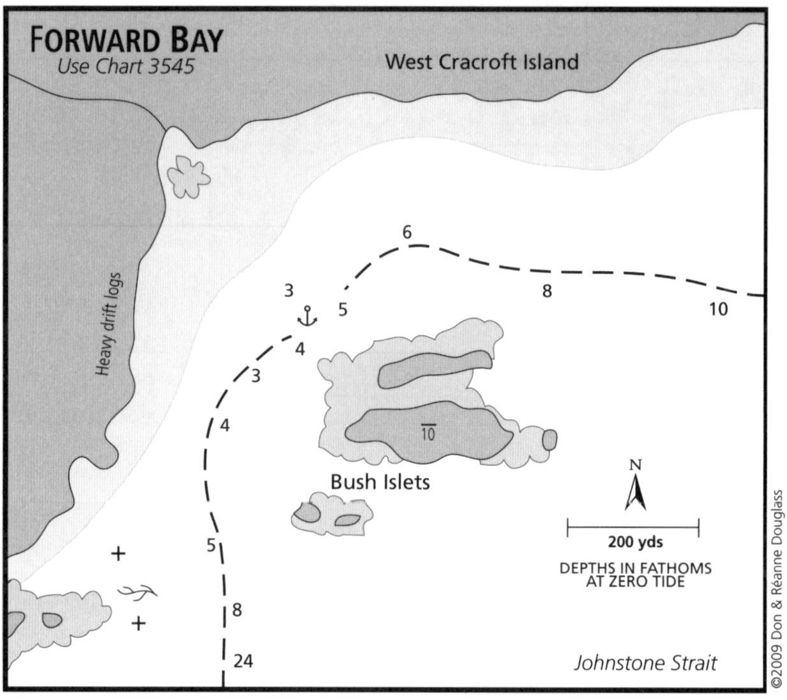

Forward Bay is strategically located on the north shore of Johnstone Strait, 3.5 miles west of Havannah Channel's south entrance. By tucking in northwest of Bush Islets, you can find fairly good protection from westerly wind and chop. Heavy drift logs on shore indicate that this spot is completely open to east winds blowing down Johnstone Strait. Even a light east wind can create an annoying swell here. Commercial fishing boats anchor in deeper water to the northeast of the site shown on the diagram.

Anchor in 4 to 5 fathoms over sand and kelp with fair-to-good holding.

Boat Bay (West Cracroft Island)

Chart 3545; 6 mi W of Forward Bay
Entrance: 50°31.28′N, 126°33.01′W
Anchor: 50°31.38′N, 126°33.81′W

> *Boat Bay affords good shelter for small craft north of the islet lying about 0.15 mile offshore. A drying rock lies about 0.15 mile south of the west extremity of the islet. A rock, with less than 2 m (6 ft) over it, lies 0.2 mile ENE of the islet.* (SD)

Offering good protection from westerlies, Boat Bay is a popular stop for cruising vessels. Although extensive kelp patches covering the rocks and reefs west of the islet cut down on westerly chop, swells and ship wake do enter the bay. The bay is also exposed to strong easterlies. Entry should be made east of the islet (44).

The campsite at the head of Boat Bay is used by kayakers; the wooden platform on

---

Orcas

Orca—the name alone brings a thrill of excitement, and watching them from the deck of a small boat is the experience of a lifetime. Sometimes called "killer whales," these striking black-and-white whales reach 20 feet in length and between 3 and 4 tons in weight. Orcas have tall dorsal fins which cut sharply through the water as they swim.

Nearly 30 different pods—extended family groups—consisting of over 300 orcas, move between Washington State and the north coast of British Columbia. Almost half of them can be found in Johnstone Strait in the summer months, where they feed on migrating salmon.

In the shallows of Robson Bight, the orcas visit their "rubbing beaches" of gravel and rock. There they can be seen rubbing their sides and bellies to rid themselves of parasites and because, apparently, it just feels good.

Whale-watching companies offer trips from Port McNeill, Port Hardy, Kelsey and Alert Bays, Sointula, and other points.

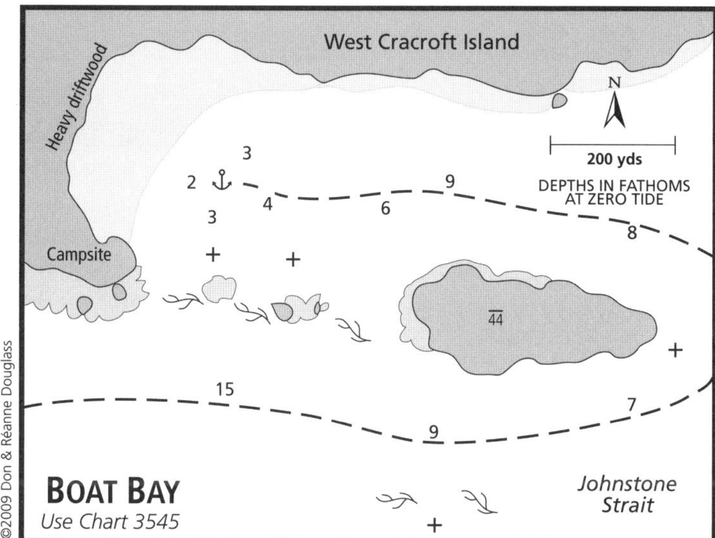

the point is used by the Robson Bight observers. From this point, with a telescope, the observers monitor the activity of boats and orcas across Johnstone Strait. The Robson Bight patrol boat protects the resident orcas in Robson Bight.

Anchor in 3 fathoms over a bottom of sand and sea lettuce with fair holding.

Robson Bight (Vancouver Island)

Chart 3545, 3546; 2 mi S of Boat Bay
Entrance: 50°29.36 N, 126°35.00'W

Robson Bight Ecological Reserve has been established to protect a core habitat of the Orcina orca (killer whale). The reserve includes a 1,248 hectare marine portion and 505 hectares of forested shoreline. Because killer whales (See http://www.comm.pac.dfo-mpo.gc.ca/publications/WhaleBook.pdf) are easily observed anywhere in northern Johnstone Strait, recreation viewing of whales should take place outside the reserve. Vessels should not enter the waters of the reserve which are patrolled. The upland portion of the reserve is closed to all entry except by permit. (SD)

Robson Bight is a favorite destination of sea kayakers who frequently camp on a beach to the west. This is the best place to observe the resident orcas (killer whales); however, it has become necessary to enforce a no-chase, no-hassle policy to ensure the continued well-being of these wonderful mammals. The bight is now closed to vessels in order to protect the orcas. Please respect this closure.

Growler Cove (West Cracroft Island)

Chart 3546; at the W end of Johnstone Strait; 12.5 mi E of Alert Bay; 21 mi W of Port Neville
Entrance (0.29 mi N of Sophia Islands): 50°32.38'N, 126°38.14'W
Anchor: 50°32.45'N, 126°36.90'W

Growler Cove … is a narrow inlet which dries at the head and has several rocks close to both shores. Small craft can obtain sheltered anchorage in 9 to 13 m (30 to 43 ft) in Growler Cove. (SD)

Growler Cove was once overrun with logbooms, but the pilings indicated on the chart have mostly been removed and nature is beginning to reestablish herself.

Although the cove is narrow with charted rocks that must be avoided, it offers good protection from southeast weather and shelter from moderate westerly chop and winds that die upon entering the cove.

Up to a dozen boats can anchor along either shore of the cove. Unfortunately, some visitors have littered the shore and bottom of the cove with empty cans and

GROWLER COVE
Use Chart 3546
200 yds
DEPTHS IN FATHOMS AT ZERO TIDE
Islet campsite
Rock face
Johnstone Strait
West Cracroft Island
©2009 Don & Réanne Douglass

bottles. Kayakers looking for an overnight campsite can find shelter on the north shore.

Growler Cove is strategically located at the west entrance to Johnstone Strait and could become a major stop for cruising boats if a little tender, loving care were expended on its behalf. Kelp is reported growing off the south entrance point.

Anchor in 3 fathoms over a mud bottom littered with bottles and cans. Holding is fair-to-good.

Blinkhorn Peninsula

Chart 3546; marks the W end of Johnstone Strait
Entrance (E): 50°32.42′N, 126°46.58′W
Anchor: 50°32.41′N, 126°46.96′W

> *Blinkhorn Peninsula, on the south side of the strait opposite the west end of Hanson Island, has drying and sunken rocks close offshore at its west end.* (SD)

Blinkhorn Peninsula has a good pebble beach with lots of drift from southeast storms. Temporary anchorage can be found close to shore on the lee side of the low spit. (See also Bauza Cove in Chapter 15.)

Cracroft Point and Blackney Passage to Blackfish Sound

Chart 3546; entered W of Cracroft Pt at the western end of Johnstone Strait
Blackney Passage (0.25 mi E of Licka Pt Light): 50°33.97′N, 126°41.21′W

> *Blackney Passage ... leads north between Hanson and Parson Islands into Blackfish Sound. Baronet Passage, north of Cracroft Point, leads east from Blackney Passage. ...*
>
> *Tidal streams in Blackney Passage attain 5 kn with heavy races off Cracroft Point on both the flood and ebb. The flood, or east-going stream, flows north and south of Hanson Island and meets near the south end of Blackney Passage causing a strong tidal race in mid-channel.* (SD)

Blackney Passage and Blackfish Sound lead north into Queen Charlotte Strait. Although Blackney Passage presents little technical challenge, there can be significant turbulence and eddies between Cracroft Point and Licka Point.

(At this point, we backtrack to Havannah Channel.)

Havannah Channel (alternate westbound route to Blackfish Sound)

Charts 3564, 3545; entered W of Broken Islands
Entrance (N, mid-ch btwn Root & Ray Pts): 50°34.66′N, 126°12.15′W
Entrance (S Pt): 50°31.70′N, 126°17.50′W
Entrance (S, 0.8 mi W of Broken Islands): 50°30.84′N, 126°19.21′W

> *Havannah Channel ... leads to Port Harvey, Call Inlet and Chatham Channel. Chatham Channel leads to Knight Inlet and is suitable for small vessels.*
>
> *The area between Broken Islands and Domville Point is filled with reefs. Hull Rock is a detached shoal rock lying west of mid-channel abreast Domville Point.* (SD)

When using Havannah Channel as an alternative to continuing west in Johnstone Strait, you head northeast, then north, connecting with Chatham Channel and Knight Inlet. This is a route to Gilford Island and the smooth-water route north along the mainland shore.

You can continue west from Minstrel Island on an interesting route that leads to the north side of Hanson Island via Clio Channel, Beware Passage, then Village or Indian channels. Or you can take Clio Channel, avoid Beware Passage, and follow Baronet Passage to the south side of Hanson Island. (Hanson Island is covered in Chapter 15.)

Open Cove (East Cracroft Island)

Charts 3564, 3545; on the N side of Harvey Pt; 1.6 mi NE of Broken Islands
Entrance: 50°32.19′N, 126°16.72′W
Anchor: 50°32.26′N, 126°16.33′W

> *Open Cove ... has marine farm facilities and affords good anchorage for small craft except in westerly winds which raise a considerable sea.* (SD)

Open Cove is a good lunch stop or fair-weather anchorage with easy access and natural scenery.

Anchor in 4 fathoms deep in the cove over mud and sand with good holding.

Port Harvey, Mist Islets

Charts 3564, 3545; an inlet that separates West & East Cracroft islands
Entrance: 50°32.35'N, 126°17.16'W
Anchor (N of Range Island): 50°33.96'N, 126°16.23'W
Anchor (N of large Mist Islet): 50°33.34'N, 126°16.18'W
Anchor (S of large Mist Islet): 50°33.01'N, 126°16.49'W

> *Port Harvey, an inlet entered west of Transit Point, affords good anchorage for small vessels NNW of Mist Islets and excellent anchorage for small craft north of Range Island.* (SD)

Port Harvey offers several well-sheltered, quiet anchorages that are perhaps the best cruising-boat anchorages the entire length of Johnstone Strait. Either of the two recommended sites north of Range Island are of easy access and have unlimited swinging room; the most popular are located at the head of the bay. When a southeasterly is forecast, we prefer to tuck in behind the northeast end of the upper Mist Islet, avoiding the several rocks off the north end of the island.

Anchor (north of Range Island) in 3 to 4 fathoms over sticky mud with very good holding.

Anchor (north of large Mist Islet) in 5 to 6 fathoms over mud and gravel with fair-to-good holding.

Anchor (south of large Mist Islet) in 3 fathoms over mud with good holding.

Boughey Bay

Charts 3564, 3545; 3.5 mi E of Port Harvey; 2.7 mi S of Chatham Channel
Entrance 50°32.69'N, 126°11.15'W
Anchor: 50°31.20'N, 126°11.05'W

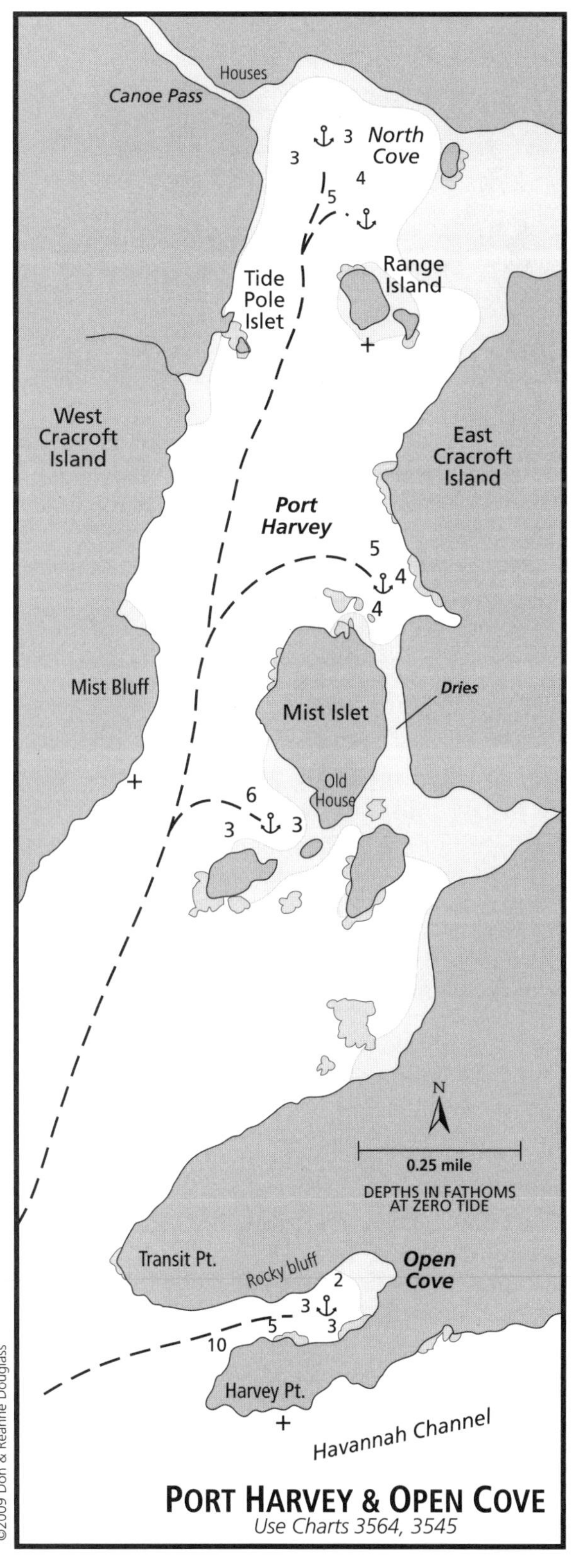

PORT HARVEY & OPEN COVE
Use Charts 3564, 3545

Float-house, Port Harvey

Boughey Shoal, an isolated rock with 5.8 m (19 ft) over it, lies in the middle of the entrance to Boughey Bay. Anchorage can be obtained in the middle of the bay. Booming grounds line its shore. (SD)

Boughey Bay is a remote quiet place with great scenery. The classic glacier-cut U-shaped valley to the south allows some winds to blow through, but with little fetch. We have found a snug anchorage here when it was howling in Johnstone Strait. Although John Chappell long ago noted williwaws here on easterly gales, we have found only occasional puffs.

Anchor deep in the bay in 3 to 4 fathoms over mud with good holding.

Burial Cove and Soderman Cove (East Cracroft Island)

Charts 3545, 3564; NW of Hull Island; just N of Soderman Cove
Entrance (Burial Cove): 50°33.57'N, 126°12.88'W
Entrance (Soderman Cove): 50°33.39'N, 126°13.15'W
Anchor (Burial Cove): 50°33.68'N, 126°13.21'W

Burial Cove ... affords good anchorage for small craft.

Soderman Cove, south of Round Island, has marine farm facilities in it. (SD)

As local residents extend their floats into the cove, Burial Cove is becoming more congested; however, good shelter can be found deep in the bay.

Anchor in 3 fathoms over mud with good holding.

Matilpi

Charts 3564, 3545; 1.5 mi N of Boughey Bay
Entrance (W): 50°33.55'N, 126°11.51'W
Anchor: 50°33.55'N, 126°11.30'W

Indian Islands lie off the abandoned Indian village Matilpi, only the ruins of one house remain. Small craft can find good anchorage behind the islands. (SD)

Matilpi is dense and overgrown except for its small white beach. (What appears to be white sand is actually a finely-crushed shell midden.) For aficionados of plant life, the shore accommodates an amazing mix of cedar, alders, broadleaf maple, gooseberry, red elderberry, salmon berry, snowberry and wild rose.

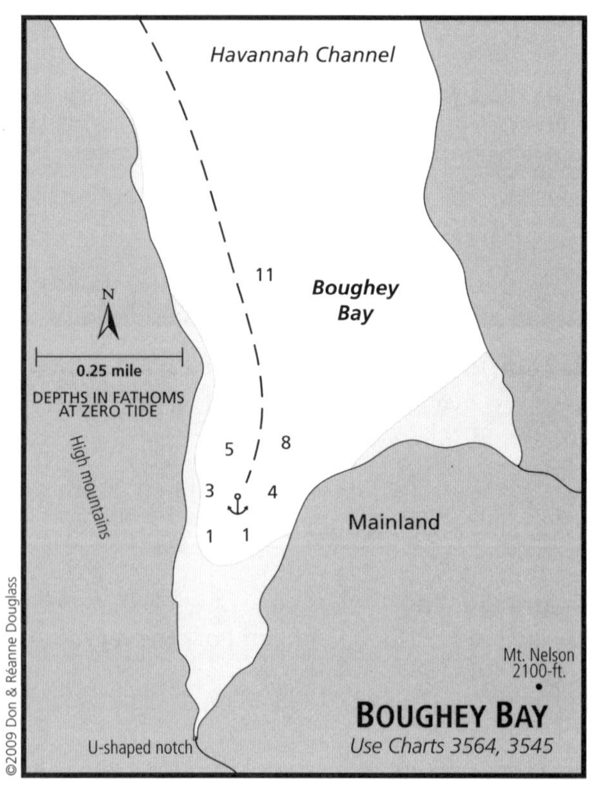

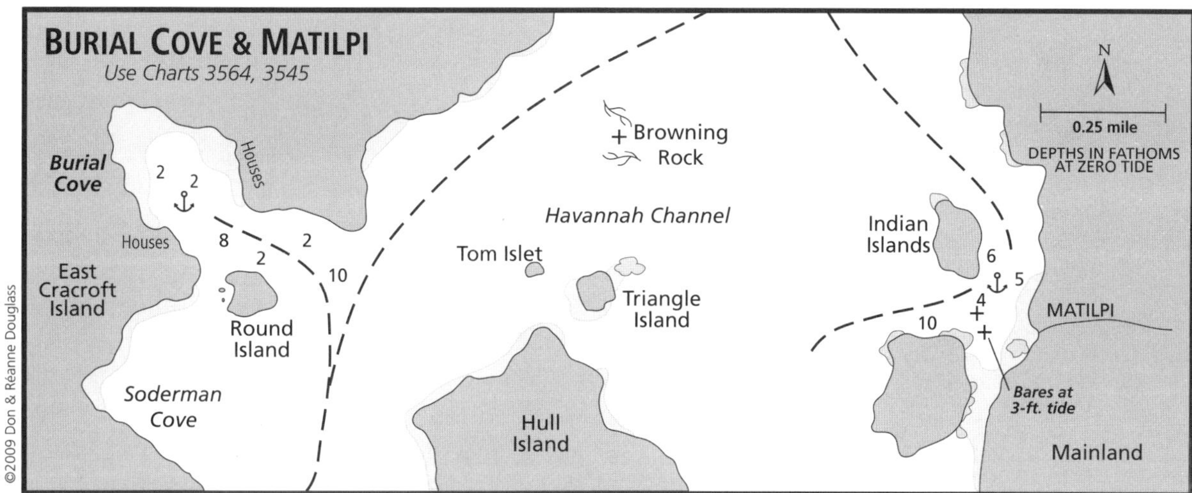

Contrary to *Sailing Directions*, we found a mixed, uneven bottom and we do not recommend it as an overnight anchorage—it makes a temporary anchor site only.

Anchor in 6 to 8 fathoms over a rocky bottom with poor holding.

Call Inlet

Charts 3564, 3545; entered N of Turn Pt; E of Chatham Channel & is 10 mi long
Entrance: 50°34.45′N, 126°11.43′W

> *The inlet is free of mid-channel dangers except for Call Shoal, with 10.7 m (35 ft) over it, lying 2 miles within the entrance.*
>
> *Depths in most places are too deep for good anchorage and east winds are reported to funnel strongly down the inlet.* (SD)

Other than the Warren Islands, Call Inlet is steep to and of little interest to cruising boats.

Warren Islands (Call Inlet)

Charts 3564, 3545; 1.25 mi E of Chatham Channel
Entrance: 50°34.91′N, 126°10.74′W

> *Warren Islands are reported to provide inadequate shelter for small craft.* (SD)

Temporary anchorage for small boats in fair weather can be found behind Warren Islands. This is a pretty and secluded area worth visiting in itself or to wait for slack water in Chatham Channel.

Chatham Channel

Chart 3564; connects Havannah Channel to Knight Inlet
Entrance (E, on range): 50°34.81′N, 126°12.46′W
Entrance (W, on range): 50°34.78′N, 126°14.13′W

> *Chatham Channel, entered between Root Point and Ray Point, leads along the north coast of East Cracroft Island and connects Havannah Channel to Knight Inlet. The channel is narrow and shallow at the east end, south of Bowers Island. A rock, with 1.5 m over it,lies in the east entrance and kelp grows almost across the channel in summer and autumn.*
>
> *Tidal streams flood to the east and have a rate at springs of 5 kn, being strongest in the first mile west of Root Point. Secondary current station Chatham Channel (Index No. 5075), referenced on Seymour Narrows, is given in the "Tide Tables, Volume 6."*
>
> *A daybeacon with a port hand daymark is on Root Point. Two daybeacons with port hand daymarks are on the south side of the channel between Root Point and Bowers Islands. A daybeacon with a starboard hand daymark is ont eh SW Bowers Island.* (SD)

Chatham Channel is a main smooth-water route between Johnstone Strait and Knight Inlet. The channel has a mind of its own though, so don't be surprised if you find

Rusting donkey, abandoned work skiff and water-logged float

the flood running east on one occasion and west on another. If the current is unfavorable, anchor to the northeast for a couple of hours, relax, then run with it when conditions are favorable. This strange behavior which is caused by occasional tidal differences between Johnstone Strait and Knight Inlet varies with local conditions, especially strong ebb tides enhanced by heavy runoff.

If you line up the ranges and watch them carefully, you should have no problem here. Mid-channel depths are 2 to 3 fathoms at low water. Avoid the shoals marked with heavy kelp.

Hadley Bay (Chatham Channel)

Charts 3564 inset, 3545; at the E end of Chatham Ch; 4.2 mi SE of Minstrel I
Entrance: 50°34.88'N, 126°12.27'W
Anchor: 50°35.02'N, 126·°12.40'W

Hadley Bay, NW of Atchison Island, has private berthing facilities and a conspicuous orange house (1981). The islet south of Atchison Island has a cliff with a white patch on it. (SD)

Hadley Bay is a good place to anchor and wait for slack water. You can anchor anywhere east of Atchison Island over a flat bottom and be out of the current stream.

Anchor in 3 fathoms over sand and gravel with fair holding.

Cutter Cove (Chatham Channel)

Chart 3545, 3564; 1.2 mi E of Minstrel Island
Entrance: 50°36.90'N, 126°16.80'W
Anchor: 50°37.27'N, 126°15.40'W

Cutter Cove provides anchorage for small vessels with good holding in mud. (SD)

Cutter Cove is a moderately large but shallow cove with good protection from all directions. Steep, high cliffs form the north shore and a wooded ridge forms the south. To the east, there is a drying mud bank. The cove has ample swinging room for a number of boats and the flat bottom makes anchoring easy. You could easily make a night or radar approach here; small Cutter Islet at the entrance is passable on either side.

If you want to be closer to the moss-covered trees, you can use as a stern tie the yellow line tied to a large tree on a small point at the south side. The bottom shoals gradually to the drying flats and the 2-fathom line is marked with a few crab pot floats.

Anchor in 3 fathoms over a mud bottom with good holding.

Minstrel Island

Charts 3564, 3545; at the N end of Clio & Chatham Channels; 1 mi N of Lagoon Cove; 11 mi NW of Port Neville
Marina float: 50°36.82'N, 126°18.23'W

The area off Minstrel Island settlement is a water aerodrome. (SD)

Rain-forest cabin near Turn Point

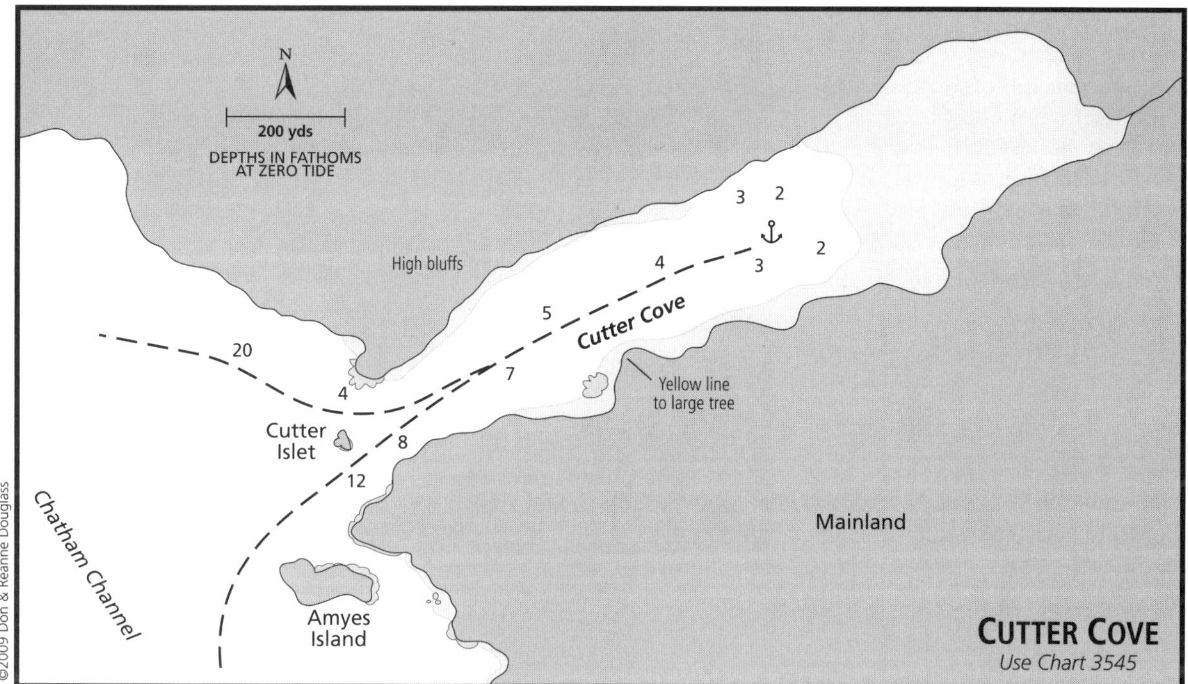

Minstrel Island, once a major stop for boats headed to Alaska, no longer has its former vibrancy. Minstrel Island Resort has long catered to sportfishing enthusiasts and once served as a fuel stop for cruising boats.

Since 1998, the resort has been for sale and, until further information is available, you should check the current situation. Lagoon Cove, one mile to the southwest, has taken over much of the former trade done at Minstrel Island Resort.

If you wish to avoid Knight Inlet, you can head west from this point through the Blow Hole to Mamalilaculla and Village Channel, then west toward Port Hardy. You can also cross Knight Inlet directly and follow the mainland coast toward Cape Caution.

Baidarka crew at Minstrel Island

The Blow Hole

Chart 3564; a narrow passage btwn Minstrel Island & East Cracroft Island
Entrance (E): 50°36.74'N, 126°18.08'W
Entrance (W): 50°36.28'N, 126°18.91'W

> *Minstrel Island is separated from East Cracroft Island by The Blow Hole, which is suitable only for small craft. It is narrow and shallow and has kelp growing almost across it in summer and autumn. A submarine pipeline crosses The Blow Hole.* (SD)

The Blow Hole is used by cruising boats as a smooth-water route to Lagoon Cove and Clio Channel. It has a minimum depth of about 1 1/2 fathoms. Avoid the large midchannel rock just east of the narrows by favoring the north shore. The rock is visible on high water.

Lagoon Cove (East Cracroft)

Chart 3564; btwn East Cracroft & Farquharson Islands; entered SW of Perley I from Clio Ch
Entrance: 50°36.03'N, 126°19.10'W
Float: 50°35.91'N, 126°18.83'W

> *Lagoon Cove ... affords sheltered anchorage, mud bottom, for small vessels.* (SD)

The store at Lagoon Cove

Lagoon Cove, with its popular Lagoon Cove Marina, is a favorite destination for most cruising boats heading north. Who would want to miss the lively and delicious shrimp pot lucks. The marina has a fuel dock (gasoline, diesel, propane, stove oil and kerosene); fishing licenses and ice can be purchased at the small store.

Anchorage can be taken anywhere in the southern part of the cove; avoiding the west shore where old cables lurk.

Anchor in 8 fathoms over a mud bottom with good holding.

⚓ **Lagoon Cove Marina** monitors VHF Ch 66A; fuel; power; restrooms; showers

Clio Channel

Chart 3545; btwn West Cracroft & Turnour islands, connects Baronet & Beware passages to Knight Inlet
Entrance (N, 0.33 mi SW of White Nob Pt): 50°37.63'N, 126°19.95'W
Entrance (W, 0.27 mi S of Nicholas Pt): 50°34.67'N, 126°29.10'W

> *A rock with less than 2 m (6 ft) over it lies midway between Klaoitsis Island and Joliffe Island. Turnour Rock lies in the approach to Turnour Bay.*
>
> *Tidal streams in Clio Channel flood to the west at about 1 kn.* (SD)

Clio Channel, 7 miles long and normally well-sheltered and smooth, is lightly used except for a few local fishing boats.

Cracroft Inlet

Chart 3545; btwn West Cracroft & East Cracroft islands; entered E of Sambo Pt
Entrance (N): 50°36.08'N, 126°21.02'W

> *Cracroft Inlet ...with Dorman Island and Farquharson Island on its NE side, is a drying gorge leading to Port Harvey.* (SD)

Cracroft Inlet is a narrow, shallow inlet that leads to a high-water passage for kayaks. The south entrance is located at the head of Port Harvey; the north entrance is one mile west of Lagoon Cove.

It may be possible to find secluded anchor-

Log ship travelling through Johnstone Strait

It's fun float fishing at Lagoon Cove

age within the first 1.5 miles of the north entrance, but swinging room here is limited. Avoid the rock awash at low water on the west end of Dorman Island, as well as a rock drying at 14 feet, 0.7 mile inside the inlet.

POTTS LAGOON
Use Chart 3545 metric

DEPTHS IN FATHOMS AT ZERO TIDE

200 yds

Bones Bay (West Cracroft Island)

Chart 3545; on the S side of Clio Channel; 2 mi W of Lagoon Cove
Entrance: 50°35.45'N, 126°21.28'W
Anchor: 50°35.12'N, 126°21.36'W

> *Bones Bay has a conspicuous abandoned cannery near its head. The charted jetty is in disrepair.* (SD)

Good shelter from southeast weather can be found in the inner bay off the old cannery ruins.

Anchor in 7 to 10 fathoms over mud with good holding.

Potts Lagoon (West Cracroft Island)

Chart 3545; at the W end of Clio Channel; 6 mi SW of Lagoon Cove; 5.5 mi SE of Mamalilaculla
Entrance: 50°33.83'N, 126°27.58'W
Anchor (Main Basin): 50°33.58'N, 126°27.09'W

> *Potts Lagoon, on the south side of the channel, and a cove on the east side of the entrance to the lagoon, offer good all weather anchorage for small craft.* (SD)

Potts Lagoon offers two very calm and secluded anchorages for cruising boats: one is the Main Basin; the other we call "East Basin."

The entrance to the lagoon is narrow and shallow with patches of kelp. Anchorage can be taken in the flat-bottomed bay southeast of island (41). This area is landlocked and protected from all weather.

Anchor (Main Basin) in 2 to 3 fathoms over mud with pieces of wood and kelp. Holding is fair-to-good.

Potts Lagoon East Basin (West Cracroft Island)

Chart 3545; 0.6 mi E of Klaoitsis Island
Entrance: 50°33.91'N, 126°27.32'W
Anchor (East Basin): 50°33.93'N, 126°27.08'W

Potts Lagoon East Basin is what we call the easy-access anchorage northeast of Potts Lagoon. It is very well-protected from all weather except strong westerlies; during such conditions, some chop curls around the point. This scenic, undeveloped basin has room where two or three boats can tuck in behind the south entrance point.

Anchor (East Basin) in 2 to 3 fathoms over sand with fair-to-good holding.

Baronet Passage

Charts 3545, 3546; btwn Harbledown & West Cracroft Islands; connects Clio Channel to Johnstone Strait
Entrance (E): 50°33.90'N, 126°29.90'W
Entrance (W, 0.4 mi NE of Cracroft Pt Light): 50°33.24'N, 126°40.29'W

Baronet Passage is partially obstructed by reefs near Walden Island and should be navigated with caution. The route thorough Baronet Passage and Clio Channel to Knight Inlet is sometimes used by small vessels.

Tidal streams flood to the west at a maximum of about 3 kn off Walden island. Secondary current station Baronet Passage (for a location 1.5 miles west of Walden Island), referenced on Seymour Narrows, is given in the Tide Tables, Volume 6.

Bell Rocks lie on the north side of the west entrance to the passage. The flood current flowing south through Blackney Passage near Bell Rocks, resulting in a counter-clockwise circulation. (SD)

Baronet Passage is the shortest, fastest way to reach Johnstone and Broughton straits. Jamieson Island can be passed on either side but Wilson Pass is the preferred route. Favor the north shore near Walden Island.

Beware Passage

Chart 3545; lies btwn Harbledown & Turnour Islands
Entrance (E, 0.12 mi NE of Kamano Island): 50°34.46'N, 126°29.77'W
Entrance (E, 0.27 mi SW of Kamano Island): 50°34.12'N, 126°30.26'W
Entrance (W, mid-ch btwn Dead & Mink Pts): 50°35.86'N, 126°34.50'W

Beware Passage is obstructed by numerous islands, rocks and shoal areas; local knowledge is recommended and it is prudent to navigate it at LW on a rising tide when underwater dangers are visible. Close attention should be paid to drift from tidal streams.

Care Rock and Beware Rock are named mid-channel dangers. Names islands are Kamano Island, Care Island and Cook Island. Karlukwees, at the SW end of Turnour Island, NW of Nicholas Point, is the site of an occasionally occupied Indian village. The wharf and float are in disrepair. (SD)

In traversing Beware Passage care must be taken to identify and avoid all the interesting rocks and reefs, especially at the west entrance. We prefer "Tugboat Pass" which is 0.35 mile southwest of Care Rock, close to the Harbledown Island shore. The Tugboat Pass route, which is about 200 yards long, keeps all the islets and difficult-to-see rocks 0.5 mile northwest of Kamano Island to the east side of the boat.

Avoid the rocks between Kamano Island and island (44) near the Harbledown Island shore by staying to their north in midchannel of Beware Passage. This should be navigated only in daylight with good visibility and lookouts posted on your bow.

Tugboat Pass has a minimum depth of about 2 fathoms at zero tide. Kelp is found along either side of the fairway. Avoid the submerged rock extending from the south shore at the north entrance. Tugboat Pass doesn't require any tricky turns or searching for unmarked rocks; it's "straight forward," but it does call for alert piloting.

Caution Cove (Turnour Island)

Chart 3545; 2.5 mi NW of Potts Lagoon; 3.2 mi SE of Mamalilaculla
Entrance: 50°34.28'N, 126°31.08'W
Anchor: 50°35.16'N, 126°30.31'W

Caution Cove, with Caution Rock in the middle

of its entrance, provides anchorage for small craft with reported good holding over mud but is open to prevailing winds. (SD)

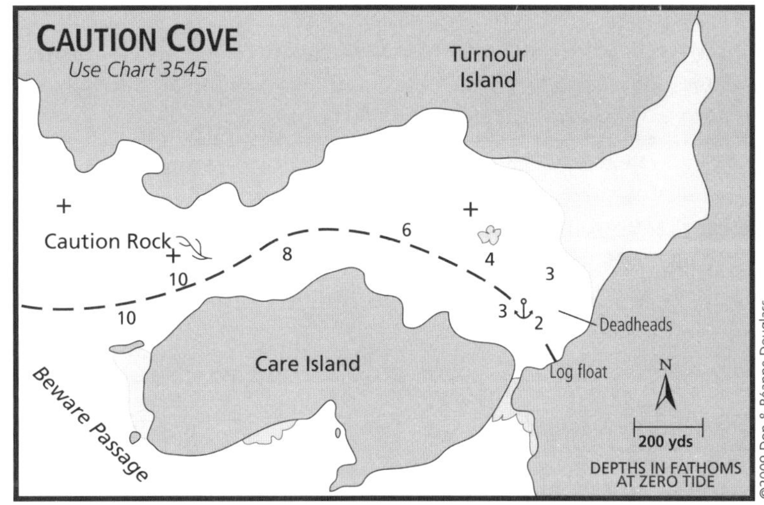

Caution Cove is well protected from east and south winds. Although open to westerlies, little chop enters the south nook. Avoid Beware Rock by remaining south of Caution Rock; on entering, favor the Care Island shore. Both rocks are marked by kelp.

Avoid also the two mid-cove rocks off the drying mud flat. The southeast corner is quiet and calm. As logging operations have retreated from the cove, its natural features are returning. Go deep into Caution Cove and anchor off the "window" on the east side of Care Island. We have found some remnants of deadheads here, so be careful. Anchorage can be found off the old unused log float.

Anchor in 2 to 3 fathom's over a mud bottom with twigs and good holding.

Beware Cove (Turnour Island)

Chart 3545; 1.2 mi NW of Caution Cove
Entrance: 50°35.57'N, 126°33.28'W
Anchor: 50°35.81'N, 126°32.52'W

Beware Cove offers protection from NW winds but is exposed to those from SE & NE.

A detached shoal with 4.9 m (16 ft) over it lies 0.4 mile south of Mink Point, and a shoal with 8.8 (29 ft) over it lies midway between Mink Point and Dead Point. (SD)

Beware Cove is a stable-weather anchorage with a number of rocks, islets and patches of kelp. During the summer, these thick patches keep out any southeasterly chop.

Anchor in 2 to 3 fathoms over sand and kelp with fair holding.

Dead Point Cove (Harbledown Island)

Chart 3545; at the W end of Beware Passage; 0.3 mi S of Dead Pt
Entrance: 50°35.55'N, 126°34.73'W
Anchor: 50°35.54'N, 126°35.15'W

Dead Point Cove, with its easy access makes a good rest stop or a place to wait out fog.

Upon entering, avoid the rocks south of Dead Point; anchor deep in the center of the cove.

Anchor in 2 fathoms over sand and mud with good holding.

Indian Channel

Charts 3545, 3546; on the N side of Harbledown Island; connects Blackfish Sound to Mamalilaculla
Entrance (E, 0.27 mi S of Cecil Islet): 50°36.19'N, 126°35.04'W
Entrance (W, 0.07 mi S of Sarah Islets): 50°35.63'N, 126°40.09'W

> *Village Channel leads along the north side, and Indian Channel, entered through Whitebeach Passage, along the south, of a group of islands which includes Berry Island, Carey Group and Hail Islets.*
>
> *Village and Indian Channels and Eliot Passage, sprinkled with unmarked dangers, are suitable only for small craft and should be navigated with caution.* (SD)

Indian and Village channels lead through the center of a well-sheltered archipelago, an area that was the center of pre-historic native activity that is believed to date back 8000 years. Throughout this small region, there are many coves and nooks suitable for exploring or anchoring.

Indian Channel connects Native Anchorage on the east to Blackfish Sound on the west via Whitebeach Passage.

Village Channel

Charts 3545, 3546; on the S side of Crease Island
Entrance (E, 0.12 mi N of Cecil Rock): 50°36.66'N, 126°35.15'W
Entrance (W, 0.08 mi W of Punt Rock): 50°35.94'N, 126°41.76'W

Village Channel connects the village of Mamalilaculla on the east to Blackfish Sound on the west via West Passage.

Eliot Passage

Charts 3545, 3546; leads N btwn Pearl & Village Islands
Entrance (S, 0.09 mi NW of Scrub Islet): 50°36.99'N, 126°36.21'W
Entrance (N, 0.37 mi SE of Clock Rock): 50°37.76'N, 126°35.13'W

Mamalilaculla (Village Island)

Charts 3545, 3546; on the W side of Village Island; 8 mi N of Robson Bight
Entrance: 50°37.34'N, 126°34.95'W
Anchor (NW cove): 50°37.42'N, 126°34.76'W

> *Mamalilaculla ... is in ruins. An Indian Reserve in the SE part of Indian Channel, on the north end of Harbledown Island, has a ruins of a jetty and several houses of the occasionally occupied Indian village.*
>
> *Small craft can find anchorage with fair shelter and good holding but limited swinging room NE of the ruins of the jetty at Mamalilaculla.* (SD)

Mamalilaculla was once a prosperous native village with handsome wooden houses, circa 1920. The village is now abandoned and nature is slowly reclaiming it. Some of the pillars of the old longhouse still stand in front of the village. The totems have fallen, but a few are in good enough condition that you can determine their form. One appears to be a bear sitting on the head of a raven; another is a sea wolf. In recent years, with increased interest from visiting boats, native caretakers sometimes take turns as summer shore guides. They are happy to give you a tour and a capsule history of Mamalilaculla's culture. (You might take note of the fact that the village is built atop 12 feet of midden!) There is an honor-system fee for visiting the village site. For information, please contact the band office in Campbell River; tel: 250-287-2955.

Much of the area around Mamalilaculla is still native territory—witness the modern-day

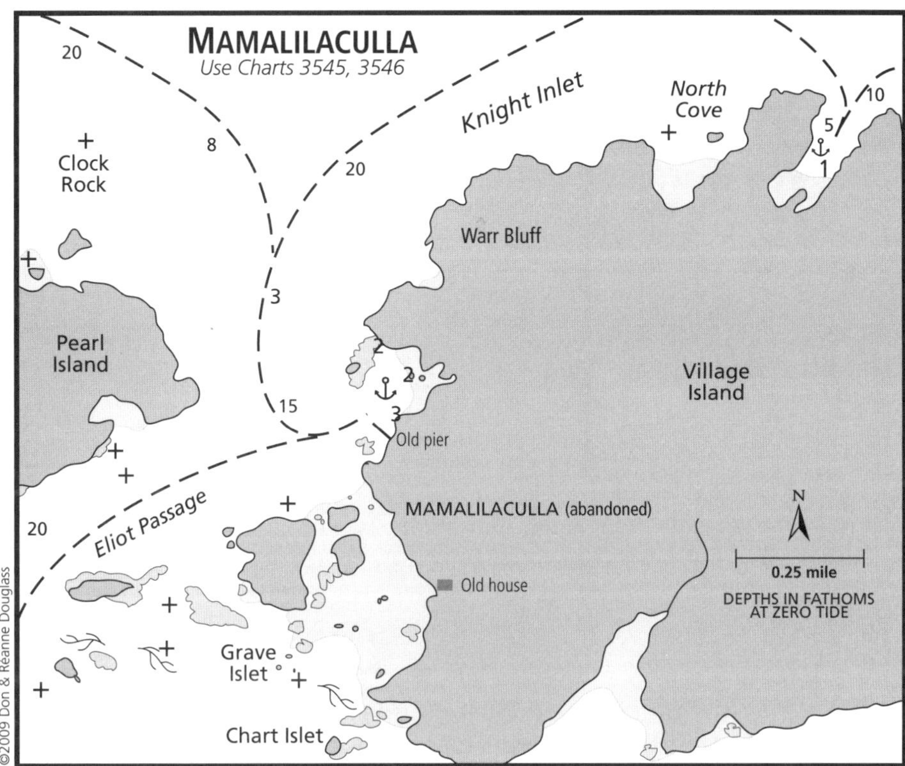

blockhouse crypts on the various islets. Please respect it!

Except for kayaks, the area in front of the village is too shallow to anchor. You can anchor in the bay a half-mile to the northwest, north of the old pier, and visit this area on the east side of Eliot Passage by dinghy.

Anchor (northwest cove) in 2 to 3 fathoms, protected by the reef; sandy mud bottom with good holding.

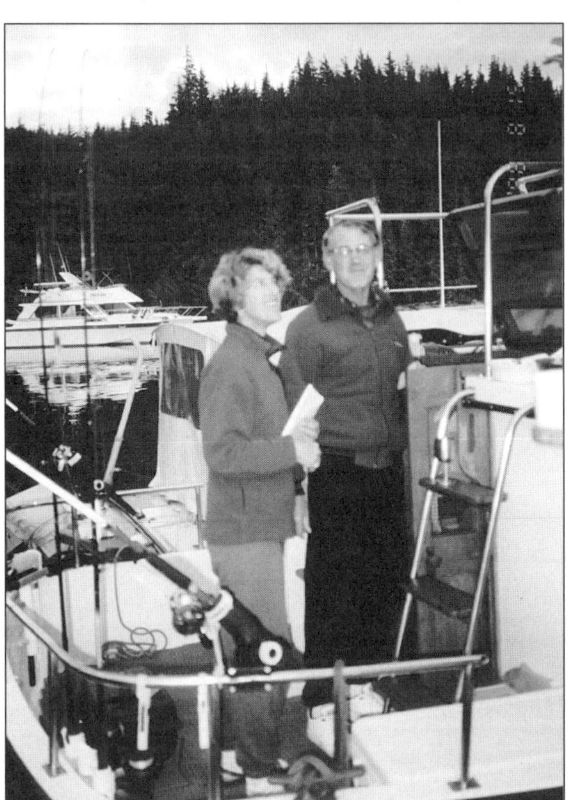

The Sangers aboard Forevergreen, *Mamililaculla*

North Cove (Village Island)

Chart 3545; 1.2 mi NE of Mamalilaculla
Entrance: 50°38.36'N, 126°33.12'W
Anchor: 50°37.88'N, 126°33.36'W

We found this cove to be a pleasant summer anchorage.

Anchor in 1 to 2 fathoms over sand and gravel with fair holding.

Remains of fallen totem at Mamalilaculla

Longhouse "survivor" at Mamalilaculla

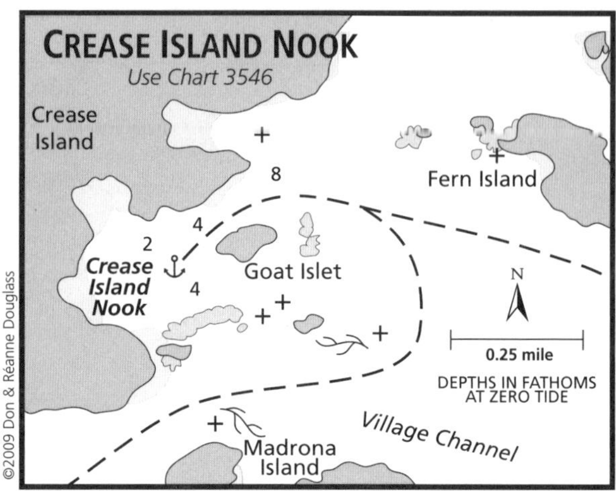

Crease Island Nook (Crease Island)

Chart 3546; on E side of Crease Island; 1.4 mi NE of Farewell Hbr
Entrance (N): 50°37.07′N, 126°38.35′W
Entrance (S): 50°36.89′N, 126°38.24′W
Anchor: 50°36.93′N, 126°38.63′W

Crease Island Cove is our name for the well-protected area behind Goat Islet. We use this site as a good base camp for exploring the area by dinghy or kayak.

The north entrance is preferable, but you can enter the cove via a shallow channel on the south side of Goat Islet. There are a number of charted and uncharted rocks and reefs in these waters, so you need to navigate carefully and keep a sharp lookout.

Anchor in 2 fathoms over mud and sand with good holding.

Farewell Harbour (Berry Island)

Chart 3546; on the W side of Berry Island; 7 mi NE of Telegraph Cove
Entrance: 50°36.07′N, 126°40.48′W
Anchor: 50°36.13′N, 126°40.38′W

> *Farewell Harbour ... affords secure anchorage for small vessels. A lodge with a float and sewer outlet submarine pipeline are on the west side of Berry Island.* (SD)

Shore facilities here belong Farewell Harbour Resort which is private.

The harbor is large enough to accommodate yachts of all sizes, with adequate swinging room for about two dozen boats. Afternoon northwest winds are sometimes felt in the bay.

Anchorage can be taken anywhere south of Kamux Island, avoiding the kelp-marked reef that extends from the southwest tip of Berry Island. The bottom is a flat 6 fathoms over a wide area.

Anchor in 6 fathoms over mud with good holding.

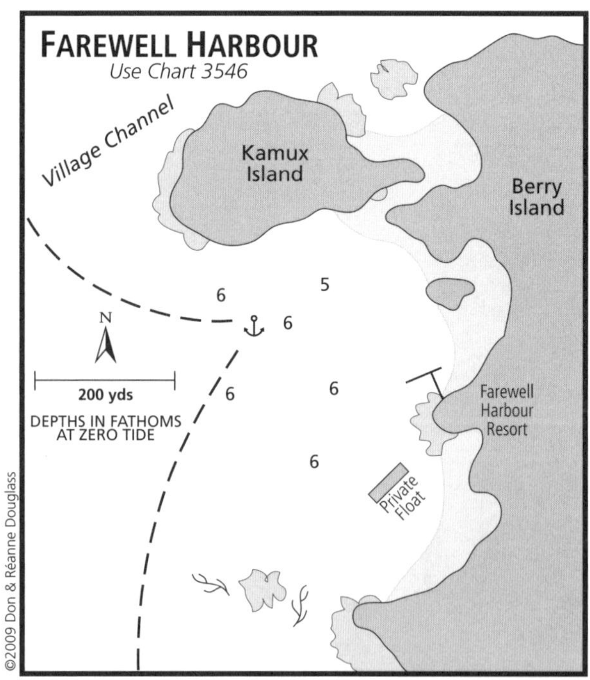

Swanson Passage

Chart 3546; lies btwn Crease & Swanson Islands
Entrance (S): 50°36.34'N, 126°40.94'W
Entrance (N): 50°37.07'N, 126°40.76'W

> *Swanson Passage, west of Crease Island, leads to Farewell Harbour. Rocks lie on both sides of the south end of the channel.* (SD)

Swanson Island Nook (Swanson Passage)

Chart 3546; W side of Crease Island; the tiny cove behind the unnamed islet 0.2 mi E of Charles Pt
Entrance (0.57 mi W of Charles Pt): 50°36.96'N, 126°41.82'W
Anchor: 50°36.85'N, 126°41.70'W

Swanson Passage is a smooth-water route between Blackfish Sound and the Broughton Archipelago to the north. Several small nooks provide shelter on either side of the entrance to Swanson Passage.

Swanson Island Nook is a small, shallow cove offering good protection in southeast weather off its drying mud flat.

Anchor (Swanson Island Nook) in 2 to 4 fathoms over sand and mud bottom with fair-to-good holding.

Crease Island Nook (Swanson Passage)

Chart 3546; located NE corner of Swanson Island; 0.6 mi SW of Charles Pt
Entrance (0.2 mi E of Charles Pt): 50°37.12'N, 126°40.79'W

Crease Island Nook is a small, scenic cove offering good protection to one boat in southeast weather; it is somewhat open to northwest winds.

Heard over VHF Radio, Channel 16 . . .

A bass voice speaking, without identifying himself or his vessel: "Has this damn fog lifted *anywhere* in Johnstone Strait?"

The reply, seconds later, from another unidentified voice: "In Farewell Harbour."

Bass voice: "Well, there may be salvation yet!"

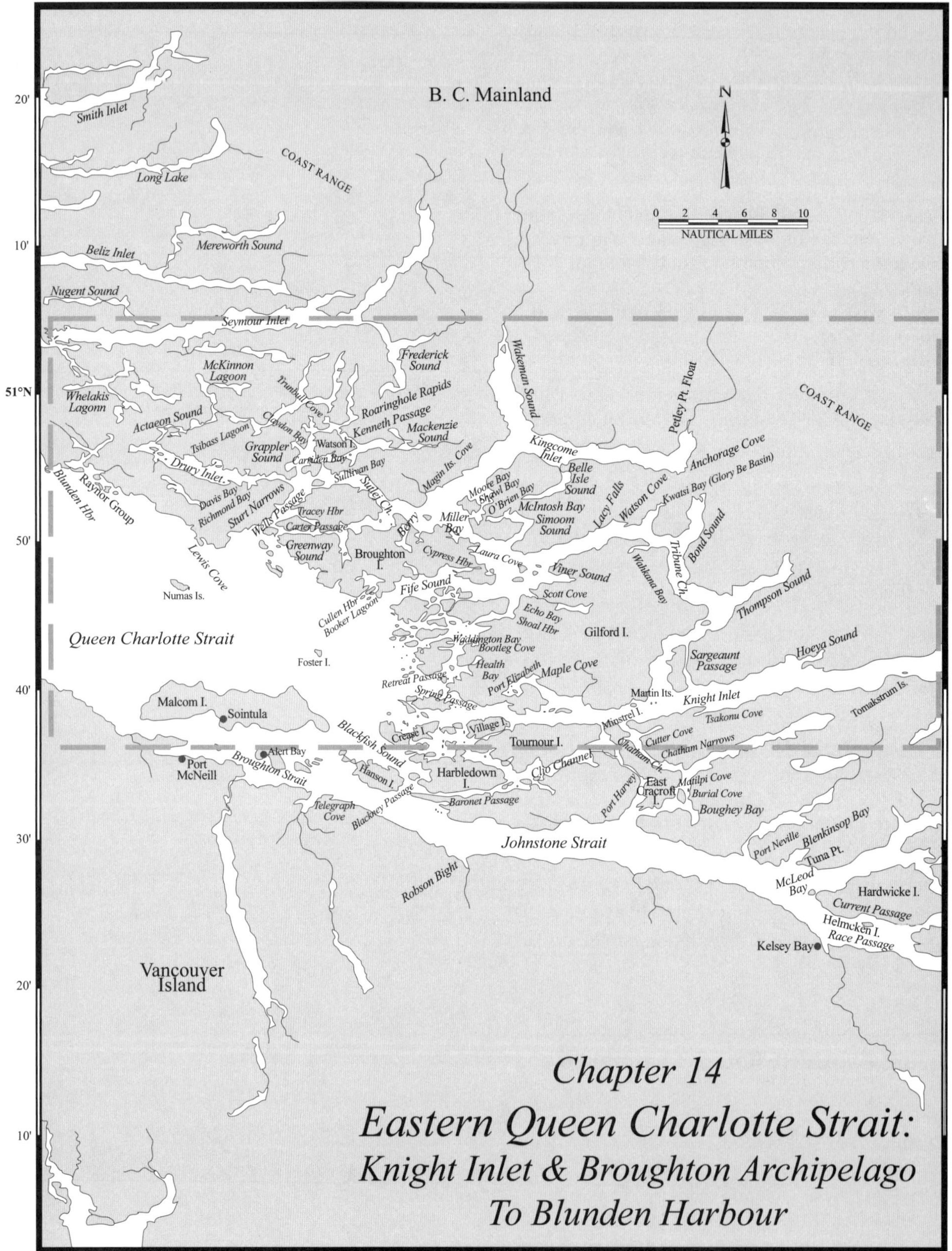

Chapter 14

Eastern Queen Charlotte Strait:

Knight Inlet & Broughton Archipelago To Blunden Harbour

14

EASTERN QUEEN CHARLOTTE STRAIT: Knight Inlet and Broughton Archipelago to Blunden Harbour

The area along the mainland shore east of Queen Charlotte Strait has some of the finest cruising and fishing grounds in the Northern Hemisphere. From Tribune Channel and Fife Sound, to remote Mackenzie Sound and Drury Inlet, opportunities exist for exploring a myriad of islands, islets, and coves within sheltered, calm waters. In the past, this recreational area was known primarily to fishing enthusiasts who flew to resorts that catered to their needs, or to intrepid kayakers crossing from Vancouver Island. However, in the past decade, cruising boaters have made this a destination area or a major stop on their way north along the Inside Passage.

These are "friendly" cruising grounds where, for the most part, the waters are protected, and where around every corner there are hundreds of pristine, secluded coves to be explored. In the past decade, as boaters venture further north, the region known as the Broughton Archipelago (or just the Broughtons) has become a popular cruising destination. Within a few miles of the wilderness Echo Bay, Pierre's Bay, Kwatsi Bay Marina, Shawl Bay, Sullivan Bay and Greenway Sound all offer a lively ambiance with varying facilities; both Echo Bay Resort and Sullivan Bay have fuel and small stores. And for full services, Port McNeill is just 25 miles from Echo Bay.

Broughton Archipelago Marine Park, a maze of small islands, islets, and narrow passages was once home to the ancestors of today's First Nation's people and, within this area you can still find mizzens that serve as an example to their existence. In our time, the Broughtons have traditionally been the playground of sea kayaks and canoes, and they still are.

In many areas of this archipelago, the islets break up the swells and chop and provide convenient haul-out beaches. The environment supports a rich marine habitat. Fishing is excellent, whales can sometimes be sighted and bear comb the brushy shores.

A number of small coves entered through smaller passages can provide temporary anchorage while you explore the area between

Knight Inlet

Bonwick and Eden islands. In some of these areas, though, currents run up to 2 knots, and the waters can hold a lot of underwater and surface kelp.

Proceding eastward and northward, many of the more remote inlets and channels recall the geology and terrain of the North Coast: deep, glacier-fed waters, high granite walls—often with snow in their crevices—and few, if any, inhabitants. Self-sufficiency, preparedness and vigilance are the keys to your enjoyment the further north you go!

Knight Inlet

Charts 3545, 3546, 3515; entered btwn Gilford Island to the N & Village Island to the S; penetrates deep into the mainland
Entrance (mid-ch btwn Warr Bluff & Slope Pt): 50°38.32'N, 126°33.91'W

Knight Inlet ... the longest inlet on the British columbia coast. Leads for much of its length between mountains with summits more than 1,500 m many snow-clad throughout the year. Depths are great with few off-lying dangers. Anchorages are few and widely separated. Winds are frequently strong, funneled by the steep sides. Large quantities of logs are shipped from the inlet. There are several logging camps but no settlements.

Tidal differences for Glendale Cove (Index No. 8310), 33 miles inside the entrance, referenced on Alert Bay, are in "Tide Tables, Volume 6."

Tidal streams between the entrance and Steep Head, 15 miles east, reach 3 kn on the ebb but considerably less on the flood. Heavy tide-rips occur in places. The turn of current occurs 1 to 2 hours after HW and LW, time being considerable affeccted by the amount of land drainage runoff.

Wind also has a considerable affect on the rate of the tidal currents. An increase of 2 kn can be expected when strong winds are blowing up or down the channel with the current.

During summer months, when there is a large land runoff, the flood stream in the upper reaches disappears entirely and there is a marked increase in the strength of the ebb stream. At this time of year there is an overlay of fresher water for a considerable distance from the head. (SD)

Knight Inlet is a classic fjord and, although "officially" 70 nautical miles long, from a practical standpoint, it is 6.5 miles longer, emptying into Queen Charlotte Strait west of Swanson and Fire islands. Many remnants of the glaciers that once cut through the inlet still cling to mountainsides high above the saltwater. Six thousand-foot peaks like Mt. Kennedy and Mt. Dyer have perpetual snowfields, and glaciers descend to within a mile and a half from the shore. Places such as Cascade Point, west of Glacier Bay, tower overhead and seem poised to tumble down as you cruise by.

In the upper reaches of Knight Inlet where depths may reach 1,500 feet or more for several miles, the glacier-cut shores are steep-to.

Upper Knight Inlet is seldom visited by cruising boats because there are no well-protected anchorages and the overriding, strong ebb currents diminish upstream progress. The west end of Knight Inlet has a number of protected anchorages; Port Elizabeth and Cutter Cove are the best. Although we feel comfortable in Tsakonu Cove, we cross to Sargeaunt Passage when strong downslope winds are expected. Tomakstum Cove, Glendale Cove, and Wahshihlas Bay are acceptable in stable weather, but are indifferent anchorages and unsafe in serious adiabatic winds. Rocky islets or shoals are few, making travel in low visibility under radar quite easy, except for an occasional floating log. Due to the high canyon walls and the geometry of the GPS satellites, you are likely to experience some loss of GPS signals. Likewise, radio reception is spotty.

Knight Inlet can be entered through Chatham and Clio channels at Minstrel Island; through Tribune, Eliot, Spring, and Sargeaunt passages at Gilford Island; or through Providence and Swanson passages or the entrance between Swanson and Owl islands. When entering or exiting Queen Charlotte Strait, we prefer to use Providence Passage.

Spring Passage

Chart 3546; N of Midsummer Island; entered btwn Sedge Islands & Canoe Islets
Entrance (W, btwn Sedge Islands & House Islet): 50°40.44′N, 126°42.27′W
Entrance (E, 0.5 mi W of Ridge Rock): 50°38.51′N, 126°35.24′W

> *Spring Passage ... provides an alternative route into Knight Inlet for small vessels., Local knowledge is advised because of numerous unmarked dangers between Midsummer and Gilford Islands.* (SD)

Spring Passage joins Knight Inlet to the fine anchorages on the west side of Gilford Island via Retreat Passage. Temporary anchorage can be found in Potts Bay. Avoid Ridge Rock and other midchannel rocks. Careful piloting and alert bow lookouts are prudent.

Potts Bay (Midsummer Island)

Chart 3546; on the S side of Spring Passage
Entrance: 50°39.14′N, 126°36.68′W

> *Potts Bay, in the NE part of Midsummer Island, has a house and float in it (1979). There are numerous rocks and shoals in this area and no aids to navigation; caution is advised.* (SD)

Potts Bay offers temporary or emergency anchorage in the head of the bay. The bottom is highly irregular, indicating a rocky bottom; we do not recommend anchoring here.

Providence Passage

Chart 3546; 1 mi E of White Cliff Islets
Entrance (W): 50°39.38′N, 126°42.34′W
Entrance (E): 50°39.48′N, 126°40.04′W

> *Providence Passage ... leads between Fire Island and Owl Island, to SW, and Cedar Island and Midsummer Island, to NE. This passage is suitable for small craft.* (SD)

Providence Passage, on the far west entrance to Knight Inlet, is the narrow, scenic channel between Midsummer Island and Owl Island and between Fire and Cedar islands. The fairway carries minimum depths of 3 to 4 fathoms with kelp and grass along both sides. Temporary anchorage in stable weather can be found for small boats midway in the passage.

Chop Bay (Gilford Island)

Chart 3545; 3 mi NE of Mamalilaculla
Entrance: 50°38.87′N, 126°30.58′W
Anchor: 50°38.93′N, 126°30.13′W

Chop Bay provides good shelter from downslope winds.

Anchor in about 5 fathoms over sand and gravel with fair holding.

Maple Cove (Port Elizabeth)

Chart 3545; on the NE shore of Port Elizabeth
Entrance (Port Elizabeth, via Lord Islet): 50°38.50′N, 126°26.89′W
Entrance (Port Elizabeth, via Lady Islands): 50°38.68′N, 126°22.66′W
Entrance (Maple Cove): 50°40.54′N, 126°28.00′W
Anchor: 50°40.78′N, 126°27.58′W

> *Port Elizabeth ... affords good anchorage in its west end for small vessels and small craft, and in Maple Cove for small vessels.* (SD)

Maple Cove, in the north east section of Port Elizabeth, which serves as a log booming area now and then, provides very good protection in all weather, but it does receive some westerly chop in the afternoon. Anchorage can be taken any where along the drying flat on its east shore, but be aware that there may be slash and sunken debris on the bottom.

Anchor (Maple Cove) in 4 to 5 fathoms over sand, mud and gravel with good holding.

Duck Cove (Port Elizabeth)

Chart 3545; at the W end of Port Elizabeth
Entrance (Duck Cove): 50°39.99′N, 126°30.31′W
Anchor (N Duck Cove): 50°39.87′N, 126°30.58′W

Although the currents of Knight Inlet do not penetrate the far west end of Port Elizabeth in Duck Cove, we have received reports from other boaters who experience heavy gusts in this site, and, with fetch over a mile, chop can build up.

The far west shore of Duck Cove is a drying mud flat that attracts both resident and migrating birds. We've seen large flocks of western grebes, hooded mergansers, sandpipers, and Barrow's goldeneye here, to mention

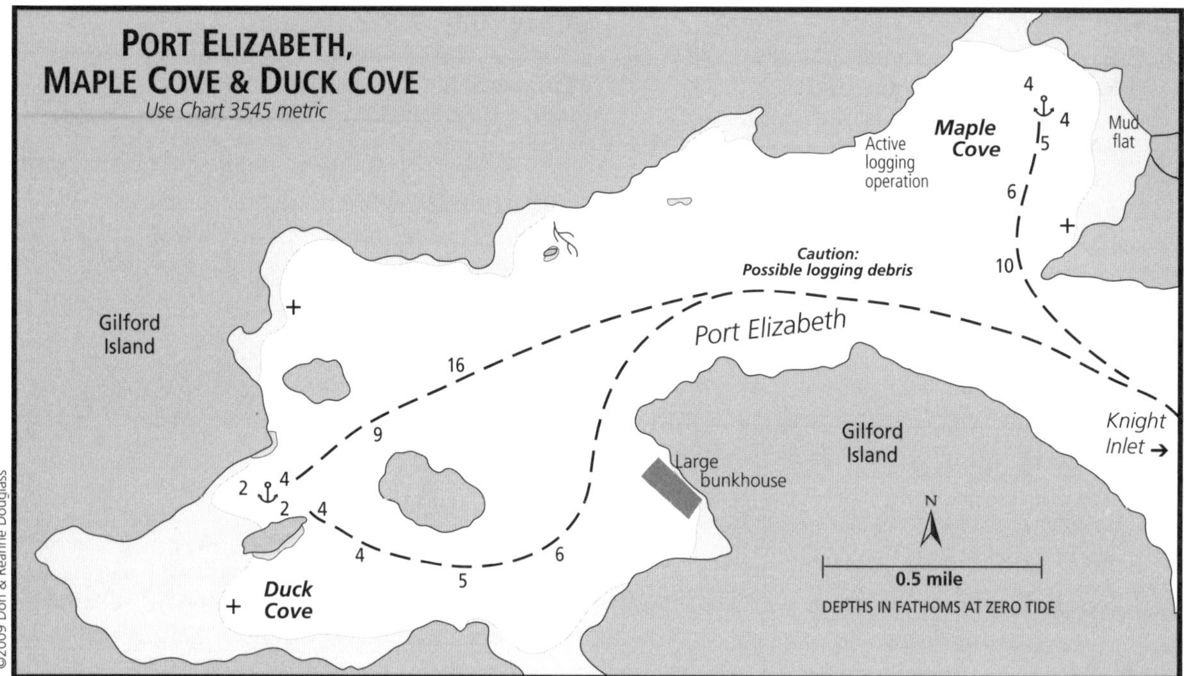

a few. We have anchored on the northern side of Duck Cove, due north of the 47-meter islet, and found the bottom somewhat rocky. Once we snagged a small nylon line. However, if you are able to set your anchor in the hard sandy spots, you should have no trouble. The lack of driftwood along shore is evidence of good protection from east and southeast storms.

Anchor (north Duck Cove) in 3 to 5 fathoms over hard sand, mud and gravel with fair to very good holding.

Gilford Bay (Gilford Island)

Chart 3545; 2.3 mi E of Gilford Pt; 2.6 mi NW of Minstrel Island
Entrance: 50°39.43'N, 126°22.95'W

> *Gilford Bay, NE of Lady Islands, has a log dump and booming grounds in it.* (SD)

Gilford Bay is open to westerlies; Maple Cove or Duck Cove in Port Elizabeth provide better shelter.

Martin Islets (Knight Inlet)

Chart 3545; on the E tip of Shewell Island; 3.5 mi NE of Minstrel Island
Entrance: 50°39.56'N, 126°14.29'W
Anchor: 50°39.47'N, 126°14.31'W

Martin Islets is the group of small islets off the east shore of Shewell Island at the south entrance to Tribune Channel. A small cove in the center of the islets offers temporary anchorage in fair weather. Martin Islets provide a scenic lunch stop, a remote, shallow bay to explore, and a place to observe conditions in Knight Inlet and Tribune Channel. Swinging room is limited.

Anchor in 1-1/2 fathoms over sand, grass and some rocks with fair-to-good holding.

Tsakonu Cove (Knight Inlet)

Chart 3545; on the S shore of Knight Inlet; 6.0 mi E of Minstrel Island
Entrance: 50°38.65'N, 126°09.37'W
Anchor: 50°38.37'N, 126°10.74'W

> *Tsakonu Cove, entered south of Protection Point, affords anchorage but is exposed to east winds.* (SD)

Alas, Taskonu Cove, which once was a favorite, has been discovered by the logging industry. In 2005, there was a big operation in the cove; how long it will remain is a guess. However, the way is clear to the head of the cove where you can anchor with good protection from

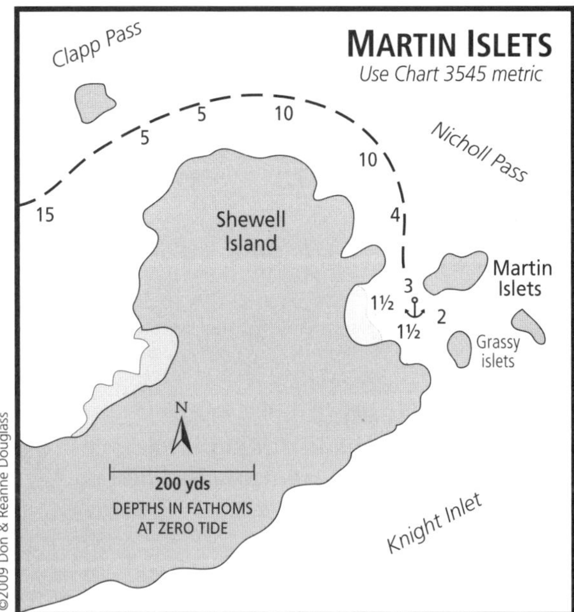

westerlies, but be sure to batten down if heavy easterlies hit. A northeast wind blowing down from Mt. Anthony creates a 2-foot chop in Knight Inlet. Tsakonu Cove lies in the wind shadow of Protection Point along the north shore. Keep an eye on the barometer when you anchor here; southeast storms tend to become east winds across this part of the coast and you may want to move before the lee shore becomes dangerous. Mt. Hawkins (4,225 ft.) is the bold, snowy peak above the south shore. This is a shrimping area, and small shrimp boats sometimes use the cove. Avoid the shoal and kelp off Protection Point.

The head of the cove has a steep-to mud flat. Do not anchor farther west than the small overhanging cave on the north shore.

Anchor in 6 to 8 fathoms over sand and mud with very good holding.

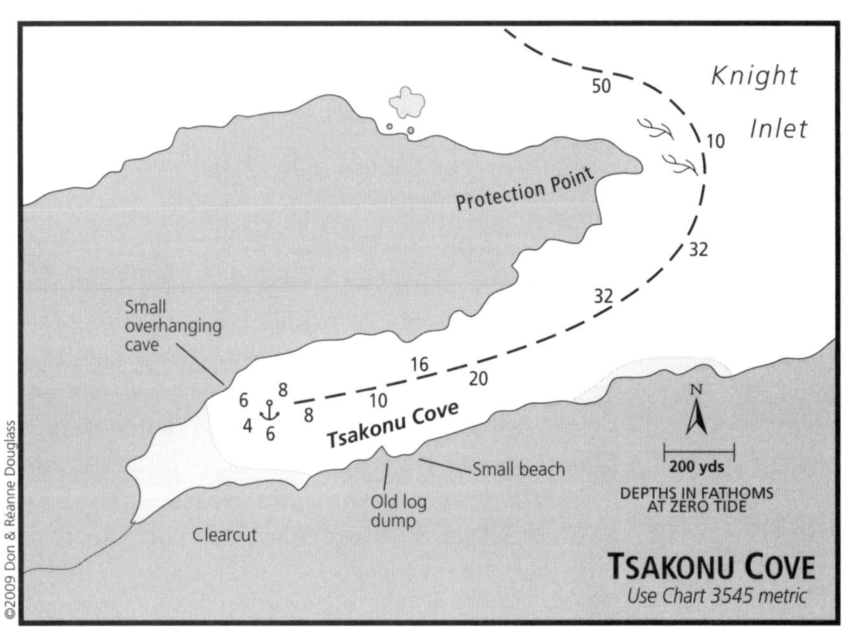

Rest Islets (Knight Inlet)

Chart 3545; on the S side of Knight Inlet; 5.5 mi E of Tsakonu Cove
Entrance: 50°39.74′N, 126°01.64′W

Rest Islets provide temporary anchorage in fair weather only.

Lull Bay (Knight Inlet)

Chart 3515; on the N side of Knight Inlet; 0.7 mi W of Hoeya Sound; 2.2 mi N of Rest Islets
Entrance: 50°41.82′N, 126°00.80′W

Lull Bay has a float and piles of a wilderness fishing camp on its west shore. (SD)

Better shelter from downslope winds can be found in Hoeya Sound.

Hoeya Sound (Knight Inlet)

Chart 3515; immediately E of Lull Bay
Entrance: 50°41.56′N, 125°59.78′W

Hoeya Sound, entered north of Hoeya Head, a relatively low headland 7 miles ENE, is too deep for anchorage. A logging camp is at the head of the sound. (SD)

Hoeya Sound, although well sheltered, is steep-to, requiring a shore tie. Williwaws from Mt. Stamp and Mt. Prideaux can be a problem. This is the beginning of the spectacular Patagonia-like scenery in Knight Inlet.

Tomaksturn Island (Knight Inlet)

Chart 3515; 1.6 mi W of Siwash Bay; 6.6 mi E of Hoeya Sound
Entrance: 50°49.99'N, 125°49.60'W

A good cove can be found on the south side of Tomaksturn Island. Enter from the west only, avoiding the submerged rocks at the head of the cove.

Siwash Bay (Knight Inlet)

Chart 3515; 1.8 mi W of Glendale Cove
Entrance: 50°41.06'N, 125°46.75'W

> *Siwash Bay is on the south side of the inlet. Anchorage is possible along the east shore.* (SD)

Siwash Bay is deep except for a small shelf at the head of the bay.

Glendale Cove (Knight Inlet)

Chart 3515; entered E of Macdonald Pt; 16.5 mi E of Tsakonu Cove
Entrance: 50°41,08'N, 125°43.75'W
Anchor: 50°40.39'N, 125°43.91'W

> *Glendale Cove ... affords anchorage, open to northerly winds, off the edge of the drying flat at its head; depths shoal rapidly. The settlement Glendale Cove is abandoned and the buildings and jetty are in ruins.* (SD)

Glendale Cove is the only moderately good shelter available east of Tsakonu Cove.

Anchor in about 10 fathoms.

Ahnuhati Point (Knight Inlet)

Chart 3515; on the W side of Knight Inlet; 13.2 mi NE of Glendale Cove
Entrance: 50°53.67'N, 125°37.72'W

> *Anchorage is available close inshore in the bay north of Ahnuhati Point, ... in Wahshihlas Bay near its head and at the head of Knight Inlet, close to the drying flat. These anchorages should be used with caution, depths shoal rapidly and are unsafe in the strong north winds common during winter months.* (SD)

Glacier Bay (Knight Inlet)

Chart 3515; on the E side of Knight Inlet; 0.5 mi N of steep-sided Mt. Kennedy Glacier & Glacier Peak; 12.8 mi NE of Glendale Cove
Entrance: 50°52.22'N, 125°33.85'W

Glacier Bay is an open roadstead offering great scenic views but no shelter.

Wahshihlas Bay (Knight Inlet)

Chart 3515; 20.9 mi NE of Glendale Cove
Entrance: 51°01.26'N, 125°35.56'W

Wahshihlas Bay, at the outlet of Sim River and a large U-shaped valley, is near large permanent icefields to the northwest.

Dutchman Head (Knight Inlet)

Chart 3515; at the head of Knight Inlet; lies btwn the Klinaklini & Franklin River deltas; 24.1 mi from Glendale Cove
Position: 51°04.62'N, 125°35.15'W

The headwaters of Knight Inlet are spectacularly scenic and overpowering, not unlike Bute Inlet. Logbooms are the only signs of man's activity. The delta is steep-to and caution is advised in traversing milky waters.

Tribune Channel

Chart 3515; leads around the E & N sides of Gilford Island
Entrance (SE, via Clapp Passage): 50°38.96'N, 126°16.48'W
Entrance (SE, via Nickoll Passage): 50°39.69'N, 126°13.27'W
Entrance (NW, via Raleigh Passage): 50°46.90'N, 126°31.31'W
Entrance (NW, via Hornet Passage): 50°46.70'N, 126°28.87'W

> *Tribune Channel ... joins Fife Sound SE of Broughton Island.* (SD)

Tribune Channel flows through steep-sided mainland fjords and enters Knight Inlet on the east side of Gilford Island. It is a smooth-water route frequently used by boats heading north. Excellent protection is available in Port Elizabeth, 5 miles west of the southern entrance to Tribune Channel. Fair protection can be found in Sargeaunt Passage. Tribune Channel is a lovely channel with several unusual anchorages.

Steep Head

Chart 3545; is the SE entrance Pt of Sargeaunt Passage
Entrance: 50°40.31′N, 126°11.10′W
Anchor: 50°40.30′N, 126°11.00′W

Steep Head offers temporary shelter from strong winds blowing down Knight Inlet. Anchor on the north side of Steep Head close off the steep-to shore. There is sometimes a fish farm or a logboom here.

Anchor in about 7 fathoms, 75 feet from shore, over a mostly rocky bottom with poor-to-fair holding. A stern tie to shore enhances your security.

Sargeaunt Passage

Charts 3515, 3545; lies btwn Viscount Island & the mainland
Entrance (S): 50°40.05′N, 126°11.35′W
Entrance (N): 50°42.86′N, 126°11.71′W
Anchor S of narrows: 50°41.60′N, 126°11.78′W
Anchor N of narrows: 50°42.02′N, 126°11.81′W

> *Sargeaunt Passage, which has a least charted depth of 6.7 m (22 ft) in its narrowest part, is frequently used by fishing vessels. It is reported that secure anchorage for small craft is available either north or south of the narrows depending upon the wind direction.* (SD)

Sargeaunt Passage, which connects Knight Inlet and Tribune Channel is a tiny, small-boat route worth doing if you're headed through Tribune Channel. The deep, dark, inner passage receives little sun and is noticeably cooler, but it provides very good protection from Knight Inlet winds and chop.

Tribune Channel in April

Depths in Sargeaunt Passage are great at the center point where minimum depths are less than those indicated on the chart. A log dump operation is located on the east shore and the passage may be slowly filling in

You can find temporary, sheltered anchorage on the south side of the narrows west of the logging float where the bottom is flatter than that of the north side; however, the log dump

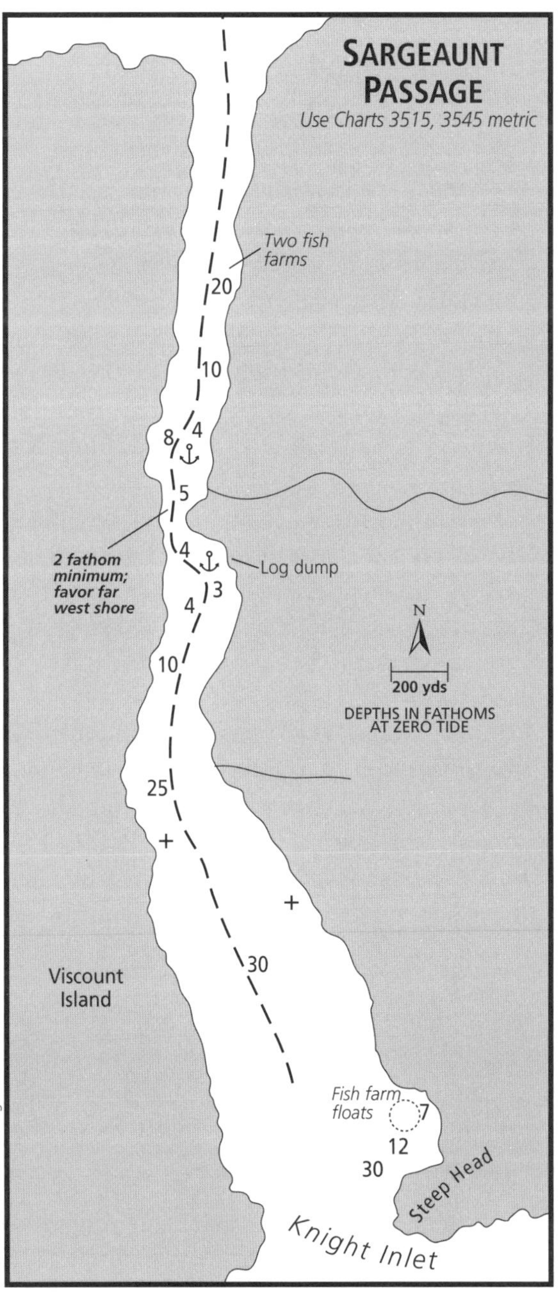

operation is putting a lot of bark and other debris into the water.

The north anchorage is steep-to and has limited swinging room. Water ebbs to the south in Sargeaunt Passage.

Anchor (south) in 3 to 4 fathoms over gravel, weeds and bark with poor-to-fair holding.

Anchor (north) in about 4 fathoms over gravel and weeds with poor-to-fair holding.

Thompson Sound

Chart 3515; N of Sackville Island; 7.4 mi SW of Wahkana Bay
Entrance: 50°45.67'N, 126°07.11'W
Anchor: 50°48.06'N, 126°00.97'W

Thompson Sound ... has indifferent anchorage with limited swinging room between the mud flats at its head. (SD)

Thompson Sound, surrounded by towering peaks, is a scenic fjord which, like the other nearby inlets, boasted a large native population when the Spanish first surveyed the area in 1792.

Snowy Mt. Francis (4,484 ft.) at the head of the sound is picturesque and typical of the coast range peaks a mile or two inland along this coast. The Kakweiken River flows through a beautiful, U-shaped, glacier-cut valley.

Tribune Channel tides meet in the vicinity of Kumlah Island. Avoid the floating logs and debris usually found here in a line from shore to shore. Northwest of Trafford Point, the water on the ebb flows west, but you may also find an ebb tide flowing north in the lower part of Tribune Channel during part of the tide cycle.

Anchorage can be found 0.4 mile north of Sackville Island on the east side of the outlet of Kakweiken River on a small, shallow shelf, although this spot may be subject to strong downslope winds.

Anchor in about 3 fathoms off the drying mud flat.

Bond Sound

Chart 3515; lies N of the NE corner of Tribune Channel
Entrance: 50°49.72'N, 126°12.24'W

Bond Sound (50°51'N, 126°11'W), entered north of Load Point, has no sheltered anchorage. (SD)

Bond Sound is very deep and steep-to. Bond Sound which is deep and steep-to has no sheltered anchorage for cruising vessels, and a prevailing northwesterly wind puts your boat on a lee shore. However, the Ahta River at the head of the sound is a wonderful place to explore. In settled weather you can anchor off the drying bar in 13 to 16 fathoms, but set your anchor well and leave a responsible person on board who can retrieve the anchor and circle around should the wind pick up.

The river is navigable only at high water, but it's well worth taking time to scout it out; you'll see wild fowl, bear and--in late season—the salmon returning to their natal waters. Along the way, there are sandy stretches where you can beach your dinghy and go ashore. But by all means, before you visit this magical place, read Billy Proctor's stirring account of his love for the river in his book *Full Moon, Flood Tide*. We agree with Billy that this beautiful river should remain just as it is—forever preserved.

Wahkana Bay (Gilford Island)

Chart 3515; on the NE corner of Gilford Island; 7 mi E of Viner Sound; 9.3 mi N of the S entrance to Tribune Channel
Entrance: 50°49.51'N, 126°15.62'W
Anchor (SE corner): 50°49.01'N, 126°17.49'W
Anchor (SW corner): 50°49.07'N, 126°17.78'W

Anchorage with good shelter for small vessels and small craft can be obtained in Wahkana Bay. A shoal lies close off Clam Point. It is reported that there has been a rockslide on the NW side of the head of the bay resulting in depths less than charted. (SD)

Wahkana Bay is a well-protected, landlocked anchorage—the best in the area—with room for a large number of boats. It has easy access and can be entered in low visibility using radar. For these reasons, it is a favorite of fishing boats transiting Tribune Channel. Wahkana Bay is a beautiful anchorage with dark granite outcroppings on its high, steep ridges.

Anchor near shore in the southeast corner of Wahkana Bay under the lee of the trees for maximum protection or on the west side where gusts sometimes blow through the low pass. Anchorage can also be found off the small creek outlet in the southwest corner.

Anchor (southeast corner) in about 6 fathoms over sand and gravel.

Anchor (southwest corner) in 2 to 5 fathoms over a mixed bottom of sand, gravel and mud with fair-to-good holding.

Kwatsi Bay

Chart 3515; 2.7 mi NE of Wahkana Bay
Entrance: 50°50.65'N, 126°16.18'W
Position (Kwatsi Bay Marina): 50°52.08'N, 126°15.03'W
Anchor (head of bay): 50°52.16'N, 126°14.08'W

Kwatsi Bay, to the north, affords less sheltered anchorage for small vessels. (SD)

Kwatsi Bay, surrounded by steep, vertical walls in every direction, is so picturesque that it brought forth shouts of joy as we entered. Adding to this beautiful and startling sight is a cascade that spills down from a high ridge above the west end of the basin at the head of Kwatsi Bay. We couldn't resist calling this "Glory Be Basin" for the emotion it produced, as well as for our expert crew member, Gloria Burke, who helped us explore this coast.

The sun rises late in Kwatsi Bay because of the high towering ridges in all directions, but this doesn't inhibit the many beautifully-colored sun starfish visible along the shores. At this point, you are only 2.3 airline miles from the headwaters of Kingcome Inlet.

Since the last edition (2nd) of our book came out, Max Knierim and Anca Fraser have built their home and the Kwatsi Bay Marina. The couple and their two children, Marieke and Russell, have developed a reputation for their warm welcome to the cruising community. In summer the floats are the gathering place for nightly potlucks and lively discussions and, as time goes by, the family improves their facility

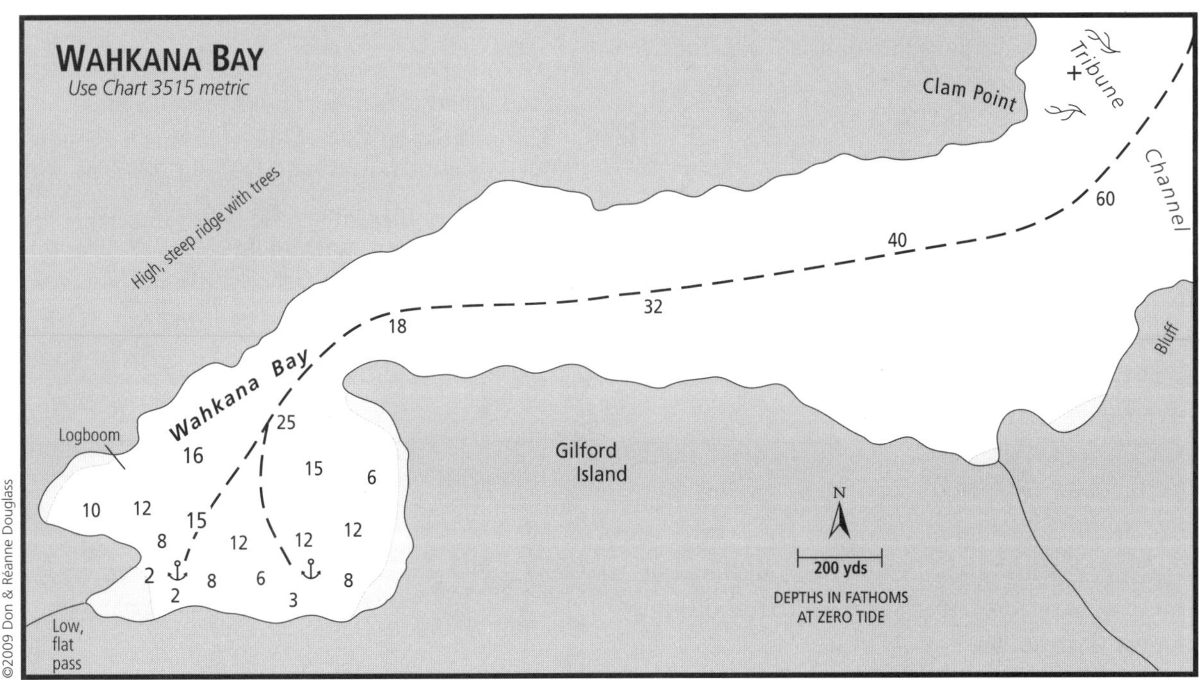

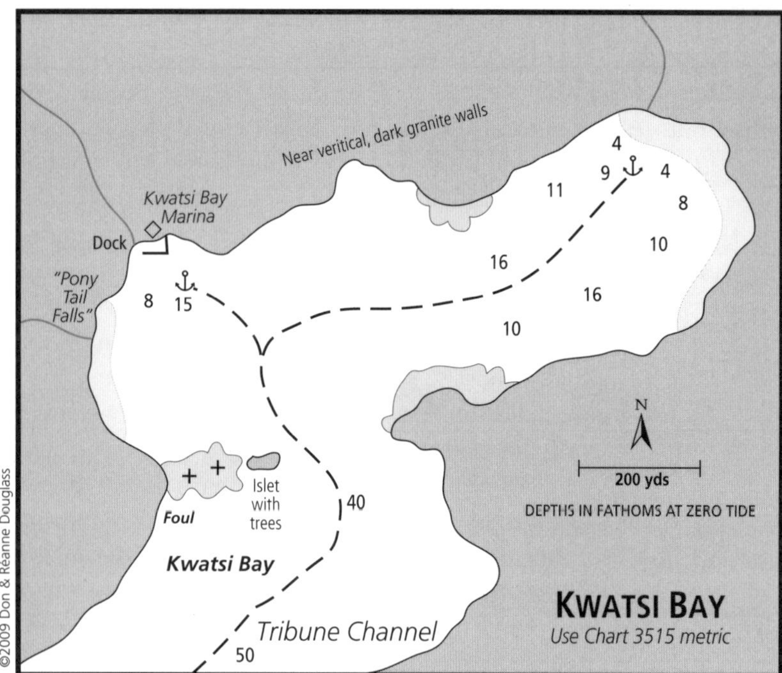

and they now have a gift store, showers and water. They monitor VHF Channel 66A.

Two anchor sites are possible in the northeast end of the bay. The first, just out of sight of the marina to the east, is in deeper water. The second, closer to the head of the cove, is in shallower water. A landslide that occurred in the far east end of the basin in winter 2006 deposited substantial underwater debris for about 60 feet from the shore. (Approximate position of the slide is 50°52.094'N, 126°14.033'W.) Tree limbs in the water and roots on shore indicate its position. Be careful to determine any hazards before you anchor.

Holding power in the basin is marginal due to its rocky bottom. In addition, winds often sweep down the mountains, creating a williwaw effect and increasing the difficulty in holding.

Anchor in about 12 fathoms (just out of sight of the marina) over a mixed, hard bottom; poor-to-fair holding.

Anchor in 5 to 8 fathoms near the NE head of the cove (caution!) over a mixed, hard bottom; poor-to-fair holding.

Anchor (Glory Be Creek) in 5 to 8 fathoms over a mixed hard bottom with poor-to-fair holding. For safety, consider using a shore tie.

⚓ **Kwatsi Bay Marina** tel: 250.949.1384; monitors VHF Ch 66A; website: www.kwatsibay.com; email: kwatsibay@kwatsibay.com; restrooms; showers

Watson Cove

Chart 3515; 1.75 mi W of Kwatsi Bay
Entrance: 50°50.80'N, 126°18.75'W
Anchor: 50°50.94'N, 126°18.30'W

Watson Cove, entered west of Gormely Point, provides sheltered anchorage for small craft. (SD)

Watson Cove is a well-sheltered cove on the north side of Tribune Channel. The entrance is protected by a rock and a large kelp patch.

The north shore has steep granite slabs where cedars have taken hold in its crevices. Beautiful Lacy Falls, which we originally named, cascades down near the entrance.

The bottom of Watson Cove, which is thin, soft, dark mud with shells, is of a consistency that does not offer good holding; in addition, it may be fouled with debris. Billy Proctor relates that there is a 15-foot diameter cedar hidden in the brush on the south shore. While we've never tried to locate it, he recommends looking.

Anchor in 8 fathoms over a soft, thin, mud bottom with poor-to-fair holding.

Lacy Falls

Chart 3515; 0.6 mi due W of Watson Cove
Position: 50°50.98'N, 126°19.55'W

Lacy Falls, Tribune Channel

Lacy Falls is our name for the magnificent waterfall that drops directly into the ocean in a series of lacy patterns. The shore here is steep-to so you can approach the falls directly.

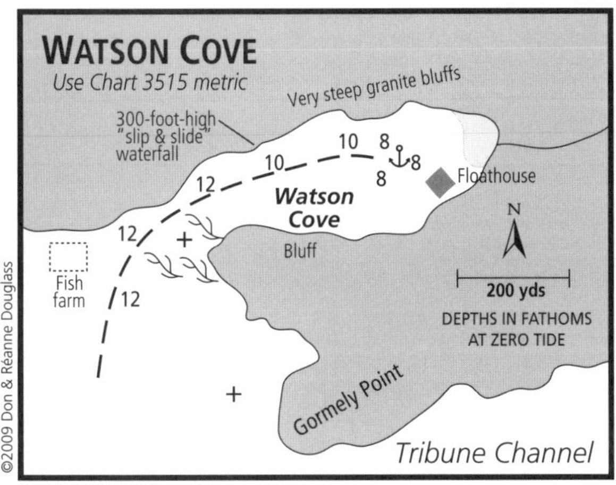

Retreat Passage

Charts 3546, 3515; btwn Bonwick & Gilford Islands; 13 mi NE of Alert Bay
Entrance (S, btwn Success Pt & Seabreeze I): 50°40.61'N, 126°38.52'W
Entrance (N, 0.35 mi NW of Bootleg Cove entrance): 50°43.21'N, 126°35.02'W

> *Retreat Passage is entered from Spring Passage between Success Point and Seabreeze Island.*
>
> *Compass errors up to 18° have been reported in Retreat Passage, particularly in the vicinity of Meade Bay.*
>
> *Gilford Rock, 0.4 mile NE of Seabreeze island, is light coloured showing white in the sun. Yellow Rock, 0.9 mile NE of Seabreeze Island, appears yellow in summer from the colour of its vegetation.* (SD)

Retreat Passage is the beginning of the main smooth-water route that leads through the labyrinth of islands on the north side of Queen Charlotte Strait. The many islands, islets, and reefs along this passage provide wonderful scenery and first-class fishing. The anchorages are usually peaceful and quiet at night. Supplies and telephones can be found at Echo Bay, Greenway Sound and Sullivan Bay; fuel is available in Echo Bay and Sullivan Bay.

(Broughton Archipelago from Echo Bay to Sullivan Bay is generally entered via Retreat Passage.)

Carrie Bay (Bonwick Island)

Charts 3546, 3515; on the SE side of Bonwick Island; 1 mi W of the Gilford Band Health Bay float
Entrance: 50°41.51'N, 126°37.62'W
Anchor: 50°41.64'N, 126°37.92'W

> *Small craft can find anchorage, open to SE, in Carrie Bay.* (SD)

Carrie Bay offers shelter from westerlies but is exposed to southeast chop.

Anchor in 4 to 6 fathoms over an unrecorded bottom.

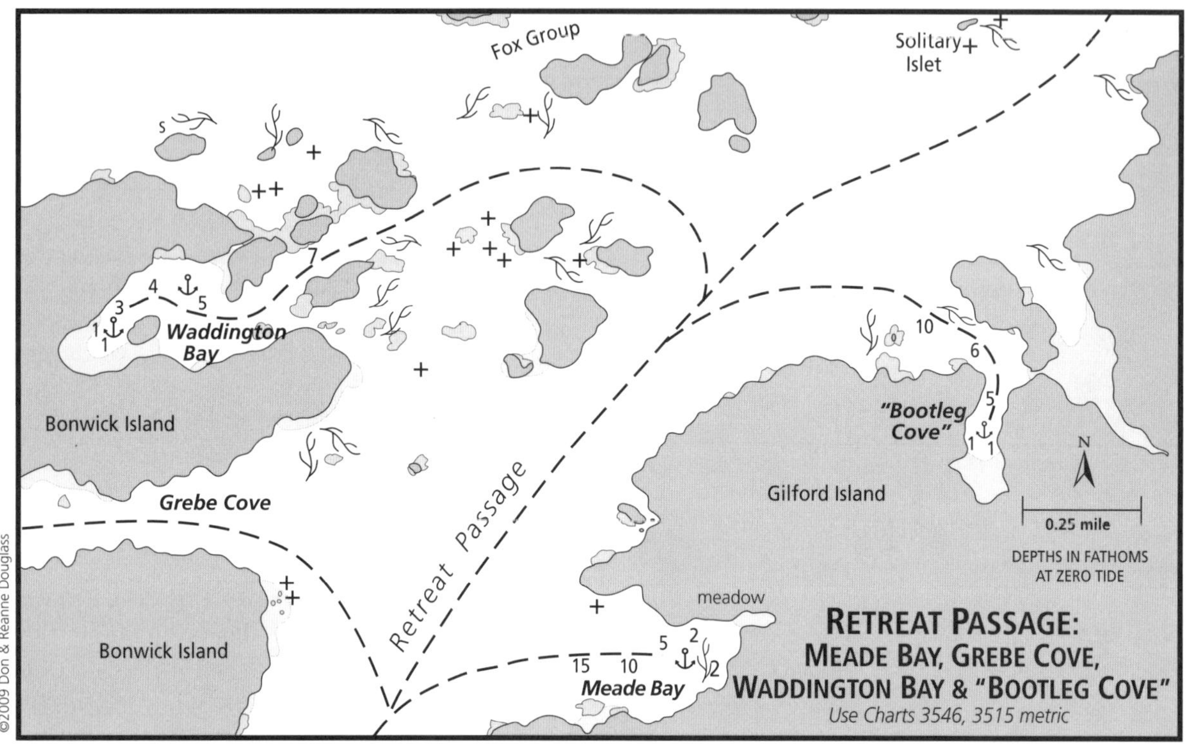

A treed islet in Retreat Passage

Health Bay (Gilford Island)

Charts 3546, 3515; the major indentation on the W side of Gilford Island
Entrance (0.38 mi E of Yellow Rock): 50°41.20'N, 126°35.44'W
Entrance (Health Lagoon): 50°41.39'N, 126°35.33'W
Anchor: 50°40.97'N, 126°34.60'W

> *Health Bay ... affords anchorage for small vessels in its mouth and for small craft farther in. A detached shoal, with 7 m (23 ft) over it, lies in midbay.* (SD)

There are many narrow passages in the Broughton Archipelago

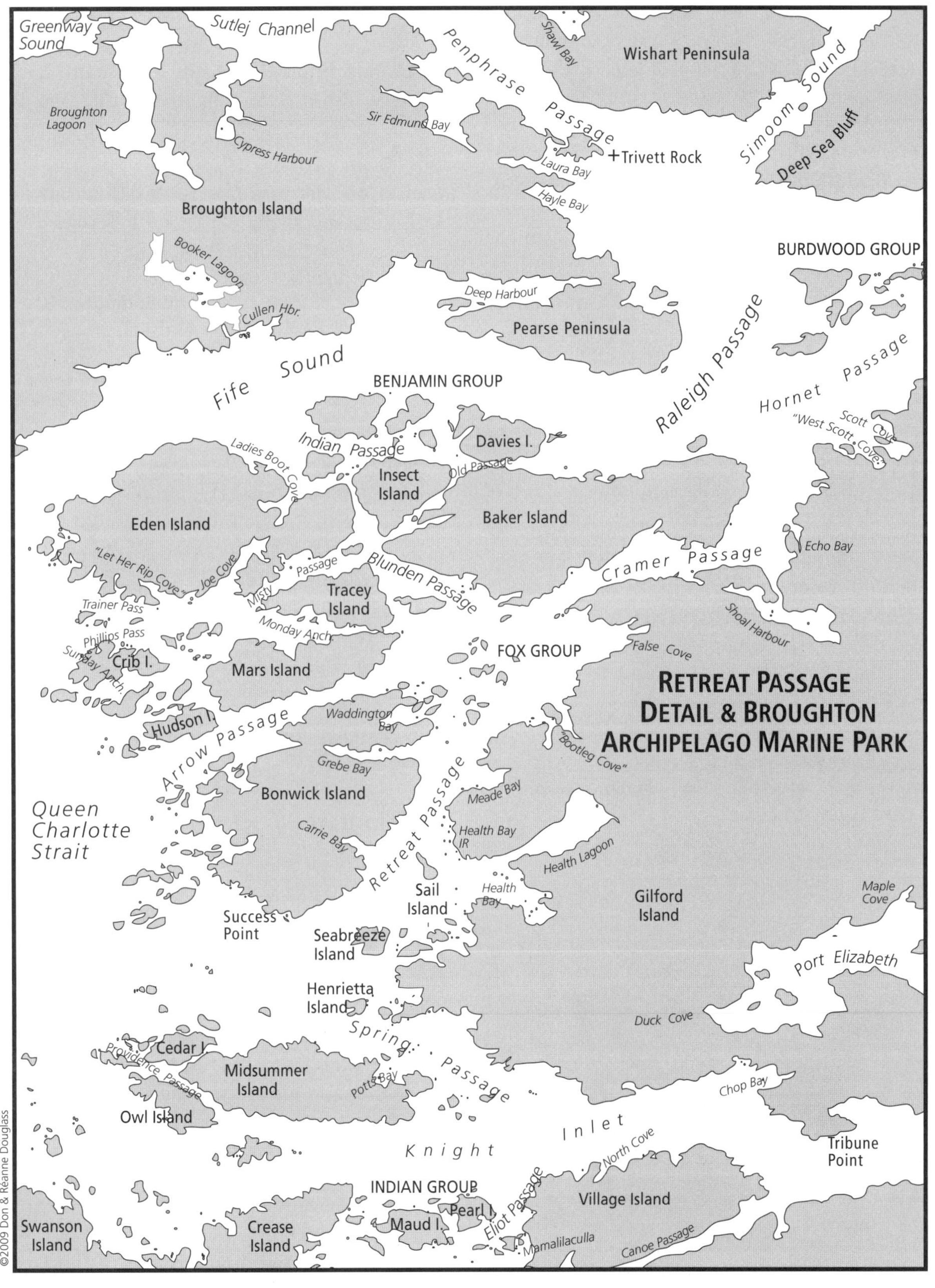
Greenway Sound
Sutlej Channel
Penphrase Passage
Shawl Bay
Wishart Peninsula
Simoom Sound
Deep Sea Bluff
Broughton Lagoon
Cypress Harbour
Sir Edmund Bay
+Trivett Rock
Laura Bay
Hayle Bay
Broughton Island
Booker Lagoon
Cullen Hbr.
BURDWOOD GROUP
Deep Harbour
Pearse Peninsula
Fife Sound
Raleigh Passage
Hornet Passage
BENJAMIN GROUP
Indian Passage
Davies I.
Scott Cove
"West Scott Cove"
Ladies Boot Cove
Old Passage
Insect Island
Eden Island
Baker Island
Echo Bay
"Let Her Rip Cove"
Joe Cove
Misty Passage
Blunden Passage
Cramer Passage
Tracey Island
Trainer Pass
Monday Anch.
Shoal Harbour
Phillips Pass
Sunday Anch.
Crib I.
Mars Island
FOX GROUP
False Cove
RETREAT PASSAGE DETAIL & BROUGHTON ARCHIPELAGO MARINE PARK
Hudson I.
Waddington Bay
Arrow Passage
"Bootleg Cove"
Grebe Bay
Bonwick Island
Queen Charlotte Strait
Meade Bay
Retreat Passage
Health Bay IR
Carrie Bay
Health Lagoon
Sail Island
Health Bay
Gilford Island
Maple Cove
Success Point
Seabreeze Island
Port Elizabeth
Henrietta Island
Duck Cove
Spring Passage
Cedar I.
Providence Passage
Midsummer Island
Potts Bay
Chop Bay
Owl Island
Knight Inlet
North Cove
Tribune Point
INDIAN GROUP
Eliot Passage
Village Island
Pearl I.
Swanson Island
Crease Island
Maud I.
Mamalilaculla
Canoe Passage
©2009 Don & Réanne Douglass

Health Bay provides well-protected anchorage deep in the bay past the two charted rocks and the south islet, north of the two small islets lying off a drying mud flat. Avoid the submerged rock on the south side of the entrance. Health Bay has more protection and less fetch than Health Lagoon immediately to the north.

There is a public float at the Gwayasdums Indian Reserve. (See next site.)

Anchor in 2 to 3 fathoms over mud and shells with good holding.

Gwayasdums Indian Reserve (Health Bay Indian Reserve) (Gilford Island)

Charts 3546, 3515; N of Health Bay; 5.2 mi SW of Echo Bay
Public dock: 50°41.69′N, 126°36.12′W

The Gilford Band (Kwakuitl) maintains a small public float (enter carefully from the north) in front of the village. By arrangement with the elders, you can take an escorted tour into their active longhouse where many beautiful masks are displayed. (Please be prepared to offer a donation to your guide.)

Meade Bay (Gilford Island)

Charts 3546, 3515; 0.8 mi N of Health Bay float; 4.6 mi SW of Echo Bay
Entrance: 50°42.37′N, 126°35.69′W
Anchor: 50°42.37′N, 126°35.21′W

Health Bay float, interview with guide

Anchorage can be obtained off Meade Bay. (SD)

Meade Bay, immediately north of Health Bay, has easy access. Although open to the west, it is well protected from easterlies or southeast storms.

Anchor off the meadow in 4 fathoms over mud, sand and shells with good holding.

Grebe Cove (Bonwick Island)

Charts 3546, 3515; 0.4 mi S of Waddington Bay; 1.0 mi NW of Health Bay float
Entrance: 50°42.61′N, 126°36.53′W
Anchor: 50°42.67′N, 126°38.22′W

Grebe Cove provides anchorage for small vessels and small craft but east and west winds are reported to blow strongly through it. (SD)

Grebe Cove is a long, thin inlet that nearly connects with Sedley Cove on the west shore of Bonwick Island. The wind is reported to whistle through Grebe Cove from the east and west. Because of limited swinging room and the reported winds, you may want to use a shore tie. For a totally landlocked cove, we recommend Waddington Bay.

Anchor in about 4 to 6 fathoms over an unrecorded bottom.

Waddington Bay (Bonwick Island)

Chart 3546; 1.5 mi NW of Health Bay float; 4.9 mi SW of Echo Bay
Entrance: 50°43.33′N, 126°36.07′W
Anchor (W of islet): 50°43.03′N, 126°37.17′W

Waddington Bay, in the NE part of Bonwick Island, is reported to provide sheltered anchorage for small craft with good holding in sticky mud. (SD)

In many ways, Waddington Bay is typical of the anchorages along the Inside Passage that are remote, tricky to enter, but offer landlocked protection from all weather. The entrance to Waddington Bay is narrow, its bottom uneven, but inside it is quiet and peaceful.

The safest entrance leads from the east, just south of the southernmost island of the Fox

Group. The rocky bottom of the outer entrance makes an echo sounder bounce up and down 2 or 3 fathoms, but have patience. Your reward is a nearly flat bottom inside.

The deep, winding cove offers total protection behind the inner island. Tree branches reaching out over the water, moss floating along the surface of the water, and natural flotsam give Waddington Bay a primeval appearance.

You can anchor either just inside the hook on the north side of the bay in about 5 fathoms, or at a second, more isolated anchorage just off the shoals west of the small islet shown near the head of the bay.

Anchor west of the islet in 1 to 3 fathoms over sticky mud with good holding.

Bootleg Cove (Gilford Island)

Charts 3546, 3515; 1.5 mi E of Waddington Bay
Entrance: 50°43.08'N, 126°34.53'W
Anchor: 50°42.80'N, 126°34.32'W

Waddington Bay, Retreat Passage

Bootleg Cove, not mentioned in *Sailing Directions*, is the unnamed cove on Gilford Island east of Waddington Bay. Its entrance cannot be seen from Retreat Passage—it looks like a dead-end bay. Chappell mentions that it is known locally as Bootleg Cove, and a better name couldn't be possible. It is landlocked, subject only to the strongest of southeast gusts, with little to disturb your peace and quiet—a perfect place to hide from authorities in the days of prohibition. Old-growth cedar, hemlock, and yew abound. Moss hangs heavy on the branches and pine pollen collects on the water. The lower limbs of the trees cut a perfectly straight line along shore, marking well the extent of high water. There is no driftwood, no chop; this is protection plus—one of the most sheltered spots on the British Columbia coast!

Anchor in 2 to 3 fathoms near the head of the bay in sand and mud with good holding.

False Cove (Gilford Island)

Chart 3515; 1.5 mi NE of the Fox Group of Islands; 2.7 mi SW of Echo Bay
Entrance: 50°43.84'N, 126°33.78'W
Anchor: 50°43.96'N, 126°32.83'W

False Cove provides good anchorage. (SD)

False Cove, open to westerlies, can provide anchorage deep in the head of the cove.

Arrow Passage (Broughton Archipelago Marine Park)

Chart 3515; on the NW side of Bonwick Island; connects Queen Charlotte Strait to Retreat Passage & Blunden & Cramer Passages
Entrance (W): 50°42.06'N, 126°42.44'W

Arrow Passage is entered from the west between Horse Rock and Evening Rocks. A rock with 7.3 m (24 ft) over it lies 0.3 mile east of Horse Rock. Spiller Passage leads north from Arrow Passage between Hudson Island and Mars Island.

Sedge Islands, Start Island and Ledge Rock are the outermost named features among the numerous islands and rocks extending 1.5 miles off the west coast of Bonwick Island; this area should not be entered without local knowledge. Shoal rocks lie up to 0.3 mile west of Sedge and Start Islands.

Misty Passage, Blunden Passage and Old Passage separate Tracey Island, Baker Island and Insect Island. These passages are narrow and shoal in places; caution is advised. (SD)

Arrow Passage provides access to the Broughton Archipelago Marine Park, a maze of small islands and islets. This amazing group of small islands and smaller passages has traditionally been the playground of sea kayaks and canoes, and it still is. The islets break up the swells and chop and provide convenient haul-out beaches. In addition, the area supports a rich marine environment. A number of small coves entered through smaller passages can provide temporary anchorage while you explore the area between Bonwick and Eden islands. Currents can run up to 2 knots, and the waters contain a lot of surface and underwater kelp.

Betty Cove and Sedgley Cove are small indentations in Bonwick Island.

Sunday Harbour (Crib Island)

Chart 3546, 3515; S of Crib Island; entered via Crib or Sunday Passages; 7.7 mi W of Echo Bay
Entrance (W, N end of Sunday Passage): 50°43.31'N, 126°42.48'W
Entrance (E): 50°43.45'N, 126°41.39'W
Anchor: 50°43.52'N, 126°41.97'W

Sunday Harbour ... affords anchorage for small vessels, with little protection from west winds.

To enter through Crib Passage, pass midway between Liska Islet and Huston Islet, taking care to avoid the rock with 4.3 m (14 ft) over it 0.1 mile west of the latter, then steer a midchannel course.

To enter east of Narrows Islet via Sunday Passage, steer for the south extremity of Angular Island, bearing 098°, to pass between 90 m (295 ft) and 0.1 mile south of Kate Islet. When Sunday Passage opens, steer a midchannel course through it. When approaching from SW, note the rock, with 6.7 m (22 ft) over it, 0.3 mile WNW of Coach Islets. (SD)

Sunday Harbour, between Crib Island and Angular Island, provides intimate surroundings and solitude at the east end of Queen Charlotte Strait. It is open to the northwest and, as the angle of the trees on shore indicates, prevailing winds here come from the northwest. Sunday Harbour can be entered by either the west or east passages. Use Chart 3546, the largest scale available.

The word "harbour," used loosely here, could well have come from a canoeist about to haul out after having paddled from Mamalilaculla on an ebb tide. Who cares about a little northwest wind when it's haul-out time!

Sunday Harbour is a great scenic lunch stop, a special place with a feeling of the outer waters and a quiet anchorage in fair weather. (Listen carefully for the beat of paddles!)

Anchor in 3 to 4 fathoms over sand with gravel and kelp with fair-to-good holding.

Gander Bay (Eden Island)

Charts 3547, 3515; indents the W end of Eden Island; 1.8 mi NW of Sunday Hbr
Entrance: 50°45.03'N, 126°43.20'W

Gander Bay is exposed to Queen Charlotte Strait, but it can be used as a haul-out spot for kayakers traversing the outer coast. The next unnamed bay to the south (which we call Let Her Rip Cove) has better shelter for kayakers or small boats. When westerlies howl in the unnamed cove, better shelter can be found northwest of Marsden Island, 1.2 miles southeast of Gander Bay.

Let Her Rip Cove (Eden Island)

Charts 3547, 3546; on the SW side of Eden Island; 0.7 mi W of Joe Cove
Entrance: 50°44.34'N, 126°41.14'W
Anchor: 50°44.46'N, 126°41.43'W

Let Her Rip Cove is the unnamed cove 1.2 miles southeast of Gander Bay. We ducked into this cove when Trainer Passage had howling westerlies and enjoyed a quiet, calm anchorage.

Anchor in 2 to 3 fathoms over sand and grass with good holding.

Joe Cove (Eden Island)

Charts 3547, 3515; 1.75 mi N of Arrow Passage; 3.5 mi SE of Cullen Hbr
Entrance: 50°44.39'N, 126°40.18'W
Anchor (S of islet): 50°44.84'N, 126°39.47'W
Anchor (head of cove): 50°44.97'N, 126°39.48'W

> *Joe Cove, in the south part of Eden Island, is reported to provide completely protected anchorage for small craft in the SE arm of its head over mud bottom.* (SD)

Joe Cove is a scenic and nearly landlocked cove that offers very good shelter from all weather at its head. It provides very good protection for one or two boats tucked in behind and south of the islet at the head of the cove. Swinging room is limited. Avoid the reef and rocks west of the islet and pass carefully between the islet and rocks. Vigilance is required to find the one-fathom hole safely. (Use Chart 3547 and an alert bow watch.)

The small float in the eastern cove was placed here in the interest of boaters by residents of Port McNeill. Please do your part to ensure its upkeep. Only small, shallow-draft vessels should try anchoring in this basin.

A slightly less secure but far easier anchorage to enter is located at the head of the cove, but be careful to avoid the rocks. Larger vessels should use this area.

Anchor (south of islet) in about 1 to 2 fathoms over good mud near the small float.

Anchor (head of cove) in 3 to 4 fathoms with more swinging room.

Monday Anchorage

Charts 3547, 3546, 3515; btwn Tracey & Mars Islands; 0.5 mi SE of Joe Cove
Entrance: 50°44.08'N, 126°39.59'W
Anchor (Second Island, N side): 50°44.14'N, 126°38.44'W

> *Monday Anchorage ... affords anchorage for small vessels in about 12 m (39 ft) with little shelter from west winds. The entrance from Queen Charlotte Strait through either Trainer Passage or Philips Passage is obstructed by rocks, particularly in the latter. Local knowledge.* (SD)

Monday Anchorage is exposed to gale force westerlies that occasionally blow directly in from Queen Charlotte Strait. However, we have found it a good fair-weather anchorage and an excellent place to stay while exploring the outside marine environment.

If the wind picks up, or if it is expected to, you can duck into either Joe Cove or fully protected Waddington Bay. Let Her Rip Cove, on the south shore of Eden Island north of Marsden Islands, also provides better shelter from westerly weather.

Small craft can transit the unnamed passage between Eden and Insect islands. Be alert for uncharted shoals and rocks. We have found about 2 fathoms minimum in the fairway at zero tide.

Lady Boot Cove (Eden Island)

Charts 3547, 3515; 1.5 mi NE of the head of Joe Cove, indents the NE shore of Eden Island & lies SW of Fly Island
Entrance: 50°45.56'N, 126°38.82'W
Anchor: 50°45.40'N, 126°39.44'W

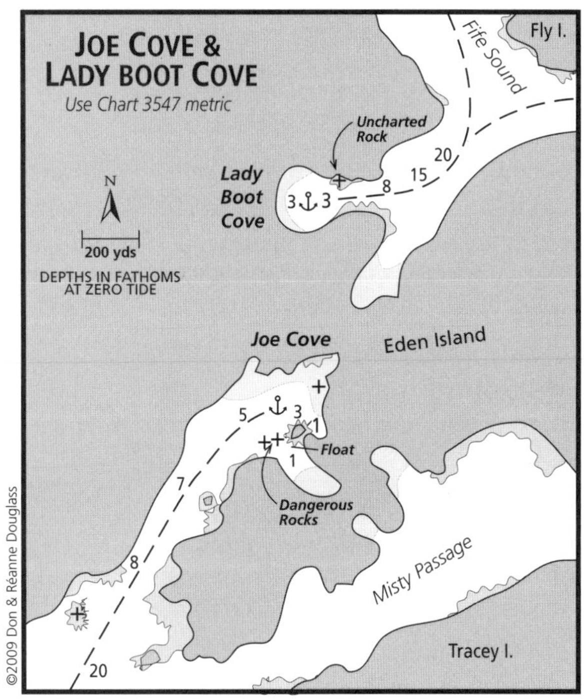

Lady Boot Cove, shaped like a lady's high-topped boot, is one of our favorite anchor sites where we like to rendezvous with friends and raft up. As in Joe Cove, there is good shelter in all weather. The heel (south cove) is shoal, but the toe (northwest cove) provides near-ideal depths for anchoring. *Caution:* An uncharted rock is off the north entrance as you enter the inner basin (top of the arch in the boot).

Anchor in about 3 fathoms over sand and gravel with good holding.

Old Passage

Charts 3547, 3515; lies btwn Insect & Baker Is
Entrance (SW): 50°45.02'N, 126°37.30'W
Entrance (NE): 50°45.78'N, 126°35.95'W
Anchor: 50°45.43'N, 126°36.32'W

Good, well-sheltered anchorage can be found in the basin in the center of Old Passage. The passage has 1-1/2 fathoms minimum in the fairway.

Anchor in 4 fathoms over sand with fair-to-good holding.

Indian Passage

Charts 3547, 3515; lies btwn Insect & Baker Islands on the S; the Benjamin Group on the N
Entrance (W): 50°46.15'N, 126°38.57'W
Entrance (E): 50°46.02'N, 126°33.68'W

Indian Passage, on the west side of Insect Island, connects to Old Passage. The fairway, which is narrow and shallow (1 fathom) is used by local runabouts and very shallow draft boats.

Fife Sound

Charts 3547, 3515; lies btwn Broughton Island on the N; Eden & Baker Islands & the Benjamin Group on the S
Entrance (W): 50°46.12'N, 126°43.80'W
Entrance (E): (0.35 mi N of Ragged I): 50°46.50'N, 126°31.57'W

> *Fife Sound, entered between Duff Islet and Gordon Point, is deep and free of midchannel dangers. A rock, with less than 2 m (6 ft) over it, lies 0.3 mile SW of Duff Islet. Gore Rock, which is 2 m (6 ft) high, and a 4.3 m (14 ft) shoal 0.4 mile west of it, are the outermost dangers on the north side of the entrance.*
>
> *Notice Point and Pym Rocks mark the east entrance of Fife Sound.* (SD)

Cullen Harbour (Broughton Island)

Chart 3547; at the entrance to Fife Sound; 9.3 mi W of Echo Bay
Entrance: 50°45.83'N, 126°44.57'W
Anchor: 50°46.27'N, 126°44.38'W

> *Cullen Harbour, entered between Gordon Point and Nelly Islet, provides well protected anchorage for small vessels and small craft; the bottom is reported to be mud.* (SD)

Cullen Harbour is the protected water at the outer entrance to Booker Lagoon. Anchorage can be found north of Olden Island or along the Broughton Island shore.

Anchor in 4 to 5 fathoms over mud with good holding.

Booker Lagoon (Broughton Island)

Chart 3547; entered through Cullen Hbr
Entrance (E, Booker Passage): 50°46.63'N, 126°44.52'W
Entrance (W, Booker Passage): 50°46.70'N, 126°44.97'W
Anchor (island 56): 50°46.85'N, 126°44.52'W

> *Booker Lagoon is entered through Booker Passage, a narrow passage with a least mid-channel depth of 6.4 m, which leads around the north end of Long Island. Tidal streams run swiftly throught the passage, enter near slack water. Marine farm facilities are reported in all four arms of the lagoon.*
>
> *Small vessels and small craft can find anchorage, clear of the marine farms, in the four arms of the lagoon, depending upon winds. Holding is reported to be good in mud.*
>
> *Anchorage, protected from west winds, in reported to be obtainable on the north side of Wicklow Point.* (SD)

Booker Lagoon is a large crab-shaped and landlocked inlet. Booker Passage is the short, narrow passage between Cullen Harbour and

Booker Lagoon where spring tides run strong (4 knots). Minimum depth is 3-1/2 fathoms with a width of 60 feet or less in the fairway. Watch for opposing traffic and give a call on VHF 16 if you're concerned about limited passing room. Booker Lagoon has one of the largest concentrations of aquacultures in any one bay.

Anchorage can be found, avoiding the aquacultures, in any of the four legs or behind island (56) in the southeast corner.

Anchor (island 56) in 5 fathoms over mud with good holding.

Deep Harbour (Broughton Island)

Chart 3515; at the SE end of Broughton Island; 4.8 mi NE of Echo Bay
Entrance: 50°47.91'N, 126°36.52'W
Anchor: 50°47.93'N, 126°33.82'W

> *Deep Harbour ... in the SE part of Broughton Island, forms the east extremity of a bay entered between Pemberton Point and Sharp Point. Jumper Island lies north of Sharp Point. Marine farm facilities lie in the centre of the harbour. Small vessels can obtain anchorage in 40 m near the head of the harbour, clear of the booming ground.* (SD)

Deep Harbour is well named. The water here is deep and the shores steep-to. The harbor is used to store logbooms and fish farms. There are some nooks east of Jumper Island close to shore where you can take advantage of the shelter afforded by Pearse Peninsula. A stern tie is advised.

Cramer Passage

Chart 3515; joins Retreat Passage to Fife Sound
Entrance (SW): 50°44.21'N, 126°34.38'W
Entrance (NE, 0.48 mi North of Baxter Shoal): 50°46.04'N, 126°30.25'W

> *Cramer Passage ... has rocks extending more than 0.1 mile from the SW entrance point. Baxter Shoal and a reef off Powell Point, the NE entrance point, are the only other dangers more than 0.1 mile offshore.*
>
> *Browne Rock, an isolated rock which dries 0.6 m (2 ft) and usually marked by kelp in summer, lies SW of Isle Point in the approach to Cramer Passage. Detached shoals lie 0.3 and 0.5 mile to the east. Solitary Islet lies in midchannel east of Fox Group. A rock which dries 2.7 m (9 ft) lies close off the south extremity of Baker Island, NNE of Steep Islet. A rock that dries 5.2 m (17 ft) lies 0.2 mile east of Steep Islet.* (SD)

Cramer Passage has excellent anchorages along Gilford Island as well as some isolated spots to explore to the west. Cliffside Moorage and Pierre's at Echo Bay Lodge and Marina all have moorage if prefer the company of other boaters.

Shoal Harbour (Gilford Island)

Chart 3515; 0.6 mi SW of Echo Bay
Entrance: 50°44.70'N, 126°30.20'W
Anchor (W): 50°44.22'N, 126°30.34'W (NAD 83
Anchor (SE): 50°44.07'N, 126°29.69'W

> *Shoal Harbour provides anchorage for small craft. The best berth is reported to be south of the islet SSW of the entrance, where there is adequate protection from west winds but not much from east winds.* (SD)

Shoal Harbour is aptly named (much of the bay is shallow), but you can find good protection here. The entrance has a shoal area that extends nearly halfway across the channel. Favor the east shore. Minimum depth is about 1 to 2 fathoms.

Small boats can hide northwest of the islet and avoid the easterlies that blow the length of the harbor. This area is very shallow, so you need to check tide levels carefully and allow plenty of swinging room.

An easier anchorage can be taken in the southeast corner of the bay 200 yards south of the floathouses over a large, flat bottom with plenty of swinging room. The water here is muskeg brown.

Anchor (southeast) in 2 to 3 fathoms over mud with good holding.

Anchor (west) in 1-1/2 fathoms over soft mud

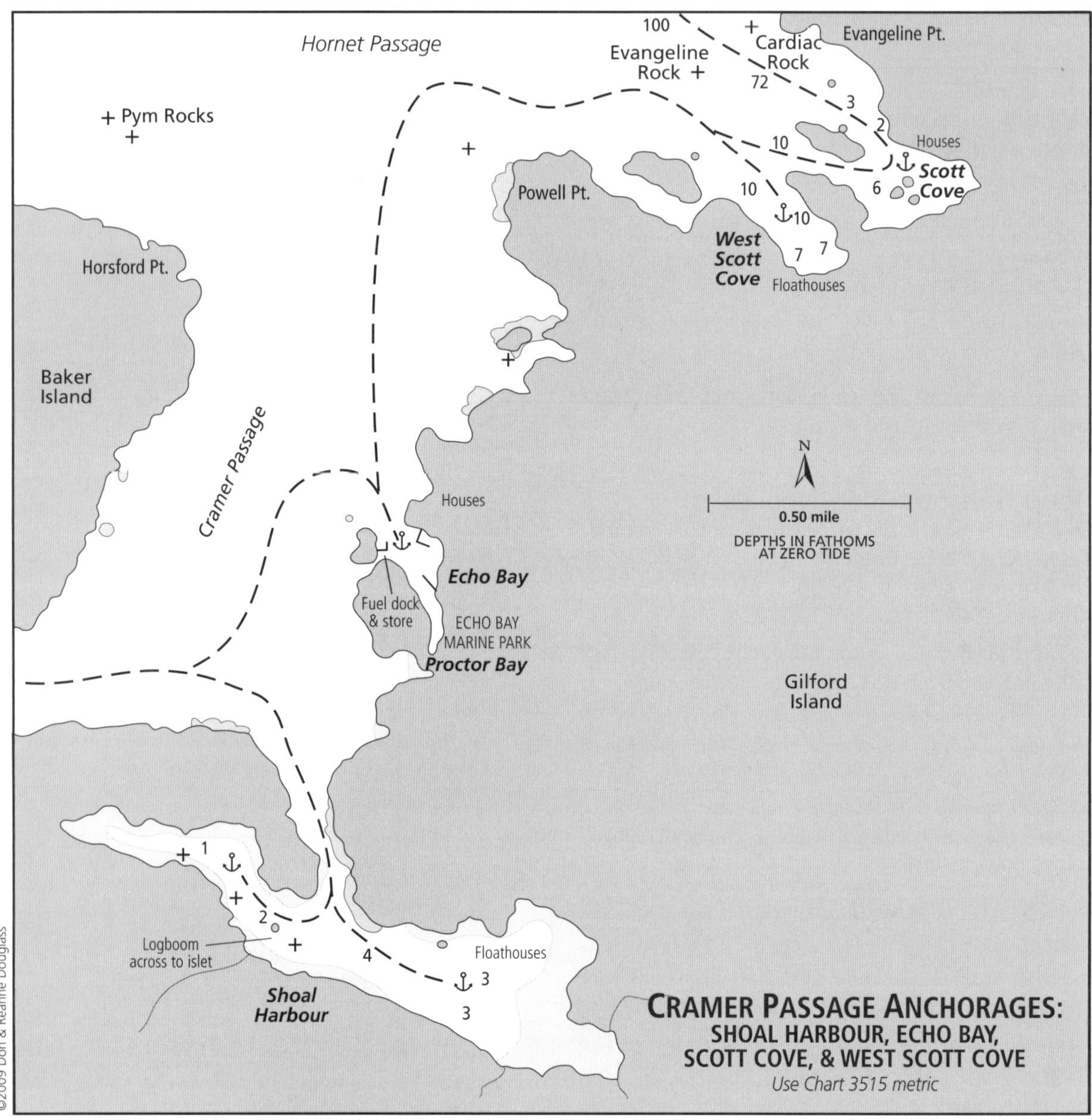

and shells with good holding.

Proctor Bay

Chart 3515; 0.5 mi S of Echo Bay
Entrance 50°44.87'N, 126°30.14'W

"Proctor Bay" is not on local charts but we suspect it will be someday. This is the home of local legend Billy Proctor and his "museum". Billy has lived in this area most of his life as a fisherman, and a variety of jobs as well as assisting his neighbors to build homes and log. In the process he has collected artifacts that have washed up or been abandoned and placed them into a building he built himself. The items form an interesting history of the last 80 years for this area and the world. The real attraction is Billy himself. Though a bit shy, he is an expert on the area and has co-authored several books that describe what life was like in this area during a period of abundant fishing and logging. There is a dock in front of the museum for Billy's boat "Ocean

Shoal Harbour

Dawn" and visiting vessels or dinghys. You can anchor in Shoal Harbour and dinghy over or use the dock if there is room. You can also reach Billy's on a trail from Pierre's at Echo Bay Lodge and Marina.

Echo Bay (Gilford Island)

Chart 3515; E of Waddington Bay; 6.7 mi SE of Shawl Bay
Entrance: 50°45.26'N, 126°29.92'W

> *Echo Bay ... is a popular destination for small craft. ... Gasoline, diesel, propane, lubricants, charts, and groceries are obtainable. Moorage with power, water, internet access, washrooms, showers, laundry, garbage disposal and haulout are abailable. There is scheduled float plane service to Seattle, Campbell River and Port McNeill.* (SD)

Pierre's at Echo Bay Lodge & Marina provides complete moorage facilities with power and water, showers, garbage disposal (small fee), fuel and propane, fish cleaning tables, tented area for barbecues, and a well-stocked store. Internet access is available to visiting boats. The resort also has shore-side rental facilities. The store sits on a section of what was originally part of Seattle's Lake Washington floating pontoon bridge. Pierre's Bay is well-known for their popular weekly Saturday night pig roasts and other events. See their website for more information.

Echo Bay Marine Park, which lies at the head of the cove (south end) has a small public float that accommodates boats under 24 feet. The float has been in poor condition for a number of years and was scheduled for repairs when we were there.

While anchorage for small boats (under 30 feet) can be found just north of the park float, avoiding the shoal area, we don't recommend it in high season when the bay is crowded.

⚓ **Pierre's at Echo Bay Lodge & Marina**
tel: 250.713.6415; monitors VHF Ch 66A; website: www.pierresbay.com; email: info@pierresbay.com; fuel; power; restrooms; showers; laundry; groceries

Echo Bay trawler

Scott Cove (Gilford Island)

Chart 3515; 1.3 mi NE of Echo Bay
Entrance: 50°46.37'N, 126°28.80'W

> *Scott Cove... Shoals lie close-off Evangeline Point and Powell Pt, and Evangeline Rock lies in the mouth of the cove. A submarine pipleine outfall extends into the cove from the logging camp.* (SD)

Scott Cove has two branches; the eastern side, once a major

Cliffside Village, Echo Bay

logging operation, had a boomstick across it, blocking entry. The western side of Scott Cove formerly was the site of Pierre's Bay Lodge and Marina.

Viner Sound (Gilford Island)

Chart 3515; E of Hornet Passage; just S of the NW entrance to Tribune Channel; 2.8 mi NE of Echo Bay
Entrance: 50°47.85'N, 126°27.05'W
Anchor (N nook): 50°47.29'N, 126°23.14'W

> *Viner Sound affords anchorage for small vessels near its head, just clear of the drying flats, and for small craft in the cove on the north side of its head. It has been reported that there is little shelter from east and west winds.* (SD)

Viner Sound is a delightfully quiet, calm inlet with a tiny nook on its north shore. Spanish moss hangs heavy from the cedar limbs, and the brown muskeg water is opaque with organic material. Weather never seems to touch this place, and if you're in the mood to contemplate the origins of the earth, this is the place to do it. Or you can leisurely explore the lagoon, enjoy summer wildflowers, or row up the mud flats at high water.

If someone else has discovered the north nook, anchorage can be taken on the 1-fathom shelf in front of the steep-to drying mud flat or on the south side as indicated in the diagram. Avoid buoys and possible float houses.

We have to call this a settled-weather anchorage because of exposure to west and east winds as noted in *Sailing Directions*. However, in prevailing settled weather, east and west winds peter out near the anchor sites.

Anchor as indicated in the diagram over sticky mud with excellent holding.

Simoom Sound

Chart 3515 inset; N of the NW entrance to Tribune Channel; 4.4 mi N of Echo Bay
Entrance: 50°49.59'N, 126°30.43'W

> *Simoom Sound ... is entered south of Pollard Point and west of Louisa Islet. Booming grounds are NNW and ENE of Louisa Islet. Esther Shoal lies in mid-channel 0.5 mile NE of Louisa Islet and detached rocks lie west of Hannant Point.*
>
> *Anchorage is obtainable NW of esther Point, in McIntosh Bay and in O'Brien Bay, entered NW of Curtis Point.* (SD)

To the northwest, Simoom Sound is dominated by Bald Mountain with its steep, high slopes and its chute of snow on the west side. In the summer of 1792, Vancouver anchored the Discovery and Chatham here while exploring the area. The sound was named after a British ship commanded by John Kingcome (Kingcome Inlet).

McIntosh Bay (Simoom Sound)

Chart 3515 inset; 2.2 mi N of the entrance to Simoom Sound
Entrance: 50°51.55'N, 126°31.30'W
Anchor (E McIntosh Bay): 50°51.79'N, 126°31.20'W
Anchor (W McIntosh Bay): 50°51.72'N, 126°31.39'W

Entrance to Viner Sound

Spanish moss, Viner Sound

Of the two McIntosh bays in Simoom Sound, East McIntosh Bay offers the safer shelter from most winds. It is steep-to and there is little swinging room, so you may want to tie a line to shore. At the head of the bay you can literally anchor under moss-laden trees.

West McIntosh Bay is not quite as pretty, but is shallower than East McIntosh.

Anchor (east McIntosh Bay) in about 7 fathoms over mud and sand with good holding.

Anchor (west McIntosh Bay) in 3 to 4 fathoms about 150 feet from the head of the bay over sand, mud, and shells with good holding.

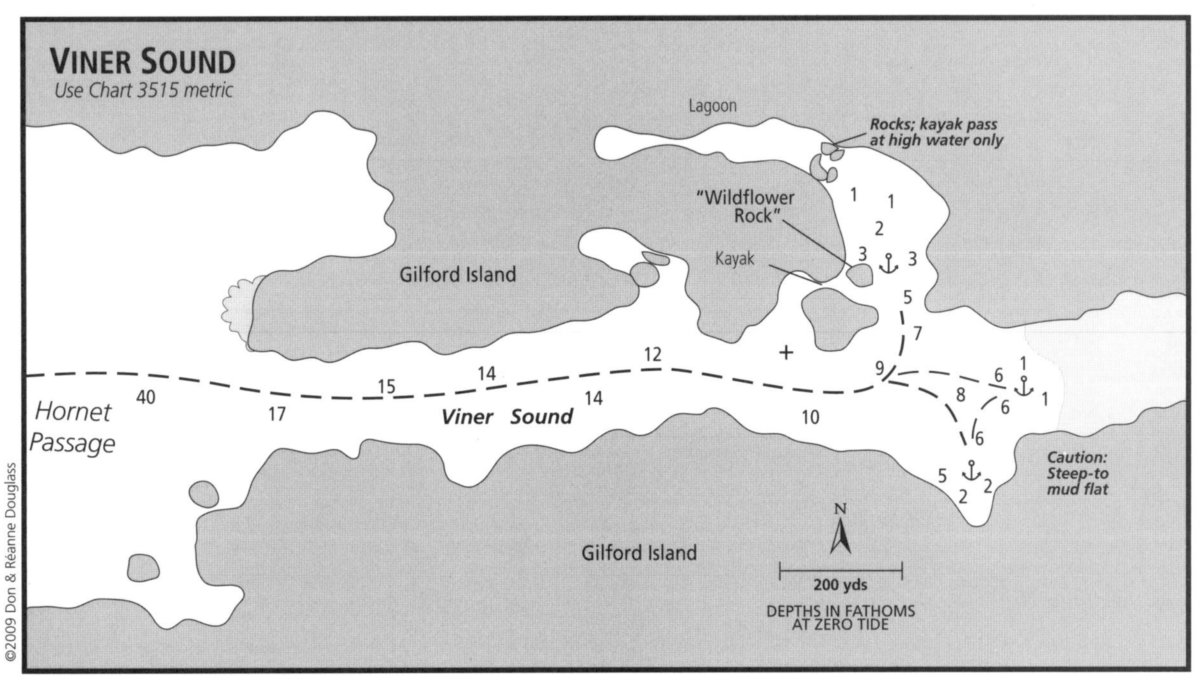

O'Brien Bay, Rusty Cove (Simoom Sound)

Chart 3515 inset; at the head of Simoom Sound
Entrance (O'Brien Bay): 50°51.31'N, 126°31.40'W
Entrance (Rusty Cove): 50°51.31'N, 126°32.85'W
Anchor (Rusty Cove): 50°51.37'N, 126°32.85'W

O'Brien Bay has easy access and you can get out of easterly winds and chop west of Curtis Point. You can anchor in most of the westerly part of the bay, but our favorite spot is the small cove in the very northwest corner. Anchoring is easier than in McIntosh Bay. Here you are protected from easterly chop by what we call Geza Point (after our crewman and former boat partner, Geza Dienes). Rusty Cove is named for Geza's spouse and partner, Russlyn "Rusty" O'Brien.

Anchor in the north end of the cove before its west bend, paying attention to an uncharted rock where the cove starts to shoal. Birds and ducks like this place as much as we do—we've spotted large numbers of surf scoters and canvasbacks.

Anchor in 5 fathoms over sand, mud, kelp and debris with good holding when your anchor is well set. (You may need to try more than once.)

Penphrase Passage

Chart 3515; connects Tribune Channel & Fife Sound to Kingcome Inlet & Sutlej Channel; 4.7 mi N of Echo Bay
Entrance (SE): 50°49.59'N, 126°32.78'W
Entrance (NW): 50°50.89'N, 126°35.74'W

> *Penphrase Passage is bounded to SE by Trivett Island, Sir Edmund Head, Nicholls Island and Hayes Point, and to NE by Steep Point and Vigis Point of Wishart Peninsula. Trivett Rock is an isolated rock in the south entrance of the passage.* (SD)

Deep Sea Bluff on Penphrase Passage's east end is worth close inspection. There are overhanging cliffs just east of the point where the water is very deep. Some echo sounders don't work well here along the cliffs because

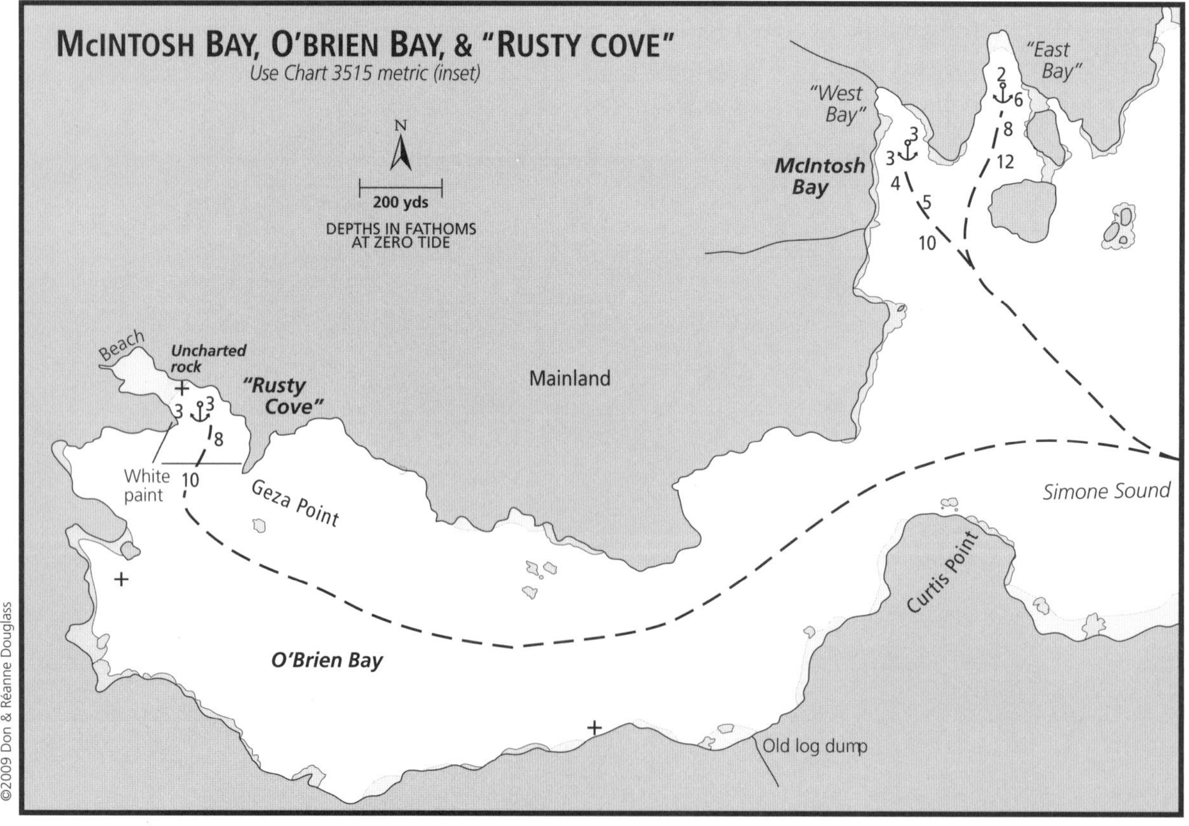

they read the distance to the underwater wall instead of to the deeper bottom. However, you can safely take your boat alongside the wall and look up 75 feet to where a tree grows out of the cliff directly above your boat!

Laura Bay and Shawl Bay have easy access from Penphrase Passage; if you want a little more solitude, consider the seldom-visited coves in Simoom Sound.

Hayle Bay (Broughton Island)

Chart 3515; 0.9 mi SW of Trivett Rock
Entrance: 50°48.83'N, 126°33.99'W

Laura Cove (Broughton Island)

Chart 3515; 0.7 mi W of Trivett Rock; 4.8 mi NW of Echo Bay
Entrance: 50°49.18'N, 126°33.68'W
Anchor (N of islet): 50°49.45'N, 126°34.09'W

> *Laura Bay (50°49'N, 126°35 W) offers anchorage with reasonable protection for small craft north of the islet in its north part. A rock awash lies 90 m ENE of the islet.* (SD)

Entrance to Rusty Cove

Although Laura Bay is a satisfactory anchor site for small boats in settled weather, it is open to easterly winds. Most small craft prefer to tuck into scenic Laura Cove on the west side of Trivett Island, although anchorage is also possible in the narrow inlet on the extreme west side of the bay.

Entering Laura Cove, pass west of the little islet with one tall triangular-shaped tree among other trees, taking care to avoid a rock off the islet. We have found this cove well protected when downslope winds kid up chop in Penphrase Passage. Swinging room, however, is limited at both sites and the bottom is hard, making set a challenge. Chappell calls Laura Cove one of the prettiest places on the coast. Tucked behind the small islet and Trivett Island, it certainly is scenic. We found this cove well protected when downslope winds were kicking up a good easterly chop outside. The center of the islet with one tall triangular-shaped tree amongst other smaller trees makes a good landmark. The only problem we have had here was in getting our anchor to bite on the hard bottom.

Anchor (north of islet) in 2 fathoms over a hard, gravel bottom with kelp and debris; poor-to-fair holding (shore tie advised).

Sir Edmund Bay (Broughton Island)

Chart 3515; 1.45 mi NW of Laura Bay
Entrance: 50°50.15'N, 126°35.43'W

> *Sir Edmund Bay, where there are ruins of an abandoned logging operation, has an isolated shoal near its centre. Numerous reefs lie between Nicholls Island and Hayes Point.* (SD)

Halfway through Penphrase Passage, northwest of Steep Point, the easterly outflow chop diminishes. Sir Edmund Bay is protected from most winds; however, it has several fish farms and floats in it. The bottom is irregular, indicating rocks, and we recommend it for emergency use only. Shawl Bay is a less difficult anchorage.

Shawl Bay

Chart 3515; on the NW side of Wishart Peninsula; 6.7 mi NW of Echo Bay
Entrance: 50°51.21'N, 126°34.85'W
Anchor (SE): 50°50.82'N, 126°33.78'W
Position (marina): 50°50.91'N, 126°33.59'W

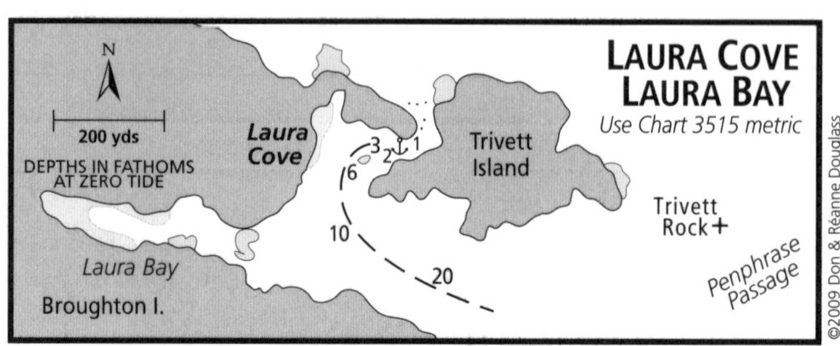

> *Shawl Bay ... is used as an achorage by fishing vessels in its south part, the north part is not recommended for anchorage. Float houses and a floating marina are in the bay. Moorage, power, water, internet access, washrooms, showers, laundry and convenience store are available. There is regular float plane service to Campbell River and Port McNeill and a water taxi to Port McNeill. A logging camp and booming ground are on the south side of the bay. The passage east of Gregory Island is reported to be frequently used by fish boats.* (SD)

Although Shawl Bay provides well-protected anchorage in most weather, its major draw for pleasure craft is Shawl Bay Marina. Lorne and Shawn Brown, owners of the marina, have made substantial improvements to the facilities in recent years. The floats (1000 feet), which have been upgraded, have water and power; a laundry and small store are also available. As with many of the resorts in the area, the B.C. government requires posting of a sign that reads: "This water is considered unfit for drinking or domestic use." (Use at your own risk.) A tented patio serves as a meeting place where boaters share pot luck and where Lorne and Shawn serve their famous complimentary pancake breakfasts daily.

Anchor (southeast) in about 2 to 4 fathoms over sand and mud with unrecorded holding.

⚓ **Shawl Bay Marina** tel; 250.483.4169; monitors VHF Ch 66A; website: www.shawlbaymarina.com; email: shawlbaymarina@hughes.net; power; restrooms; showers; laundry

Kingcome Inlet

Chart 3515; entered btwn Bradley Pt & Magin Islets; 8.3 mi NW of Echo Bay
Entrance: 50°52.20'N, 126°37.16'W

> *Kingcome Inlet ... has no off-lying dangers and is deep to about 1.5 miles from its head, where it shoals gradually and then abruptly to a drying mud flat.* (SD)

Kingcome Inlet has some of the most spectacular high country along this stretch of the mainland coast. Although much of its shoreline is too steep and its waters too deep, you can find fair-weather shelter in several places. At the outlet, you can find good shelter in Shawl Bay, and in Moore Bay, in the bight southwest of Thief Island (although holding in this site is marginal—see below). Kingcome Village, located on the Kingcome River, a mile beyond the head of the inlet, was the setting for the poignant novel, *I Heard the Owl Call My Name.*

At the entrance to Wakeman Sound, you'll notice a 2,000-foot scar on Mt. Plowden, caused by a climax avalanche that took the soil down to bedrock; vegetation has again taken hold. An even more spectacular slide on the south, toward Tarease Point has occurred in the recent past.

Magin Islets Cove (Kingcome Inlet)

Chart 3547; at the W entrance to Kingcome Inlet; 2.8 mi NW of Shawl Bay
Entrance (SW of Magin Islets): 50°52.28'N, 126°38.84'W
Anchor: 50°52.48'N, 126°39.63'W

Magin Islets Cove is our name for the cove

between Philips Point and Reid Bay. This small, scenic cove can be used as a lunch stop or temporary anchorage in stable weather. Westerly winds can gust through the U-shaped notch at the head of the cove which communicates to Sutlej Channel. Logs on shore suggest that the off-lying Magin Islets give only partial shelter against downslope or southeast winds. Anchorage can be taken in the head of the cove, avoiding drift logs and occasional deadheads.

Magin Islets Cove has a large shoal area and two rocks that extend from its south shore. Depths are less than the chart indicates, so favor the north shore. You gain entrance into Magin Islets Cove by staying either south or north of the islets. Avoid the rock and reef west of Magin Islets.

Anchor in 3 to 5 fathoms over a soft bottom with poor-to-fair holding.

"Low bridge," Hornet Passage

Reid Bay (Kingcome Inlet)

Chart 3515; immediately N of Magin Islets Cove
Entrance: 50°52.78'N, 126°38.87'W

> *Reid Bay ... has an isolated shoal near its centre. It is not recommended for anchorage because of depths and limited swinging room.* (SD)

Moore Bay (Kingcome Inlet)

Chart 3515; 1.6 mi NE of Shawl Bay
Entrance: 50°52.87'N, 126°33.87'W
Anchor (E): 50°52.40'N, 126°32.50'W
Anchor (W): 50°52.25'N, 126°33.95'W

> *Moore Bay ... is generally too deep for satisfactory anchorage. ... can be found in the bay east of the easternmost island in Moore Bay. A B.C. Forest Service Float is in the NE part of the bay.* (SD)

Moore Bay can be entered at sufficient tide level through the shallow and narrow passage which connects to Shawl Bay. Although we have found two anchor sites in this bay, both have a hard, rocky bottom that makes anchoring somewhat difficult. We prefer Magin Islets Cove for a temporary stop.

Entrance to Kingcome Inlet

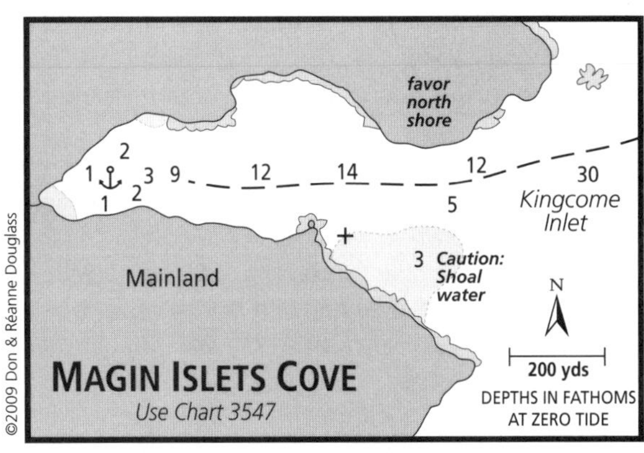

McKenzie Cove (Kingcome Inlet)

Chart 3515; just N of Olivia Pt on the NW side of Kingcome Inlet; 2.9 mi N of Shawl Bay
Entrance: 50°54.08'N, 126°35.13'W

McKenzie Cove is a shallow bight useful only for temporary anchorage in fair weather. Moore Bay, although preferred for its shelter, has marginal holding as noted above.

Ellen Cove (Kingcome Inlet)

Chart 3515; NE of McKenzie Cove
Entrance: 50°54.87'N, 126°33.61'W

> *Ellen Cove, on the west side of the inlet, has a log dump and booming grounds.* (SD)

Ellen Cove, like McKenzie Cove, is useful in fair weather only.

Wakeman Sound

Chart 3515; on the N side of Kingcome Inlet; entered E of Upton Pt; 6.4 mi NW of Shawl Bay
Entrance: 50°56.57'N, 126°29.37'W

> *Wakeman Sound ... does not offer good anchorage and terminates in the estuary of Wakeman River. The runoff from the snow-clad mountains makes the water quite fresh near the head at LW and gives it a dull, milky appearance.* (SD)

Wakeman Sound cuts deep cut into the coast range with magnificent scenery. Wakeman River at the head of the sound drains a number of glaciers from miles inland; the wide U-shaped valley is a classic glacier-cut. The sound is quite deep and steep-to with no significant opportunities for anchoring.

Belleisle Sound

Chart 3515; on the S side of Kingcome Inlet; 6.8 mi NE of Shawl Bay
Entrance: 50°54.47'N, 126°25.37'W

> *Belleisle Sound ... is generally too deep to afford satisfactory anchorage, except in a few places near shore for small craft, and is reported to provide little protection from west winds.* (SD)

Kingcome Village (Gwa' yi)

Kingcome Village was immortalized by Margaret Craven in her 1967 novel, *I Heard the Owl Call My Name* (published in the U.S. in 1973). In her memoir, *Again Calls the Owl* (G.P. Putnams's Sons, 1980) she gives a nonfiction account of her research for the novel. More recently, Judith Williams has written about the area in her book, *Two Wolves at the Dawn of Time*. These books comprise an impressive literary legacy for a tiny and remote village also known by its native name, Gwa' yi. In fact, it's so remote you might want to curl up on the deck with the aforementioned books instead of attempting to visit!

I Heard the Owl Call My Name describes the village Mark Brian was sent to as a young vicar. It's a lyrical and profound tale of life, death and cultural change in a setting as exquisite as it is harsh. Craven explains the burial, marriage and potlatch customs of the native people; and how they make their living from forest, sea and river. Problems such as alcohol and the departing young people are also confronted in the novel.

Early on in the story Craven recounts the creation myth featuring two brothers who borrowed a wolf's skin. They came to "a small and lovely valley on a river's edge, surrounded by high mountains." One brother left and the other established the tribe: "The elder built his house, and in his dances he moved right as even now the dancers move right because the wolf moved right, and on his totem he carved a wolf as one of the crests of his tribe."

Williams's book is a nonfiction account of rock art around Kingcome Inlet, not only historical but modern as well. In 1998, artist Marianne Nicolson completed a gigantic pictograph on a sheer rock face near Petley Point. In bold red pigment, she depicted a ceremonial shield, or copper, with an image of Kawadilikala, the Wolf. Nicolson grew up in Gwa' yi and wanted to leave an enduring symbol of her Dzawada' enuxw heritage, a culture that has survived despite the Canadian government's efforts at assimilation.

You can't miss the 28 by 38-foot painting as you pass the head of Kingcome Inlet en route to the village. Before visiting, you should obtain permission from the band manager (250-974-3013). This is a place of dangerous waters, killer whales, landslides and burial sites. You can see remains of shell middens as well as totems and dwellings being reclaimed by nature. Going upriver, you must avoid snags and shifting sandbars. There's no dock at the village, so you'll have to wade ashore. You can still see the whitewashed Church of St. George and the long house mentioned in Craven's books.

Belleisle Sound, off-the-beaten-path, gives the feel of more intimacy than that of Kingcome Inlet, and it affords relief from the chop when there is a blow outside. It is entered through a narrow but deep entrance channel south of Edmond Islet. Tidal flow is restricted into Belleisle Sound, so the water is several degrees warmer than the glacier-fed waters of Kingcome Inlet.

Temporary anchorage can be taken off the islet next to the Indian Reserve; swinging room is limited.

Anchorage Cove (Kingcome Inlet)

Chart 3515; near the head of Kingcome Inlet; 14.9 mi E of Shawl Bay
Entrance: 50°54.45'N, 126°12.11'W

> *Anchorage Cove ... affords anchorage near shore for small vessels but is open to north and west winds.* (SD)

Under the overhangs at Deep Sea Bluff

Anchorage Cove, a small bight on the southeast shore of the inlet, may offer temporary anchorage with limited swinging room. Reported to be sheltered in east winds, it is exposed to sudden north winds. It is sometimes used as an anchorage to allow a shore party to explore the river delta. Since the cove is exposed to both upslope and downslope winds, your boat should not be left unattended.

Petley Point Float (Kingcome Inlet)

Chart 3515; on the N shore near the head of Kingcome Inlet; 1.5 mi NW of Anchorage Cove
Float: 50°55.72'N, 126°13.18'W

> *Petley Point ... has public floats secured to shore, accessible only by water. Float plane service operates to Port Hardy. A logging camp, the Indian village Kingcome and the Kingcome Inlet Post Office are about 1 mile up the Kingcome River. The river is navigable only by small craft.* (SD)

The small float at Petley Point is used extensively by residents of Kingcome Village and for commercial activities as a transfer point between supply boats and small boats capable of maneuvering the river up to the village and logging camp. Its use is not recommended for visiting cruising boats.

Although village runabouts regularly use the river, unannounced visits by cruising boat tenders are not advised. Check with local guides if you're interested in visiting the village.

The pictographs to the southwest of the float, which reportedly dated back to the 1930s, are defaced with graffiti. While the huge modern pictograph of a copper northeast of the float may startle the first-time viewer, there's no doubt that it is impressive. Much controversy surrounded (and continues) Native artist Marianne Nicolson's decision to paint the copper where it is.The channel of the river is reported to favor the west shore, past a booming ground, then midchannel past the old Halliday farm, homesteaded at the end of the 19th century, and north one mile to the logging camp; from this point to the village, the current flows at about 3 knots or more, and entry becomes more difficult. Glacier melt in the water reduces visibility and a sharp lookout is required.

Sutlej Channel

Charts 3547, 3515; joins Wells Passage to Kingcome Inlet
Entrance (E, 0.95 mi NE of Stackhouse I): 50°51.65'N, 126°37.14'W
Entrance (W, Patrick Passage): 50°53.75'N, 126°50.23'W

> *Sutlej Channel, entered from west through Patrick Passage, connects Wells Passage to Kingcome Inlet. Surgeon Islets, in the west approach to the passage, have shoals lying up to 0.2 mile east of them.* (SD)

Stackhouse Island can be passed on its south side via Sharp Passage or on its north side via Pasley Passage.

Harry Bay (Broughton Island)

Chart 3547; S of Moore Pt; 0.7 mi E of Cypress Hbr
Entrance: 50°50.48'N, 126°38.60'W

Harry Bay is an open roadstead too deep for convenient anchorage. Cypress Harbour offers good shelter.

Cypress Harbour, Miller Bay (Broughton Island)

Chart 3547; 3.2 mi W of Shawl Bay
Entrance (Cypress Hbr): 50°50.45'N, 126°39.65'W
Anchor (Miller Bay): 50°50.24'N, 126°39.57'W

> *Cypress Harbour is entered between Donald Head and Fox Rock, a drying reef extending from Woods Point.*
>
> *Sheltered anchorage for small vessels in 26 m (85 ft), mud, is available off Harbour Point, and for small craft in Miller Bay or Berry Cove, depending upon wind direction. Note the 5.8 m (19 ft) shoal in the entrance to Miller Bay.* (SD)

Miller Bay is the first anchorage in Cypress Harbour on the east shore immediately south of Donald Head. You can get excellent protection from easterlies south of a large fish farm in Miller Bay. There is a grassy beach at the head of the bay.

Anchor in 2 to 3 fathoms over a mixed bottom with good holding.

Berry Cove (Broughton Island)

Chart 3547; on the W side of Cypress Hbr
Anchor: 50°50.13'N, 126°40.30'W

> *Berry Cove offers excellent protection from westerlies, but it is partially exposed to easterlies that shoot down Kingcome Inlet.*

Anchor in 4 to 5 fathoms in the center of the cove over a mixed bottom with fair-to-good holding.

Stopford Bay (Cypress Harbour)

Chart 3547; at the head of Cypress Hbr
Entrance: 50°49.88'N, 126°39.91'W

Stopford Bay is a large drying sand and gravel flat, too shallow for anchorage except for small boats, north of Cawston Point.

Greenway Sound

Chart 3547; Greenway Sound & Carter Passage separate Broughton Island from North Broughton Island; 4.2 mi SE of Sullivan Bay; 7.4 mi W of Shawl Bay; 11.8 mi NW of Echo Bay
Entrance: 50°51.73'N, 126°43.33'W
Marina float: 50°50.30'N, 126°46.46'W

> *Greenway Sound Marine Resort, on the east side fo the bay east of Greenway Point, has marina Facilities. Moorage is available late May to mid September, and resaurant available mid June to end of August. Washrooms, laundry, garbage drop, power, convenience store and boat sitting services are available. Float plane service can be arranged. A dingy dock, at the south end of the bay, allows access to a BC forest Service Picnic area and hiking trails to Broughton Lake.*
>
> *Dangers.—A rock which dries 0.3 m lies in mid-sound west of Greenway Point, and 8.2 and 6.1 m) shoals lie off the north and west sides of the point.* (SD)

Greenway Sound, as a major cruising destination for years, has been synonymous with the Marine Resort owned by Tom and Ann Taylor. The resort, located on the south shore of Greenway Sound, has full and elegant services for cruising boats, including telephones, showers, laundry, groceries and an excellent restaurant; no fuel. Direct air service to points south is also available. A hiking trail leads from the resort southeast to Broughton Lake.

Temporary anchor sites can be found behind Cecil Island at the east side of Greenway Sound or behind Broughton Point inside Carter Passage on the west side of the sound, or in the southern part of the sound, south of Simpson Island.

Note: In 2009, the resort was for sale, but still in full operation. For updated information, check their website www.greenwaysound.com or one of the annual publications, such as the Waggoner Guide.

⚓ **Greenway Sound Marine Resort** tel: 604.629.9838 or 360.466.4751 (winters); monitors VHF Ch 66A; power; restrooms; website: www.greenwaysound.com; email: greenwaysound@seanet.com; showers; laundry

Cecil Island (Greenway Sound)

Chart 3547; at the E end of Greenway Sound
Entrance: 50°50.71′N, 126°43.08′W
Anchor (SE corner): 50°50.56′N, 126°42.59′W

Cecil Island, at the entrance to Greenway Sound, offers temporary anchorage with shelter from all but northwest winds. You can tuck in behind the southeast side of Cecil Island, avoiding the small islet and rocks off this side. The north entrance to Broughton Lagoon, lies just east of Cecil Island and the suggested anchor site. The narrow entrance to the 2.5-mile long lagoon has a reversing tidal rapids that can be entered by inflatable about an hour or so after high flood tide; you then have about 20 minutes to check it out before the tide reverses. Tom Taylor, who has guided many a boater into the lagoon, does not recommend entering unless you have local knowledge, but many boaters who have, laud Broughton Lagoon's beauty. Tuck in behind Cecil Island and the small islet and rocks off the southeast corner, just southwest of the lagoon's smaller exit.

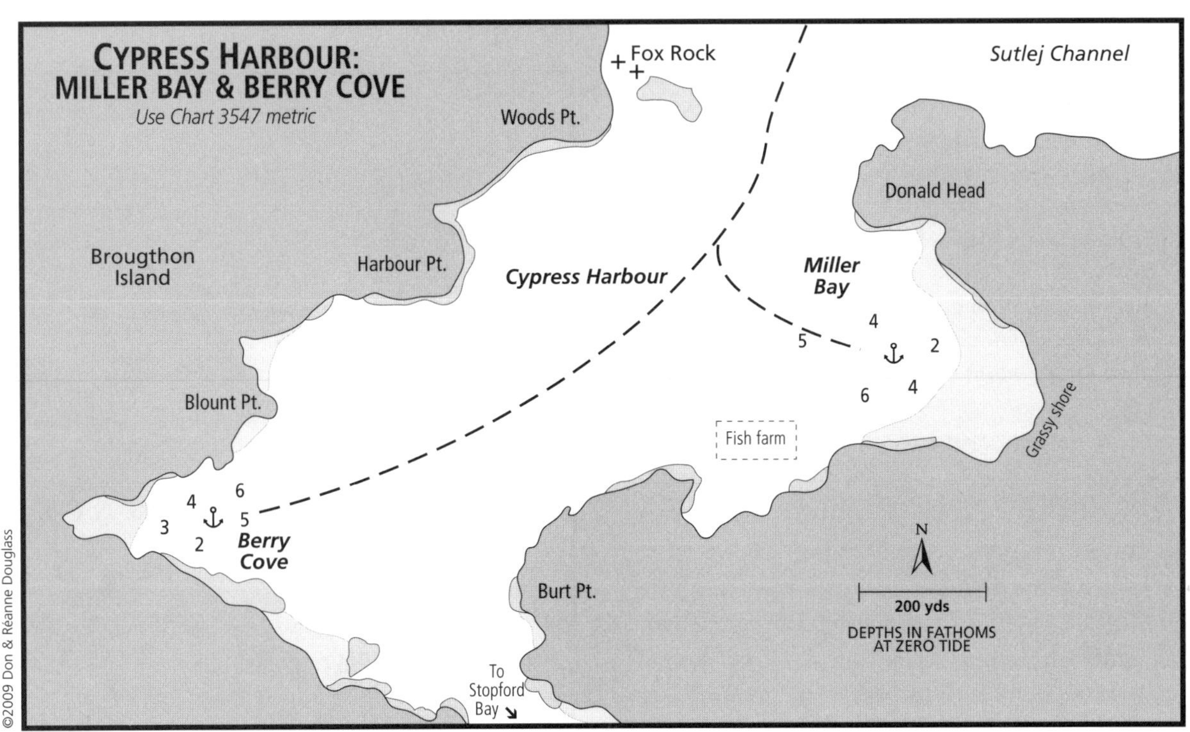

Floating marine resort, Greenway Sound

Just east of Cecil Island is the entrance to Broughton Lagoon, a 2.5 mile-long saltwater lagoon separated by very narrow tidal rapids from Greenway Sound; it can be entered by inflatables near high-water slack.

Carter Passage

Chart 3547; btwn the W ends of Broughton & North Broughton Islands; connects Wells Passage to Greenway Sound
Entrance (E): 50°50.30'N, 126°48.82'W
Entrance (W): 50°50.20'N, 126°54.54'W
Anchor: 50°50.32 N, 126°49.02'W

> *The fairway dries about 2.5 miles east of the west entrance and has boulders in it that dry 3.7 m (12 ft); it can only be attempted by small craft at HW and local knowledge is required.*
>
> *Tidal streams attain 5 to 7 kn at the entrance, which should be navigated only near HW slack.*
>
> *From Wells Passage it is approached south of Bourmaster Point and a group of rocks lie close west of the entrance. The west entrance has a least depth of 3 m (10 ft) and narrows to about 15 m (50 ft) north of some rocks on the south side.*
>
> *Anchorage for small craft with good protection is reported to be obtainable in Carter Passage.* (SD)

Sheltered temporary anchorage is reported to be located just inside the eastern entrance to Carter Passage. To enter Carter Passage, favor the south shore until past the islet. Turn north and anchor behind the islet in scenic surroundings. Westerlies may blow through the passage.

Additional anchor sites are reported along the shore north of Simpson Island and at the head of the two major bights.

Cartwright Bay (North Broughton Island)

Chart 3547; on the S side of Sutlej Channel; 2.0 mi E of Sullivan Bay & 2.3 mi W of the entrance to Greenway Sound
Entrance: 50°53.03'N, 126°46.38'W
Anchor: 50°52.81'N, 126°46.47'W

> *Cartwright Bay affords anchorage for small craft but provides protection from south and west winds only.* (SD)

Cartwright Bay, on the northeast side of North Broughton Island, provides shelter in all but northeast winds when you tuck into the head of the bay close to the drying mud bank. We feel it makes a good temporary anchorage in settled weather and it has easy access. Cartwright Cove is surrounded by old-growth forest and is quite scenic. The creek can be explored by dinghy at high tide. However, we have received reports that the cove was being used as log-boom storage, but that a boat could tie to the booms.

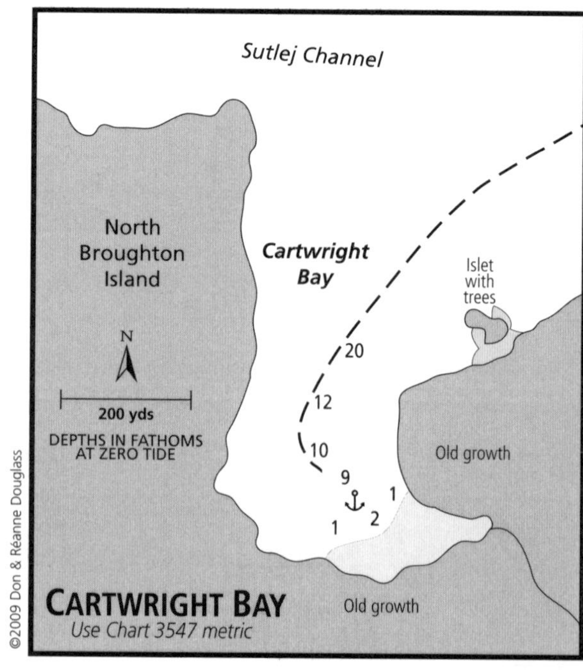

Anchor in about 5 fathoms over soft mud with fair-to-good holding.

Sullivan Bay (North Broughton Island)

Chart 3547; 2 mi W of Cartwright Bay; 15.2 mi NW of Echo Bay
Entrance: 50°53.34'N, 126°49.86'W
Float: 50°53.15'N, 126°49.58'W

Sullivan Bay settlement, in Sullivan Bay ... has a store, post office (V0N 3H0) and lodge, all built on floats secured to shore. Supplies, water, gasoline, diesel fuel and berthing space are obtainable. Regular air service is available. On entering the bay note the rocks fringing Atkinson Island and the shoal patches off the east entrance point of the bay. (SD)

Sullivan Bay is "the zany last bastion of civilization," we wrote in our last edition of this guidebook; and, there are still the decided touches of the comical (such as The Brig), built by Sullivan Bay's former owners, Pat Finnerty and Lynn Whitehead. (The marina even made the front page of the Travel Section of the Los Angeles Times in 2003!) Its 3,500 feet of transient floats with names such as Market Street, Main Street, Fish Alley house the marina's full services which include the fuel dock, the store, the laundry, showers, power and water, a covered fish cleaning station, and an excellent restaurant; the liquor agency is located inside the store; pay phone (satellite) available.

The restaurant, which opened in summer of 2004, has internet access for mooring customers. Upscale floats houses (including one with a helicopter on its rood) continue to be added in "Halibut Heights," along the southwest side of the marina. Both Canada Day and the American 4th of July are celebrated at this resort.

Regularly scheduled float plane service is available to Sullivan Bay Marina almost daily during the high season from Port McNeill, Campbell River, Vancouver and Seattle.

Although some boats anchor at the east end of the drying passage between Atkinson Island and North Broughton Island, Pat and Lynn don't advise it; the bottom is "too steep and mushy." As you enter Sullivan Bay from the west, be careful to avoid the rock off the east end of Atkinson Island; a number of boats have left bottom paint on the rock.

Note: If you haven't yet read Lynn's "Sully the Seal and Alley the Cat" for children, ask to buy a copy.

⚓ **Sullivan Bay Marina Resort**
tel: 604.629.9900; monitors VHF Ch 66A; website: www.sullivanbay.com; email: sullivanbaymarina@gmail.com; fuel; power; restrooms; showers; laundry; store; restaurant (open June to mid-Sept); internet; reservations advised in July-August

Patrick Passage

Chart 3547; btwn Kinnaird & Atkinson Islands; W entrance to Sutlej Channel
Entrance (E, at Sutlej Channel): 50°53.75'N, 126°50.23'W
Entrance (W): 50°53.66'N, 126°51.69'W

Grappler Sound

Chart 3547; entered from Wells Passage btwn Pandora Head & Kinnaird Island; 2.4 mi NW of Sullivan Bay
Entrance (S, 0.3 mi S of Kinnaird Rock): 50°54.26'N, 126°52.99'W

Grappler Sound ... has Kinnaird Rock in the middle of its entrance. (SD)

Fuel stop, Sullivan Bay

Grappler Sound has some great areas to explore with well-sheltered anchorages.

Carriden Bay

Chart 3547; immediately N of Pandora Head;
3 mi NW of Sullivan Bay
Entrance: 50°54.65'N, 126°53.68'W
Anchor: 50°54.42'N, 126°54.53'W

> *Carriden Bay, south of Linlithgow Point, offers good anchorage for small vessels, and in good weather, for small craft, but is exposed to easterly winds and seas.* (SD)

Carriden Bay affords good protection from prevailing westerlies but it is open to easterly wind and chop. It appears to us that it may offer protection from southeast storms, since the summer waters are stagnant and still (small debris, moss, and yellow sea sponges float on the surface).

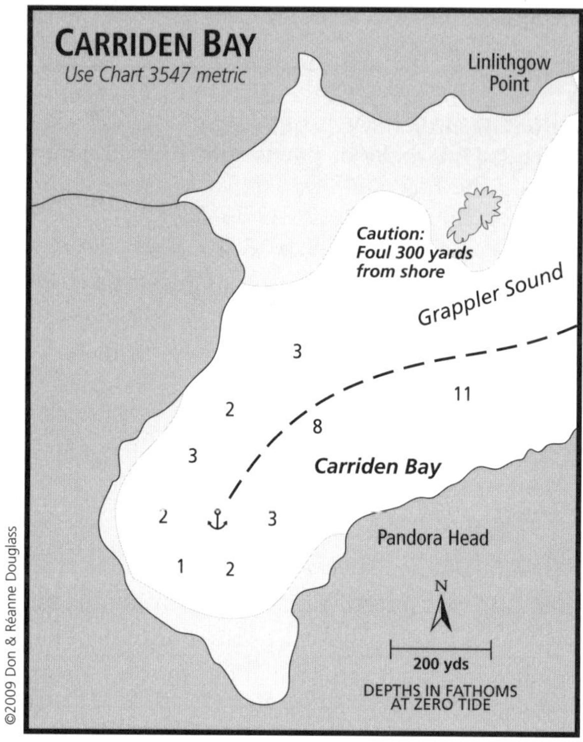

Floating marine resort, Sullivan Bay

Favor the south shore when entering Carriden Bay, since foul ground extends about 300 yards from the reef which partly dries on a 13-foot tide. Pandora Head, on the south side of the entrance, makes a good landing point.

Anchor in 2 to 3 fathoms over a thick mud and clam bottom with good swinging room and very good holding.

Dunsany Passage

Chart 3547; connects Sutlej Channel to Hopetown Passage & Grappler Sound;
1.5 mi NW of Sullivan Bay
Entrance (S): 50°54.06'N, 126°50.00'W
Entrance (N): 50°54.85'N, 126°50.64'W

Hopetown Passage

Chart 3547; S of Watson Island; extends E from Grappler Sound
Entrance (W): 50°55.04'N, 126°49.48'W
Entrance (E): 50°55.33'N, 126°47.87'W

> *[The] east end of the passage is obstructed by a drying reef and can be navigated only by shallow draught craft at HW.* (SD)

Hoy Bay (Watson Island)

Chart 3547; immediately E of Hopetown Pt & on the S side of Watson Island; 2.1 mi N of Sullivan Bay
Entrance: 50°55.41'N, 126°49.97'W
Anchor: 50°55.36'N, 126°50.15'W

> *Anchorage with mud bottom and good shelter is available in Hoy Bay.* (SD)

Hoy Bay offers moderate temporary shelter on the east side of Grappler Sound, on the south side of Watson Island. Hopetown Point offers partial shelter from westerlies and the fetch east is somewhat limited by Hopetown Passage. Six houses and a float are located in the Indian Reserve on the east side of Hoy Bay.

Anchor south of the old log dump and rusting tractor, avoiding the bare rocks on the south shore.

Anchor in 5 fathoms over a mixed bottom of rocks and young mud with shells. The holding is poor to fair.

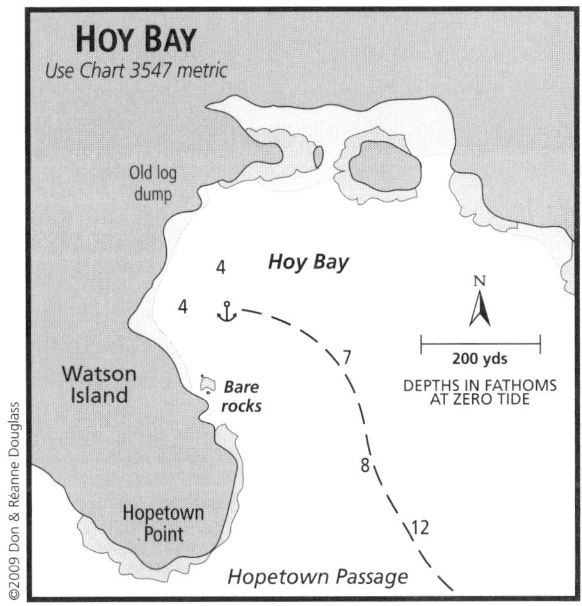

Claydon Bay (Grappler Sound)

Chart 3547; 3.2 mi NW of Sullivan Bay
Entrance: 50°55.53'N, 126°53.00'W
Anchor (N cove): 50°56.28'N, 126°53.44'W

> *Claydon Bay, between Morton Point the rocks in its entrance, affords good anchorage for small vessels in its south part and for small craft in its north arm.* (SD)

Claydon Bay is a popular anchorage, offering very good protection from all directions. The north cove (the preferred anchor site) is landlocked and has swinging room for several boats.

Thick cedar forests line the shores and the bay is popular with seals, blue herons and loons, We've heard reports that crabbing is good here, too.

Favor the west shore on entering to avoid both the rocks awash at 5 feet, as well as a large bare rock. To enter the north basin, favor the west shore to avoid the islet and offlying reefs. The north cove has a shallow flat bottom of thick, sticky mud.

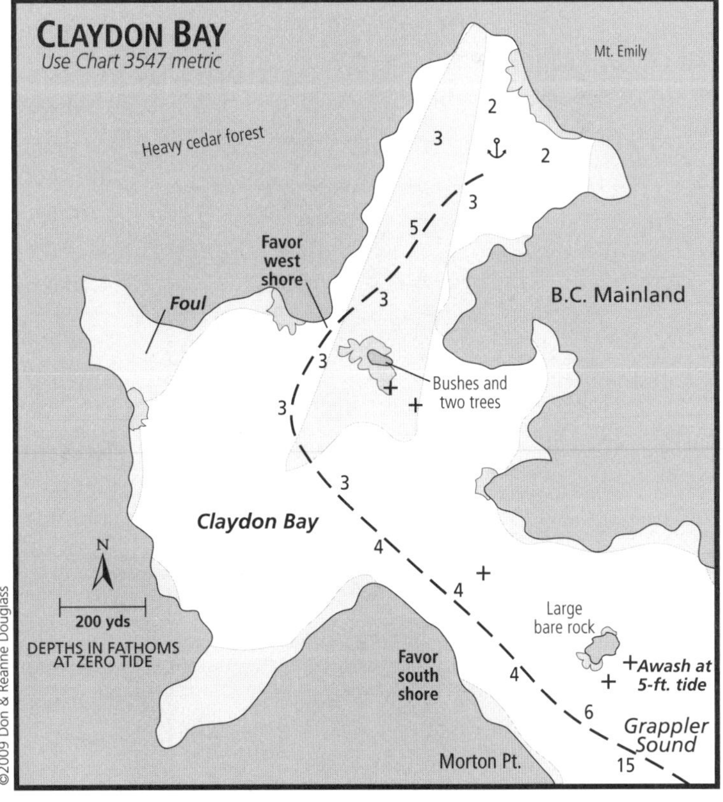

Anchor (north cove) in 2 to 3 fathoms over thick, sticky mud with very good holding.

Woods Bay (Watson Island)

Chart 3547; at the W end of Watson Island; 1.2 mi NE of Claydon Bay
Entrance: 50°56.04'N, 126°51.31'W
Anchor: 50°56.06'N, 126°51.10'W

Woods Bay is a small bay with easy access and a gently-sloping bottom. There is room for a couple of boats to anchor near the drying beach. This is a fair-weather anchorage only since the bay is rather open to westerlies.

Anchor in 2 fathoms over sand and gravel with fair holding.

Embley Lagoon

Chart 3547; at the N end of Grappler Sound; 1.5 mi N of Claydon Bay
Position: 50°56.97'N, 126°52.14'W

Embley Lagoon would make a perfect anchorage except that it is nearly filled with drying mud flats. The narrow entrance of Overflow Basin, 0.6 mile north of Embley Lagoon, becomes a 3-foot high waterfall with lots of white water on ebb tides.

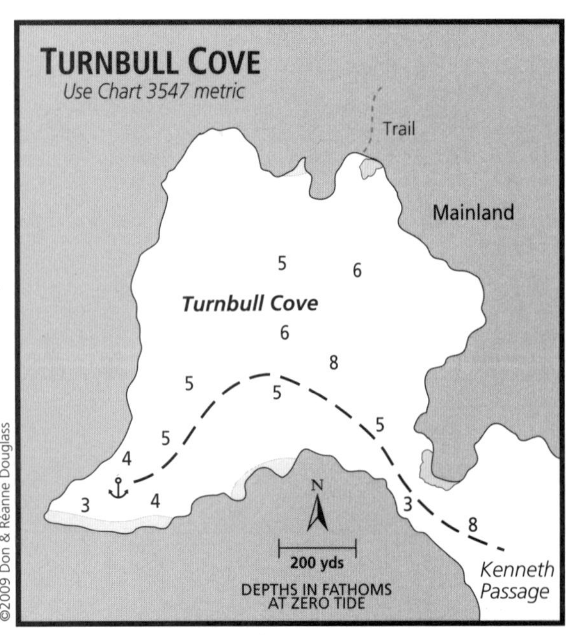

Turnbull Cove

Chart 3547; lies off the NW entrance to Kenneth Passage; 2.8 mi NE of Claydon Bay
Entrance: 50°57.38'N, 126°49.78'W
Anchor: 50°57.44'N, 126°50.54'W

> *Turnbull Cove affords anchorage for small vessels. It is reported that the holding is excellent in mud, but winds in a SE gale circle the cove at full force.* (SD)

Turnbull Cove offers the best protection in the area and, although *Sailing Directions* report the effect of southeast gales, we like the fact that there is little fetch from the southeast. We have a heavy Bruce anchor, that sets well in the sticky mud and has kept us well feathered into heavy east wind, although we've never ridden out a full gale inside Turnbull.

A number of boats can anchor over a fairly large areas. Since our last edition, the Forest Service has developed what was once a primitive trail to Huaksin Lake. Although *Sailing Directions* report the effect of southeast gales, we like the fact that Turnbull Cove has little fetch to the southeast, a wide flat bottom of sticky mud, and unlimited swinging room that allows excellent scope ratios.

Logging floathouses formerly located here are gone and only two small green buoys remain on the north side.

Turnbull Cove is quiet and calm; seals swim by placidly and time passes slowly.

Anchor in 4 fathoms over sticky mud with excellent holding.

Roaringhole Rapids (Nepah Lagoon)

Chart 3547 inset; the entrance to Nepah Lagoon; 3.2 mi NE of Claydon Bay
Position: 50°57.23'N, 126°48.70'W

> *... navigation of this rapid should be attempted only at HW slack.* (SD)

Roaringhole Rapids is just that—roaring! At low-water spring tides, roostertails extend over an area 100 yards from the 60-foot wide waterfall, and a thick blanket of foam fills the entire bay. The charted minimum depth of Roaringhole Rapids is 3 feet, with a second shoal of 7 feet at the inner end of the narrows. We have been too mesmerized to enter, but entry is reported possible at high water slack. Reconnoiter before entering, and verify by closely monitoring the current of the rapids, since times of slack water vary and are short in duration. Review the inset on Chart 3547, as well as the notes regarding times of slack water.

The scenery backing Nepah Lagoon is spectacular. The water inside is deep and the shores are steep-to. Yuki Bay, 1.2 miles from the rapids on the east shore, may offer some temporary anchorage, but it appears unsheltered from williwaws.

Kenneth Passage

Chart 3547 inset; 0.25 mi S of Roaringhole Rapids; 3 mi NE of Claydon Bay
Entrance (NW): 50°57.00'N, 126°48.85'W
Entrance (SE): 50°55.96'N, 126°46.49'W

> *Kenneth Passage is obstructed by an island and reefs abreast Kenneth Point; the channel leads SW of Jessie Point, which has a shoal rock close south of it; caution is advised.* (SD)

Roaringhole Rapids at slack water

Kenneth Passage fronts some very high and rugged snow-clad peaks. Current and turbulence are strong at spring tides. Caution is required off Jessie Point because of the eddies and a submerged rock. The fairway east of island (70) has an unreported bottom with a minimum depth of about 6 fathoms.

Steamboat Bay (Watson Island)

Chart 3547 inset; on the S side of Kenneth Passage; 1.5 mi SE of Turnbull Cove
Entrance: 50°56.39'N, 126°48.26'W
Anchor: 50°56.18'N, 126°48.24'W

> *Steamboat Bay ... affords anchorage for small craft.* (SD)

Steamboat Bay is a pretty, quiet bay in Kenneth Passage that makes a good base camp from which to fish or explore Mackenzie Sound. The bay is well sheltered and out of the current that flows through Kenneth Passage. Its bottom slopes gently to the very small landing beach.

Enter through the center and avoid the two rocks to the east that dry at 5 feet.

Anchor in 2 to 3 fathoms over mud, sand, eel grass and clam shells with fair-to-good holding.

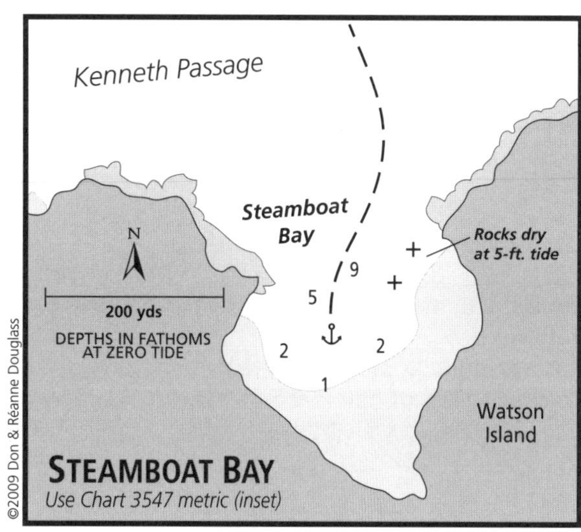

Roaringhole Rapids, start of ebb tide

Mackenzie Sound

Chart 3547; lies E of Watson Island
Entrance: 50°55.95'N, 126°46.56'W

> *Mackenzie Sound is free of offshore dangers except for shoal areas between Turner Island and Stirling Point and NE of Nimmo Islet. The entrance to Nimmo Bay is obstructed by drying ledges; local knowledge is required for entry.* (SD)

Mackenzie Sound is a remote and pristine cruising ground. Long strands of Spanish moss hang from tree limbs and the shores are ruled by grizzly bears.

Except for a fly-in fishing resort in Little Nimmo Bay, Mackenzie Sound seems a long way from the Pacific Ocean.

Burly Bay (Mackenzie Sound)

Chart 3547; S of the W entrance to Mackenzie Sound; 2.6 mi SE of Turnbull Cove; 2.7 mi NE of Sullivan Bay
Entrance: 50°55.37'N, 126°47.19'W
Anchor (head of bay): 50°54.68'N, 126°47.29'W

> *Burly Bay, entered SW of Claypole Point, affords anchorage for small vessels near its head in about 20 m (66 ft), but is reported to offer little protection from strong SE winds. Small craft can obtain anchorage nearer the head of Burly Bay ...* (SD)

Burly Bay appears to be well-sheltered with room for a number of boats at the head of the bay. The low isthmus to the south may funnel southeast winds through the pass. The bottom is said to be gravel with poor-to-fair holding.

Anchorage is also reported on the west side of Blair Islet with more pleasing surroundings; however, there is exposure to both east and west wind at the east entrance to Hopetown Passage.

Little Nimmo Bay (Mackenzie Sound)

Chart 3547; 3.2 mi E of Kenneth Passage
Entrance: 50°56.19'N, 126°41.47'W
Anchor: 50°56.30'N, 126°40.90'W

> *Small craft can obtain anchorage ... with local knowledge, in Little Nimmo Bay ... but shelter from west winds ... is not good. The floats and buildings of a fishing lodge are on the north side of Little Nimmo Bay.* (SD)

Little Nimmo Bay is reported to offer fair shelter and a scenic environment. The entrance, however, is shallow and choked with rocks. Enter when the tide is rising.

Anchor in about 4 fathoms over an unrecorded bottom.

The head of Mackenzie Sound appears to offer easy anchorage but is open to westerlies.

Landlocked Richmond Bay, Drury Inlet

Drury Inlet

Chart 3547; W of Wells Passage & Grappler Sound, entered btwn Compton Pt & Pandora Head
Entrance (0.13 mi NE of Morris Islet): 50°53.62'N, 126°53.75'W

> *Drury Inlet ... leads 12 miles west between low hills. Depths through most of the inlet and the connecting waters are less than 40 m (131 ft) and there are many dangers. Caution is advised.* (SD)

Drury Inlet covers a large, low, cedar-forested area near the coast leading to remote Actaeon Sound and Tsibass Lagoon. Except for some heavy logging activity, it is seldom visited.

The low tree-covered hills along this inlet are a decided contrast to the high, rugged peaks and the fjords of the coast range. This is a lovely area, but once in a while chain saws disturb the quiet. No williwaws blow here, but you might expect low clouds and drizzle to hang around forever.

Helen Bay (Drury Inlet)

Chart 3547; 1.4 mi NW of the entrance to Drury Inlet
Entrance: 50°54.28'N, 126°55.89'W
Anchor: 50°54.15'N, 126°56.17'W

Helen Bay offers good temporary anchorage in its northwest corner out of the current stream; you can wait here for slack water in Stuart Narrows if necessary.

Anchor in 4 fathoms over sand and gravel with poor-to-fair holding.

Stuart Narrows (Drury Inlet)

Chart 3547 inset; 1.6 mi W of the entrance to Drury Inlet
Entrance (E): 50°53.83'N, 126°56.23'W
Entrance (W, 0.1 mi NW of Leche Islet): 50°53.82'N, 126°58.22'W

> *Stuart Narrows ... is obstructed by Morris Islet and several rocks in its entrance, by Welde Rock in its central part, and by Leche Islet, as well as some isolated shoals off and within Richmond Bay, near its west end.*
>
> *Tidal differences for Stuart Narrows (Entrance), referenced on Alert Bay, are given in the Tide Tables, Volume 6.*
>
> *Tidal streams in Stuart Narrows attain 7 kn on the ebb and 6 kn on the flood. Secondary current station Stuart Narrows, Drury Inlet, referenced on Alert Bay, is given in the Tide Tables, Volume 6.* (SD)

Stuart Narrows has strong current and turbulent water on spring tides. Caution is required in the vicinity of Welde Rock; the fairway is close on the south side of Welde Rock and north of the unnamed islet off Restless Bay. The passage south of this unnamed islet is foul with rocks and kelp.

Restless Bay (Stuart Narrows)

Chart 3547 inset; immediately S of the rapids in the narrows; 1.8 mi from the entrance to Drury Inlet
Entrance: 50°53.68'N, 126°56.63'W

Restless Bay is a temporary stop only to watch the action in the rapids.

Richmond Bay (Stuart Narrows)

Chart 3547 inset; on the S side of the W entrance to Stuart Narrows; 3.1 mi W of the entrance to Drury Inlet
Entrance: 50°53.41'N, 126°58.70'W
Anchor (SW): 50°53.04'N, 126°58.74'W

> *Stuart Narrows ... is obstructed by ... some isolated shoals off and within Richmond Bay, near its west end.* (SD)

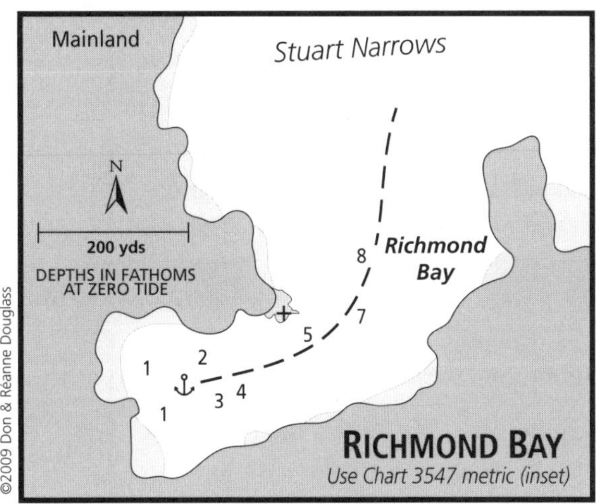

Enter Richmond Bay by passing north of Leche Islet (heavy trees), and by clearing either side of the several rocks in the central portion of the bay.

Richmond Bay offers two anchor sites on the south shore. The east cove has a rocky bottom with poor holding and is not advised. The southwest cove is almost landlocked and offers very good protection from all weather. Swinging room is limited. This is an intimate anchorage with moss-covered trees whose lower limbs dip into the water at high tide. Multi-pronged silvery snags contrast vividly with the living cedars. Bald eagles soar above, and seals come and go.

Anchor (southwest) in 1-1/2 fathoms over mud and shells with excellent holding.

Bughouse Bay (Drury Inlet)

Chart 3547 inset; on the N side of the inlet; W of Stuart Narrows
Entrance: 50°53.94'N, 126°58.90'W

Bughouse Lake is 150 yards north of the creek outlet into Bughouse Bay.

Tancred Bay (Drury Inlet)

Chart 3547; on the S side of the inlet; just W of Richmond Bay & E of Davis Bay
Entrance: 50°53.37'N, 126°59.97'W

Davis Bay (Drury Inlet)

Chart 3547; on the S shore of the inlet; 1.5 mi W of Richmond Bay
Entrance: 50°53.35'N, 127°01.33'W
Anchor: 50°53.33'N, 127°00.83'W

Davis Bay is a small, well-protected anchorage. The entrance south of Davis Islet is narrow with dangerous rocks off its south shore. The bottom is irregular and there is limited swinging room. A shore tie (or two) can make this otherwise marginal anchorage secure.

Anchor in 2 to 3 fathoms over a rocky mixed bottom with poor holding. A shore tie is advised.

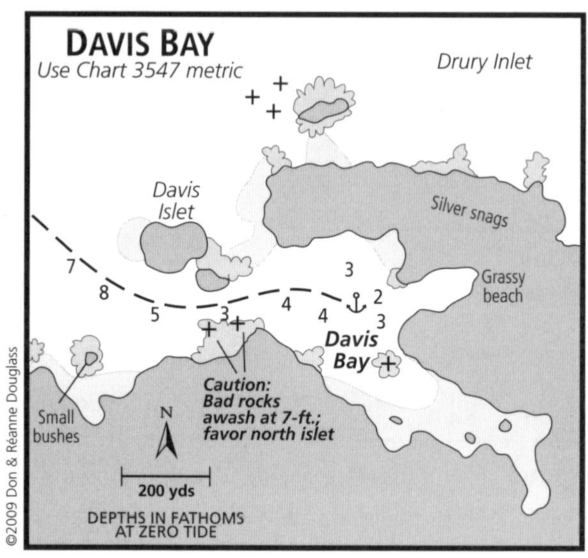

Jennis Bay (Drury Inlet)

Chart 3547; on the N shore of the inlet; entered on either side of Hooper Island; 1.3 mi N of Davis Bay
Entrance (E): 50°54.28'N, 127°01.47'W
Entrance (W): 50°54.45'N, 127°02.26'W
Anchor: 50°54.88'N, 127°02.06'W

A wharf, float and boathouse are on the north shore of Jennis Bay. (SD)

Jennis Bay, a sheltered bay, was chiefly a loggers' residence and is now another wonderful resort run by Allyson and Tom Allo with their children. Moss floats serenely on the

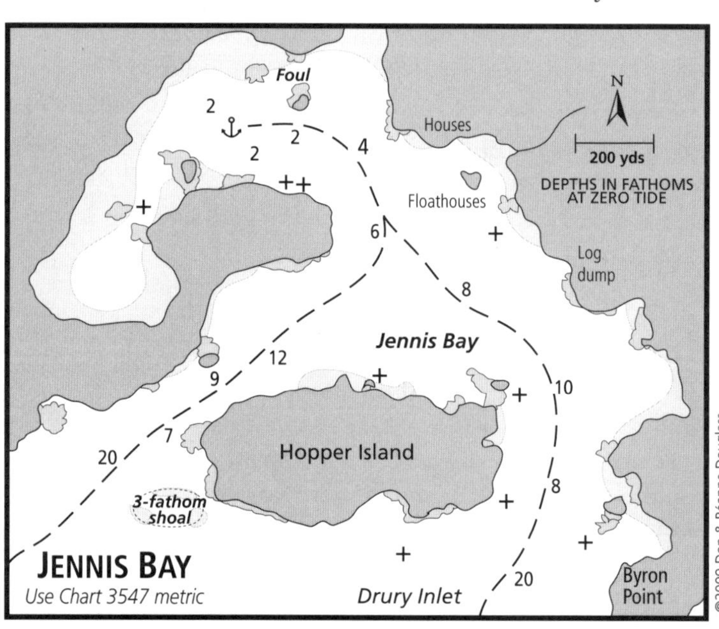

surface of the water and no current is felt here. Anchor on the west side of the bay or moor at the docks.

See the website for the full list of guest activities.

Anchor in 2 fathoms over sand and mud with good holding.

⚓ **Jennis Bay Extreme Expeditions Ltd.,** tel: 250.949.0203; monitors VHF Ch 66A; website: www.jennisbay.com; email: jennisbay@hughes.net; restrooms; showers; guest room and gift shop

Collinson Bay (Drury Inlet)

Chart 3547; on the N side of the inlet; 2.3 mi W of Jennis Bay
Entrance: 50°55.13'N, 126°05.25'W

Collinson Bay is open and offers only marginal anchorage.

Sutherland Bay (Drury Inlet)

Chart 3547; at the head of Drury Inlet; 5.5 mi W of Jennis Bay
Entrance: 50°55.60'N, 127°10.23'W
Anchor: 50°55.67'N, 127°10.98'W

> *The channel leading north of Muirhead Islands, near the west end of the inlet, has several detached shoals in midchannel.*
>
> *Sutherland Bay, farther west, is reported to afford good anchorage over mud for small craft, sheltered from all but strong easterly winds.* (SD)

Sutherland Bay, the largest area of shallow water in Drury Inlet, has unlimited swinging room. Entrance is made through the main channel north of Muirhead Islands. Although the bay is not long enough for fetch to build up, it is open to easterly winds.

The bay makes a good base from which to explore, by kayak or dinghy, scenic Muirhead Islands and the rock-filled Actress Passage.

Sutherland Bay is less than two airline miles from Whelakis Lagoon which can be reached by small cruising boats via Nakwakto Rapids.

Davis Bay, Drury Inlet

Anchor in 1-1/2 fathoms over a mud bottom of reported good holding.

Actaeon Sound

Chart 3547; extends NE from the head of Drury Inlet & Actress Passage; 9.5 mi W of the Drury Inlet entrance
Entrance (0.25 mi SW of Charlotte Pt): 50°55.82'N, 127°08.43'W

> *Dove Island lies in the entrance of Actress Passage, which leads to Actaeon Sound. This sound, encumbered with islets and rocks, is suitable only for small craft and should not be attempted without local knowledge. There is a slight tidal stream in the entrance to the sound, but not much current within it.* (SD)

Entry to Actaeon Sound is via Actress Passage, with a very narrow fairway which requires avoiding numerous hazardous rocks and reefs. To avoid the strong currents and to maximize water depths, transit at high-water slack. You can pass on either side of Dove Island.

Work boats tend to take the east channel because they know how to "read" the private sticks and poles marking the various rocks. Follow Chart 3547 carefully and avoid kelp patches and turbulent water. The difficult part of Actress Passage, found between Skeene Point and Bond Peninsula, is known locally as Snake Pass. The recommended route passes the midchannel rock off Charters Point, favoring the west shore, then heads northeast toward Bond Peninsula and the first of a series of private white markers. Remain on the north side along Bond Peninsula, watching for drying rocks, then changing to a more westerly course, while crossing the eddies on a course pointing for Skeene Bay. From Skeene Bay, take a northeast midchannel course until the sound opens up and the current decreases.

Skeene Bay (Actaeon Sound)

Chart 3547; W of Bond Peninsula; 1.1 mi N of the entrance to Actaeon Sound
Entrance: 50°56.93'N, 127°08.25'W

> *The section of channel leading from Charters Point around Bond Peninsula, known locally as Snake Pass, requires extra caution, particularly through the shoals off Skeene Point.* (SD)

Bond Lagoon (Actaeon Sound)

Chart 3547; 3.4 mi NW of Jennis Bay
Entrance: 50°56.80'N, 127°06.00'W

Bond Lagoon has a very narrow entrance with about a 2-foot depth at zero tide. While good anchorage at reasonable depths can be found inside the lagoon, we recommend that boats anchor just outside the entrance to the east in Hand Bay and explore the lagoon by dinghy.

Author along Blunden Harbour, beach fronting ruins of longhouse

Hand Bay (Actaeon Sound)

Chart 3547; immediately E of Bond Lagoon
Entrance: 50°56.72'N, 127°05.42'W

Hand Bay is a small bay out of the mainstream.

Creasy Bay (Actaeon Sound)

Chart 3547; 1.2 mi NE of Bond Lagoon
Entrance: 50°57.42'N, 127°04.42'W

> *Creasy Bay has booming grounds and an abandoned logging camp with a jetty on its west shore.* (SD)

Creasy Bay was full of logbooms at last report.

Tsibass Lagoon (Actaeon Sound)

Chart 3547; at the head of Actaeon Sound; 2.7 mi NE of Bond Lagoon
South entrance: 50°58.28'N, 127°02.55'W

Tsibass Lagoon has a narrow channel in a rock-strewn pass that carries about 2 feet at zero tide. Enter only at high-water slack using an inflatable. The head of Tsibass Lagoon is about two airline miles from Seymour Inlet.

Wells Passage

Chart 3547; lies to the NW of the Broughton Is
Entrance (N 0.3 mi S of Kinnaird Rock): 50°54.26'N, 126°52.99'W
Entrance (S, 0.7 mi E of Boyles Pt): 50°49.09'N, 126°59.78'W

> *Wells Passage, entered east of Boyles Point, is generally deep but has occasional depths near midchannel of 27 to 37 m (89 to 121 ft). Compton Point and Providence Point form its north end.*
>
> *Tidal streams in Wells Passage reach up to 3 kn.*
>
> *A drying rock lies 0.4 mile SSW of Boyles Point. Lewis Rocks, described in Chapter IX, lie 1 mile farther SW. A rock with 3.4 m (11 ft) over it lies near midchannel 0.6 mile south of*

James Point. Rocks extend more than 0.1 mile into the channel from Ommaney Islet, and the area SE and eastward of this islet is filled with dangers. A rock, with 7.9 m (26 ft) over it, lies 0.15 mile south of Popplewell Point. A 7.3 m (24 ft) shoal lies 0.2 mile off Providence Point. (SD)

Wells Passage is the main channel leading from the Sullivan Bay area to Queen Charlotte Strait via Labouchere Passage.

Wehlis Bay (Wells Passage)

Chart 3547; on the W side of Wells Passage; 4.0 mi SW of Sullivan Bay
Entrance: 50°51.85'N, 126°55.43'W

Wehlis Bay ... is not recommended for anchorage. (SD)

The next bay south of Wehlis Bay is Kenneth Bay (3.5 miles southwest), a drying sand and gravel flat with no anchorage.

Tracey Harbour, Napier Bay (North Broughton Island)

Chart 3547; with Napier Bay at its head, indents the W shore of North Broughton Island; 3 mi SW of Sullivan Bay
Entrance: 50°51.42'N, 126°53.25'W
Anchor: 50°50.98'N, 126°51.12'W

Good anchorage for small vessels is available in Napier Bay, mud bottom; stay well clear of the submarine pipeline crossing the bay. (SD)

Tracey Harbour and Napier Bay are good places to seek shelter before heading out into Labouchere Passage and Queen Charlotte Strait. Easy to enter, Tracey Harbour's only obstruction is its north wall; however, watch for drifting logs or trees with limbs. Napier Bay to the north of Carter Point is well sheltered from all seas and most winds. There are several floathouses in the bay, with a submerged pipeline between them, as shown on

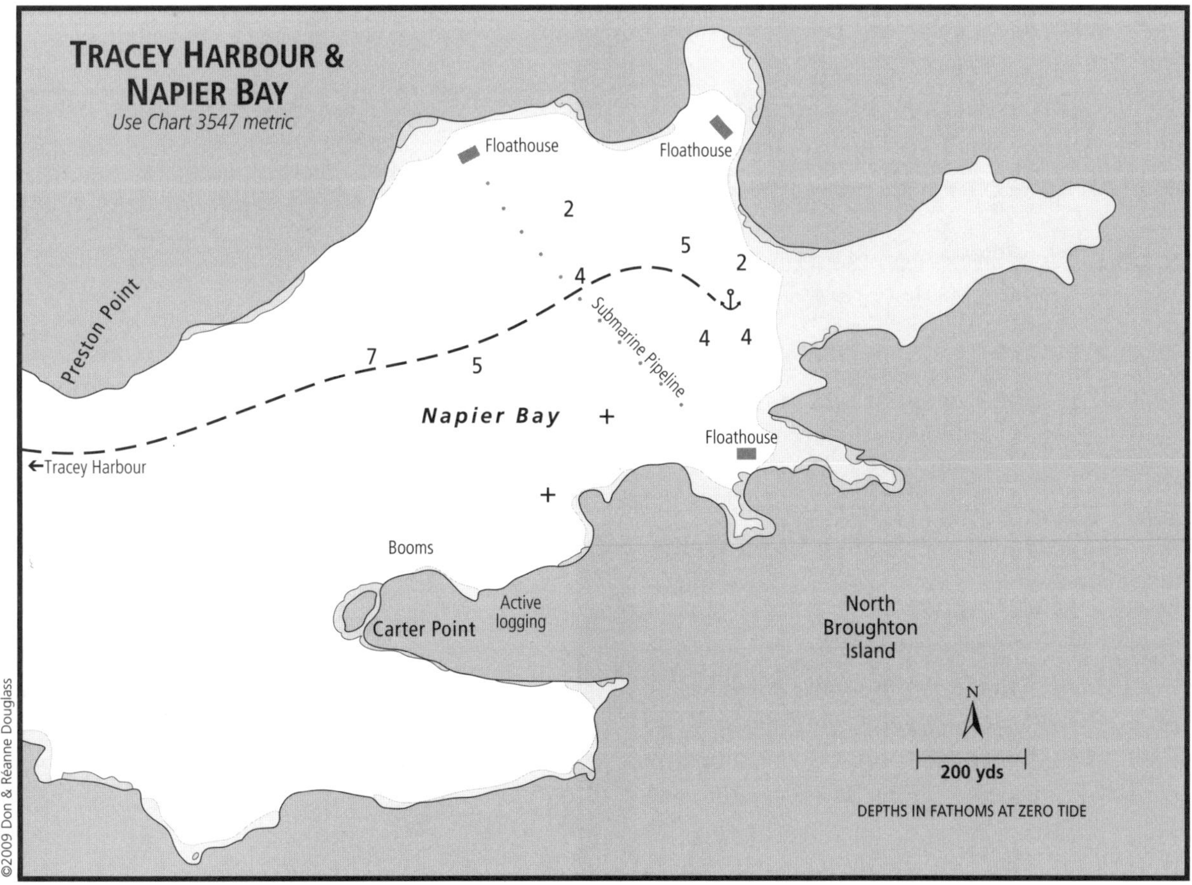

the diagram. The logging operation on Carter Point is busy and noisy, but you can find an out-of-the-way spot by anchoring off the creek shoal.

Anchor in 2 fathoms off the creek outlet over a thin layer of sand, gravel, mud and rocks with log debris; good holding if you[r] anchor's well set. Some drag has been reported.

Ralph Bay and Aimee Bay (Broughton Island)

Chart 3547; near the far W end of Broughton Island; lie NE of Polkinghorn Islands; 5 mi SW of Sullivan Bay
Entrance (both bays): 50°49.22'N, 126°54.60'W

Cockatrice Bay (Broughton Island)

Chart 3547; 2.8 mi SE of Ralph & Aimee bays
Entrance: 50°47.58'N, 126°51.10'W

> *Dobbin Bay and Cockatrice Bay, which has rocks extending from its south shore, are too exposed for anchorage. A wreck lies in the cove at the head of Cockatrice Bay.* (SD)

The entrance to Cockatrice Bay is open to the southwest, but some shelter can be found at the head of the bay avoiding old pilings.

Dobbin Bay (Broughton Island)

Chart 3547; on the N side of Nowell Channel; 1.6 mi SE of Cockatrice Bay
Entrance: 50°46.54'N, 126°48.77'W

Dobbin Bay offers temporary anchorage at the head of the bay in fair weather.

Lewis Cove (Labouchere Passage)

Chart 3547; NE of Numas Islands; 5.4 mi SW of Tracey Hbr
Entrance: 50°49.25'N, 127°02.92'W
Anchor: 50°49.37'N, 127°03.10'W

Lewis Cove is the last windward mark before you turn northwest into the semi-open waters of central Queen Charlotte Strait. Several groups of dangerous rocks lie off Lewis Cove and caution is advised. Because of the difficulty in locating all the rocks visually, you may want to remain outside all of them, or pass close inside them. In fair weather, passing inside doesn't present difficulty—the hazards are marked by heaping or breaking waves—and you profit from the lee effect of Lewis Rocks for another mile or so.

Although Lewis Cove is not considered an anchorage, and is not found in *Sailing Directions*, we have included it as a temporary fair-weather anchorage because, from here, you can get a good idea of what's happening on the outside. You can duck in for a short time, study conditions in the strait, then head back into Wells Passage if you don't like what you see.

Lewis Cove gives temporary protection from westerlies only. The west shore of the cove, a bold, rocky headland of light granite, is covered with windswept trees. The head of the bay is shoal with two or three above-water rocks, one of which has a tree on it. Two rocks mark the shallow water on the east side of the

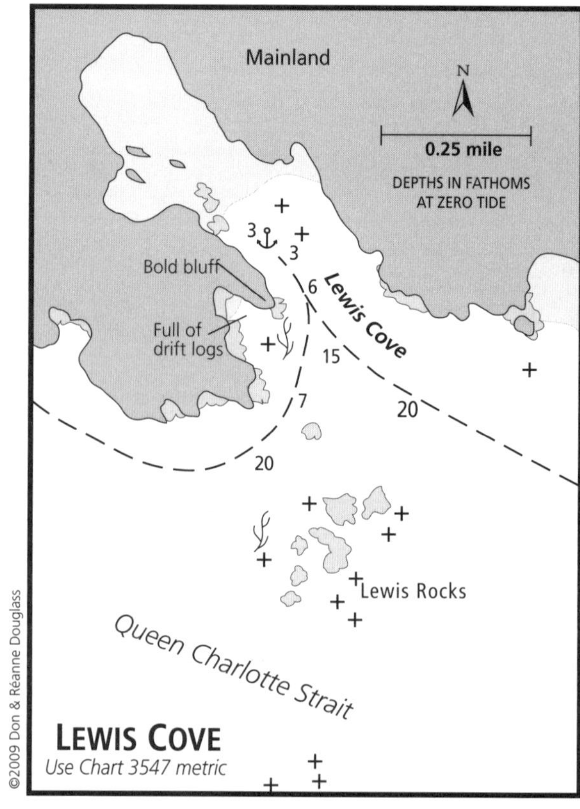

cove. Large drift logs along shore indicate that the cove is subject to heavy weather from the south. Watch out for deadheads—we found a nasty one in line with the rocks on the left side of the cove.

If you are heading north, you can exit between the cove and Lewis Rocks, keeping the 2-meter rock to port, and the bold bluff to starboard. The fairway has a flat bottom with about 9 fathoms.

Anchor in 4 fathoms over sand and gravel with fair holding.

Raynor Group, Cohoe Bay (Queen Charlotte Strait)

Chart 3548 metric; lies close offshore btwn Akam Pt & Cohoe Bay; 9 mi NW of Wells Passage
Entrance (S, 0.46 mi SE of Akam Pt): 50°52.55′N, 127°12.24′W
Entrance (N, off Cohoe Bay): 50°53.86′N, 127°14.99′W

> *Gillot Rock, 0.2 mile south of the SE island in the group, dries 5.5 m (18 ft). Brandon Rock, 0.1 mile west of the westernmost island, is 2 m (7 ft) high.* (SD)

The Raynor Group is full of rocks and reefs. Anchor sites for temporary stops can be found among the islands in surprisingly calm water during fair weather. The best spot is on the south side of Cohoe Bay on the north side of island (43).

Blunden Harbour (Queen Charlotte Strait)

Chart 3548 inset; 11.5 mi NW of Wells Passage; 16.7 mi W of Sullivan Bay
Entrance: 50°54.14′N, 127°16.15′W
Anchor: 50°54.45′N, 127°17.36′W

> *Blunden Harbour, entered between Shelf Head and Edgell Point, is separated into two arms by the Augustine Islands which are connected to one another and joined to the north shore by a drying mud flat on which there are numerous boulders. An abandoned Indian village is on the north shore, NW of Augustine Islands.*
>
> *A narrow channel suitable for small craft, lies to the west and north of these islands* [Julia Island and Frost Islands] *and leads to rapids at the entrance to Bradley Lagoon. This rapids can only be passed at HW slack.*
>
> *Anchorage in the outer part of Blunden Harbour can be obtained south of the north Augustine Island in a depth of about 13 m (43 ft), mud bottom. In the inner part a good anchorage is SW of Moore Rock in 6 m (20 ft), mud bottom. Both anchorages afford good shelter.*
>
> *If proceeding to the inner anchorage care must be taken to avoid the drying reefs and rock with less than 2 m (6 ft) over it extending south from Augustine Islands and the drying reef close north of Bartlett Point.* (SD)

Blunden Harbour is a wonderful, well-sheltered anchorage and a favorite of cruising boats that follow the mainland coast. To enter, follow a midchannel route. Once you're inside, the bay is shallow but holding is good.

Traditional backcountry float house, Port Neville

Modern float house, Wells Passage

Another peaceful anchorage

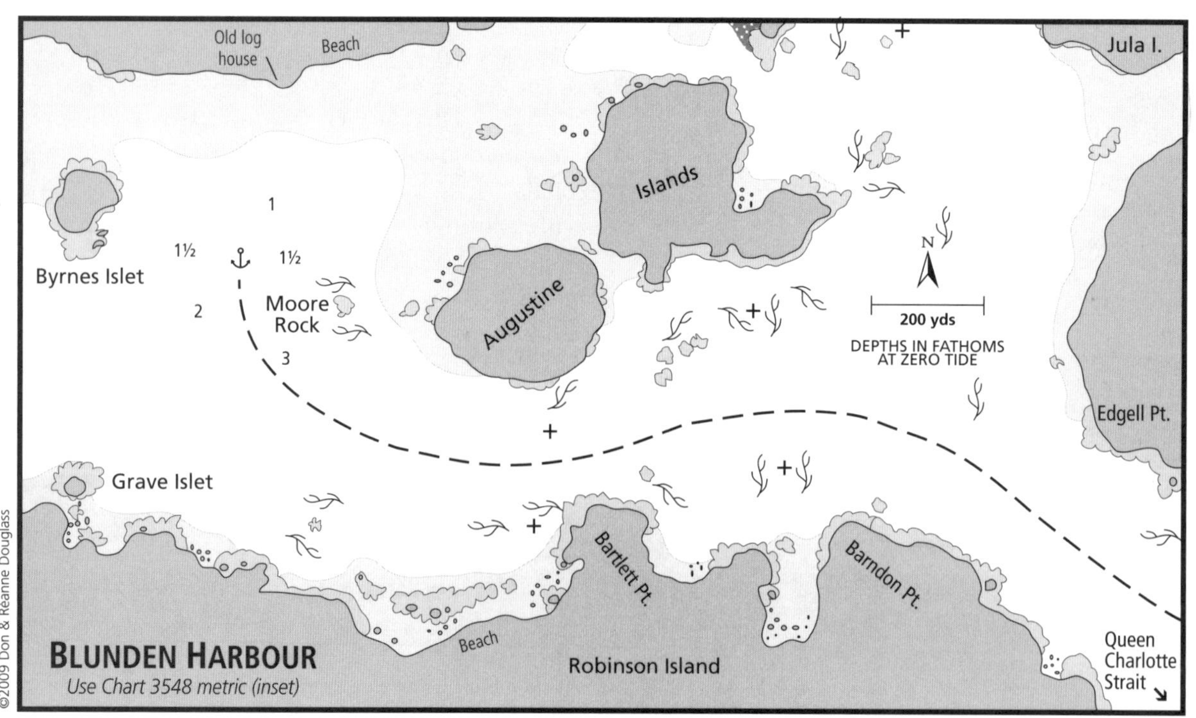

A thriving native culture once existed in this area. Giant logs on shore—the remains of a longhouse—and an extensive midden indicate once-successful native residency.

The narrow entrance to Bradley Lagoon dries at 11 feet, and while we know of one cruising boat that entered the lagoon on a high spring tide and anchored overnight, it is advisable to reconnoiter the narrows first by inflatable. Slack water at the narrows lasts for just a short time before it reverts to a rapids and becomes a waterfall once again. Needless to say, turning room at this point is restricted! On the east side just short of the narrows there is an old grid used by fishing boats to haul out.

Anchor in 1-1/2 fathoms over mud with very good holding.

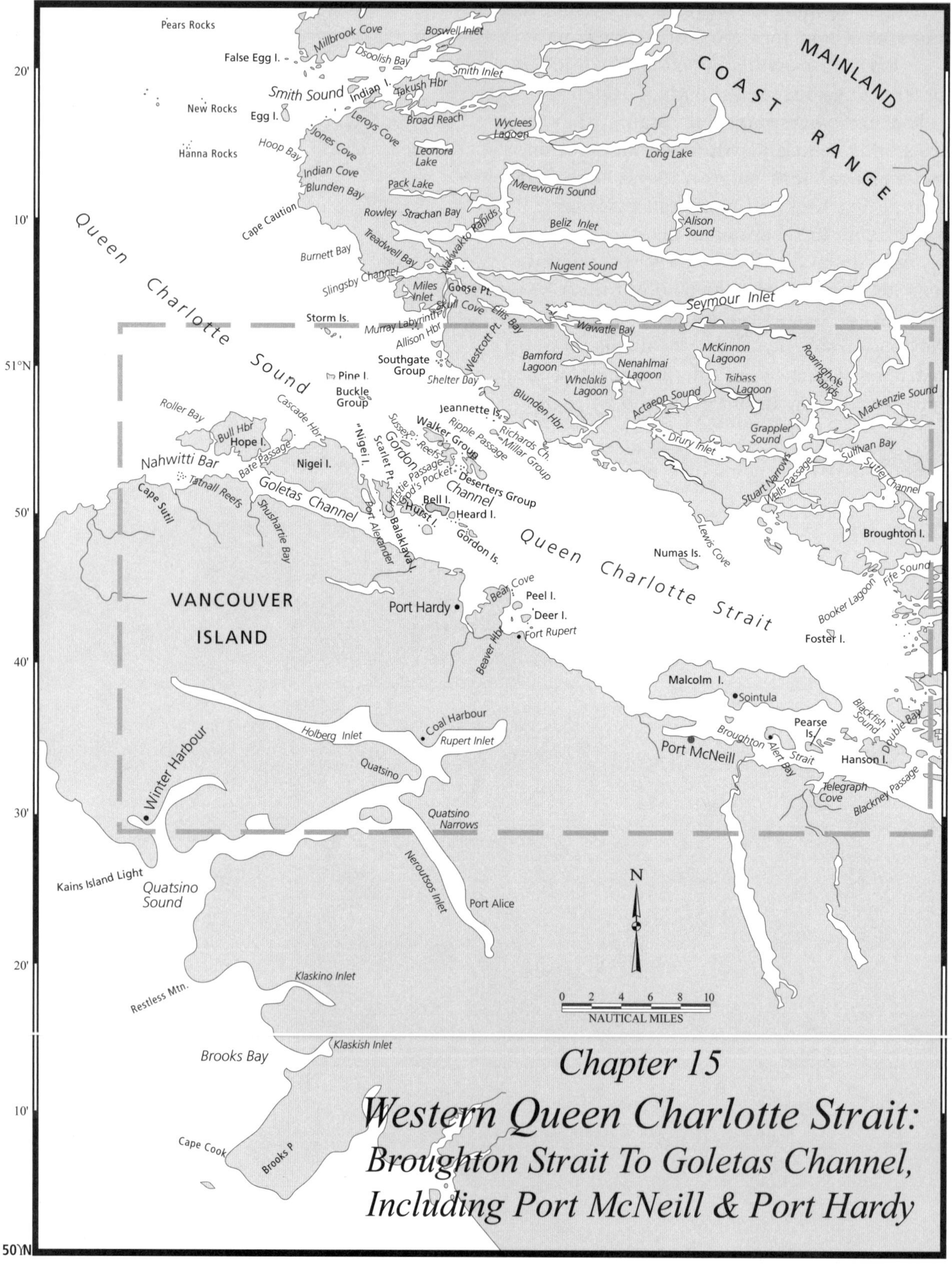

Chapter 15

Western Queen Charlotte Strait:

Broughton Strait To Goletas Channel, Including Port McNeill & Port Hardy

15

WESTERN QUEEN CHARLOTTE STRAIT: Broughton Strait to Goletas Channel, including Port McNeill and Port Hardy

Broughton Strait (the continuation of Johnstone Strait) and twenty-three-mile-long Goletas Channel mark the final link between "civilization" and the wilderness to the north. Here the coast takes on the windswept appearance so typical of Vancouver Island's west coast—stunted trees, wide sandy beaches and, as you enter Queen Charlotte Sound, rolling seas.

The area often buzzes with activity as sportfishing, cruising and commercial fishing boats ply these water. Trailerable boats and kayaks are putting in with increasing numbers at convenient locations such as Port McNeill and Port Hardy—the two most important supply centers on Vancouver Island's north coast. Large cruise ships and ferries also funnel through these channels on their way to Prince Rupert or Alaska.

The northern end of Queen Charlotte Strait has an unfavorable reputation because it is here that the initial force of "outside" swells is felt. Much of this has to do with winter storms; during late spring and summer, however, Broughton Strait, Alert Bay and Port McNeill in the lee of Malcolm Island usually enjoy pleasant, mild weather.

PASSAGES BETWEEN BROUGHTON, JOHNSTONE AND QUEEN CHARLOTTE STRAITS

Orca watching, Cormorant Channel

Blackney Passage

Chart 3546; leads N btwn Hanson & Parson Is into Blackfish Sound
Entrance (S, 0.25 mi W of Cracroft Pt): 50°32.98'N, 126°41.10'W
Entrance (N, 0.4 mi E of Burnt Pt): 50°34.62'N, 126°41.77'W

Tidal streams in Blackney Passage attain 5 kn with heavy races off Cracroft Point on both the flood and ebb. The flood, or east-going stream, flows north and south of Hanson Island and meets near the south end of Blackney Passage causing a strong tidal race in midchannel.

Secondary current station Blackney Passage, referenced on Johnstone Strait

(Central), is given in the Tide Tables, Volume 6. (SD)

Blackney Passage, entered west of Cracroft Point, is the passage of choice for northbound ships and cruising boats. Turbulence and eddies are strong here on spring tides. The passage which is marked with two navigation lights is the easiest route to follow in low visibility or under radar.

Weynton Passage

Chart 3546; btwn Pearse & Plumper Islands; joins Johnstone Strait to Cormorant Channel & Blackfish Sound
Entrance (S, 0.47 mi SW of Weynton I): 50°34.10'N, 126°48.22'W
Entrance (N, 0.35 mi S of Stubbs I): 50°35.82'N, 126°49.03'W

The fairway, which is deep, has a minimum width of 0.7 mile.

Tidal streams in Weynton Passage attain 6 kn at times and set over and across the shoals extending from Stephenson Islet. The flood sets south and the ebb north through Weynton Passage. There are heavy tide-rips at times near both shores and in the vicinity of Stubbs Island. Times and rates of maximum current and the time of slack water are predicted and tabulated as daily tables for current station Weynton Passage in the Tide Tables, Volume 6. (SD)

Kayaker stops for a rest

Weynton Passage is an alternative to Blackney Passage. Due to the nearby reefs, it has upwellings and strong turbulence on spring tides. Keep a lookout for fast-moving sportfishing boats in this area.

Pearse Passage

Chart 3546; btwn Cormorant Island & Pearse Islands; joins Broughton Strait to Cormorant Channel
Entrance (S): 50°34.37'N, 126°53.95'W
Entrance (N): 50°35.18'N, 126°53.76'W

Pearse Passage ... is about 0.7 mile wide. Gordon Rock, in the middle of Pearse Passage, has two drying heads. The passage is narrowed by drying and above-water rocks lying off the east side and by shallow depths off the west shore. The best channel is to the west of Gordon Rock, but neither is recommended.

Tidal streams set obliquely through Pearse Passage and attain 5 kn at times. (SD)

Pearse Passage, which has strong turbulence and upwellings on spring tides, is unmarked and requires careful navigation. Avoid mid-channel Gordon Rock. The passage is used principally by fast sportfishing boats.

Parson Bay (Harbledown and Parson Is)

Chart 3546; indents the W end of Harbledown Island
Entrance: 50°34.84'N, 126°40.83'W

Parson Bay [is] entered between Parson Island and Red Point. Harris Shoals lie in the middle of the entrance. (SD)

Parson Bay is open to prevailing northwest winds and chop. This large bay is out of the current of Blackney Passage and is easy to enter during foggy weather. Temporary anchorage can be found at the head of the bay.

Double Bay (Hanson Island)

Chart 3546; on the N side of Hanson Island; 4 mi NW of Blackney Passage
Entrance (W): 50°35.40'N, 126°45.92'W
Entrance (E): 50°35.40'N, 126°45.42'W
Anchor (E bight): 50°35.16'N, 126°45.49'W

> *Double Bay, west of Spout Islet, is used by commercial fishermen and congested during fishing season.* (SD)

Double Bay offers shelter for small boats on its west side. During fishing season the floats inside the bay are used primarily by commercial fishing boats and the bay itself may be too crowded to be interesting to cruising vessels.

By anchoring in the small east bight you can escape the busyness at the floats or resort. The east bay dries almost entirely at low water; however, you can find good anchorage just off the beach with moderate swinging room.

Double Bay is a sportfishing center for both Weynton Passage and Blackfish Sound. It is also a good base from which to explore the Plumper Islands by kayak or dinghy; these islands are excellent for fishing and interesting to explore. The current can run rapidly in the narrow passages between the islands and islets, so it's a good idea to carry a hand-held VHF transceiver when you go dinking around. Cruising boats regularly use the narrow passage between Hanson Island and the Plumper Islands, but currents are strong and there is local turbulence.

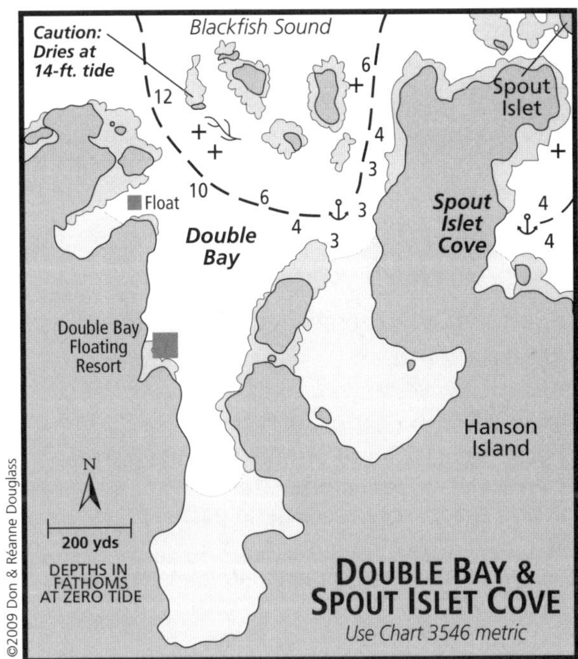

Anchor (east bight) in 1 to 3 fathoms over sand and gravel with fair holding.

The cove to the east, behind Spout Island, offers good protection and is less used.

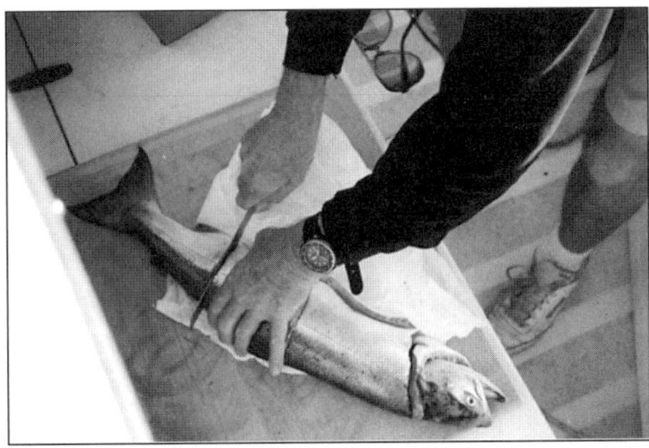

"Get the barbecue ready!"

Spout Islet Cove (Hanson Island)

Chart 3546; 0.6 mi E of Double Bay
Entrance: 50°35.39'N, 126°44.73'W
Anchor: 50°35.15'N, 126°45.00'W

> *Spout Islet lies close off the north coast of Hanson Island. The bay south of Spout Islet offers good anchorage and shelter in 5 to 10 m (16 to 33 ft).* (SD)

Spout Islet Cove is what we call the cove south of Spout Islet. It is easier to enter than Double Bay and is less crowded. While open to the northeast, Spout Islet Cove has good protection from all other directions. Swinging room is adequate for several boats.

The best shelter from prevailing northwest winds is found in the southwest corner off the small beach north of the islet near shore. Spout Islet Cove is close to fishing activity in Blackfish Sound and, from here, you have a good view of conditions outside. The islets along the north shore of Hanson Island are full of marine life and are fun to explore. The cove immediately east also appears to offer good protection for one or two boats.

Anchor in 4 fathoms over sand and gravel with fair holding.

Bauza Cove (Vancouver Island)

Chart 3546; 1.2 mi W of Blinkhorn Peninsula; W entrance to Johnstone Strait
Entrance (E of Bauza Islet): 50°32.76′N, 126°47.68′W
Entrance (W of Bauza Islet): 50°32.93′N, 126°48.57′W
Anchor: 50°32.62′N, 126°49.13′W

Bauza Cove can be entered on either side of Bauza Islet; it affords anchorage to small vessels in a depth of about 20 m (66 ft). (SD)

Scenic Bauza Cove offers good protection from westerly wind and swell. Its location near the west end of Johnstone Strait makes it a good temporary rest or lunch stop. Avoid the Bauza Islets when entering. Anchor close to the sandy beach.

Anchor in 8 fathoms over sand with fair holding.

Telegraph Cove (Vancouver Island)

Chart 3546; E side of Beaver Cove; 0.8 mi W of Bauza Cove
Entrance: 50°32.88′N, 126°50.04′W

Telegraph Cove, 0.3 mile SW of Ella Point ... has an entrance approximately 60 m (197 ft) wide. There is a marina, launching ramp, booming ground, sawmill, store and post office (V0N 3J0). It has a population of 28 (1986). (SD)

Telegraph Cove, which began as a telegraph station in 1912, has come a long way in the past decade. There are two marinas in the cove: Telegraph Cove Marina and Telegraph Cove Resort.

Telegraph Cove Marina has undergone substantial renovation with power, water, showers and laundry, RV Park and a lodge.

Empty log ship returns for another load

Moorage at Telegraph Cove Resort consists of 130 slips for vessels up to 65 feet. The resort has lodging, showers and laundry. Both marinas have launch ramps that are popular with sportfishermen and are often used by kayakers that set out to explore the Cormorant Channel Marine Park (Pearse Islands) and the Broughtons.

The cove has an excellent pub and restaurant, a Whale Interpretive Centre and a whale watching company.

There is no anchorage in the cove.

⚓ **Telegraph Cove Marina** tel: 250.928.3163 or 877.835.2683; fax: 250.928.3162; monitors VHF Ch 66A; website: www.telegraphcove.ca; email: reservations@telegraphcove.ca; power; showers; laundry

⚓ **Telegraph Cove Resorts** tel: 250.928.3131; website: www.telegraphcoveresorts.com; email: tcrltd@islands.net

Beaver Cove (Vancouver Island)

Chart 3546; enter btwn Ella & Lewis Pts
Entrance: 50°33.09′N, 126°50.67′W

Extensive booming grounds with numerous dolphins, piles and mooring buoys are in the SW part of the cove. Extensive booming grounds lie along the east shore and along the north shore fronting Englewood.

Temporary anchorage can be obtained in about 55 m (180 ft). (SD)

Beaver Cove, a large bay with a major log storage and processing area, is completely filled with logbooms, pilings and private mooring buoys.

The cove is well out of the current and chop of Johnstone Strait,; emergency moorage or anchorage can be found close to shore among the various complexes.

Cormorant Channel Marine Park

(Broughton Strait)
Chart 3546; lie btwn Weynton & Pearse Passages; 2.5 mi E of Alert Bay
Entrance (S, Pearse Passage): 50°34.49'N, 126°53.97'W
Entrance (E, Pearse Narrows): 50°34.94'N, 126°51.17'W

> *Pearse Islands are a group of ten thickly wooded islands. Do not attempt to pass between these islands and Stephenson Islet without the aid of local knowledge because of islets and rocks. A reef runs parallel to and about 0.1 mile south of the south shore of the main island.* (SD)

Exploring Cormorant Channel Marine Park

Cormorant Channel Marine Park, which incorporates most of the Pearse and Plumper islands, is a kayaker and small-boat heaven. The tide pools, small beaches and kelp beds that dance to the ebb and flow of the current and winds invite exploration. Underwater visibility is up to 25 feet, so you can easily spend hours studying the sea life. What we call Pearse Narrows Anchorage offers good shelter, out of the turbulence of surrounding

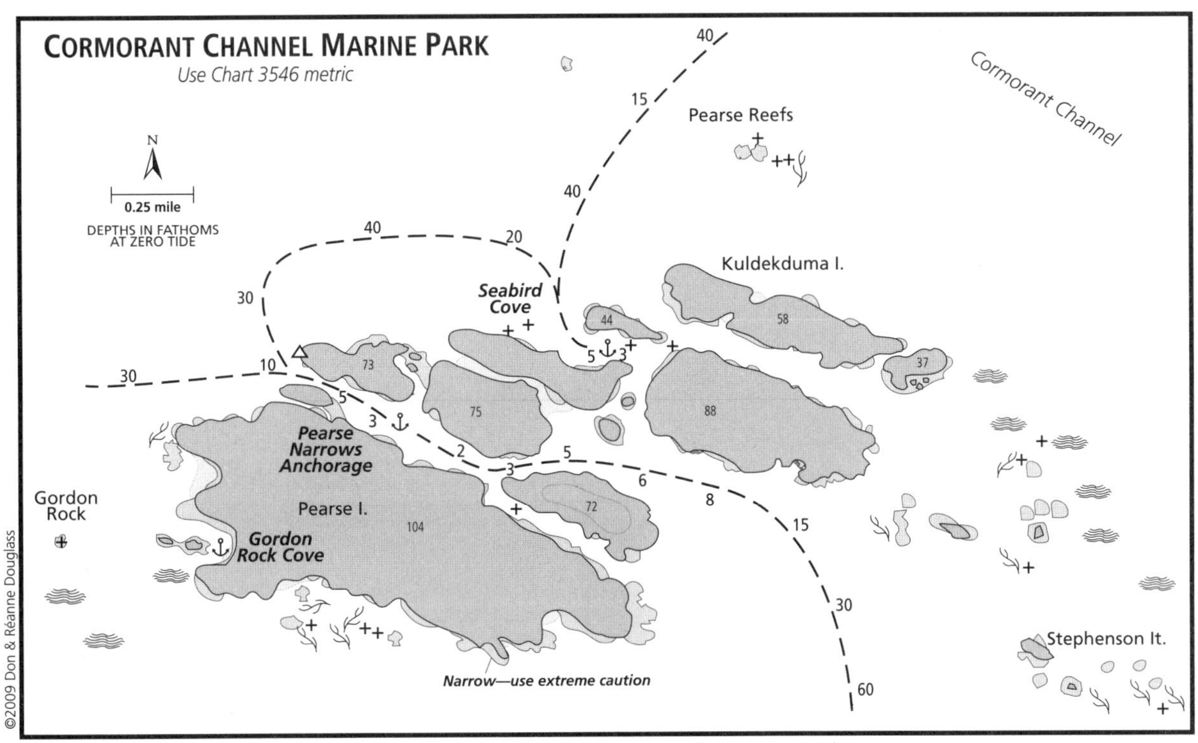

The entrance to the Pearse Islands group

Navigating through Pearse Narrows

waters. Space is limited, however, so proceed slowly as you enter, paying careful attention to reefs and isolated rocks.

Seabird Cove (Pearse Islands)

Chart 3546; N side of the Pearse Islands
Entrance: 50°35.36′N, 126°51.63′W
Anchor: 50°35.26′N, 126°51.46′W

Seabird Cove is our name for the small cove on the south side of island (44) [see diagram]. The cove is well protected from southeast weather and has easy access from Cormorant Channel. The cove makes a good base from which to explore the local bird life and orca pods frequently found around the Pearse Islands.

Avoid the rocks and foul area west of the entrance point. Swinging room is limited, here, and the north shore is steep-to, so a shore-tie is a good idea.

Anchor in about 5 fathoms over sand with fair holding.

Pearse Narrows Anchorage (Pearse Is)

Chart 3546; lies on the N side of the largest of the Pearse Islands
Entrance (W): 50°35.21′N, 126°52.78′W
Entrance (E): 50°34.93′N, 126°51.15′W
Anchor: 50°35.03′N, 126°52.21′W

Pearse Narrows Anchorage is well protected from all weather with a large, shallow bottom allowing anchorage for a number of boats. It can be entered from either end. The center basin is a calm pool with a 3-to-4-fathom bottom clearly visible.

The east entrance is quite narrow with a fairway that carries 3 fathoms. Avoid the charted rock at the east entrance.

Anchor in 3 fathoms over sand with some kelp; good holding.

Gordon Rock Cove (Pearse Islands)

Chart 3546; 1.8 mi E of Alert Bay
Entrance (S): 50°34.69′N, 126°53.15′W
Entrance (N): 50°34.80′N, 126°53.26′W

Gordon Rock Cove is located on the southwest corner of the largest of the Pearse Islands, 0.4 mile east of Gordon Rock. Small craft can find shelter from easterly winds tucked behind the small islet in the center of the cove in 2 to 4 fathoms.

Mitchell Bay (Malcolm Island)

Chart 3546; on the SE side of Malcolm Island; at the E end of Cormorant Channel
Public float: 50°37.83′N, 126°51.09′W
Anchor: 50°37.94′N, 126°51.49′W

Mitchell Bay, close west of Donegal Head, is deep but shallows gradually toward a shingle beach at its head. The bay is free of off-lying dangers and sheltered from all but south winds. The public float, on the east side of the bay, is 12 m (39 ft) long with a depth of about

5.8 m (19 ft) alongside. During the fishing season a fish camp supplies some facilities. (SD)

Mitchell Bay is a fair-weather anchorage that can be easily entered in poor visibility or under radar. It is exposed to southerlies, and the east side of the bay is susceptible to an afternoon westerly chop.

The public float here is rather small but it allows access to the road for those who like to hike or jog. We were blown off the public float (broadside to an 18-inch westerly chop!), but after anchoring in the northwest corner of the bay, we had a sound night's sleep. The road along Mitchell Bay makes an interesting walk. (Several tiny log-tugs that lie rusting ashore are slowly being overgrown by brush.) When anchoring, avoid the rock on the north side which dries at 4 feet.

Anchor in 2 to 3 fathoms over sand and gravel with fair-to-good holding.

Alert Bay (Cormorant Island)

Chart 3546 inset; on the S side of Cormorant I
Entrance: 50°35.04'N, 126°56.33'W
Breakwater light: 59°35.39'N, 126°55.98'W
Public float (S side): 50°35.02'N, 127°55.76'W

Alert Bay breakwater light (548), on the NW extremi ty of the breakwater, has a starboard hand daymark.

A privately operated light and radar reflector are on a dolphin at the ferry landing.

Good, well protected anchorage can be obtained in Alert Bay, about 0.3 mile SW of the breakwater light, in depths of about 13 m [43 ft], sand bottom. (SD)

Alert Bay, on the west side of Cormorant Island, has become a popular stop for cruising boaters as well as for tourists who come by cruise ship or ferry from Europe and Asia to enjoy the ambiance of this small town and learn about the First Nations' culture. The lovely U'Mista Cultural Center and the Ceremonial Big House are big draws or benefit from the quiet—in off-season—or the lively summer activities.

The Alert Bay Boat Harbour, owned by the Municipality, has embarked on a plan to upgrade its facilities. A floating breakwater added to the north end of the rock mound breakwater gives added protection to the boat harbor; floats and power (15 & 30 amp) were upgraded in 2005. A pump out station will be installed in 2006, and plans for future improvements are on the drawing boards. Although the harbor is still home to many fishing vessels, it welcomes transient pleasure craft. In off-season you can choose your moorage anywhere there's room; in high-season, float B is reserved for transients; however, arrive plan to arrive early or you may have to raft.

The fuel dock was closed in 2005, and Alert Bay Shipyards, long a magnet of service and interest run by the Gullstrom family, closed since our last edition. A newly constructed entrance for the B.C. Ferries dock, with a car- and passenger-waiting area is expected to be

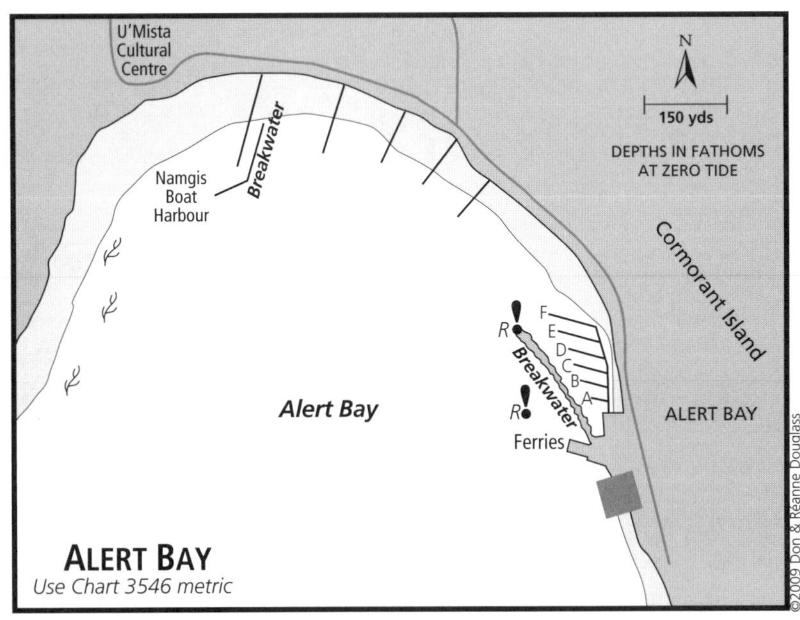

ALERT BAY
Use Chart 3546 metric

Rendezvous with Forevergreen *for fresh fish dinner*

in place by 2006. Small boats can moor at the double-sided municipal float at the south end of town, but this site is open to chop, wind and current, and can be uncomfortable; there are no facilities at this site.

The town, itself, has an attractive waterfront walkway, featuring lamplights decked with hanging flowerpots. New lodgings are slowing springing up. Cormorant Island is ringed with 20 kilometers of hiking and biking trails, which makes a call here especially appealing. The residents are proud of their deep-well water (which does not need treatment) and their sewage treatment plant. For provisioning you have Shop Rite market, a liquor store, a beer and wine store, a pharmacy; two laundries (one was "on vacation" the last time we were there) and several nice restaurants.

Alert Bay Attractions

The 'Namgis First Nation (pronounced num-kees—formerly Nimpkish) has strong presence in Alert Bay. Between 1914 and 1920, as happened elsewhere, the authorities banned potlatches and forced the Natives to surrender their ceremonial possessions such as masks, totem poles, and "coppers." (The latter were flat copper sheets, 15 centimeters to nearly a meter in size, beaten into the shape of shields.) A substantial portion of the potlatch material was sold without authorization to a New York museum in 1921 for just $291. In the 1970s, many of these artifacts were returned and placed in the U'Mista ("the return of something important") Cultural Center, Alert Bay's tastefully designed and executed museum.

One of the world's tallest totems, 53 meters high, carved in 1973, can be seen outside the Ceremonial Big House. The Big House, completed in 1999 after the band's Long House burned, is the maximum size for this type of structure—it holds 2000 people!

Also worth visiting: the Alert Bay Library and Museum, old Christ Church, and the 'Namgis Burial Grounds (no photos, please). Gator Gardens, an ecological park, contains rain forest, cedar marsh, and abundant bird life.

⚓ **Alert Bay Boat Harbour** tel: 250.974.5727; fax: 250.974.5470; monitors VHF Ch 66A; website: www.alertbay.ca; email: boatharbour@alertbay.ca; power

Nimpkish River (Vancouver Island)

Chart 3546; SW of Cormorant Island; 1.4 mi SW of Alert Bay
Entrance (0.23 mi SW of Kish Rock): 50°34.67'N, 126°58.17'W
Anchor (0.15 mi S of Green Islet): 50°34.30'N, 126°57.60'W

Nimpkish Bank extends from the south shore of Broughton Strait across the mouth of the Nimpkish River and dries in places ... The Nimpkish River is barred by rapids, overhead power cables and a highway bridge. It can only be ascended by small craft for a short distance above its mouth. Flats covered with boulders are on either side of the river mouth, between which the channel is narrow.

Anchorage can be obtained off the mouth of the Nimpkish River in 20 m (66 ft), out of the

Geza pilots Baidarka

tidal stream, with Green Islet bearing 110°, distant 0.5 mile. (SD)

Nimpkish River delta extends well into Broughton Strait, forming a sand bank a mile offshore. Cruising boats can find temporary limited shelter in a slot west and south of Green Islet.

Anchorage is reported off the drying flat west to south of Green Islet.

Anchor in 3 to 4 fathoms over sand and gravel with fair holding.

The Blueberry *docks at Port McNeill*

Haddington Passage

Chart 3546; on the N side of Haddington Island
Waypoint (mid-ch btwn Haddington Island & Haddington Reefs): 50°36.43'N, 127°00.97'W

Haddington Passage ... is the westbound traffic lane in the Broughton Strait/Haddington Island Traffic Separation Scheme. (SD)

Haddington Passage is the main channel for boats headed north. A traffic separation scheme (mandatory for ships) is in effect. Northwest-bound vessels pass north of Haddington Island and southeast-bound vessels cross south of Haddington Island.

If you are headed to Port Hardy via Broughton Strait or Cormorant Channel, you should give Haddington Reefs a wide berth and avoid the shoal extending from Dickenson Point as well as Leonard Rock. If you are heading for Port McNeill and you want to avoid Alert Rock and Nimpkish Reef, follow the Vancouver Island shore off Broad Point directly to Port McNeill.

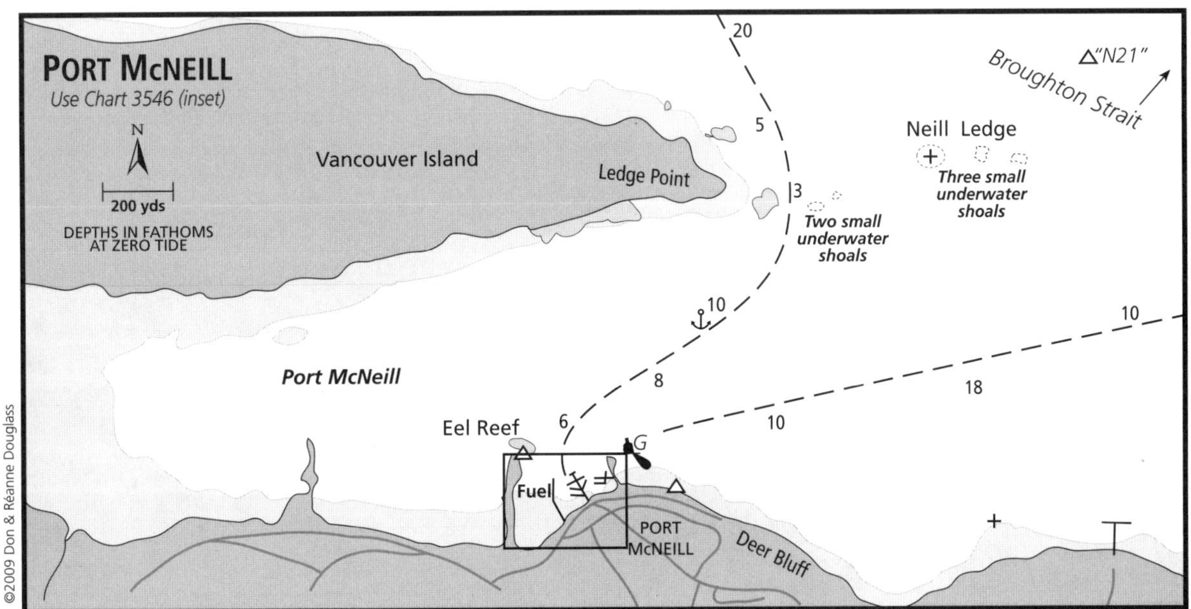

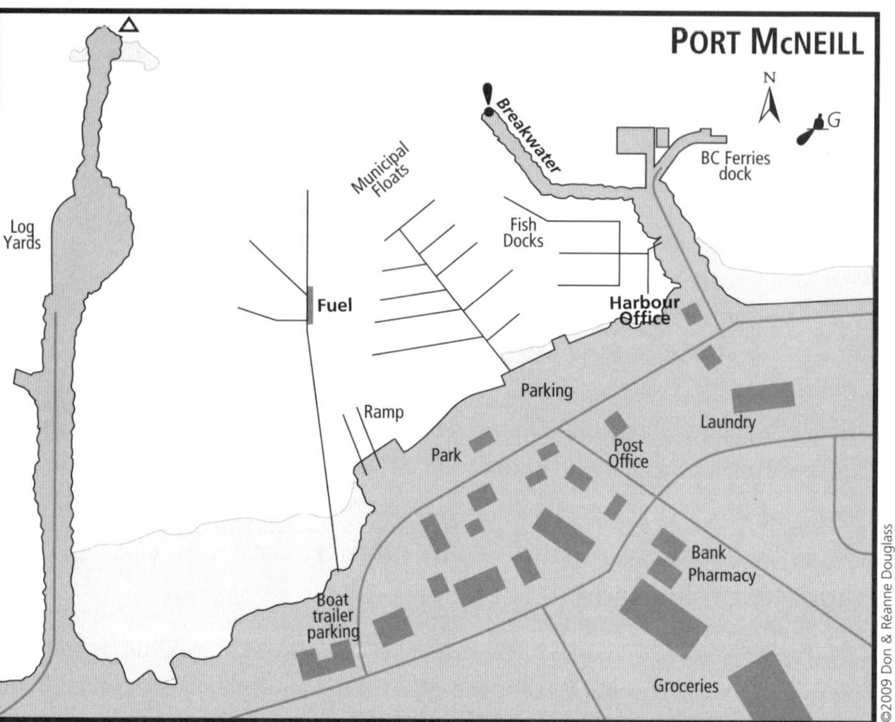

If you are returning from the Port Hardy area bound for Johnstone Strait, pass north of Neill Rock and south of Haddington Island. In the latter case, if you want to stop at Port McNeill, take the fishing boat route through the narrow, unmarked channel and cut across Neill Ledge in deeper water, close east of the rock off Ledge Point.

In summer, Neill Ledge is covered with kelp. The unofficial channel that crosses just west of Ledge Point Rock (at the 7.3-meter-mark on Chart 3546) is frequently clear of kelp. It can be helpful to set your GPS for the crossing point. To cross the bar, we set our GPS position at lat 50°36.215'N, long 127°04.329'W.

Port McNeill (Vancouver Island)

Chart 3546 inset, 3548; 5 mi W of Alert Bay
Entrance (harbour): 50°35.80'N, 127°04.65'W
Entrance (marina): 50°35.56'N, 127°05.36'W
Anchor: 50°35.80'N, 127°05.55'W

Public floats at Port McNeill

Steam donkey, Port McNeill park near marina

Nine-foot butt-cut section, old-growth tree, Port McNeill park

The town of Port McNeill is on the south shore west of Deer Bluff. Caution should be used as the harbour is becoming congested particularly with logboom and floatplane traffic.

Port McNeill has a post office, an RCMP detachment, hospital with heliport, doctors, dentists, stores and accommodation. An asphalt airstrip is 732 m long. A daily bus service operates to Port Hardy and Campbell River. A passenger and vehicle ferry provides scheduled service to Sointula and Alert Bay. Gasoline and diesel fuel are obtainable.

Eel Reef, 0.4 mile WNW of Deer Bluff, dries 4 m and is connected to the south shore by a causeway. It is marked by a daybeacon with a port hand daymark.

Anchorage, sheltered from north and west winds, can be obtained 0.4 mile NE of Deer Bluff to 10 to 16 m. anchorage can also be obtained farther east, south of Neill Ledge, in 16 to 38 m but there is less shelter from north winds.

Port McNeill breakwater light (551.5) is on the outer end of the rock breakwter.

The waters of Port McNeill are a water aerodrome. (SD)

Port McNeill, according to some boaters has the best facilities on the North Coast of Vancouver Island, and Hiltje Binner, its Harbour Manager, has been instrumental in assuring the efficient operation of the marina and offering a warm welcome to pleasure boaters. Facilities include water and power (20 to 100 amp), showers, internet access, pumpout, garbage disposal and a fuel dock (gasoline, diesel and propane). In high-season, it's a good idea to phone or radio ahead to verify space availability.

The harbor is conveniently located close to all services; for groceries Super Valu is just up from the marina, and IGA, two blocks west, has a sophisticated selection of foods, deli and bakery goods, a welcome addition over the past decade; a new laundromat is just across the road from the pleasure craft floats and the post office is next door. Marine supplies, galleries, boutiques, restaurants and a swimming pool (and yes, there's a golf course) round out the list of tourist attractions. Bus service to points north and south and the airport near Port Hardy make it easy to meet friends or drop off crew. Ferry service runs to both Sointula and Alert Bay.

The area offers myriad possibilities for active people: fishing, hiking, climbing, kayaking and canoeing;bicycle up the Island Highway to take a look at the "world's largest burl."

Anchorage can be found 0.4 mile northwest of the marina over a large, flat sand and mud bottom with good holding.

⚓ **Port McNeill Boat Harbour** tel: 250.956.3881; monitors VHF Ch 66A; email: pmharbour@telus.net; power; restrooms; showers; pumpout

⚓ **Port McNeill Fuel Dock and Marina** tel: 250.956.4044; monitors VHF Channel 66A; fuel; power

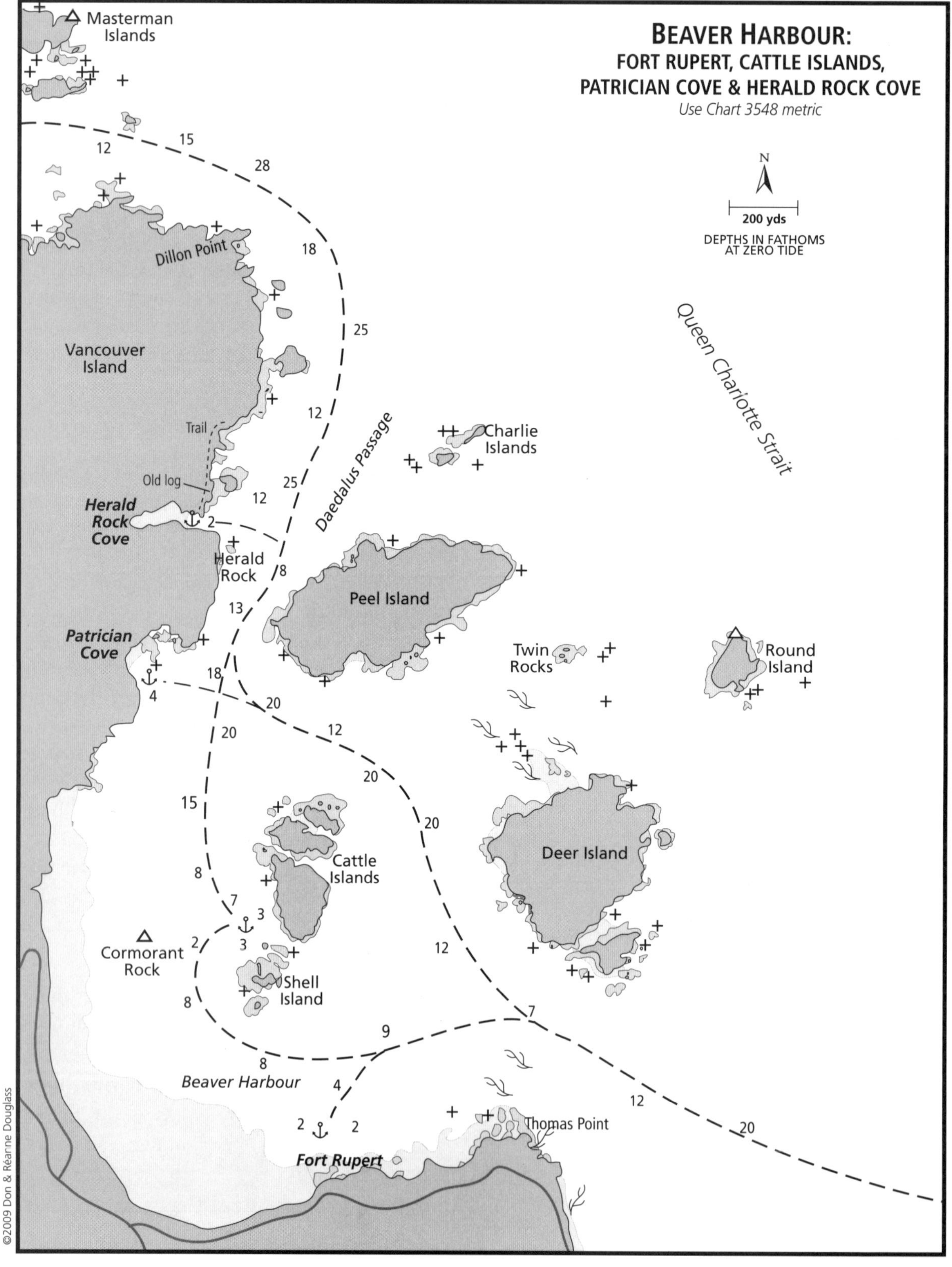
BEAVER HARBOUR:
FORT RUPERT, CATTLE ISLANDS, PATRICIAN COVE & HERALD ROCK COVE
Use Chart 3548 metric
N
200 yds
DEPTHS IN FATHOMS AT ZERO TIDE
Masterman Islands
Dillon Point
Vancouver Island
Trail
Old log
Herald Rock Cove
Herald Rock
Patrician Cove
Daedalus Passage
Charlie Islands
Queen Charlotte Strait
Peel Island
Twin Rocks
Round Island
Deer Island
Cattle Islands
Cormorant Rock
Shell Island
Beaver Harbour
Fort Rupert
Thomas Point
©2009 Don & Réanne Douglass

Sointula (Malcolm Island)

Chart 3546; on the S side of Malcolm Island btwn Dickenson Pt & Rough Bay
Malcolm I Lions Hbr: 50°38.47'N, 127°01.97'W

Sointula ... is a farming and fishing settlement with a population of 692 (1986).

Sointula breakwater light, on the outer end of the rock breakwater at the small craft harbour, has a starboard hand daymark.

The waters fronting Sointula are a water aerodrome.

Anchorage, suitable for small vessels, can be obtained about 0.3 mile SW of the breakwater light in 13 to 18 m (43 to 59 ft). Large vessels can anchor farther south in a depth of about 30 m (98 ft) but this position is exposed to the west.

The public wharf, 1 mile SSE of the small craft harbour, has a berthing length of 15 m (49 ft) and depths of 8.5 to 10 m (28 to 33 ft) alongside its head. The north face of the wharf is 43 m (141 ft) long with depths of 3 to 7.6 m (10 to 25 ft) alongside and has several floats extending north from it. The ferry landing, with berthing dolphins, is at the NE corner.

The Sointula Co-op has a food store near the head of the public wharf and a marine hardware store near the head of the small craft harbour. Two repair yards and postal (V0N 3E0) service are available. Diesel fuel, gasoline, lubricants and fresh water can be obtained. Charter aircraft are available. A passenger and automobile ferry provides connection with Alert Bay and Port McNeill. Water taxi service is also available. (SD)

Sointula, a friendly, picturesque village of 1,000 people, is on the east arm of Rough Bay. The settlement was begun in 1900 by Finnish immigrants working in the mines near Nanaimo. Matti Kurikka, a Finnish socialist and pacifist, was invited by these miners, who had been inspired by his utopian writings, to head a new community.

Settlers arrived on Malcolm Island in 1901 and established Sointula, which means harmony in the Finnish language.

A few years later, in 1904, Kurikka left, taking almost half of the population with him. Although the original colony was liquidated, many of those who remained retained some of Kurrika's utopian ideas. Despite many other waves of immigrants, the Finnish influence can still be seen today.

Pulteney Point Light Station

The town has colorful painted buildings, a museum, stores, the original co-op store, and a fascinating old cemetery. Nearby Bere Point Regional Park offers camping, picnic areas, firepits. A variety of birds can be seen on the Rough Bay mud flats.

Malcolm Island Lions Harbour Authority, the village's small craft harbor, lies a mile to the northwest in Rough Bay. The harbor floats are separated into the north and south docks. Facilities include power (20 & 30 amp), water, showers, laundry, garbage disposal and pay phones. Showers, washrooms, laundry and harbor office are at the north dock. The Co-op Marine Hardware is located at the head of the south dock.

To provision, you need to head back to the co-op in town. It's a bit of a stretch to carry a load of groceries back to the harbor, but chances are someone will give you a lift-it's a friendly community!

⚓ **Malcolm I. Lions Harbour Authority** tel: 250.973.6544; website: www.sointula.com; email: nilha@island.net; power; restrooms; showers; laundry

Rough Bay (Malcolm Island)

Chart 3546; immediately NW of Sointula
Entrance: 50°38.24′N, 127°02.22′W
Harbor entrance: 50°38.46′N, 127°02.02′W

The small craft harbour, protected by a rock breakwater, is at the north end of Sointula in Rough Bay. (SD)

Pulteney Point (Malcolm Island)

Chart 3546; at the SW extremity of Malcolm I
Waypoint (0.3 mi S of Pulteney Pt Light): 50°37.53′N, 127°09.30′W

Pulteney Point has a classic, colorful lighthouse. The sand spit is a good place to stop for lunch, anchoring temporarily on the lee side in fair weather.

Beaver Harbour (Vancouver Island)

Chart 3548; 10 mi NW of Pulteney Pt; 3 mi E of Port Hardy
Entrance (S): 50°42.27′N, 127°22.60′W
Round Island Light: 50°43.58′N, 127°21.93′W

Beaver Harbour, between Thomas Point and Dillon Point, is protected by several islands in its entrance and affords good anchorage.

Anchorage west of Cattle Islands in Beaver Harbour is well protected in 20 to 25 m (66 to 82 ft), mud. Small craft can anchor closer to Cattle Islands in 5 to 10 m (16 to 33 ft). (SD)

Beaver Harbour generally provides good shelter over a large area; it has easy access and is a convenient anchorage for cruising boats heading north or those that want to provision in Port Hardy.

Anchorage in Beaver Harbour can be found off Fort Rupert, west of Cattle Islands, in Patrician Cove, or in what we call "Herald Rock Cove."

Fort Rupert (Vancouver Island)

Chart 3548; on the S shore of Beaver Hbr
Anchor: 50°42.02′N, 127°24.16′W

Fort Rupert ... has a population of 33 (1986). The south and SW shores are fronted by extensive drying flats, which on the SW side, are composed of sand and shingle and on the south side, in front of Fort Rupert, are composed of white shells and shingle. (SD)

An open and somewhat exposed temporary anchorage can be found off Fort Rupert, 0.7 mile west of Thomas Point. The drying flat in front of Fort Rupert has a wide, 1-to 21/2-fathom shelf that provides a lot of winging room and easy access.

Cattle Islands (Beaver Harbour)

Chart 3548; in the center of the harbor; lie S of Peel Island & W of Deer Island
Anchor: 50°42.68′N, 127°24.50′W

Cattle Islands ... are connected to one another by drying reefs and have three drying reefs close off their NW side. Shell Island, SW of Cattle Islands, is surrounded by a conspicuous white shell beach and has drying reefs close south and NE of it. Cormorant Rock, 0.4 mile WNW of Shell Island, dries 4.3 m (14 ft). (SD)

The Cattle Islands provide good shelter in most conditions. Entry can be made on either side of Cormorant Rock (its east side has 12 feet minimum), and there is good swinging room. If you want more protection from westerlies, consider Patrician Cove.

Anchor in 3 fathoms over sand and gravel with fair holding.

Patrician Cove (Vancouver Island)

Chart 3548; 0.7 mi NW of Cattle Islands
Entrance: 50°43.47′N, 127°24.96′W
Anchor: 50°43.48′N, 127°25.05′W

Patrician Cove, 0.5 mile SSW of Herald Rock, has a drying rock in its centre. (SD)

Patrician Cove named for the motor vessel, *Patrician*, that caught fire and sank in the cove several decades ago, gives good protection from westerlies tucked off the small beach on its south side. The center of the cove is filled with a large reef and a rock off its south end, so take care to avoid this hazard if you anchor.

Anchor in 4 to 5 fathoms over sand and gravel with fair holding.

Daedalus Passage

Chart 3548; along the NW side of Beaver Hbr
Entrance (S): 50°43.52'N, 127°24.60'W
Entrance (N): 50°44.37'N, 127°23.83'W

> *Daedalus Passage ... is formed on its east side by Charlie Islands, which are bare, and Peel Island which is wooded. Herald Rock, on the west side of the passage, has 2.4 m (8 ft) over it with drying rocks between it and the shore. A detached shoal, with 4.6 m (15 ft) over it, lies on the east side of the passage, 0.1 mile SW of the west extremity of Peel Island.* (SD)

Herald Rock Cove (Vancouver Island)

Chart 3548; in Daedalus Passage; 0.25 mi W of submerged Herald Rock
Entrance: 50°43.97'N, 127°24.49'W
Anchor: 50°43.94'N, 127°24.76'W

Herald Rock Cove provides good protection from westerlies, but shelter from southeasterlies is only fair, due to the lee of Peel Island.

The head of the cove dries and, since swinging room is limited, we advise use of a shore tie. As you enter, avoid the rock off the south point and the rocks along shore inside the cove.

This is a picturesque nook, and it's fun to take a kayak or dinghy along the shore to the north. An old trapper's trail follows the bluff above, dropping down into the small bight a few hundred yards north of Herald Rock Cove.

Anchor in 1 to 2 fathoms over sand, mud and gravel with fair-to-good holding.

Explorers, Herald Rock Cove

Goletas Channel

Chart 3549; one of four chs connecting Queen Charlotte Strait with Queen Charlotte Sound
Entrance (SE, 0.8 mi N of Duval Pt): 50°46.98'N, 127°29.18'W
Entrance (NW, 0.65 mi S of Nahwitti Pt): 50°53.64'N, 127°59.12'W

> *Nahwitti Bar, at the west end, generally prevents high seas rising in Goletas Channel during west gales. Tide-rips and overfalls on Nahwitti Bar can be dangerous to small craft.*
>
> *Small vessels can also obtain anchorage between Heard and Bell Islands, in Shushartie Bay and in Bull Harbour.* (SD)

Goletas Channel—straight and deep—points directly toward Queen Charlotte Sound. At the channel's northwest end, Nahwitti Bar and Tatnall Reefs act as a barrier to keep out the swells from Queen Charlotte Sound.

Although Goletas Channel has moderate current, its flow is laminar (non-turbulent). Generally calm, the channel can easily be transited in low visibility by using radar.

Crossing Nahwitti Bar has traditionally been a major concern for skippers heading to the west coast of Vancouver Island, or for sailboats that want to use it to get a better tack across Queen Charlotte Sound to Calvert Island. Several strategies are discussed later in this chapter to help make your transit of the bar as safe and comfortable as possible.

Port Hardy

Chart 3548 inset; 17 mi NW of Port McNeill; 21 mi SE of Cape Sutil
Entrance (Outer, midway btwn Duval Island & Masterman Islands): 50°45.80'N, 127°27.60'W
Entrance (Middle, 0.4 mi E of red light off of Tsulquate River): 50°43.80'N, 127°28.35'W
T-float public wharf: 50°43.37'N; 127°29.24'W
Entrance (inner boat basin, 0.1 mi E of Buoy "N28"): 50°43.13'N, 127°28.83'W
Quarterdeck Marina: 50°42.82'N, 127°29.35'W

> *Port Hardy ... is a municipality with a population of 5,389 (1986). There are hotels, motels, a shopping centre, liquor store, and a post office (V0N 2P0). Medical services, including a hospi-*

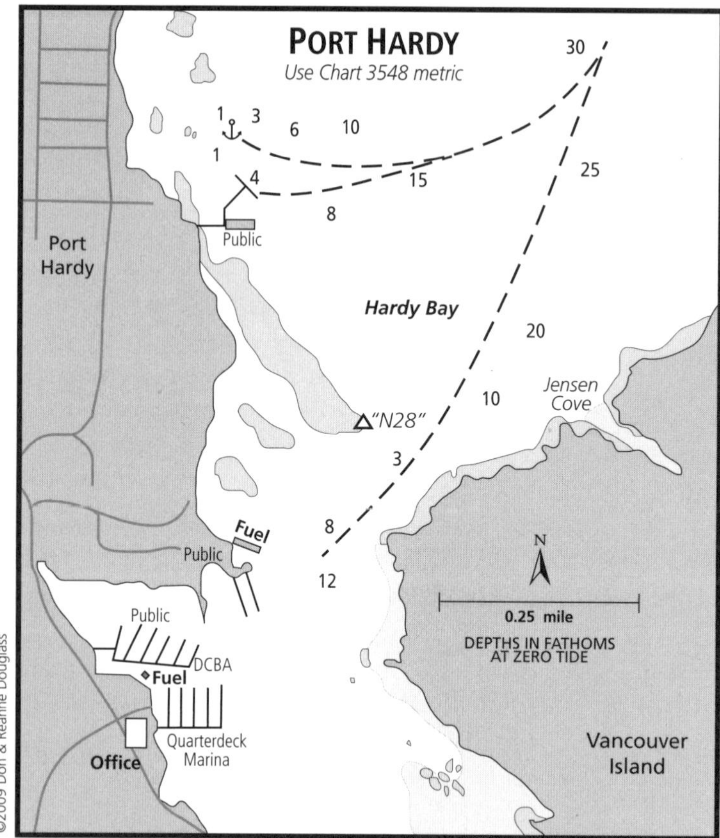

tal with a heliport, are available. Radio station CFNI broadcasts on a frequency of 1240 kHz and station CBRW on a frequency of 630 kHz.

The public wharf, 0.5 mile SSW of Hardy Bay light, is 61 m (200 ft) long. A T-shaped float, attached to its north side, has a least depth of 3.5 m (11 ft) alongside. Fresh water is available at the wharf.

The boat basin, 0.3 mile SW of Hardy Bay Inner light, with a depth of 3 m (10 ft) in the entrance, is protected by breakwaters extending from its north and south sides. The public floats in the boat basin have depths of 3.2 m (11 ft) alongside. Power and water are available at these floats. A marina is at the south end of the boat basin.

A tidal grid, a launching ramp, and a boat hoist with a capacity of 2.2 tonnes are in the boat basin and a launching ramp is in Bear Cove.

A scheduled bus service operates between Port Hardy and Victoria. Scheduled air services operate from Port Hardy Airport which has an asphalt runway 1,524 m (5,000 ft) long. The B.C. Ferry Corporation operate a scheduled ferry service between Port Hardy and Prince Rupert. (SD)

Port Hardy, the northernmost town on Vancouver Island relies on its natural resources—fishing, logging, and mining—as well as tourism, for its economic well-being.

The town has a full range of recreational facilities and convenient services. Since we frequently have crew changes in Port Hardy, we prefer to tie up at the public wharf and floats at the foot of town, within walking distance of all services. The bus station, market, hardware store, bank, and laundromat are just a few blocks from the wharf. For provisioning, Overwaitea is four blocks away; Giant Foods, just up from the wharf, opens at 0600 in July and August and at 0900 the rest of the year. Overnight and long-term moorage for pleasure vessels is available at Quarterdeck Marina in the inner harbor; full services are provided and reservations are a good idea in the summer months.

Public floats, Port Hardy

Baidarka *at Coal Harbour*

Recreational activities include bird and whale watching, swimming, hiking, and fishing. There is a small museum which focuses on the natural and cultural history of the area. According to archaeologists, the site was first occupied some 8,000 years ago, and there are exhibits of ancient tools and artifacts. If you walk along the sea wall in Kinsmen Park, you will see ancient petroglyphs on the flat rocks. Visit nearby Fort Rupert where you can see traditional native art.

Fish buyers and large boats anchor 200 yards north of the Port Hardy public wharf. Fishing boats anchor in the boat basin alongside the logbooms and work-floats off the drying flats at the head of the bay.

To the west, Coal Harbour, Holberg in Holberg Inlet and Cape Scott are accessible by road.

By Road from Port Hardy

COAL HARBOUR

Twenty minutes from Port Hardy, you will find the small town of Coal Harbour on the shore of Holberg Inlet, located on the west side of Vancouver Island. Coal mining began in 1883, but the coal was of poor quality and the mining gradually ceased. An open-pit copper mine that has operated there for years was scheduled to close in 1995.

Coal Harbour was also the site of the most recent whaling operations on the Pacific Coast; the whaling station there closed as late as 1967, when whales had become too scarce. You can see what is called the world's largest jawbone—from a blue whale—which is over 20 feet in length, displayed in the harbor area. The village was also an RCAF seaplane and reconnaissance station during World War II, and many reminders of that era can still be seen.

HOLBERG

Along the road from Port Hardy to Holberg, you pass through an area of bright blue lakes and thickly-forested valleys. There is a good chance to see bear and deer along the way. Driving past Kains Lake, you will see the "shoe tree," an old cedar snag where, since 1989, people have been hanging a wild variety of shoes, sandals, and boots.

Holberg, once a floating logging camp, is now situated on the land. Attractions include the annual Logger Sports Day, Ronning Gardens—with exotic plants from all over the world—and the famous, if incongruous, Elephant Crossing.

WINTER HARBOUR

Winter Harbour is a small, typically "west coast" port. It was badly damaged by a tidal wave in 1960 after the Chilean earthquake, and by the 1964 Alaska quake. This small village features a post office and store, and a seasonal restaurant. Bird watching here is superb, and you may see eagles, puffins, ducks, herons, murres, and murrelettes. At Kwaksistah Park, there are campsites, fire pits, and a boat launch.

CAPE SCOTT PROVINCIAL PARK

Located on the northwest corner of Vancouver Island, Cape Scott Provincial Park has trails that wind for 27 kilometers through spectacular scenery. There are wide, sandy beaches, deep forest, and open uplands. Deer, elk, otters, cougars, wolves and bears can be seen. Along the coast, there are seals, sea lions, and whales.

First occupied by coastal native tribes, there are still two Nahwitti reserves within the park boundaries. This is a wilderness area with no facilities of any kind. Be prepared for wet weather.

⚓ **Port Hardy Harbour Authority**
tel: 250.949.6332; fax: 250.949.6037; monitors VHF Ch 66A; email: phfloats@cablerocket.com; power; restrooms; pumpout

⚓ **Quarterdeck Inn and Marina Resort**
tel: 250.949.6551; fax:250.949.7777; monitors VHF Ch 66A;website: www.quarterdeckresort.net; email: info@quarterdeckresort.net; fuel; power; liquor; restrooms; showers; laundry; and 60-ton Travelift

⚓ **W.C. Fuels Ltd. Petro Canada Bear Cove**
tel:250.949.9988; fax 250.949.9987; monitors VHF Ch 09; fuel; restrooms; showers

God's Pocket

"Thar she blows" is often heard in the waters of Christie Passage, 12 miles north-northeast of Port Hardy. Pods of whales, dolphins and abundant sea life forms can be seen in this area. Two government mooring buoys frequented by fishing vessels are located just inside the calm waters of a bay to the north on Hurst Island—charted as God's Pocket—and limited private moorage with no services is available on a first-come basis at God's Pocket Resort. Home-cooked meals may be enjoyed here with advance notice. Contact the resort on VHF 73. Be aware of tidal shallows at the extreme head of this dock. An established hiking path from God's Pocket Resort garden provides wonderful views of the bay. Alternatively, there is a path marked for pets leading in the general direction of a helicopter pad. Air for divers' tanks is on hand and nearby, famous Browning Passage provides a plethora of scuba diving experiences. If God's Pocket is full, you may elect to try nearby Port Alexander anchorage located at the western end of Browning Passage.

God's Pocket, a popular "jumping off" spot for crossing Queen Charlotte Strait, allows assessment of current weather conditions. Passing scenic Scarlett Point Lighthouse at the northeast side of Christie Passage, you can obtain visual or foghorn sound bearings. Note: Harlequin Bay, charted nearby, is rocky and anchorage is not advised. **—Linda Schreiber**

Goin' cruising

Bear Cove

Chart 3548 inset; 1.0 mi NE of the Port Hardy public floats
Entrance: 50°43.50'N, 127°27.90'W
Anchor: 50°43.45'N, 127°27.55'W

Bear Cove offers very good protection in heavy southeast weather. Fishing boats anchor off the reefs and rocks of the east shore (marked by buoy "N25"), between the fuel dock on the south and the B.C. Ferry landing to the north.

Gordon Islands (Goletas Channel)

Chart 3549; 5 mi N of Port Hardy
Safety position: 50°48.80'N, 127°28.70'W

> *Gordon Islands, Heard Island, Bell Island and Hurst Island lie along the south side and at the east end of Gordon Channel.* (SD)

Temporary safety anchorage from southeast winds can be found in the cove northeast of Miles Cove. There is a fish farm located here.

Heard Island (Goletas Channel)

Chart 3549; 3 mi E of God's Pocket
Safety position: 50°48.88'N, 127°30.92'W

> *The passage between the north end of Gordon Islands and Heard Island has two rocks with less than 6 feet (1.8 m) over them; they lie about 0.1 mile east of Heard Island. The passage between Heard and Bell Islands is encumbered by rocks.* (SD)

Temporary safety anchorage from southeast winds can be found in the cove on the west side of Heard Island. A fish farm lies to the west.

Harlequin Bay (Hurst Island)

Chart 3549; on the NE side of Hurst Island
Entrance: 50°50.37'N, 127°34.01'W

Harlequin Bay ... is very shallow and its approach is encumbered with islets and rocks. (SD)

Harlequin Bay is a difficult place to enter safely. Although we consider it picturesque, Chappell thought this to be one of the ugliest places on the coast. Entrance lies along the south shore at high water when the channel is 20 feet wide. The center of Harlequin Bay is 1-1/2 to 2 fathoms deep.

God's Pocket (Hurst Island)

Chart 3549; 8 mi NW of Port Hardy
Entrance: 50°50.40'N, 127°35.90'W
Buoys: 50°50.42'N, 127°35.62'W

God's Pocket, a local name for the small cove on the west side of Hurst Island, provides good shelter to small craft from all winds. Two public mooring buoys and a small fishing resort are in the cove. (SD)

God's Pocket has long been the traditional jumping-off point for boats wanting to get an early start across Queen Charlotte Sound. The advantages to the "Pocket" are its easy access (particularly for making an early morning exit or when visibility is limited), and its two convenient mooring buoys. Its disadvantages, on the other hand, are busyness, restricted space, considerable depths for a small-craft anchorage, and frequent annoying chop or wake. God's Pocket Resort has limited private moorage only.

Increasingly, sailboats have been using Bull Harbour as an anchorage, and exiting via Nahwitti Bar to get a better tack on the prevailing wind and a smoother, faster ride. We find that "Walker Group Cove" is a little closer to Cape Caution and a good alternative to the old standard.

Deserters Group

Charts 3548, 3549; lies btwn Gordon Channel & Ripple Passage
Position: 50°52.65'N, 127°29.28'W

Deserters Group consists of Wishart Island, Deserters Island, McLeod Island and several smaller islands and rocks. The passage between Wishart Island and Deserters Island is reported to have a rock in its south entrance and is only suitable for small craft. The passage between Deserters and McLeod Islands is foul. Castle Point, the SE extremity of Deserters Island, is steep-to. (SD)

Temporary anchorage from southeast winds can be found in the cove on the west-central coast of Wishart Island, inside the fish farm located there.

Shelter Passage

Chart 3549; separates Deserters Group from Walker Group
Entrance (S): 50°52.54'N, 127°30.82'W
Entrance (N): 50°53.94'N, 127°30.15'W

Shelter Passage ... is entered west of Bleach Rock and Race Island. It leads north from Gordon Channel to Ripple Passage and, although 0.2 mile wide and relatively deep, is not recommended except for small vessels. (SD)

Walker Group Cove

Charts 3549; located on the N side of the channel btwn Kent & Staples islands
Entrance (W channel): 50°53.86'N, 127°32.27'W
Entrance (E channel): 50°54.11'N, 127°31.06'W
Anchor: 50°53.93'N, 127°31.91'W
Anchor (fishing boats): 50°54.00'N, 127°31.33'W

Staples Island, the south island of Walker Group, is densely wooded and hilly.

Anchorage for small craft is reported to be good in the shallow 2 fathom (3.7 m) basin formed by the north side of Staples Island, the SE end of Kent Island, and the west side of the large unnamed island. Kelp usually grows in both entrances but no dangers have been reported. (SD)

Word is getting out about Walker Group Cove, one of our favorite anchorages. An alternative to God's Pocket, this small cove is quiet, fairly easy of access, and offers great all-weather protection.

The cove is entirely landlocked and its

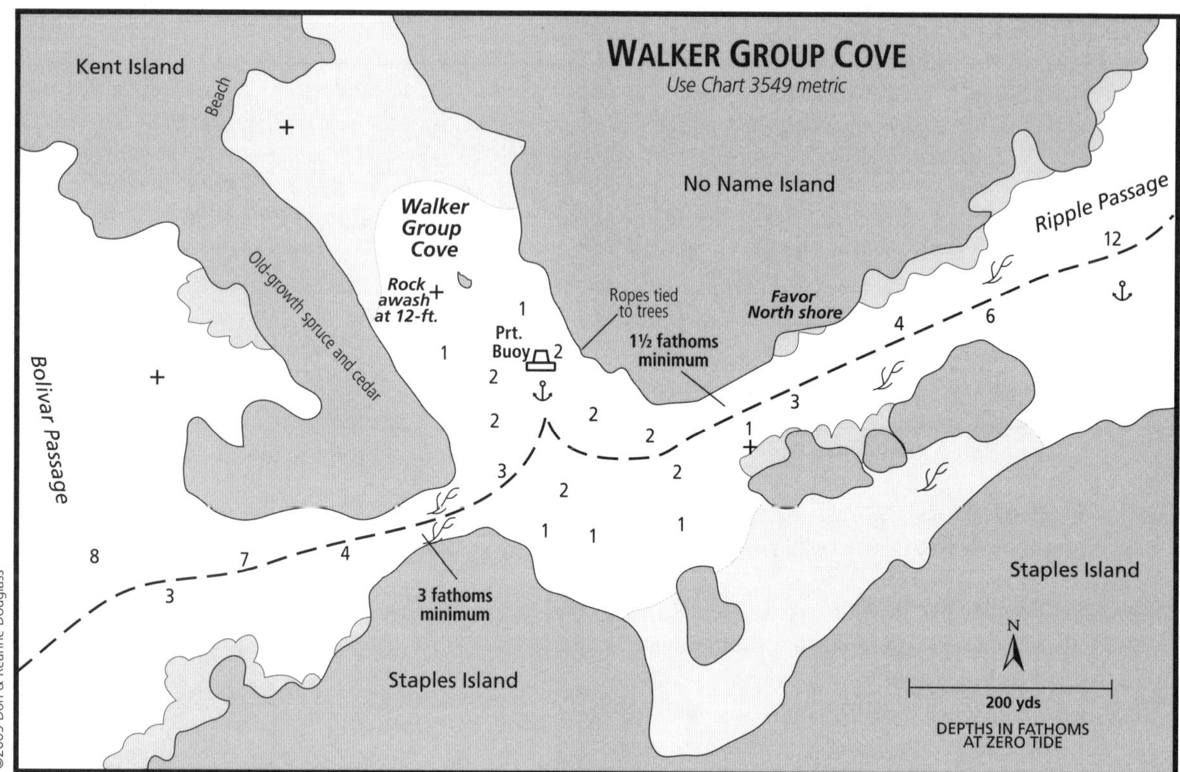

shores are covered with old-growth cedar and spruce. There are small beaches where you can land and stretch your legs, and river otters and loons provide hours of entertainment. With no evidence of driftwood on the beaches or saltwater damage to the vegetation, this seems one of the most protected areas close to Queen Charlotte Sound. The overhanging trees with their windblown tops do indicate strong northwest winds aloft, but the shallow water means you can have good anchor scope and be comfortable in any gusts that hit the surface. Favor the north shore when entering the cove. Avoid the reported private buoy near the anchor site. Limited swinging room; shallow.

Watching the River Otter

It's high tide and the river otter comes out of hiding again. He swims toward the stern of Baidarka, dives down for a second then surfaces with a sanddab held firmly in his teeth. He shakes his head, jiggling the fish around and around until he can get it in his mouth. He throws his whiskered chin upward, crunches the still-wriggling creature, swallows, crunches again. It takes eight bites for the sanddab to disappear.

The otter swims toward the swim step again, as if he plans to hop aboard. Maybe he thinks it's a tree branch.

"Hello there," I say softly. He turns his satiny body around and looks at me. His whiskers twitch, as if he's giving me a signal. Who is this human who's been watching and photographing him all day?

After thirty minutes of diving and surfacing, he swims to shore, climbs on a vertical rock and rubs himself in a mossy depression.

"It's early." I say to the captain. "He doesn't observe our dinner hours."

"No, he doesn't; he's definitely not a French river otter."

The river otter—a mustelid of the family of weasels, wolverines, minks, sea otters—has a muscular tail one-third its total body length and can dive to depths of 60 feet!

Anchor in 2 fathoms over sand, shells, and grass with good holding.

Pine Island

Chart 3575; lies on the N side & W end of Gordon Channel
Pine Island Light: 50°58.54'N, 127°43.69'W

> [Pine Island] *is heavily wooded, level topped and its south and west sides are steep-to.*
>
> *Pine Island light (576), on the SW point of the island, is shown at an elevation of 93 feet (28.3 m) from a white tower, 32 feet (9.7 m) high. The light is obscured by high land on its east side. It has a radio beacon, an emergency light and a heliport. The fog signal consists of two blasts on two horns every minute.* (SD)

Current weather conditions are reported on VHF weather channels which will give you a good idea of the wind force and sea state at the west end of Queen Charlotte Strait.

Browning Passage

Chart 3549; lies btwn Balaklava & Nigei Islands
Entrance (N): 50°52.90'N, 127°39.60'W
Entrance (S): 50°49.75'N, 127°38.30'W

> *Browning Passage ... provides an alternative route from Goletas Channel to Gordon Channel and is convenient for vessels leaving Port Alexander.* (SD)

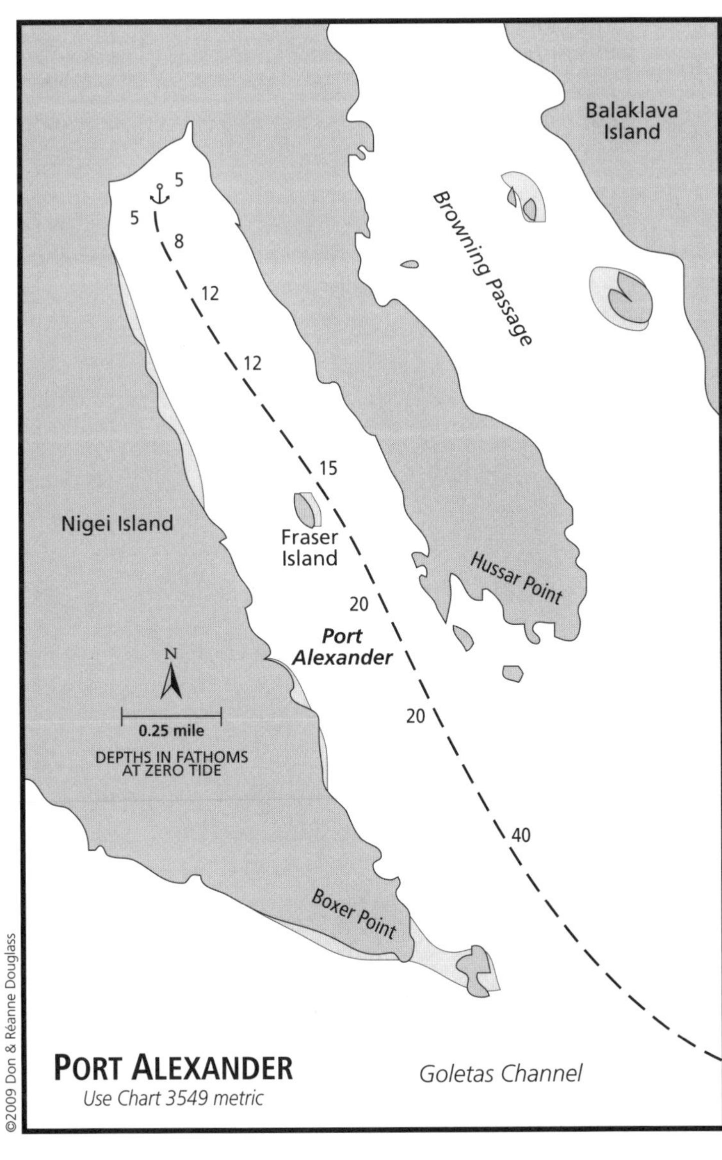

Those wishing to avoid Nahwitti Bar can enter Queen Charlotte Sound directly by using Browning Passage then following a route to Cape Scott on the north side of Nigei and Hope islands.

Browning Passage can also be used in southeast weather to provide access to good protection in Clam Cove or Cascade Harbour.

Port Alexander (Goletas Ch)

Chart 3549; on the SW side of Browning Passage; 2 mi W of God's Pocket
Entrance: 50°50.20'N, 127°38.80'W
Anchor: 50°51.45'N, 127°39.95'W

> *Port Alexander penetrates the SE side of Nigei Island. It is easy of access and affords good anchorage sheltered from all but SE winds.*
>
> *Anchorage in Port Alexander can be obtained north of Fraser Island in 11 to 12 fathoms (20 to 22 m).* (SD)

Port Alexander is a large bay useful in stable weather but exposed to the southeast. High bluffs rise above the east and west shores. Early clear-cutting shows considerable re-growth, but logging is visible on the north side of the hill above the beach. The gray gravel beach at the head of the bay is a good place for walking. The abundance of driftwood on the beach indicates its exposure to southerly storms. However, it escapes the brunt of the winds that flow out of Goletas Channel.

The water is clear to 3 fathoms and giant white sea-stars are visible on the bottom. The water shoals rapidly and is steep-to.

Strong northwest winds in Goletas Channel show up as a northerly breeze inside Port Alexander. There is lots of swinging room over a flat bottom.

Anchor (the head of the bay) in about 8 fathoms, sand and gravel with good holding.

Loquillilla Cove (Goletas Channel)

Chart 3549; 3.5 mi W of Port Alexander; 8 mi SE of Bull Hbr
Entrance: 50°50.25'N, 127°44.70'W
Anchor: 50°51.67'N, 127°45.45'W

Loquillilla Cove, on the south side of Nigei Island, affords shelter to small craft during west winds. (SD)

Loquillilla Cove is conveniently placed on the north side of Goletas Channel. It is exposed to southeast winds but offers good shelter from westerlies if you tuck deep in the cove. In southeast weather we advise using Clam Cove or Cascade Harbour.

Anchor in 6 to 8 fathoms over sand, mud and some gravel.

Clam Cove (Nigei Island)

Chart 3549; at the N end of Browning Passage; 1 mi NW of Port Alexander
Entrance (E): 50°52.64'N, 127°40.13'W
Entrance (N): 50°52.72'N, 127°40.23'W
Anchor (inner basin): 50°52.07'N, 127°40.35'W

Clam Cove, a local name, is entered between two groups of wooded islets 0.7 mile SSE of Hougestal Point. A rock, with less than 6 feet (1.8 m) over it, lies in midchannel 0.2 mile south of the entrance. Anchorage for small craft can be obtained near the head of the cove but there are deadheads and sunken piles. (SD)

Clam Cove, which formerly we called Nigei Island East Cove, is a bombproof shelter with good swinging room for several boats. Clam Cove is hidden by a number of small islands and islets along the east side of Nigei Island in Gordon Channel. The cove can be entered in both strong northwesterly or southeasterly winds. Look for a small bay 0.77 mile southwest of Hougestal Point and 0.6 mile due west of Cardigan Rocks at the north end of Browning Passage. The east entrance is marked by a small sign "Clam Cove" and white marks on the rocks. The north

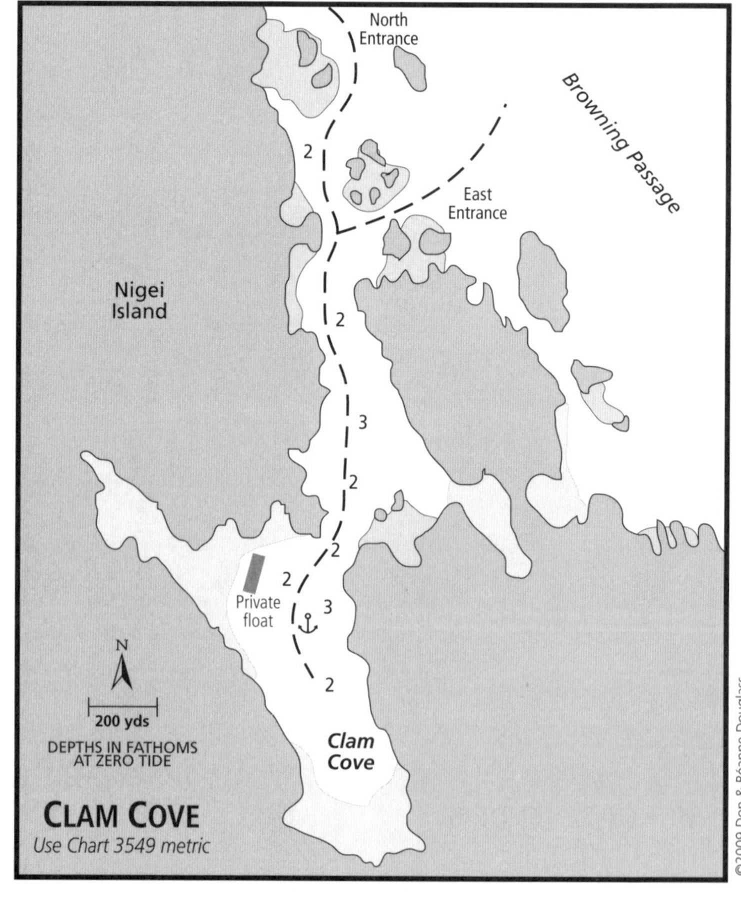

CLAM COVE
Use Chart 3549 metric

entrance is 200 yards northwest of the east entrance by way of a narrow channel marked 3.6 meters on Chart 3549. Both the east and north entrances lead into a north/south narrow channel which is a half-mile long. At the south end of this channel, Clam Cove opens up into a flat-bottom bay providing total shelter from the seas of Gordon Channel. Minimum depth in the fairways of both the east and north entrances is between 1 and 2 fathoms at zero tide.

Fishermen use both the middle bay and inner basin for anchoring; however, we prefer the greater swinging room found in the south end of Clam Cove.

Deep inside the lovely cove is a float camp still used for logging. The islands are very scenic with old growth, but the hills to the west have been clearcut. Because of the extensive logging in this area, the bottom may be full of slash and/or old cables, but we have not had a problem anchoring here. From the inner cove, you can view Cape Caution through a "window" to the north.

Anchor (inner basin) in 2 to 3 fathoms over mud, sand and shells with good holding.

Hougestal Point Cove (Nigei Island)

Chart 3549; 0.3 mi NW of Hougestal Pt
Entrance: 50°53.61'N, 127°41.06'W

There is a tiny cove immediately west of the small peninsula on the north side of Hougestal Point. This cove offers temporary protection for small craft from southerly weather. On our last visit it had a floathouse with a sign on the islet that says Private. When entering, avoid the rock (34) which is 0.15 mile north of the entrance.

Cascade Harbour (Nigei Island)

Chart 3549; 4.5 mi NW of Port Alexander;
7.5 mi W of Bull Hbr
Entrance: 50°54.93'N, 127°44.47'W
Anchor: 50°54.42'N, 127°44.35'W

Cascade Harbour usually has a heavy swell entering it, particularly during summer when NW winds prevail. It is reported that small craft can obtain protection from the swell by anchoring close to the south part of the island on the west side of the harbour. The harbour is used by fishing vessels. (SD)

Cascade Harbour is on the northern tip of Nigei Island within easy view of Pine Island. Although exposed to northwest wind and swell at its entrance, reasonable anchorage can be obtained deep in the lee of Malei Island shown on the chart as island (55). An opening on the west side of Malei Island is choked with kelp but would be a good window to conditions outside.

The harbor offers very good protection from southeast storm winds. Avoid the pile of rocks at the north end of the island at Greeting Point.

On the west shore just north of the creek is an old camp with a cabin and dock in ruins. A beautiful new home stands on the west side of island. A dock with a float on the south side says Malei Island Dive and Fishing Lodge.

Anchor south of the Malei Island Dive and Fishing Lodge float avoiding the old jetty on the west side of the bay.

Anchor in 4 to 6 fathoms over gravel with sandy patches and some kelp; fair-to-good holding depending on anchor set.

Bate Passage

Chart 3549; lies btwn Nigei & Hope Islands
Entrance (SW): 50°53.10'N, 127°51.70'W
Entrance (NE): 50°55.30'N, 127°44.80'W

Bate Passage leads NE from Goletas Channel to Gordon Channel; it lies between Nigei Island on the SE and Hope and Vansittart Islands on the NW. The fairway is straight, not less than 0.5 mile wide, and can be taken with safety. (SD)

Bate Passage connects Cascade Harbour and Gordon Channel to Goletas Channel.

Shadwell Passage Bight (Hope Island)

Chart 3549; 3.5 mi E of Bull Hbr
Entrance (S): 50°54.30'N, 127°49.20'W
Entrance (N): 50°55.90'N, 127°49.35'W
Anchor: 50°54.94'N, 127°50.45'W

> *Shadwell Passage, entered from Bate Passage between Pivot Point and Vansittart Island, leads north to Gordon Channel. The passage is not recommended owing to several dangers lying within it. A heavy swell is usually present at the north end of the passage.* (SD)

Shadwell Passage Bight is a large flat shallow area on the east side of Hope Island offering good protection in westerlies. Avoid the submerged rocks to the south and the 4-foot shoal to the north when entering and the many reefs and rocks on the west side of Vansittart Island.

Anchor approximately 0.25 mile offshore of a wide sand and gravel beach at the head of the bay about 1.0 mile south of Cape James.

Anchor in 2 to 4 fathoms over sand and gravel with fair-to-good holding.

Kalect Island Cove (Bate Passage)

Chart 3549; 4.5 mi SW of Cascade Hbr
Entrance: 50°53.84'N, 127°50.81'W
Anchor: 50°53.98'N, 127°51.12'W

> *Kalect Island lie[s] close off the coast of Hope Island at the south end of Bate Passage. The bay north of Kalect Island is mainly foul. The site of the former Indian village on the east entrance point of the bay can be identified by a conspicuous clearing.* (SD)

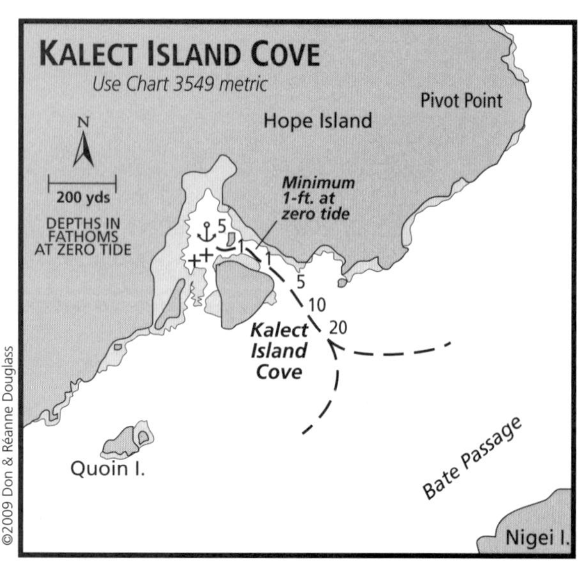

Kalect Island Cove lies between the north side of Kalect Island and the southwest side of Hope Island and is tiny but scenic. A bar with 1 to 2 feet at zero tide lies across the entrance. Inside the bar is a 2- to 4-fathom hole which affords good protection. The entrance on the west side of Kalect Island should not be attempted; it is foul and can be used by shallow draft boats only.

Anchor in the center of the 4-fathom hole over sand and grass with fair holding.

Willes Island Cove (Willes Island)

Chart 3549; 2 mi NE of Shushartie Bay
Entrance (SW): 50°52.87'N, 127°50.92'W
Anchor: 50°52.97'N, 127°50.52'W

> *Willes Island is separated from the west extremity of Nigei Island by a narrow channel, encumbered with rocks.* (SD)

The tiny cove on the southeast side of Willes Island offers good protection from southeast winds. Avoid the submerged rocks; there is limited swinging room, and you may have to share the cove with a floathouse. The cove is subject to strong winds out of the west.

Anchor in about 5 fathoms over gravel and rocky bottom with poor-to-fair holding. A shore tie may be advisable.

Shushartie Bay

Chart 3549; 7.5 mi W of Port Alexander; 4 mi SE from Bull Hbr
Entrance: 50°51.50'N, 127°51.70'W
Anchor (S of Halstead Islet): 50°51.29'N, 127°51.36'W

> *Shushartie Bay is fairly sheltered and offers anchorage, with limited space, in the centre of the bay SW of Dillon Rock light in 24 to 27 fathoms (44 to 49 m).* (SD)

Shushartie Bay, although out of the afternoon chop, has a large drying flat at its head with a bottom that drops off abruptly. Depths are too great for convenient small-craft anchorage. The bay can be used as a temporary lunch stop but overnight anchorage is not advised. Along the steep-to shore, holding is poor and swinging room is limited.

Fair protection from southeasterlies can be taken, using a stern tie, in the tiny cove south of Halstead Islet, 0.16 mile southeast of Dillon Rock, off the remains of an old pier.

Bull Harbour (Hope Island)

Chart 3549 inset; 21 mi NW of Port Hardy; 5 mi NE of Cape Sutil
Entrance: 50°53.80'N, 127°56.30'W
Public float (0.13 mi NE of Norman I): 50°54.76'N, 127°55.81'W
Anchor (0.25 mi N of Norman I): 50°55.05'N, 127°56.13'W

Bull Harbour, entered between Jones and Godkin points, is an indentation on the south side of Hope Island. During SE gales winds gust through the harbour; when Pine Island was reporting SE winds at 70 km, measured gusts within Bull Harbour were 55 kn. West gales are generally of lower velocity within the harbour but they can blow quite strongly. Norman Island lies 0.8 mile north of Jones Point and close to the west shore; the fairway passes east of it. A drying mud and sand flat fills the head of the harbour.

Anchorage with good holding ground in heavy mud can be obtained for small vessels in Bull Harbour. Above Norman Island anchorage is secure but with limited scope. The south part of the bay is reported to be fouled with old chain and cable; the bottom is reported to be less foul toward the head of the bay. When strong winds are forecast ensure that the anchor has adequate scope. (SD)

Heading for the West Coast, Forevergreen *in Bull Harbour*

Bull Harbour, a secure anchorage named for the large bull sea lions found here in the early 19th century, is a rendezvous point for vessels crossing Nahwitti Bar.

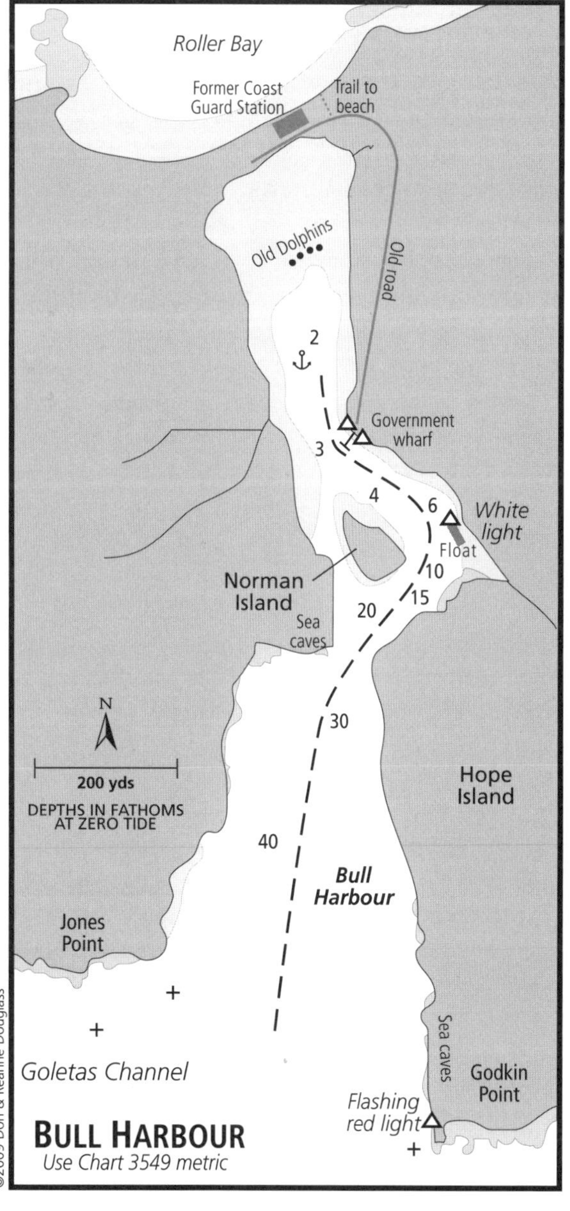

Nature is slowly reclaiming Bull Harbour. The Coast Guard station of earlier days has been closed for a number of years, and just one or two native families now make their permanent home here. During fishing openings, the harbor is used extensively by fishing boats and space for anchoring or tying to floats may be limited. It's a good idea to keep your anchor light on all night since some vessels arrive after dark.

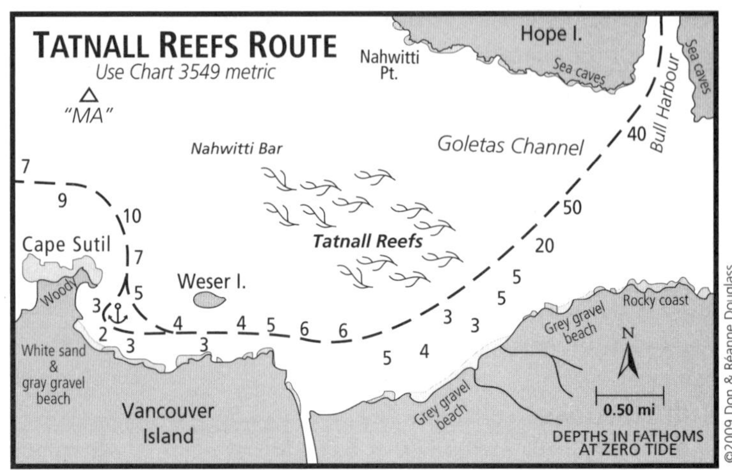

As you enter Bull Harbour, pass east of Norman Island and anchor anywhere in the center of the bay well north of the government wharf. There is now a float south of the government dock; we observed a sandhill crane there on our most recent visit.

For a little exercise, you can land your dinghy on the east shore near the wharf and walk along the old road across the sand spit to Roller Bay on the north side of Hope Island. The beach is covered with polished stones made round from incessant wave action. Since winds can kick up quite a blow across the low spit, be sure to have sufficient scope out before you leave your boat.

Anchor in 2 to 3 fathoms over heavy mud with good holding.

Tatnall Reefs (Goletas Channel)

Chart 3549; 2.5 E of Cape Sutil; 3 mi SW of Bull Hbr

Tatnall Reefs, on the south part of Nahwitti Bar, extend NW from Vancouver Island. The fairway north of Tatnall Reefs is about 0.8 mile wide with depths of 6 fathoms (11 m). Depths on the seaward side of the bar increase very gradually but on the inside they increase suddenly to about 40 fathoms (73 m). A swell is nearly always present on the bar and, in bad weather with a west wind opposing a strong west-going tidal stream, there is a very heavy sea on it which breaks and is dangerous to small vessels. In strong west gales the sea breaks across the bar and it is then dangerous to attempt crossing the bar. (SD)

Tatnall Reefs, 2 miles southwest of Jones Point on the south side of Nahwitti Bar, are covered with kelp. The shape of the reef forces the bulk of the ebb current of Goletas Channel to the north side of Nahwitti Bar.

We have found the current west of Tatnall Reefs to be less than half that of Goletas Channel's main stream. For this reason, the swells do not heap up as much as they do east of the entrance buoy "Mo(A)", and they are less threatening to a small, low-powered boat.

The strategy of using Tatnall Reefs to cross Nahwitti Bar was first brought to cruising boaters' attention in an article by experienced sailor June Cameron (Pacific Yachting,

Southeast Storm Winds

Southeast storm winds have been known to pick up quickly in the vicinity of Queen Charlotte Strait, blowing fiercely across the sound and hitting Egg Island [lighthouse station] with terrifying results.

Egg Island lightkeepers, Judy and Stan Westhaver, report having experienced southeast storm winds that rose from 8 knots to 80 knots within just 15 minutes during an unpredicted storm in 1984. At that time, two boats—one a fishing boat the other a sailboat—were lost, while the Westhavers stood by on the radio unable to go to their aid.

September 1992). June circumnavigated Vancouver Island in her 25-foot sloop with a small outboard motor and used Tatnall Reefs to advantage.

From Jones Point, make good a course of 196° magnetic, crossing Tatnall Reefs in 2 to 3 fathoms minimum. The current on the west side of the reef is less than half that of the northeast side, and the seas are not as high. After leaving the kelp of Tatnall Reefs, continue along Vancouver Island shore, following the 5- to 6-fathom curve until you reach the vicinity of Cape Sutil. From here you can observe the Nahwitti Bar buoy to gauge sea conditions. We spent one September afternoon crisscrossing Nahwitti Bar and found much less current and swell height in the area between Tatnall Reefs and Cape Sutil. The route across Tatnall Reefs is slightly longer than the conventional one, which follows the center of Goletas Channel, but it can be shorter if you are bucking an incoming current.

The bull kelp in Tatnall Reefs, easily avoided in daylight (it is not matted or bunched together), can truly be called "old growth." Its

Great blue heron enjoys the Bull Harbour wharf

Basic Strategies for a Safe Crossing of Nahwitti Bar

1. Cross at high water slack. Slack occurs when the water stops moving; note that slack varies somewhat from local high or low water according to runoff, tide levels and weather conditions. If you choose this option, you have about 30 minutes to push through the big swells. As you cross the bar, you will experience little current. Once past the bar, you will have up to 3 knots of current with you all the way to Cape Scott.

2. Cross at low water slack. The disadvantage of this option is that the inflowing current of 2 to 3 knots will be against you all the way to Cape Scott (and perhaps around the Cape as well).

3. Follow the advice and timing of responsible local fishing boats similar in size and speed to your vessel. Do as they do and follow at a safe distance behind them! Note: The maximum current at the bar of 5.5 knots occurs during periods of large tidal differences but is frequently less for smaller tides. Often fishing boats try to catch the last hour or two of flood in the early morning when conditions are likely to be the smoothest.

4. In exercising any of the options above, close all port lights and stow your dinghy on deck. Towing a dinghy on any outside passage—especially at Nahwitti Bar—can be an extremely risky proposition. Pleasure boats frequently ignore this recommendation, and many a derelict dinghy has been found washed up on shore along the coast.

5. Arrive ahead of predicted slack time and study the conditions firsthand until you are satisfied that slack water has begun—good practice in crossing any bar. The flood at Nahwitti Bar occurs 25 minutes before low water at Alert Bay; duration of high water slack is 12 minutes. Ebb occurs 20 minutes before high water at Alert Bay, and duration of low water slack is 17 minutes. (See *Canadian Tide and Current Tables,* Vol. 6, and *Sailing Directions,* Vol. 1, South Portion).

The North Coast wilderness is just a day or two away

bulbs are six inches in diameter and its blades are sometimes 20 feet long!

Once you are off Skinner Creek, you can follow the coast either inside small Weser Island, at about the 4-fathom curve, to Cape Sutil, or stay outside Weser Island in 5 to 6 fathoms until you reach the cape.

Avoid the rocks 0.7 mile southeast of Weser Island near shore. As noted below and in the diagram above, Cape Sutil can provide temporary anchorage.

Nahwitti Bar (Goletas Channel)

Chart 3549; at the W end of Goletas Channel; 2 mi NE of Cape Sutil; 2.5 mi SW of Bull Hbr
W entrance, Buoy "Mo(A)" (1.5 mi NE of Cape Sutil): 50°54.15'N, 128°02.52'W
Entrance (E, 1 mi NE of Tatnall Reef): 50°53.55'N, 127°58.45'W

The shortest route to Cape Scott from the east is via Goletas Channel and the infamous Nahwitti Bar. The problem for skippers is that the bar is quite shallow (about 7 fathoms) with a maximum ebb current at spring tides of 5.5 knots. The prevailing northwest swell heaps up, and if a wind blows at the same time, rising seas can become heavy and dangerous for small craft.

During strong westerly gales when giant eastbound rollers break over the bar, small vessels should not venture near Nahwitti Bar. Fortunately, Bull Harbour is less than 2.5 miles from the bar and you can wait there for conditions to stabilize.

Most fishing boats heading out beyond Cape Scott use Bull Harbour as an overnight anchorage then leave early in the morning to cross the bar under calm-water conditions. Once you are west of the bar itself, a lighted whistle buoy "Mo(A)" in the fairway gives you an indication of your progress. When you are abeam Cape Sutil, you are in the waters of Queen Charlotte Sound. Turn southwest and cruise along the coast following the 15-fathom curve for 16 miles to Cape Scott.

Cape Sutil

Chart 3549; 5 mi SW of Bull Hbr; 15.3 mi NE of Cape Scott
Anchor: 50°52.20'N, 128°02.90'W

Cape Sutil ... the north tip of Vancouver Island, is a low promontory. (SD)

Temporary anchorage in fair weather can be found off the south side of Cape Sutil close to shore. From this vantage point, you can watch sea conditions at the entrance to Nahwitti Bar, as well as enjoy the view of Cape Sutil's lovely, wide sandy beach.

Local fishing boats use the bight due south of Cape Sutil to wait for northwesterlies to die down or as a fair-weather anchorage. We would not hesitate to anchor here in stable weather.

From 080°M to 340°M you are in the lee of the land and you have a good view of the entrance whistle buoy "Mo(A)." You can use it to judge the height of the swell building across Nahwitti Bar. In settled weather, you can easily land on the light-colored beach and take a walk.

Temporary anchorage can be found a quarter-mile south of Cape Sutil, 200 yards off the beach just outside the kelp line.

Anchor in 3 fathoms over sand with fair-to-good holding.

Queen Charlotte Sound

Charts 3549, 3598, 3625; lies btwn the N end of Vancouver Island & the Queen Charlotte Is

If you want to avoid crossing Nahwitti Bar altogether, you can use either Bate, Browning or Christie passages to enter Gordon Channel. Once you pass north of Hope Island, follow the 50-fathom curve into Queen Charlotte Sound. When Pine Island bears due east, turn west and continue along the 50-fathom curve until you intersect a course line from Egg Island to Cape Scott. At this point, turn southwest and cross Cook Bank in about 30 fathoms.

This route takes you about 9 miles west of Nahwitti Bar. The prevailing swells, while not menacing, are still impressive. Although this route is about 12 miles longer, it largely eliminates the need to wait for slack water at Nahwitti Bar. You may even be able to get a nice boost if you can catch the full current ebbing out of Queen Charlotte Strait. Monitor the weather reports from Pine Island for an idea of what to expect.

Boats heading out to the West Coast on their way south from upper B.C. turn southwest at Egg Island and take a course on a direct line to Cape Scott (36 miles).

Each summer a few hardy sailboats take advantage of the brisk tail wind and cross the entire width of Queen Charlotte Sound (110 miles) on their way south from Queen Charlotte Islands.

The routes into or across Queen Charlotte Sound should be attempted only when weather forecasts call for near-calm or moderating conditions. Unfortunately, calm conditions may bring bouts of fog. Monitor weather reporting stations, especially the offshore buoys at Pine and Egg islands, and have a safe alternative planned in case conditions deteriorate. Don't be afraid to call Comox Coast Guard Radio on Channel 16 at any time for a weather update and to consult with them on possible alternatives if conditions are not what were forecast.

During southeast gales in Queen Charlotte Strait, large pockets of kelp occasionally break

---

Seeking Shelter in Queen Charlotte Strait

If you were to be caught unexpectedly in a brisk southeaster in or near Queen Charlotte Strait, you should seek protection without delay.

Were this to happen to us (it hasn't in over a decade), we would head down-wind, if possible, and seek shelter in the following places (coordinates are for safety position):

From Goletas Channel or Gordon Channel:

Gordon Island, cove on the west side:
50°48.80′ N, 127°28.70′ W
Heard Island, cove on the west side:
50°48.88′ N, 127°30.92′ W
Hurst Island, God's Pocket; buoys:
50°50.42′ N, 127°35.62′ W
Nigei Island, Clam Cove (formerly "Nigei Island East Cove"): 50°52.13′ N, 127°40.37′ W
Hope Island, Bull Harbour: 50°55.05′ N, 127°56.13′ W

From Bolivar Passage or Ripple Passage:

"Walker Group Cove:"
50°53.94′ N, 127°31.88′ W
Deserters Island, cove west of Wishart Island:
50°52.63′ N, 127°29.30′ W

From Ripple Passage or Richards Channel:

Shelter Bay (mainland), northeast of Wallace Islands:
50°58.08′ N, 127°25.33′ W
Nigei Island, Cascade Harbour:
50°54.42′ N, 127°44.35′ W

If we were caught farther north, we would head for Miles Inlet: 51°04.03′ N, 127°34.82′ W

(All safety positions listed above are NAD 83, except Miles Inlet which is NAD 27.)

loose and blow west into Queen Charlotte Sound. One summer, as we followed the Egg Island to Cape Scott route after a gale, we were obliged to change course 10 miles north of Cape Sutil to avoid kelp patches more than a half-mile wide.

Each year, for many well-found small boats, the trip around the top of Vancouver Island turns out to be a routine experience, rather anticlimactic after all the preparation and anxiety involved. We can't overemphasize good preparation and execution—the keys to enjoying your passage!

16

OUTER PASSAGES—British Columbia

Exploring the Outer Passages

The northern end of Vancouver Island marks the end of this book and, unfortunately, the upper cruising limit for many pleasure craft. It is just the beginning, however, for those who appreciate the wilderness that lies beyond Queen Charlotte Sound. The exciting cruising areas beyond Nakwakto Rapids, the excellent sportfishing in Smith Sound and Rivers Inlet, the pristine and newly-charted area of Fish Egg Inlet, the seldom-visited Queens Sound—all are just a day or two away across Queen Charlotte Sound.

Farther north, the newly charted (1996) Spiller Channel area encompasses several hundred square miles along the southern border of Fjordland Park, beckoning those who appreciate wilderness. B.C.'s seldom-explored north coast, with its deep inlets and thousands of islands reaching to the Alaskan border, and the beautiful Queen Charlotte Islands—historical home of the Gwaii Haanas—all call to the adventurous traveller. Discover the thrill of exploring these remote places for yourself.

Exploring the North Coast of British Columbia, the next in this series of Fine Edge guidebooks, covers the destinations north of Blunden Harbour and Queen Charlotte Sound. We hope you can join us there soon. Until that time, we have other ideas to suggest for your cruising pleasure.

Instead of retracing your southbound itinerary as you return, we encourage you to visit places you missed on your way north. Why not follow the south shore of Johnstone Strait and watch the orcas off Robson Bight, test some of the rapids you missed, or visit the quiet area on the north side of Quadra Island? If you followed the mainland shore on your northbound trip, you might follow the Vancouver Island shore on your return.

If—after having tasted the cruising areas of Queen Charlotte Strait—you're still not ready to take the "cruise ship freeway" and you'd like to prolong your time in this quiet, beautiful environment, consider rounding Cape Sutil and Cape Scott. From there you can follow the west coast of Vancouver Island all the way back to Juan de Fuca Strait, enjoying seclusion, excellent fishing, and outstanding natural beauty.

Every year, more cruising boats discover the "West Coast Outer Passage," the route that uses the lee of the smaller islands extending from Glacier Bay to Victoria. This route, which parallels the traditional Inside Passage used by ferry boats and cruise ships, is more scenic and less congested.

The western shores of all the larger islands—Chichagof, Baranof, Prince of Wales, Porcher, Pitt, Princess Royal, and Vancouver Island—offer more sheltered coves and inlets, and more interesting things to see than do their eastern shores. For detailed information covering the West Coast Outer Passage from Queens Sound north to Glacier Bay, please see our companion cruising guide, *Southeast Alaska*,.

The west coast of Vancouver Island itself has five great sounds, sixteen major inlets, and over 200 islands, all of which offer a variety of wild and magnificent scenery. Forty percent of all the coves listed in Canadian *Sailing Directions,* Volume 1 (from the U.S. border to Cape Caution), are located on the west coast of the island. Except for a few exposed but relatively short day-passages, you can find protected waters and a snug, calm anchorage every night. (Study a large-scale chart and see how many small islands and reefs you can keep to windward!) Because there are nearly 200 anchor sites on Vancouver Island's West Coast, it is beyond the scope of this book to provide the information you need for such a trip. Please consult our companion cruising guide, the second edition of *Exploring Vancouver Island's West Coast,* Second Edition.

We hope you enjoy your cruises along the South Coast of British Columbia and that you can sense the joy and pleasure we've had in documenting so many wonderful places. We would like to hear your suggestions for improving subsequent editions.

Please check our website www.FineEdge.com for supplemental information.

Smooth sailing, Checleset Bay, Vancouver Island's west coast

Appendices and References

APPENDIX A

Principal Distances within the Inside Passage between Vancouver Island and the Mainland

From *Sailing Directions*, used with permission

	Victoria (Ogden Point) (See Note 1)	New Westminster	Vancouver (Brockton Point)	Nanaimo	Nanoose Bay (Richards Point)	Northwest Bay	Halfmoon Bay	Pender Harbour (Entrance) (See Note 2)	Blubber Bay	Powell River	Comox	Campbell River	Seymour Narrows	Stuart Island (Settlement) (See Note 3)	Kelsey Bay	Port Neville (Entrance)	Broken Islands (See Note 4)	Blinkhorn Peninsula	Pulteney Point	Blunden Harbour	Alison Harbour	Port Hardy	Bull Harbour (Entrance)	Pine Island Lt. Ho. brg. 050°, 1 mile	Cape Scott Lt. Ho. brg. 150°, 1.3 miles
New Westminster	72																								
Vancouver (Brockton Point)	73	40																							
Nanaimo	76	46	34																						
Nanoose Bay (Richards Point)	81	53	40	13																					
Northwest Bay	88	59	46	20	12																				
Halfmoon Bay	85	54	35	21	18	18																			
Pender Harbour (Entrance) (See Note 2)	95	65	48	30	25	21	11																		
Blubber Bay	117	87	70	52	46	37	35	25																	
Powell River	118	88	70	52	46	41	35	26	5																
Comox	122	94	79	54	48	37	52	42	18	21															
Campbell River	143	114	99	75	69	58	62	53	29	31	33														
Seymour Narrows	151	122	107	83	77	66	70	61	37	39	41	8													
Stuart Island (Settlement) (See Note 3)	156	126	109	91	85	75	74	64	42	39	54	33	41												
Kelsey Bay	186	157	142	118	112	101	105	96	72	74	75	43	34	36											
Port Neville (Entrance)	193	164	148	125	118	108	112	102	78	81	82	50	41	43	7										
Broken Islands (See Note 4)	200	171	156	132	126	116	120	110	86	88	90	57	49	50	15	8									
Blinkhorn Peninsula	219	190	175	151	145	134	138	129	105	107	109	76	68	69	34	27	19								
Pulteney Point	234	205	190	166	160	150	154	144	120	123	124	91	83	85	49	42	34	15							
Blunden Harbour	252	223	208	184	178	168	172	162	138	141	142	109	101	103	67	60	52	33	18						
Alison Harbour	264	235	220	196	190	180	184	174	150	153	154	121	113	115	79	72	64	45	30	16					
Port Hardy	251	222	207	183	177	167	171	161	137	140	141	108	100	102	66	59	51	33	17	14	21				
Bull Harbour (Entrance)	269	240	225	201	194	184	188	179	154	157	158	126	117	119	84	77	69	50	34	29	21	22			
Pine Island Lt. Ho. brg. 050°, 1 mile	265	236	221	197	191	180	184	174	151	153	155	122	114	115	80	73	65	46	31	20	9	20	11		
Cape Scott Lt. Ho. brg. 150°, 1.3 miles	289	260	245	221	215	204	208	199	175	177	179	146	138	139	104	97	89	87	55	49	39	43	20	30	
Cape Caution Light brg. 078°, 2.2 miles	277	248	232	208	202	192	196	186	162	165	167	133	125	127	91	85	76	58	42	27	16	32	22	12	32

	Blinkhorn Peninsula	Beaver Cove	Alert Bay	Port McNeill	Sointula
Beaver Cove	3				
Alert Bay	7	5			
Port McNeill	12	10	6		
Sointula	12	10	6	4½	
Pulteney Point	15	14	9	7½	5

APPENDIX A

Distances in Juan de Fuca Strait, Admiralty Inlet, Puget Sound and the S.E. Part of the Strait of Georgia

From *Sailing Directions,* used with permission

	Cape Flattery, Wash. (Tatoosh Id. Lt. Ho. brg. 140°, 3.5 miles)	Noah Bay, Wash.	Port Renfrew, B.C.	Sooke Harbour, B.C. (Entrance)	Race Rocks Lt. Ho. brg. 000°, 1.5 miles	Port Angeles, Wash.	Victoria, B.C. (Ogden Point)	Point Wilson Lt. Ho. brg. 225°, 1 mile	Port Townsend, Wash.	Port Ludlow, Wash.	Port Gamble, Wash.	Everett, Wash. (See Note 3)	Eagle Harbour, Wash.	Seattle, Wash.	Bremerton, Wash.	Tacoma, Wash.	Olympia, Wash.	Anacortes, Wash.	Bellingham, Wash.	Blaine, Wash.	New Westminster, B.C.	Nanaimo, B.C.
Noah Bay, Wash.	10																					
Port Renfrew, B.C.	16	14																				
Sooke Harbour, B.C. (Entrance)	43	35	36																			
Race Rocks Lt. Ho. brg. 000°, 1.5 miles	51	43	44	10																		
Port Angeles, Wash.	61	54	54	21	12																	
Victoria, B.C. (Ogden Point)	61	53	54	20	10	19																
Point Wilson Lt. Ho. brg. 225°, 1 mile	84	76	77	43	33	29	31															
Port Townsend, Wash.	87	79	80	46	36	32	34	3														
Port Ludlow, Wash.	100	92	93	59	49	45	47	16	16													
Port Gamble, Wash.	105	97	98	64	54	50	52	21	21	10												
Everett, Wash. (See Note 3)	118	110	111	77	67	63	65	34	34	25	28											
Eagle Harbour, Wash.	124	116	117	83	73	69	71	40	40	32	34	29										
Seattle, Wash.	124	116	117	83	73	69	71	40	40	32	34	29	8									
Bremerton, Wash.	133	125	126	92	82	78	80	49	49	41	44	38	13	14								
Tacoma, Wash.	144	136	137	103	93	89	91	60	60	52	55	49	25	25	29							
Olympia, Wash.	168	160	161	128	117	113	115	84	84	76	79	73	50	50	50	34						
Anacortes, Wash.	92	84	85	51	41	42	35	26	29	42	47	49	66	66	75	86	110					
Bellingham, Wash.	106	98	99	65	55	55	49	40	43	56	61	63	80	80	89	100	124	16				
Blaine, Wash.	111	103	104	70	60	65	53	55	58	71	76	78	95	95	104	115	139	35	37			
New Westminster, B.C.	138	130	131	97	87	91	79	88	91	104	109	111	128	128	137	148	172	69	70	47		
Nanaimo, B.C.	143	135	136	102	92	100	85	94	97	110	115	116	134	134	143	154	178	74	74	53	46	
Vancouver, B.C. (Brockton Point)	138	130	131	97	87	92	80	89	92	105	110	111	129	129	138	149	173	68	70	47	40	34

Bibliography & References

Anderson, Hugo. *Secrets of Cruising the New Frontier, British Columbia Coast and Undiscovered Inlets.* Anacortes: Anderson Publishing Company, 1995.

Cameron, June. *Destination Cortez Island.* Surrey, B.C.: Heritage House and Bishop, CA: Fine Edge, 1999.

Canadian Tide and Current Tables, Pacific Coast, Vols. 5 and 6 [issued annually]. Ottawa: Department of Fisheries and Oceans.

Chappell, John, *Cruising Beyond Desolation Sound.* Vancouver: Naikoon Marine, rev. ed. 1987.

Drushka, Ken. *Against Wind and Weather, The History of Towboating in British Columbia.* Vancouver: Douglas & McIntyre Ltd., 1991.

Graham, Donald. *Keepers of the Light, A History of British Columbia's Lighthouses and Their Keepers.* Madeira Park: Harbour Publishing, 1990.

Hale, Robert, ed. *Waggoner Cruising Guide.* Bellevue: Weatherly Press, published annually.

Hill, Beth. *Seven-Knot Summers.* Victoria: Horsdal & Schubart, 1994.

Marine Weather Hazards Manual, a guide to local forecasts and conditions, 2nd Edition. Vancouver: Environment Canada, 1990.

McGee, Peter, ed. *Kayak Routes of the Pacific Northwest Coast.* Vancouver, Douglas & McIntyre, 1998.

Minister of Supply and Services, *Marine Weather Hazards Manual, a guide to local forecasts and conditions,* 2nd Edition. Vancouver: Environment Canada, 1990.

Northwest Boat Travel. Anacortes: Anderson Publishing Company [published annually].

Pinkerton, Kathrene. *Three's a Crew.* Ganges: Horsdal & Schubart, 1991 (original copyright 1940).

Renner, Jeff. *Northwest Marine Weather, From the Columbia River to Cape Scott.* Seattle: The Mountaineers, 1993.

Sailing Directions British Columbia Coast (South Portion). Ottawa: Department of Fisheries and Oceans, Communications Directorate for the Canadian Hydrographic Service, Vol. 1.

Small Craft Guide, British Columbia, Vancouver Island, Port Alberni to Campbell River, Including the Gulf Islands. Department of Fisheries and Oceans, Institute of Ocean Sciences, Sidney, B.C., Vol. 1.

Small Craft Guide, British Columbia, Boundary Bay to Cortes Island. Department of Fisheries and Oceans, Institute of Ocean Sciences, Sidney, B.C., Vol. 2.

Snively, Gloria. *Exploring the Seashore in British Columbia, Washington and Oregon, A Guide to Shorebirds and Intertidal Plants and Animals.* West Vancouver: Gordon Soules Book Publishers Ltd., 1978, sixth printing 1985.

Stooke, Philip. *Landmarks and Legends of the North Island.* Port Hardy: North Island Gazette Ltd., 1978.

Thomson, Richard E., *Oceanography of the British Columbia Coast.* Ottawa: Department of Fisheries and Oceans, 1981.

Walbran, Captain John T.B.C., *British Columbia Coast Names.* Vancouver: Douglas & McIntyre, 1971.

Washburne, Randel. *The Coastal Kayaker, Kayak Camping on the Alaska and B.C. Coast.* Chester, Connecticut: Globe Pequot Press, 1983.

Wolferstan, Bill. *Gulf Islands, Cruising Guide to British Columbia,* Vol. 1. Vancouver: Whitecap Books, 1987, with 1997 Addenda.

________. *Desolation Sound and the Discovery Islands, Cruising Guide to British Columbia,* Vol. 2. Vancouver: Whitecap Books, 1987, first paperback edition 1989.

________. *Sunshine Coast, Cruising Guide to British Columbia,* Vol. 3. Vancouver: Whitecap Books, 1982, second paperback edition 1994.

Wood, Charles E. *Charlie's Charts North to Alaska, Victoria B.C. to Glacier Bay, Alaska.* Surrey, B.C.: Charlie's Charts, 1995 (revised edition).

Index

Please Note: Names in italics refer to sidebars

About the Authors

Authors **Don Douglass and Réanne Hemingway-Douglass** have logged more than 170,000 cruising miles over the past 35 years—from 60°N to 63°S latitude. Since 1991, they have spent their summers cruising on their trawler, *Baidarka*, gathering data for new titles and updating their acclaimed *Exploring* series of nautical guidebooks. Together they have documented 6,000 anchor sites between San Diego and the Alaska Peninsula.

Don began exploring Alaskan waters as a youth living in Ketchikan. He has sailed the West Coast and the Inside Passage on everything from a 21-foot sailboat to a commercial fishing boat and a Coast Guard icebreaker. He holds a BSEE degree from California State University and a Masters in Business Economics from Claremont Graduate University. Don is an honorary member of the International Association of Cape Horners and, as the author of several mountain biking guidebooks and a father of the sport, he was elected to the Mountain Biking Hall of Fame.

Réanne, who holds a BA degree in French from Pomona College, attended Claremont Graduate University and the University of Grenoble, France. Sailor, writer, cyclist and language teacher, Réanne's articles have appeared in numerous outdoor magazines. Her classic, *Cape Horn: One Man's Dream, One Woman's Nightmare* has been published in French and Italian. Réanne led the first women's bicycling team to cross Tierra del Fuego at the tip of South America. In 2008, she finally signed the register atop Cape Horn Island during Don's second visit.

Anne Vipond, of Vancouver, B.C., is a writer-photographer, a regular contributor to *Pacific Yachting,* and author of the best-selling guidebook *Alaska by Cruise Ship.* Anne often collaborates with her husband and journalist William Kelly.

Enjoy these other publications from Fine Edge

Exploring Southeast Alaska

Dixon Entrance to Skagway

Don Douglass and Réanne Hemingway-Douglass

Second Edition of the best-selling reference book, covers in unique detail every harbor and cove between Dixon Entrance and Skagway. "This book is the authority for Southeast Alaska Cruising...." "A classic guidebook series...The book is stunning."

Exploring the San Juan and Gulf Islands

Cruising Paradise of the Pacific Northwest

Don Douglass and Réanne Hemingway-Douglass

All the anchor sites in the paradise that straddles the U.S.-Canadian border, bounded by Deception Pass and Anacortes on the south, Nanaimo on the north, Victoria on the west, and Bellingham on the east.

Exploring Vancouver Island's West Coast

Don Douglass and Réanne Hemingway-Douglass

With five great sounds, sixteen major inlets, and an abundance of spectacular wildlife, the largest island on the west coast of North America is a cruising paradise.

Exploring the Pacific Coast—San Diego to Seattle

Don Douglass and Réanne Hemingway-Douglass

All the places to tie up or anchor your boat from the Mexican border to Victoria/ Seattle. Over 500 of the best marinas and anchor sites, starting from San Diego to Santa Barbara—every anchor site in the beautiful Channel Islands, the greater SF Bay Area, the lower Columbia River, and the greater Puget Sound.

Exploring the North Coast of British Columbia

Blunden Harbour to Dixon Entrance, Including Queen Charlotte Islands

Don Douglass and Réanne Hemingway-Douglass

Describes previously uncharted Spiller Channel and Griffin Passage, the stunning scenery of Nakwakto Rapids and Seymour Inlet, Fish Egg Inlet, Queens Sound, and Hakai Recreation Area. Helps you plot a course for the beautiful South Moresby Island of the Queen Charlottes.

Cruising the Virgin Islands

Joe Russell and Mark Bunzel

This cruising guide for the British and U.S. Virgin Islands features all the well-known anchorages, as well as many you have not seen before. Most shown with aerial photos, anchorage diagrams and GPS waypoints to make navigation in this cruising paradise easy.

Available at nautical bookstores, West Marine and www.FineEdge.com

FINE EDGE

Nautical & Recreational Publishing

Enjoy these other publications from Fine Edge

THE DREAMSPEAKER SERIES

BY ANNE & LAURENCE YEADON-JONES

Volume 1: Gulf Islands & Vancouver Island

Volume 2: Desolation Sound & Discovery Islands

Volume 3: Vancouver, Howe Sound & the Sunshine Coast

Volume 4: The San Juan Islands

Volume 5: The Broughtons

Volume 6: The West Coast of Vancouver Island

Ann and Laurence Yeadon-Jones' Dreamspeaker series are not only valuable resources filled with delightful hand-drawn maps, photos and important cruising information, they're also infused with a little bit of fun which makes them stand out from the others.
—Peter A. Robson, editor, *Pacific Yachting Magazine*

ANNE & LAURENCE YEADON-JONES
are experienced offshore and inshore sailors who voyaged from Southampton, England, in 1985 on their first adventure across the Atlantic Ocean. Over the last 17 years they have logged thousands of cruising hours charting, recording and photographing their travels, and exclusively along the beautifully rugged coastline and islands of the Pacific Northwest. Through their writing, charting and photography they endeavour to promote safe and enjoyable boating while profiling the uniqueness of coastal life.

Available at nautical bookstores, West Marine and www.FineEdge.com

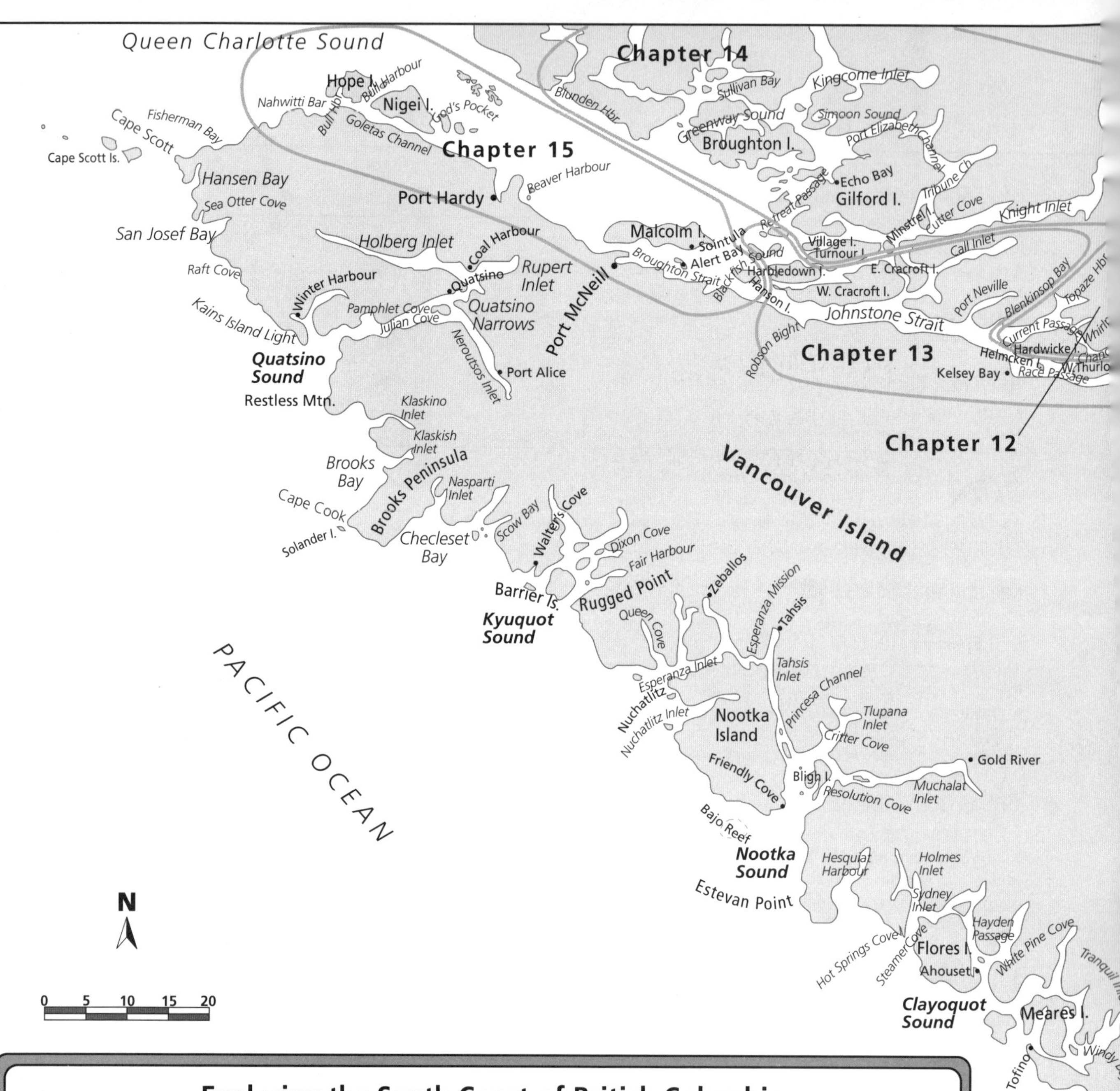

Exploring the South Coast of British Columbia

1. **Victoria to Saanich Inlet**
2. **Boundary Pass to Active Pass**
   Plumper Sound and Swanson Channel
3. **Satellite Channel to Sansum Narrows**
   Saltspring Island, Prevost and Portland Islands
4. **Trincomali Channel**
   Montague Harbour to Valdes Island
5. **Stuart Channel**
   From Sansome Narrows to Dodd Narrows
6. **Gabriola Passage**
   From Valdes Island to Nanaimo
7. **Sunshine Coast**
   Vancouver to Howe Sound
8. **Sunshine Coast**
   Sechelt Peninsula and Inlet
9. **Sunshine Coast**
   Jervis Inlet
10. **Northern Strait Of Georgia**
    Newcastle Island Passage to Copeland Islands
11. **Desolation Sound**
    Malaspina Inlet and Sutil Channel to Bute Inlet
12. **Campbell River to Wellbore Channel**
    Seymour Narrows and the Inside Rapids
13. **Johnstone Strait**
    Chatham Point to Minstrel I. and Blackfish Sound
14. **Eastern Queen Charlotte Strait**
    Knight Inlet & Broughton Arch. to Blunden Hbr.
15. **Western Queen Charlotte Strait**
    Broughton Strait to Goletas Channel
16. **Outer Passages—British Columbia**